RMAN Recipes for Oracle Database 11*g*

A Problem-Solution Approach

Darl Kuhn, Sam Alapati, and Arup Nanda

Apress®

RMAN Recipes for Oracle Database 11*g*: A Problem-Solution Approach

Copyright © 2007 by Darl Kuhn, Sam Alapati, Arup Nanda

ISBN-13 (pbk): 978-1-59059-851-1

ISBN-10 (pbk): 1-59059-851-2

Printed and bound in the United States of America 9 8 7 6 5 4 3 2 1

Trademarked names may appear in this book. Rather than use a trademark symbol with every occurrence of a trademarked name, we use the names only in an editorial fashion and to the benefit of the trademark owner, with no intention of infringement of the trademark.

Lead Editor: Jonathan Gennick
Technical Reviewer: Bernard Lopuz
Editorial Board: Steve Anglin, Ewan Buckingham, Gary Cornell, Jonathan Gennick,
    Jason Gilmore, Jonathan Hassell, Chris Mills, Matthew Moodie, Jeffrey Pepper,
    Ben Renow-Clarke, Dominic Shakeshaft, Matt Wade, Tom Welsh
Project Manager: Richard Dal Porto
Copy Edit Manager: Nicole Flores
Copy Editor: Kim Wimpsett
Assistant Production Director: Kari Brooks-Copony
Production Editor: Lori Bring
Compositor: Diana Van Winkle, Van Winkle Design Group
Proofreader: Dan Shaw
Indexer: Broccoli Information Management
Artist: Diana Van Winkle, Van Winkle Design Group
Cover Designer: Kurt Krames
Manufacturing Director: Tom Debolski

Distributed to the book trade worldwide by Springer-Verlag New York, Inc., 233 Spring Street, 6th Floor, New York, NY 10013. Phone 1-800-SPRINGER, fax 201-348-4505, e-mail orders-ny@springer-sbm.com, or visit http://www.springeronline.com.

For information on translations, please contact Apress directly at 2855 Telegraph Avenue, Suite 600, Berkeley, CA 94705. Phone 510-549-5930, fax 510-549-5939, e-mail info@apress.com, or visit http://www.apress.com.

The information in this book is distributed on an "as is" basis, without warranty. Although every precaution has been taken in the preparation of this work, neither the author(s) nor Apress shall have any liability to any person or entity with respect to any loss or damage caused or alleged to be caused directly or indirectly by the information contained in this work.

The source code for this book is available to readers at http://www.apress.com in the Source Code/ Download section. You will need to answer questions pertaining to this book in order to successfully download the code.

To Heidi, Lisa, and Brandi. —Darl Kuhn

To my wife Valerie; for her enormous support and sacrifice. —Sam Alapati

To Anu and Anish. —Arup Nanda

Contents at a Glance

Contents

■CHAPTER 6   **Using the Recovery Catalog** 149

■CHAPTER 7   **Making Backups with RMAN** 177

■CHAPTER 8 **Maintaining RMAN Backups and the Repository** 225

■CHAPTER 9 **Scripting RMAN** 257

■CHAPTER 10   Restoring the Control File 295

■CHAPTER 11   Performing Complete Recovery 313

▪CHAPTER 12 Performing Incomplete Recovery

▪CHAPTER 13 Performing Flashback Recovery

■CHAPTER 14 Handling Online Redo Log Failures 427

■CHAPTER 15 Duplicating Databases and Transporting Data 443

Foreword

What skills set the database administrator (DBA) apart from other technologists? Of the many responsibilities laid upon a DBA, which cannot be performed by someone else? Adding database accounts? Creating tables and indexes? Installing and configuring databases? Optimizing the database and the applications that access and manipulate it?

All of these tasks are regularly performed by people who do not consider themselves database administrators. They consider themselves to be programmers/analysts, to be application developers, or to be managers and directors, and they do all these things just to be able to move forward with their own jobs. Most application developers know how to run the Oracle Universal Installer—it's just another graphical application, and accepting all the default choices is a perfectly valid way to get the job done these days. Adding database accounts? That's easy! Granting database privileges? Just give 'em `dba` or `sysdba` and no more problems! Creating tables and indexes? C'mon, that's more of a developer's job than the DBA's job, isn't it? Tuning Oracle databases is mostly about crafting efficient SQL statements, and although this job often falls to DBAs, it is best handled by the developers and programmers who write the SQL in the first place.

Although many of these duties are correctly assigned to a DBA, they are not a hallmark of the job.

Think about the people flying airliners. With the degree of automation in aircraft cockpits now, it can be argued (with a lot of merit) that the planes can fly themselves, from take-off through navigated flight to touchdown. So, what are the pilots for?

If something goes wrong with the plane, you want the best pilots at the controls of that plane. That's because when things go wrong, they go wrong in a hurry, and it takes somebody who knows exactly what all that PlayStation gadgetry is really controlling in that cockpit, and it takes somebody who can intelligently take control and land the thing safely when dozens of lights are flashing and dozens of alarms are buzzing. It's not too hard to justify the presence of pilots on airplanes in the end.

Likewise, 50 years ago, at the dawn of the American space program, a debate was underway then, as there is now: should space flights be *manned* or *unmanned*? There were good arguments in favor of the latter. The first astronauts weren't human—they were dogs and chimps. When humans were finally included, the spacecraft engineers assured them they were redundant; they were just "spam in a can" went the gallows humor.

But it didn't take long to prove those people wrong. The presence of a well-trained and comprehensively knowledgeable pilot in the spacecraft has proven its worth, time and time again. A classic example is the final two minutes of the historic Apollo 11 moon landing, when Neil Armstrong looked out the window of the Eagle lunar module and realized that their automated descent, controlled from Houston via computer, was dropping them into a boulder field. Only a few hundred meters from the lunar surface, Armstrong flipped the controls to manual and pushed the lunar module higher, seeking a more viable landing site. While Houston nervously and repeatedly queried for status, Armstrong calmly replied, "Hold, Houston," until, with only 30 seconds of fuel remaining, he set the lunar module down and declared that the Eagle had landed.

That why we have human astronauts. This is what sets "spam in a can" apart from a pilot. This is why airliners, although heavily automated, have highly trained pilots at the controls.

And that brings us back to database administrators…I hope!

What sets a DBA apart from an ambitious programmer or a developer doing what needs to be done to move forward?

It is the ability to prepare for trouble and recover from it. Database recovery in the event of failure or mishap is the most vital skill in a DBA's toolkit.

The Oracle RDBMS has been around now for about 30 years. The internal mechanisms for backup and recovery have changed very little in the past 20 years. Of course there have been enhancements, but the mechanism for basic "hot" or online backups has changed very little.

However, it is the mechanism for restore and recovery that took a great leap forward 10 years ago, when Oracle Recovery Manager (RMAN) was introduced with Oracle 8. In a world where misnomers abound, Recovery Manager is quite aptly named. The focus of the product is not on automating backups, but rather on automating the steps of restore and recovery as much as possible. Much of the early reluctance to adopt RMAN came about not from any failings in the product, but rather from disappointment that the product did not make the job of performing backups any easier. Since backups are the operation that DBAs see most often, what RMAN does for recovery operations was not fully appreciated.

As I teach people how to use RMAN, I attempt to stress the mind-set that RMAN is not just about performing backups. Rather, it is about "feeding" the RMAN recovery catalog. Backups are not ends in themselves but simply entries in the recovery catalog used by RMAN during restore and recovery operations. If a DBA considers it their duty to *feed the recovery catalog* with backup operations and other maintenance such as cross-checks, then you have someone who is truly preparing for the eventuality, not just the remote possibility, of restore and recovery. Someone understands the tool and is not just applying a different tool to bang in nails the same old way.

The knowledge and capability to recover a database from catastrophic failure is what separates a real DBA from someone who found the installer or who knows how to do the clickety-clickety thing in Oracle Enterprise Manager—and not just once, by luck, but knows how to use RMAN to its full advantage in order to work around those confusing and misleading error messages and to verify backups and maintain and protect the recovery catalog(s) so as to virtually guarantee recoverability, each and every time.

It is this protective mind-set, liberally seasoned with caution and pessimism, that separates DBAs from other technologists. Systems administrators and network administrators have much the same tendencies, but only databases administrators are made responsible for *never* losing data. Systems and networks can be made redundant, and if they fail, it is only a matter of bringing them back to service, but data loss is forever and is never forgiven.

Years ago, I worked with a very no-nonsense vice president. She didn't want to know the details of my job and rightly so. She simply stated, very clearly, "Failures happen, but don't *ever* tell me that you could not recover my data." Message received.

This book was written by seasoned professionals who have been using RMAN since its inception. They have recognized that RMAN can be confusing, and they think everyone should not have to go through the same learning curve in order to arrive at the same conclusions. So they have gathered together their best practices and tried-and-true procedures and compiled them into this wonderful book.

If you are an Oracle database administrator, this could very well be the most important book you read. Technology books are famous for becoming *shelfware*, pristine and unopened books adorning shelves everywhere. This book will be the exception—the book that is dog-eared and worn, the cover falling off and pages smudged, found more often opened face down on a desk than perched serenely on a shelf. The information within this book is the very essence of the job of the Oracle DBA, the most important facet of the job, and I am grateful to Darl, Sam, and Arup for sharing.

Tim Gorman
Evergreen, Colorado
July 2007

About the Authors

DARL KUHN is a senior DBA with Sun Microsystems. Before joining Sun, his work as a consultant ranged from database administration to custom application development. Darl is the coauthor of *Oracle RMAN Pocket Reference* and has written several articles for *Oracle Magazine*. In addition, he is an affiliate professor at Regis University where he teaches Oracle courses for the graduate department of computer information technology. For the past 10 years, Darl has served as a volunteer DBA and developer for the Rocky Mountain Oracle Users Group. Darl has a master's degree from Colorado State University and currently lives near Aguilar, Colorado.

SAM ALAPATI manages Oracle databases for the Boy Scouts of America at its National Office in Los Colinas, Texas, where he performs both DBA tasks as well as some HP Unix system administration work. Before this, Sam worked for Sabre in Dallas and Lewco Securities in New Jersey. Prior to that, Sam worked at Lehman Brothers and ABC in New York City as a senior principal consultant for Oracle Corporation. Sam is the author of two previous books for Apress about Oracle9*i* Database and Oracle 10*g* Database administration. Sam also wrote two Oracle certification books for Oracle Press. Sam lives in the town of Flower Mound near Dallas, Texas, with his wife, Valerie; daughter, Nina; and sons, Shannon and Nicholas.

ARUP NANDA has been an Oracle DBA since 1993, when the world was slowly turning its attention to a big force to reckon with—Oracle 7. But he was not so lucky; he was entrusted with a production Oracle database running Oracle 6. Since then, he has never been out of the Oracle DBA career path—weaving several interesting situations from modeling to performance tuning to backup/recovery and beyond, with lots of gray hairs to document each ORA-600. He has written articles for publications such as *Oracle Magazine* and for Oracle Tech Net, he has presented at conferences such as Oracle World and IOUG Live, and he has coauthored three other books. In 2003, Oracle chose him as the DBA of the Year. He lives in Danbury, Connecticut, with his wife, Anu, and their son, Anish.

About the Technical Reviewer

BERNARD LOPUZ is a senior technical support analyst at Oracle Corporation, and he is an Oracle Certified Professional (OCP) in Oracle database versions 8, 8*i*, 9*i*, and 10*g*. Bernard holds a bachelor's degree in computer engineering from the Mapúa Institute of Technology in Manila, Philippines, and he is currently pursuing a master's degree in computer information technology at Regis University in Denver, Colorado. He was born in Iligan, Philippines, and now lives in Toronto, Canada, with his wife, Leizle, and two daughters, Juliet and Carol. Aside from tinkering with computers, Bernard loves to play soccer and basketball.

Acknowledgments

Special thanks go to Jonathan Gennick, the seasoned chef in our virtual kitchen, who kept us focused on ensuring the recipes were clear and concise. Jonathan's vision and deft skills with assembling and coaching have made this book a much greater sum than its unedited pieces. This book simply would not have been possible without Jonathan.

We also owe huge thanks to Bernard Lopuz, the technical editor for this book. Bernard enthusiastically joined this project and made countless suggestions and modifications that greatly contributed to the quality of the final product. His in-the-trenches experience with backup and recovery have truly added grit to this book.

We're very thankful to Richard Dal Porto for being a kind and efficient project manager for the book. We also wish to acknowledge the contributions of Dominic Shakeshaft, copy edit manager Nicole Flores, production editor Lori Bring, copy editor Kim Wimpsett, assistant production director Kari Brooks-Copony, and the entire production and marketing team at Apress for all the effort they put into producing the final book. Of course, our names indeed appear on the cover of the book, but the entire Apress team worked with great diligence and dedication, and they deserve as much credit as the authors for the final product.

From Darl

A special thanks goes to Heidi Kuhn; she read every page before it went through the edit process. Thanks also to Shawn Heisdorffer, who helped me work through (in tandem) many of the original scenarios. Thanks to Carlos Gonzalez, a former student who asked for better examples. Thanks also to Don Gritzmacher, Will Thornburg, Dona Smith, Jeff Sherard, Mike Tanaka, Gary Schut, and Roy Backstrom, for all of their sage system administration advice.

Thanks also to my recent team of DBAs: Sujit Pattanaik, Mehran Sowdaey, Janet Bacon, Doug Davis, Margaret Carson, Nehru Chacha Kaja, Tim Colbert, Inder Ganesan, Dan Fink, Guido Handley, Lou Ferrante, John Liu, Ken Roberts, Sue Wagner, Mike Perrow, Roger Murphy, Moya Cleaver, and Stan Yellott.

From Sam

Writing a book is always a team effort, although this fact isn't easily evident to the reader, and I'm grateful to the wonderful Apress team that helped make this book a reality. I owe an enormous debt of gratitude to the brilliant contributions of lead editor Jonathan Gennick, who strove tirelessly and with great insight to help us make this book as good as possible. His painstaking review of my chapters helped me immeasurably improve the technical content as well as the writing style. Jonathan turned out to be a one-stop resource for all my editorial questions. He line edited the (truly) rough first drafts and gently prodded me to do my best. Jonathan is a throwback to the classic book editor of yore, the type who has become rarer than a triple-billed woodpecker in today's publishing world. Besides the strictly editorial role, Jonathan played the far more important role of an advisor, mentor, and friend throughout the long process of writing this book.

Our technical editor, Bernard Lopuz, was, to put it simply, magnificent. Bernard unstintingly went through two drafts of every chapter, testing everything, conscientiously looking for any possible error, and asking very thoughtful questions. I benefited immensely from Bernard's reviews, and I am in his debt.

It has been a special pleasure to work with my two coauthors—Darl Kuhn and Arup Nanda. Working with both was a sheer delight because of their exceptional skills as DBAs as well as the keen sense of humor they displayed throughout the project.

I owe a round of thanks to my colleagues and friends at the Boy Scouts of America: Lance Parkes, Stan Galbraith, Rob Page, Steven Graves, Bill Ritchie, Royce Allen, Nate Langston, Dan Nelson, Chris Wolfe, Tom Hulcy, Inga Gurova, Carla Wallace, Sabrina Kirkpatrick, and Linda Almanza. They've made my work life at the Boy Scouts so enjoyable and productive. Belinda Potter, Lynn (RajCoomarie) Adcock, and Debra Kendrew have been very solicitous and caring during a crisis while I was in the middle of the book-writing process—I'm grateful for their kindness. Thanks also to Lee Mullins and Bob Woods for their support during a difficult time. Lashonda Spencer was very helpful at a critical time, and I want to acknowledge her help. Dabir Haider has been a true friend and brought my PC back to life (a better one) when I really needed it. Thanks also to Josh Maske for prompt and competent help when I almost lost everything on my PC.

David Jeffress, with his exceptional perceptiveness and his capacity to see the funny side of things, has made for a terrific working environment at the Boy Scouts. David Campbell, as always, is a fount of wisdom and unwavering support for all of us in the operations group at the Boy Scouts. My thanks to Dave, who is one manager who doesn't need to read any of the million books out there on how to manage people.

I'm deeply grateful to Mark Potts for the many things he helped me with over the past year. Dr. Michael Atchley has been a true friend during a difficult period, and I appreciate his kind help.

Although I'm geographically separated from my parents, Appa Rao and Swarna Kumari, and brothers, Hari Hara Prasad and Siva Sankar Prasad, they are always close to my heart and play a big factor in all my endeavors. I thank my family for their encouragement and interest in my work. My family, including sisters-in-law Aruna and Vanaja, nephews Teja and Ashwin, and nieces Aparna and Soumya, have always sustained me with their enthusiastic support and belief in me. I'm grateful for the enormous affection and love they have shown me over the years.

It was my wife Valerie's selfless and strong support that enabled me to write this book, and I thank her for that. Nina and Nicholas, as usual, were supportive and helpful during my writing efforts—they both contributed this time around by placing the "bullets" for me in most of the chapters and both had a constant supply of good cheer. I owe a lot to my son Shannon (who helped me place some of the notes to the proofreader during the final stages of the writing) for all his help during the writing of the book.

From Arup

First and foremost, I thank my wife, Anindita, and son, Anish, for letting me pound away on the keyboard, especially Anish, who must have missed his Daddy playing with him, although he was very considerate for his ripe old age of 3! Thank you, my father, Ajay, and mother, Asha, for guiding my life and making me what I am today.

Beyond my immediate family, I sincerely thank my extended family of friends, colleagues, customers, and associates for enriching me and my professional life. Thank you to the team that started me off in Oracle Database management: Kanchan Ray, Akbar Patel, T.R.S. Subramaniam, Nandita Saigal, Ravi Varadharajan, and others from the ISBS crew. Thank you Lance Tucker and the rest of the DBA team at Boston College; Serge Nikulin and the team at IntraLinks; Daniel Lyakavesky, Robert Vittori, and others at McKesson; Henry Thomson, Jim Roland, Nick Yelashev, Celine Hatch, and the others at Cigna; Jonas Rosenthal, Matt Augustine, Scott Uhrick, Mladen Gogala, and the awesome team at United Healthcare; Alan Patierno, Bob Kess, Bonnie Majeski, and others at Lucent; Barry Sergeant and the rest of the Financials team at Priceline; and Tom Urban, Chris Overbey, Dave Hallman, and others at Blue Cross Blue Shield of VA for believing in me and supporting me whenever and wherever they could. Last but not the least, Bill Camp, Brad Carr, Christos Kotsakis, Steve Golinski, Athy Pandy, Ravi Kumar, and my own special DBA team of Harish Patel, Arun Rao, Ajay Thotangare, and others at Starwood Hotels, thank you for the believing in me and pushing and challenging me to explore new frontiers.

Many thanks to Tom Kyte, Jonathan Lewis, Tim Gorman, and Jeff Maresh for shining on the path less traveled and gently pushing me back on track whenever I veered off; Tony Jedlinski, George Trujillo, David Teplow, Mike Abbey, and others at Independent Oracle Users Group; Paul Dorsey, Mike LaMagna, Rob Edwards, Mike Olin, Caryl Lee Fisher, Jeff Bernknopf, and others at New York Oracle User Group; Lyson Ludvic, Jameson White, and the wonderfully appreciated crowd at Boston DBA SIG; Jeff McCormick and Lucas Lukasiak at CTOUG; Reed Overby, Kim Marie Mancusi, Donna Cooksey, Tim Chien, Mughees Minhas, Len Len Tang, Erick Peterson, Krishna Telikicherla, and many others at Oracle whose help and support I have counted on and received. I can't express my thanks enough to Tom Haunert and Justin Kestelyn for bringing the best out of my writing and reiterating their faith in me every day; Don Burleson for making me an author for the first time; Steven Feuerstein for continuing that; Robert Freeman for extending the trust and now; Darl and Sam for welcoming me into the team; Jonathan for making me look good while being completely in the background; and the rest of the crew at Apress for making this book a reality.

But, above all, thank *you*, dear reader, for that ultimate support you have shown that makes every keystroke worthwhile.

Introduction

Every company relies on data to efficiently operate. Protecting corporate data is a critical task. One major responsibility of a DBA is to ensure that information stored in corporate databases is safe and available. This is what makes a database administrator valuable.

Oracle is a leading vendor of database technology. Many companies use Oracle databases to store mission-critical data. Recovery Manager (RMAN) is Oracle's flagship database backup and recovery solution. A DBA's job security depends on being able to back up and safely recover databases. Therefore, RMAN is a tool that every Oracle DBA *must* be proficient with.

RMAN can be used out of the box for simple backup and recovery needs or can be configured to meet the most sophisticated requirements. When implementing RMAN backups, sometimes it can be difficult to find clear examples of how to accomplish a specific task. *Or worse*, you find yourself in a stressful recovery situation, and you can't quickly find a solution to get your mission-critical database restored and available.

In those hectic circumstances, you don't want to wade through pages of architectural discussions or complex syntax diagrams. Rather, you require a solution right then and there. You want a quick step-by-step cookbook example that is easy to read and to the point.

This book provides you with task-oriented, ready-made solutions to both common and not so common backup and recovery scenarios. You do not need to read this book cover to cover. You can pick and choose whatever topic requires your attention. Whether you just need to brush up on an old backup and recovery subject or whether you want to implement an RMAN feature that is new in Oracle Database 11*g*, this book allows you to focus on a topic and its corresponding solution.

Audience

This book is for any DBA who quickly wants to find accurate solutions to their RMAN backup and recovery operations. Any database administrator from rookie to expert can leverage the recipes in this book to implement RMAN's features and resolve troublesome issues.

This book is also for system administrators. System administrators are responsible for keeping the overall system backed up and available. The delineation line between system administration tasks and database administration tasks is often nebulous. This is especially true when troubleshooting and tuning disk, tape, hardware, and network issues. System administrators and database administrators *must* work together to ensure that the database servers are backed up, scalable, and highly available.

Using This Book

Problem

You often find yourself thinking "Gosh darn it, I just want to see a good example and explanation of how to implement this RMAN feature...."

Solution

Use this book to locate a recipe that matches your scenario, and then use the corresponding example solution to solve your problem.

How It Works

RMAN Recipes for Oracle Database 11g is a cookbook of solutions for a wide variety of backup and recovery scenarios. The recipe titles act as an index to the task you need help with. You should be able to search for the recipe that fits your scenario and then find a concise answer that you can use to solve the issue you face. Each recipe starts with a description of the *problem*, followed by a to-the-point *solution*, and then a thorough explanation of *how it works*.

What This Book Covers

This book covers the gamut of RMAN backup and recovery subject matter. Major topics included are as follows:

- Backing up your database
- Performing complete and incomplete recovery
- Using flashback database technology
- Implementing a media management layer
- Troubleshooting and tuning RMAN
- Differences between Unix and Windows environments
- Using Enterprise Manager with RMAN
- Using new RMAN features in Oracle Database 11g

Where appropriate, we highlight the differences between RMAN in Oracle Database 11g and older versions (these recipes go to 11). There have been significant improvements to RMAN with each new release of Oracle. Where relevant, we point out in what version the particular RMAN feature was introduced.

Conventions Used in This Book

The following typographical conventions are used in this book:

- *Italics* is used to highlight a new concept or word.
- `Monospaced` font is used for code examples and to denote utility names.
- **Code that is bold** is used to highlight the statements being discussed.
- UPPERCASE indicates view names, column names, and column values.
- < > is used where you need to provide input, such as a filename or password.
- C:\> is used to denote the DOS command-line prompt.
- $ is used to denote the Unix command-line prompt.

Comments and Questions

We value your input. We'd like to know what you like about the book and what you don't like about it. You can send us comments via email to feedback@apress.com. When providing feedback, please make sure you include the title of the book in your note to us.

We've tried to make this book as error free as possible. However, mistakes happen. If you find any type of an error in this book, whether it be a typo or an erroneous command, please let us know about it. Please email the problem to support@apress.com. Your information will be validated and posted on the errata page to be used in subsequent editions of the book. The corrigendum can be viewed on the book's web page at http://www.apress.com.

Contacting the Authors

You can contact the authors directly at the following email addresses:

Darl Kuhn: darl.kuhn@gmail.com

Sam Alapati: salapati@netbsa.org

Arup Nanda: arup@proligence.com

CHAPTER 1

■■■

Backup and Recovery 101

Oracle *backup and recovery* refers to the theory and practice of protecting a real-life Oracle database against data loss and recovering data after a loss. You can lose data either because of a technical problem such as media failure (such as a disk drive breaking down) or because of errors made by the users (such as a wrong update or an overeager sysadmin or DBA deleting the wrong file). Oracle backup is the set of concepts, strategies, and steps to make copies of a database so you can use them to recover from a failure/error situation. Backups in this sense refer to physical backups of database files, control files, and archived redo log files. Oracle recovery is the set of concepts, strategies, and steps to actually recover from a system/user error or a potential data loss due to media-related problems such as the loss of a disk drive.

Ideally, we all like to never have any data loss or downtime because of a database failure. However, the constraints of both humans and machinery such as disk drive technology means that there's bound to be some type of failure during the course of your life as a practicing DBA, since you're the one in charge of maintaining and tuning databases that support the business. Here is your more realistic set of goals then:

- Protect the database from as many types of failure as possible.

- Increase the mean time between failures.

- Decrease the mean time to recover.

- Minimize the loss of data when there is a database failure.

Recovery Manager (RMAN) is Oracle's main backup and recovery tool and is a built-in component of the Oracle server. You don't have to pay additional licensing fees to use RMAN, as is the case when you use other Oracle products such as the Enterprise Manager Grid Control, for example. Since its introduction as part of the Oracle 8 release, RMAN has improved considerably to the point where it has become the most powerful tool to back up and recover Oracle databases, with its wide array of sophisticated and powerful capabilities. You can still use traditional user-managed backup and recovery techniques, but the powerful backup and recovery features offered by RMAN mean you won't be taking full advantage of your Oracle server software if you don't use RMAN. This book provides comprehensive coverage of RMAN's backup and recovery capabilities.

Before starting our discussion of how to perform backup and recovery tasks with RMAN, it's important to get an overview of key backup- and recovery-related concepts. We discuss the following topics in this chapter before turning to a detailed discussion of RMAN backup and recovery techniques starting in Chapter 2:

- Types of database failures

- Oracle backup and recovery concepts

- Backup types

- Recovery types

- An introduction to RMAN

- Backup and recovery best practices

We use the Oracle Database 11*g* release throughout this book, thus providing you with cutting-edge RMAN backup and recovery solutions. Most of what we say, however, applies equally to Oracle Database 10*g*. We specifically mention whenever we're discussing a feature not available in Oracle Database 10*g*.

Types of Database Failures

Since database backups are made to protect against a database failure, let's quickly review the types of database failures that can occur. A database can fail, either entirely or partially, because of various reasons. You can recover from some types of database failure with scarcely any effort on your part, because the Oracle database can recover automatically from some types of failures. The more critical types of failures require you to go in and "recover" the database by using your backups. You can divide database failures into the categories covered in the following sections.

Statement Failure

A typical example of a statement failure is when a program attempts to enter invalid data into an Oracle table. The statement will fail because of the checks built into the data insertion process. The solution here is to clean up the data by validating or correcting it. Sometimes, a program may fail to complete successfully because of programmatic logical errors. You must then refer the problem to the development group for corrections.

It is fairly common for a long data insertion job or a data import job to fail midway because there is no more room to put the data in. If you haven't already invoked the *resumable space allocation* feature, you must add space to the tablespace that contains the table that ran out of space. Another common cause of a statement failure is not having the proper privileges to perform a task. Your task as a DBA is to simply grant the appropriate privileges for the user who invoked the failed SQL statement.

User Process Failure

Sometimes, a user process may be terminated abruptly because of, say, the user performing an abnormal disconnect or performing a terminal program error and losing the session connection. As a DBA, there is not much you need to do here: the Oracle background processes will roll back any uncommitted changes to the data and release the locks that were held by the abnormally disconnected user session. The user will have to reconnect after the abrupt termination.

Network Failure

A network failure can also cause a database failure. Network failures can occur because the Oracle Net listener, the network interface card (NIC), or the network connection has failed. The DBA must configure multiple network cards and a backup network connection and backup listener to protect against these errors. In addition, you can use the connect-time failover feature to protect against a network failure.

Instance Failure

You experience an Oracle instance failure when your database instance comes down because of an event such as a hardware failure, a power failure, or an emergency shutdown procedure. You may also experience an instance shutdown when the key Oracle background process such as pmon shuts down because of an error condition.

Following an instance failure, first you check the alert log and trace files for any potential hints about the cause of the instance failure. Following this, you can just restart the database instance by using the Oracle command startup from the SQL*Plus command line.

Since the database wasn't cleanly shut down and the database files aren't synchronized, Oracle will perform an automatic instance or crash recovery at this point. Oracle will automatically perform a rollback of the uncommitted transactions by using data from the undo segments and will roll forward the committed changes it finds in the online redo log files. You don't need to use any sort of backup when restarting the database instance following an instance failure. Once the uncommitted changes are backed out and the committed changes are rolled forward, the datafiles are in sync again and will contain only committed data.

User Error

Inadvertently dropping a table is every DBA's nightmare. In addition to accidentally dropping a table, users can also wrongly modify or delete data from a table. You can use techniques such as the flashback table feature to restore a table to a previous point in time. You can use the flashback drop feature to recover an accidentally dropped table. Of course, if the transaction isn't committed yet, you can simply roll back the unwanted changes. Oracle's LogMiner tool also comes in handy in situations like this.

Media Failure

Media failure occurs when you lose a disk or a disk controller fails, hindering access to your database. A head crash, file corruption, and the overwriting or deletion of a datafile are all examples of a media failure. In general, any failure to read from or write to a disk constitutes a media failure. Although the first four types of failures don't require you to resort to a backup, media failure in most cases would require performing a media recovery with the help of backups of the datafiles and archived redo logs.

Each type of media failure may have a different solution as far as recovery is concerned. For example, if a control file copy is accidentally deleted, you won't have to go to your backups. On the other hand, deleting a datafile most likely requires you to restore the datafile from a backup as well as use the archived redo logs to bring the database up-to-date. If only a few blocks in a datafile are corrupt, you may use RMAN's block media recovery feature instead of restoring datafiles and performing media recovery.

In this book, we are mostly concerned with problems caused by media failures and how to recover from them. For this reason, let's analyze how database failures can occur because of media problems. Once your Oracle database instance is running in open mode, it could crash because of the loss of several types of files. For example, the database will crash if any of the following are true:

- Any of the multiplexed control files are deleted or lost because of a disk failure. You must restore the missing control file by copying from an existing control file and restarting the instance.

- Any datafile belonging to the system or the undo tablespace is deleted or lost because of a disk failure. If you lose one of these files, the instance may or may not shut down immediately. If the instance is still running, shut it down with the `shutdown abort` statement. You then start up the database in mount state, restore the lost datafile, and recover it before opening the database for public access.

- An entire redo log group is lost. If you have at least one member of the redo log group, your database instance can continue to operate normally. Restore the missing log file by copying one of the other members of the same group.

The database won't crash if any of the following are true:

- Any nonsystem or undo tablespace datafile is lost. If you lose a nonsystem or undo tablespace file, also known as a noncritical datafile from the point of view of the Oracle server, you must first restore and then recover that datafile. The database instance can continue operating in the meanwhile.

- At least a single member of each redo log group is available, although you might have lost other members of one or more groups.

Oracle Backup and Recovery Concepts

Before you jump into Oracle backup and recovery concepts, it's a good idea to review the basic Oracle backup and recovery architecture. Oracle uses several background processes that are part of the Oracle instance, and some of these background processes play a vital role in backup and recovery tasks. For a quick understanding of the Oracle background processes involved in backup and recovery, please see Figure 11-1 (in Chapter 11). Oracle also has several physical structures that are crucial components of backup and recovery, which we discuss in the following sections.

Backup and Recovery Instance Architecture

The Oracle instance consists of the system global area (SGA), which is the memory allocated to the Oracle instance, and a set of Oracle processes called the *background processes*. The Oracle processes start when you start the instance and keep running as long as the instance is alive. Each of the Oracle background processes is in charge of a specific activity, such as writing changed data to the datafiles, cleaning up after disconnected user sessions, and so on.

We'll briefly review the key Oracle background processes that perform critical backup and recovery–related tasks, which are the checkpoint process, the log writer process, and the archiver process.

The Checkpoint Process

The checkpoint process does three things:

- It signals the database write process (DBWn) at each checkpoint.

- It updates the datafile headers with the checkpoint information.

- It updates the control files with the checkpoint information.

The Log Writer Process

Oracle's online redo log files record all changes made to the database. Oracle uses a "write-ahead" protocol, meaning the logs are written to before the datafiles are. Therefore, it is critical to always protect the online logs against loss by ensuring they are multiplexed. Any changes made to the database are first recorded in the redo log buffer, which is part of the SGA.

Redo log files come into play when a database instance fails or crashes. Upon restart, the instance will read the redo log files looking for any committed changes that need to be applied to the datafiles. Remember, when you commit, Oracle ensures that what you are committing has first been written to the redo log files before these changes are recorded in the actual datafiles. The redo log is the ultimate source of truth for all changes to the data in an Oracle database, since an instance failure before the changes are written to the datafiles means that the changes are only in the redo log files but not in the datafiles.

The log writer (LGWR) process is responsible for transferring the contents of the redo log buffer to the online redo log files. The log writer writes to the online redo files under the following circumstances:

- At each commit

- Every three seconds

- When the redo log buffer is one-third full

The important thing to remember here is that the log writer process writes before the database writer does, because of the *write-ahead* protocol. Data changes aren't necessarily written to datafiles when you commit a transaction, but they are always written to the redo log.

■**Note** In fact, some esoteric features in the Oracle database allow you to make changes without generating redo log entries. Such features are helpful, for example, when loading large amounts of data. However, their benefits do not come without additional risk. The important point to take away from this section is that unless you are specifically using a feature that disables logging, any changes you commit are first written to the redo log files, and it is the log writer process that does the writing.

The Archiver Process

The archiver (ARCn) is an optional background process and is in charge of archiving the filled online redo log files, before they can be overwritten by new data. The archiver background process is used only if you're running your database in archivelog mode.

Physical Database Structures Used in Recovering Data

You need to deal with four major physical database structures during a database recovery:

- Datafiles

- Redo logs (archived and online)

- Control files

- Undo records

In a basic database recovery situation, you'd need to first restore datafiles by using backups (from a past period, of course). Once the restoration of the datafiles is completed, you issue the recover command, which results in the database rolling forward all committed data and thus bringing the database up-to-date. The database also rolls back any uncommitted data that's recorded in the undo segments that are part of the undo tablespace. The database server automatically performs the rollback of uncommitted data by using undo records in the undo tablespace to undo all uncommitted changes that were applied to the datafiles from the redo logs during the recovery process. This rolling back of uncommitted data takes place by using the information about all the changes made since the last database start-up. Oracle records all changes made to the database in files called the *online redo log files*. Since Oracle uses a round-robin method of writing the online redo log members, it is critical that you save the filled online redo logs before they are written. The process of saving the filled redo log files is called *archiving*, and the saved redo log files are termed *archived redo log files*. A media recovery process uses both the archived redo log files and the online redo log files.

The control file is essential for the Oracle instance to function, because it contains critical information concerning tablespace and datafile records, checkpoints, redo log threads in the current online redo log, log sequence numbers, and so on.

RMAN lets you back up all the files you need for a database recovery, including datafiles, control files, and archived redo logs. RMAN also lets you make image copies of both datafiles and control files, in addition to the standard RMAN-formatted backup pieces. You should never back up online redo log files; instead, always duplex these files to protect against the loss of an online redo log.

Archivelog and Noarchivelog Mode of Operation

You can operate your Oracle database in either *archivelog* mode or *noarchivelog* mode. In noarchivelog mode, Oracle will overwrite the filled online redo logs, instead of archiving (saving) the online redo logs. In this mode, you're protected only from instance failures, such as those caused by a power failure, for example, but not from a media failure. Thus, if there is a media failure, such as a damaged disk drive, the changes that were overwritten are gone forever, and the database won't be able to access those data modifications to recover the database up to the current point in time. The transactions made since the last backup are lost forever, and you can restore the database only to the point of the last backup you made.

If you are running your database in noarchivelog mode and you happen to lose a datafile, for example, you follow these steps to get back to work again:

1. If the instance isn't already shut down, first shut it down.

2. Restore the entire database (datafiles and control files) from the backups.

3. Restart the database by using the startup (open mode) command.

4. Users lose any data that was changed or newly entered in the database since you took the backup that was just restored. You can enter the data if you have a source, or you're going to have a data loss situation.

If you are running a production database—or if you want to make sure that all the data changes made to any database, for that matter, are always protected—you must operate your database in archivelog mode. Only a database running in archivelog mode can recover from both instance and media failures. You can't perform a media recovery on a database running in noarchivelog mode.

If you're running the database in noarchivelog mode, remember that you can make a whole-database backup only after first shutting the database down. You can't make any online tablespace backups in such a database. A database in noarchivelog mode also can't use the tablespace point-in-time recovery technique. Make sure you take frequent whole-database backups if an important database is running in noarchivelog mode for some reason.

Flashback Technology

Traditionally, restoring backed-up datafiles and recovering the database with the help of archived redo logs was the only way you could rewind the database to a previous point in time or view older data. Oracle's *flashback* technology offers new techniques that let you recover from several types of errors without ever having to restore backup files. The key idea behind the flashback technology is to improve database availability while you're fixing logical data errors. While you're correcting the logical data errors in one or more errors, all the other database objects continue to be available to the users unhindered. Flashback technology actually consists of a half dozen specific features, most but not all of which rely on the use of undo data to undo the effect of logical errors:

Oracle flashback query (uses undo data): This feature lets you view results from a past period in time. You can choose to use this query to retrieve lost or wrongly deleted data.

Oracle flashback version query (uses undo data): This feature lets you view all versions of a table's rows during a specific interval. You can use this feature for retrieving old data as well as for auditing purposes.

Oracle flashback transaction query (uses undo data): This feature enables you to view all the changes made by one or more transactions during a specified period of time.

Oracle flashback transaction backout (uses undo data): This new Oracle Database 11g feature lets you back out unwanted transactions by using compensating transactions.

The Oracle flashback table (uses undo data): This feature lets you recover a table (online) to a previous point in time. You can recover a table or a set of tables to a past point in time by using the contents of the undo tablespace. The database can remain online during this time, thus enhancing its availability. All of a table's constraints, triggers, and indexes are restored during the recovery, while the database remains online. You don't have to restore from a backup when you perform a flashback table operation. Since you're using undo data to restore the table instead of media recovery, you'll get done faster, and with less effort to boot.

Oracle flashback drop feature (uses the recycle bin): This relies on the concept of a recycle bin and lets you restore a dropped table. When you accidentally drop a table with the drop table statement, information about the purged table is saved in the recycle bin (which is actually a data dictionary table) under a system-assigned name. Actually, the table's contents remain intact and in place, but the data dictionary marks the table as having been dropped. You can then "undrop" the table at a later time by using the flashback table ... to before drop statement, which recovers the dropped object from the recycle bin. The flashback table feature relies entirely on the recycle bin concept.

A new feature of the Oracle Database 11g release, the *flashback data archive* lets you use the previously described flashback features to access data from a period of time that's as old as you want. By using a flashback data archive, you overcome the limitation of a short undo retention time in the undo tablespace.

The *Oracle flashback database* feature serves as an alternative to traditional database point-in-time recovery. You use this feature to undo changes made by logical data corruption or by user errors. The essential point to understand here is that the opposite of flashback is to *recover*. In normal database recovery, you update the backups by applying logs forward. In flashback, you rewind the database by applying flashback logs backward. Thus, in most cases, a flashback database operation will take much less time than the time it takes to restore and recover during the traditional alternative, which is a database point-in-time recovery. The flashback database feature takes the database back in time, essentially rewinding it to a past point in time by undoing all changes made to the database since that time. Unlike traditional point-in-time recovery, you don't have to perform a media recovery by restoring backups. You simply use the new flashback logs (stored in the flash recovery area) to access older versions of the changed data blocks. In addition, the database makes use of the archived redo logs as well.

■**Note** The flashback database feature is useless in dealing with cases of lost datafiles or damaged media. You can use this feature to undo the changes made to an Oracle database's datafiles only by reverting the contents of the datafiles to a previous point in time.

When you enable flashback logging so that you can use the flashback database feature, you may not always be able to return to a specific point in time, if the flashback logs for that period aren't available. Oracle's *guaranteed restore points* feature lets you specify an system change number (SCN) to which you can always restore the database. That is, the database will ensure that the flashback logs from the specific SCN on are saved, no matter what. Thus, guaranteed restore points, which are an adjunct to the flashback database feature, let you ensure that you'll be at least able to recover until the specified SCN, even if you aren't necessarily able to recover up to the current SCN.

Backup Types

When we talk about a database backup, your first thought might be that it is simply a copy of all the database physical files. However, an Oracle database offers several types of backups. We summarize the main types of backups in the following sections.

Physical and Logical Backups

When you make a copy of a database file using an operating system utility such as cp, for example, you are making an actual physical copy of the database file. You can use this file to restore the database contents if you happen to lose the disk containing that file. Physical backups are simply physical copies of the files used by the database, such as datafiles, redo logs, and control files. However, making exact physical copies of the database file isn't the only way to copy the contents of an Oracle database. You can also make a logical backup by using Oracle's Data Pump Export tool wherein you copy the definitions and contents of all of the database's logical components such as tables and so on. You can use Oracle's Data Pump Import utility to later import the logical data into the same or another Oracle database. Logical backups are, however, not a complete backup and recovery solution; they serve as a secondary means of backing up key tablespaces or tables in some situations.

Whole and Partial Backups

A *whole-backup* of a database is the backup of the *entire* database; this is the most commonly made type of Oracle database backup. A whole-database backup includes all the datafiles plus the control files. A *partial backup* refers to backups of a tablespace or datafile in a database. A datafile backup will include only a single operating system file. A tablespace backup includes all the datafiles that are part of that tablespace. You can also back up the control file just by itself by making either a text or a binary copy of it. The control file is a crucial part of the recovery process, since it contains key information about various recovery-related structures.

Online and Offline Backups

RMAN supports both *offline* and *online* backups. An offline backup, also called a *cold backup*, is one made after shutting down the database using the shutdown command or the shutdown command with the immediate or transactional clause. An offline backup, provided you make one after the database is shut down gracefully, is always consistent, whether you're operating in archivelog or noarchivelog mode. When making an offline backup with RMAN, you must, however, start the database you want to back up in the mount mode.

An online backup, also called a *hot* or *warm* backup, is one made while the database instance is still open. By definition, an online backup is always inconsistent. During a recovery, the application of the necessary archived redo logs will make the backup consistent. Thus, you can make online backups of any database you're operating, and the resulting inconsistent backups can be made consistent with the application of archived redo logs. However, for databases running in noarchivelog mode, open inconsistent backups aren't recommended.

Full and Incremental Backups

A full backup of a database will contain complete backups of all the datafiles. Incremental backups contain only the changed data blocks in the datafiles. Obviously, then, incremental backups can potentially take a much shorter time than full backups. You can make incremental backups only with the help of RMAN—you can't make incremental backups using user-managed backup techniques.

Consistent and Inconsistent Backups

To understand the crucial difference between consistent and inconsistent backups, you must first understand the concept of the system change number (SCN). The SCN is an Oracle server–assigned number that indicates a committed version of the database. It's quite possible that different datafiles in the database might have a different SCN at any given point in time. If the SCNs across all the datafiles are synchronized, it means that the data across the datafiles comes from a single point of time and, thus, is consistent.

During each checkpoint, the server makes all database file SCNs consistent with respect to an identical SCN. In addition, it updates the control file with that SCN information. This synchronization of the SCNs gives you a consistent backup of your database. Not only does each of the datafiles in the database have the same SCN, it must also not contain any database changes beyond that common SCN.

If you back up your database while it's running, you may end up with backups of the various datafiles at various time points and different SCNs. This means your backups are inconsistent, since the SCNs aren't identical across all the datafiles.

If you're operating the database in noarchivelog mode, you can use only consistent backups to restore your database. If you're operating in archivelog mode, however, you can use consistent or inconsistent backups to restore the database. If you're using a consistent backup, you can open a whole-database backup without recovery and without using the open resetlogs command. If you're using inconsistent backups, however, you must use archived redo logs to make the data current and synchronize the SCNs across the datafiles.

The key fact here is that the recovery process will make your inconsistent backups consistent again by using the data from the archived redo logs and the online redo log files to apply all the necessary changes across the datafiles to make them all consistent with reference to a single SCN.

If you're running the database in noarchivelog mode, the recommended approach to backing up the database is to shut down the database cleanly first and then to back up all the datafiles. If you're using RMAN to perform an offline backup, the database must be mounted before you can actually perform the RMAN backup. This is because RMAN needs to update the target database control file.

When you follow the approach suggested in the previous paragraph, you'll be backing up a consistent database. It's not recommended that you back up an inconsistent database resulting from an abrupt shutdown using the shutdown abort command, for example.

If you're running the database in archivelog mode, you can back up a whole database in any of the following ways:

- Closed and consistent

- Closed and inconsistent

- Open and inconsistent

The ability to back up a database while it is open and in use is a key benefit of running a database in archivelog mode.

Recovery Types

There are several methods of recovering data, and the particular recovery strategy you adopt will depend on your backup strategy to a large extent. For example, if you are operating in noarchivelog mode, then in most cases you can't go perform a complete recovery. You can restore only the latest backup and will lose all the data that was entered since the time of the backup. In the following sections, we'll briefly describe the major recovery techniques you can use. Similarly, the flashback database technique offers a much faster means of restoring a database to a previous point in time than traditional media recovery, but of course, you can't avail yourself of this wonderful feature if you haven't configured and used a flashback recovery area (to store the flashback logs).

Database Recovery and Consistent vs. Inconsistent Backups

If you shut down your database using either shutdown normal (same as the shutdown command), shutdown immediate, or shutdown transactional, you'll have a *consistent* database. A shutdown following each of the previously mentioned variations of the shutdown command will result in the following actions:

- All uncommitted changes are rolled back first.

- The contents of the database buffer cache are written to the datafiles on disk.

- All resources such as locks and latches are released.

Since the database was cleanly shut down, when you restart the database, there is no need for an instance recovery, which is the main implication of performing and using a consistent backup.

If you shut down your database using either the shutdown abort or shutdown force command or if there is an instance failure, you'll end up with an *inconsistent* database, wherein the database is said to be in a "dirty" state. Once the shutdown command is issued or the instance is terminated abruptly because of some reason, the following things will be true:

- Any committed changes are *not* rolled back automatically.

- Changes made to the database buffers aren't written to the datafiles on disk.

- All resources such as locks and latches are still held and aren't released.

In other words, there is simply no time to perform a graceful and tidy closure of the database. Your database instance is simple terminated, even though it may be in the middle of processing user transactions and hasn't properly recorded all the modified data to the datafiles. Upon restarting your database, the Oracle database instance will do the following things first:

- Use the information in the online redo logs to reapply changes.

- Use the undo tablespace contents to roll back the uncommitted changes to data.

- Release the resources held.

The work that the Oracle database performs upon a restart following an inconsistent shutdown is known as *instance recovery*. Instance recovery is thus mandatory and entirely automatic, with the database itself performing all the work without any intervention by the DBA.

Crash Recovery and Media Recovery

As noted in the previous section about instance or crash recovery, if your Oracle instance crashes, because of a power failure, for example, you don't have to perform a media recovery of the database, which requires that you restore backups of the database and bring them up-to-date with the help of the archived redo logs. The Oracle server will perform an automatic crash recovery when you restart the instance. However, if you lose a disk drive, for example, or you can't access the disk's contents because of some kind of media failure, you may have to restore your backups and bring them up-to-date using the archived redo logs.

Crash Recovery

Crash recovery or instance recovery is the automatic recovery of the database by the Oracle server, without any intervention by the DBA. For example, if a power outage brings down your database instance, when the power supply resumes, you only need to restart the database instance. You don't have to perform any restore or recovery tasks, because the server will use the information in the undo tablespace to perform automatic instance recovery by rolling back uncommitted transactions in the database. The server uses the online redo logs to record in the datafiles the changes that were committed before the outage but couldn't be written to the database files before the occurrence of the failure.

The Oracle server automatically performs crash recovery whenever you open a database whose files were not cleanly synchronized before shutting down. Since an abrupt shutdown doesn't provide a chance to synchronize the datafiles, it is a given that, in most cases, an instance recovery will be performed by the Oracle server when you restart the Oracle instance. The Oracle server will use the information saved in the online redo log files to synchronize the datafiles. Instance recovery involves the following two key operations:

Rolling forward: During this operation, the Oracle server will update all datafiles with the information from the redo log files. The online redo log files are always written to before the data is recorded in the datafiles. Thus, an instance recovery may usually leave the online log files "ahead" of the datafiles.

Rolling back: During this operation, uncommitted changes that were added to the datafiles during the rollforward operation are rolled back. Oracle does this by using the undo tablespace contents to return uncommitted changes to their original states. At the end of the rollback stage, *only committed data* at the time of the instance failure is retained in the datafiles.

During instance recovery, in the first rollforward operation, the database server must apply all transactions between the last checkpoint and the end of the redo log to the datafiles. Thus, in order to tune instance recovery, you control the gap between the checkpoint position and the end of the redo log. You use the Oracle initialization parameter `fast_start_mttr_target` to specify the number of seconds you want the crash recovery to take. Oracle will try to recover the instance as close as possible to the time that you specify for the `fast_start_mttr_target` parameter. The maximum value of this parameter is 3,600 seconds (1 hour).

Media Recovery

When a disk drive fails and you can't access the contents of an Oracle datafile, you're looking at a potentially much more serious situation than a crash recovery, since the server won't be able to automatically recover from such a catastrophe. You must provide the lost datafiles from backup. Since it's likely that data has changed in the meanwhile, you must provide the changes stored both in the archived redo log files and in the online redo log files. When the Oracle database issues an error indicating media problems, you must first find which files you must recover by querying the V$RECOVER_FILE view, which lists all files that need media recovery.

RMAN completely automates the process of media recovery. You use two basic commands—`restore` and `recover`—to perform media recovery. The `restore` command restores the necessary datafiles from RMAN's backup sets or image copies to the same or an alternative location on disk. The `recover` command performs the recovery process by applying necessary archived redo logs or incremental backups to the restored datafiles. You must do the following as part of a media recovery operation:

- Restore the necessary datafiles from backup, either to the old or to an alternative location.

- Rename the datafiles, if necessary, so the database will know about their new location.

- Recover the datafiles (bring them up to date), if necessary, by applying redo information to them.

To open the database after a successful restore and recovery, the following must be true:

- You must have synchronized copies of all the control files.

- You must have synchronized online datafiles.

- You must have at least one member of each redo log group.

If all these are true, you can open the recovered database.

Complete and Point-in-Time Recovery

You perform a complete recovery when you bring a database, a tablespace, or a datafile up-to-date with the most current point in time possible. It's important to emphasize that complete recovery isn't synonymous with recovering the complete database. Rather, completeness here alludes to the completeness of the entire database or part of it (tablespace or datafile) with reference to the time element. If you update the database tablespace or datafile completely by applying all changes from the archived redo logs to the backup files, you're performing a complete backup. In other words, complete recovery will ensure that you haven't lost any transactions. Note that when using RMAN, you may also use incremental backups as well, in addition to archived redo logs, during the recovery process.

When you perform media recovery, it isn't always the case that you can or should bring the database up-to-date to the latest possible point in time. Sometimes you may not want to recover the database to the current point in time. Following a loss of a disk or some other problem, the complete recovery of a database will make the database current by bringing all of its contents up to the present. A *point-in-time recovery*, also known as *incomplete recovery*, brings the database to a specified time in the past. A point-in-time recovery implies that changes made to the database after the specified point may be missing. On the face of it, a point-in-time recovery may seem strange. After all, why would you recover your database only to a past period in time and not bring it up-to-date? Well, there may be situations where a point-in-time recovery is your best bet, as in the following examples:

- You lose some of the archived redo logs or incremental backups necessary for a complete recovery following a media failure.

- The DBA or the users delete data by mistake or make wrong updates to a table.

- A batch job that's making updates fails to complete.

In all of these situations, you can use either point-in-time recovery or Oracle's flashback technology to get the database back to a previous point in time. Prior to the introduction of the flashback technology, a database point-in-time recovery (DBPITR) and a tablespace point-in-time recovery (TSPITR) were the automatic solutions when confronted by situations such as an erroneous data entry or wrong updates. Flashback technology offers you the capability to perform point-in-time recovery much quicker than the traditional point-in-time recovery techniques that rely on media recovery. The flashback database feature is the alternative to traditional database point-in-time recovery, while the flashback table feature lets you avoid having to perform a media recovery in most cases.

Deciding on the Appropriate Recovery Technique

Fortunately for the Oracle database administrators, several recovery techniques are available, such as media recovery, Oracle flashback, and so on, each geared toward recovering from a certain type of problem. Here's a summary of when to use the various types of recovery techniques:

- Use media recovery if you're confronted with damaged, missing, or inaccessible datafiles.

- If a user drops a table or commits a major data entry error, you can perform a point-in-time media recovery, but the best option is to use the `flashback drop` feature. You can also import the affected table using the Data Pump Import utility or have users reenter data in some situations.

- If you run into logical errors, perform a TSPITR or consider using an appropriate flashback technique to make a point-in-time recovery.

- If you have data corruption in a few blocks in a datafile or a set of datafiles, use block media recovery. Again, there's no need to perform a media recovery and make the rest of the database inaccessible.

- If a user error affects a large set of tables or the entire database, use the flashback database feature to revert the database to a previous "good" time by undoing all the changes since that point in time.

- Use the flashback table feature to revert to a previous state of a table in order to undo unwanted changes.

RMAN Architecture

You can start performing backups with RMAN without installing or configuring a thing. Simply invoke the RMAN client by using the RMAN executable (named rman) from the $ORACLE_HOME/bin directory, and you're ready to go. Just specify the target database you want to work with at the command line, and that's it. You can perform backup and recovery actions with RMAN through the RMAN client or through the Enterprise Manager GUI.

In addition to the RMAN client, you may use additional optional components to make your backup and recovery strategy robust and easy:

The recovery catalog: The target database control file will always store the RMAN repository, which is the set of RMAN-related backup and recovery information. This data is also referred to as RMAN's *metadata*. However, it's smarter to use a dedicated database to store the RMAN repository. You can then create a special schema called the *recovery catalog* in this dedicated database and have RMAN store its repository in it, thus avoiding the risk of the critical metadata being overwritten when the control file runs out of space. As you'll see in Chapter 6, using a recovery catalog, which is optional, has several other advantages.

The flash recovery area: This is a location on disk where the database will store the backup and recovery–related files. This is also optional but highly recommended. See Chapter 3 for a detailed discussion of the flash recovery area.

Media management layer: As mentioned earlier, RMAN can directly interact only with disk drives. If you want to use tape drives to store your backups, you'll need a media management layer in addition to RMAN, since RMAN can't directly interact with the tape drives. You can use any of several Oracle-certified third-party media management layers. Oracle also provides Oracle Secure Backup, which it claims is the "most well-integrated media management layer for RMAN backups." Together, RMAN and Oracle Secure Backup provide a complete end-to-end backup solution for all Oracle environments. Chapter 18 deals with the media management layer.

An RMAN session in Unix/Linux systems consists of the following processes:

- The RMAN client process.

- A default channel, which is the connection to the target database.

- Additional channels you allocate and the corresponding target connection to each of the target databases.

- If you're using the recovery catalog, there will be a catalog connection to the recovery catalog database.

- During database duplication or TSPITR operations, there will be an auxiliary connection to the auxiliary instance.

- By default, RMAN makes one polling connection to each of the target databases to help monitor the execution of RMAN commands on the different allocated channels.

Benefits of Using RMAN

You can perform basic backup and recovery tasks using operating system utilities and standard SQL commands. However, there are several drawbacks to using these so-called user-managed backup and recovery techniques. For example, you can't perform incremental backups using user-managed techniques. In general, user-managed backup and recovery techniques require you to manually keep track of your backup files, their status, and their availability. You must write your own SQL and operating system scripts to manage the backup and recovery operations. In addition, you must provide the necessary datafiles and archived log files during a database recovery operation. If the database is operating during your backups (online or hot backups), you must place the database files in the backup mode before performing the actual file backups.

Oracle explicitly states that you can use user-managed techniques to perform backup/recovery activities. Oracle actually states that both user-managed techniques and RMAN are alternative ways of performing backup and recovery tasks. However, Oracle strongly recommends using RMAN to make your backups and perform database recovery, because of the tool's strengths and powerful features. Although you can perform a basic backup and recovery task with user-managed techniques without ever having to even start the RMAN interface, you should make RMAN your main backup and recovery tool for several reasons. Several important backup and recovery features are available to you only through RMAN.

Here's a brief description of the important benefits of using RMAN instead of user-managed backup and recovery techniques:

- You can take advantage of the powerful Data Recovery Advisor feature, which enables you to easily diagnose and repair data failures and corruption (Chapter 20 discusses the Data Recovery Advisor).

- There are simpler backup and recovery commands.

- It automatically manages the backup files without DBA intervention.

- It automatically deletes unnecessary backup datafiles and archived redo log files both from disk and tape.

- It provides you with detailed reporting of backup actions.

- It provides considerable help in duplicating a database or creating a standby database.

- It lets you test whether you can recover your database, without actually restoring data.

- It lets you verify that available backups are usable for recovery.

- It lets you make incremental backups, which isn't possible by any other means of backup.

- It lets you perform database duplication without backups by using the network-enabled database duplication feature, also known as *active duplication*.

- It automatically detects corrupt data blocks during backups, with the corruption relevant information recorded in the V$DATABASE_BLOCK_CORRUPTION view.

- When only a few data blocks are corrupted, you can recover at the data block level, instead of recovering an entire datafile.

- You can take advantage of the unused block compression feature, wherein RMAN skips unused data blocks during a backup.

- Only RMAN provides the ability to perform encrypted backups.

- You can use RMAN with a variety of third-party storage systems.

- You can use a powerful yet easy-to-use scripting language, which lets you write custom backup and recovery scripts quickly.

Backup and Recovery Best Practices

To successfully recover from unforeseen database mishaps, you must of course be fully conversant with the Oracle recovery techniques and concepts. In addition, you must ensure you are following certain basic steps to make sure you can successfully carry out the database recovery when you're pressured for time.

In addition, you must always document your backup and recovery procedures. You must have a detailed recovery plan for each type of failure you anticipate. If possible, you must write scripts to automate the execution of the recovery plan during a crisis. You must also update the written backup and recovery procedures on a regular basis and communicate these changes to all the personnel involved in the backup and recovery process in your organization. The following is a summary of basic Oracle backup and recovery best practices that will ensure that your database recovery efforts are successful.

Configure a Flash Recovery Area

It's common for backed-up datafiles and archived redo logs to be archived to tape storage. However, the problem is that when you're recovering a database, tape drives are rather slow media to copy to disk. Oracle strongly supports *automatic disk-based backup and recovery*, wherein all the necessary backup files are stored on disk itself. You make the initial copy of the necessary datafiles and archived redo log files to the flash recovery area and, from here, copy them to tape so you can store them off-site in a secure location.

Oracle recommends using the *flash recovery area* to store the entire set of backup and recovery–related files. The flash recovery area is simply a location on a server where you decide to store backup and recovery–related files such as RMAN's backup pieces, copies of control files and the online redo log files, and so on. At the minimum, Oracle recommends that you size the flash recovery area large enough to hold all archived redo logs that have not yet been copied to tape. It's easy to maintain the flash recovery area—all you have to do is specify the size of the area and the retention policy, which dictates when RMAN will discard unnecessary files from the flash recovery area. It's RMAN's job to keep the maximum number of backups possible in the flash recovery area, while discarding both obsolete backups and the backup files already copied to tape.

Oracle recommends that you size the flash recovery area large enough so it equals the sum of the size of the database plus the size of the archived redo logs not yet copied to tape and the size of any incremental backups.

Although the flash recovery area is by no means mandatory, Oracle recommends that you use one. You must have activated a flash recovery area in order to avail of the flashback database or the guaranteed restore point feature. In addition, using a flash recovery area means you're reducing your recovery time, since necessary backups and archived redo logs can be kept on disk instead of having to recover from tape backups. Since obsolete backups are automatically deleted when space is needed for fresh files, you won't be running the risk of accidentally deleting necessary files.

Make and Protect a Database Redundancy Set

You may have to perform a database recovery when you lose or can't access (because of a media problem) any of these three types of Oracle database files: datafiles, online redo log files, and control files. Oracle recommends that you maintain a *database redundancy set*, which is a set of files that'll help you recover any of the three key types of Oracle files when they become unavailable to the database. This essential set of recovery-related files, called the *redundancy* set, will enable you to recover your database from any contingency. Here are the components of the redundancy set:

- Most recent backups of all datafiles plus the control file

- All archived redo logs made after the last backup

- Current control files and online redo file copies

- Oracle database-related configuration file copies (spfile, password file, tnsnames.ora and listener.ora files, for example)

To maintain the database redundancy set described here, you must duplex the control file as well as the online redo log files *at the database level*. That is, although a mirrored disk setup means that a copy of the redo log files and the control file will be automatically made at the operating system level, that doesn't provide you with complete safety.

Although you can mirror the online redo files at the operating system level, Oracle advises against this. Follow these Oracle best practices for protecting your database files:

- Multiplex the online redo log file at the database level. If you're using the flash recovery area, make this the destination for the duplexed copies of the online redo log file.

- Ensure that you use hardware or software (OS) mirroring to duplex the control file. This way, the database will always continue to operate following the loss of one control file.

- Mirror the datafiles in the database so you don't have to perform media recovery for simple disk failures.

- Keep more than one set of backups so you can withstand a database corruption issue.

- Consider making more than one copy of the redundancy set on tape if you aren't going to be using a disk-based recovery plan.

Oracle recommends that you use at least two disk drives on all production systems (one for the redundancy set and the other for the datafiles) and completely separate them by using different volumes, file systems, disk controllers, and RAID devices to hold the two sets of files: database files and the files in the redundancy set. One way to do this is to simply use the Oracle recommended flash recovery area. In fact, Oracle recommends the flash recovery area as a logical candidate to keep a copy of all the files belonging to the redundancy set (which includes the most recent database backup) on disk.

Create Powerful Backup Strategies

The strength of your backup strategy determines the strength of your recovery strategy. No backups, no recovery! Your backup strategies are derived entirely from your recovery strategies. Ideally, you must plan your recovery strategy based on the potential types of database failures you might encounter. The more types of database failures you want to guard against, the more complex your backup strategy will be.

Schedule Regular Backups

Schedule your backups on a regular basis, thus reducing your exposure to media failures. You, of course, can recover any database from a backup made at any remote time in the past, provided you have all the archived redo logs from that point forward. But can you imagine applying all those archived redo logs to the backups and suffering a horrendous downtime?

Create Regular Backups of the Control File

Back up a database's control file after any structural change to your database, such as creating a new tablespace or adding or renaming a datafile or an online redo log member. The best way to do this is to issue the RMAN command `configure controlfile autobackup on`. By default, the automatic backup of the control file is turned off. By turning control file autobackups on, you make sure that at the end of every RMAN `backup` command, RMAN automatically backs up the control file. When you make some changes via SQL*Plus, even though you're outside the purview of RMAN, the control file is automatically backed up, if you set the control file autobackup feature on. Using the control file autobackup, you can restore RMAN's backup and recovery information (called RMAN's *repository*), when you lose all your control files and aren't using the optional recovery catalog.

Run the Database in Archivelog Mode

To be able to restore a database completely (that is, bring them up-to-date with all the changes ever made to that database), you must run the database in archivelog mode. Only development and test databases where data loss isn't an issue should be run in noarchivelog mode.

Multiplex the Control File

Since the control file is absolutely necessary during a recovery, use the following guidelines to safeguard the control file:

- Keep the Oracle-recommended three copies of the control file.

- Put each copy of the control file on a separate disk.

- Place at least one of the three copies on a separate disk controller.

Multiplex the Redo Log Groups

If you lose your online redo logs, you may not be able to recover all committed changes to your database following a media failure and subsequent recovery. You must always duplex the online redo logs, using the following guidelines:

- Have a minimum of two members in each redo log group.

- Place each member on a separate disk drive.

- Place each redo log member on a separate disk controller.

Adopt the Right Backup Storage Strategy

Where you store your backups is quite critical to your recovery strategy, since different storage strategies have different implications for recovery time. If you use a flash recovery area, of course, the backups are all on disk, and consequently, you can recover with the least amount of elapsed time. If you store your backups only on tape or you store them off-site, it means you have to endure a longer interval to restore and recover your database.

Plan Your Backup Retention Duration

One of the key questions every backup strategy must address is how long you want to keep a backup. Although you can specify that a backup be kept forever without becoming obsolete, it's not common to follow such a strategy, unless you're doing it for a special reason. Instead, backups become obsolete according to the retention policy you adopt. You can select the retention duration of backups when using RMAN in two ways. In the first method, you can specify backup retention based on a *recovery window*. That is, all backups necessary to perform a point-in-time recovery to a specified past point of time will be retained by RMAN. If a backup is older than the point of time you chose, that backup will become obsolete according to the backup retention rules. The second way to specify the retention duration is to use a *redundancy-based* retention policy, under which you specify the number of backups of a file that must be kept on disk. Any backups of a datafile greater than that number will be considered obsolete.

You can set a default retention policy for all files that RMAN backs up. Once you do this, you can choose to delete any files that are obsolete under that retention policy using simple RMAN commands. The files you delete may be on disk or on tape storage. When you delete the obsolete files using RMAN commands, RMAN will remove the relevant information from its metadata. If, however, you're using the flash recovery area to store your backups, RMAN will automatically delete all obsolete files as and when it needs space for accommodating newer datafile backups or archived redo logs in the flash recovery area.

Plan Your Backup Schedules

Determining a backup schedule means how often you use RMAN to back up your database files, as well as what files you back up. Do you perform nightly or weekly backups, or do you back up different files at different intervals? How frequently you create a backup will, of course, depend on how fast the data in your database is changing. If your database performs a very large number of DML operations on a daily basis, you must back it up on a daily basis rather than a weekly basis, for example. If, on the other hand, a database is being mostly used for lookup purposes, with minimal DML changes, you can back up at a more infrequent interval, say on a weekly basis. An incremental backup strategy may be especially apt in a case such as this, because of the small amount of changes.

Validate Your Recovery Strategy

A key part of a backup and recovery strategy is the validation of your backups. Merely backing up the database regularly doesn't guarantee that you can recover your database successfully with those backups. You must choose a method to regularly validate the backups you take with RMAN. Since the only goal in creating database backups is to use them in a recovery situation, you must make sure you regularly validate your backups and test your data recovery strategy. RMAN provides commands that let you validate the database files you're planning to back up by reading those files without actually backing them up.

Conduct Regular Trial Recoveries

Another key part of a solid backup and recovery strategy is to schedule regular trial recoveries using your current recovery plan and the latest backups for various simulated scenarios. In addition to verifying that your backups are being made correctly, you'll also get plenty of practice with the recovery techniques and commands. Aside from that, it is only during the test restore/recovery that you'll know the duration of a restore/recovery and, therefore, how fast you can perform the actual restore/recovery.

It's much better to get acquainted with the recovery techniques this way rather than to try them for the first time after a production database runs into problems and you're under the gun to recover it fast.

■**Note** You can configure the `nls_date_format` environment variable to include the date and time format, such as DD-MON-RRRR HH24:MI:SS (in the Korn shell, use the command `export nls_date_format=` YYYY-MM-DD:`HH24:MI:SS`) because by default only the data is displayed in the RMAN log. This is helpful when troubleshooting, because most often you want to know the exact date and time a specific problem or error occurred. Furthermore, this will also display the date/time of the RMAN backup completion and datafile checkpoints.

Record Accurate Software and Hardware Configuration

Always keep handy vital information that you might have to send to the Oracle Support personnel, such as the following:

- Server model and make

- Operating system version and patch number

- Oracle database version number and patch release

- Database identifier (DBID)

- Names and location of all your datafiles

- Version of the recovery catalog database and the recovery catalog schema, if you're using one

- Version of the media management software you are using

Of course, it's always a good idea to keep the complete RMAN log file generated during the RMAN backup (even though this is already captured in the V$RMAN_OUTPUT), which is useful when you lose the control file or recovery catalog that has information about the RMAN backups you want to restore from.

In this introductory chapter, we have provided a quick review of the essentials of Oracle backup and recovery concepts and have defined key terms. We also introduced the Recovery Manager tool and explained its basic architecture and an overview of its important features. Later chapters, of course, delve into the intricacies of using RMAN to perform backup and recovery.

CHAPTER 2

■ ■ ■

Jump-Starting RMAN

This chapter is for those who are fairly new to Oracle and RMAN. The purpose of this chapter is to show you how simple it can be—even for a novice—to back up, restore, and recover a database using RMAN. You'll see that it's possible to use RMAN with little or no training. This chapter will walk you through critical tasks such as how to connect to your database, start it, enable archiving, and then perform basic backup and recovery tasks.

If you're a seasoned Oracle DBA and are already somewhat familiar with RMAN, then this chapter is not for you. As an experienced DBA, the recipes that come after this chapter contain the information you need.

This chapter starts with simple SQL*Plus examples of how to connect to your database, how to start/stop it, and how to enable archiving. Once your database is in archivelog mode, then you can use RMAN to start, stop, back up, and recover your target database.

■Note This chapter does not cover how to install the Oracle binaries. You should already have Oracle installed on your server and should have already created a database.

2-1. Connecting to Your Database

Problem

You're new to Oracle and wonder how to connect to your database via SQL*Plus so that you can perform basic commands such as starting and stopping your database and enabling archivelog mode.

Solution

Before you connect to an Oracle database, you need to establish the following:

- Operating system (OS) environment variables

- Access to a privileged OS account or schema with sysdba privileges

The OS environment variables are usually set when you log on to your database server. Minimally, you need to set ORACLE_SID to the name of your target database and ORACLE_HOME to the directory where you installed the Oracle RDBMS software (binaries). Your PATH variable should also include ORACLE_HOME/bin. In a Unix environment, Oracle provides an oraenv script for the Korn and Bourne shells and coraenv for the C shell to set the required OS variables.

In a Windows environment, ORACLE_SID and ORACLE_HOME are set as variables in the Windows registry. These variables are set for you as part of the installation of the Oracle software on your computer. Normally you don't need to modify these variables after you install Oracle. If the need arises, you can override these settings by establishing OS environment variables from the command line.

■**Note** See Oracle's installation guide for the OS you are using. The OS installation guide will have instructions on how the OS variables should be configured for your environment.

After you've established your operating system variables, you now need to connect to the database with either sysdba or sysoper privileges. You can do this one of two ways.

Using OS Authentication

If your Unix account is a member of either the dba or oinstall group (your installation might use different group names, but those are the most common), then you can connect to your database via SQL*Plus by virtue of being logged into your Unix account. On Windows, the OS user must be part of either the ora_dba group or the ora_oper group. This example uses OS authentication to connect to your database as the user sys:

```
$ sqlplus / as sysdba
```

The slash (without a schema/password) tells SQL*Plus to use operating system authentication.

■**Tip** Starting with Oracle Database 10*g*, you no longer need to enclose the OS-authenticated connect string in double quotes.

You can verify that you have connected as sys by issuing the following:

```
SQL> show user
USER is "SYS"
```

Using a Password File

The alternative is to authenticate to your database by giving a username and password. When you provide a username/password and attempt to connect with sysdba privileges, this type of authentication uses a password file. A password file allows you to do the following from SQL*Plus or RMAN:

- Connect to your database with sysdba/sysoper privileges as a non-sys user

- Connect to your database via Oracle Net

This example shows the syntax for using a password file:

```
$ sqlplus <username>/<password>@<database connection string> as sysdba
```

Here you connect to sys with a password of hathi with a database connection string of BRDSTN:

```
$ sqlplus sys/hathi@BRDSTN as sysdba
```

How It Works

Before you can connect to Oracle, you need to have the proper OS variables set and also have access to either a privileged OS account or a privileged schema. Connecting as a privileged user (either sysdba or sysoper) allows you to perform administrative tasks such as starting, stopping, and creating databases. You can use either OS authentication or a password file to connect to your database as a privileged user.

The concept of a privileged user is important also to RMAN backup and recovery. Like SQL*Plus, RMAN uses OS authentication and password files to allow privileged users to connect to the rman utility. Only a privileged account is allowed to back up, restore, and recover a database.

Explaining OS Authentication

OS authentication means that if you can log on to an authorized OS account, then you are allowed to connect to your database without the requirement of an additional password. OS authentication is administered by assigning special groups to OS accounts.

When you install the Oracle binaries in a Unix environment, you are required to specify at installation time the names of the OS groups (usually named oinstall or dba) that are assigned the database privileges of sysdba and sysoper. In a Windows environment, an OS group is automatically created (typically named ora_dba) and assigned to the OS user who installs the Oracle software.

The sysdba and sysoper privileges allow you to perform administration tasks such as starting and stopping your database. The sysoper privilege contains a subset of the sysdba's privileges. Table 2-1 details which privileges sysdba and sysoper contain.

Table 2-1. *Privileges of* sysdba *and* sysoper

System Privilege	Authorized Operations
sysdba (all privileges of the sys schema)	Start up and shut down, alter database, create and drop database, toggle archivelog mode, recover database
sysoper	Start up and shut down, alter database, toggle archivelog mode, recover database

Any OS account assigned to the authorized OS groups can connect to the database without a password and perform administration operations. In Unix, it's common to create an oracle OS account and assign its primary group to be either oinstall or dba. Here's an example of displaying the user and group ID information with the Unix id command and then connecting to the database using OS authentication:

```
$ id
uuid=100(oracle) gid=101(oinstall)
$ sqlplus / as sysdba
```

In Windows environments, you can verify which OS users belong to the ora_dba group as follows: select Start ➤ Control Panel ➤ Administrative Tools ➤ Computer Management ➤ Local Users and Groups ➤ Groups. You should see a group named something like ora_dba. You can click that group and view which OS users are assigned to it.

Additionally, for OS authentication to work in Windows environments, you must have the following entry in your sqlnet.ora file:

```
SQLNET.AUTHENTICATION_SERVICES=(NTS)
```

Explaining Password File Authentication

You can also use a password file to authenticate users connecting to the database as sysdba or sysoper. To implement a password file, you need to perform the following steps:

1. Create the password file with the orapwd utility.

2. Set the initialization parameter remote_password_file to EXCLUSIVE.

In a Unix environment, you can use the orapwd utility to create a password file as follows:

```
$ cd $ORACLE_HOME/dbs
$ orapwd file=orapw<ORACLE_SID> password=<sys password>
```

In a Unix environment, the password file is usually stored in ORACLE_HOME/dbs, and in Windows, it's typically placed in the ORACLE_HOME\database directory. The format of the filename that you specify in the previous command may vary by OS. For example, on Windows the format is PWD<ORACLE_SID>.ora. The following shows the syntax in a Windows environment:

```
c:\> cd %ORACLE_HOME%\database
c:\> orapwd file=PWD<ORACLE_SID>.ora password=<sys password>
```

To enable the use of the password file, set the initialization parameter remote_login_passwordfile to EXCLUSIVE. Setting this value to EXCLUSIVE instructs Oracle to allow only one instance to connect to the database and also specifies that the password file can contain schemas other than sys. Table 2-2 details the meanings of the possible values for remote_login_password.

Table 2-2. *Values for* remote_login_passwordfile

Value	Meaning
EXCLUSIVE	One instance can connect to the database. Users other than sys can be in the password file.
SHARED	Multiple databases can share a password file; sys is the only user allowed in the password file. Oracle will throw an ORA-01999 if you attempt to grant sysdba to a user when the value is set to SHARED.
NONE	Oracle ignores the password file. Only local privileged accounts can connect as sysdba.

Once the password file is created and enabled, you can then log into SQL*Plus as sys as follows:

```
$ sqlplus sys/<sys password> as sysdba
```

One potential issue with the previous example is that in Unix environments you can see the password by inspecting the process description via the ps command as follows:

```
$ ps -ef | grep sqlplus
```

To prevent people from viewing the password in the process description, you can alternatively connect to sys after you've started SQL*Plus as follows:

```
$ sqlplus /nolog
SQL> connect sys/<sys password> as sysdba
```

You can add users to the password file via the grant sysdba command. The following example grants the sysdba privilege and adds the user heera to the password file:

```
SQL> grant sysdba to heera;
Grant succeeded.
```

Enabling a password file also allows you to connect to your database remotely with sysdba privileges via an Oracle Net connection. This allows you to do remote maintenance that would otherwise require you to physically log on to the database server.

■**Tip** You can query the V$PWFILE_USERS view to display users granted sysdba and sysoper privileges.

2-2. Starting and Stopping Your Database

Problem

You want to start or stop your Oracle database.

Solution

Connect to the database with a privileged user account, and issue the startup and shutdown statements. If you're not sure which account you should use, refer to recipe 1-2 for details on connecting to your database. The following example uses OS authentication to connect to the database:

```
$ sqlplus / as sysdba
```

After you are connected as a privileged account, you can now start up your database as follows:

```
SQL> startup;
```

However, if the parameter file (pfile or spfile) is not located in ORACLE_HOME/dbs for Unix or in ORACLE_HOME\database for Windows, then you have to include the `pfile` clause as follows:

```
SQL> startup pfile=C:\temp\initORCL.ora
```

You should then see messages from Oracle indicating that the system global area (SGA) has been allocated and the database is mounted and then opened:

```
ORACLE instance started.
Total System Global Area  289406976 bytes
Fixed Size                 11235813 bytes
Variable Size              31415926 bytes
Database Buffers          192937984 bytes
Redo Buffers                1235711 bytes
Database mounted.
Database opened.
```

You can use the `shutdown immediate` statement to stop a database. The `immediate` parameter instructs Oracle to halt database activity and roll back any open transactions:

```
SQL> shutdown immediate;

Database closed.
Database dismounted.
ORACLE instance shut down.
```

For a detailed definition of the parameters available with the `shutdown` statement, refer to Table 2-3. In most cases, `shutdown immediate` is an acceptable method of shutting down your database.

Table 2-3. *Parameters Available with the* shutdown *Command*

Parameter	Meaning
NORMAL	Wait for users to log out of active sessions before shutting down.
TRANSACTIONAL	Wait for transactions to finish and then terminate the session.
IMMEDIATE	Immediately terminate active sessions; open transactions are rolled back.
ABORT	Instance terminates immediately; transactions are terminated and are not rolled back.

How It Works

Starting and stopping your database is a fairly simple process. If the environment is set up correctly, you should be able to connect to your database and issue the appropriate `startup` and `shutdown` statements. You should rarely need to use the `shutdown abort` statement. Usually `shutdown abort` is required only when you can't shut down your database with one of the other options.

■**Note** Stopping and restarting your database in quick succession is known colloquially in the DBA world as *bouncing your database.*

2-3. Toggling Archivelog Mode

Problem

You attempted to use RMAN to back up your database and received this error message:

```
RMAN-03009: failure of backup command on ORA_DISK_1 channel
ORA-19602: cannot backup or copy active file in NOARCHIVELOG mode
```

This message indicates that before you can create an RMAN online backup, you need to place your database into archivelog mode.

Solution

To place your database in archivelog mode, perform the following steps:

1. Connect as sysdba.

2. Shut down your database.

3. Start up in mount mode.

4. Alter the database into archivelog mode.

5. Open your database for use.

If you want to disable archivelog mode, then you would execute all the previous steps, with one change; in step 4, you will need to use the noarchivelog parameter (instead of archivelog mode).

Enabling Archivelog Mode

You first need to connect to your database with a schema that has sysdba privileges (usually the sys schema). The following example connects as sys and then issues the commands to enable archivelog mode:

```
SQL> connect sys/chaya as sysdba
SQL> shutdown immediate;
SQL> startup mount;
SQL> alter database archivelog;
SQL> alter database open;
```

Disabling Archivelog Mode

If for some reason you want to disable archiving, issue these commands:

```
SQL> connect sys/chaya as sysdba
SQL> shutdown immediate;
```

```
SQL> startup mount;
SQL> alter database noarchivelog;
SQL> alter database open;
```

■Note If you have enabled the flashback database feature, you must first disable it before you can disable archivelog mode.

Displaying Archive Information

After you have changed the archivelog mode of your database, you might want to verify that the mode has been set properly. To display the status of archiving, you can query V$DATABASE as follows:

```
SQL> select log_mode from v$database;
LOG_MODE
--------------------
ARCHIVELOG
```

The SQL*Plus archive log list command displays a useful summary of the archiving configuration of your database. As shown in the following output, it includes information such as the archivelog mode, automatic archiving, archive destination, and log sequence numbers.

```
SQL> archive log list;
Database log mode              Archive Mode
Automatic archival             Enabled
Archive destination            /ora_archive/smtst3
Oldest online log sequence     87950
Next log sequence to archive   87952
Current log sequence           87952
```

Enabling archivelog mode is a prerequisite for online backups. The previous commands give you a quick way to verify the archivelog mode status of your database.

How It Works

Your database is required to be in archivelog mode for online backups. This is because RMAN will return an error if you attempt to take an online backup when your database isn't in archivelog mode.

Archivelog mode is the mechanism that allows you to recover all committed transactions. This mode protects your database from disk failure because your transaction information can be restored and recovered from the archived redo log files. Archivelog mode ensures that after every online redo log switch that the contents of the logs are successfully copied to archived redo log files.

When in archivelog mode, Oracle will not allow an online redo log file to be overwritten until it is copied to an archived redo log file. If Oracle cannot copy an online redo log file to an archived redo log file, then your database will stop processing and hang. Therefore, it's critical that you have a strategy to manage the available free space where the archived redo log files are being stored.

Prior to Oracle Database 10*g*, you were also required to enable automatic archiving. Automatic archiving tells Oracle to automatically create an archived redo log file when the online redo log file becomes full. With Oracle Database 10*g* and newer, it is no longer necessary to enable automatic archiving via setting the `archive_log_start` parameter. The `archive_log_start` parameter has been deprecated, and automatic archiving in Oracle Database 10*g* is enabled by default.

■**Tip** Enabling archivelog mode is like making an immutable rule that the commode must be flushed before it can be used again. Enabling automatic archiving is like putting in place the flushing mechanism and automatically having the commode flush after it has been filled.

2-4. Connecting to RMAN

Problem

You want to connect to RMAN and prepare to perform backup and recovery tasks.

Solution

To connect to RMAN, you need to establish the following:

- OS environment variables

- Access to a privileged operating system (OS) account or schema with `sysdba` privileges

These are the same conditions that need to be in place before connecting to your database and that are described in recipe 2-1. If you haven't already done so, review recipe 2-1 and ensure that you have the proper OS variables set and that you have access to a privileged account.

You can connect to RMAN either through the operating system command-line interface or through Enterprise Manager (EM). Using EM for backup and recovery is covered in Chapter 19 of this book. This chapter uses the command-line interface for its examples.

■**Tip** Even if you use the EM GUI, it's useful to understand the RMAN commands used for backup and recovery operations. This knowledge can be particularly useful when debugging and troubleshooting problems.

The following example assumes you have logged on to a Unix server using the `oracle` account. You can then invoke RMAN and connect to the target database as follows:

```
$ rman target /
```

You should see output that is similar to the following:

```
Recovery Manager: Release 11.1.0.4.0 - Beta on Fri May 11 15:24:55 2007
Copyright (c) 1982, 2005, Oracle.  All rights reserved.
connected to target database: ORCL (DBID=1109210542)
```

If you're using a password file, then you might need to specify the username and password:

```
$ rman target sys/<sys password>
```

If you're accessing your target database remotely via Oracle Net, then you will need to specify a connection string as follows:

```
$ rman target sys/<sys password>@<database connection string>
```

You can also invoke RMAN and then connect to your target database as a second step, from the RMAN prompt:

```
$ rman
RMAN> connect target /
```

■**Note** When connecting to RMAN, you do not have to specify the `as sysdba` clause. This is because RMAN *always* requires that you connect as a user with `sysdba` privileges. Therefore, you must connect to RMAN with either a user that is OS authenticated or a username/password that is in the password file. This is unlike SQL*Plus, where you have the option of connecting as a nonprivileged user. In SQL*Plus, if you want to connect as a user with `sysdba` privileges, you are required to specify the `as sysdba` clause.

While connected as RMAN, you can start up and shut down your target database:

```
RMAN> startup
RMAN> shutdown immediate
```

To exit RMAN, enter the `exit` command as follows:

```
RMAN> exit
```

How It Works

Before you can connect to RMAN, you need to ensure that you have the proper OS variables set and that you have access to an account with `sysdba` privileges. Once those are in place, then you can start RMAN and connect to your target database via the `rman` command-line utility.

You can also issue commands to start up and shut down your database directly from RMAN. This saves you the inconvenience of having to jump back and forth between SQL*Plus and RMAN. You'll see in other recipes throughout the book that many SQL*Plus commands can be run directly from within RMAN.

2-5. Backing Up Your Database

Problem

You're new to RMAN, and you want to back up your database. You just need to get a backup created, and you want to take the simplest possible approach.

Solution

Start the rman utility, connect to your target database, and use the backup command to back up your entire database:

```
$ rman target /
RMAN> backup database;
```

You should now see a list of RMAN messages displaying information about which files are being backed up and to which file and location. Here's an abbreviated portion of that output:

```
Starting backup at 19-OCT-06
using target database control file instead of recovery catalog
allocated channel: ORA_DISK_1
channel ORA_DISK_1: sid=152 devtype=DISK
channel ORA_DISK_1: starting full datafile backupset
channel ORA_DISK_1: specifying datafile(s) in backupset
```

To display information about your backup, use the list backup command as follows:

```
RMAN> list backup;
```

Here's a partial snippet of the output that you can expect to see:

```
List of Backup Sets
===================
BS Key  Type LV Size       Device Type Elapsed Time Completion Time
------- ---- -- ---------- ----------- ------------ ---------------
391     Full   106.04M    DISK         00:00:49     19-OCT-06
        BP Key: 392    Status: AVAILABLE  Compressed: NO  Tag: TAG20070311T19474
```

■**Tip** By default RMAN displays the date information only. To include the time information in the RMAN output, we recommend that you set the NLS_DATE_FORMAT=DD-MON-RRRR HH24:MI:SS at the OS level prior to running RMAN. This is useful especially when checking the exact RMAN backup completion date and time as generated in the RMAN log.

How It Works

Backing up a database with RMAN was designed to be simple. All the required configuration settings are automatically set to sensible defaults. Therefore, you can perform basic backup and recovery tasks without any configuration of your RMAN environment.

By default RMAN will allocate a channel and backup to a default location on disk. The default location is operating system dependent. The list backup command will show you where the backup files are located.

If you want to specify a location for your backup pieces, you can specify this either by enabling a flash recovery area as described in recipe 3-1 or by specifically setting the backup location through the format command described in recipe 5-13.

2-6. Simulating a Failure

Problem

You want to simulate a failure as a prelude to testing RMAN's restore and recovery capabilities.

Solution

To simulate a failure, perform the following steps:

1. Ensure you have a backup.

2. Determine the location and name of a datafile to rename. You will simulate failure by renaming a datafile so that it appears to have been lost.

3. Stop the database.

4. Rename a datafile at the OS level (simulates media failure).

5. Attempt to start the database.

Before simulating a media failure, ensure that you're in a noncritical test database environment and that you have a good RMAN backup of your database. Run the following command in your target database, and ensure that you have a good backup:

```
RMAN> connect target /
RMAN> list backup;
```

■**Caution** If no backup information is listed, then stop here. You need to ensure that you have a good backup of your database before you simulate media failure.

Determine the location of a target database datafile so that you can rename it to simulate media failure:

```
RMAN> report schema;
```

Shown next is an abbreviated portion of the output of the previous command. This shows the name of the file that you're going to rename.

```
File Size(MB) Tablespace          RB segs Datafile Name
---- -------- ------------------- ------- --------------------------
4    22       USERS               ***     C:\ORA01\BRDSTN\USERS01.DBF
```

Note the location and name of a datafile in your target database for which you want to simulate media failure. Next, shut down your target database, and rename the datafile.

```
RMAN> shutdown immediate;
RMAN> exit
```

This example uses the Windows move command to rename the users01.dbf datafile:

```
C:\> move c:\ora01\BRDSTN\users01.dbf  c:\ora01\BRDSTN\users01.bk
```

If you were in a Unix environment, you would use the Unix mv command to rename the datafile as follows:

```
$  mv /ora01/BRDSTN/users01.dbf  /ora01/BRDSTN/users.bk
```

Once the datafile has been renamed, attempt to start your database as follows:

```
RMAN> connect target /
RMAN> startup
```

You should see a message similar to the following:

```
RMAN-03002: failure of startup command at 10/19/2006 16:13:07
ORA-01157: cannot identify/lock data file 4 - see DBWR trace file
ORA-01110: data file 4: 'C:\ORA01\BRDSTN\USERS01.DBF'
```

How It Works

To simulate media failure, you can rename a datafile at the OS level on your target database server. After the datafile has been renamed, when Oracle starts up, it reads the control file and compares the information to all the datafile headers. If Oracle can't find a datafile, it will display a message indicating that it can't find the file. You won't be able to open your target database until you restore and recover your database.

2-7. Restoring and Recovering Your Database

Problem

You've experienced a failure and want to use RMAN to restore and recover your database. You have a current and good backup in the default location, and all needed control files, archived redo log files, and online redo log files are available.

Solution

Connect to RMAN, and use the following commands to restore and recover your database. In this recipe you'll perform the following steps:

1. Connect to the target database.

2. Mount the database.

3. Restore the database.

4. Recover the database.

5. Open the database.

To keep this example as simple as possible, we'll show how to restore and recover the entire database.

```
RMAN> connect target /
RMAN> startup mount;
RMAN> restore database;
```

You'll see several lines of output as RMAN tells you what it is restoring. It should look something like the following:

```
Starting restore at 19-OCT-06
allocated channel: ORA_DISK_1
channel ORA_DISK_1: sid=156 devtype=DISK
channel ORA_DISK_1: specifying datafile(s) to restore from backup set
restoring datafile 00001 to C:\ORA01\BRDSTN\SYSTEM01.DBF
restoring datafile 00002 to C:\ORA01\BRDSTN\UNDOTBS01.DBF
restoring datafile 00003 to C:\ORA01\BRDSTN\SYSAUX01.DBF
restoring datafile 00004 to C:\ORA01\BRDSTN\USERS01.DBF
```

Next recover your database as follows:

```
RMAN> recover database;
```

You should see a message similar to this:

```
Starting recover at 19-OCT-06
using channel ORA_DISK_1
starting media recovery
media recovery complete, elapsed time: 00:00:07
Finished recover at 19-OCT-06
```

You can now open your database for use with the alter database open command:

```
RMAN> alter database open;
database opened
```

How It Works

If you have a good backup of your database, it's fairly simple to use RMAN to restore and recover your database. RMAN uses information stored in the control file to determine where to retrieve backups and which files to restore and recover.

Restore and recovery are two separate steps. *Restore* is the process of copying back datafiles from the backup files. *Recovery* is the process of applying transaction information to the datafiles to recover them to the state they were in just before the failure occurred.

■Tip Restore and recovery are analogous to the healing process when you break a bone. Restoring is similar to the process of setting the broken bone back to its original position. This is like restoring the datafiles from a backup and placing them in their original locations. Recovering a datafile is similar to the healing process that recovers the bone back to its state before it was broken. When you recover your datafiles, you apply transactions (stored in the redo files) to get the datafiles back to the state they were in before the media failure took place.

RMAN ships with practical default values that allow you to use it immediately to back up, restore, and recover your database. Although these default settings are reasonable, you'll want to read the subsequent chapters in this book for best practices on how to configure RMAN for an industrial-strength backup and recovery strategy.

CHAPTER 3

■■■

Using the Flash Recovery Area

In Chapter 2 you learned how to take an RMAN backup to a storage location on the disk. Disk-based backup offers significant benefits over backing up to tape, such as a considerably faster backup (and an even faster recovery), the ability to merge backups to make the recovery quicker, the constant validation of incremental backups, and so on. In subsequent chapters, you will learn more about those operations.

One of the important considerations in the process of setting up a disk-based backup is the location of the backup. You can choose any location, such as a filesystem, a directory on a filesystem or an ASM disk group, or a directory under a disk group. The only requirement is that the location must be visible to and writable by the instance performing the backup.

Another important consideration is the management of the space inside the disk-based backup location. You, as the DBA, must ensure that the location has enough free space to hold all the backups required—backups of datafiles, archivelogs, and so on. When new backups require more space, it's your responsibility to make sure the space is available, which you can archive by either adding space or deleting redundant backups. If you choose the latter, you must decide which files are redundant.

What if Oracle Database did all the work for you? It can, if you let it know the location to use. In Oracle Database 10*g* Release 1 and newer, you can define a special area on disk called the *flash recovery area* (FRA) that is used by the database as a backup location. By default, RMAN creates backups of all types—regular backup sets, image copies, and archivelogs—in that area. Since RMAN knows about the existence of this area, it automatically deletes unneeded backups (based on redundancy and retention periods) to make room for new backups.

In addition to backups, the flash recovery area can also store online redo log files, archived redo log files, and control files. Again, these are optional; you can always define the location of those files to be anywhere, not necessarily inside the flash recovery area. Since the flash recovery area is generally used for backup files, you should consider creating it on disks different from your main database disks. Doing so helps protect you from losing both your main database and your backup files from a single failure. You can further take advantage of this probability by putting one member of the redo log group or one control file on the flash recovery area. This reduces the possibility of all members of a redo log group or all control files getting damaged at the same time.

3-1. Creating the Flash Recovery Area

Problem

You want to create the flash recovery area for your database.

Solution

Before creating the flash recovery area, you should decide the following:

- Where you want the FRA to be created

- How much space should be allocated to the FRA

Having the answers to these questions in mind, you can then use the following process to create the flash recovery area:

1. Disable the parameters log_archive_dest and log_archive_duplex_dest, if they are set in the database. You can do that by issuing the following commands:

```
alter system set log_archive_duplex_dest = '';
alter system set log_archive_dest = '';
```

2. Log on as a user with the sysdba role (such as the user sys) in preparation to create the flash recovery area:

```
sqlplus / as sysdba (if logged in as the Oracle software owner)
sqlplus sys/<PasswordOfUserSys> as sysdba
```

3. Issue the following commands to size and create the flash recovery area:

```
alter system set db_recovery_size = 4G;
alter system set db_recovery_dest = '/home/oracle/flasharea';
```

The sequence of these commands is important; you have to issue them in that order, not the reverse. However, do replace the size and path name with the values you have chosen for your system.

That's it; the flash recovery area is ready for operation.

How It Works

The issues of location and size are key to creating a flash recovery area. The location issue is straightforward if you use a single-instance database. Any location, as long as it's a directory (or a filesystem) should be acceptable as the FRA. If you use ASM, you can use a disk group as the FRA as well. You can also use the same disk group you use for the database files. However, you cannot use a raw device.

To decide the size of the FRA, use the detailed analysis shown in recipe 3-16.

As a best practice, you should avoid putting the flash recovery area and the database files on the same mount point (if a filesystem) or disk group (if on ASM). This way a failure in the underlying physical disks will not affect both the database files and the FRA files at the same time. You thus ensure your ability to quickly recover from a failure by again pointing the damaged datafile to the copy in the flash recovery area.

Remember, you can always define a different location for archived redo logs. If you use a different location, then you can't just erase the values of the parameters log_archive_dest and log_archive_duplex_dest, as suggested in the earlier solution:

```
alter system set log_archive_duplex_dest = '';
alter system set log_archive_dest = '';
```

To place your log files elsewhere than the flash recovery area, you should use a different parameter to specify the archived redo log location; use log_archive_dest_1 instead of log_archive_dest. Suppose log_archive_dest used to be /dbarch. You can use log_archive_dest_1 to specify the same location for archived redo logs.

First, check the value of the parameter log_archive_dest:

```
SQL>show parameter log_archive_dest
```

NAME	TYPE	VALUE
log_archive_dest	string	/dbarch

The current setting of the archived redo log destination is /dbarch. Next, set the log_archive_dest_1 parameter to that location:

```
SQL> alter system set log_archive_dest_1 = 'location=/dbarch';
```

Note the different syntax for this parameter; it has a location clause. Now, set log_archive_dest to NULL:

```
SQL> alter system set log_archive_dest = '';
```

If you have set the two parameters—log_archive_dest and log_archive_duplex_dest—in the initialization parameter file, you should edit the file to remove these two parameters completely. Remember to recycle the database after editing the file for the changes to take effect.

3-2. Writing Regular RMAN Backups to the FRA

Problem

Now that you have configured a flash recovery area, you want RMAN to use it when creating disk-based backups.

Solution

You can easily make RMAN store backups in the flash recovery area. Here are the steps to follow:

1. Start RMAN:

```
$ rman
Recovery Manager: Release 10.2.0.1.0 - Production on Fri Sep 29 01:20:19 2006

Copyright (c) 1982, 2005, Oracle.  All rights reserved.

RMAN>
```

2. Connect to the target database:

```
RMAN> connect target /
connected to target database: PRODB2 (DBID=524826567)
```

3. Now, initiate a backup without specifying a format option:

```
RMAN> backup database;
Starting backup at 09-OCT-06
starting full resync of recovery catalog
full resync complete
allocated channel: ORA_DISK_1
channel ORA_DISK_1: sid=134 devtype=DISK
channel ORA_DISK_1: starting full datafile backupset
channel ORA_DISK_1: specifying datafile(s) in backupset
input datafile fno=00001 name=/home/oracle/oradata/PRODB2/SYSTEM.dbf
input datafile fno=00003 name=/home/oracle/oradata/PRODB2/SYSAUX.dbf
input datafile fno=00005 name=/home/oracle/oradata/PRODB2/EXAMPLE.dbf
input datafile fno=00002 name=/home/oracle/oradata/PRODB2/UNDOTBS1.dbf
input datafile fno=00004 name=/home/oracle/oradata/PRODB2/USERS.dbf
channel ORA_DISK_1: starting piece 1 at 09-OCT-06
channel ORA_DISK_1: finished piece 1 at 09-OCT-06
piece handle=/home/oracle/flasharea/PRODB2/backupset/2006_10_09/➡
o1_mf_nnndf_TAG20061009T200113_2lorpcgq_.bkp tag=TAG➡
20061009T200113 comment=NONE
channel ORA_DISK_1: backup set complete, elapsed time: 00:01:57
Finished backup at 09-OCT-06

Starting Control File Autobackup at 09-OCT-06
piece handle=/home/oracle/flasharea/PRODB2/autobackup/2006_10_09/➡
o1_mf_n_603403392_2lort11n_.bkp comment=NONE
Finished Control File Autobackup at 09-OCT-06

RMAN>
```

Note the command in step 3 carefully; you issued just the backup database command. You specified nothing else—no channel creation, no format, nothing. Since you have defined a flash recovery area, the backups go in there by default. Of course, you can issue a format command and use channels to redirect the backup to a different location, but the flash recovery area provides greater control if you choose to place the backups there.

How It Works

The solution in this recipe creates backup sets under the directory specified as the flash recovery area. Note the output carefully and, more specifically, the following line:

```
handle=/home/oracle/flasharea/PRODB2/backupset/2006_10_09/o1_mf_nnndf_➥
TAG20061009T200113_2lorpcgq_.bkp tag=TAG20061009T200113
```

This line of output shows the file created by the RMAN backup process. The file is named o1_mf_nnndf_TAG20061009T200113_2lorpcgq_.bkp, which is a pretty strange name in any language. This is what is known as an *Oracle managed file*. Ordinarily, you don't need to worry about the name since Oracle manages the file on your behalf—it creates the file with a unique name, deletes the file when not needed, and so on. Since you don't deal with it, the daunting name does not sound so daunting after all.

Also note the directory in which the backup file was stored. Remember, you set the flash recovery area in recipe 3-1 to /home/oracle/flasharea. The RMAN backup process created a subdirectory called PRODB2, the same name as the database you are backing up. This way, you can use the same flash recovery area for as many databases as you want. Under the directory corresponding to a database name, Oracle creates several other directories:

backupset: This subdirectory is for RMAN regular backups.

datafile: This subdirectory is for RMAN image copies.

autobackup: This subdirectory is for control file autobackups.

flashback: If your database runs in flashback mode, you will see flashback logs in this subdirectory.

archivelog: Archived redo logs can optionally be stored in the FRA (recipe 3-6). If so, they go in this subdirectory.

controlfile: The control file, if configured to go to the flash recovery area (recipe 3-8), goes in this subdirectory.

onlinelog: Online redo logs can also be made to go to the flash recovery area (recipe 3-9). In that case, they go in this subdirectory.

Under each of the directory's backupset, autobackup, and archivelog, Oracle also creates a subdirectory named per the date of the backup in the format YYYY_MM_DD (2006_10_06, in this case indicating October 6, 2006). So on another day, the backup goes into a different directory. Oracle creates all these directories and subdirectories automatically.

■**Note** Even if you see that the flash recovery area is filled up close to the size you specified in the initialization parameter db_recovery_file_dest_size (4GB in this case), never delete files manually to make room. Oracle automatically removes any files unnecessary for a subsequent recovery operation. Later in this chapter you will learn how to see the contents of the flash recovery area.

3-3. Freeing FRA Space in an Emergency

Problem

The flashback recovery area has run out of space. You see a message in the alert log similar to the following:

```
Can not open flashback thread because there is no more space in flash recovery area
```

If the database has aborted earlier because of any flashback errors and you attempt to start it, you get the following error:

```
SQL> alter database open;
alter database open
*
ERROR at line 1:
ORA-38760: This database instance failed to turn on flashback database
```

You want to correct the problem, or at least shut the flashback down so that the normal database operations can continue.

There are three solutions. Which to choose depends upon the nature of the emergency and the resources you have at your disposal.

Solution 1: Increase Space

You can increase the size of the flashback area dynamically. To increase it to, say, 10GB, you would issue the following:

```
SQL> alter system set db_recovery_file_dest_size = 10G;
```

By the way, the converse is also possible; you can reduce the FRA size using this command, although that will not solve the problem addressed in this recipe.

Solution 2: Remove Restore Points

The alternative to increasing the size of the flashback area is to remove some of the older restore points that you no longer need. The following is a query to list the restore points you currently have:

```
SQL> col name format a25
SQL> select name, storage_size
  2* from v$restore_point;

NAME                      STORAGE_SIZE
------------------------- ------------
RP0                          207028224
RP1                                  0
RP2                          915701760
PRE_TEST1                            0
POST_TEST1                           0
GOOD_ONE                             0
QA_GOLD                              0
```

```
BRANCH_1                        0
AFTER_BRANCH_2                  0
AFTER_BRANCH_3                  0

10 rows selected.
```

These results show that restore points RP0 and RP2 have storage associated with them. This is because they are *guaranteed restore points* (see "How It Works" for an explanation of what that means). You should remove them to make some room in the flash recovery area. To remove a restore point, issue a `drop restore point` command:

```
SQL> drop restore point rp2;

Restore point dropped.

SQL> drop restore point rp0;

Restore point dropped.
```

Dropping restore point should clear up space, and you may be able to start the database.

Solution 3: Disable Flashback

If solutions 1 and 2 fail or are not applicable, you may want to disable flashback in the database temporarily. First shut down the database (if not down already):

```
SQL> shutdown immediate
Database closed.
Database dismounted.
ORACLE instance shut down.
```

Then start the database in mount mode:

```
SQL> startup mount
ORACLE instance started.

Total System Global Area  167772160 bytes
Fixed Size                  1218316 bytes
Variable Size              67111156 bytes
Database Buffers           96468992 bytes
Redo Buffers                2973696 bytes
Database mounted.
```

Then disable flashback in the database:

```
SQL> alter database flashback off;
Database altered.
```

This will stop the flashback operations and will stop generating flashback logs. This should reduce the space requirement on the flash recovery area. To free up some space, you may want to delete some more files such as archived redo logs, unneeded backups, and so on. In RMAN, delete these:

```
$ rman target=/
Recovery Manager: Release 10.2.0.1.0 - Production on Mon Oct 2 09:46:55 2006

Copyright (c) 1982, 2005, Oracle.  All rights reserved.

connected to target database: DBA102 (DBID=950528201, not open)
RMAN> delete noprompt archivelog all;
allocated channel: ORA_DISK_1
channel ORA_DISK_1: sid=41 devtype=DISK

List of Archived Log Copies
Key      Thrd Seq      S Low Time    Name
------- ---- ------- - --------- ----
75       1    10       A 08-AUG-06 +USERDG3/dba102/archivelog/➥
2006_10_02/thread_1_seq_10.536.602760807
74       1    11       A 09-AUG-06 +USERDG3/dba102/archivelog/➥
2006_10_02/thread_1_seq_11.504.602760809
… and so on …
deleted archive log
archive log
filename=+USERDG3/dba102/archivelog/2006_10_02/thread_1_seq_10.536.60276➥
0807 recid=75 stamp=602760817
deleted archive log
archive log
filename=+USERDG3/dba102/archivelog/2006_10_02/thread_1_seq_11.504.60276➥
0809 recid=74 stamp=602760813
… and so on …
```

Similarly, you may want to delete copies of the database and backup sets:

```
RMAN> delete noprompt backup of database;
RMAN> delete noprompt copy of database;
```

Now, open the database. Logging in as sys in SQL*Plus, issue the following:

```
SQL> alter database open;
Database altered.
 SQL> exit
```

The database is now fully functional, but without the flashback ability. If you want to reenable flashback later, you can do so. Because you've cleared unneeded files, the flash recovery area is fully usable whenever you choose to again enable flashback. Until then, you can always back up the database using RMAN without a flashback recovery area.

How It Works

The first solution is easy to understand. It merely increased the flash recovery area's size to accommodate the new contents.

In the second solution, you removed restore points. Restore points are created by executing SQL statements such as the following:

```
SQL> create restore point rp1;
```

This statement creates a named point in time to which you can flash back the database, through the SQL statement (provided, of course, that you have turned on the flashback for the database). Once you have a restore point, you can rewind or flash back to that point in time using a statement such as this:

```
SQL> flashback database to rp1;
```

There are two types of restore points—*normal* and *guaranteed*. The preceding example of creating a restore point creates a normal one. You may be able to flash back to that point, provided enough flashback logs are available. If the flashback logs are not available (perhaps because the space in the flashback recovery area ran out and Oracle had to delete some flashback logs to make room for the newer occupants), then your flashback operation will fail. The solution—a guaranteed restore point. To create a guaranteed restore point, you will have to specifically ask for the guarantee:

```
SQL> create guaranteed restore point rp1;
```

A guaranteed restore point stores information needed to flash back in a special way. When space pressures in the flash recovery area force the database to remove the unneeded files, flashback logs are the first to go, unless these are for a guaranteed restore point. The flashback logs of the guaranteed restore points are stored even when the flash recovery area runs out of space. The only way to reclaim the space is to drop the guaranteed restore point. Dropping the guaranteed restore points frees up that space.

■**Note** Disabling flashback on the database does not remove the space occupied by the guaranteed restore points. Once the damaging situation has been cleared, you will want to start the flashback option again.

3-4. Checking Space Usage in the FRA

Problem

After setting up the flash recovery area, you want to check on the types of files that are present inside, and you want to report on the space occupied by each type of file.

Solution

The data dictionary view V$RECOVERY_FILE_DEST shows the sum of various types of files in the flash recovery area in terms of percentages of the total space. It has only one row. Here is an example of how you can use the view:

```
SQL>select * from v$recovery_file_dest;

NAME
-------------------------------------------------------------

SPACE_LIMIT SPACE_USED SPACE_RECLAIMABLE NUMBER_OF_FILES
----------- ---------- ----------------- ---------------
/home/oracle/flasharea
 2147483648 1359345152           7487488              50
```

To see space used by different types of files in the flash recovery area, you should check the view V$FLASH_RECOVERY_AREA_USAGE. Here is an example of how you can see the contents of the flash recovery area:

```
SQL> select * from v$flash_recovery_area_usage;

FILE_TYPE     PERCENT_SPACE_USED PERCENT_SPACE_RECLAIMABLE NUMBER_OF_FILES
------------- ------------------ ------------------------- ---------------
CONTROLFILE                    0                         0               0
ONLINELOG                      0                         0               0
ARCHIVELOG                  6.07                         0               6
BACKUPPIECE                   .7                       .35               2
IMAGECOPY                  48.58                         0               5
FLASHBACKLOG                8.14                      7.95              37
```

Note the number of files of each category. The sum of the total number of files (6 + 2 + 5 + 37) equals 50, as shown in the previous example querying V$RECOVERY_FILE_DEST.

V$FLASH_RECOVERY_AREA_USAGE shows the percentages of the total space consumed, not the space itself. You may want to join it to V$RECOVERY_FILE_DEST to see the total space occupied by each type of file, as shown here:

```
select
  file_type,
  space_used*percent_space_used/100/1024/1024 used,
  space_reclaimable*percent_space_reclaimable/100/1024/1024 reclaimable,
  frau.number_of_files
from v$recovery_file_dest rfd, v$flash_recovery_area_usage frau;

FILE_TYPE          USED RECLAIMABLE NUMBER_OF_FILES
------------- --------- ----------- ---------------
CONTROLFILE         .00         .00               0
ONLINELOG           .00         .00               0
ARCHIVELOG       664.86      547.20              34
```

BACKUPPIECE	573.23	520.73	16
IMAGECOPY	.00	.00	0
FLASHBACKLOG	6.07	.00	1

The report generated by this example may prove to be a more useful display of the space occupancy inside the flash recovery area compared to information in the view V$FLASH_RECOVERY_AREA_USAGE. The key is to understand how much space is left as reclaimable. By observing this view for a while, you should be able to figure out how much space is necessary for a day's backup. If that much space is not available as reclaimable, then you may run out of space later. If you detect an impending shortage of space, you can mark some of the old backups as expired, or you can extend the space in the flash recovery area.

How It Works

Table 3-1 and Table 3-2 describe the columns in the two V$ views used in the solution. Both the views display useful information, but they are not useful individually. For instance, the view V$FLASH_RECOVERY_AREA_USAGE displays information on the percentage of space used, but not the value whose percentage is referred. That total value is found in V$RECOVERY_FILE_DEST, in the column PERCENT_SPACE_USED. Joining the two views yields more useful information than either does separately.

Table 3-1. *Columns of the View V$RECOVERY_FILE_DEST*

Column Name	Contents
NAME	This is the directory used as the flash recovery area. In case an ASM disk group is used, then this is the name of the disk group.
SPACE_LIMIT	This is the total space allocated to the flash recovery area.
SPACE_USED	This is the total space used right now.
SPACE_RECLAIMABLE	When all the space is consumed in the flash recovery area, Oracle must remove the redundant files to make room for the newer backups. The total space contained in these redundant files is shown here.
NUMBER_OF_FILES	This is the total number of files present in the flash recovery area.

Table 3-2. *Columns of the View V$FLASH_RECOVERY_AREA_USAGE*

Column Name	Contents
FILE_TYPE	This is the type of the files, such as a control file.
PERCENT_SPACE_USED	This is the total space occupied by that type of file as a percentage of the total space allocated to the flash recovery area.
PERCENT_SPACE_RECLAIMABLE	Of the total space, this is how much (a percentage) is reclaimable because of the redundant backups.
NUMBER_OF_FILES	This is the total number of files of that type.

3-5. Expanding or Shrinking the FRA

Problem

From time to time you may need to expand your flash recovery area. Expansion may be required because of a variety of reasons—the size of the database keeps increasing, or you may want to increase the retention period, leaving more backups in the flash recovery area and reducing the reclaimable space.

Solution

To increase space in the flash recovery area, just use the command shown in the following example:

```
SQL> alter system set db_recovery_file_dest_size = 2G;

System altered.
```

This example sets the maximum size of flash recovery area to 2GB. You can use the same command to reduce space as well. For example:

```
alter system set db_recovery_file_dest_size = 1G;
```

The flash recovery area size has now been reduced from 2GB to 1GB.

How It Works

The alter system set db_recovery_file_dest_size command expands or shrinks the allocated space in the flash recovery area. There is something important you have to know, though: if you are shrinking the flash recovery area and if the total space occupied in the flash recovery area is more than your new, lower target value, then the command to shrink succeeds; however, the files in the flash recovery area are not deleted, keeping the total space occupied at more than the new target.

Returning to the example shown in this recipe's solution, the following query illustrates the shrinkage issue we've just described. Remember, flash recovery space has just been reduced to 1GB:

```
SQL> select * from v$recovery_file_dest;

NAME
-----------------------------------------------------------

SPACE_LIMIT SPACE_USED SPACE_RECLAIMABLE NUMBER_OF_FILES
----------- ---------- ----------------- ---------------
/home/oracle/flasharea
 1073741824 1391670784                 0              59
```

Note the column SPACE_USED is about 1.3GB, whereas the column SPACE_LIMIT is 1GB, which is less than the space actually used. Also note that the column SPACE_RECLAIMABLE, which shows the space that can be freed up should the new backups need space, is zero, indicating that there is no room for any additional backup. At this time, if you decide to take any backup, however small, you will receive an error, as shown in the following attempt to get a backup of the tablespace users:

```
RMAN> backup as copy tablespace users;

Starting backup at 10-OCT-06
allocated channel: ORA_DISK_1
channel ORA_DISK_1: sid=146 devtype=DISK
channel ORA_DISK_1: starting datafile copy
input datafile fno=00004 name=/home/oracle/oradata/PRODB2/USERS.dbf
RMAN-00571: ===========================================================
RMAN-00569: =============== ERROR MESSAGE STACK FOLLOWS ===============
RMAN-00571: ===========================================================
RMAN-03009: failure of backup command on ORA_DISK_1 channel at 10/10/2006 00:08:53
ORA-19809: limit exceeded for recovery files
ORA-19804: cannot reclaim 5242880 bytes disk space from 1073741824 limit
```

Note the error ORA-19804: cannot reclaim 5242880 bytes disk space from 1073741824 limit. To reclaim space from the flash recovery area at this time, you have to delete the redundant backups yourself. For example:

```
RMAN> report obsolete;

RMAN retention policy will be applied to the command
RMAN retention policy is set to redundancy 1
Report of obsolete backups and copies
Type                 Key    Completion Time    Filename/Handle
-------------------- ------ ------------------ --------------------
Archive Log          5442   08-OCT-06
/home/oracle/oracle/product/10.2.0/db_1/flash_recovery_area/PRODB2/archivelog/➥
2006_10_08/o1_mf_1_40_2lmkv9mo_.arc
Datafile Copy        5461   27-SEP-06                /home/oracle/orabackup/Copy_data➥
 D-PRODB2_I-3053038066_TS-SYSTEM_FNO-1_5ehubk8h
Datafile Copy        5462   27-SEP-06                /home/oracle/orabackup/Copy_data➥
 D-PRODB2_I-3053038066_TS-UNDOTBS1_FNO-2_5hhubkbs
Datafile Copy        5463   27-SEP-06                /home/oracle/orabackup/Copy_data➥
 D-PRODB2_I-3053038066_TS-SYSAUX_FNO-3_5fhubka9
Datafile Copy        5464   27-SEP-06                /home/oracle/orabackup/Copy_data➥
_D-PRODB2_I-3053038066_TS-USERS_FNO-4_5ihubkbv
Datafile Copy        5465   27-SEP-06                /home/oracle/orabackup/Copy_data➥
_D-PRODB2_I-3053038066_TS-EXAMPLE_FNO-5_5ghubkbc
```

To create even more space in the flash recovery area, you may want to remove the old backups. The RMAN command delete obsolete does the trick:

```
RMAN> delete obsolete ;
RMAN retention policy will be applied to the command
RMAN retention policy is set to redundancy 1
using channel ORA_DISK_1
```

```
Deleting the following obsolete backups and copies:
Type                  Key    Completion Time    Filename/Handle
--------------------  -----  -----------------  --------------------
Archive Log           5442   08-OCT-06                /home/oracle/oracle/product/➥
10.2.0/db_1/flash_recovery_area/PRODB2/archivelog/➥
2006_10_08/o1_mf_1_40_2lmkv9mo_.arc
Datafile Copy         5461   27-SEP-06                /home/oracle/orabackup/Copy_data➥
 D-PRODB2_I-3053038066_TS-SYSTEM_FNO-1_5ehubk8h
Datafile Copy         5462   27-SEP-06                /home/oracle/orabackup/Copy_data➥
_D-PRODB2_I-3053038066_TS-UNDOTBS1_FNO-2_5hhubkbs
Datafile Copy         5463   27-SEP-06                /home/oracle/orabackup/Copy_data➥
 D-PRODB2_I-3053038066_TS-SYSAUX_FNO-3_5fhubka9
Datafile Copy         5464   27-SEP-06                /home/oracle/orabackup/Copy_data➥
_D-PRODB2_I-3053038066_TS-USERS_FNO-4_5ihubkbv
_Datafile Copy        5465   27-SEP-06                /home/oracle/orabackup/Copy_data➥
D-PRODB2_I-3053038066_TS-EXAMPLE_FNO-5_5ghubkbc
```

At this time, RMAN will display the following message:

```
Do you really want to delete the above objects (enter YES or NO)?
```

Answer YES at the prompt. RMAN will delete the files:

```
deleted archive log
archive log
filename=/home/oracle/oracle/product/10.2.0/db_1/flash_recovery_area/PRO➥
DB2/archivelog/2006_10_08/o1_mf_1_40_2lmkv9mo_.arc recid=64 stamp=603330732
deleted datafile copy
datafile copy filename=/home/oracle/orabackup/Copy_data_D-PRODB2_I-305303➥
8066_TS-SYSTEM_FNO-1_5ehubk8h recid=72 stamp=602266180
deleted datafile copy
datafile copy filename=/home/oracle/orabackup/Copy_data_D-PRODB2_I-305303➥
8066_TS-UNDOTBS1_FNO-2_5hhubkbs recid=73 stamp=602266180
deleted datafile copy
datafile copy filename=/home/oracle/orabackup/Copy_data_D-PRODB2_I-305303➥
8066_TS-SYSAUX_FNO-3_5fhubka9 recid=74 stamp=602266180
deleted datafile copy
datafile copy filename=/home/oracle/orabackup/Copy_data_D-PRODB2_I-305303➥
8066_TS-USERS_FNO-4_5ihubkbv recid=75 stamp=602266180
deleted datafile copy
datafile copy filename=/home/oracle/orabackup/Copy_data_D-PRODB2_I-305303➥
8066_TS-EXAMPLE_FNO-5_5ghubkbc recid=76 stamp=602266180
Deleted 6 objects
```

If you want to delete the files without being prompted, you can issue the following command:

```
delete noprompt obsolete;
```

When you include the noprompt option, RMAN will delete the files without prompting you. This might open up enough space inside the flash recovery area for future backups. If it does not, then you have to add some more space to the flash recovery area (as shown at the beginning of this recipe's solution).

■Caution As this recipe illustrates, reducing the size of the flash recovery area may not result in a reduction of the actual space consumed. When you reduce the size, Oracle tries to remove the nonessential backups to reduce the space consumed; however, if the backups are considered essential, then they are not removed, and the flash recovery area may consume more than what you had requested it to be shrunk to. As a best practice, check the actual space consumed after a resize operation.

3-6. Configuring Archived Redo Logs to Go to FRA

Problem

You want to configure your database so that archived redo log files are written to the flash recovery area.

Solution

When you run the database in archivelog mode, you have to configure a location to which the archived redo logs are written when they are generated. The default location for archived redo logs is $ORACLE_HOME/dbs. Of course, you can always configure a specific location by executing the command alter system set log_archive_dest_1. In this recipe, you will see how to use the flash recovery area as the destination of the archived redo logs.

Here are the steps to follow to send archived redo logs to the flash recovery area:

1. Configure the flash recovery area with adequate space (recipe 3-1).

2. If the flash recovery area is already defined, then make sure you have enough space to hold at least one archived log (recipe 3-4).

3. Log on to the database as a user with the sysdba privilege (such as sys), and issue the following command:

   ```
   alter system set log_archive_dest_1 = 'LOCATION=USE_DB_RECOVERY_FILE_DEST';
   ```

   This command instructs the database to use the flash recovery area as the destination for archived redo logs.

4. Make sure the archived redo log destination 1 is enabled. By default it's enabled, but someone may have disabled it. Issue the following SQL:

   ```
   SQL>show parameter log_archive_dest_state_1
   ```

NAME	TYPE	VALUE
log_archive_dest_state_1	string	ENABLE

   The presence of ENABLE confirms that the destination is enabled.

5. If the destination is not enabled, enable it now by issuing this:

```
alter system set log_archive_dest_state_1 = enable;
```

6. Check the correct setting by issuing an archive log list command at the SQL prompt:

```
SQL>archive log list
Database log mode              Archive Mode
Automatic archival             Enabled
Archive destination            USE_DB_RECOVERY_FILE_DEST
Oldest online log sequence     47
Next log sequence to archive   49
Current log sequence           49
```

Note the line Archive destination USE_DB_RECOVERY_FILE_DEST, which confirms that the archived redo log destination is set to the flash recovery area.

7. Check the operation by issuing a log switch that forces the generation of an archived redo log:

```
alter system switch logfile;
```

Execution of this command should come back with the message "System altered." If you see any other message, then you will get a clue for your next action from the message itself. For instance, a common message is as follows:

```
ORA-00257: archiver error. Connect internal only, until freed.
```

This message indicates that the location specified for archived redo logs is possibly full, so you need to address that, as shown in recipe 3-5.

8. Confirm that an archived redo log was created in the flash recovery area. Oracle will automatically create a directory called archivelog in the FRA and also a subdirectory under that named as the day's date specified in the format YYYY-MM-DD. You can go to that directory and check for the existence of a new, archived redo log file.

9. Alternatively, or in addition to checking for the physical presence of the file, you can check the database for the existence of the archivelog:

```
SQL>select name from v$archived_log
  2  order by completion_time;
NAME
--------------------------------------------------------------------------------
--
/home/oracle/oracle/product/10.2.0/db_1/dbs/arch1002.arc
… and so on …
/home/oracle/oracle/product/10.2.0/db_1/dbs/arch1002.arc
/home/oracle/flasharea/PRODB2/archivelog/2006_10_10/o1_mf_1_49_2lr2mhv8_.arc
```

This shows the last archived redo log was created in the flash recovery area as an Oracle managed file (note the *long* name).

10. Now the archived redo log destination is set to the flash recovery area.

How It Works

Before you start on this recipe, ask yourself whether you really want to direct the archived redo logs to the flash recovery area. Let's see the pros and cons of doing so.

The following are the benefits of directing archived redo logs to the flash recovery area:

- Doing so allows Oracle to back up the archived redo logs and to delete them when a space shortage occurs.

- Using the single command `backup recovery area` (recipe 3-15), you can back up everything, including archived redo logs, to tape at once.

- You have one location where the database recovery-related files are kept. You can make this location very reliable through the use of RAID structures.

- You can monitor the space easily.

And the disadvantage is only one:

- Since all the recovery-related files are in one place, a disaster in that filesystem or ASM disk group will make everything unavailable for recovery. This is a practical consideration and can't be ignored.

■**Caution** As a best practice, we do *not* advise that you put the archived redo logs in the flash recovery area. When a disaster makes the disks inoperable and you need to recover the datafiles, archived redo logs are very important. If you miss an archived redo log, you can't recover beyond that point. Sometimes you can't even perform an incomplete recovery when an archived redo log is missing, since that archived redo log may contain some changes to the system tablespace. Even in the case when a datafile has no backup, you can re-create it if you have all the archived redo logs generated since the creation of the datafile. Therefore, archived redo logs are far more important than datafile backups. Also, they sometimes compensate for each other's absence. Because of this, you should place the archived redo logs and datafile backups in two different locations so that at least one of them is available. We recommend keeping the datafile backups, but not the archived redo logs, in the flash recovery area. Use the parameter `log_archive_dest_1` to set an explicit location for the archived redo logs. You should, however, place *backups* of archived redo logs in the flash recovery area.

3-7. Using the Same FRA for Two Databases with the Same Name

Problem

In the preceding recipes, you learned that the different files are placed inside the flash recovery area in the following directory structure:

```
<Flash Recovery Area>/<Database Name>/<Type of File>/<Date>
```

For instance, the archived redo logs for database PRODB2 for November 10, 2006, are stored here:

```
/home/oracle/flasharea/PRODB2/archivelog/2006_11_10
```

The structure allows several databases to share the same flash recovery area. However, you may wonder, what happens when two databases with the same name want to share the same flash recovery area? They can't have two directories with the same name.

Solution

The solution is rather simple. The directory for <Database Name> does not refer to the database name; rather, it refers to the *unique name* of the database. To check the unique name, use the following query:

```
SQL> select db_unique_name
  2  from v$database;


DB_UNIQUE_NAME
------------------------------
PRODB2
```

By default, the unique name of a database is the same as the database name. If you want to use the same flash recovery area for two databases, you must use different unique names. Unfortunately, you can't change this dynamically. You have to put the following parameter in the initialization file and restart the database:

```
db_unique_name = <Unique Name of the Database>
```

Once done, the RMAN backups are automatically created in the appropriate directory.

How It Works

This solution has some caveats. This solution works fine in most cases but not all. For instance, suppose you had a database called PRODB2 and the unique name was also PRODB2. The backups go in the directory /home/oracle/flasharea/PRODDB2/backuppiece/2006_10_10. Later you configure another database also called PRODB2 to share the same flash recovery area. Of course you have to use a different unique name, but for which database? You have two choices:

- Change the unique name of the new database to PROD2, and let the old one keep the unique name PRODB2.

- Change the unique name of the old database to PROD2, and let the new one have the unique name PRODB2.

If you choose the former, then a new subdirectory, PROD2, will be created in /home/oracle/flasharea, and all the backups of the new database will go there. This is the easiest and the least intrusive option. We recommend this, if you have a choice. In most cases, this will be possible.

However, sometimes it may not be possible to give a new unique name to the new database. You may have to change the unique name of the old database. This will also create a new subdirectory—PROD2—in the flash recovery area. But here is the problem. Prior to renaming the unique name, the backups of the old database were going to the following directory:

```
/home/oracle/flasharea/PRODB2/backuppiece/2006_11_10
```

After renaming, however, the backup pieces go in this directory instead:

```
/home/oracle/flasharea/PROD2/backuppiece/2006_11_10
```

However, the backup pieces taken earlier will be still in /home/oracle/flasharea/ PRODB2/backuppiece/2006_11_10, along with the backup pieces of the new database PRODB2. This may cause some confusion. Therefore, instead of leaving the backup pieces there, you may want to move them to the newly created directory—/home/oracle/flasharea/ PROD2/backuppiece/2006_11_10. You can do this by using the unix mv command. For ASM files, you can either use dbms_file_transfer package or use FTP (only on Oracle Database 10g Release 2).

The RMAN repository will not be aware of the move, so it will continue to report the existence of the backup pieces in the old directory. So, you have to make the repository know that the location of the backup piece has changed. You can accomplish that by simply uncataloging and recataloging the backup pieces in their appropriate directories. Here are the steps:

1. First, check the backup pieces in the old location:

```
RMAN> list backup of database;


List of Backup Sets
===================

BS Key  Type LV Size       Device Type Elapsed Time Completion Time
------- ---- -- ---------- ----------- ------------ ---------------
159     Full    796.63M    DISK        00:01:57     10-NOV-06
        BP Key: 153   Status: AVAILABLE  Compressed: NO  Tag:➥
TAG20061110T175734
        Piece Name: /home/oracle/flasharea/PRODB2/backupset/2006_11_10/➥
o1_mf_nnndf_TAG20061110T175734_2ob0yzgp_.bkp
   List of Datafiles in backup set 159
   File LV Type Ckp SCN    Ckp Time  Name
   ---- -- ---- ---------- --------- ----
   1       Full 3350546    10-NOV-06 /home/oracle/oradata/PRODB2/SYSTEM.dbf
   2       Full 3350546    10-NOV-06 /home/oracle/oradata/PRODB2/UNDOTBS1.dbf
   3       Full 3350546    10-NOV-06 /home/oracle/oradata/PRODB2/SYSAUX.dbf
   4       Full 3350546    10-NOV-06 /home/oracle/oradata/PRODB2/USERS.dbf
   5       Full 3350546    10-NOV-06 /home/oracle/oradata/PRODB2/EXAMPLE.dbf
   6       Full 3350546    10-NOV-06 +DG2/accdata_01.dbf

BS Key  Type LV Size       Device Type Elapsed Time Completion Time
------- ---- -- ---------- ----------- ------------ ---------------
161     Full    796.65M    DISK        00:01:45     10-NOV-06
        BP Key: 155   Status: AVAILABLE  Compressed: NO  Tag:➥
```

```
TAG20061110T180848
        Piece Name: /home/oracle/flasharea/PROD2/backupset/2006_11_10/➥
                    o1_mf_nnndf_TA
G20061110T180848_2ob1n1ol_.bkp
  List of Datafiles in backup set 161
  File LV Type Ckp SCN    Ckp Time  Name
  ---- -- ---- ---------- --------- ----
   1      Full 3353618    10-NOV-06 /home/oracle/oradata/PRODB2/SYSTEM.dbf
   2      Full 3353618    10-NOV-06 /home/oracle/oradata/PRODB2/UNDOTBS1.dbf
   3      Full 3353618    10-NOV-06 /home/oracle/oradata/PRODB2/SYSAUX.dbf
   4      Full 3353618    10-NOV-06 /home/oracle/oradata/PRODB2/USERS.dbf
   5      Full 3353618    10-NOV-06 /home/oracle/oradata/PRODB2/EXAMPLE.dbf
   6      Full 3353618    10-NOV-06 +DG2/accdata_01.dbf
```

2. From the previous output, you can see that the backup piece with the name
/home/oracle/flasharea/PRODB2/backupset/2006_11_10/o1_mf_nnndf_
TAG20061110T175734_2ob0yzgp_.bkp is in the old place. Using the usual mv
command, move it to the right directory:

```
mv o1_mf_nnndf_TAG20061110T175734_2ob0yzgp_.bkp /home/oracle/➥
flasharea/PROD2/backupset/2006_11_10
```

3. Now that the backup piece is in the right directory, you must tell RMAN. First you need
to remove the identity of the backup piece from the RMAN repository using a process
generally known as *uncataloging*:

```
RMAN> change backuppiece
'/home/oracle/flasharea/PRODB2/backupset/2006_11_10➥
/o1_mf_nnndf_TAG20061110T175734_2ob0yzgp_.bkp' uncatalog;

uncataloged backuppiece
backup piece handle=/home/oracle/flasharea/PRODB2/backupset/2006_11_10/➥
o1_mf_nnndf_TA G20061110T175734_2ob0yzgp_.bkp recid=153 stamp=606160655
Uncataloged 1 objects
```

4. Then catalog the piece again with the correct file:

```
RMAN> catalog backuppiece
'/home/oracle/flasharea/PROD2/backupset/2006_11_10/o1_mf_n➥
nndf_TA G20061110T175734_2ob0yzgp_.bkp';

cataloged backuppiece
backup piece handle=/home/oracle/flasharea/PROD2/backupset/2006_11_10/➥
o1_mf_nnndf_TA G20061110T175734_2ob0yzgp_.bkp recid=157 stamp=606163369
```

5. Test whether RMAN knows this file is a backup piece of the database:

```
RMAN> list backup of database;


List of Backup Sets
===================

BS Key  Type LV Size       Device Type Elapsed Time Completion Time
------- ---- -- ---------- ----------- ------------ ---------------
159     Full    796.63M    DISK        00:01:57     10-NOV-06
        BP Key: 157   Status: AVAILABLE  Compressed: NO  Tag:➥
TAG20061110T175734
        Piece Name: /home/oracle/flasharea/PROD2/backupset/➥
2006_11_10/o1_mf_nnndf_TA G20061110T175734_2ob0yzgp_.bkp
  List of Datafiles in backup set 159
  File LV Type Ckp SCN    Ckp Time  Name
  ---- -- ---- ---------- --------- ----
  1       Full 3350546    10-NOV-06 /home/oracle/oradata/PRODB2/SYSTEM.dbf
  2       Full 3350546    10-NOV-06 /home/oracle/oradata/PRODB2/UNDOTBS1.dbf
  3       Full 3350546    10-NOV-06 /home/oracle/oradata/PRODB2/SYSAUX.dbf
  4       Full 3350546    10-NOV-06 /home/oracle/oradata/PRODB2/USERS.dbf
  5       Full 3350546    10-NOV-06 /home/oracle/oradata/PRODB2/EXAMPLE.dbf
  6       Full 3350546    10-NOV-06 +DG2/accdata_01.dbf

BS Key  Type LV Size       Device Type Elapsed Time Completion Time
------- ---- -- ---------- ----------- ------------ ---------------
161     Full    796.65M    DISK        00:01:45     10-NOV-06
        BP Key: 155   Status: AVAILABLE  Compressed: NO  Tag:➥
TAG20061110T180848
        Piece Name: /home/oracle/flasharea/PROD2/backupset/2006_11_10/➥
o1_mf_nnndf_TA G20061110T180848_2ob1n1ol_.bkp
  List of Datafiles in backup set 161
  File LV Type Ckp SCN    Ckp Time  Name
  ---- -- ---- ---------- --------- ----
  1       Full 3353618    10-NOV-06 /home/oracle/oradata/PRODB2/SYSTEM.dbf
  2       Full 3353618    10-NOV-06 /home/oracle/oradata/PRODB2/UNDOTBS1.dbf
  3       Full 3353618    10-NOV-06 /home/oracle/oradata/PRODB2/SYSAUX.dbf
  4       Full 3353618    10-NOV-06 /home/oracle/oradata/PRODB2/USERS.dbf
  5       Full 3353618    10-NOV-06 /home/oracle/oradata/PRODB2/EXAMPLE.dbf
  6       Full 3353618    10-NOV-06 +DG2/accdata_01.dbf

RMAN>
```

As you can see, the backup piece is correctly displayed as /home/oracle/flasharea/ PROD2/backupset/2006_11_10/o1_mf_nnndf_TAG20061110T175734_2ob0yzgp_.bkp, just the way you intended. Now all backup pieces are located properly and also recorded accurately in the repository.

You can use this technique in cases where two databases share the same flash recovery area and have the same name.

3-8. Placing a Control File in the FRA

Problem

You want to create a database and have one of the control file mirrors placed into the flash recovery area, or you have an existing database and want to create a control file mirror in the flash recovery area.

Solution

The control files are created only once—during the database creation. Later, the control files can be re-created from either a backup or a script possibly produced by a control file trace. So, there are only three occasions when the control files could be placed in the flash recovery area:

- When the database is created for the first time

- When the control file is re-created through a SQL script to recover from a failure, just prior to restoring the backup

- When the control file is restored from a backup

During any one of these cases, you make the database create one of the control files in the flash recovery area by making the required changes to the initialization parameter file. You have two options:

- Place the control files parameter explicitly in the initialization parameter file, taking care to place at least one control file in a location different from the flash recovery area. For instance, if the flash recovery area is /home/oracle/flasharea, you put the following entry in the initialization parameter file:

  ```
  control_files = ('/home/oracle/flasharea/PRODB2/controlfile/control01.ctl', ↦
  '/home/oracle/oradata/control02.ctl')
  ```

- The second option is to let the database guess the control file location in the flash recovery area:

  a. Specify the flash recovery area location and size (recipe 3-1)

  b. Put the following parameters in the initialization parameter file:

  ```
  DB_CREATE_FILE_DEST = '/home/oracle/oradata'
  ```

  c. Check that these two parameters are not in the initialization parameter file:

  ```
  db_create_online_log_dest_1
  db_create_online_log_dest_2
  ```

If they exist, remove them.

In either option, one control file is created in the flash recovery area.

How It Works

While deciding where to place the control file, the database uses a decision plan, as shown here. Essentially, the decision is based on which initialization parameters are set. Table 3-3 shows the location of the control files based on the settings of the various initialization parameters. The headings are the abbreviations of the initialization parameters.

DCOL1: db_create_online_log_dest_1

DCOL2: db_create_online_log_dest_2

DCFD: db_create_file_dest

DRFD: db_recovery_file_dest

Table 3-3. *Decision for Location of the Control File*

DCOLD1	DCOLD2	DCFD	DRFD	Location of Control File(s)
Set	Set	Not Set	Not set	Two members created, one each in db_create_online_log_dest_1 and db_create_online_log_dest_2.
Not set	Not set	Set	Set	Two members created, one each in db_create_file_dest and the flash recovery area.
Not set	Not set	Set	Not set	Only one member is created in db_create_file_dest.
Not set	Not set	Not set	Set	Only one member is created in the flash recovery area.

As you can see, the only cases where control files are created in the flash recovery area is the case where parameter db_recovery_file_dest is set and db_create_online_log_dest_1 and _2 are not set. So, to make sure the control file is created there, you should specify the flash recovery area (assumed true since we are talking about that in this whole chapter). Make sure these parameters are not set by issuing the following SQL statement:

```
SQL> show parameter db_create_online_log_dest
```

```
NAME                                 TYPE        VALUE
------------------------------------ ----------- ------------------------------
db_create_online_log_dest_1          string
db_create_online_log_dest_2          string
```

The output shows nothing as values of these parameters, which is what we expect. When the conditions of these two parameters being NULL and the flash recovery area being set are met, at least one control file will be created in the flash recovery area when the database is created or the control file is re-created.

Before implementing this recipe, it's wise to consider the pros and cons of placing a control file in the flash recovery area.

Advantages

The easiest advantage to understand is the visibility across all instances of a real application cluster (RAC) database. Since the flash recovery area must be visible to all the nodes of the RAC database (recipe 3-1), it makes a perfect location for a control file, which must be visible to all the nodes as well. Only one control file should be placed there. The rest should be placed in other locations.

It's the other advantage that is more significant, one that relates to availability. If their primary database fails and you need to recover (or restore, whatever is appropriate), the flash recovery area is used, which has the backups of the database. So, technically, you have positioned the flash recovery area on such areas of the storage that the placement reduces the probability of failure at the same time as the failure of the primary database. For instance, you may have put your database disks on a SAN different from where the flash recovery area disks are. So, the chances of both disks (the database and the flash recovery area) going down at the same time are substantially reduced. If the primary database files are down and you have access to the most current online redo log files, you may avoid the possibility of an incomplete recovery, since you have a control file and will not need to start a recovery using a backup control file. If you don't have a control file on the flash recovery area, then there is a fair chance you will have to resort to a backup control file during recovery, which means an incomplete recovery, even if you have access to the current redo log files. So, there is a strong argument for placing one control file in the flash recovery area.

Disadvantages

It's not a slam-dunk argument; there is a significant disadvantage that you should consider. In a more practical situation, you probably have limited resources (read: *money* to buy disks) and want to maximize your investment for performance and reliability. So, you probably made the storage location of the main database files on RAID level 0+1, have a more reliable SAN, and so on. And, you may have placed the flash recovery area on a less reliable (and less expensive) SAN, even on a NAS, and perhaps with RAID 5 or even no RAID at all. The latter is not advisable but is not unusual. So, the chance of failure in the flash recovery area is greater compared to the main database disks. If the flash recovery area fails, then you lose one of the control files. This, by itself, is not the end of the world. Let's hope you have been prudent in putting the other control files in other locations. So, when the database comes down after the control file in the flash recovery area suddenly becomes inaccessible, all you have to do is to remove that control file from the control file parameter in the initialization parameter file and restart the database. There is no data loss; you will have an interruption of service, since the database is unavailable from the time the flash recovery area is unavailable and the database is back up after removing the control file from the initialization parameter.

Choice

Here comes the tough question: should you put a control file in the flash recovery area? If your flash recovery area is in a storage location as reliable as the main database storage, then we strongly urge you to put one control file there.

If that is not true (and most likely the case), decide how important complete recovery is to you. If you must have a complete recovery after a failure regardless of other consequences including a possible interruption in service, then put one control file in the flash recovery area. If the potential service interruptions in case of the flash recovery area failure are not acceptable, do not use it as a location for even one control file.

Without knowing your exact circumstances, it's not easy for us to recommend one solution over the other. In general, however, we find it safer not to put even one control file in the flash recovery area. Under no circumstances should you put all your control files in the flash recovery area.

3-9. Placing Online Redo Log Files in FRA

Problem

You want to create online redo logs in the flash recovery area.

Solution

Online log files are not created by default in the flash recovery area. It's possible to place them there, however, and you can do so when creating the database or when adding a new logfile group. Furthermore, when adding a new logfile group, you have two choices regarding the placement of online redo logs in the flash recovery area:

- Creating both members of the group in the flash recovery area

- Creating only one member in the flash recovery area and creating the other member in the regular datafile location

The following sections cover the two scenarios just described.

During Database Creation

During database creation, Oracle creates the online redo log files in the locations specified in the initialization parameter file. The parameters that affect the placement are db_create_online_log_dest_1 and db_create_online_log_dest_2.

1. Put the following lines in the initialization parameter file:

```
db_create_online_log_dest_1 = '/home/oracle/flasharea'
db_create_online_log_dest_1 = '/home/oracle/flasharea'
```

When the database is created, Oracle will create two members of each online redo log group and both members in the flash recovery area.

2. If the parameter db_create_file_dest is set in the initialization parameter file, either remove it or set it to '' (null string), as shown here:

```
db_create_file_dest = ''
```

3. After the database is created, confirm the creation of online redo log files by selecting the member names from the data dictionary view V$LOGFILE:

```
SQL> select member
  2  from v$logfile
  3  where group# = 1;
```

```
MEMBER
-----------------------------------------------------------------------------
/home/oracle/flasharea/PRODB2/onlinelog/o1_mf_1_2psd26ox_.log
/home/oracle/flasharea/PRODB2/onlinelog/o1_mf_1_2lpsd285q_.log
```

Note how the online redo log files were created in the flash recovery area.

Adding a New Logfile Group: Both Members in the FRA

Follow these steps to place both members of an online redo log group in the flash recovery area. We're assuming you have already defined the flash recovery area (recipe 3-1).

1. Make sure the flash recovery area is set:

```
SQL> show parameter db_recovery_file_dest
```

```
NAME                                TYPE          VALUE
------------------------------------ ----------- ----------------------------
db_recovery_file_dest               string        /home/oracle/flasharea
```

2. Also make sure that the parameters db_create_file_dest and db_create_online_log_dest_* are all set to NULL. For example:

```
SQL> show parameter db_create_online_log_dest
```

```
NAME                                TYPE          VALUE
------------------------------------ ----------- ----------------------------
db_create_online_log_dest_1         string
db_create_online_log_dest_2         string
db_create_online_log_dest_3         string
db_create_online_log_dest_4         string
db_create_online_log_dest_5         string
SQL> show parameter db_create_file_dest
```

```
NAME                                TYPE          VALUE
------------------------------------ ----------- ----------------------------
db_create_file_dest                 string
```

3. Now, add the logfile group with the appropriate number. For example, to add a logfile group 4, do this:

```
SQL> alter database add logfile group 4;
```

```
Database altered.
```

The logfile group is created in the flash recovery area in the subdirectory onlinelog, in a naming convention for Oracle managed files. The logfile created this way is 100MB.

4. Confirm placement of the new member in the flash recovery area by selecting the member names from the data dictionary view V$LOGFILE:

```
SQL> select member
  2  from v$logfile
  3  where group# = 4;

MEMBER
----------------------------------------------------------------------------

/home/oracle/flasharea/PRODB2/onlinelog/o1_mf_4_2lrt26ox_.log
```

5. Optionally check for the member's existence in the onlinelog directory at the flash recovery area destination:

```
$ cd /home/oracle/flasharea/PRODB2/onlinelog
$ ls -l
total 205016
-rw-r-----   1 oracle   oinstall 104858112 Oct 10 23:43 o1_mf_4_2lrt26ox_.log
```

This has a small problem, however. As you can see, there is only one log file member for that group. Best practices suggest that there should be at least two members per group to eliminate any single point of failure. You can accomplish this by specifying two additional parameters for the online redo log creation, shown in the following steps:

1. Set the parameters db_create_online_log_dest_1 and db_create_online_log_dest_2 to the flash recovery area location:

```
SQL> alter system set db_create_online_log_dest_1 = '/home/oracle/flasharea';

System altered.

SQL> alter system set db_create_online_log_dest_2 = '/home/oracle/flasharea';

System altered.
```

2. Now add the logfile group without mentioning any specific file or directory names:

```
SQL> alter database add logfile group 5;

Database altered.
```

3. Confirm the creation of online redo log files by selecting the member names from the data dictionary view V$LOGFILE:

```
SQL> select member
  2  from v$logfile
  3  where group# = 5;

MEMBER
----------------------------------------------------------------------------

/home/oracle/flasharea/PRODB2/onlinelog/o1_mf_4_2lrt26ox_.log
/home/oracle/flasharea/PRODB2/onlinelog/o1_mf_4_2lrt285q_.log
```

This confirms that two members were created for the logfile group, not one.

4. Optionally, you can also verify that these files were created in the flash recovery area destination:

```
$ cd /home/oracle/flasharea/PRODB2/onlinelog
$ ls -l
total 205016
-rw-r-----    1 oracle   oinstall 104858112 Oct 10 23:43 o1_mf_4_2lrt26ox_.log
-rw-r-----    1 oracle   oinstall 104858112 Oct 10 23:43 o1_mf_4_2lrt285q_.log
```

Using the following command, you can add a logfile group quickly without specifying anything else, such as the group number:

```
alter database add logfile;
```

This will create a new logfile group at a sequence of one more than the last logfile group sequence. So, if currently the group number of the last added logfile group is 6, the previous command will add a group 7 with just one file in the Oracle managed file format. You can check that through the following query:

```
SQL> select member
  2  from v$logfile
  3  where group# = 7;

MEMBER
----------------------------------------------------------------

/home/oracle/flasharea/PRODB2/onlinelog/o1_mf_6_2lrvlth1_.log
```

Adding a New Logfile Group: Only One Member in the FRA

If you want only one member of the group in the flash recovery area and the other one in the regular database file location, you should define two parameters—the flash recovery area and db_create_file_dest. This parameter determines where a datafile should be created if no location is given.

1. Set the parameter where you want to create the first member of the online redo log groups. To specify the location, such as the ASM disk group DG1, issue the following SQL statement:

```
SQL> alter system set db_create_file_dest = '+DG1';

System altered.
```

2. Ensure that the parameter db_create_file_dest is set:

```
SQL> show parameter db_create_file_dest

NAME                                 TYPE        VALUE
------------------------------------ ----------- ----------------------------
db_create_file_dest                  string      +DG1
```

Like the flash recovery area, the directory you specify as a location of the previously mentioned parameter must already exist. Oracle will not create it for you.

3. Make sure the flash recovery area is set:

```
SQL> show parameter db_recovery_file_dest
```

```
NAME                                 TYPE        VALUE
------------------------------------ ----------- -----------------------------
db_recovery_file_dest                string      /home/oracle/flasharea
```

With this configuration, if you decide to add a log file group, the group will be created with two members, and they will be in the flash recovery area and the directory specified by db_create_file_dest. Let's see how that is done:

1. First add a logfile group:

```
SQL> alter database add logfile group 7;
```

2. Check how many members are created and where:

```
SQL>  select member
  2   from v$logfile
  3   where group# = 7;
```

```
MEMBER
--------------------------------------------------------------------------------
+DG1/prodb2/onlinelog/group_7.256.606165125
/home/oracle/flasharea/PRODB2/onlinelog/o1_mf_7_2ob5bw2j_.log
```

3. In the physical flash recovery area location and in the view V$LOGFILE, verify the existence of the new redo logfiles.

How It Works

One of the lesser known features of Oracle database administration is the ability to create datafiles, online redo log files, and so on, without specifying filenames and locations. You do this by specifying some locations in the initialization parameter file as the location for these files. These locations could be ASM disk groups or filesystems or directories under filesystems. The location must be available to all instances in case of a Real Application Cluster (RAC) database. Please note that the directory you specify as a location must already exist. Oracle will not create it for you. If you have defined the flash recovery area, the redo logs will be created there.

You must carefully decide whether you really want to create redo logs in the flash recovery area. The arguments pro and con are the same as for the question of putting the control file in the FRA (see recipe 3-8). Read up on those arguments, and arrive at your own conclusion.

Advantages of Putting Redo Log Members in the FRA

In summary, the argument for putting at least one member of a redo log group in the flash recovery area hinges on the assumption that the flash recovery area and the main database disks are located in such a way that the probability of both going down at the same time is very slim, almost to the point of being negligible. You attain that probability by putting the flash recovery area disks on a SAN or NAS other than where the main database is located. Even if the flash recovery area and main database are both on the same SAN (or NAS), if they do not share the same physical disks, then it further reduces the probability of simultaneous failure. The idea is to make sure that whatever causes the main database disks to go down will not affect the flash recovery area disks. This way, should the main database disks get corrupted, you can still access the backup of the database files in the flash recovery area.

With the assumption we've just described, the idea of putting one member of an online redo log group on the flash recovery area ensures that at least one member of the group will still be available in case the main database disks experience a failure. For instance, suppose your database has three log groups, each with two members, and one member of each group is on the flash recovery area, as shown in Figure 3-1.

The members in Figure 3-1 are named in the following form: g<group#>m<member#>. Since the database is in archivelog mode, each logfile group can be in one of three states:

Current: The online redo log group is the current group. If the group fails, the database immediately aborts with an error. If all the members of the group are damaged, then you need to perform an incomplete recovery from previous backups.

Active: The group is not the current one, but it was earlier. Now it's being archived, and that operation is not completed yet. If the group fails, the database is not halted, but the logfile will not have been archived, and any subsequent recovery operation will stop at this group. When an active group fails, you should take a fresh backup of the database so that you do not need to roll forward from a previous backup with archived redo logs. You don't want the rollforward operation to be dependent upon a failed group.

Inactive: The group is not current now, and it has already been archived. The loss of this group does not affect database operations, and it doesn't affect any recovery that you might perform in the future.

Having these explanations in mind, now assume that the status of the online redo log groups in Figure 3-1 is as follows:

Group 1: Current

Group 2: Active

Group 3: Inactive

With this information, suppose one member (or even both) of the online redo log group is damaged. Let's see the consequences. You can find a more detailed description of the redo log failure in Chapter 14; we will look at only one scenario here. Member g3m1 of Group 3 gets damaged. Since this member is INACTIVE, it has no impact on the database operation. But when the current log group gets filled, Group 3 must be available, so we need to fix the damaged member now. The solution is really simple. Since the other member of the group—g3m2—is in a different part of our storage, in the flash recovery area, that is most likely intact. We can copy it over the damaged file and be on our way:

```
$ cp g3m2 g3m1
```

No other action is required. Had g3m2 been on the same storage area as g3m1, then the probability of g3m2 being intact would have been much less because it would have been prone to the same failure that affected g3m1. So, there is a strong reason to place redo log group members on different storage areas, even if one of them is not the flash recovery area. Since we are assuming in case of database failure that the flash recovery area might survive, keeping one member of the redo log groups will reduce the chances of failure of both members of the online redo log group.

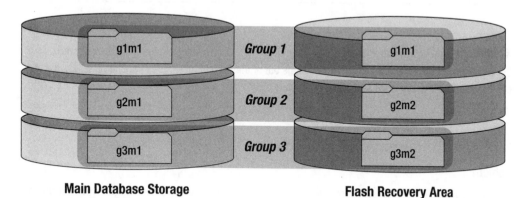

Figure 3-1. *Ideal placement of redo log members if FRA is used as a location*

Disadvantages of Placing One Member of the Online Redo Log Group in FRA

Putting members of the redo log groups in the flash recovery area is not a slam-dunk decision either. Let's revisit the scenario in Figure 3-1. Suppose that one member—g1m1—of Group 1 fails. Since the group is now current, the failure of the member will cause a failure in the database, and the database instance will abort.

You can correct the situation by copying the intact member of the online redo log group to the damaged member and starting the database. Since we describe the process of recovery in case of redo log failure in detail in Chapter 14, we will skip the details here. The important point to understand is that the sole reason of success in re-creating the redo log member was because we had an intact copy. Keeping one member of the logfile group in the flash recovery area improves the odds of that, as shown in the previous section. However, on the flip side, the failure of a current redo log member temporarily shuts the database down, even if you can repair it and bring the database up quickly. This creates a denial-of-service situation and should be avoided at all costs. Prevention of the loss is the key, not the repair afterward. The flash recovery area is usually built on cheaper, less reliable disks and is more prone to failure than the more reliable database disks. Therefore, putting even one member of the redo log group there increases your chances of failure.

So, in summary, you should decide to place a member of the redo log group on the flash recovery area with care. You can use the decision grid shown in Table 3-4 to support your decision.

Table 3-4. *Decision Grid to Decide Placement of One Redo Log Member on the FRA*

Reliability of the Disk Under the Flash Recovery Area	Risk of Temporary Database Failure	
	Acceptable	Not Acceptable
Low	Yes	No
High	Maybe	Yes

■**Caution** We do not recommend creating all members of online redo logs in the flash recovery area. As a best practice, we recommend keeping the redo logs out of the flash recovery area in general, unless the reliability of the area is pretty close to the main database disks.

3-10. Sending Image Copies to the FRA

Problem

You have configured the flash recovery area, and you want to make sure image copies of the datafiles go there.

Solution

There is no special command to specify the flash recovery area as the target of the image copies. All you have to do is to make sure of the following:

- The flash recovery area is configured.

- The RMAN script does not have any format command in the channel configuration.

Once these two conditions are met, you can issue a simple backup as copy database, and the image copies will go there. Here is a sample command and output:

```
RMAN> backup as copy database;

Starting backup at 11-NOV-06
using channel ORA_DISK_1
channel ORA_DISK_1: starting datafile copy
input datafile fno=00001 name=/home/oracle/oradata/PRODB2/SYSTEM.dbf
output filename=/home/oracle/flasharea/PRODB2/datafile/o1_mf_system_➥
2obvhdcc_.dbf tag=TAG20061111T013004 recid=131 stamp=606187848
channel ORA_DISK_1: datafile copy complete, elapsed time: 00:00:45
channel ORA_DISK_1: starting datafile copy
input datafile fno=00003 name=/home/oracle/oradata/PRODB2/SYSAUX.dbf
output filename=/home/oracle/flasharea/PRODB2/datafile/o1_mf_sysaux_➥
2obvjskv_.dbf tag=TAG20061111T013004 recid=132 stamp=606187883
channel ORA_DISK_1: datafile copy complete, elapsed time: 00:00:35
channel ORA_DISK_1: starting datafile copy
```

```
input datafile fno=00005 name=/home/oracle/oradata/PRODB2/EXAMPLE.dbf
output filename=/home/oracle/flasharea/PRODB2/datafile/o1_mf_example_➥
2obvkx07_.dbf tag=TAG20061111T013004 recid=133 stamp=606187895
channel ORA_DISK_1: datafile copy complete, elapsed time: 00:00:15
channel ORA_DISK_1: starting datafile copy
input datafile fno=00006 name=+DG2/accdata_01.dbf
output filename=/home/oracle/flasharea/PRODB2/datafile/o1_mf_accdata_➥
2obvld5f_.dbf tag=TAG20061111T013004 recid=134 stamp=606187909
channel ORA_DISK_1: datafile copy complete, elapsed time: 00:00:15
channel ORA_DISK_1: starting datafile copy
input datafile fno=00002 name=/home/oracle/oradata/PRODB2/UNDOTBS1.dbf
output filename=/home/oracle/flasharea/PRODB2/datafile/o1_mf_undotbs1_➥
2obvlvh8_.dbf tag=TAG20061111T013004 recid=135 stamp=606187923
channel ORA_DISK_1: datafile copy complete, elapsed time: 00:00:15
channel ORA_DISK_1: starting datafile copy
input datafile fno=00004 name=/home/oracle/oradata/PRODB2/USERS.dbf
output filename=/home/oracle/flasharea/PRODB2/datafile/o1_mf_users_➥
2obvmbs6_.dbf tag=TAG20061111T013004 recid=136 stamp=606187931
channel ORA_DISK_1: datafile copy complete, elapsed time: 00:00:01
Finished backup at 11-NOV-06
```

As you can see in the resultant output, the image copies are now in the flash recovery area.

How It Works

The solution should be self-explanatory. When the RMAN image copy command is given, the database makes the copies and places them in the flash recovery area. The image copies are placed in the directory /home/oracle/flasharea/PRODB2/datafile, that is, <flash recovery area>/<DB Unique Name>/datafile. As we explained earlier, Oracle will now manage these files—deleting redundant ones to make room for new ones, and so on.

3-11. Deleting Backup Sets from the FRA

Problem

Recall from the earlier discussion that one of the biggest appeals of using the flash recovery area is that Oracle automatically deletes the unnecessary files from this location whenever additional space is needed. So, you may not need to delete files manually. However, in some rare occasions you may want to delete backup sets, such as cleaning up under space constraints, where you are forced to remove some nonredundant backup set.

Solution

Like archived redo logs, there is no special command to delete backup sets from the flash recovery area. You delete a backup set in the same way as you would have deleted one while not using a flash recovery area. Here's the process to follow:

1. First check the backup sets existing in the RMAN repository:

```
$ rman target=/

Recovery Manager: Release 10.2.0.1.0 - Production on Wed Nov 8 00:20:58 2006

Copyright (c) 1982, 2005, Oracle.  All rights reserved.

connected to target database: PRODB2 (DBID=3053038066)

RMAN> list backupset;

using target database control file instead of recovery catalog

List of Backup Sets
===================

BS Key  Type LV Size       Device Type Elapsed Time Completion Time
------- ---- -- ---------- ----------- ------------ ---------------
157     Full    7.14M      DISK        00:00:01     14-OCT-06
        BP Key: 151    Status: AVAILABLE  Compressed: NO  Tag:➥
TAG20061014T233415
        Piece Name: /home/oracle/flasharea/PRODB2/autobackup/2006_10_14/➥
                    o1_mf_n_6038
48055_2m3c1r1s_.bkp
    Control File Included: Ckp SCN: 1909037     Ckp time: 14-OCT-06
```

2. Now, to delete a backup set, let's say number 157, issue a delete backupset command:

```
RMAN> delete backupset 157;

allocated channel: ORA_DISK_1
channel ORA_DISK_1: sid=144 devtype=DISK

List of Backup Pieces
BP Key  BS Key  Pc# Cp# Status      Device Type Piece Name
------- ------- --- --- ----------- ----------- ----------
151     157     1   1   AVAILABLE   DISK
/home/oracle/flasharea/PRODB2➥
/autobackup/2006_10_14/o1_mf_n_603848055_2m3c1r1s_.bkp

Do you really want to delete the above objects (enter YES or NO)? yes
deleted backup piece
backup piece handle=/home/oracle/flasharea/PRODB2/autobackup/2006_10_14/➥
                    o1_mf_n_6038
48055_2m3c1r1s_.bkp recid=151 stamp=603848056
Deleted 1 objects
```

The backup set is now removed.

How It Works

This process is no different than deleting the backup sets from any other location. When you give a `delete backupset` command, RMAN knows about all the available backup sets and deletes the one specified by the user. However, please note that RMAN must know about the existence of the backup set. If the backup set is removed from the catalog, then RMAN does not know about it, and the delete operation will not work.

3-12. Deleting Archived Redo Logs from the FRA

Problem

You want to delete archived redo logs from the flash recovery area, possibly to free up space quickly to avoid running out of room.

Solution

One strong motivation for using the flash recovery area as the archivelog destination is the automated way redundant archivelogs are deleted by Oracle so you do not need to worry about the redundant archivelogs. Therefore, you may not ever need to delete them manually, and this recipe may not be required on a regular basis. In some rare circumstances, however, you may want to delete the archived redo logs in the flash recovery area. One case could be that you have taken the backup of the archived redo logs to a different location, which is not yet cataloged in the RMAN repository, and you are running out of space in the flash recovery area. To quickly make room, you may want to delete some archived redo logs, such as those you've backed up somewhere else, from the flash recovery area. Here are the steps to follow:

1. First, find out the archived redo logs to delete. List all archived redo logs like so:

   ```
   RMAN> list archivelog all;
   ```

   Here is the output:

   ```
   using target database control file instead of recovery catalog


   List of Archived Log Copies
   Key     Thrd Seq     S Low Time  Name
   ------- ---- ------- - --------- ----
   70      1    46      A 09-OCT-06 /tmp/1_46_599877236.dbf
   102     1    78      A 09-NOV-06 /home/oracle/flasharea/➥
   PROD2/archivelog/2006_11_10/o1_mf_1_78_2obh633f_.arc
   103     1    79      A 10-NOV-06 /home/oracle/flasharea/PROD2/➥
                                    archivelog/2006_11_12/
   o1_mf_1_79_2ofdltnv_.arc
   ```

2. To delete the archived log sequences 78 and 79, you can use the following commands:

   ```
   RMAN> delete archivelog from logseq=78 until logseq=79;
   ```

   The output comes back as follows:

   ```
   allocated channel: ORA_DISK_1
   ```

```
    channel ORA_DISK_1: sid=134 devtype=DISK

    List of Archived Log Copies
    Key     Thrd Seq     S Low Time   Name
    ------- ---- ------- - ---------- ----
    102     1    78        A 09-NOV-06
    /home/oracle/flasharea/PROD2/archivelog/2006_11_10/➥
    o1_mf_1_78_2obh633f_.arc
    103     1    79        A 10-NOV-06
    /home/oracle/flasharea/PROD2/archivelog/2006_11_12/➥
    o1_mf_1_79_2ofdltnv_.arc

    Do you really want to delete the above objects (enter YES or NO)? yes
    deleted archive log
    archive log
    filename=/home/oracle/flasharea/PROD2/archivelog/2006_11_10/o1_mf_1_78_2➥
    obh633f_.arc recid=102 stamp=606175250
    deleted archive log
    archive log
    filename=/home/oracle/flasharea/PROD2/archivelog/2006_11_12/o1_mf_1_79_2➥
    ofdltnv_.arc recid=103 stamp=606270875
    Deleted 2 objects
```

```
    RMAN>
```

3. Verify in the directory that the archived redo logs got deleted. For instance, in Unix,
    you can do this using the standard ls command.

How It Works

Just like any other backups, the Oracle database knows where the archived redo logs are
stored. The delete archivelog command deletes the archived redo logs pretty much the same
way it would have done if the archived redo logs were stored in any other directory.

3-13. Reinstating a Damaged Datafile from an Image Copy

Problem

One of the database files has been damaged, and you have to repair the file quickly to bring
the associated tablespace back online. Instead of restoring the datafile from backup, you want
to use the image copy in the flash recovery area.

Solution

When a database file fails and you need to repair the file, you can just reinstate the image copy of the file from the flash recovery area instead of actually repairing it. This reduces the time to operation significantly.

1. First check the files of the database:

```
RMAN> report schema;

using target database control file instead of recovery catalog
Report of database schema

List of Permanent Datafiles
===========================
File Size(MB) Tablespace          RB segs Datafile Name
---- -------- ------------------- ------- ----------------------------
1    480      SYSTEM              ***     /home/oracle/oradata/PRODB2/SYSTEM.dbf
2    200      UNDOTBS1            ***     /home/oracle/oradata/PRODB2/UNDOTBS1.dbf
3    280      SYSAUX              ***     /home/oracle/oradata/PRODB2/SUSAUX.dbf
4    7        USERS               ***     /home/oracle/oradata/PRODB2/USERS.dbf
5    70       EXAMPLE             ***     /home/oracle/oradata/PRODB2/EXAMPLE.dbf

List of Temporary Files
=======================
File Size(MB) Tablespace          Maxsize(MB) Tempfile Name
---- -------- ------------------- ----------- --------------------
1    26       TEMP                32767       home/oracle/oradata/PRODB2/TEMP.dbf
```

Suppose file 5, /home/oracle/oradata/PRODB2/EXAMPLE.dbf, has been damaged.

2. Check for the existence of image copies of the damaged datafile:

```
$ rman target=/

Recovery Manager: Release 10.2.0.1.0 - Production on Sun Nov 12 15:03:42 2006

Copyright (c) 1982, 2005, Oracle.  All rights reserved.

connected to target database: PRODB2 (DBID=3053038066)

RMAN> list copy of datafile 5;
```

```
List of Datafile Copies
Key      File S Completion Time Ckp SCN   Ckp Time        Name
-------  ---- - --------------- ---------- --------------- ----
133      5    A 11-NOV-06       3374753    11-NOV-06       /home/oracle/➥
flasharea/PROD2/datafile/o1_mf_example_2obvkx07_.dbf
```

As you can see from the output, there is an image copy of the damaged file in the flash recovery area (o1_mf_example_2obvkx07_.dbf).

3. Take the damaged datafile offline, if not offline already:

```
RMAN> sql 'alter database datafile 5 offline';

sql statement: alter database datafile 5 offline
```

4. Now, instruct the database to make the copy of the file in the flash recovery area, the production datafile:

```
RMAN> switch datafile 5 to copy;

datafile 5 switched to datafile copy "/home/oracle/flasharea/PROD2/datafile/➥
o1_mf_example_2obvkx07_.dbf"
```

5. Recover the copy to make it consistent with the current state of the database:

```
RMAN> recover datafile 5;

Starting recover at 12-NOV-06
using channel ORA_DISK_1

starting media recovery
media recovery complete, elapsed time: 00:00:06

Finished recover at 12-NOV-06
```

6. Bring the recovered datafile online:

```
RMAN> sql 'alter database datafile 5 online';

sql statement: alter database datafile 5 online
```

When you bring the datafile back online, the tablespace will be brought online as well. The tablespace is now operational. Don't leave the database using a file in the flash recovery area, though, especially not for the long term. When you have some time, follow the steps in recipe 3-14 to switch to the original datafile.

How It Works

It is important to contrast this recipe's approach to recovery with the traditional Oracle database recovery technique. If one of your database datafiles fails, the traditional solution is to restore the datafile from your RMAN backup and then recover it. In summary, the steps are roughly as follows:

1. Take the tablespace offline (if not already).

2. Restore the datafile from RMAN backup.

3. Apply the incremental backups.

4. Recover the datafile by applying archived redo logs.

5. Bring the tablespace online.

These steps will recover the datafile, but note the steps carefully. Steps 2 and 3 involve actual data transfer from the RMAN backup to the original datafile location, and those transfers will take a considerable amount of time, depending on the type of RMAN storage, the speed of the connection, the other load on the SAN at the time, and so on. During these steps, the tablespace remains offline, and data in the tablespace remains inaccessible.

Now consider the approach shown in this recipe. If you took datafile image copies in RMAN, you can switch to using the copy of the damaged datafile instead of restoring from that copy. The advantage here is that pointing to a different file is for all practical purposes an instant operation—you save all the time you would normally spend copying from a backup. Figure 3-2 should make the concept easier to understand. For simplicity, assume the database has only three datafiles—File1, File2, and File3. The RMAN backups are done as image copies, which are made in the flash recovery area.

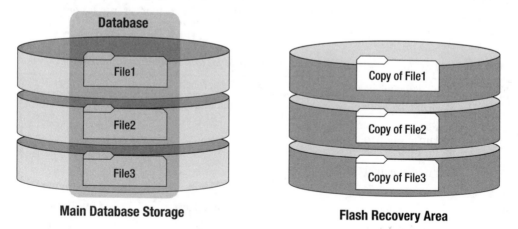

Figure 3-2. *Presence of image copies in the flash recovery area*

Suppose now File1 gets damaged. Ordinarily, you would resort to restoring the file from the image copy and recovering it. However, the image copy is actually a copy of the datafile File1, and it can be used as a substitute. Of course, the copy was taken at some point in the past, so it's not up-to-date, and it must be updated before being used. You do this update by applying the archived redo logs to the image copy. Finally, after the image copy is current, you used the `switch` command to make the datafile copy part of the database.

Now you are running the database with one file in the flash recovery area. Figure 3-3 depicts the datafiles being used now.

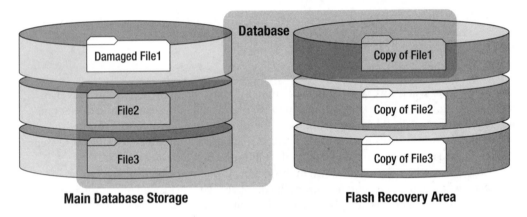

Figure 3-3. *Use of image copy of datafile File1*

As an illustration, Table 3-5 compares the elapsed times under both approaches. The time estimates are highly approximate and depend on your specific conditions such as hardware, disk speed, and so on. It is shown as an illustration for the relative analysis, not for empirical establishment of elapsed times.

Table 3-5. *Comparison of Elapsed Times During Traditional and Image Copy Switch Approaches*

Step	Original Approach	Switch Approach	Time
1	Make datafile offline	Make datafile offline	1 minute
2	Restore copy of datafile from the backup location to the main data file location	N/A	2 hours
3	Apply incremental backup	N/A	30 minutes
4	N/A	Switch to copy	1 minute
5	Recover datafile	Recover datafile	30 minutes
6	Make datafile online	Make datafile online	1 minute

As you can see from the comparison in Table 3-5, the switch approach eliminates steps 2 and 3, saving 2.5 hours (your time savings will vary). The switch approach takes about 33 minutes to get a tablespace back online, while the original approach takes more than 3 hours. (Again, your timesavings may vary from this example.) If time to return to service is a priority, then you should seriously consider this recipe's approach as a recovery strategy.

3-14. Switching Back from an Image Copy

Problem

You've followed recipe 3-13 in order to quickly get back online after a datafile failure. You did that by having your database switch to the image copy of the failed file in the flash recovery area. Now you have some time, and you want to undo that switch.

Solution

Begin by creating a copy of the datafile at the main location. Then switch to using that copy. Here are the steps to follow:

1. Check the datafiles once again:

```
RMAN> report schema;

using target database control file instead of recovery catalog
Report of database schema

List of Permanent Datafiles
===========================
File Size(MB) Tablespace          RB segs Datafile Name
---- -------- -------------------- ------- ------------------------
1    480      SYSTEM              ***     /home/oracle/oradata/PRODB2/SYSTEM.dbf
2    200      UNDOTBS1            ***     /home/oracle/oradata/PRODB2/UNDOTBS1.dbf
3    280      SYSAUX             ***     /home/oracle/oradata/PRODB2/SUSAUX.dbf
4    7        USERS              ***     /home/oracle/oradata/PRODB2/USERS.dbf
5    70       EXAMPLE            ***     /home/oracle/flasharea/PROD2/datafile➥
/o1_mf_example_2obvkx07_.dbf
List of Temporary Files
=======================
File Size(MB) Tablespace          Maxsize(MB) Tempfile Name
---- -------- -------------------- ----------- --------------------
1    26       TEMP                32767       home/oracle/oradata/PRODB2/TEMP.dbf
```

   Note how datafile 5 is in the flash recovery area. You want to move it to its original location.

2. Remove the file at the OS level from the original location, if present. The file is unused, so it can be removed without any effect on the database. This is an example in Unix:

```
$ rm /home/oracle/oradata/PRODB2/EXAMPLE.dbf
```

3. Connect to RMAN:

```
$ rman target=/
```

4. Create an image copy of the file, in this case file 5. Place that image copy in the file's *original* location:

```
RMAN> backup as copy datafile 5 format='/home/oracle/oradata/PRODB2/EXAMPLE.dbf';

Starting backup at 12-NOV-06
using channel ORA_DISK_1
channel ORA_DISK_1: starting datafile copy
input datafile fno=00005
name=/home/oracle/flasharea/PROD2/datafile/o1_mf_example_2obvkx07_.dbf
output filename=/home/oracle/oradata/PRODB2/EXAMPLE.dbf tag=➥
TAG20061112T181248 recid=142 stamp=606334379
channel ORA_DISK_1: datafile copy complete, elapsed time: 00:00:15
Finished backup at 12-NOV-06

Starting Control File Autobackup at 12-NOV-06
piece handle=/home/oracle/flasharea/PROD2/autobackup/2006_11_12/➥
1_mf_n_606334383_2ohbn0wd_.bkp comment=NONE
Finished Control File Autobackup at 12-NOV-06
```

5. Take the datafile offline:

```
RMAN> sql 'alter database datafile 5 offline';

sql statement: alter database datafile 5 offline
```

6. Switch the datafile to the copy you just placed in the original location:

```
RMAN> switch datafile 5 to copy;

datafile 5 switched to datafile copy "/home/oracle/oradata/PRODB2/EXAMPLE.dbf"
```

7. Recover the datafile to bring it up-to-date with changes that occurred between step 4 and step 5:

```
RMAN> recover datafile 5;

Starting recover at 12-NOV-06
using channel ORA_DISK_1

starting media recovery
media recovery complete, elapsed time: 00:00:03

Finished recover at 12-NOV-06
```

8. Bring the datafile online:

```
RMAN> sql 'alter database datafile 5 online';

sql statement: alter database datafile 5 online

RMAN>
```

9. Check the location of the file once again:

```
RMAN> report schema;

using target database control file instead of recovery catalog
Report of database schema

List of Permanent Datafiles
===========================
File Size(MB) Tablespace           RB segs Datafile Name
---- -------- -------------------- ------- ------------------------
1    480      SYSTEM               ***     /home/oracle/oradata/PRODB2/SYSTEM.dbf
2    200      UNDOTBS1             ***     /home/oracle/oradata/PRODB2/UNDOTBS1.dbf
3    280      SYSAUX               ***     /home/oracle/oradata/PRODB2/SUSAUX.dbf
4    7        USERS                ***     /home/oracle/oradata/PRODB2/USERS.dbf
5    70       EXAMPLE              ***     /home/oracle/oradata/PRODB2/EXAMPLE.dbf

List of Temporary Files
=======================
File Size(MB) Tablespace           Maxsize(MB) Tempfile Name
---- -------- -------------------- ----------- --------------------
1    26       TEMP                 32767       home/oracle/oradata/PRODB2/TEMP.dbf
```

The file is in the proper location now.

10. As a best practice, you should now create a fresh image copy of the file and place it in the flash recovery area:

```
RMAN> backup as copy datafile 5;

Starting backup at 12-NOV-06
using channel ORA_DISK_1
channel ORA_DISK_1: starting datafile copy
input datafile fno=00005 name=/home/oracle/oradata/PRODB2/EXAMPLE.dbf
output filename=/home/oracle/flasharea/PROD2/datafile/o1_mf_example_➥
2ohbslqx_.dbf tag=TAG20061112T181602 recid=144 stamp=606334572
channel ORA_DISK_1: datafile copy complete, elapsed time: 00:00:15
Finished backup at 12-NOV-06
```

This step creates a new image copy of the file in the flash recovery area. Now you are well prepared for any future failure involving that same file.

How It Works

Although a quick switch to an image copy in the flash recovery area can get you back up and running with a minimal loss of time after a datafile failure, running with a datafile in the flash recovery area offers its own problems. The flash recovery area, by definition, is for backups. Many sites choose to put their flash recovery area on disks that are not as reliable as those used for the main database files. Perhaps those disks are not mirrored or are slower. You may not want to keep your now main datafiles there for long.

Even if your flash recovery area is on reliable disks, consider the implications of another failure. By design, you have strived to separate the storage of the main database and the flash recovery area to reduce the possibility of failure in both locations simultaneously. Keeping one datafile in the flash recovery area violates that principle. You should move the datafile back to the original location as soon as possible.

3-15. Backing Up the FRA to Tape

Problem

You want to back up the contents of the flash recovery area to tape to be shipped offsite and reuse the storage in the flash recovery area.

Solution

The flash recovery area is, after all, a disk location. This location is prone to the same failures as any other disk-based location. Again, because the Oracle Database 10g knows about the special purpose of the flash recovery location, it knows how to back it up to tape using just one command. Just define a channel to tape, and issue the special RMAN command backup recovery area:

```
RMAN> run {
2>    allocate channel c1 type sbt_tape;
3>    backup recovery area;
4> };
```

This run block backs up the entire flash recovery area to tape.

How It Works

This recipe first creates a channel based on tape. A lot of details have been omitted here on the channel allocation for tape drive. These details rely heavily on the type of media management library used. We discuss media management libraries used in tape backups in Chapter 18.

After the channel creation, the next command in the script backs the flash recovery area to tape using a single command. RMAN knows the existence of the various types of files in the flash recovery area. After the backup to tape, RMAN marks the backed-up files as redundant and as candidates for deletion in the event that space needs to be freed. For instance, suppose your retention policy is that only one version of a backup is to be retained, and the backup of the files in the flash recovery area are themselves backed up to tape. Those backup files will be made obsolete. If there is no room on the flash recovery area and new backups need space, Oracle deletes those obsolete backup files since they are already available on the tape.

3-16. Sizing the Flash Recovery Area

Problem

While setting up the flash recovery area, you have to specify its size. If you specify a very low setting, backups will fail, and a high setting will waste space without adding a real value. How can you determine the correct size?

Solution

Sizing the flash recovery area is a rather complex topic, and getting to a reasonable size will require some analysis on your part. In this recipe, you will see how to use a worksheet to arrive at the optimal size of the flash recovery area for your database.

Here are the different files you are concerned with:

- Copy of all datafiles

- Incremental backups, as used by your chosen backup strategy

- Flashback logs (if enabled)

- Online redo logs

- Archived redo logs not yet backed up to tape

- Control files

- Control file autobackups (which include copies of the control file and spfile)

Since flashback logs are created only when the database runs in flashback mode, we will not include the space for those in this calculation. Decide how many versions to keep for each type, and determine how big each version of each file will be. You can get the size of each version by watching it for a few days. For instance, if the control file is 10MB, then you can assume that the control file autobackup will also be 10MB per backup set. For image copies, the size of the backups will be the same as the size of datafiles. For regular RMAN backups, you should observe the backup sets for a few days to get an idea about their sizes.

Once you determine the size of each type of file and have decided how many versions you should keep, you are ready for the next step. In this step, you decide what type of backup you will use. Your choices are as follows:

Regular RMAN backups: You back up incrementally (Level 1) every day and create a full backup (Level 0) at a longer frequency, say once a week. In this case, you will need to keep at least the prior Level 0 backup and all the Level 1 backups until the next Level 0 backup. However, you must keep the first Level 0 backup intact until the second Level 0 backup successfully completes. If the second Level 0 backup fails, you will need the first one to recover. For archived redo logs, you can back up and delete them after you create an incremental Level 1 backup. So, here is the minimum number of files you should plan for:

- Two copies of Level 0 backup

- Six days of incremental Level 1 backups

- Two days of archived redo logs

Of course, these are minimums. If you plan to have redundancy in the backups or you plan to retain longer for the purpose of doing a point-in-time recovery, you will need more space for more files, and you'll need to increase the numbers given here to values appropriate for your plans.

RMAN image copies: The frequency is similar to the regular backup option. You'll take a Level 0 backup every week and a Level 1 backup every day. Again, here are the minimum files counts:

- Two copies of Level 0 backup

- Six days of incremental Level 1 backups

- Two days of archived redo logs

RMAN image copies with the merge backup option: Here you can take an incremental backup every day but merge that with the Level 0 backup already present. This option does not need the incremental backups to be kept, since they are merged with the Level 0 backup. You need space for only one incremental backup and only one Level 0 backup. Here are the minimum quantities of files that you need to keep:

- One Level 0 image copy

- One incremental Level 1 backup

- Two days of archived redo logs

Once you decide the exact alternative to choose from the preceding list, figure out the size of the following components:

RMAN regular backup set Level 0 backup: You can get the size of this component by watching the space it takes from one RMAN run. Since RMAN regular backups skip the unused blocks, the size will be less than the total database size, and you can determine that by watching a Level 0 backup set. Assume it's 2,500GB.

RMAN image copies: Getting the size of these files is simple. Just add up the size of all the datafiles. The following query shows it:

```
SQL> select sum(bytes)/1024/1024
  2  from dba_data_files;

SUM(BYTES)/1024/1024
--------------------
         3188263.55
```

Now you know that each Level 0 image copy of the database takes about 3,188,263.55MB, or 3TB.

RMAN incremental Level 1 backup: This is something you have to determine by watching how big each incremental Level 1 takes. Assume it's 200GB.

Archived redo logs for a day: You can get the total size of the archived redo logs generated and the count by issuing the following query:

```
select count(1), avg(blocks*block_size)/1024 MB
from v$archived_log
where completion_time between sysdate-1 and sysdate
```

Suppose the output comes back as follows:

```
  COUNT(1)                      MB
---------- ----------------------
        10             103657472
```

From the output, you know every day the database generates about ten archived redo logs of the total size 103,657,472KB, or about 100GB.

Size of the control file: Assume it to be 200MB for this example's purposes.

Taking the numbers you've come up, you can use the worksheet shown in Table 3-6 to arrive at the size of the flash recovery area.

Table 3-6. *Worksheet to Calculate the Size of the FRA*

Type	Size per File or Set	Total per Cycle (Week)	Total	Description
Full backup set				Put how many of the Level 0 backup sets are required and the size of each.
Image copies				If you use image copies instead of backup sets, use this instead.
Archived redo logs				Calculate how many archived redo logs are needed. If you take a daily incremental Level 1 or Level 0 backup, you need about two days of archived redo logs. Remember, this is the archived redo log backups, not the archived redo logs themselves.
Incremental copy of the datafiles				Size of incremental Level 1 RMAN backup.
Control file autobackup				Put the size of the control file autobackup.
Total space required				Count the sum of the space needed.

How It Works

Sizing a flash recovery area is simple in concept. Decide on a backup strategy. Work through each file type to determine how much flash recovery space each file type needs. Total everything up. Allocate that amount of space. The key to success is to carefully think through the details.

By the way, in this recipe we have assumed that the flash recovery area to be sized will be used for only one database. If you have more than database to back up to the same area, calculate the space for each database, and sum the resulting values to arrive at a size that will suffice for a combined flash recovery area serving all the databases.

Tables 3-7 through 3-9 show several working examples of our sizing worksheet. There's one example for each of the three backup strategies that we listed earlier in the solution section. Our file sizes and counts won't match yours of course, but you can see how the different values in the worksheets ultimately lead to a size recommendation for the flash recovery area.

Table 3-7. *Sizing the FRA for Regular RMAN Backup*

Type	Size per File or Set	Total per Cycle (Week)	Total	Description
Full backup set	2,500	2	5,000	We need 2 Level 0 backups per cycle, that is, a week.
Image copies	0	0	0	We take RMAN backup sets in this option, so this is not required.
Archived redo logs	100	2	200	Two days worth of archived redo logs backup.
Incremental copy of the datafiles	200	6	600	
Control file autobackup	0.20	7	1.40	
Total space required			**5,801.40**	

Table 3-8. *Sizing the FRA for RMAN Image Backup*

Type	Size per File or Set	Total per Cycle (Week)	Total	Description
Full backup set	0	0	0	We use image copies, so this is zero.
Image copies	3,000	2	6,000	We need 2 Level 0 backups per cycle, that is, a week.
Archived redo logs	100	2	200	Two days worth of archived redo logs backup.
Incremental copy of the datafiles	200	6	600	
Control file autobackup	0.20	7	1.40	
Total space required			**6,801.40**	

Table 3-9. *Sizing the FRA for RMAN Image Backup with Merge*

Type	Size per File or Set	Total per Cycle (Week)	Total	Description
Full backup set	0	0	0	We use image copies, so this is zero.
Image copies	3,000	1	3,000	We need only one Level 0 backup per cycle, that is, a week, which is updated every day by merging the incremental.
Archived redo logs	100	2	200	Two days worth of archived redo logs backup.
Incremental copy	200	1	200	Since we merge the Level 1 incremental backups with the Level 0 one, we will not need six of them; only one will be present at any point.
Control file autobackup	0.20	2	0.4	There is no need to control file backups since each day the incremental is merged with the Level 0.
Total space required			3,400.40	

CHAPTER 4

■■■

Using RMAN

You can start using RMAN to back up and recover your databases with very little fanfare. When you install the Oracle server software, you'll automatically install RMAN as well. You only absolutely need two things to start using RMAN: the database you want to back up (referred to as the *target database*) and the RMAN client, which is the interface you use to interact with the RMAN server processes that perform the actual backup and recovery tasks.

When you use RMAN to back up and recover your database files and objects, you use the RMAN client to interact with the database. The RMAN client interprets the RMAN commands you issue and starts up the necessary server sessions to process those commands. The term *RMAN repository* refers to the record of RMAN metadata about all backup and recovery actions on the target database. RMAN relies on this metadata when it performs backup and recovery operations.

By default, RMAN always stores a copy of the RMAN repository in the target database's control file. Optionally, you can also use a *recovery catalog* for long-term storage of the RMAN repository. Whenever there is a change in the database structure, archived redo logs, or backups, RMAN updates the recovery catalog with the new information from the target database control file. This way, you have an alternate source for the all-important RMAN repository data if you lose or can't access the control file of the target database. In addition, the recovery catalog provides a long-term storage capacity for all RMAN backup and recovery information, whereas such older data is liable to be overwritten in the control file. The recovery catalog exists as a separate database schema, located ideally in a database separate from the target database(s). You can simplify your RMAN administration by using a single recovery catalog for all your Oracle databases.

You start up the RMAN client using the RMAN executable rman, which you'll find in the $ORACLE_HOME/bin directory. In addition to the rman executable, RMAN also comes with two other internal components: one a set of PL/SQL procedures in the target database and the other a file named recover.bsq. RMAN turns the backup and recovery commands you issue into PL/SQL procedure calls using the recover.bsq file to construct the calls. After you start the RMAN client, you must log in using either operating system credentials or database authentication. After logging in, you can issue backup and recovery instructions either by entering RMAN commands at the command line or by executing a script file that contains RMAN commands. You can also issue several types of SQL commands from the RMAN command line. After you finish your backup and recovery session, you exit the RMAN client.

In addition to the target database and the RMAN client, the RMAN environment can have other optional elements. If you follow the Oracle's backup and recovery recommendations (see Chapter 1), you may also have a flash recovery area. In addition, you must have a media management layer (MML) to interact with tape drives, since RMAN can't work directly with the tape drives. RMAN can use either a third-party MML or Oracle's own backup and recovery offering, called Oracle Secure Backup. The MML accesses and controls the tape libraries and manages the loading and unloading of tapes.

Finally, if you plan on working with several databases, it may be a smart idea to use an RMAN catalog database, which is a separate Oracle database dedicated to storing the recovery catalog. Although the recovery catalog isn't mandatory, it provides two important advantages over using the database control file to store the RMAN metadata relating to backup and recovery activity: you can store vastly greater amounts of data in the recovery catalog as compared to a control file, and you can store RMAN scripts inside the recovery catalog. By default, all RMAN-related records in the target database's control file are overwritten after seven days, but you can control the length of retention by setting a higher value for the initialization parameter `control_file_record_keep_time`.

One may argue that since the control file can record all of RMAN's metadata, there is no need to create and manage a separate recovery catalog database to store RMAN metadata. However, consider a situation where you lose all your control file copies at once. You can, of course, rebuild the control file quickly using the output of a recent `alter database backup controlfile to trace` command. However, when you re-create the control file using the output of that command, the one thing you do not get back is all the RMAN metadata that used to be stored in the control file! This and the fact that Oracle may always overwrite even useful RMAN metadata in the control file means you should seriously consider using the recovery catalog. Oracle recommends using a recovery catalog in order to provide redundancy for your RMAN metadata. Chapter 6 discusses the recovery catalog in detail.

4-1. Starting the RMAN Client

Problem

You want to start working with the RMAN tool and need to use the RMAN client.

Solution

Invoke the RMAN executable, which is named `rman`, in order to start the RMAN client. The RMAN executable file is always in the $ORACLE_HOME/bin directory. If you've set your ORACLE_HOME environment variable, you'll be able to invoke RMAN from any directory by simply entering the command `rman` at the command prompt:

```
$ rman
Recovery Manager: Release 11.1.0.1.0 - Beta on Mon Apr 2 06:31:11 2007
Copyright (c) 1982, 2005, Oracle.  All rights reserved.

RMAN>
```

When the RMAN prompt is displayed, you aren't connected to a target database or the recovery catalog. You must of course connect to the target database, the recovery catalog, or the auxiliary database (or sometimes all of them) to perform backup and recovery tasks. Once you finish working with RMAN, you shut down the Recovery Manager by using the command exit at the RMAN prompt:

```
RMAN> exit
```

You can also use the `quit` command to terminate your RMAN session, as shown here:

```
RMAN> quit
```

How It Works

The command `rman` starts the RMAN client. Once the RMAN prompt is displayed, you can choose to connect to the target database, the recovery catalog, or an auxiliary database. If you issue any RMAN command at this stage, RMAN will use the RMAN repository in the default nocatalog mode. You can't use the `connect catalog` command to connect to the recovery catalog after having issued RMAN commands in the nocatalog mode—you must first exit RMAN before you can restart and make a connection to the recovery catalog.

Even if you've set the Oracle-specific operating system environment variables correctly, you may find that absolutely nothing happens when you execute the `rman` command, as shown in the previous example. If you have a problem with starting the client, simply specify the complete path to the RMAN executable when you invoke RMAN:

```
$ $ORACLE_HOME/bin/rman
```

The reason you may need to specify the full path names is that in some operating systems, the command `rman` may be pointing not to the Recovery Manager executable but to another executable on Linux with an identical name (`rman`). You can verify whether that's the case by issuing the `which` command in Linux (and Unix), which tells you which particular version of an executable is being executed. For example, the following command will reveal the exact RMAN executable that's executed:

```
$ which rman
/usr/bin/X11/rman
$
```

In this case, the executable being shown is in the /usr/bin/X11 directory, and it is a binary that belongs to the XFree86 operating system. Since XFree86 has nothing to do with Oracle RMAN, you must use the command `$ORACLE_HOME/bin/rman` to invoke Oracle's RMAN client. An even easier way to get around this problem would be to place the $ORACLE_HOME/bin location at the beginning of the PATH environmental variable.

4-2. Issuing RMAN Commands

Problem

You'd like to start working with RMAN and issue the various RMAN commands to back up your database and to manage those backups.

Solution

RMAN uses a free-form command language. Each RMAN command statement starts with a keyword, is followed by specific arguments, and ends with a semicolon. A command can be one line or multiple lines. For example, the following single-line command initiates a backup of the target database:

```
RMAN> backup database;
```

If you enter a partial command and hit Enter, RMAN will prompt you to continue the input and provides a line number as well. In the following example, the command requests RMAN to back up the database along with its control file:

```
RMAN> backup database
   2> include current
   3> controlfile
   4> ;
```

You can add comments to your RMAN commands, which makes it easy to follow the logic of your RMAN commands when you use several of them inside a command file (we discuss RMAN command files later in this chapter). Each comment must be preceded by the # sign. Here's an example of an RMAN command file that performs an incremental backup of the database:

```
# this command will be run daily
backup incremental level 1
for recover of copy  # uses incrementally updated backups
database;
```

How It Works

When you begin entering a command, RMAN buffers every line that you enter until you end a line with a semicolon. Any text on a line following a # sign is considered commentary and is ignored. When you enter the terminating semicolon, RMAN executes the command that you've entered. Although you aren't supposed to use reserved keywords as part of the arguments you supply to RMAN commands, you can, if you want, use reserved keywords by simply enclosing them within double quotes, as shown in the following example, which allocates an RMAN channel named backup (which is an RMAN reserved word):

```
RMAN> allocate channel 'backup' device type disk;
```

In general, it's probably best to avoid using RMAN keywords for things such as channel names.

4-3. Saving RMAN Output to a Text File

Problem

You want to save the output of an RMAN session to a text file.

Solution

You can save RMAN output to a text file by issuing the spool command and specifying the name of the log file. You don't have to create the log file beforehand. Here's an example showing how to use the spool command:

```
spool log to '/tmp/rman/backuplog.f';
backup datafile 1;
spool log off;
```

RMAN will create the log file if it doesn't already exist. If a file with the same name exists, RMAN will overwrite the older file.

How It Works

The spool command works the same way as it does in SQL*Plus. If the file with the same name you specify already exists, RMAN will overwrite the file, unless you specify the append option. For example:

```
spool log to '/tmp/rman/backuplog.f' append.
```

The previous spool command will add the new contents to the end of the log file named backuplog.

4-4. Logging Command-Line RMAN Output

Problem

You want to log the output of RMAN commands you issue in command-line mode.

Solution

If you want RMAN to log all its output when you use RMAN from the operating system command line, just add the keyword log to the command line, and supply the name of the log file to use. For example:

```
$ rman target / cmdfile commandfile1.rcv  log /u01/app/oracle/outfile.txt
```

In this case, RMAN will write the output of the RMAN commands in the command file named commandfile.rcv to the log file outfile.txt. If you later want to run another set of RMAN commands and want to append the log messages to the same log file, you can do this by using the append option along with the log option. Here's an example:

```
$ rman target / cmdfile commandfile2.rcv log /u01/app/oracle/outfile.txt append
```

The previous command will append the output from executing the command file commandfile2.rcv to the text file outfile.txt.

How It Works

The command-line argument log causes RMAN to send all its output to the log file you specify. Failure to add the keyword append when referring to an already existing log file will result in the overwriting of that older log file.

If you are running RMAN interactively and you want to see output on your terminal screen as well as have it written to a log file, you can take advantage of the Unix/Linux tee command. The tee command sends output both to a text file and to the terminal. Here's how you use the tee command:

```
$ rman | tee rman.log
RMAN>
```

All is not lost if you don't specify a log file to capture the RMAN output. The view V$RMAN_OUTPUT returns detailed information about RMAN jobs in progress. For example, if your media manager runs into a problem with a tape drive, RMAN records the associated error messages in V$RMAN_OUTPUT and also outputs the message to the terminal or to a log file. As with all dynamic performance views, the contents of the V$RMAN_OUTPUT view are refreshed when you restart the database. The V$RMAN_STATUS view contains information about completed RMAN jobs as well as all RMAN jobs in progress.

4-5. Connecting to a Target Database from the RMAN Prompt

Problem

You want to connect to your target database from the RMAN prompt.

Solution

After you invoke the RMAN client, you can connect to a target database from the RMAN prompt in order to perform backup and recovery tasks. A target database is the database where you want to perform RMAN backup or recovery actions. You can connect only to a single target database at a time. You can connect with operating system authentication, or you can connect by validating your password against a password file. You must have the sysdba privilege to connect to the target database. However, you do not use the as sysdba clause that you have to use in SQL*Plus when connecting to a database with sysdba privileges. RMAN automatically expects that you have the sysdba privilege and attempts the database connection with that privilege.

You can connect to a target database either by using an operating system authentication method or by supplying the database credentials (provided you use a password file). Here's an example showing how to make a connection using operating system authentication (first make sure you have set the correct ORACLE_SID variable):

```
$ rman
RMAN> connect target /
Connected to target database:  NINA  (DBID=922224687)
RMAN>
```

And here's an example showing how to log in using a database username and password that are authenticated against the password file:

```
$ rman

Recovery Manager: Release 11.1.0.1.0 - Beta on Mon Apr 2 08:31:11 2007

Copyright (c) 1982, 2005, Oracle.  All rights reserved.

RMAN> connect target sys/sammy1@nina
```

This method of connection is also called the *Oracle Net password file* authentication method.

How It Works

To use operating system authentication rather than database authorization to connect to a target database, you must first set your environment correctly so that the ORACLE_SID points to the correct database. Having done that, you can specify `target /` to connect to the target database. As long as you belong to the `dba` group in Unix/Linux or to the `ora_dba` group on Windows, you can connect to the database without specifying a username and password.

When you're using password file authentication, the keyword `target` must specify a database connection string, such as `target sys/sammyy1@mydb`. If you want to make a privileged database connection from RMAN, you must have already created an Oracle password file. The username and password that you give to RMAN must match those recorded in the password file.

■**Note** See the sidebar "Creating an Oracle Password File" for help creating such a file.

CREATING AN ORACLE PASSWORD FILE

You can easily create an Oracle password file with the help of the `orapwd` utility. Just type `orapwd` at the operating system command line to view the syntax of the command:

```
$ orapwd
Usage: orapwd file=<fname> password=<password> entries=<users> force=<y/n>
        ignorecase=<y/n> nosysdba=<y/n>

   where
     file - name of password file (required),
     password - password for SYS (required),
     entries - maximum number of distinct DBA (required),
     force - whether to overwrite existing file (optional),
     ignorecase - passwords are case-insensitive (optional),
     nosysdba - whether to shut out the SYSDBA logon (optional Database Vault only).

   There must be no spaces around the equal-to (=) character.
5
```

Of the six options for the `orapwd` utility, the `file`, `password`, and `entries` options are mandatory. You can create a simple Oracle password file using the following syntax:

```
$ orapwd file=mydb_pwd password=sammyy1 entries=20
```

This command will create an Oracle password file. The default location for the password file is the $ORACLE_HOME/dbs directory. Once you create the password file, edit your init.ora file or your spfile in the following manner:

```
remote_login_passwordfile = 'EXCLUSIVE'
```

Once your restart your database after this, you'll be able to log in as the `sys` user.

4-6. Connecting to a Target Database from the Operating System Command Line

Problem

You want to invoke the RMAN client and connect to the target database from the operating system command line.

Solution

You can make a connection to the target database from the operating system by using the same two methods of connection you use to connect to a target database from within RMAN. That is, you can use either operating system authentication or Oracle Net authentication.

Here's an example showing how to connect to a target database from the command line using operating system authentication:

```
$ rman target /
```

You can also connect to the target database from the command line using Oracle Net password file authentication, as shown here:

```
% rman target sys/<sys password>@trgt
```

How It Works

Once you see the RMAN prompt, you're ready to issue the RMAN commands. RMAN always attempts a database connection assuming you are connecting with the sysdba privilege. If you're having problems connecting to a target database, first check that you can connect to the database from SQL*Plus using the sysdba privilege, as shown in this example:

```
SQL> connect sys/<sys password>@trgt as sysdba
```

4-7. Executing Operating System Commands from Within RMAN

Problem

You've invoked the RMAN client, and now you need to issue some operating system commands.

Solution

Use the RMAN command host to invoke an operating system subshell. You can execute this command in two ways: you can issue it from the RMAN prompt, or you can execute it from inside a run block, which is a group of RMAN commands executed as a single unit. If you issue the host command stand-alone, without any parameters, RMAN will take you to the operating system command line. Thus, the host command works the same in RMAN as it does from within SQL*Plus. If you issue the command host followed by a valid operating system command as a parameter, then RMAN will execute that operating system command and continue to process the rest of the commands in the run block, if there are any.

In the following example, we use the host command to list all files ending with *dbf,* after backing up a datafile from the RMAN prompt:

```
RMAN> shutdown immediate;
RMAN> startup mount;
RMAN> backup datafile '/u01/app/oracle/oradata/targ/system01.dbf'
      format  '/tmp/system01.dbf';
RMAN> host  'ls -l /tmp/*dbf';
RMAN> alter database open;
```

The following example uses the host command with no parameters to temporarily escape to the operating system level during an interactive RMAN session:

```
RMAN> backup datafile 3 format '/u01/app/oracle/oradata/targ_db/dbs01.cpy';
RMAN> host;
    $ ls $ORACLE_HOME/oradata/dbs01.cpy
      /net/oracle/oradata/dbs01.cpy
    $ exit
RMAN>
```

How It Works

As you can see in the two examples, you can use the host command with or without an operating system command as a parameter. If you run the host command as part of a series of RMAN commands, RMAN executes the host command and continues with the rest of the commands. When you execute the host command by itself, RMAN displays the operating system command prompt and resumes after you exit the command-line subshell.

4-8. Scripting RMAN

Problem

You want to automate an RMAN process by executing a set of commands that you've placed into a script file. You don't want to type each command one at a time. You want to start the entire sequence of commands and walk away while they execute. You may even want to execute your script periodically via a job scheduler such as cron.

Solution

It's common practice to include RMAN backup scripts within an operating system shell script. Doing so allows you to schedule your backup jobs via cron to run automatically. The following is an example of an operating system shell script to back up a database. The script executes various RMAN backup commands to perform an incremental backup of a database as well as delete all expired archivelogs.

Notice the <<- EOF notation in lines 2 and 5 and the corresponding EOF markers in lines 4 and 18. Use <<- EOF to tell the shell interpreter that input to the command in question is to be read from the shell script file until an EOF marker is encountered. You can replace the letters EOF with any sequence that you like, but you really should stick with the universally recognized convention of EOF.

```
#!/bin/ksh
1 export ORACLE_SID=$1
2 rman target / catalog rman/rman@rcat > ${LOGFILE} <<- EOF
3 sql 'alter system archive log current';
4 change archivelog all crosscheck;
5 allocate channel for maintenance type disk;
6 delete noprompt expired archivelog all;
7 run {
8 allocate channel ch1 type disk format
9 '${BACKUP_DIR}/%d_level${LEVEL}_${TIMESTAMP}_%s_U%U.bak';
10 set limit channel ch1 kbytes=2000000;
11 backup incremental level ${LEVEL} (database);
12 release channel ch1;
13 resync catalog;
14 }
15 EOF
```

When this script executes, whether it is run from the command line or fired off as a `cron` job, the script will start up RMAN, connect to the target database, and execute the commands to back up that database.

Alternatively, you can write RMAN files that are sequences of RMAN commands. Then you can invoke RMAN from the command line to execute those files. For example, suppose you have a file called full_backup.rman consisting of the following `run` block:

```
run {
   allocate channel d1 type disk;
   backup full database format '/export/rman/rman_%n_%T_%s_%p.bus';
   }
```

You can then invoke RMAN from the operating system command line to execute this file as follows:

```
$ rman target / @full_backup.rman
```

The use of @ followed immediately by the filename causes RMAN to read and execute commands from the specified file.

How It Works

The full benefits of RMAN come when you use it to automate your backup and recovery tasks. Key to doing that is the ability to define sequences of commands that you can execute on demand or on a regular schedule. The solution section shows two general approaches you can take:

- You can embed your RMAN scripts within shell scripts. The advantage here is that you have all commands—both shell and RMAN commands—in one place.

- You can place your RMAN scripts into their own files. This approach works on non-Unix systems, such as Windows. It also enables you to execute those files interactively from the RMAN client.

The solution shows @ as a command-line parameter to RMAN. You can also use @ from within RMAN to interactively execute a file. For example, you can run the following three scripts to first shut down the database, then perform a full backup of the database, and finally open the database after the backup is completed:

```
RMAN> @close_database
RMAN> @full_backup.rman
RMAN> @open_database
```

The @ parameter works from within a run block as well as directly from the RMAN prompt. You can substitute the command cmdfile for @, but most DBAs use @ because it's easier to type and because @ has a long history of being used to invoke scripts in Oracle.

4-9. Executing RMAN Command Files

Problem

You want to automate an RMAN process by executing a set of commands you've placed into a script file. You don't want to type each command one at a time. You want to start the entire sequence of commands and walk away while they execute.

■Note This recipe shows you how to execute a file containing just RMAN commands. This differs from the solution in recipe 4-7, which shows you how to embed RMAN commands in operating system shell scripts.

Solution

Instead of entering each command piecemeal, you can create a *command file* with a number of commands and execute the command file. Use the keyword cmdfile to let RMAN know that it must execute the commands inside the script file command. The individual commands in the command file will execute as if they were entered from the command line. Here's an example showing how to execute a command file named commandfile.rcv:

```
$ rman target / cmdfile commandfile.rcv
```

In this example, the commandfile.rcv file is in the same directory from which you're executing the cmdfile command. If the command file is elsewhere, you must provide the complete path name to access that file. For example:

```
$ rman target / cmdfile /oracle/dbs/cmd/commandfile.rcv
```

You can also execute a command file by placing the @ sign in front of the command file, as shown in the following example:

```
$ rman target / @commandfile.rcv
```

You aren't limited to invoking command files from the command line, though that is very useful when using cron to automate your work. You also have the option of running command files interactively from the RMAN prompt:

```
$ rman target /
RMAN> @commandfile.rcv
RMAN>
```

This approach is useful when you want to execute a script of RMAN commands and then do more work from the RMAN command line. After executing the command file, you'll be back at the RMAN prompt.

Once RMAN finishes executing the contents of the command file you specify, control returns to RMAN once again, and you'll see the following comment on the screen:

```
RMAN>  **end-of-file**
```

You'll still be at the RMAN command line after the command file finishes executing.

How It Works

The RMAN session will terminate immediately after the command file finishes executing. There's an important difference to be aware of regarding how RMAN reacts to syntax errors in command files. The difference depends upon whether you invoke RMAN to execute a command file from the operating system prompt or whether you invoke a command file interactively from the RMAN prompt. Here's what you need to know:

- When you run an RMAN file from the operating system line, RMAN will first try to parse all the RMAN commands in the file. Then RMAN will start executing each in a sequential fashion. If RMAN encounters any errors at the parse stage or during the execution phase, it'll immediately exit.

- On the other hand, when you run an RMAN file from the RMAN prompt, RMAN executes each command separately and will exit only after it attempts the execution of the last command in the file.

In addition to executing a command file from the RMAN prompt, you can also call a command file from within another command file. Use the double at (@@) command for that purpose. When you issue the @@ command inside a command file, RMAN will look for the file specified after the @@ command in the same directory that contains the parent command file. For example:

```
$ rman @$ORACLE_HOME/rdbms/admin/dba/scripts/cmd1.rman
```

In this example, the command @@cmd2.rman is specified within the cmd1.rman command file. Once you execute the main or parent command file (cmd1.rman), RMAN will look for and execute the cmd2 command file in the directory $ORACLE_HOME/rdbms/admin/dba/scripts/, the same directory that holds the parent command file. The @@ command is useful when you have a set of related command files, because you can place all those files into one directory and they can all find each other automatically after that point.

4-10. Creating Dynamic Command Files

Problem

You want to create dynamic command files that can be used for multiple jobs by passing substitution variables.

Solution

You can create dynamic shell scripts by using substitution variables in the RMAN command files inside the shell scripts. You can specify values for use in substitution variables through the new using clause when calling an RMAN command file. You use the *&integer* syntax (&1, &2, and so on) to indicate to which variable your substitution values should be assigned, just as in SQL*Plus.

Let's review an example that shows how to create a dynamic backup shell script.

1. Create the RMAN command file that uses two substitution variables:

```
#backup.cmd
connect target sys/<sys_password>@prod1
run {
backup database
tag &1
format  &2
}
exit;
```

The command file shown here will back up the database using two substitution variables (&1 and &2), one for the backup tag and the other for the string value in the format specification.

2. Create the shell script to run the backup command file you created in step 1:

```
#!/bin/tcsh
# script name: nightly_backup.sh
set tag=$argv(1)
set format=$argv[2]
rman  @backup.cmd using  $tag $format
```

3. Now that you have created a dynamic shell script, you can specify the arguments for the tag and format variables on the command line, thus being able to modify them for different jobs. Here's an example:

```
$ nightly_backup.sh longterm_backup back0420
```

The example shows how to execute the shell script nightly_backup.sh with two dynamic parameters, longterm_backup (tag) and back0420 (format string).

How It Works

The ability to use substitution variables in RMAN scripts is new in Oracle Database 11*g*. The use of substitution variables in RMAN scripts is similar to the way you specify substitution variables in operating system and SQL*Plus scripts. Specifying substitution variables lets you use the same command file by modifying it appropriately for different backup tasks, thus making the command file dynamic.

4-11. Connecting to an Auxiliary Database

Problem

You need to connect to an auxiliary database to duplicate a database or to perform a tablespace point-in-time recovery.

Solution

You can connect to an auxiliary instance either from the operating system command line or from the RMAN prompt. To connect to an auxiliary database instance from the operating system command line, simply replace the usual keyword target with the keyword auxiliary, as shown here:

```
$ rman auxiliary sys/<sys_password>@aux
```

You can also start the RMAN client first and then connect to the auxiliary instance from the RMAN prompt, as shown in this example:

```
$ rman
RMAN> connect auxiliary sys/<sys_password>@aux
```

How It Works

You mostly connect to an auxiliary database to perform a duplicate command or to perform a tablespace point-in-time recovery (TSPITR) operation. The syntax is the same as for connecting to a target database, except that you specify the keyword auxiliary rather than target.

Note that you can't connect to the three types of databases—auxiliary, target, and catalog database—with one connection string once you're working from the RMAN command prompt, whereas you can connect to all three types from the operating system prompt. Once you're operating from an RMAN prompt, you have to connect using separate connect commands for each of the three databases, one after the other, as shown in the following examples:

```
RMAN> connect target sys/<sys_password>@trgt
RMAN> connect catalog rman/<rman_password>@catalog
RMAN> connect auxiliary sys/<sys_password>@aux
```

The following example shows how you can connect to all three types of database in one go from the operating system command line:

```
% rman target sys/oracle@trgt catalog rman/cat@catalog auxiliary sys/aux@aux
```

As you'll see in Chapter 15, when creating a duplicate database, you may not be able to connect to all three instances at once in this fashion, since the auxiliary database may not be open and hence may not permit the use of a connection string to connect to it.

4-12. Executing Multiple RMAN Commands As a Single Unit

Problem

When you are setting up the environment for some RMAN backup and recovery commands from the command line, you'll sometimes need to execute multiple RMAN commands as one atomic operation. That is, you want all commands to be run sequentially if they are syntactically correct but want the entire operation to fail if any of the commands in the group aren't valid.

Solution

You use the RMAN special syntax known as the run block when you want to group a set of RMAN commands into a block and execute the commands serially. RMAN will treat the entire set of commands as one single block, which it'll execute sequentially. The series of commands is enclosed within a beginning and an ending set of curly braces, and the entire set of commands is called a run block.

A common use to which you can put the run block is to override one or more default configuration settings for the duration of a backup job. For instance, you can use a run block to allocate channels using the allocate command in order to override the automatic channels that you configured using the configure command. In the following example, the run block first manually allocates two channels for the disk devices and then backs up the database:

```
run
{
  allocate channel t1 device type disk format '/disk1/%U';
  allocate channel t2 device type disk format '/disk2/%U';
  backup database;
}
```

Here's one more example, this time showing how you use the set command to temporarily change the value of a parameter within a run block. Let's say you configured datafile copies to three using the following command:

```
RMAN> configure datafile backup copies for device type sbt to 3;
```

You can override the default of three copies by using the following run block, where the set command sets the number of backup copies to only two. You'll thus get two copies of each datafile and archived log that's part of the backup.

```
run
{
  allocate channel  dev1 device type sbt;
  set backup copies = 2;
  backup datafile 1,2,3,4,5;
  backup archivelog all;
}
```

Once the `run` block finishes executing, the datafile copies for tape devices will be set to three again, per your configured settings.

How It Works

You can execute a `run` block from the RMAN command line by entering each line sequentially, but it's more common to employ the `run` block from inside a command file. You can then execute the command file from the RMAN prompt or use it inside a cron job. The `run` block is useful when you want to schedule RMAN jobs, say through the `cron` facility. Once RMAN completes checking the syntax of the input lines in the `run` block, it'll execute each statement sequentially.

When RMAN encounters the closing brace of a `run` block, it groups the commands into one or more job steps and starts executing the job step(s) immediately. Frequently, you use a `run` block to override the default configured channels or other parameters for a certain task and then reset the channels or parameters to their original values before finishing the `run` block. RMAN uses the `allocate channel` and `release channel` commands to override the default configured channels for a task. You use the `set` command to change other parameters. You can specify the allocate channel and set commands within a `run` block to override the default values of key RMAN backup and recovery settings for a particular job.

You can use some RMAN commands only within a `run` block. These commands, such as `allocate channel` and `set newname for datafile`, are typically used to set the execution environment for the other RMAN commands within the `run` block. Conversely, you can't use some of the RMAN commands dealing with configuration and environmental settings within a `run` block. For example, you can't use the following commands from within a `run` block:

```
connect, configure
create catalog, drop catalog, upgrade catalog
create script, delete script, replace script
list
report
```

Note that you can use any of the commands listed previously inside a command file, as long as you don't enclose them inside a `run` block. In Chapter 9 you'll learn about storing RMAN scripts, known as *stored scripts*, within the recovery catalog. Since all commands inside a stored script must be enclosed in a `run` block, it means you can't use any of the commands listed here in a stored script as well.

When you invoke an RMAN script, you must do so only within a `run` block, as shown in the following example, where the script backup_db is executed using a `run` block:

```
 run {execute script backup_db; }
```

We discuss RMAN scripting in detail in Chapter 9.

4-13. Issuing SQL Statements from the RMAN Client

Problem

You're using RMAN to issue backup and recovery commands, and you find that you need to issue some SQL statements as well.

Solution

It's easy to execute a SQL statement from RMAN. All you need to do is type the keyword SQL followed by the actual SQL statement. Make sure you enclose the actual SQL statement inside single or double quotes. For example:

```
RMAN> SQL 'alter system archive log all';
```

You can execute SQL statements from within a run block too. The following run block restores and then recovers the tablespace tools:

```
run
{
  SQL "alter tablespace tools offline immediate";
  restore tablespace tools;
  recover tablespace tools;
  SQL "alter tablespace tools online";
}
```

The example shown here illustrates how you can interleave SQL statements and RMAN commands within a single run block. The first SQL statement takes the tools tablespace offline. Following this, the two RMAN commands first restore and then recover the tools tablespace. The final SQL statement at the end of the run block brings the tools tablespace online.

How It Works

Usually, you use the RMAN command line or a RMAN script to issue RMAN backup and recovery commands. However, from time to time, you may need to issue some SQL commands from within the RMAN interface.

■Note Although you can issue SQL commands from within RMAN, you are limited to commands that don't return data—you can't issue a select statement from within RMAN.

If you're passing filenames with the SQL string you use from the RMAN prompt, you must remember to do the following:

- Enclose the entire SQL string in double quotes.

- Enclose the filename in duplicate single quotes.

Here's an example that shows how to specify a filename in a SQL command issued from the RMAN prompt. Note the use of *two* single quotes inside the SQL statement:

```
SQL "create tablespace test1
    datafile ''/u01/app/oracle/oradata/mydb/test01.dbf''
    size 100m temporary";
```

You can execute PL/SQL blocks in the same manner as SQL statements. Remember that a block includes the begin and end keywords, as shown here:

```
SQL 'begin rman.rman_purge; end;';
```

Similarly, you can execute a PL/SQL block from within a run block, as illustrated for SQL in recipe 4-13.

4-14. Starting and Shutting Down a Database with RMAN

Problem

You need to start and shut down the Oracle database from the RMAN client during a backup and recovery–related task.

Solution

You can both shut down and start up a database using the equivalent of the usual SQL*Plus startup and shutdown commands from the RMAN client. The following sections show how to issue the startup and shutdown commands from RMAN.

Starting a Database

You can use the startup command with several options. Here's an example that shows how the database is opened using the startup command:

```
RMAN> startup
```

RMAN enables you to do more with the nomount option, however. In the following example, you can see how you can go through all the steps of opening a database—starting the instance, restoring the control file, mounting the control files, recovering the database, and, finally, opening the database. The example shows how to restore the control file while connected to the recovery catalog. After restoring the control file, the database is mounted with the alter database mount command. Next you see the recover command, which is mandatory after restoring a control file. Finally, the database is opened with the open resetlogs option:

```
RMAN> connect target /
RMAN> connect catalog rman/rman@catdb
RMAN> startup nomount;
RMAN> restore controlfile;
RMAN> alter database mount;
RMAN> recover database;
RMAN> alter database open resetlogs;
```

The nomount option also comes in handy when you lose your spfile or are forced to start the instance without a spfile (and any init.ora file). You can then use the nomount option to start up the database with a dummy parameter file. For example:

```
set DBID 1296234570;
startup force nomount; # RMAN will start the instance with a dummy parameter file
```

Once RMAN starts the database with the dummy parameter file, you can restore the actual spfile from the autobackup:

```
restore spfile from autobackup; # restore a server parameter file
startup force; # restart instance with the new server parameter file
```

After restoring the spfile, you can start the database using that spfile.

You can also use the dba option with the shutdown command to restrict access only to those users who've been granted the restricted session privilege. Here's how to do that:

```
RMAN> startup dba pfile=/tmp/initprod1.ora;
```

The database is now open, but only users with the restricted session privilege will be able to connect. Typically, DBAs give the restricted session privilege only to each other. It gives you a way to do work in the database while ensuring that no business users are connected.

Shutting Down a Database

Issue the shutdown command to close down the database and stop the instance. All the standard SQL*Plus options you can use with the shutdown command—normal, immediate, abort, and transactional—have the same effect and meaning when used from within RMAN. Here's an example:

```
RMAN> shutdown immediate;
RMAN> startup mount;
RMAN> backup database;
RMAN> alter database open;
```

This example shuts down the database, kicking off any current users as soon as their currently executing SQL statements finish. The database is then backed up and reopened for use.

How It Works

All the shutdown and startup commands shown here pertain only to the target database. You can't start and stop the recovery catalog instance from RMAN. The only way to start up and shut down the recovery catalog instance is by connecting to the recovery catalog database as the target database and by issuing the relevant commands to start or stop the instance.

4-15. Checking the Syntax of RMAN Commands

Problem

You want to check the syntax of your RMAN commands without actually executing the commands.

Solution

To check the syntax of RMAN commands, you must start the RMAN client with the operating system command-line argument checksyntax. You can easily check the syntax of commands prior to their execution either by entering them at the command prompt or by reading in the commands through a command file. Here's how you check the syntax of a single RMAN command (run {backup database;}) by first starting the RMAN client with the checksyntax argument:

```
$. /rman checksyntax
Recovery Manager: Release 11.1.0.1.0 - Beta on Mon Apr 2 08:31:11 2007

Copyright (c) 1982, 2005, Oracle.  All rights reserved.
RMAN> run {backup database;}

The command has no syntax errors
RMAN>
```

In this example, there were no errors in the syntax of the simple run block, and RMAN confirms that. You can also use the checksyntax argument to check the syntax of RMAN commands that are part of a command file. Simply specify the checksyntax argument before invoking the command file that consists of the RMAN commands. In the following example, the file goodcmdfile contains a couple of restore and recovery commands:

```
$ rman checksyntax @/tmp/goodcmdfile
Recovery Manager: Release 11.1.0.1.0 - Beta on Mon Apr 2 08:31:11 2007

Copyright (c) 1982, 2005, Oracle.  All rights reserved.

 RMAN> #  file with legal syntax
    2> restore database;
    3> recover database;
    4>
The cmdfile has no syntax errors
 Recovery Manager complete.
$
```

You can also open an RMAN session solely for the purpose of checking the syntax of commands that you type interactively:

```
$ rman checksyntax
```

An important point about the checksyntax argument is that you can't use it after starting RMAN. That is, you can't include the checksyntax argument from the RMAN command line. You must pass checksyntax as an argument to the rman command when you start the RMAN client and without connecting to any target or recovery catalog.

How It Works

When you either execute an RMAN command file by preceding it with the checksyntax argument or enter any RMAN commands after starting RMAN with the checksyntax argument, RMAN won't actually execute any RMAN commands. RMAN will check and report only on the syntax of those commands. If the RMAN commands that you type at the command line or that you include as part of a command file have no errors, you get the "the command (cmdfile) has no errors" message from RMAN. Otherwise, RMAN will issue an error, as shown in the following example:

```
$ rman checksyntax @/tmp/badcmdfile
Recovery Manager: Release 11.1.0.1.0 - Beta on Mon Apr 2 08:31:11 2007

Copyright (c) 1982, 2005, Oracle.  All rights reserved.

RMAN> #  file with illegal syntax
RMAN> run (backup database);

RMAN-00571: ===========================================================
RMAN-00569: =============== ERROR MESSAGE STACK FOLLOWS ===============
RMAN-00571: ===========================================================
RMAN-00558: error encountered while parsing input commands
RMAN-01009: syntax error: found "(": expecting one of: "{"
RMAN-01007: at line 1 column 5 file: standard input

RMAN>
```

The output of the checksyntax command reveals there is a syntax error in your run block. The checksyntax command is handy for checking scripts for syntax errors. With RMAN, there's no need for a script to fail unexpectedly because you mangled the syntax of a command. If you're surprised by an error, it's because you didn't test with checksyntax first.

4-16. Hiding Passwords When Connecting to RMAN

Problem

You want to hide the database passwords when connecting to the RMAN client.

Solution

One of the easiest ways to prevent others from gleaning sensitive database passwords by looking over your shoulder is simply to never type a password directly at the operating system level when starting the RMAN client. One approach is to pass only your username on the command line, letting RMAN prompt for your password:

```
$ rman target sys@nick
Recovery Manager: Release 11.1.0.1.0 - Beta on Mon Apr 2 08:31:11 2007

Copyright (c) 1982, 2005, Oracle.  All rights reserved.

target database Password:
connected to target database: NICK (DBID=2561840016)

RMAN>
```

When RMAN prompts you for the target database password, it won't echo the characters you type to the terminal, and thus your password is safe from prying eyes.

If you're using a command file that employs database credentials (username and password), you must ensure that the connection string doesn't get written to any log files that capture the RMAN output. One good way to prevent the Oracle user password from being captured by an

RMAN log file is to run command files using the @ command-line option. In the following example, the command file backup.rman contains the following lines:

```
connect target sys/syspassword@trgt
backup database;
```

Execute the backup.rman command file by using the @ option at the command line:

```
$ rman @backup.rman
```

When the command file executes, the connect command will make the connection to the target database using the database credentials you supplied, but it won't reveal the database password. RMAN replaces the connection credentials (username and password) with an asterisk, as shown here:

```
$ rman
Recovery Manager: Release 11.1.0.1.0 - Beta on Mon Apr 2 08:31:11 2007

Copyright (c) 1982, 2005, Oracle.  All rights reserved.

RMAN> connect target *...
```

In this case, the command file issued a connect target command. That command included a password. RMAN displays the command, but with an asterisk in place of the password.

How It Works

An important fact to remember is that you'll be exposing the database credentials when you connect to RMAN from the operating system command line. For example, a scan of the Unix processes using ps -ef will reveal any RMAN command lines, including passwords. You can avoid this problem by always using the connect string from the RMAN prompt to connect to the recovery catalog, the target database, and the auxiliary database.

■Note Anyone with read permissions on the command file containing the connect string with the password will be able to read that file and obtain the password. For this reason, you should look to secure that file, limiting read access to only DBAs.

4-17. Identifying RMAN Server Sessions

Problem

RMAN performs all its backup and recovery tasks using server sessions. You want to know more about these server sessions, such as how many server sessions are created and how to identify them.

Solution

You can find out the number of RMAN server sessions using this formula:

```
Number of sessions = C+N+2
```

where the following is true:

- C is the number of channels allocated.

- N is the number of "connect" options used in the allocate channel commands (if no connect options are used, N has the value of 1).

If you're using a recovery catalog, there are always at least two sessions, one for connecting to the recovery catalog and the other for the default connection to the target database. The default connection is needed to perform tasks such as applying archived redo logs during a recovery task.

You can find out exactly who is currently running the RMAN client by issuing a command such as ps -ef on a Unix system:

```
$ ps -ef | grep rman
oracle      9255      9012     0    Mar18  pts/4     00:00:01  rman  target  /
oracle      6856      6834     2    Mar18  pts/2     00:00:01  rman  target  /
$
```

Having a list of RMAN client sessions like this, you can pick one in which you're interested. Say that you're interested in the session for process ID 9255. You can then issue the following command, which will find all the child processes associated with that instance of the client:

```
$ ps -ef | grep 9255
oracle      9255      9012     0    Sep18  pts/4     00:00:01  rman   /oracle
/oracle/product/10.2.0/db_1/bin/rman    target  /
oracle      92600     9255     0    Sep18  ?         00:00:00  rman   oraclenina
(DESCRIPTION=(LOCAL=YES)
(ADDRESS=(PROTOCOL=beq)))
 oracle     9255      9012     0    Sep18  pts/4     00:00:00  rman   oraclenina
(DESCRIPTION=(LOCAL=YES)
(ADDRESS=(PROTOCOL=beq)))
```

To identify the Oracle session ID of the RMAN session, look for the following types of messages in the RMAN log:

```
channel ch2: sid=12 devtype=SBT_TAPE
```

On a Windows server, you can use the Task Manager to identify the RMAN client sessions. Then you can drill down into associated server processes by clicking the Process tab and clicking the relevant server process under the process list.

How It Works

Identifying RMAN server sessions is crucial for tasks such as terminating an unwanted RMAN session. The best way to terminate an RMAN session that's executing commands is to simply use the Ctrl+C combination. You can kill a server session corresponding to an RMAN channel by executing the SQL statement alter system kill session.

4-18. Dropping a Database using the RMAN Client

Problem

You are planning to drop a database and want to make sure you drop all the datafiles, online logs, and control files pertaining to the database. Of course, you can drop a database from SQL*Plus using the drop database command. However, if you can't access SQL*Plus, you can drop a database from RMAN instead.

Solution

Use the drop database command to drop a database from the RMAN prompt. Here are the steps to follow:

1. Start up the database in mount exclusive mode:

   ```
   SQL> startup mount exclusive;
   Database mounted.
   SQL> exit
   ```

2. From the RMAN interface, use the following command to drop the database:

   ```
   RMAN> drop database;
   Database name is "NINA" and DBID is 922224687.
   ```

3. RMAN will require a confirmation from you that you really do want to drop the database. Respond with yes, if that's what you intend to do:

   ```
   Do you really want to drop the database (enter YES or NO)? yes
   Database dropped.
   RMAN>
   ```

Note how RMAN prompts you if you really want to drop the target database. By using the optional keyword noprompt, you can prevent such a message. However, considering how critical the dropping of a database is, you may simply ignore the noprompt keyword.

The drop database command drops only the datafiles, the online redo log files, and the control files. You can get rid of all the backups and copies in one fell swoop by adding the including backups option to the drop database command:

```
RMAN> drop database including backups;
```

Needless to mention, you should use this command with the utmost care.

How It Works

RMAN will ensure that all datafiles, online redo logs, and control files belonging to the database are removed from the operating system file system. Optionally, you can also specify that all the archive logs, backups, and copies that belong to the database be dropped as well.

CHAPTER 5

■■■

Configuring the RMAN Environment

To work with RMAN, you must configure several things, such as the default backup type (disk or tape), the number of channels, and the degree of parallelism. For simple backup tasks, you probably can get by with RMAN's default configuration settings. However, for complex jobs involving sophisticated backup strategies, you need to customize one or more of RMAN's configuration settings.

Broadly speaking, you can configure the RMAN environment in two ways:

- Make the configuration settings persistent across different RMAN sessions.

- Manually modify configuration settings for only a particular backup or recovery job.

You can also set different persistent configuration settings for each of the target databases registered in your recovery catalog if you are using a recovery catalog. Thus, you can configure different backup retention policies, for example, for different databases. In this chapter, we'll look at several important recipes that show you how to configure the RMAN backup and recovery environment, including configuring the backup device type, configuring the backup type, generating the backup filenames, and creating backup retention polices.

■Note Chapter 3 discusses configuring the flash recovery area. Configuring RMAN to make backups to a media manager is an important part of RMAN configuration. We discuss how to configure a media manager in Chapter 18.

5-1. Showing RMAN Configuration Settings

Problem

You want to see your current RMAN configuration settings. For example, you may be seeing unexpected RMAN behavior, or you may be encountering performance issues because of how you've configured RMAN in your environment.

Solution

Use the RMAN command show to view the current value of one or all of RMAN's configuration settings. The show command will let you view the value of a specified RMAN setting. For example, the following show command displays whether the autobackup of the control file has been enabled:

```
RMAN> show controlfile autobackup;
RMAN configuration parameters are:
CONFIGURE CONTROLFILE AUTOBACKUP OFF;
RMAN>
```

The show all command displays both settings that you have configured and any default settings. Any default settings will be displayed with a # default at the end of the line. For example, the following is the output from executing the show all command:

```
RMAN> connect target /
RMAN> show all;
RMAN configuration parameters are:
CONFIGURE RETENTION POLICY TO REDUNDANCY 1; # default
CONFIGURE BACKUP OPTIMIZATION OFF; # default
CONFIGURE DEFAULT DEVICE TYPE TO DISK; # default
CONFIGURE CONTROLFILE AUTOBACKUP OFF; # default
CONFIGURE CONTROLFILE AUTOBACKUP FORMAT FOR DEVICE TYPE  DISK TO '%F';   # default
CONFIGURE DEVICE TYPE DISK PARALLELISM 1 BACKUPTYPE TO BACKUPSET;    # default
CONFIGURE DATAFILE BACKUP COPIES FOR DEVICE TYPE DISK TO 1;  # default
CONFIGURE ARCHIVELOG BACKUP COPIES FOR DEVICE TYPE DISK TO 1;  #  default
CONFIGURE MAXSETSIZE TO UNLIMITED; # default
CONFIGURE ENCRYPTION FOR DATABASE OFF; # default
CONFIGURE ENCRYPTION ALGORITHM 'AES128'; # default
CONFIGURE COMPRESSION ALGORITHM 'ZLIB'; # default
CONFIGURE ARCHIVELOG DELETION POLICY TO NONE; # default
CONFIGURE SNAPSHOT CONTROLFILE NAME TO
'C:\ORACLE\PRODUCT\11.1\DB_1\DATABASE\SNCFORCL.ORA'; # default
RMAN>
```

Table 5-1 lists all the parameters you can use with the show command and describes each parameter.

Table 5-1. *Parameters to RMAN's* show *Command*

Parameter	Description
all	Shows all parameters.
archivelog deletion policy	Shows the archivelog deletion policy.
archivelog backup copies	Shows the number of archivelog backup copies.
auxname	Shows the auxiliary database information.
backup optimization	Shows whether optimization is on or off.

Parameter	Description
[auxiliary] channel	Shows how the normal channel and auxiliary channel are configured.
channel for device type [disk | <media device>;	Shows the characteristics of the channel.
controlfile autobackup	Shows whether autobackup is on or off.
controlfile autobackup format	Shows the format of the autobackup control file.
datafile backup copies	Shows the number of datafile backup copies being kept.
default device type	Shows the default type (disk or tape).
retention policy	Shows policy for datafile and control file backups and copies that RMAN marks as obsolete.
encryption algorithm	Shows the encryption algorithm currently in use.
encryption for [database | tablespace]	Shows the encryption for the database and every tablespace.
exclude	Shows the tablespaces excluded from the backup.
maxsetsize	Shows the maximum size for backup sets. The default is unlimited.
retention policy	Shows the policy for datafile and control file backups and copies that RMAN marks as obsolete.
snapshot controlfile name	Shows the snapshot control filename.
compression algorithm	Shows the compression algorithm in force. The default is the ZLIB algorithm.

■**Note** You can also display nondefault RMAN configuration settings by querying the V$RMAN_
CONFIGURATION view.

How It Works

The show command queries the target database control file to retrieve RMAN configuration settings. Configuration settings are stored in the target database control file regardless of whether you are using a recovery catalog. Once configured, settings persist until you change them again. Because RMAN settings are stored in the control file, your target database must be mounted or open when issuing the show command.

The show all command reveals the present configuration regarding several important RMAN backup and recovery settings. The following list summarizes the meaning of the most important of these settings, shown by issuing the show all command:

- configure retention policy to redundancy 1 means that RMAN retains only one set of backup copies.

- configure backup optimization off means that by default RMAN won't skip the backing up of unchanged data blocks in the datafiles.

- `configure default device type to disk` means that by default RMAN sends backup output to a disk drive.

- `configure controlfile autobackup off` means that by default RMAN doesn't automatically back up the control files when it performs a backup task.

- `configure device type disk parallelism 1 backup type to backupset` means that the default RMAN backup type is a backup set (and not an image copy) and the degree of parallelism is 1.

- `configure datafile backup copies for device type disk to 1` means that by default RMAN doesn't make multiple copies of a backup file.

- `configure maxsetsize to unlimited` means that there's no limit on the size of a backup set by default.

- `configure encryption for database off` means that by default RMAN backups aren't encrypted.

Notice that the output of the `show all` command shows the existing RMAN configuration in the form of RMAN commands to re-create that configuration. Therefore, if you are planning to use the same type of configuration on a different database, just save the output from the `show all` command to a text file that you can then execute from the RMAN command line after connecting to the target database to which you're planning to migrate those settings.

You can view information about RMAN's persistent configuration settings by querying the V$RMAN_CONFIGURATION view, as shown here:

```
SQL> select * from v$rman_configuration;
    CONF# NAME                                     VALUE
---------- ------------------------------  ------------------------
        1 RETENTION POLICY                         TO REDUNDANCY 3
        2 BACKUP OPTIMIZATION                      ON
        3 DEFAULT DEVICE TYPE TO                   sbt_tape
        4 CONTROLFILE AUTOBACKUP                   ON
        5 DEVICE TYPE                              DISK PARALLELISM 2
```

5 rows selected.

The NAME column in the V$RMAN_CONFIGURATION view shows the type of RMAN configuration, and the VALUE column shows the present `configure` command setting for that type, for example, `configure retention policy to redundancy 3`.

5-2. Configuring RMAN

Problem

You want to configure RMAN to suit the requirements of the particular backup and recovery strategy you choose to implement in your organization.

Solution

You can create or modify any of RMAN's persistent configuration settings affecting backup and recovery by using the configure command. The general format of the configure command is as follows:

```
RMAN> configure [<parameter> <syntax>];
```

If you want, you can script an entire set of configuration changes and run it from within a run block. Alternatively, you may execute the configure command from the RMAN command prompt in order to change a single parameter at a time. The following example changes many settings all at once from within a run block:

```
run
{
configure retention policy to 1 redundancy 2;
configure backup optimization off;
configure default device type to disk;
configure controlfile autobackup on;
configure controlfile autobackup format for device type disk to
'/proj/11/backup/%F';
configure device type disk parallelism 2;
configure datafile backup copies for device type disk to 1;
configure archivelog backup copies for device type disk to 1;
configure maxsetsize to unlimited;
configure snapshot controlfile name to '/proj/11/backup/snapf_prod11.f';
 }
```

It's quite common to specify the configure command within backup and recovery scripts to change the default settings for one or more RMAN persistent configuration settings.

How It Works

Use the configure command to configure persistent settings for backup, restore, duplication, and maintenance jobs. Once set, the settings will apply to all future RMAN sessions until you clear or modify those settings by using the configure command again. RMAN stores the configuration for each of the target databases in that database's control file. The recovery catalog, if you're using one, contains the configuration for all the databases that are registered in the catalog.

You must connect to the target database, which must be in mount or open state, since RMAN configuration settings are stored in the control file. In Chapter 15, you'll learn about the configure auxname command, which lets you rename files when you're duplicating databases using RMAN.

5-3. Restoring Default Parameter Settings

Problem

You want to restore RMAN's default settings after performing a special task that required you to modify some parameters.

Solution

If you don't explicitly use the `configure` command to specify the value of any RMAN parameters, RMAN will use default values for those parameters. By using the `configure ... clear` command, you can return an individual configuration setting to its default value, as shown in the following example:

```
RMAN> configure backup optimization clear;
RMAN> configure retention policy clear;
```

The first example shows how to turn off backup optimization, since by default the backup optimization is set to off. The second example sets the retention policy to the default value of `redundancy 1`.

How It Works

You can't clear individual parameters affecting a particular RMAN component by using the `configure ... clear` command. For example, you may have configured several options using the `configure channel ...` command. However, you can't erase the individual options by using the `configure ... clear` command. That is, you can't run a command such as the following, which attempts to clear only the individual option `maxpiecesize`:

```
RMAN> configure channel device type sbt maxpiecesize 100m clear;
```

However, you can use the following command successfully:

```
RMAN> configure channel device type sbt clear;
```

The previous command will clear the permanent setting for the device type and set it back to the default setting of disk.

5-4. Enabling and Disabling Automatic Control File Backups

Problem

You want to configure RMAN so it automatically backs up the control file and the server parameter file whenever RMAN repository data in the control file changes, since those changes critically affect the ability of RMAN to restore the database.

Solution

To enable automatic control file backups, use the `autobackup` clause with the `configure` command as follows:

```
RMAN> configure controlfile autobackup on;
```

If for any reason you want to disable automatic control file backups, run the following command:

```
RMAN> configure controlfile autobackup off;
```

An alternative way to disable automatic control file backups is to *clear* (see recipe 5-3 for instructions on clearing configured RMAN settings) the autobackup setting. For example:

```
RMAN> configure controlfile autobackup clear;
```

This command will set the control file autobackup to off, which is the default setting.

How It Works

By default, automatic control file backups are disabled. Even when the autobackup feature is disabled, RMAN will back up the current control file and the server parameter file whenever any backup command includes datafile 1 from the datafiles that belong to the target database. In an Oracle database, datafile 1 is always part of the system tablespace, which contains the data dictionary. You can configure RMAN to automatically back up the control file following *every* backup and any database structural change by using the configure command. We highly recommend you configure automatic control file backups for two reasons:

- To ensure that the critical control file is backed up regularly following a backup or structural change to the database

- To simplify the scripts used to back up your database

■**Note** Oracle recommends you enable the control file autobackup feature if you aren't using a recovery catalog.

Once you configure automatic control file backup, RMAN will automatically back up your target database control file, as well as the current server parameter file, when any of the following events occurs:

- Successful completion of either a backup or copy command

- After a create catalog command from the RMAN prompt is successfully completed

- Any structural changes to the database modify the contents of the control file

After a backup or copy command completes and the recovery catalog—if you are using one—is successfully updated, RMAN will then back up the control file to its own backup piece. In addition, any changes to the physical structure of your database, even if they are made through SQL*Plus, will trigger a control file autobackup. (For example, the following actions will trigger an autobackup of the control file: adding a tablespace or datafile, dropping a datafile, placing a tablespace offline or online, adding an online redo log, and renaming a datafile.) When automatic backup is triggered by a structural change, an Oracle server process (not an RMAN process) will automatically create the autobackup of your control file.

■**Note** If you are using a binary server parameter file (spfile), it will also be automatically included in the control file backup piece.

Why back up the control file after database structure changes? Having a backup of the control file that reflects the current physical structure of the database simplifies your recovery process. Without such a control file, you'll have to re-create your control file using the `create controlfile` statement with the updated physical structure of the database.

The autobackup of the control file is independent of any backup of the current control file that you may make as part of a `backup` command. The automatic control file backup that follows a database structural change is always a back up to a disk location. See recipe 5-5 to learn how to specify that location. Automatic control file back ups that occur after a datafile backup can be created on disk or on tape, however.

Once you configure autobackup of the control file, RMAN can recover a database even if the current control file, the recovery catalog, and the server parameter file all turn out to be inaccessible. The following are the steps RMAN takes in recovering the database:

1. RMAN will first restore the server parameter file from the location where the file was automatically backed up to by RMAN.

2. RMAN will start the instance with the help of the server parameter file it restored in step 1.

3. RMAN will restore the control file from the same autobackup.

4. Once the control file is mounted, RMAN will connect to the target database in the `nocatalog` mode and use the RMAN repository available in the control file to restore the data files and then recover the database.

5. At this point, you may re-create a new recovery catalog and register your target databases in it.

6. Finally, RMAN will copy all the RMAN repository records from the target database control files to the new recovery catalog.

This recovery sequence shows the importance of configuring the autobackup of the control file.

5-5. Specifying the Autobackup Control File Directory and Filename

Problem

You've just enabled the autobackup of the control file feature, but you don't know where the files are physically being written. You want to ensure that these critical backups are being written to a location you know about so that you can maintain and monitor that location.

Solution

You can override where RMAN will write the autobackup control file and its name using the `configure` command. For example, the following `configure` command changes both the directory where RMAN stores the autobackup of the control file and the filename of the autobackup:

```
RMAN> configure controlfile autobackup format
    for device type disk to 'c:\rback\prod1\autobackup\controlfile_%F';
```

To set the directory and file format back to the default value, run this command:

```
RMAN> configure controlfile autobackup format for device type disk clear;
```

You can use the command set control file autobackup format, either within a run block or at the RMAN prompt (the run block has precedence over the RMAN prompt), to override the configured autobackup format for the duration of an RMAN session.

How It Works

If you have enabled a flashback area as well as the autobackup of the control file, then RMAN will write the backup to the directory defined for the flashback area. By default, RMAN creates these files as Oracle managed files.

When specifying a filename as well as a target directory, you must include the format variable %F in the filename. The format variable %F yields a unique combination of the database ID, day, month, year, and sequence.

When you clear the control file autobackup format for disk as shown in the "Solution" section for this recipe, the control file will be backed up to the flash recovery area, provided you have enabled it first. If you haven't enabled a flashback area, RMAN will create the autobackups in an operating system–specific location ($ORACLE_HOME/dbs on Unix and %ORACLE_HOME%\database on Windows).

You can also configure the autobackup to back up the control file to an automatic storage management (ASM) disk group, as shown in the following example:

```
RMAN> configure controlfile autobackup
      for device type disk to '+dgroup1/%F';
```

The control file autobackup will be stored in the disk group +*dgroup1* when you execute this configure command.

5-6. Specifying the Snapshot Control Filename and Location

Problem

RMAN occasionally creates a special control file called the *snapshot control file*. You want to specify your own name for this file as well as the location for storing it.

Solution

Use the configure snapshot controlfile to ... command to change the snapshot control filename and the directory in which it is stored:

```
RMAN> configure snapshot controlfile name to 'c:\rback\prod1\snct.ctl';
```

To reset the snapshot control filename and location to the default values, use the configure command as follows:

```
RMAN> configure snapshot controlfile name clear;
```

Use the show command to display the current location of the snapshot control file:

```
RMAN> show snapshot controlfile name;
RMAN configuration parameters are:
CONFIGURE SNAPSHOT CONTROLFILE NAME TO
'C:\ORACLE\PRODUCT\11.0.1\DB_1\DATABASE\eleven.ORA'; # default

RMAN>
```

The output of the show snapshot controlfile name command reveals that the current location, which is actually $ORACLE_HOME\database, is the default location. On a Linux/Unix system, the default location is the $ORACLE_HOME/dbs directory.

How It Works

RMAN requires a consistent view of the control file under two circumstances:

- When resynchronizing with the recovery catalog

- When making a backup of the control file

■**Note** Oracle allows only one RMAN session to access the snapshot control file at a time. This ensures that multiple RMAN sessions do not concurrently write and read from the snapshot control file.

To achieve these two goals, RMAN creates a temporary backup copy of the control file called the *snapshot control file*, which enables RMAN to resynchronize with the recovery catalog or back up the control file, using a read-consistent version of the control file. The default location and name of the snapshot control file is operating system dependent. On Windows XP, the default location is ORACLE_HOME/database, and the default name of the snapshot control file is of the form SNCF<database name>.ORA. On Unix the default directory is $ORACLE_HOME/dbs, and the default name is snapcf_<database name>.f.

■**Note** RMAN uses the default snapshot directory and name regardless of whether you have configured a flash recovery area.

5-7. Specifying the Retention Period for RMAN History

Problem

You're using only a control file, and not the recovery catalog, to record RMAN's backup and recovery activity. You want to change the length of time for which the Oracle server will retain history data in the control file before overwriting it.

Solution

Use the `control_file_record_keep_time` initialization parameter to specify the minimum length of time that RMAN history is saved in the control file before being overwritten. Here's an example showing how to set the retention period to 15 days:

```
SQL> alter system set control_file_record_keep_time=15;
System altered.
SQL>
```

The `alter system` statement in this example specifies that all reusable records in the control file be kept for at least 15 days before they are eligible for overwriting.

How It Works

The control file contains two types of sections: reusable and nonreusable. The `control_file_record_keep_time` parameter applies only to the reusable section of the control file. If RMAN needs to add new backup and recovery–related records to the control file, any records that expired as per the `control_file_record_keep_time` parameter are overwritten. If there are no eligible records to be overwritten, the reusable section of the control file (and therefore the control file itself) expands.

The default value of the `control_file_record_keep_time` parameter is seven days. You can dynamically change the value of the parameter through the `alter system` statement as shown in the previous example. The range of values you may use can be anywhere from 0 to 365 days. If you set the retention time to zero, it means the reusable sections of the control file will not expand when there aren't any more empty reusable records and the database starts overwriting the existing records as and when it needs them.

The Oracle database records all RMAN backup information in the control file, whether you use a recovery catalog or not. If there is no limit to the number of days that information can be kept, the control file will keep growing without a limit. To avoid letting the control file grow without limit, the Oracle database overwrites backup records that are older than a threshold you specify.

If you choose the default value of seven days for the parameter, for example, any reusable records older than seven days can be overwritten by the Oracle server when it needs space to write new history. If no reusable record is old enough to be overwritten and yet more space is needed for new history, then Oracle will expand the control file's size. If space limitations preclude the expansion of the control file, Oracle will be forced to overwrite the oldest reusable record in the control file anyway, even if that record's age is less than the value of the `control_file_record_keep_time` parameter.

The `control_file_record_time` initialization parameter controls the overwriting of only the circularly reusable records such as the archive log records and the backup records. The value for the parameter has no bearing on the control file records pertaining to datafiles, tablespaces, and redo thread records, which are reused only after the relevant object is dropped from the database. The V$CONTROLFILE_RECORD_SECTION view provides information about the control file record sections.

5-8. Configuring the Default Device Type

Problem

You want to change the default backup device from disk to tape or from tape to disk.

Solution

By default, *disk* is the default device type for all automatic channels. However, you can use the `configure` command with the `default device type` option to make a tape device the default device type instead. The following example shows how to do this:

```
RMAN> configure default device type to sbt;
```

You can use the `clear` option to return the default device type to disk again:

```
RMAN> configure default device type clear;
```

You can also explicitly reset the default device type to disk, as shown here:

```
RMAN> configure default device type to disk;
```

Once you configure the default device type to disk, all backups will be made to disk.

How It Works

You can override RMAN's default device type settings by specifying the backup device type as a part of the `backup` command itself, as shown in the following two commands, the first backing up to a tape device and the second to a disk device:

```
RMAN> backup device type sbt database;
RMAN> backup device type disk database;
```

When you issue a `backup` command, RMAN will allocate channels of the default device type only. For example, let's say you configure automatic channels for both disk and tape (sbt), but you set the default device type to disk. When you subsequently issue a `backup database` command, RMAN will allocate only a disk channel, and not an sbt channel, for the backup job.

The following example illustrates this point. The first command configures a channel for a tape device (sbt). The second command sets the default device type to tape (sbt). The third command backs up the archived logs through the default sbt channel that you set through the second command. Finally, the last command backs up the database to disk, rather than to the default tape device (set by the second command). Thus, the `backup device type disk ...` command overrides the default device type setting of sbt.

```
RMAN> configure channel device type
sbt parms='sbt_library=/mediavendor/lib/libobk.so
env=(nsr_server=tape_svr,nsr_client=oracleclnt,
nsr_group=ora_tapes)';
RMAN> configure default device type to sbt;
RMAN> backup archivelog all;
RMAN> backup device type disk database;
```

You can also override RMAN's behavior regarding the default device type, which is to manually allocate a specific channel within the run command, as shown here:

```
RMAN> run
    {
    allocate channel c1 device type disk maxpiecesize 1G;
    backup database plus archivelog;
    }
```

The previous command will make a backup to disk, even if the default device type is a tape device.

Here's an example showing how you can first make a backup to a default disk device and then back up the resulting backup sets to tape for safekeeping off the premises:

```
RMAN> run
    {
    backup database plus archivelog;
    backup device type sbt backupset all;
    }
```

You only ever need to worry about overriding the default device type when issuing a backup command. The default device type is not an issue with the restore command. That's because the restore command will allocate channels of both configured device types, no matter what the default device type is. RMAN works this way because you may be restoring files from both disk-based and tape-based backups.

5-9. Configuring the Default Backup Type

Problem

You want to change the default backup type to image copies from the default backup type, which is a backup set.

Solution

The default backup type in RMAN, whether you're backing up to disk or to tape, is a backup set. You can change the default backup type to an image copy by using the following command:

```
RMAN> configure device type disk backup type to copy;
```

You can revert to the original setting of backup set backup type by using either of the following two commands:

```
RMAN> configure device type disk clear;
RMAN> configure device type disk backup type to backupset;
```

How It Works

You have the option to set image copies as your backup type only when making backups to disk. If you're using a tape device, you don't have an image copy option—you can make backups only in the form of a backup set when using a tape device.

5-10. Making Compressed Backup Sets the Default

Problem

You want to make compressed backups using RMAN in order to save storage space and reduce the network traffic.

Solution

By default, all RMAN backups are made in a noncompressed format. You can, however, configure RMAN to make compressed backup sets, both for disk-based as well as for tape-based backups. Here's the command for specifying the compression of a disk-based backup:

```
RMAN> configure device type disk backup type to compressed backupset;
using target database control file instead of recovery catalog
new RMAN configuration parameters:
CONFIGURE DEVICE TYPE DISK BACKUP TYPE TO COMPRESSED BACKUPSET PARALLELISM 1;
new RMAN configuration parameters are successfully stored
RMAN>
```

And here's how you specify compression when making backups to a tape device:

```
RMAN> configure device type sbt backup type to compressed backupset;
new RMAN configuration parameters:
CONFIGURE DEVICE TYPE 'SBT_TAPE' BACKUP TYPE TO COMPRESSED BACKUPSET PARALLELISM
 1;
new RMAN configuration parameters are successfully stored

RMAN>
```

Both in the case of disk and tape backups, you can revert to the default noncompressed backup format by omitting the keyword compressed in the two commands shown in this solution.

How It Works

RMAN uses binary compression to produce compressed backup sets. Since a compressed backup means fewer bytes are transmitted across the network, it makes it a lot easier for you to safely schedule a daily backup of the database without adversely affecting other users of your network. Of course, even compression may not permit you to back up a very large database during the backup window.

When you restore a compressed backup set, RMAN can read the backup set directly, without having to first uncompress it, thus saving you a considerable amount of time. If you compress backup sets through some other means, such as the Unix/Linux tar command, then you'll incur significant overhead in time and in disk space when uncompressing them.

When using the RMAN compression feature, you can choose among different compression algorithms. You can query the view V$RMAN_COMPRESSION_ALGORITHM to view the compression algorithms available to you, as shown here:

```
SQL> select algorithm_name,algorithm_description, is_default
     from v$rman_compression_algorithm;

ALGORITHM    ALGORITHM DESCRIPTION                            IS_
-------------------------------------------------------------- ---
ZLIB                fast but little worse compression ratio        YES

BZIP2              good compression ratio but little slower     NO


SQL>
```

As the query shows, the ZLIB compression algorithm offers speed but not a good compression ratio. The alternate compression algorithm, BZIP2, is slower but provides a better compression ratio. You can use the show command to check the current compression algorithm in use, as shown here:

```
RMAN> show compression algorithm;

RMAN configuration parameters are:
CONFIGURE COMPRESSION ALGORITHM 'ZLIB'; # default

RMAN>
```

■**Note** If you set the compatible initialization parameter to 11.1 or newer, ZLIB will be the default compression algorithm. You can't choose the compression algorithm if you set the compatible parameter to anything older than 11.0—-your only option then will be to use the default algorithm, which is BZIP2.

The show command reveals that RMAN is using the ZLIB compression, which also happens to be the default compression algorithm. You can use the configure compression algorithm to bzip2 command to switch to the BZIP2 compression algorithm. Remember that the choice of the compression algorithm is available only in Oracle Database 11g. In earlier versions of the database, you only have a single choice—the default algorithm BZIP2.

5-11. Configuring Multiple Backup Copies

Problem

You want to initiate a backup (as a backup set) and have RMAN automatically make multiple copies of the resulting backup sets. You do not want to make any persistent configuration changes to your RMAN environment.

Solution

RMAN provides a backup *duplexing* feature under which you can direct RMAN to make multiple copies of the backup pieces inside a backup set. Using a single backup command, you can make up to four copies of each backup piece in a *backup set* on four separate devices. *Copy* in this context means an exact copy of each of the backup pieces in a backup set.

You can use the copies parameter with the configure command to specify the duplexing of backup sets. Here's an example showing how to use the configure ... backup copies command:

```
RMAN> configure datafile backup copies for device type disk to 2;
```

The configure ... backup copies command shown here specifies that RMAN must make two copies of each backup piece for all types of backups (archived redo logs, datafiles, control files) made to a disk device.

You can configure the number of backup set copies for each type of device—disk and tape—separately. The following example shows how to configure multiple copies when backing up to a tape device:

```
RMAN> configure datafile backup copies for device type sbt to 2;
```

Use the format option of the backup command to specify the multiple destinations for the multiple backups you're making when duplexing backups. With the format option when using a disk channel, you can specify that multiple copies be sent to different physical disks. For example, if you want to place one copy of a backup set in three different locations on disk, you would configure RMAN as follows:

```
RMAN> configure channel device type disk format '/save1/%U','/save2/%U','save3/%U';
```

■**Note** You can't make duplex backups to the flash recovery area.

When you next execute a backup command, RMAN will place one copy each of the resulting backup piece in the /save1, /save2, and /save3 directories. For tape backups, if your media manager supports version 2 of the SBT API, RMAN will automatically place each copy on a separate tape.

How It Works

You can use the configure ... backup copies command to specify how many copies of each backup piece should be made on a specified type of device. Not only can you specify the number of copies, but you can also specify the type of backup file, such as datafile, archived redo, log, or control file. Using the configure command this way specifies a new default level of duplexing. The original default level of duplexing is set to 1, meaning that RMAN will make only a single copy of each backup piece.

You must understand that when duplexing backups, RMAN produces multiple identical copies of each backup piece in a backup set, rather than producing multiple backup sets. There's only one backup set with a unique backup set key with multiple copies of its member backup pieces.

You can check the current configuration for multiple backup copies by using the show ... backup copies command. For example, the following command shows the configuration of the datafile backup copies setting:

```
RMAN> show datafile backup copies;

RMAN configuration parameters are:
CONFIGURE DATAFILE BACKUP COPIES FOR DEVICE TYPE
 DISK TO 1; # default
CONFIGURE DATAFILE BACKUP COPIES FOR DEVICE TYPE
SBT_TAPE TO 1; # default
RMAN>
```

By replacing the keyword *datafile* with *archivelog*, you can view the current configuration for multiple backups of archived logs, as shown here:

```
RMAN> show archivelog backup copies;
RMAN configuration parameters are:
CONFIGURE ARCHIVELOG BACKUP COPIES FOR DEVICE TYPE DISK TO 1; # default
RMAN>
```

Note that the backup duplexing feature is limited only to backups made as backup sets—you can't direct RMAN to make multiple simultaneous copies of image copies—you have to first make a single image copy before you can make multiple copies of it. Also note that you can't use the flash recovery area as one of the destinations for a duplexed copy.

Ideally, you should keep the multiple backup copies on multiple media. For example, say you want to keep one copy on disk and another on tape. Instead of making persistent configuration changes to make multiple backup copies as shown in this recipe, you can specify the number of copies only for a specific backup job using the backup copies and set backup copies commands. Please refer to Chapter 7 to learn how to use the copies parameter in the set and backup commands to specify multiple copies when using the backup command.

5-12. Skipping Previously Backed Up Files

Problem

You want to use the *backup optimization* feature of RMAN to save on backup time by making RMAN skip those files that it has already backed up.

Solution

By default, backup optimization is set to off, meaning RMAN will back up every file, whether an exactly identical copy was backed up previously or not. You can configure backup optimization by using the following command:

```
RMAN> configure backup optimization on;
```

From here on out, RMAN will attempt to avoid backing up files that have already been backed up to the specified device type.

How It Works

By enabling backup optimization, you can make RMAN skip those files that it has already backed up. The backup optimization feature applies to three types of files: datafiles, archived redo logs, and backup sets. Optimizing backups can lead to a considerable reduction in the time it takes to back up a database. For the backup optimization to work, you must satisfy the following conditions after first turning backup optimization on using the `configure` command, as described in the "Solution" section of this recipe:

- You must run a `backup database`, a `backup archivelog` command with the `all` or `like` options, or the `backup backupset all` command. You can also execute a `backup backupset all`, `backup recovery area`, `backup recovery files`, or `backup datafilecopy` command.

- You must not mix both disk and sbt channels in the same `backup` command—all channels must be of the same type.

You can turn off backup optimization during a particular RMAN session and force RMAN to back up a file regardless of whether it's identical to a previously backed up file by specifying the `force` option with your `backup` command, as shown here:

```
RMAN> backup database force;
```

By using the `force` option, you make RMAN back up all the specified files, even if the backup optimization feature is turned on. To turn off backup configuration on a more permanent basis, use the `configure` command, as shown here:

```
RMAN> configure backup optimization off;
```

RMAN also provides *restore optimization*, which lets it avoid restoring datafiles wherever possible. If, after checking a datafile's file headers, RMAN concludes that the header contains the correct information and that the data file is in the correct location, it will skip the restoration of that datafile from backup.

Once you configure backup optimization, RMAN will skip backing up previously backed-up files if they are exactly identical to their previously backed-up versions (that is, if they haven't changed at all since the last backup). The following example shows the result of trying to back up the database immediately after a backup of that database was made, assuming you've turned backup optimization on:

```
RMAN> backup database;

Starting backup at 09-NOV-06
using channel ORA_DISK_2
using channel ORA_DISK_1
using channel ORA_DISK_3
skipping datafile 1; already backed up 2 time(s)
skipping datafile 1; already backed up 2 time(s)
skipping datafile 1; already backed up 2 time(s)
skipping datafile 1; already backed up 2 time(s)
```

```
skipping datafile 1; already backed up 2 time(s)
finished backup at 09-NOV-06
```

RMAN>

RMAN uses specific rules for each type of file it backs up to determine whether the file is identical to a previously backed up version. For example, a datafile must have the same DBID and checkpoint SCN as a previously backed up file to be deemed identical to it. Similarly, an archived redo log must have the same DBID, thread, and sequence number as a previously backed up version, and a backup set must have the same backup set record ID and stamp.

The fact that a datafile, archived redo log, or backup set is identical to a previously backed up file doesn't mean that RMAN will automatically skip backing up that file. When RMAN detects an identical file, that file initially is deemed only a *candidate* for optimization. Once RMAN determines that an identical file (datafile, archived redo log file, or a backup set) has already been backed up, that file becomes a candidate for backup optimization. RMAN must consider the retention policy in force at the time and the backup duplexing feature before determining whether it has sufficient backups on the specified device to let it skip the particular file.

RMAN uses a backup optimization algorithm to determine whether it should skip backing up a previously backed up file. The optimization algorithm takes into account two factors: the retention policy currently in use and RMAN's backup duplexing feature. The rules specified by the optimization algorithm vary, depending on the type of file or whether you're dealing with the backing up of a backup set. We summarize the rules of the optimization algorithm for datafiles, archived redo logs, and backup sets in the following sections.

Datafiles

The key determinant of how RMAN decides to treat the backup optimization issue for a datafile depends on whether you have a retention policy in use and, if so, the type of retention policy in effect. Here's a brief summary of how RMAN approaches backup optimization under different circumstances.

- If you're using a recovery window–based retention policy, then the backup media type determines whether RMAN will skip a datafile. If you are making tape backups, RMAN will make another backup of a datafile even if it has a backup of an identical file, if the latest backup is older than the configured recovery window. That is, RMAN ignores the backup optimization policy you've configured. For example, let's say today's date is April 1, and we're dealing with the backup of a read-only tablespace whose contents don't change by definition. If the last backup of this read-only tablespace was made on March 15 and you have configured a recovery window of seven days, it means that the backup is older than the recovery window. RMAN will make another backup of that tablespace, even though its contents haven't changed a bit. If you're backing up to disk instead, RMAN will not back up a datafile if the backup of an identical file is already on disk. It doesn't matter whether the latest disk backup is older than the beginning of RMAN's recovery window.

- If you're using a redundancy-based retention policy (and, say, the redundancy is set to *r*), RMAN will skip backing up a file if *n* (defined as r+1) copies of an identical file exist on the specified device, whether it's disk or tape.

- If you don't have a retention policy in effect, RMAN skips a backup if n number of copies of that file exist on the specified backup device. RMAN determines the value of n in the following order of precedence, with higher values on the list overriding the lower values:

    1. The number of backup copies when using the `backup ... copies` n command

    2. The number of backup copies when using the `set backup copies` n command

    3. The number of backup copies configured by using the `configure datafile backup copies for device type ... to n` command

    4. $n=1$

Accordingly, if the number of backup copies is set to the default number of 1, after you make two identical copies of a datafile, RMAN will skip that datafile in future backups.

Archived Redo Logs

In the case of archived redo logs, RMAN will determine the value of n according the following order of precedence and will skip backing up a file if at least n backups already exist on the specified device:

1. The number of backup copies when using the `backup ... copies` n command

2. The number of backup copies when using the `set backup copies` n command

3. The number of backup copies configured by using the `configure datafile backup copies for device type ... to n` command

4. $n=1$

Suppose the value of n in your `backup ... copies` command is 2 and you issue the following command first:

```
RMAN> backup device type sbt copies 3 archivelog all;
```

Let's say you turn on backup optimization some time later with the following command:

```
RMAN> configure backup optimization on;
```

Issue the following command to back up the archived redo logs:

```
RMAN> backup device type sbt copies 2 archivelog all;
```

RMAN will set the value of n to 2 in this case, and RMAN will back up only those archivelogs that haven't been backed up more than twice. That is, all archived redo logs that were backed up by the very first `backup` command will be skipped during the second `backup` command. However, RMAN will make two copies of any archived redo logs produced subsequent to the first backup when you issue the second `backup` command.

Backup Sets

RMAN uses the following order of precedence to determine n, which is the number of copies of a backup set that must already exist if RMAN is to skip backing up that backup set:

1. The number of backup copies when using the backup ... copies *n* command

2. The number of backup copies when using the set backup copies *n* command

By default, n = 1. To be considered eligible for backup optimization, a backup set must have an identical record ID and stamp as another existing backup set.

■Caution Media managers may have their own expiration policies. Therefore, RMAN may sometimes skip a backup according to its optimization algorithm, but the media manager may have already discarded the older backup stored to tape that formed the basis for RMAN's decision to skip the backup. To avoid a discrepancy between RMAN's metadata and that of a media manager, you must issue the crosscheck command frequently to synchronize the RMAN repository with the media manager's metadata.

5-13. Specifying Backup Piece Filenames

Problem

You want to specify your own names for RMAN backup pieces.

Solution

You can specify your own meaningful names for backup pieces using the format option in the backup command. You can provide substitution variables for use in the generation of unique filenames for image copies and backup pieces.

Here's how you incorporate the format parameter within a backup command when using backup pieces:

```
RMAN> backup tablespace users format = '/tmp/users_%u%p%c';
```

RMAN uses the substitution variables you provide to create meaningful names for the backup pieces.

How It Works

If you don't use the format option within your backup command to generate names for the backup pieces, RMAN will automatically generate a unique name for each of those backups in the default backup location. If you're using a media manager, check your vendor documentation for specific restrictions on using the format parameter, such as the length of the name, for example.

■Note In addition to the format option, you can also use the db_file_name_convert parameter to generate unique filenames for RMAN image copies. The db_file_name_convert parameter is a database initialization parameter that you set either in the database parameter file or by issuing an alter database command. You use the same syntax to set the db_file_name_convert parameter as you use when specifying the format option.

5-14. Generating Filenames for Image Copies

Problem

You want to set meaningful names for image copies instead of letting RMAN generate its own default names.

Solution

You can use the `format` parameter to generate unique names for RMAN image copies. The default format `%U` is defined differently for image copies of datafiles, control files, and archived redo logs, as shown in Table 5-2.

Table 5-2. *Default Formats for Various Types of Files*

Type of File	Meaning of %U
Datafile	`data-D-%d_id-%I_TS-%N_FNO-%f_%u`
Archived log	`arch-D_%d-id-%I_S-%e_T-%h_A-%a_%u`
Control file	`cf-D_%d-id-%I_%u`

You can specify up to four values for the `format` parameter, but the second through fourth values are used only if you're making multiple copies. That is, the second, third, and fourth format values are used when you execute the `backup copies`, `set backup copies`, or `configure ... backup copies` command.

For image copies, you can also use the `db_file_name_convert` option of the `backup` command to generate your own filenames for RMAN image copies. When you use this option, you must provide a pair of filename prefixes to change the names of the output files. The first filename prefix refers to the filenames of the files that are being copied by RMAN. The second filename prefix refers to the filenames for the backup copies. In the following example, we use the `db_file_name_convert` option to specify that the backup copies of a file that starts with /u01/oradata/users are prefixed with /backups/users_ts:

```
RMAN> backup as copy
      db_file_name_convert=('/u01/oradata/users','/backups/users_ts')
      tablespace users;
```

The `db_file_name_convert` option to set the image copy filenames is useful in situations where you may want to direct the backups of tablespaces to different locations, as shown in the following example:

```
RMAN> backup as copy device type disk
      db_file_name_convert = ('/u01/app/oracle/table',
      '/u05/app/oracle/copy_table',
      '/u01/app/oracle/index','/u05/app/oracle/copy_index')
      tablespace data, index;
```

This example shows how you can easily direct the image copies of the data and index tablespaces to different locations on disk.

How It Works

When you use the db_file_name_convert option within a backup command when creating image copies, RMAN will first try to use the pair of names (for the original file and backup copy) you provide to convert filenames. If it fails to do this, RMAN will try to name the image copy according to any format parameter values you may have specified. If you didn't use the format parameter within the backup command, RMAN will use the default format %U.

5-15. Tagging RMAN Backups

Problem

You want to name your RMAN backup pieces and image copies with symbolic names so that it's easy to refer to them.

Solution

You can assign a character string called a *tag* to either a backup set or an image file. A tag is simply a symbolic name such as nightly_backup, for example, that helps you identify the contents of a backup file. Once you associate a tag with a backup, you can refer to just the tag later in RMAN commands. For example, when executing a restore command, you can specify the tag nightly_backup instead of having to specify the actual backup filename.

The following example shows how to associate a tag with a backup set:

```
RMAN> backup copies 1 datafile 5 tag test_bkp;
```

The following example shows how to associate a tag with an image copy:

```
RMAN> backup as copy tag users_bkp tablespace users;
```

To copy an image copy with a specific tag, you can use the following command format:

```
RMAN> backup as copy
    copy of database
    from tag=full_cold_cpy
    tag=new_full_cold_cpy;
```

In the following example, we show how you can create backup sets of image copies of the tablespace users, which has the tag weekend_users, and the tablespace system, which has the tag weekend_system. Note that both of the new backup sets you're creating are given the same tag, new_backup.

```
RMAN> backup as backupset tag new_backup
    copy of tablespace users from tag weekend_users
    copy of tablespace system from tag weekend_system;
```

Tags are case-insensitive. Even if you specify a tag in lowercase, RMAN will store and display the tag in uppercase.

How It Works

The main benefit in using tags for backups is that a tag can clearly tell you what a given backup's purpose is. For example, you can have two copies of a backup, one with the tag switch_only and the other with the tag for_restore_only. During a restore/recovery situation, you can use the first tag if you're using the switch command and the second if you are restoring the actual file.

You can use tags to identify backups taken for a specific purpose or at a specific time. Examples of such tags are tags such as weekly_incremental and 2006_year_end. It's common to use tags to distinguish among a set of backups that are part of a backup strategy, such as an incremental backup strategy. If you back up a backup set, you can provide a different tag for the new copy of the backup set.

Even if you don't expressly specify a tag using the keyword tag, Oracle assigns a default tag to every backup except for control file backups. The default tag is of the format TAGYYYYMMDDTHHMMSS, where YYYY refers to the year, MM to the month, DD to the day, HH to the hour, MM to the minutes, and SS to the seconds. For example, a backup of datafile 1 made on November 15, 2006, will receive the tag TAG20061115T062822.

5-16. Configuring Automatic Channels

Problem

You want to configure channels for use with either a disk device or a tape on a persistent basis for all RMAN sessions.

Solution

Use the configure command to cause RMAN to automatically allocate channels. Automatic channel allocation lets you configure persistent channels for use in all RMAN sessions.

■**Note** Remember that any specification of automatic channels using the configure command can be overridden by manually setting different channels within a run block.

You can configure the degree of parallelism, the default device type, and the default device type settings for your RMAN channels by using the options configure device type ... parallelism, configure default device type, and configure channel [n] device type, respectively. Let's look at the three channel configure command options in more detail.

Specifying a Default Device Type

You can specify a default device type for automatic channels by using the configure default device type command, as shown here:

```
RMAN> configure default device type to sbt;
```

The result of configuring the device type to sbt (tape drives) in this example is that RMAN will use only the sbt type channels for backups, because sbt (tape) was selected as the default device. As you learned earlier, the default device type for automatic channels is disk.

Specifying the Degree of Parallelism for Channels

The degree of parallelism for a specific device type controls the number of server sessions that will be used for I/O for a specific device type. You use the `configure device type ...` `parallelism` command to specify the number of automatic channels to be assigned for both types of device types—disk and tape. The default degree of parallelism is 1. It's best to allocate only one channel for each physical device on the server. That is, if you have only a single disk drive, don't set the degree of parallelism (default is 1).

You can use the `show device type` command to see the current parallelism settings:

```
RMAN> show device type;
RMAN configuration parameters are:
CONFIGURE DEVICE TYPE DISK PARALLELISM 1 BACKUP TYPE TO BACKUPSET;
RMAN>
```

You can use the following set of commands to back up to a media manager by using three tape drives in parallel:

```
RMAN> configure device type sbt parallelism 3;
RMAN> backup device type sbt database plus archivelog;
```

Each of the three tape channels that you configured will back up roughly a third of the database files and archivelogs.

You can configure a maximum of 255 channels, with each channel capable of reading 64 files in parallel. The number of channels you specify for use with a particular device determines whether RMAN writes (or reads, if it's a recovery) to this device in parallel when performing a backup. If you configure three tape channels, for example, each channel may back up more than one file, but a single file won't be backed up simultaneously by the three channels. For RMAN to use multiple channels to back up a datafile, you must use the new Oracle Database 11*g* feature called *multisection backups*, which is explained in detail in Chapter 7.

Specifying the Maximum Backup Piece Size

You can specify the maximum size of a backup piece by using the `maxpiecesize` option, as shown here (1g stands for 1 gigabyte):

```
RMAN> configure channel device type disk
      maxpiecesize 1g;
```

The previous command will limit the size of an individual backup piece to 1 gigabyte.

■**Note** RMAN allocates only a single type of channel—disk or sbt—when you execute a `backup` command. However, when you issue a `restore` command (or a `maintenance` command such as `delete`), RMAN allocates all necessary channels, including both disk and sbt.

Generic Settings for Automatic Channels

If you don't specify a number (up to *nn*) while allocating a channel, RMAN configures a *generic channel*. You use the `configure channel device type` command to configure a template of generic parameter settings for all automatic channels that belong to either the disk or the sbt type. Here's an example that shows how you can specify the disk rate and format settings for backup pieces, assuming that the default device type is set to disk:

```
RMAN> configure channel device type disk rate 5m format="?/oradata/%U";
```

As another example, look at the following command, where all backups using a tape device will use the channel settings specified:

```
RMAN> configure channel device type sbt parms='ENV=(NSR_SERVER=bksvr1)';
```

If you don't explicitly configure settings for a specific named channel, the generic settings will come into play. Thus, generic channel settings are applied to all channels you don't explicitly configure. Whenever you reconfigure a generic channel of either disk or tape, any previous settings for that device type are erased. In the following example, the format setting in the second command erases the maxpiecesize value set by the first configure command:

```
configure channel device type sbt maxpiecesize 1G;
configure channel device type sbt format 'bkup_%U';
```

Configuring Specific Channels for a Device Type

Sometimes you want to control each channel's parameters separately instead of using generic channel settings for all your channels. By assigning channel numbers to a channel, you can configure a specific channel for each device type. Note that if you want to use a specific channel for a device, you must specify at least one channel option such as maxpiecesize or format for that channel. In the following example, we use three specific channels to send disk backups to three separate disks:

```
RMAN> configure channel 1 device type disk format '/disk1/%U';
RMAN> configure channel 2 device type disk format '/disk2/%U';
RMAN> configure channel 3 device type disk format '/disk3/%U';
```

How It Works

When you send a command to the target database through the RMAN interface, the command is sent through an RMAN *channel*. An RMAN channel is simply a connection that RMAN makes from itself to the server session on the target database for performing a backup or recovery task. Each connection will initiate a database server session on the target or auxiliary database. This server session is the one that actually performs the backup and recovery tasks for RMAN. Each server session that performs a backup, restore, or recovery job relies on an RMAN channel representing a stream of data *to a particular device type* such as a disk or a tape drive. Thus, an RMAN channel is simply an input or output channel for RMAN backup and recovery jobs. Since each RMAN channel works on a single backup set or image copy at a given time, by allocating multiple channels you can have RMAN execute some commands in parallel. That is, different server sessions can be instructed to concurrently execute the same remote procedural call (RPC). RMAN will read or write multiple backup sets or copies in parallel when you allocate multiple channels for a job. Each of the allocated channels will work on a separate backup set or disk copy.

You can have two different types of RMAN channels—disk and sbt. Using a disk channel, a server process can read and write to a disk. Similarly, the sbt channel will let the server process read or write from a tape device. Note that regardless of the channel type (disk or tape), RMAN can always read from or write to a disk by default, and RMAN always allocates a single disk channel for all backup and recovery operations.

You must either manually allocate a channel (explained in the next recipe) or preconfigure channels for automatic allocation before you can execute any of the following RMAN commands:

- backup

- recover

- restore

- duplicate

- create catalog

- validate

For each RMAN channel, a connection is made to the target database. That is, each channel will spawn a separate process. It is important to understand that there's only a single RMAN session that corresponds to multiple server sessions, each for a different channel. If you're using disk devices only, you don't have to configure automatic channels, since RMAN preconfigures a disk channel for you by default. If you're using tape drives, you'll have to configure the channels whether explicitly in the RMAN run blocks or by using automatic channel configuration. Automatic channel configuration is the way to go in most cases; it makes life easy for you because you don't have to manually allocate the channels each time you perform a backup, restore, or recovery task.

You can configure persistent channel settings to simplify your usage of RMAN by using the configure channel commands shown earlier in this recipe. These persistent channel settings are stored in the RMAN repository, thus making it unnecessary for you to use the allocate channel command with each RMAN backup, recovery, restore, or maintenance command. RMAN first looks for any generic settings you might have set for any channel you don't explicitly configure. If you haven't manually set any channel configurations, RMAN will use the automatic channel configuration.

You use the clear option with the configure command to clear any automatic channel settings. You must use a separate configure ... clear command to set the configuration back to its default value. Here are some examples:

```
RMAN> configure default device type clear;      # reverts to the default
device type (DISK)
RMAN> configure channel device type sbt clear;   # erases all
options that were set for the sbt channel
RMAN> configure channel 1 device type disk clear;   # erases
configuration values set specifically for channel 1.
```

There is a difference between how RMAN treats a backup or copy command and a restore command when it comes to the allocation of channels. Even if you configure automatic channels for sbt, if your default disk type is disk, RMAN will allocate only disk channels when you run a backup or copy command. If you want RMAN to use the sbt channel, you have to use one of the following two methods:

- Use the allocate channel command in a run block to allocate the sbt channel.

- Specify the device type as disk directly within the backup command.

By default, RMAN sends all backups to the flash recovery area if you've already configured one. That is, you don't have to expressly specify the location by using the format option of the configure channel command. However, sometimes you may want to bypass the flash recovery area and send the RMAN backups elsewhere to disk. You can do so by explicitly configuring a backup device type with a specific format option. In the following example, we show how you can use the configure channel device type disk format command to specify that all RMAN disk backups be made to the /backup directory:

```
RMAN> configure channel device type disk format '/backup/ora_df%t_s%s_s%p';
```

In the format specification:

- %t stands for four-byte time stamp.

- %s stands for the backup set number.

- %p stands for the backup piece number.

If you use the configure command as shown in the previous example, all RMAN backups will be made in the /backup directory, even if you've configured a flash recovery area and there is plenty of free space in it. Thus, you must be prepared to lose the benefits of having the flash recovery area when you use the configure channel device type disk format command shown previously.

You can also send the backups to an automatic storage management (ASM) disk group, as shown in the following example:

```
RMAN> configure channel device type disk format '+dgroup1';
```

All backups will now be stored in the ASM disk group +dgroup1.

5-17. Manually Allocating RMAN Channels

Problem

You want to manually allocate RMAN channels for a specific backup or recovery command within a run block.

Solution

You can manually specify channels inside a run block by using the allocate channel command as shown here, where we allocate a single channel that we named c1, for the backup:

```
run
{
  allocate channel c1 device type sbt;
  backup database plus archivelog;
}
```

The use of the channel ID, which is c1 in the previous example, is optional. Oracle will use the channel ID when reporting input and output errors during the execution of an RMAN job.

The following example shows how to use multiple RMAN channels to spread a backup over multiple disk drives:

```
run
{
  allocate channel disk1 device type disk format '/disk1/backups/%U';
  allocate channel disk2 device type disk format '/disk2/backups/%U';
  allocate channel disk3 device type disk format '/disk3/backups/%U';
  backup database plus archivelog;
}
```

Each of the three allocate channel commands allocates a separate disk channel for each of three disk drives and also employs the format option to specify filenames that point to the different disk drives.

How It Works

You can use all options of the configure channel command when you use the allocate channel command to manually allocate RMAN channels. You can use the allocate channel command only within a run block. A manually allocated channel applies only to the run block in which it's issued. If you don't manually allocate channels during any RMAN job, automatic channels will apply to that job. Manual channels override automatic channels. You can manually allocate channels for a backup, copy, or restore task.

■**Note** Once you specify manual channels, you can't specify either the backup device type or restore device type command to use automatic channels.

Since a manually allocated works only within a run block, as soon as the run block finishes executing, RMAN automatically releases the manually allocated channels. However, you can release a channel manually by using the same identifier as you used when allocating a channel.

In the following example, we show how to use the ability of manually releasing channels to configure different options (format and maxpiecesize) for tape backups:

```
run {
    allocate channel c1 device type sbt format 'bkup_%U';
    allocate channel c2 device type sbt maxpiecesize = 5M;
    backup channel c1 datafile 1,2,3;
    release channel c1;
    backup datafile 4,5,6;
    }
```

The first backup command backs up the datafiles numbered 1, 2, and 3 to a tape drive using channel c1. Once these three datafiles are backed up, the release channel command releases channel c1. The second `backup datafile` command will then use the only remaining open channel, channel c2, to back up datafiles 4, 5, and 6.

5-18. Allocating an RMAN Maintenance Channel

Problem

You want to allocate a channel in order to perform maintenance tasks such as deleting obsolete RMAN backups.

Solution

Use the `allocate channel for maintenance` command to allocate a maintenance channel before running a `change`, `delete`, or `crosscheck` command. Suppose you've already backed up to a tape device and sent offsite all RMAN backups you made to a tape device first. You now want to delete permanently the original backups on tape so you can reuse those tapes for future backups space. Assume you've configured only a disk device by default. You can then allocate a maintenance channel as a preparatory step to deleting those backups you don't need on tape any longer:

```
RMAN> allocate channel for maintenance device type sbt;
RMAN> delete backup of database completed before 'sysdate-30';
```

The `allocate channel` command allocates the previously unallocated tape channel to perform the deletion of the backups.

How It Works

The `allocate channel for maintenance` command is meant to be used for maintenance tasks such as a `change`, `delete`, or `crosscheck` operation. You can use maintenance channels only at the RMAN prompt. That is, you can't use maintenance channels within a `run` block. You can also allocate a maintenance channel automatically. Whether you allocate a maintenance channel manually or automatically, you can't use it for a backup or restore operation. You won't have to allocate a maintenance channel when executing a `maintenance` command such as `crosscheck`, `change`, or `delete` against a disk-based file (such as an archived redo log, for example), because RMAN preconfigures an automatic disk channel for those operations.

■**Note** As long as you configure at least one channel for each device type you're using, you don't need to use maintenance channels. RMAN recommends preconfiguring the channels of tape and disk instead of using the maintenance channel command. Since RMAN always comes configured with a disk channel, this means you must configure the tape channel as well in order to avoid using the `allocate channel` command in each `run` block in preference to configuring persistent settings for the channels.

Suppose your current backup strategy uses only disk, but you have several old tape backups you want to get rid of. You can allocate a maintenance channel for performing the deletion of the tape backups by using the dummy sbt API (because the media manager isn't available any longer). You can then use the `delete obsolete` command to remove the tape backups. Here's an example showing how to do those things:

```
RMAN> allocate channel for maintenance device type sbt
      parms 'SBT_LIBRARY=oracle.disksbt,
      ENV=(BACKUP_DIR=/tmp)';
RMAN> delete obsolete;
```

Although the media manager isn't available any longer, RMAN simulates a callout to the media management layer (MML) and successfully initiates the `maintenance` command to delete the old tape backups you want to get rid of.

5-19. Creating a Backup Retention Policy

Problem

You're in charge of coming up with a backup retention policy for your enterprise. You want to create a retention policy to optimize storage space and other expenses involved in retaining backups.

Solution

You can specify a backup retention policy in two ways:

- Use a recovery window (based on the length of time to retain backups).

- Use the concept of redundancy (number of backup copies to retain) .

In both cases, you use the `configure` command to set the backup retention policy.

Backup Retention Policy Based on a Recovery Window

You can decide that you want your backups to be retained in the flash recovery area for a specific number of days. After the specified number of days, RMAN will mark the backups as obsolete, making them eligible for deletion. By using a recovery window, you're assuring that you can recover your database to any point within the recovery window. For example, if your recovery window is configured to be seven days, you can recover the database to any day and time within the last week.

Here's how you use the `configure retention policy ...` command to set a recovery window–based backup retention policy:

```
RMAN> configure retention policy to recovery window of 7 days;
```

This command specifies that RMAN must retain all backups for the duration of seven days before marking them obsolete. Any backup file that's older than seven days is marked obsolete by RMAN. If you're using RMAN incremental backups, the retention period will be greater than seven days, since RMAN has to consider not only the incremental level 0 backup but all the incremental level 1 backups as well in this case. In such a situation, the actual retention period for the backups will exceed the configured retention period of seven days.

Backup Retention Policy Based on Redundancy

By default, RMAN keeps a single copy of each backed-up datafile and control file. However, you can specify that RMAN retain more than a single copy of a backed-up datafile or control file by using the redundancy parameter of the configure retention policy command. RMAN will mark any additional copies of a datafile backup or a control file that exceed the value of the redundancy parameter as obsolete.

In the following example, we set the backup redundancy value at 2:

```
RMAN> configure retention policy to redundancy 2;
```

Let's say you make five backups of a specific datafile, one on each day of the workweek, starting on a Monday. Thus, on Friday, you end up with five different backups of that datafile. However, the first three days backups of the datafile are deemed obsolete by RMAN, since you've set your backup redundancy value at 2. That is, only the Thursday and Friday backups are considered nonobsolete backups.

How It Works

Storing backups indefinitely isn't impossible, but it's impractical—you clearly don't need to save very old backups. However, you must guard against the opposite problem of not retaining enough backups. For one reason or another, all your most recent backups may become unusable. You then have no recourse but to use older backups to perform a database recovery.

By using RMAN's backup retention policies, you can direct RMAN to retain specific backups of the database and archived redo logs in the flash recovery area. Any backup files or archived redo logs that aren't covered by the backup retention policy guidelines are automatically declared obsolete, making them candidates for deletion if space requirements demand it.

To view the current backup retention policy in effect, use the show retention policy command, as shown in this example:

```
RMAN> show retention policy;
RMAN configuration parameters are:
CONFIGURE RETENTION POLICY TO REDUNDANCY 2;
RMAN>
```

The output of this show retention policy command shows that RMAN is currently using a redundancy-based retention policy and that the redundancy is set to 2 copies.

RMAN marks any backups that fail to meet the backup retention policy constraints as *obsolete* backups. This, of course, means that the other backups that meet the retention policy criterion are considered not obsolete. The distinction between obsolete and nonobsolete backups is quite crucial, since RMAN will always retain all archived redo logs and incremental backups necessary to recover just the nonobsolete backups. It's important to understand that RMAN won't automatically delete obsolete backup files—that job falls to the DBA, who must delete the obsolete files explicitly with the delete obsolete command. Use the report obsolete command first to see which files are marked obsolete by RMAN. You can also query the V$BACKUP_FILES view to check on obsolete backups.

■**Note** Explicitly setting the retention policy to neither a window nor a redundancy-based policy (configure retention policy to none) completely disables a backup retention policy. This isn't the same as using the command configure retention policy clear, which resets the retention policy to its default value, which is redundancy 1.

RMAN uses a redundancy-based backup retention policy by default, with a default redundancy of 1. By using the command configure retention policy to none, you can specify that RMAN follows no retention policy whatsoever. This means RMAN will never consider any backup as obsolete. If you're using a flash recovery area, this means RMAN can't delete a file from the flash recovery area until you first back up the file to either disk or tape. You therefore run the risk of running out of room in the flash recovery area because of the unavailability of any reclaimable space, and eventually you'll receive an ORA-19809 error (limit exceeded for recovery files). In most cases, an ORA-19809 error results in a hung database.

5-20. Configuring an Archived Redo Log Deletion Policy

Problem

You want to configure an archived redo log deletion policy so that you can make unnecessary archived redo logs eligible for deletion.

Solution

By default, RMAN doesn't use an archived redo log policy. However, you can specify your own archived redo log deletion policy using the configure command. After connecting to the target database, issue the configure archivelog deletion policy ... command, as shown in the following example:

```
RMAN> configure archivelog deletion policy to
   2> backed up 2 times to sbt;

new RMAN configuration parameters:
CONFIGURE ARCHIVELOG DELETION POLICY TO BACKED UP 2 TIMES TO 'SBT_TAPE';
new RMAN configuration parameters are successfully stored

RMAN>
```

The preceding configure command specifies that once an archived redo log has been backed up twice to tape, it's eligible for deletion from all archived redo log locations, including the flash recovery area. The configuration of an archived redo log deletion policy is a new feature introduced in the Oracle Database 11g release.

How It Works

The configure archived redo log deletion policy command specifies only which archived redo logs are *eligible* for deletion—it doesn't automatically delete all those archived redo logs. RMAN automatically deletes only those archived redo logs in the flash recovery area that become eligible as per this deletion policy. Any archived redo logs that exist in other locations will remain there, even after becoming eligible for deletion, until you manually delete them.

In Chapter 8, where you learn about manually deleting archived redo logs using the `delete input` and `delete all input` commands, you'll see that those commands can't violate any configured archived redo log policies you may have set, unless you specify the `force` option when using those commands. By using the `force` option with either archived redo log deletion command, you can override any configured archived redo log deletion policy.

Note that the archived redo log deletion policy you set through the `configure` command doesn't affect the archived redo logs in backup sets. The deletion policy applies only to local archived redo logs. Foreign archived redo logs, meaning those received by a logical standby database for a LogMiner session, aren't affected by the deletion policy.

5-21. Limiting the Size of Individual Backup Pieces

You want to restrict the size of each individual backup piece produced by RMAN. For example, you want to limit backup piece size to something that will fit on a single backup tape.

Solution

To limit the size of a backup piece, you must specify the `maxpiecesize` option of the `configure channel` or `allocate channel` commands. The following example illustrates how you can limit the maximum size of a backup piece to 1 gigabyte:

```
RMAN> configure channel device type disk maxpiecesize = 1g;
RMAN> backup as backupset tablespace users;
```

The first command configures an automatic disk channel and limits the maximum size of a backup piece to 1 gigabyte. The second command backs up the users tablespace.

How It Works

One reason to limit the size of backup pieces is to accommodate physical limitations inherent in your storage devices. For example, if it looks like backup pieces are going to be greater in size than the capacity of a single tape drive, assuming you are backing up to tape, you can use the `maxpiecesize` parameter to ensure that a single backup piece isn't larger than the tape drive's capacity. Then, if the backup of a datafile or tablespace is larger than the configured maximum size of a backup piece, RMAN will create as many backup pieces as necessary to conform to the `maxpiecesize` value you set.

5-22. Configuring the Maximum Size of Backup Sets

You want to limit the size of an individual backup set because your operating system won't support files larger than a certain size.

Solution

Use the `maxsetsize` parameter in either the `configure` or `backup` command to set the maximum size of backup sets created on disk or tape devices. A maximum backup set size you set using the `configure` command will serve as the default for all backups performed using whatever channel you are configuring. You can set the maxsetsize parameter in units of bytes, kilobytes (K), megabytes (M), and gigabytes (G). By default, maxsetsize is set in bytes. Here's an example that shows how to set the maximum backup set size to 1 gigabyte:

```
RMAN> configure maxsetsize to 1g;
```

The second way to configure the maximum size of backup sets is to specify the maxsetsize parameter directly within a backup command, as shown here:

```
RMAN> backup database maxsetsize=1g;
```

The backup command first sets the maxsetsize parameter to 1 gigabyte before backing up the database.

How It Works

The size of a backup set made using RMAN equals the sum of the bytes in each of the backup pieces that are part of that backup set. By default, the maximum size of a backup set is unlimited, as you can see by issuing the following command:

```
RMAN> show maxsetsize;
RMAN configuration parameters are:
CONFIGURE MAXSETSIZE TO UNLIMITED; # default
RMAN>
```

The configure maxsetsize command applies to both disk and tape backups.

■**Note** You can't specify the number of backup pieces in a backup set.

Since your backup will fail if a large file in the database being backed up is larger than the value of the maxsetsize parameter, make sure the value of this parameter is at least as large as the largest datafile being backed up by RMAN. If you're backing up to tape, you run the risk of losing all your data even if just one of the tapes fails. Using the maxsetsize parameter, you can force RMAN to back up each backup set to a separate tape, thus limiting the damage to the contents of only the single failed tape.

Finally, know that the maxsetsize parameter doesn't give you absolute control over the size of the backup set that RMAN will create. The maxsetsize parameter is only one of the factors determining the size of backup sets. In addition to the setting of the maxsetsize parameter, RMAN takes into account the following factors when determining the sizing of RMAN backup sets:

- Number of input files specified in each backup command.

- Number of channels you allocate. Each allocated channel that's not idle will produce at least one backup set. RMAN also aims to divide work so all allocated channels have roughly an equal amount of work to do.

- Default number of files in each backup set.

- Default number of files that a single channel reads simultaneously (eight).

■**Note** You can't limit the size of image copies. By definition, an image copy must be identical to the original data file, so you really don't have a choice here regarding the size of a copy—it'll simply be the same size as the original data file.

In Chapter 8, you'll learn about RMAN's restartable backups feature. Following a backup failure, RMAN will back up only that data that wasn't backed up before. That is, once it's backed up, the same data won't be backed up again if a backup fails midway. Using the maxsetsize parameter of your backup command, you can make smart use of this restartable backup feature. For example, if you set maxsetsize to 10MB for a backup, RMAN produces a new backup set after every 10MB worth of backup output. Let's say your backup failed after backing up 12 backup sets. Following a restart of the backup after a backup failure, RMAN won't have to back up the data already backed up to the 12 backup sets before the backup failure.

CHAPTER 6

■ ■ ■

Using the Recovery Catalog

A *recovery catalog* is an optional database schema consisting of tables and views, and RMAN uses it to store its repository data. The control file of each target database always serves as the primary store for the repository, but you may want to create a recovery catalog as secondary storage for the repository, thus providing redundancy for the repository. For most small databases, you can get away with using just the control file to store the RMAN metadata. However, the recovery catalog provides a larger storage capacity, thus enabling access to a longer history of backups, and it is an ideal solution when dealing with a large number of databases. In addition, you can create and store RMAN scripts in the recovery catalog. Any client that can connect to the recovery catalog and a target database can use these stored scripts. Recovery catalog–based stored scripts aren't the same as operating system scripts that invoke RMAN or RMAN command scripts, which are available only if the RMAN client can access the filesystem. (See Chapter 9 for details on invoking RMAN from operating system scripts.) You can execute a *local* stored script only in the target database you're connected to from RMAN. You can execute a *global* stored script against any of the databases you register (enroll) with the recovery catalog. We discuss how to create and use RMAN-stored scripts in Chapter 9.

■Note Even when you choose to use a recovery catalog, backup information will continue to be stored in the control file as well by default.

The recovery catalog contains information about both RMAN backups and the target database. More specifically, the recovery catalog contains the following:

- RMAN configuration settings

- RMAN-stored scripts that you create

- Target database tablespace and datafile information

- Information pertaining to datafile and archived redo log backup sets and backup pieces, as well as datafile and archived redo log copies

The recovery catalog isn't a default entity—you must create it manually. Since the recovery catalog instance is a regular Oracle database like any other, you must also regularly back up this critical database. Sometimes you may have to export and import or restore and recover the recovery catalog. The recipes in this chapter show you how to create, use, merge, move, upgrade, and drop the recovery catalog. In addition, you'll also learn how to restrict access to the central or base recovery catalog by creating *virtual private recovery catalogs.*

Using a recovery catalog requires you to create and maintain a recovery catalog schema in an Oracle database. Your first task will be choosing an Oracle database in which to create the recovery catalog. You may create the recovery catalog in an existing Oracle database or create it in a new Oracle database created for that purpose. If you have anything approaching a decent number of databases to manage, we recommend creating a dedicated recovery catalog database. If you're creating a new database for housing the recovery catalog, you must create that database with a set of tablespaces such as these:

- System tablespace

- Sysaux tablespace

- Temporary tablespace

- Undo tablespace

- Recovery catalog tablespace

You can create the recovery catalog in a target database that you want to back up using the recovery catalog, but that's an unwise choice! In such a case, losing the target database means you've lost the recovery catalog as well, thus making recovery much harder or even impossible.

Back up your recovery catalog database just as you would any other production database by making it part of your regular backup and recovery strategy. It's a good policy to back up the recovery catalog right after you back up the target databases. This way, you can secure the most recent backup information records of all your production databases. Always run the recovery catalog instance in the archivelog mode, and try to make at least one backup on disk and on tape each time you back up the catalog database.

■**Note** In this book, when we use the words *recovery catalog*, we are referring to the *base* recovery catalog.

The owner of a recovery catalog, called the *recovery catalog owner*, can grant restricted access of the recovery catalog to other users. The main or central recovery catalog that acts as the repository for all databases is called the *base recovery catalog* to distinguish it from a restricted user's access to the metadata of one or more databases, called a *virtual private catalog*. The owner of the base recovery catalog determines which databases the virtual catalog owner can access. This way, there can be multiple virtual catalogs but only one base recovery catalog.

■**Note** Oracle recommends creating one central recovery catalog to act as the repository for all your databases.

6-1. Creating the Recovery Catalog

Problem

You are planning to use a recovery catalog, have already created a recovery catalog database, and want to create a recovery catalog in that database.

Solution

Creating the recovery catalog consists of two major steps. First, you must create the recovery catalog owner or schema in the database where you want to house the recovery catalog. Second, once you successfully create the recovery catalog schema, you must create the recovery catalog itself.

Creating the Recovery Catalog Owner

Follow these steps to create the recovery catalog owner:

1. Using SQL*Plus, connect as the user sys to the database where you want to create the recovery catalog. For example:

```
SQL> connect sys/oracle@catdb as sysdba
```

2. Create a default tablespace for the RMAN recovery catalog owner you're about to create. Otherwise, the system tablespace may be used by default to hold the recovery catalog structures, and it's not a smart idea to let that happen. This example creates a tablespace named cattbs:

```
SQL>  create tablespace cattbs
        datafile '/u10/oradata/catdb/cattbs_01.dbf' size 500M;
   Tablespace created.
SQL>
```

3. Create the recovery catalog owner. This example creates a user named rman to own the catalog:

```
SQL> create user rman identified by rman
        temporary tablespace temp
        default tablespace cattbs
        quota unlimited on cattbs;
User created.
SQL>
```

The default tablespace of the recovery catalog owner in this example is the cattbs tablespace created in the previous step.

4. Once you create the recovery catalog owner, you must grant that user the recovery_catalog_owner privilege in order for that user to have the authority to work with the recovery catalog you'll create in the next step. This recovery catalog owner is named rman, so grant the recovery_catalog_owner privilege to that user:

```
SQL> grant recovery_catalog_owner to rman;
SQL> exit;
```

Now that you have created the recovery catalog user, it's time to create the recovery catalog, as shown in the next section.

Creating the Recovery Catalog

Once you've created the recovery catalog schema, your next step is to create the recovery catalog. You must connect to the recovery catalog, but not to a target database, when you do this. Here are the steps you must follow to create the recovery catalog:

1. Connect to the RMAN catalog database by starting up the RMAN client and using the `connect catalog` command. You must connect as the recovery catalog owner you created in the previous section.

   ```
   RMAN> connect catalog rman/cat@catdb
   connected to recovery catalog database
   RMAN>
   ```

2. Using the `create catalog` command, create the recovery catalog. RMAN will create the recovery catalog in the default tablespace of the recovery catalog owner. For example:

   ```
   RMAN> create catalog;
   recovery catalog created
   RMAN>
   ```

You're now ready to use RMAN with the recovery catalog, which will store RMAN's backup and recovery metadata.

How It Works

Whether you decide to create a new recovery catalog using the database or merely create a recovery catalog schema in an existing database, you must configure the size of the default tablespace for the recovery catalog owner (schema). Several factors determine the sizing of the recovery catalog owner's default tablespace. The most important factors are as follows:

- The size of the databases you need to back up and recover with RMAN

- The frequency of the RMAN backups

- The number of databases you are planning to back up

- The number and size of the archived redo logs the database(s) will produce

- The number and size of the scripts you plan to save in the recovery catalog

Each backup piece you create with RMAN will require an entry in the backup piece table, stored in the recovery catalog. So, the amount of space you'd need to allocate to the recovery catalog schema will depend on the size of a database. This means the number of datafiles in a database is a key determinant of the size of the recovery catalog.

The most important factor when determining the size of the recovery catalog is the frequency of backups. Even if you have a large database with a huge number of datafiles, if you are backing it up only infrequently, say, once a month, the amount of space taken up in the recovery catalog over time won't be significant. However, if you're making daily backups of even a medium-sized database with hundreds of datafiles, you'll end up needing a lot more space in the recovery catalog.

Another key determinant of the size of the recovery catalog is the number of archived redo logs produced by the database. If a database is churning out archived redo logs every few seconds, the recovery catalog will require more space to record metadata about these archived logs. On the other hand, a database with few DML operations won't put out too many archived redo logs and, consequently, would take up very little space in the recovery catalog.

In practical terms, Oracle suggests that if you perform a daily RMAN backup of a target database with about 100 datafiles, it takes roughly 60MB of storage space. Assuming the same amount of space for storing metadata for the archived redo log backups, you'll need about 120MB for the recovery catalog tablespace for the year. If you aren't making a daily backup, your storage requirements would, of course, be considerably lower. You can allocate minimal space for the temp and undo tablespaces in the recovery catalog database, since those tablespaces are sparingly used.

6-2. Granting Restricted Access

Problem

You want to grant restricted recovery catalog access to some users, granting them access to only some of the databases registered in the base recovery catalog.

Solution

You can grant a user restricted access to the base recovery catalog by granting that user read/write access only to that user's RMAN metadata, also known as a *virtual private catalog*. Creating a virtual private catalog actually encompasses two tasks—first you must create the virtual private catalog owner and grant that user the `recovery_catalog_owner` role and the `catalog for database` privilege. Then the virtual private catalog owner must connect to the base recovery catalog and create the virtual catalog.

In our example, we've registered three databases—orcl11, eleven, and newdb. We want to grant a restricted view of the base recovery catalog by granting a user access to the metadata for only one database, orcl11. The following are the basic steps for creating a virtual private catalog:

1. If the user who will own the new virtual private catalog doesn't exist yet in the database, then create the user (in our example, the username is `virtual1`):

```
SQL> create user virtual1 identified by virtual1
  2   temporary tablespace temp
  3   default tablespace vp_users
  4    quota unlimited on vp_users;

User created.
SQL>
```

Once you create the new user, you must grant the `recovery_catalog_owner` role to that user.

2. Grant the new user the recovery_catalog_owner role, just as you do when you create a
base recovery catalog:

```
SQL> grant recovery_catalog_owner to virtual1;

Grant succeeded.

SQL>
```

User virtual1 now has the privileges to work with a recovery catalog.

3. Connect to the recovery catalog database as the base recovery catalog owner, and grant
the new user virtual1 restricted access (virtual private catalog access) to just one database, orcl11, from the base recovery catalog. You grant the catalog for database
privilege to the new user in order to do this:

```
$  rman

Recovery Manager: Release 11.1.0.1.0 - Beta on Sun Apr 8 13:19:30 2

Copyright (c) 1982, 2005, Oracle.  All rights reserved.

RMAN> connect catalog rman/rman@nick

connected to recovery catalog database

RMAN> grant catalog for database orcl11 to virtual1;

Grant succeeded.
RMAN>
```

The catalog for database privilege allows the user virtual1 to access the catalog
metadata pertaining to the orcl11 database.

4. Now that the virtual private catalog owner has the catalog for database privilege, that
user can log in to the base recovery catalog and create the virtual private catalog:

```
RMAN> connect catalog virtual1/virtual1@nick

connected to recovery catalog database

RMAN> create virtual catalog;

found eligible base catalog owned by RMAN
created virtual catalog against base catalog owned by RMAN

RMAN>
```

You can confirm that the user `virtual1` can access only the orcl11 database (and not the other two registered databases in the base recovery catalog) by issuing the following command:

```
RMAN> list incarnation;

List of Database Incarnations
DB Key  Inc Key DB Name  DBID             STATUS   Reset SCN  Reset Time
------- ------- -------- ---------------- -------- ---------- ----------
1       15      ORCL11   3863017760       PARENT   1          22-NOV-06
1       2       ORCL11   3863017760       CURRENT  909437     03-MAR-07

RMAN>
```

If you log in as the owner of the base recovery catalog owner and issue the list incarnation command, you'll see the other two databases in the base recovery catalog as well, as shown in the following output:

```
RMAN> list incarnation;

List of Database Incarnations
DB Key  Inc Key DB Name  DBID             STATUS   Reset SCN  Reset Time
------- ------- -------- ---------------- -------- ---------- ----------
192     207     ELEVEN   3481526915       PARENT   1          22-NOV-06
192     193     ELEVEN   3481526915       CURRENT  909437     13-MAR-07
1       15      ORCL11   3863017760       PARENT   1          22-NOV-06
1       2       ORCL11   3863017760       CURRENT  909437     03-MAR-07
12      150     TESTDB   3533598612       PARENT   1          10-MAR-07
12      150     TESTDB   3533598612       CURRENT  909437     15-APR-07

RMAN>
```

You can see that only the owner of the base recovery catalog can view the metadata for all the databases registered in that catalog, unlike the owner of the virtual private catalog, who is restricted to a specific database or databases.

How It Works

The virtual private catalog is really a set of views and synonyms based on the central or base recovery catalog. These views and synonyms are copied to the schema of the virtual catalog owner.

The virtual private catalog is a subset of the base recovery catalog to which you can grant access to users in the recovery catalog database. You can create multiple recovery catalog users, but by default, only the creator of the base recovery catalog has access to all its metadata. A virtual recovery catalog owner has no access to the metadata of the entire base recovery catalog.

■**Note** By default, the virtual recovery catalog owner can't access the base recovery catalog.

You must be familiar with the RMAN command grant, which lets you assign privileges to database users for a virtual private catalog. You must first create a virtual private catalog before you can use the grant command to assign privileges on that private catalog to users. The grant command lets you grant two important virtual recovery catalog–related privileges, register database and catalog for database, which we explain next.

The catalog for database privilege shown here grants the virtual catalog user access to a database already registered in the base recovery catalog:

```
RMAN> connect catalog rman/rman@catdb
RMAN> grant catalog for database prod1 to virtual1;
```

By granting the register database privilege as shown in the following example, you grant a user the ability to register new databases in the virtual private catalog and, implicitly, in the base recovery catalog as well:

```
RMAN> connect catalog rman/rman@catdb
RMAN> grant register database to virtual1;
```

The register database privilege automatically grants the user the catalog for database privilege as well. Once you grant a user the register database privilege, that user has the ability to register *new databases* in the recovery catalog. The virtual private catalog owner can register new databases—that is, databases that aren't part of the base recovery catalog—by issuing the register database command. Any databases that the virtual private catalog owner registers in this way are also registered automatically in the base recovery catalog.

Even if the virtual private catalog owner has registered a particular database, the base recovery catalog owner can always unregister that database from the central recovery catalog and thus from the virtual recovery catalog, which is a subset of the main catalog.

Just as the grant command lets you grant various privileges to the recovery catalog users, the revoke command lets you take those rights away. Here's a summary of the revoke command's usage:

- By using the catalog for database clause, you can revoke recovery catalog access to a database from a user, as shown in the following example:

  ```
  RMAN> revoke catalog for database prod1 from virtual1;
  ```

- The register database clause lets you revoke the ability of a recovery catalog user to register new databases.

- The all privileges from clause, as shown in the following example, helps revoke both the catalog and the register privileges from a user:

  ```
  RMAN> revoke all privileges from virtual1;
  ```

If you're using an Oracle 10.2 or older release of RMAN, you must perform the following steps in order to use a virtual private catalog. Connect to the base recovery catalog as the virtual catalog owner, and execute the create_virtual_catalog procedure as shown here:

```
SQL> execute base_catalog_owner.dbms_rcvcat.create_virtual_catalog;
```

If all your target databases are from an Oracle Database 11.1*g* or newer release, you can omit the previous step. The step is necessary only if you're planning to use a virtual private catalog with an Oracle Database 10.2*g* or older release. The step doesn't create a virtual private catalog—you've created the private catalog already. You need to execute this step before you can use a database belonging to an older release.

6-3. Connecting to the Catalog from the Command Line

Problem

You want to connect to the recovery catalog and the target database directly from the operating system command line.

Solution

You always use Oracle Net authentication information to connect to the recovery catalog database, but you can connect to the target database using either operating system authentication or Oracle Net authentication. The following example shows how to connect from the operating system command line using operating system authentication for the target database connection and Oracle Net authentication for the recovery catalog:

```
$ rman  target /  catalog rman/rman@catalog_db
```

In the example, we're assuming that you've already created the rman schema in the catalog database, as we described in recipe 6-1. Since you must always connect to the recovery catalog as the owner of the catalog schema, you must, in this case, connect as the recovery catalog database user rman; whatever username you connect with in your environment should be the owner of your recovery catalog.

Instead of using operating system authentication with your target database, you can use Oracle Net credentials to connect to *both* the target database and the recovery catalog, as shown here:

```
$ rman target sys/sammyy1@target_db catalog rman/rman@catalog_db
```

Just make sure that your tnsnames.ora file, if you're using one, lists both the catalog database and the target database to which you're connecting.

How It Works

The catalog connection connects you to the recovery catalog database, and the target connection connects you to the target database you want to back up or recover. You must make some changes in the tnsnames.ora file on the server from which you're connecting to the recovery catalog, before trying the operating system–level commands shown in this solution. For example, if your recovery catalog database(catdb) is running on the server prod1, you must add the following entry in your tnsnames.ora file in the $ORACLE_HOME/network/admin directory:

```
catdb =
(DESCRIPTION =
    (ADDRESS_LIST =
        (ADDRESS =  (PROTOCOL = TCP) (HOST = prod1) (PORT=1521))
        )
    (CONNECT_DATA =
        (SERVICE_NAME = prod1)
    )
)
```

You must also add the following entry to the listener.ora file on the server where the recovery catalog instance is running. The listener.ora file is also located in the $ORACLE_HOME/ network/admin directory on Unix/Linux systems and the ORACLE_HOME\network\admin directory on Windows servers.

```
(SID_DESC =
    (ORACLE_HOME = /u01/app/oracle/db/prod1)
    (sid_name=catdb)
)
```

The portion of the listener.ora file shown here includes the protocol address, which is the network address of any object on the network, in this case the Oracle database cat_db. The Oracle listener service will accept connection requests for all databases listed in the listener.ora file.

Don't forget to specify your catalog database when invoking RMAN. Otherwise, RMAN will use the control file by default, since the recovery catalog is only an optional construct. If you don't specify catalog or nocatalog when you make a connection to the target database, you'll be using the control file as the source of all repository information. Make one mistake, and you will have permanently broken the link between target and catalog. The following example demonstrates this:

```
$ rman
RMAN> connect target sys/sys_passwd@prod1;
RMAN> backup datafile 1;

Starting backup at 25-NOV-06
using target database file instead of recovery catalog
...
Finished backup at 25-NOV-06

RMAN> connect catalog rman/rman@catdb
RMAN-00571: =========================
RMAN-00569: ===============
ERROR MESSAGE STACK FOLLOWS

 ====================================
RMAN-06445: cannot connect to recovery catalog
 after NOCATALOG has been used
RMAN>
```

This example connects only to the target database. Notice the message given by RMAN in response to the backup command (using target database ...). That message alerts you that you've just broken the link to your catalog database. Notice the error given next when a connection to the catalog is subsequently attempted. Just making that one backup without connecting to the catalog first has severed the link between catalog and target.

In the example shown previously, your failure to first connect to the recovery catalog before performing the backup of the target database means the recovery catalog won't have a record of this backup. The entire metadata for this backup will be absent from the recovery catalog, which is something that'll cost you dearly if you have to restore the database using RMAN. Not to worry, because you can always update or synchronize the recovery catalog from the contents of the control file. Recipe 6-8 shows how to perform a resynchronization of the recovery catalog.

6-4. Connecting to the Catalog from the RMAN Prompt

Problem

You have invoked RMAN without connecting to anything, you are sitting at the RMAN prompt, and now you want to connect to your target and catalog databases.

Solution

An easy solution is to connect to each database as a separate step. You can use operating system authentication to connect to the target database in the following way:

```
RMAN> connect target /
```

You can then use Oracle Net authentication to connect to the recovery catalog:

```
RMAN> connect catalog rman/rman@catalog_db
```

And, of course, you can issue the `connect auxiliary` command to connect to an auxiliary database, should you need to do so.

How It Works

Connecting to the target database and the recovery catalog (and to the auxiliary database) from the RMAN interface is a good way to keep key passwords from being revealed to other users in the system. If you connect directly from the operating system prompt, you'll be exposing your passwords to everyone, because they are (often) visible in the results from a `ps` command. However, the `ps` command does not "see" what you type after you invoke RMAN.

6-5. Registering Target Databases

Problem

You want to use a recovery catalog to manage the RMAN repository data for a new database.

Solution

To use a recovery catalog to store RMAN repository data concerning any target database, you must first *register* the target database with that catalog. The following steps show how to register a database in a recovery catalog:

1. Make a connection to the recovery catalog, as well as to the target database you want to register:

   ```
   % rman target / catalog rman/rman@catdb
   ```

2. If the target database isn't mounted yet, start it in the mount state:

   ```
   RMAN> startup mount;
   ```

3. Issue the register database command to register the target database to which you are currently connected:

```
RMAN> register database;

database registered in recovery catalog
starting full resync of recovery catalog
full resync complete

RMAN>
```

You can ensure that you have successfully registered the target database by issuing the list incarnation command. Here's an example:

```
RMAN> list incarnation;


List of Database Incarnations
DB Key  Inc Key DB Name  DBID             STATUS   Reset SCN  Reset Time
-------  ------- -------- ---------------- -------- ---------- ----------
1        15      ORCL11   3863017760       PARENT   1          22-NOV-06
1        2       ORCL11   3863017760       CURRENT  909437     03-MAR-07

RMAN>
```

The list incarnation command is actually meant to show the various incarnations of a database, but we're using it here to confirm database registration in the recovery catalog by using the DB_NAME and DB_ID columns.

How It Works

When you register a new target database in your recovery catalog, RMAN reads the control file of the target database and copies the RMAN metadata into tables in the recovery catalog. After registration, the control file and the recovery catalog will contain identical information regarding RMAN backups.

■**Note** Should your target database control file ever become out of sync with your recovery catalog, as it will when there are structural changes in the database, see recipe 6-7 for instructions on how to resynchronize the two.

You can register multiple target databases in the same recovery catalog. Conversely, you can register the same target database in multiple recovery catalogs. If you have several target databases that you plan to register in a given recovery catalog, you must connect to each of them separately and register them one at a time. Make sure that each of the target databases has a unique database ID (DBID). Usually that is the case; however, if you copy a database, you might end up with multiple databases with the same DBID. Because RMAN relies on the

DBID to distinguish between databases, you won't be able to register the source database and the copied database in the same recovery catalog unless you change the DBID of the copied database.

■**Tip** In the event you do find yourself with two databases having the same DBID, first change the DBID of one of the databases using the dbnewid utility. Then you can register that database in the recovery catalog.

6-6. Unregistering a Database

Problem

You want to remove a target database from the recovery catalog because you have decided to rely instead on the control file to hold backup and recovery metadata.

Solution

You can remove a target database's information from a recovery catalog and stop RMAN from tracking a target database's activity in that catalog by using the unregister database command. Here are the steps for unregistering a database from the recovery catalog:

1. Connect both to the recovery catalog and to the target database:

```
$ rman target  /  catalog  rman/rman@catdb

connected to target database: RDBMS (DBID=1237603294)
connected to recovery catalog database
RMAN>
```

2. Issue the unregister database command to unregister the target database to which you're currently connected:

```
RMAN> unregister database;
database name is "TENNER" and DBID is 922224687
Do you really want to unregister the database (enter YES or NO)? yes
database unregistered from the recovery catalog
RMAN>
```

You may also explicitly specify the name of the database you want to unregister from the recovery catalog, along with the unregister command, as in unregister database tenner, for example.

How It Works

When you unregister a target database from the recovery catalog, the backups pertaining to that database aren't affected—you now rely on the control file, instead of the recovery catalog, to store the history of those backups. Just a reminder—prior to the Oracle Database 10*g* release, you were required to execute the dbms_rcvcat.unregisterdatabase(db_key, db_id) procedure from SQL*Plus to unregister a database from the recovery catalog.

Prior to unregistering a database, it's a smart idea to record the complete set of backups known to the recovery catalog by issuing the commands list backup summary and list copy summary. Then, if you later decide to reregister the database, you'll know exactly which backups are not recorded in that database's control file. You'll need to recatalog those backups. Recipe 6-6 shows you how.

You may someday find yourself in the situation of needing to unregister a database that no longer exists. In such a case, you can't, of course, connect to the nonexistent database in order to unregister it. The solution is to connect to your catalog database independently and issue an unregister command specifying exactly which database it is that you want to unregister. For example:

```
RMAN> unregister database testdb;
```

It is further possible that you might have another database of the same name, perhaps because it is running on a different server. In such a case, use the set dbid command to specify the particular database that you want to unregister. The following example shows how to remove a specific database named testdb when multiple databases named testdb are registered:

```
RMAN> run
       {
         set dbid 1234567899;
         unregister database testdb;
       }
```

In the event that you need to issue a set dbid command, you can easily determine the DBID to use. Whenever you connect to a target database, RMAN displays the DBID for that database. In addition, you can query the recovery catalog or check the filenames of the control file autobackup to find the DBID for a database. To find out how to determine the database identifier (DBID), please refer to recipe 10-3.

6-7. Cataloging Older Files

Problem

You have some image copies, some RMAN backup pieces, and some archived redo log files from before your recovery catalog was created. You want to make all these part of the recovery catalog so that information about them is available to RMAN.

Solution

You can catalog any existing datafile copies, backup pieces, or archived redo logs by using the catalog command, as shown in the following example, which catalogs an operating system–based copy of a datafile:

```
RMAN> catalog datafilecopy '/u01/app/oracle/users01.dbf';
cataloged datafile copy
datafile copy filename=/u01/app/oracle/users01.dbf recid=2 stamp=604202000
RMAN>
```

Similarly, you can use the following two commands to catalog an RMAN-made backup piece and an archivelog, respectively:

```
RMAN> catalog backuppiece '/disk1/backups/backup_820.bkp';
RMAN> catalog archivelog '/disk1/arch_logs/archive1_731.dbf',
                '/disk1/arch_logs/archive1_732.dbf';
```

The files you want to catalog can exist only on disk and not on tape, and they must belong to one of the following types:

- Datafile copy

- Control file copy

- Archived redo log

- Backup piece

Cataloging a Datafile Copy As an Incremental Backup

You can use the `catalog` command to catalog a datafile copy that you want to use as a level 0 incremental backup. Simply add `level 0` to the `catalog datafilecopy` command, as shown here:

```
RMAN> catalog datafilecopy '?/oradata/users01.bak' level 0;
```

Once you catalog a datafile copy as a level 0 backup, you can then perform an incremental backup by using that copy as your base.

Cataloging Sets of Files

If you have a whole bunch of files you need to record in the recovery catalog, you can save time and effort by using the `catalog start with` command. After the keywords `catalog start with`, you specify a string pattern. The command catalogs all valid backup sets, datafile copies, archived redo logs, and control file copies whose names start with the string pattern you specify. The string pattern can refer to an OMF directory, an ASM disk group, or part of a filename.

RMAN will automatically catalog all the backups found in the locations that match the string pattern that follows the `catalog start with` command. For example, to catalog all files in the /disk1/arch_logs directory, use this:

```
RMAN> catalog start with '/disk1/arch_logs/';
```

In this case, the `catalog start with` command will catalog an entire directory of archived redo logs. By default, RMAN will prompt you after each match to verify that you want the item to be cataloged. You can skip this prompting by using the additional keyword `noprompt`, as shown here:

```
RMAN> catalog start with '/disk1/arch_logs/' noprompt;
```

The previous command will let RMAN perform the Cataloging without prompting after each match.

Cataloging the Flash Recovery Area

You can also use the `catalog start with` command to catalog the contents of the flash recovery area. All the backup sets, archived redo logs, and datafile copies that are part of the active flash recovery area will be cataloged. Here's how to do that:

```
RMAN> catalog recovery area;
```

You can optionally use the `noprompt` keyword if you don't want RMAN to prompt before Cataloging each object it finds in the flash recovery area.

How It Works

The `catalog` command comes in handy when you want to record information pertaining to backup-related files that were created outside the context of the recovery catalog. It's important to understand that this `catalog` command is completely different from the `connect catalog` command used when connecting to the recovery catalog.

When you create a recovery catalog, an initial automatic synchronization occurs. During this synchronization process, RMAN gets all backup-related data from the current control file and stores the data in its own internal tables. However, as you probably are aware by now, the control file doesn't necessarily save *all* the older backup-related data. It's quite likely that some of the older backup data has aged out of the control file because of space limitations. You can make all the aged-out, older backup data available to RMAN by explicitly using the `catalog` command to register the older backups, recording them in your recovery catalog.

6-8. Updating the Recovery Catalog

Problem

The recovery catalog is sometimes not available when issuing certain RMAN commands. In addition, RMAN updates of the recovery catalog may be made infrequently under some conditions. You want to make sure the recovery catalog is updated with all the current backup information.

Solution

You use the `resync catalog` command in order to update or resynchronize a recovery catalog. You must connect to the recovery catalog as well as to the target database in order to perform the resynchronization. First, start the target database in mount mode:

```
RMAN> startup mount;
```

Next, once you connect to the target database, issue the `resync catalog` command:

```
RMAN> resync catalog;
  starting full resync of recovery catalog
  full resync complete
RMAN>
```

■**Note** Full resynchronization uses a snapshot of the target database control file as the source to resynchronize the recovery catalog.

How It Works

To update the recovery catalog using the current control file information, RMAN will first create a snapshot control file. It'll then compare the contents of the recovery catalog to the contents of the snapshot control file and update the recovery catalog by adding the missing information and modifying the changed backup- and schema-related records.

How often you must use the `resync catalog` command will depend on your backup frequency as well as the number of archived redo logs and online log switches produced by the target database. At the least, you must ensure that you resynchronize the recovery catalog often enough that the data in the control file gets transferred to the recovery catalog before that data is overwritten because the control file is full. This means you must keep the value of the initialization parameter `control_file_record_keep_time` longer than your backup interval. This is also a good reason why you must never set the value of this parameter to 0.

Two basic types of records get updated in the recovery catalog during the resynchronization process. The first type of records consists of mostly archive log and backup–related data such as the following:

- Online log switch information

- Archived redo log information

- Backup history, such as backup sets, backup pieces, and proxy copies

- Database incarnation history

The other major type of recovery catalog data that's updated is data relating to the *physical schema*, such as data relating to datafiles and tablespaces, for example. If the target database is using a backup control file or a newly created control file or if you're using the `resync catalog from controlfilecopy` command, the physical schema data in the recovery catalog will not be updated. That is, you must be using the current control file for the target database in order for the physical schema to be updated with the `resync` command. In other words, to perform a full synchronization of the dataset, you must use the current control file.

When you issue certain RMAN commands such as the `backup` command, RMAN automatically performs a resynchronization. A resynchronization involves the comparison of the recovery catalog to the current control file and the updating of the recovery catalog with the missing information that is either missing or changed. A resynchronization is said to be *partial* when RMAN updates only information about archived redo logs and new backups. During a *full* synchronization, in addition to the backup-related information, RMAN also updates metadata about the physical schema, such as tablespaces, datafiles, online redo logs, and undo segments. Thus, RMAN performs a full resynchronization whenever the schema metadata is changed; otherwise, it does only a partial synchronization.

Although RMAN automatically resynchronizes the recovery catalog pursuant to most RMAN commands such as `backup` and `delete`, it is easy to think of situations when you may not be able to avail of this feature. For example, you may decide to perform the backups of a database without connecting to the catalog database, or you may be prevented from connecting to the recovery catalog database before the backup of a target database. Clearly, in such cases, the control file will contain the backup information but not the recovery catalog, since you weren't even connected to the recovery catalog during the backup of the target database. In cases such as these, you must connect to the recovery catalog when you get a chance and perform a resynchronization using the `resync catalog` command.

Another scenario requiring you to resort to the manual resynchronization of the recovery catalog is when you don't perform frequent backups such as a nightly backup but instead perform, say, a weekly or monthly backup. If you were to perform a daily backup, RMAN would've automatically synchronized the recovery catalog as part of the `backup` command. However, since you aren't performing a nightly backup, the recovery catalog gets updated only once a week or once a month, depending on the frequency of your backups. If you're running your database in archivelog mode and the database churns out a million of these between backups, the recovery catalog won't contain the information relating to these archived redo logs, although the control file will. The same will also be true of all online redo log switches—data regarding what is stored only in the control file but not propagated automatically to the recovery catalog. In situations such as these, manually resynchronizing the recovery catalog with the help of the `resync catalog` command is the only way to update the catalog.

If you've never backed up the recovery catalog or if you've backed it up but are missing some necessary archived redo logs, you can use the `resync catalog` command to bail yourself out. If you don't have a backup of the recovery catalog or you can't recover the recovery catalog for some reason from the backups, you must re-create the recovery catalog. You can use the `resync catalog` command to update the newly re-created recovery catalog with the information from the control file of the target database. However, you'll be missing the metadata for those records that have aged out of the control file. You can then use the `catalog start with` ... command to enter any available older backup information in the freshly re-created recovery catalog.

6-9. Dropping the Recovery Catalog

Problem

You decide to do away with your base recovery catalog, because you've decided that the control file is adequate to maintain your RMAN backup and recovery needs. Or, you want to remove just a particular virtual private catalog but keep the base recovery catalog intact.

Solution

To drop the base recovery catalog, you must drop the recovery catalog schema from the recovery catalog database by using the `drop catalog` command. Here are the steps to follow:

1. Connect to the base recovery catalog before you can use this command. You don't need to be connected to a target database to drop the recovery catalog. Here's how to connect:

```
RMAN> connect catalog rman/rman@catdb
Connected to recovery catalog database
```

2. Issue the drop catalog command. For example:

```
RMAN> drop catalog;

recovery catalog owner is RMAN
enter DROP CATALOG command again to confirm catalog removal
```

RMAN will force you to enter the drop catalog command a second time to ensure that you really do want to drop the recovery catalog. You want to drop the catalog for sure, so issue the drop catalog command again:

```
RMAN> drop catalog;
recovery catalog dropped
RMAN>
```

The steps for dropping a *virtual* private catalog are identical to those for the base recovery catalog. You must first connect to the appropriate virtual private catalog before issuing the drop catalog command.

■**Caution** When you drop the base recovery catalog, you lose the backup information for all databases registered in the base recovery catalog.

How It Works

The drop catalog command will remove all RMAN backup metadata from the base recovery catalog or the virtual private catalog database. You thus lose the ability to use any of the backups formerly registered in the catalog if the backups were recorded in the dropped recovery catalog but not in the control file. If you've backed up your recovery catalog prior to dropping it, you can restore it and access the backup metadata. The only other way to make those backups available to RMAN again is to create a new recovery catalog and then manually use the catalog command to record those backups in the new recovery catalog.

You can drop a virtual private catalog by logging in as the base catalog owner or the virtual catalog owner. If you drop the base recovery catalog but don't drop any virtual private catalogs defined on the parent catalog, the virtual private catalogs will be unusable. Dropping a virtual catalog has no impact on the base recovery catalog.

6-10. Merging Recovery Catalogs

Problem

You have multiple recovery catalogs, each for a different version of your Oracle databases. You want to merge all of these recovery catalogs into one.

Solution

Use the import catalog command to merge recovery catalog schemas. In the following example, the destination recovery catalog schema, owned by user rman11, is located in the recovery catalog database eleven. This recovery catalog currently has two databases registered with it, as shown by the following list incarnation command:

```
RMAN> list incarnation;
List of Database Incarnations
DB Key  Inc Key DB Name  DBID             STATUS   Reset SCN  Reset Time
------- ------- -------- ---------------- -------- ---------- ----------
192     207     ELEVEN   3481526915       PARENT   1          22-NOV-06
192     193     ELEVEN   3481526915       CURRENT  909437     13-MAR-07
1       15      ORCL11   3863017760       PARENT   1          22-NOV-06
1       2       ORCL11   3863017760       CURRENT  909437     03-MAR-07
RMAN>
```

You also have another 10.2 recovery catalog schema owned by the user rman10, with one database registered in it, as shown by the following list incarnation command:

```
RMAN> list incarnation;

List of Database Incarnations
DB Key  Inc Key DB Name  DBID             STATUS   Reset SCN  Reset Time
------- ------- -------- ---------------- -------- ---------- ----------
1       8       TENNER   1166569509       PARENT   1          30-AUG-05
1       2       TENNER   1166569509       CURRENT  534907     13-MAR-07

RMAN>
```

Your goal is to merge the 10.2 release recovery catalog into the 11.1 release recovery catalog, thus creating a consolidated recovery catalog schema with all three databases registered in that catalog. To do this, connect to the destination catalog, and issue the import catalog command, as shown in the following example:

```
$ rman
RMAN> connect catalog rman/rman@eleven
RMAN> import catalog rman10/rman10@tenner;

Starting import catalog at 08-APR-07
connected to source recovery catalog database
import validation complete
database unregistered from the source recovery catalog
Finished import catalog at 08-APR-07
RMAN>
```

In the previous command, you must specify the connection string for the source catalog whose metadata you want to import into the destination catalog. Issue the list incarnation command again to ensure that all three databases are now part of the single consolidated recovery catalog:

```
RMAN> list incarnation;

List of Database Incarnations
DB Key  Inc Key DB Name  DBID            STATUS    Reset SCN   Reset Time
------- ------- -------- --------------- --------  ----------  ----------
1411    1418    TENNER   1166569509      PARENT    1           30-AUG-05
1411    1412    TENNER   1166569509      CURRENT   534907      13-MAR-07
192     207     ELEVEN   3481526915      PARENT    1           22-NOV-06
192     193     ELEVEN   3481526915      CURRENT   909437      13-MAR-07
1       15      ORCL11   3863017760      PARENT    1           22-NOV-06
1       2       ORCL11   3863017760      CURRENT   909437      03-MAR-07

RMAN>
```

You'll find that there are no databases registered in the source database any longer:

```
RMAN> list incarnation;

RMAN>
```

You don't see any databases registered in the source database, since RMAN automatically unregisters all databases from the source recovery catalog after importing the contents of that catalog into the destination recovery catalog. If you don't want RMAN to unregister the databases from the source catalog after importing the metadata for the databases registered in that catalog, issue the following import catalog command, with the no unregister option:

```
RMAN> import catalog rman10/rman10@tenner no unregister;
```

In cases where you want to re-create a recovery catalog from a source catalog, you will not want to unregister all databases from the source catalog.

How It Works

Importing a catalog into another and merging it with the destination catalog all takes place without connecting to a target database. You simply need to connect to the source and destination recovery catalogs with the RMAN client.

The import catalog command will import the metadata for all the databases that are currently registered in the source catalog schema into the destination catalog schema. If you'd rather import a specific database(s), you can do so using the following variation on the import catalog command wherein you specify the DBID or database name of the database you want to import:

```
RMAN> import catalog rman10/rman10@tenner dbid = 123456, 123457;
RMAN> import catalog rman10/rman10@tenner db_name = testdb, mydb;
```

If a database is registered in both the source and destination target recovery catalogs, first unregister that database from one of the catalogs before proceeding. You can't perform an import when a database is simultaneously registered in both the source and destination catalogs.

You can issue the import catalog command only if the source database's version is identical to the version of the RMAN client you're using. If the source recovery catalog schema belongs to an older version, upgrade that catalog schema first using the upgrade catalog command, shown in recipe 6-10.

6-11. Moving the Recovery Catalog to Another Database

Problem

You want to move a recovery catalog from one database to another.

Solution

You can move a recovery catalog to a different database from the present recovery catalog database by using the import catalog command. Here are the steps to move a recovery catalog:

1. Create a new recovery catalog in the target database, but don't register any databases in it.

2. Use the import catalog command in RMAN after connecting to the target database:

```
$ rman
RMAN> connect catalog rman/rman@target_db
RMAN> import catalog rman10/rman10@source_db;
```

The import catalog command will import the source recovery catalog contents into the target recovery catalog.

How It Works

Moving a recovery catalog to another database is similar to merging recovery catalogs discussed in the previous recipe, since both use the import catalog command to import a recovery catalog from one database to another.

6-12. Creating a High-Availability Recovery Catalog

Problem

You have registered a large number of databases in a single recovery catalog and want to ensure that the recovery catalog is always available to perform backup and recovery tasks. That is, you want a high-availability solution for the RMAN recovery catalog.

Solution

The solution is to maintain multiple, redundant recovery catalogs. If you're using the recovery catalog to manage the backup and recovery tasks for a large number of production databases, maintaining high availability becomes critical. You can ensure high availability of the recovery catalog just as you would any other Oracle database—by using a *standby* recovery catalog instance. In the case of recovery catalogs, however, you really don't use a special standby database for the alternate recovery catalog instance—you simply maintain a *secondary recovery catalog* that can take over from the primary recovery catalog in the event disaster strikes.

Here's a simple outline of the strategy for using a standby recovery catalog:

1. Create a secondary recovery catalog in a separate Oracle database.

2. Register all databases—all that you have registered in your primary catalog—in the secondary recovery catalog.

3. The primary recovery catalog is synchronized automatically during the normal backups of the target databases.

4. Synchronize the secondary recovery catalog manually with the `resync catalog` command after connecting to each of the target databases registered in the catalog.

5. Switch to the secondary catalog as the primary recovery catalog when necessary after resynchronizing it first. Switching to the secondary catalog is as easy as can be. Simply connect to that catalog instead of to the primary one. The secondary catalog will be now your primary catalog.

How It Works

It's important to synchronize the secondary recovery catalog manually on a frequent basis so the catalog remains current. This way, when you are forced to fall back on the secondary catalog, it'll have all the backup metadata you need.

You must back up the secondary recovery catalog database just as you would the primary catalog database to provide high availability.

6-13. Viewing Backup Information

Problem

You want to access information stored in the recovery catalog. You know you can use the database views in the individual target databases to find out information about their backups, but you'd like to get data about all your target databases from the recovery catalog itself.

Solution

The recovery catalog comes with its own special set of dynamic views that are analogous to the database performance views (V$ views). These recovery catalog views have the prefix RC_. Each such recovery catalog view contains information for all the target databases registered in the recovery catalog.

Most of the RC_ views use the DB_KEY column to uniquely identify a target database registered in the recovery catalog. That is, the DB_KEY column is the primary key in each of the recovery catalog views or RC_ views. To obtain the DB_KEY for a database, first identify the DBID for that database. Each DBID is mapped to a unique database and is connected to a single DB_KEY value. You can find out the DBID of a database with the following query:

```
SQL> connect / as sysdba
SQL> select DBID from v$database;

DBID
--------
6325412
```

Once you have the DBID for a database, you can get the DB_KEY from the RC_DATABASE view after first connecting to the recovery catalog database:

```
SQL> connect rman/cat@catdb
SQL> select db_key from rc_database where dbid = &dbid_of_target;
```

The following are brief descriptions of the most important recovery catalog views:

RC_STORED_SCRIPT: This view lists information about RMAN scripts stored in the recovery catalog.

RC_UNUSABLE_BACKUPFILE_DETAILS: This view shows the unusable backup files recorded in the recovery catalog.

RC_RMAN_STATUS: This view is similar to the V$RMAN_STATUS view and shows the status of all RMAN operations. This view doesn't contain information about any operations that are currently executing.

RC_RMAN_CONFIGURATION: This view provides information about persistent configuration settings.

RC_DATAFILE: This view shows all datafiles registered in the recovery catalog.

RC_DATABASE: This view shows the databases registered in the recovery catalog.

RC_ARCHIVED_LOG: This view provides historical information on both archived as well as unarchived redo logs.

How It Works

Remember that you can also use RMAN commands such as `list` to view the information stored in the recovery catalog tables. It's often far easier to use commands than to query the views. For example, we find it generally easier to issue a `list script names` command than it is to write a `select` statement against the RC_STORED_SCRIPT view. Unlike normal V$ views, the recovery catalog views described in this recipe aren't normalized, since they exist mainly for the use of RMAN and Enterprise Manager. Owing to the joining of multiple tables to build each of the recovery catalog views, you see a lot of redundant information when you query these views.

6-14. Uncataloging RMAN Records

Problem

You want to remove information from the recovery catalog, perhaps pertaining to a deleted backup or to a file that you have deleted with an operating system utility.

Solution

Use the `change ... uncatalog` command to alter or remove specific RMAN repository records. The following are two examples of the usage of this command. The first one deletes the record of a control file copy, and the second deletes the record of a datafile copy:

```
RMAN> change controlfilecopy '/u01/app/oracle/rman/backup/control01.ctl' uncatalog;
RMAN> change datafilecopy '/u01/app/oracle/rman/backup/users01.ctl' uncatalog;
```

If you want, you can query the RC_DATAFILE_COPY and RC_CONTROLFILE_COPY views to confirm deletions such as these.

How It Works

Use the change ... uncatalog command for two specific purposes:

- To update a deleted backup record's status to *deleted* in the control file repository.

- To delete a backup record from the recovery catalog. For example, if you delete an archived redo log through an operating system command instead of deleting it through RMAN, you can use the change archivelog ... uncatalog command to remove the record of that now-deleted archived redo log from the recovery catalog.

When you execute the change ... uncatalog command, RMAN doesn't remove any physical files—it merely removes references to the specified file from the recovery catalog. Only the records pertaining to the uncataloged files are removed from the recovery catalog.

6-15. Using a Release 11.*x* Client with Older Catalogs

Problem

You've installed the new Oracle 11.*x* release RMAN software. When you try to connect to an RMAN recovery catalog you created with the Oracle 10.2 release, you get an error.

Solution

If you try to connect to older versions of the recovery catalog schema using the new Oracle 11 release RMAN client, you'll receive an error saying the recovery catalog is too old. The solution is to upgrade the recovery catalog to the newer version required by the RMAN client using the upgrade catalog command. The following is a set of examples that shows how you get an error and what to do about it.

First check the version of your recovery catalog by issuing the following command from SQL*Plus after logging in as the recovery catalog owner:

```
SQL> select * from rcver;

VERSION
------------
10.02.00.00

SQL>
```

The preceding query shows that your recovery catalog is release 10.2.*version*. Now, try connecting to this recovery catalog by invoking your Oracle 11 release RMAN client, as shown in the following example:

```
$ rman

Recovery Manager: Release 11.1.0.1.0 - Beta on Sun Apr 8 16:30:09 2007

Copyright (c) 1982, 2005, Oracle.  All rights reserved.

RMAN> connect catalog rman10/rman10@tenner

connected to recovery catalog database
PL/SQL package RMAN10.DBMS_RCVCAT version 10.02.00.00
in RCVCAT database is too old

RMAN>
```

To be able to connect to the older recovery catalog, you must upgrade the recovery catalog in the following manner (you'll have to issue this command twice, as shown in the example, by using the upgrade catalog command):

```
RMAN> upgrade catalog;

recovery catalog owner is RMAN
enter UPGRADE CATALOG command again to confirm catalog upgrade

RMAN> upgrade catalog;

recovery catalog upgraded to version 11.01.00.01
DBMS_RCVMAN package upgraded to version 11.01.00.01
DBMS_RCVCAT package upgraded to version 11.01.00.01

RMAN>
```

After the catalog is successfully upgraded, confirm the version of the recovery catalog in SQL*Plus, again logging in as the recovery catalog owner, as shown in this example.

```
SQL>  select * from rcver;

VERSION
------------
11.01.00.01

SQL>
```

You've successfully upgraded your 10.2 version of your recovery catalog schema to the 11.1 release version.

How It Works

Not all catalog schema versions are usable with all target database releases. Please check the compatibility matrix provided by Oracle to learn about which recovery catalog schema versions are compatible with a particular version of RMAN. You can also refer to recipe 6-12, which deals with the resolution of RMAN compatibility issues.

The RMAN client you're using can't be a more recent version than the target or auxiliary database to which you're connecting. The recovery catalog schema version must be at least the same as the RMAN client version or greater.

You can't upgrade a virtual private catalog with the upgrade catalog command—you must upgrade the base recovery catalog. When RMAN connects to the virtual private catalog the next time, it automatically performs any necessary changes in the virtual private catalog.

CHAPTER 7

■■■

Making Backups with RMAN

You can use the backup command to back up datafiles, archived redo logs, or control files. You can also use the backup command to make copies of datafiles and backups of backup sets. Since RMAN provides (since the Oracle9*i* Database release) the default configuration for all backup-related parameters such as devices, formats, and tags, you can, if you want, back up your entire database by simply typing the command backup database at the RMAN prompt. You must, of course, first connect to the target database before backing it up, and the database must be in mount or open state if it's running in archivelog mode and must be the mount state if it's operating in noarchivelog mode.

Before we discuss various RMAN backup-related recipes in this chapter, it helps to quickly review key RMAN backup-related concepts before jumping into the mechanics of performing the backups.

Backup Sets and Image Copies

The backup command lets you make two types of RMAN backups: *backup sets* and *image copies*. By default, all RMAN backups are in the form of backup sets. Each backup set contains one or more backup pieces, which are files in an RMAN-specific format. Backup sets are the default backup type for both disk- and tape-based backups.

A backup set is a logical structure that consists of a minimum of one *backup piece*, which is a physical, RMAN-specific format file that actually contains the backed-up data. A backup set can contain data from one or more datafiles, archived redo log files, or control files. By default, a backup set contains just one backup piece. However, you can limit the size of a backup piece by using the maxpiecesize parameter. If you do this and the backup set size is larger than the backup piece size specified by the maxpiecesize parameter, there'll be multiple backup pieces within that backup set.

Each of the objects you back up with the backup command—database, tablespace, archived redo logs, and so on—will result in at least one backup set if you specify backup set as the backup type. RMAN determines the number of backup sets for a backup according to an internal algorithm. However, you can limit the size of a backup set by specifying the maxsetsize parameter. You can also indirectly control the number of backup sets made by RMAN for each backup by specifying the filesperset parameter, which limits the number of input files (datafiles, archived redo log files, and so on) that can be backed up into a single backup set.

The key difference between an image copy and a backup set is that RMAN can write blocks from many files into the same backup set (known as *multiplexing*) but can't do so in the case of an image copy—an image copy is identical, byte by byte, to the original datafile, control file, or archived redo log file. An RMAN image copy and a copy you make with an operating system copy command such as dd (which makes image copies) are identical.

■**Note** RMAN treats all user-made backups as image copies.

Since RMAN image copies are identical to copies made with operating system copy commands, you may use user-made image copies for an RMAN restore and recovery operation after first making the copies "known" to RMAN by using the catalog command, as shown in recipe 6-7. After this point, there's no difference between those image copies made by you and those made by RMAN. During a restore operation, if you have both image copies and backup sets from the same time period, RMAN prefers to use an image copy over a backup set. This is because there is more overhead involved in sorting through a backup set to get the files to restore. In addition, image copies offer yet another benefit during a restore and recovery operation. If you need to restore a current datafile and happen to have an image copy of that datafile available, you can use the switch command to simply point the database to the replacement file instead of the original datafile. This eliminates the need to restore the datafile, thus speeding up database recovery considerably.

RMAN Backup Modes

A control file or an archived redo log file is always backed up completely and in a consistent fashion. A datafile, however, may be backed up partly or completely. You can also make consistent or inconsistent backups with datafiles. The various backup types are as follows:

Full vs. incremental backups: A full backup is a backup of a datafile that includes every allocated block in that file. Note that an image copy backup of a datafile will always include every block in that file. A backup of a datafile as a backup set, however, may skip data blocks that aren't in use. An incremental backup can be one of two different levels: a level 0 backup including all blocks in the datafile except those blocks compressed because they have never been used or a level 1 backup including only those blocks that have changed since the parent backup.

Consistent vs. inconsistent backups: A backup taken after a database was shut down gracefully (as opposed to using the shutdown abort command or a shutdown following an abrupt database crash) and restarted in mount state is said to be *consistent*. A consistent backup doesn't require recovery after you restore the database. A backup taken while the database is online or after it was brought into mount state after being shut down abruptly is called an *inconsistent* backup. An inconsistent backup always needs recovery to make the backup consistent.

If you're running in archivelog mode, the target database must be mounted or be open before you can issue an RMAN backup command. If you're running the database in noarchivelog mode, the database must first be shut down cleanly and started up in mount state before you can use RMAN for backups. If the database was abruptly shut down and restarted, RMAN can't make the backups. You mustn't back up a database running in noarchivelog mode while the database is open.

■Note Starting with the Oracle Database 11*g* release, RMAN excludes the backup of undo in the undo tablespace, which is not necessary for recovering an RMAN backup. Unlike the backup optimization feature, you have no control over whether to use this feature—it works by default, and you can't disable it.

By default, all RMAN backups—whole database, tablespace level, and so on—are full backups. That is, all data blocks in the datafiles that were ever used, even if they are currently empty, are included in the backup. You can specify the command backup full database, for example, to start a whole-database backup, but it's not necessary to do so. Just use the command backup database to do the same thing. However, when you are performing an incremental RMAN backup, you must specify the keyword incremental in your backup commands since it isn't the default backup type.

Types of Files That RMAN Can Back Up

RMAN lets you back up all the files you'd need for a database recovery, such as the following:

- Datafiles

- Control files

- Archived redo logs

- Image copies of datafiles and control files, including those made by RMAN

- Backup pieces that contain RMAN backups

The Oracle database uses three types of "live" files during its operation: datafiles, online redo log files, and control files. Of these three types of files, RMAN backs up only the datafiles and the control files. You can't use RMAN to back up the online redo log files. If you're operating in noarchivelog mode, then you won't need the online redo logs, since the database files are always consistent when you back up the database using the only permitted modes of backing up a database in noarchivelog mode, which are closed whole backups. You won't need the online redo log backups if you're operating in archivelog mode either, since RMAN is continually backing up all your archived redo logs. However, you must make sure you always multiplex the online redo log so you won't lose all members of a group and thus all the committed changes as yet unrecorded in the datafiles.

In addition to the previously mentioned types of files, RMAN also can back up the server parameter file, or *spfile*, which contains the initialization parameter for starting up your database. You *can't*, however, back up the following types of files using RMAN:

- External files

- Network configuration files

- Password files

- Any Oracle home-related files

Use normal operating system copy utilities to back up any of these four types of files.

RMAN Backup Destinations

RMAN can back up to the following destinations:

- Any disk directory, including an automatic storage management (ASM) disk group.

- A media management library (tape device).

- A flash recovery area, which is the heart of Oracle's disk-based backup and recovery strategy. The flash recovery area is a disk area reserved entirely for backup and recovery purposes as well as for storing flashback logs used to support the flashback database feature.

■**Note** RMAN places all backups of the datafiles, archived redo logs, and control files in the flash recovery area by default.

7-1. Specifying Backup Options

Problem

You want to back up your database using the backup command but want to override some of the default options for the backup command as well as some of the preconfigured persistent settings made with the configure command.

Solution

To back up anything using RMAN, you use the backup command, as shown in the following example, which backs up the entire database:

```
RMAN> backup database;
```

Although the simple command backup database would suffice to perform a whole-database backup, it's smart to understand the most common options that you can specify with the backup command.

Specifying Channels

By default, RMAN comes with a single disk channel preconfigured, starting with the Oracle9*i* release of the database. So, if you're backing up to a disk, you don't have to manually allocate a channel. However, if you're backing up to tape, you must either configure an automatic channel for the tape device or manually allocate a tape (sbt) channel as part of the backup commands you issue. The following example shows how to set a channel for a tape device before making a backup of the database:

```
run {
    allocate channel c1 device type sbt;
    backup database;
    }
```

You can use the `allocate channel` option to specify the channel to use when creating backups. RMAN also uses the channel ID you provide to report I/O errors. You can use a meaningful name such *ch1* or *dev1* as the channel name. If you don't use the channel parameter, RMAN dynamically assigns the backup set to one of the available channels.

Specifying the Output Device Type

As you saw in Chapter 5, you can configure the backup device (disk or tape drive) by using the `configure` command. However, you can use the `device type` clause with the `backup` command to specify whether you want a disk device or tape device for a specific backup. The device type you specify with the `device type` clause will override the persistent configuration setting you created for the device type. The following example shows how to specify a tape device for a backup instead of the default disk device:

```
RMAN> backup
      device type sbt
      database;
```

Note that you must first run the `configure device type` command for a tape device before you can choose tape as the backup device type in the previous `backup` command.

Specifying Image Copy or Backup Set Output

When you're backing up to a disk, you have the choice of creating backups as *backup sets* or *image copies*. If you don't specify whether RMAN should make an image copy or a backup set, RMAN will make a backup set, which is the default backup type. You can use the `as copy` and `as backupset` clauses with a `backup` command to override the configured default device type.

You can explicitly specify that a backup be made as a backup set by using the `as backupset` clause within the `backup` command:

```
RMAN> backup as backupset
      database;
```

The following command shows how to specify a tape device as the backup destination and specify that the backup be made as a backup set:

```
RMAN> backup as backupset
      device type sbt
      database;
```

To make image copies of the database, use the `as copy` clause instead, as shown here:

```
RMAN> backup as copy
      database;
```

You can make image copies only on disk but not on a tape device. Therefore, you can use the `backup as copy` option only for disk backups, and the `backup as backupset` option is the only option you have for making tape backups.

Specifying a Backup Format

Backup format refers to the naming of the RMAN backup files. There are several ways in which you can specify the backup filename. Here are the set of rules governing the filenames in order of precedence:

- Specify the `format` clause in the `backup` command to generate the backup filename.

- Configure a `format` setting for the specific channel that you use in the backup.

- Configure a `format` setting for the device type used in the backup.

- If you enabled a flash recovery area, RMAN will generate a name for the backups in the flash recovery area if you don't specify the `format` clause.

If none of the four formatting rules applies, then RMAN will name the backups and store them in locations based on operating system–specific rules. Since the `format` clause is at the top of the formatting rules in order of precedence, let's look at that clause in detail in this section.

You can specify the `format` option with the `backup` command to direct the RMAN backup output to a specific location. In the following example, RMAN's backup output is directed to the /u01/backup/ directory, and the backup files are stored with unique names generated by the random string generator `%U`:

```
RMAN> backup
    database
    format= '/u01/backup_%U ';
```

If your default backup device is a disk, by default all RMAN backups are sent to the flash recovery area (if you've configured it) and stored there with automatically generated filenames. If you don't specify the `format` option and you haven't configured a flash recovery area, the backups are stored in an operating system–specific default location.

You may also use an ASM disk group as the destination for the RMAN backups, as shown in the following example:

```
RMAN> backup
    database
    format '+dgroup1';
```

The database backups will be stored in the diskgroup +dgroup1.

Specifying Tags for Backup Output

You can use the `tag` option to make RMAN assign a unique name to each of the backups that you make. In the following example, the `tag` parameter of the `backup` command specifies that the backup must be tagged with the identifier `weekly_backup`:

```
RMAN> backup
    database
    tag  'weekly_backup';
```

If you don't use the `tag` parameter to assign your own customized tag, RMAN will attach a default tag to every backup it creates. Chapter 4 discusses RMAN tags.

How It Works

If you're operating the target database in archivelog mode, the database must be mounted or be open before you can issue an RMAN backup command. If you are running the database in noarchivelog mode, the database must first be shut down cleanly and started up in mount state before you can use RMAN for backups. If the database was abruptly shut down and restarted, RMAN can't make the backups. You mustn't back up a database running in noarchivelog mode while the database is open.

You can use RMAN's backup command to back up the following entities:

- Tablespaces

- Datafiles (current or copy)

- Control file (current or copy)

- Spfiles

- Archived logs

- Backup sets

In this recipe, we showed how to use the most common options that control the types, naming, and formatting of RMAN's backup output files. However, you don't need to use all those options. Since RMAN uses default values for all those options, your backups will still be made successfully without you specifying values for each possible option. You need to specify an option only when the default value is not something you like.

The following are the key points you must remember about the basic RMAN options described in this recipe:

- The backup set is the default backup type.

- The default device is disk.

- RMAN assigns default tags if you omit the tag clause in your backup commands.

- You can't set the number of backup pieces in a given backup set—that's something RMAN will determine based on an internal algorithm.

- If you don't use the device type clause in your backup command, RMAN will back up to the currently configured default device type.

- You can't back up a backup set from tape to another tape or from tape to disk, although you can go from disk to tape.

7-2. Backing Up the Control File

Problem

You want to back up the control file often so that your backup copy always reflects the current structure of the database.

Solution

In recipe 5-3, you learned how to use the `configure` command to enable automatic backups of the control file:

```
RMAN> configure controlfile autobackup on;
```

From here on out, RMAN will create a backup of the control file (as well as the server parameter file) whenever you perform any backup with RMAN or make structural database changes.

If you prefer not to configure automatic control file backups, you can use the `backup` command's `current controlfile` clause to perform a manual backup of the current control file, as shown here:

```
RMAN> backup current controlfile;
```

You also have the option to manually include the control file with any other backup that you make. You do that by adding the `include current controlfile` option to any `backup` command. For example, you can back up the control file as part of a tablespace backup operation:

```
RMAN> backup tablespace users include current controlfile;
```

If you make any backup that includes datafile 1, RMAN automatically backs up both the control file and the server parameter file. You can use the `include current controlfile` clause with a `backup database` command as well.

In addition to the just-described manual techniques, you can also use the RMAN `sql` command to issue the SQL `alter database backup controlfile` command. For example:

```
RMAN> sql "alter database backup controlfile to ''/orabac/prod1/cf_back.ctl''";
```

Issuing an `alter database backup controlfile` command is probably the least desirable method for backing up the control file. Unlike a control file autobackup, this backup doesn't have the metadata for the previous backup, which is essential for database recovery. Thus, you have to manually keep track of when and where such a backup took place.

■Note See recipe 5-4 for a complete description of enabling/disabling the `controlfile autobackup` feature.

How It Works

You can have RMAN automatically back up the control file as part of regular database backups, or you can explicitly issue commands whenever you want to back up your control file. We strongly recommend using the autobackup feature for control file backups, as explained in Chapter 5.

When you issue the `backup current controlfile` command, RMAN will create a backup set that contains a copy of the control file. If you are using a server parameter file (spfile), RMAN includes it in the same backup set. If you are using a flash recovery area, RMAN will place the backup piece in the location specified by the initialization parameter `db_recovery_file_dest`. If you aren't using a flash recovery area, the control file is backed up to an

OS-dependent directory under ORACLE_HOME. For example, with Windows the default directory is ORACLE_HOME/database. From then on, RMAN will back up the control file anew whenever you initiate a backup operation from RMAN that includes datafile 1.

RMAN actually backs up the control file whenever you back up datafile 1, regardless of the autobackup setting. If you haven't set the control file autobackup to on, RMAN will include the control file as well as the server parameter file (if you have started the instance with a server parameter file) as part of the backup of datafile 1. If, on the other hand, you've configured the control file autobackup to on, RMAN won't include the control file as part of the datafile 1 backup, but it generates a separate control file autobackup piece for it.

The control file autobackups contain metadata about the previous backup. RMAN makes a control file autobackup after every backup command you issue from the command line and after every backup command in a run block that's not followed by another backup command. Control file autobackups are significant because RMAN can restore the control file even if you lose both the control file and the recovery catalog.

7-3. Backing Up the Server Parameter File

Problem

You want to make a copy of the database's server parameter (spfile) file using RMAN so that you have a record of the most recent database configuration.

Solution

Use the backup spfile command to back up the server parameter file, as shown here:

```
RMAN> backup spfile;
```

The previous command backs up the server parameter file currently in use by the database instance.

How It Works

To successfully back up a given server parameter file through RMAN, you must first make sure you start the database with that server parameter file. You don't want to have used the text-based, init.ora style of parameter file. If you start the database using an init.ora file instead of an spfile, RMAN won't back up the spfile, since it really isn't currently in use by the instance.

■**Note** RMAN can't make backups of the multiple server parameter files you may have on the server. It backs up only the *current* server parameter file.

7-4. Backing Up Datafiles

Problem

You have a large database with thousands of datafiles, and you don't have the resources to take a daily backup of your database. You therefore need to implement a strategy that can back up a subset of the database by copying a set number of datafiles each day.

Solution

RMAN gives you the option of backing up individual datafiles. You can back up a datafile either by using the datafile number or by using the datafile name. The following example shows how to back up datafiles by specifying their numbers. The `format` option specifies the format of each backup piece filename:

```
RMAN> backup datafile 1,2,3,4
      format '/u01/app/oracle/rman/%d_%U.bus';
```

Instead of specifying a datafile number, you can specify the names of the datafiles you want to back up. In the following example, the first command configures a channel with a specific filename format, and the second command backs up two datafiles:

```
RMAN> configure channel device type disk format '/oraback/prod1/%d_%U.bus';
RMAN> backup datafile '/u01/app/oracle/oradata/system01.dbf',
      '/u01/app/oracle/oradata/users01.dbf';
```

■Note Once you configure a channel, there is no need to specify it in other backup commands unless you need to change it. These configuration settings are persistent.

You can also take *incremental backups* of datafiles. The following example takes an incremental level 1 backup of datafile 5:

```
RMAN> backup incremental level 1 datafile 5;
```

You can use RMAN to make a physical copy, also called an *image copy*, of a datafile. The next example makes an image copy of the datafile system01.dbf and uses the `format` parameter to specify the backup filename. The name of the original file is /ora01/testdb/system01.dbf, and the image copy is named /oraback/system01.bk.

```
RMAN> backup as copy datafile '/ora01/testdb/system01.dbf'
      format '/oraback/system01.bk';
```

```
Starting backup at 13-NOV-06
using channel ORA_DISK_1
channel ORA_DISK_1: starting datafile copy
input datafile fno=00004 name=/ora01/testdb/system01.dbf
output filename=/oraback/system01.bk tag=TAG20061113T062822 recid=3
 stamp=606378503
channel ORA_DISK_1: datafile copy complete, elapsed time: 00:00:01
Finished backup at 13-JUN-07
RMAN>
```

The `as copy` clause directs RMAN to make an image copy instead of the default backup sets.

How It Works

The backup datafile command is fairly straightforward. RMAN will back up the specified datafiles and put them into backup pieces. If autobackup of the control file is disabled and datafile 1 (SYSTEM) is backed up, RMAN will create a backup of the control file. If the auto-backup of the control file is disabled and the system tablespace isn't included in the tablespace list, then no backup of the control file is created.

When you perform a full datafile backup (as against an incremental datafile backup), RMAN reads every block that has ever been used in a datafile into the input buffer and eventually backs it up to the specified device. RMAN skips all data blocks in a datafile that have never been used. That saves space and is unlike an image file backup, which makes a byte-per-byte copy of the source file.

Only never-used data blocks are skipped to save on space. Even if a previously used data block is currently empty because the data was deleted at some point, RMAN still backs up the data block. The reason for this seemingly odd behavior is because RMAN was designed to back up data even when the database isn't open when you can't access the data dictionary to check whether a specific data block is on the freelist (blocks get on the freelist once all data has been deleted from them).

If you haven't configured a format for the location and name of the backup pieces, RMAN will write files to the flash recovery area. If the flash recovery area is not configured, then it is operating system dependent on where the backup pieces are written.

If you're using the backup as copy command and don't specify a destination for the image copies, RMAN chooses the storage locations according to the following criteria:

- If the output channel has a default configure ... format setting, that setting will be the basis for the output filenames.

- If you configure a flash recovery area, the backups will be sent there.

- If you haven't configured a flash recovery area, an operating system–specific default format is used (that is, the format parameter, which includes a %U for the generation of unique filenames, is used).

You can view datafile numbers and datafile names in the V$DATAFILE, V$DATAFILE_COPY, or V$DATAFILE_HEADER view. For example, to view datafile numbers and datafile names in your database, issue this SQL command:

```
SQL> select file#, name from v$datafile;
```

You can also issue the RMAN report schema command to display datafile names and numbers. Once you know the name or number for each file you want to back up, you can use the backup datafile command to perform the actual backup operation.

7-5. Backing Up Tablespaces

Problem

You want to back up one or more tablespaces, either as a part of a regular backup schedule or for some special purpose.

Solution

Use the backup tablespace command to back up one or more tablespaces. The following example shows how to back up two tablespaces, users and tools:

```
RMAN> backup tablespace users, tools;
```

Since we didn't specify an image copy, RMAN will create a backup set containing the two specified tablespaces.

The following example shows how to specify the format parameter in a backup tablespace command:

```
RMAN> backup tablespace system format '/ora01/prod1/%d_%U.bus';
```

This next example shows how to make an image copy of a tablespace:

```
RMAN> backup as copy tablespace users;
```

If you want to take an incremental backup of a tablespace, include the incremental clause in the backup command:

```
RMAN> backup incremental level 1 tablespace example;
```

The previous command performs a level 1 incremental backup of the tablespace named example.

How It Works

In Oracle a tablespace is a logical grouping of datafiles. Sometimes you'll need the flexibility to back up these logical subsets of your database. Using the backup tablespace command provides you with an easy way to back up parts of your database. You can use the backup tablespace command to back up both read/write and read-only tablespaces.

■Tip If you're using an Oracle Database 11.1*g* or newer release, transportable tablespaces don't have to be in read/write mode. You can't, however, perform a backup of read-only transportable tablespaces if you're dealing with older databases.

When backing up tablespaces, RMAN will back up all datafiles that belong to those tablespace(s). RMAN takes each tablespace name and translates it into the corresponding datafile names. RMAN then copies the datafile blocks to the backup pieces. If autobackup of the control file is disabled (the default) and the system tablespace is backed up, RMAN automatically creates a backup of the control file.

If you don't specify the location and name of the backup pieces by using the format option or by using the configure command, RMAN will write files to the flash recovery area. If you haven't configured the flash recovery area, the backup pieces are written to an operating system–dependent location.

7-6. Making a Whole-Database Backup

Problem

You want to back up the entire database.

Solution

You can perform a whole-database backup with the database started in mount state or the database open. Issue the simple `backup database` command, as shown here:

```
RMAN> backup database;
```

The `backup database` command will back up all datafiles. And, assuming you've set `configure controlfile autobackup` to on, it'll back up the current control file and the current server parameter file as well at the end of the backup.

To make sure you have a complete set of archived redo logs through the time of the backup, it is common practice to archive the current online redo log, as shown in the following example:

```
RMAN> backup database;
RMAN> SQL "alter system archive log current";
```

The first of these commands backs up the database. The second archives the current redo log right after the backup completes.

How It Works

The `backup database` command backs up all datafiles and the control file but not the archived redo logs. If you take a consistent backup of the database, you can later use this backup to restore and recover without performing media recovery. That is, you won't have to apply any changes from the archived redo logs before opening the database.

To take a consistent backup, you must satisfy the following two conditions:

- You must first shut down the database normally, that is, use one of the following statements: `shutdown`, `shutdown normal`, `shutdown immediate`, or `shutdown transactional`.

- You must start up the database in mount state before taking the backup.

If you're recovering a database using inconsistent backups, you must first make the database consistent through applying the archived redo logs before you can open it. Backups taken under the following conditions are inconsistent:

- If you create a backup of a database after restarting a database that was shut down abruptly (say, because of a power failure) or with the `shutdown abort` command

- If you create a backup of the database while the database is open

There's nothing wrong with inconsistent backups—by definition, all open database backups are inconsistent. You can safely use inconsistent backups as the foundation of your backup and recovery strategy. Since database uptime is critical, most production databases depend on inconsistent backups. All you have to do is to make sure you're running your database in archive log mode and that you're backing up your archived redo logs along with your datafiles.

7-7. Backing Up Archived Redo Logs

Problem

You want to back up the archived redo logs by themselves.

Solution

Use the `backup archivelog` command to back up archived redo logs. To back up one copy of each log sequence number for all the archived redo logs, for example, you can issue the following command:

```
RMAN> backup archivelog all;
```

The `backup archivelog` command shown in this example will back up only a single copy of each of the archived redo logs, even if there are multiple copies of those logs. That is, the command will back up a single copy of each distinct log sequence number.

The following example shows how to use the `archivelog like` clause with the `backup` command to back up one archived redo log for each unique log sequence number:

```
RMAN> backup device type sbt
      archivelog like '/disk%arc%'
      delete all input;
```

Let's say you have two archiving destinations, one called /disk1/arch/ and the other called /disk2/arch/. If a certain archived redo log, say log 9999, is in both directories, RMAN will back up only one of the copies, not both of them. The `delete all input` clause deletes all archived redo logs from all (in this case, two) destinations after the backup.

You can limit the backup of the archived redo logs based on a specific time, SCN, or log sequence number. In the following example, the clauses `from time` and `until time` limit the range of the archived redo log backups:

```
RMAN> backup archivelog
      from time "sysdate-15" until time "sysdate-7";
```

The previous command uses a specified time period to direct the backing up of all archivelogs generated between two weeks ago and last week. To back up archived redo logs based on specific log sequence numbers, use the keyword `sequence` and provide either a specific log sequence number or a range for the sequence numbers. Here are some examples:

```
RMAN> backup archivelog sequence 99
      delete input;       # specifies a particular log sequence number

RMAN> backup archivelog sequence between 99 and 199 thread 1
      delete input;       # specifies range of records by log sequence numbers
```

In both examples, the `delete input` clause directs RMAN to delete the backed-up archived redo log files after they're successfully backed up.

How It Works

You can make a backup of the archived redo logs using any of the following clauses with the backup command:

- archivelog all

- plus archivelog

- archivelog from ...

When you issue the backup command with the archivelog all or plus archivelog clause, either of these commands will back up the archived redo logs, and RMAN first directs the database to switch the current online redo log group. After this, all unarchived redo logs, including the one the database just switched out of, are archived. This process guarantees that the backup contains all the redo information generated until the backup started.

When you use the backup database plus archivelog command to back up archive logs as part of another backup, RMAN will perform the following operations in the sequence listed here:

1. Run the alter system archive log current command.

2. Run the backup archivelog all command.

3. Back up the rest of the datafiles specified by the backup database command.

4. Run the alter system archive log current command.

5. Back up the new archive logs generated during the backup operation.

The sequence of operations listed here means that RMAN will have all the necessary archived redo log information that it'll need down the road if it has to perform a complete recovery of the database.

▓**Note** The backup database plus archivelog command will back up the entire database and all the archived redo logs as well as the current control file in a single command. See the next recipe for details.

Instead of backing up archive logs specifically by using the backup archivelog command, you can back up the archive logs as part of a database backup or some other datafile backup. The following recipe shows how you can back up the database, along with all the archivelogs, using a single command, backup database plus archivelog.

7-8. Backing Up Everything

Problem

You want to create a backup of the entire database, meaning all the datafiles, the archived redo logs, and the control file.

Solution

To make sure the control file is backed up automatically as part of the database backup, first make sure you have configured automatic control file backups by using the following command:

```
RMAN> configure controlfile autobackup on;
```

Then you can issue the backup database plus archivelog command to back up the database along with the archived redo logs:

```
RMAN> backup database plus archivelog;

Starting backup at 21-APR-07
current log archived
allocated channel: ORA_DISK_1
channel ORA_DISK_1: sid=143 devtype=DISK
channel ORA_DISK_1: starting piece 1 at 21-APR-07
channel ORA_DISK_1: finished piece 1 at 21-APR-07
...
Finished backup at 21-APR-07

Starting backup at 21-APR-07
using channel ORA_DISK_1
channel ORA_DISK_1: starting full datafile backupset
input datafile fno=00001 name==/u01/app/oracle/product/10.2.0/oradata/nina/
system01.dbf
...
channel ORA_DISK_1: starting piece 1 at 21-APR-07
channel ORA_DISK_1: finished piece 1 at 21-APR-07
piece handle=/u01/app/oracle/product/10.2.0/db_1/flash_recovery_area/NINA/
backupset/2007_04_21/01_mf_nnndf_ATAG2007_04_21T044741_2p5ls1_.bkp tag=
TAG200721T044741 comment=NONE
Finished backup at 21-APR-07

Starting backup at 21-APR-07
current log archived
using channel ORA_DISK_1
channel ORA_DISK_1: starting archive log backupset
channel ORA_DISK_1: specifying archive log(s) in backupset
...
Finished backup at 21-APR-07

Starting Control File and spfile Autobackup at 21-APR-07
piece handle=/u01/app/oracle/product/10.2.0/db_1/flash_recovery_area/NINA/
autobackup/2007_04_21/01_mf_s_607063775_2p5lxj4v_.bkp comment=NONE
Finished Control File and spfile Autobackup at 21-APR-07

RMAN>
```

The backup command shown in this example backs up the datafiles, the archived redo log files, and the control file (because control file autobackup is on), as well as the current server parameter file (spfile). If you issue the list backup by file command now, you can see that RMAN has a record of all the backed-up files, sorted by the backup file type (datafiles, archived logs, control files, and the spfile). For example:

```
RMAN> list backup by file;

List of Datafile Backups
===============================================================================
File  Key  TY LV  S  Ckp  SCN  Ckp Time   #Pieces #Copies Compressed       Tag
----  ---- -- --  -  -------- ---------- ------- ------- ---------- ------------
1     1404 B  F   A  21116038 21-NOV-06  1       1       NO         TAG20061121t044741
...
List of Archived Log Backups
===============================
Thrd Seq  Low SCN  Low Time  BS Key S  #Pieces #Copies Compressed Tag
---- ---- -------  --------  ------ -  ------- ------- ---------- ---------------
1    410  21096803 21-NOV-06 1403   A  1       1       NO         TAG20061121T044737
1    410  21116022 21-NOV-06 1425   A  1       1       NO         TAG20061121T044930

List of Control File Log Backups
=============================

CF Ckp SCN Ckp Time  BS Key  S  #Pieces  #Copies   Compressed  Tag
---------- --------  -------  -  --------  -------- ----------  ------------------
21116154   21-NOV-06 1445     A  1         1        NO          TAG20061121T044935

List of spfile Backups
=============================

Modification Time  BS Key S  #Pieces #Copies Compressed  Tag
-----------------  ------ -  ------- ------- ----------  ------------------
21-NOV-06          1445   A  1       1       NO          TAG20061121T044737

RMAN>
```

The list backup by file command shows you the datafiles, the archived redo logs, the control file, and the spfile that was backed up with the backup database plus archivelog command.

How It Works

You can use the backup database command to make a backup of all the datafiles in a database. The backup database command by itself can back up only datafiles and control files but not the archived redo log files. You must add the plus archivelog clause to back up the archived redo logs.

If the control file autobackup feature is turned off, RMAN *won't* automatically include the control file in the database backup. To force RMAN to include a backup of the current control file in the backup in such a situation, you must add the `include current controlfile` clause to your backup command, as shown here:

```
RMAN> backup database
   2> include current controlfile;
```

The previous command will back up all the datafiles, the control file, and the spfile. You can't add the `include current controlfile` clause to a backup that includes the archived redo logs. You can use the clause only in a datafile backup.

7-9. Backing Up Flash Recovery Files

Problem

You want to back up all the recovery files located in the flash recovery area of a database so that you can store them offline on tape.

Solution

Use either the `recovery area` clause or the `db_recovery_file_dest` clause with your backup command to back up all the recovery files for a database (*recovery area* and db_recovery_ file_dest are synonymous). To back up the recovery files in the flash recovery area, use the following command (you must first configure sbt as the backup channel):

```
RMAN> backup recovery area;
```

The previous command will back up recovery files that were created not only in the current flash recovery area but also in all previous flash recovery area locations.

If you want to back up the recovery files located in all locations, not merely the flash recovery area, use the following command instead after configuring a tape backup channel:

```
RMAN> backup recovery files;
```

The previous command backs up *all* recovery files on disk, whether they're part of the flash recovery area or are stored elsewhere.

How It Works

Recovery files include full and incremental backup sets, control file autobackups, archived redo logs, and datafile copies. Recovery files do not include files such as flashback logs, the current control file, and the online redo log files. If the flash recovery area isn't currently enabled, RMAN will back up eligible recovery files from previously configured and enabled flash recovery area destinations.

When RMAN is backing up the flash recovery area, it has the capability to fail over to alternate archiving destinations if necessary. For example, if an archived redo log in the flash recovery area is missing or corrupted, RMAN will instead back up a good archived redo log from the alternative location.

It's important to remember that you must specify a tape device when backing up any flash recovery area files. By default, RMAN turns backup optimization on during a flash recovery area backup, even if that feature is currently turned off. You may, however, override this behavior by adding the `force` option when configuring backup optimization.

7-10. Performing Incremental Backups

Problem

Instead of making a complete backup of your database every night, you want to be able to back up only the changed data in order to complete backups within the time interval provided by your backup window and also to save storage space.

Solution

An *incremental backup* includes only changed data blocks instead of entire datafiles, as normal full backups do. You can make two types of incremental backups with RMAN—*differential incremental backups* and *cumulative incremental backups*—and both of these types are explained in the following sections.

■**Note** If you don't specify either the full or the incremental option during a backup, RMAN will perform a full backup by default.

Differential Incremental Backups

A *differential incremental backup* is an incremental backup of all data blocks that changed subsequently to a level 0 or a level 1 backup. RMAN first looks for a level 1 backup and, in its absence, looks for a level 0 backup and backs up all changes since that level 0 backup. Here's an example of a differential incremental level 0 backup:

```
RMAN> backup incremental level 0 database;
```

Incremental level 0 backups can be made as image copies or backup sets.

Here's how you'd perform a level 1 differential incremental backup that backs up the data blocks changed since the most recent level 0 or, if there's no level 0 backup, a level 1 backup:

```
RMAN> backup incremental level 1 database;
```

■**Note** Backup sets are the only choice you have for creating level 1 incremental backups to either a tape device or a disk device.

Since a level 1 incremental backup backs up only the changed blocks, it tends to be faster than a level 0 backup in most cases. You can make backups of the backup set type only when making a level 1 incremental backup.

■**Note** RMAN makes differential incremental backups by default if you don't specify the incremental backup type.

Cumulative Incremental Backups

A *cumulative incremental backup* is an incremental backup of *all* data blocks that changed subsequently to the most recent level 0 incremental backup. The following command shows how to make a cumulative incremental backup of a database:

```
RMAN> backup incremental level 1 cumulative database;
```

The previous command backs up all data blocks that have changed since the last *level 0* backup.

How It Works

An incremental backup is designed to make shorter and faster backups of your datafiles by backing up only changed data blocks instead of all the data blocks in a datafile. RMAN uses the SCNs present in each of Oracle's data blocks in every datafile as the basis of its incremental backup policy. If the SCN of a data block in the datafile that's a backup candidate is the same or greater than the SCN of the parent incremental backup, RMAN will back up that data block. Otherwise, RMAN will exclude that data block from the incremental backup.

The basis for all incremental backups is the parent backup, also called a *level 0* backup. A level 0 backup includes all the data blocks in all the datafiles and serves as the base or foundation for future incremental backups. Note that even though a full backup also includes all data blocks, it can't serve as the basis for future incremental backups—you can use a level 0 backup only as the parent for incremental backups.

Often, the choice between a cumulative differential and incremental differential backup comes down to a trade-off between space and recovery time. If you use cumulative backups, you'll use more storage space, but you can recover faster, since you'll need to apply fewer incremental backups. Differential incremental backups, on the other hand, take less space to store, but you'll take more time to recover with them, because you'll, in most cases, need to apply a lot more of these than the cumulative differential backups.

When you issue the following command to perform a differential incremental backup, if neither a level 1 nor a level 0 incremental backup is available, RMAN will back up all blocks changed since the creation of that datafile and save the backup as a level 1 backup (for database compatibility greater than or equal to 10.0.0).

```
RMAN> backup incremental level 1 database;
```

Here's an example of how the default differential incremental backup works in an Oracle database:

1. Let's say you take an incremental level 0 backup on a Sunday night. This backup will include all the blocks in the database that were used and will serve as the foundation for future incremental backups.

2. On Monday, you take a differential incremental level 1 backup that backs up all changed blocks since the level 0 backup on Sunday.

3. From Tuesday through Saturday, you take a level 1 differential backup that copies all changed blocks since the level 1 backup the day before.

4. If you have to recover the database on a Saturday morning, you'll need the previous Sunday's level 0 backups plus all the differential incremental level 1 backups from Monday through Friday.

A cumulative level 1 backup always takes longer than a differential backup, since it backs up all changed blocks since the last level 0 incremental backup. Thus, cumulative backups need more time as well as space, since they "repeat" or "duplicate" the copying of changed blocks. Differential backups, on the other hand, don't duplicate the work performed by previous backups at the same level—a differential incremental level 1 backup done on a given day is always distinct from the same level backup done the day before.

You can perform incremental backups of any of the following:

- Datafile

- Datafile copy

- Tablespace

- Database

You *can't* perform an incremental copy of a control file, archived redo log, or backup set.

While incremental backups do, in general, take significantly less time to complete than a full backup of the same files, you can't be absolutely sure that this is always true. This is because of how RMAN checks data blocks for changes. Even during an incremental backup (at a greater than level 0 incremental backup), RMAN still reads all data blocks in a datafile into the memory to check the block's SCN number. Any block with an SCN more recent than the SCN of the level 0 incremental backup is moved from the input buffer to the output buffer, and from there it's written to the backup piece.

■Note If you want fast incremental backup performance, use the block change tracking feature, where RMAN doesn't scan all the data blocks to see whether they've changed, to determine whether they are candidates for the incremental backup.

You can't use an incremental backup directly during a database restore operation since it's only a complement to a full backup and can't be "restored." It's only to provide a faster recovery time (faster mean time to recovery, or MTTR). The following example serves to demonstrate this point:

```
RMAN> run
      {
       restore datafile 7;
       recover datafile 7;
      }
```

Once RMAN restores datafile 7 from the latest level 0 incremental backup, it has two choices. It can use incremental level backups since the most recent level 0 backup and add any necessary archivelogs to recover the database to the present point in time. Alternatively, RMAN can choose to use archived logs only from the level 0 backup time to recover. RMAN always prefers using incremental backups to archivelogs.

7-11. Reducing Incremental Backup Time

Problem

You want to reduce the time it takes to perform incremental backups.

Solution

Implement RMAN's *block change tracking* feature to reduce the time it takes to make an RMAN incremental backup. By default, the block change tracking feature is disabled. Use the following command to create a change tracking file in the specified location (if you leave out the location, RMAN creates the block change tracking file in the location specified by the db_create_file_dest initialization parameter).

1. First, make sure the db_create_file_dest parameter is set. If it isn't, set it using the alter system command, as shown in this example:

```
SQL> alter system set
    db_create_file_dest='/u01/app/oracle/dfiles'
    scope= both;
```

2. Enable block change tracking by using the following alter database statement:

```
SQL> alter database enable block change tracking;
Database altered.

    SQL>
```

If you want, you can create the block changing file in a location you specify, as shown here:

```
SQL> alter database enable block change tracking using file
    '/u05/app/oracle/change_track.txt';

Database altered.

SQL>
```

You can *disable* block change tracking by using the following command:

```
SQL> alter database disable block change tracking;
```

The change tracking file is automatically deleted when you execute the previous command.

How It Works

RMAN uses a binary file referred to as the *block change tracking file* to record the changed blocks in each datafile in a database. When you perform an incremental backup, RMAN refers to this change tracking file instead of scanning all the data blocks in all the datafiles in the database, thus making the incremental backups finish faster. You can use the `alter database` statement to change the name of the change tracking file.

The V$BLOCK_CHANGE_TRACKING view shows whether change tracking is enabled as well as other things such as the change tracking filename.

If you need to move the change tracking file, use the following procedure:

1. Determine the current location of the change tracking file with the following command:

   ```
   SQL> select filename from v$block_change_tracking;
   ```

2. Shut down the database.

3. Move the change tracking file to the new location using the following command:

   ```
   $ mv /u05/app/oracle/change_trck.f  /u10/app/oracle/change_track.f
   ```

4. Start up the database in mount mode:

   ```
   SQL> startup mount
   ```

5. Use the `alter database rename file` command to rename the change tracking file in the Oracle database:

   ```
   SQL> alter database rename file
           '/u05/app/oracle/change_track.f' to
           '/u10/app/oracle/change_track.f';
   ```

6. Open the database:

   ```
   SQL> alter database open;
   ```

If you can't shut down the database for some reason, you have to first disable change tracking and then reenable it after you rename the change tracking file, as shown here:

```
SQL> alter database disable block change tracking;
SQL> alter database enable block change tracking using file
        '/u10/app/oracle/change_track.f';
```

■**Note** You can turn block change tracking on in a physical standby database, thus making the incremental backups of the standby database run faster.

As a result of directing output to the new change tracking file without shutting down the database, you'll lose the contents of the original change tracking file. RMAN will scan the entire file as a result until the next time you perform a level 0 incremental backup.

The size of the change tracking file is not proportional to the number of updates in the database. Instead, the size of the file depends on how large the database is, the number of datafiles, and how many threads of redo are enabled. Initially, the change tracking file starts at 10MB and grows in 10MB increments. Since RMAN allocates 320KB of space in the change tracking file for each datafile in the database, a database with a very large number of datafiles would require a larger allocation of space for the change tracking file than a database with a small number of datafiles.

7-12. Creating Multiple Backup Sets

Problem

You want to initiate a backup and have RMAN automatically make multiple copies of the resulting backup set. You don't want to make any persistent configuration changes to your RMAN environment.

Solution

You can specify the making of multiple copies (duplexing) of backup sets by using the backup command's copies option or by issuing the set backup copies clause in a backup command. The following example shows how to use the copies option to make multiple backup copies. Of course, you need to tell RMAN where the multiple destinations for the duplexed backups are by using the format option. Here's our example:

```
RMAN> backup
      copies 2
      database
      format  '/u01/app/oracle/backup/db_%U',
              '/u02/app/oracle/backupdb_%U';
```

In the example shown here, the copies parameter produces two backups of the database, each on a different disk, with disk locations being specified by the format parameter.

The next example shows how to use the set backup copies command to make two backup copies of the database:

```
run
{
  allocate channel c1 device type sbt;
  parms 'env=(ob_device_1=testtape1,ob_device_2=testtape2)';
  set backup copies = 2;
  backup database  plus archivelog;
}
```

■**Note** If you want to duplex your backups when using a tape device, you must enable the backup_tape_io_slaves initialization parameter on the target database you are backing up.

Assuming you are using a media manager that supports version 2 of the SBT API, the media manager will automatically write the two identical backup copies resulting from the previous run block to different tape drives. If you're using a disk channel instead, you must specify the format parameter to direct the copies to their destination physical disk locations.

When you use the set command from the RMAN command line by using a command such as set backup copies=2, the configuration specified by the set command will remain in force until the end of the session. If you use the same set command in a run block, the configuration will be in force until the run block completes executing.

How It Works

Whenever RMAN creates a backup set (but not an image copy), you can take advantage of RMAN's built-in *duplexed backup set* feature to make multiple copies of that backup set. You can specify a maximum of four copies of each backup piece in a backup set. This applies to backups of datafiles, archived redo log files, and control files. You can use the configure ... backup copies command to persistently configure backup duplexing, as explained in recipe 5-11. If you'd rather not persistently configure multiple backup copies, you can use either of the two commands shown in the "Solution" section of this recipe—set backup copies or backup copies—to configure duplexed backup sets. By default, the configure ... backup copies is set to 1 for both disk and tape backups. You can use the configure command to change the default duplexing level of 1 for all future backups. You can also use either the backup copies command or the set backup copies command to override the configured setting for multiple copies.

Here's the order of precedence for the three ways in which you can configure RMAN backup duplexing, with settings higher in the list overriding the others:

```
backup copies
set backup copies
configure ... backup copies
```

You can't use the as copy option when duplexing, since you can duplex only backup sets and not image copies. You also can't use duplexing when creating backup files in the flash recovery area. However, this is true only when making image copies (using the backup as copy command). You can duplex backups as a backupset when the flash recovery area is the destination. The following example shows this:

```
RMAN> run {
      allocate channel d1 type disk;
      set backup copies = 2;
      backup
      as backupset
      datafile 12
      format '+BACKUP',
      '+BACKUP';
      release channel d1;
      }
allocated channel: d1
channel d1: SID=124 device type=DISK
executing command: SET BACKUP COPIES
```

```
Starting backup at 03-JUN-2007 23:02:43
...
Finished backup at 03-JUN-2007 23:02:51

Starting Control File and spfile Autobackup at 03-JUN-2007 23:02:51
piece handle=+BACKUP/db11g/autobackup/2007_06_03/s_624322971 comment=NONE
Finished Control File and spfile Autobackup at 03-JUN-2007 23:02:58

released channel: d1
RMAN>
```

If you don't specify the `format` parameter and you haven't configured a flash recovery area, RMAN will still make the multiple copies and send them to operating system–specific locations. For example, on a Windows-based system, the backups are sent to the $ORACLE_HOME/database directory.

Note that when you specify the duplexing of a backup set, RMAN doesn't produce multiple *backup sets*—it produces multiple copies of the *backup pieces* in that backup set. That is, if you set duplexing to the maximum of four, for example, RMAN will produce only one back up set and then generate four copies of each backup piece in that backup set.

You can't back up from a tape device to another tape device. You also can't back up from a tape device to disk. You can, however, use the `backup ... backupset` command with the `device type sbt` clause in order to back up disk-based backups to a tape device.

7-13. Making Copies of Backup Sets

Problem

You have previously made backups in the form of backup sets and want to make copies of these backups for offsite storage and other purposes.

Solution

Use the `backup ... backupset` command to back up a previously made backup set. Here's an example showing how to use the `backup ... backupset` command:

```
RMAN> backup device type sbt
        backupset
        completed before 'sysdate-30'
```

The `backup ... backupset` command shown here backs up to tape all backup sets more than a month old.

How It Works

The `backup ... backupset` command is useful in moving backup sets from disk to a tape storage device. The command comes in handy when you want to save storage space by removing older backup sets from disk after first copying them to tape for long-term storage. It's especially important to free up space in the flash recovery area for new backups by moving the older backups from disk to tape.

It's important to understand that the backup ... backupset command produces only additional copies of the backup pieces in the backup set but doesn't create a new backup set itself with a different backup set key.

7-14. Making Copies of Image Copy Backups

Problem

You want to make copies of image copy backups you've already made using RMAN.

Solution

Use the backup as copy or backup as backupset command to make copies of image copies made by RMAN. Here are some examples:

```
RMAN> backup as copy copy of database;
RMAN> backup as backupset copy of tablespace users;
RMAN> backup as backupset copy of datafile 4;
```

The first backup as copy command makes an image copy of an image copy of the database. The second command, backup as backupset, creates a backup set from an image copy of a tablespace. The third command, backup as backupset, creates a backup set from an image copy of a datafile.

The following example shows how to copy two datafiles using the tag weekly_copy. The example creates the datafile copies in a new location and names them using substitution variables:

```
RMAN> backup as copy
      copy of datafile 2,3
      from tag 'weekly_copy'
      format '/backup/datafile%f_Database%d';
```

In the previous example, the format parameter uses the percent sign (%) as a wildcard that means zero or more characters. Use an underscore (_) instead of the percent sign to refer to exactly one character. The syntax element f refers to the absolute file number, and the syntax element d specifies the name of the database.

The following example shows how to make an image copy of a database copy to the default destination:

```
RMAN> backup as copy
      copy of database
      from tag "test";
```

The previous command will create new copies of the original image copy of the database with the tag test.

How It Works

You can use either the copy of database, copy of tablespace, or copy of datafile clause to make a backup of an image copy of a database, tablespace, and datafile, respectively. Note that the output of any of these commands can be either an image copy or a backup set.

> ■**Note** If you happen to have multiple image copies of a datafile and you issue an RMAN backup command with the copy of database clause, RMAN uses the most recent image copy of that datafile to make the backup.

As shown in the examples, you can refer to a file by its name or by its file number. You may also specify copies by their tag names and let RMAN find the specified files from those tags.

7-15. Making Tape Copies of Disk-Based Image Copies

Problem

You've already made an image copy of a datafile on disk and want to move it to a tape drive for offsite storage.

Solution

You can use either the backup datafilecopy or backup ... copy of command to back up image copies from disk to tape (you can use either command to back up an image copy from disk to disk as well). Here's how you use the backup datafilecopy command:

```
RMAN> backup device type sbt datafilecopy '/u05/app/oracle/system01.dbf';
```

The previous command backs up the image copy of the /u05/app/oracle/system01.dbf datafile to a tape drive. Instead of the actual datafile name as shown in this example, you can alternatively specify a backup *tag* to identify the input image copies. This makes it easy for you to specify the input datafile copy when you happen to have multiple backups of that datafile. The following command backs up all datafile copies that have the tag whole_db:

```
RMAN> backup datafilecopy from tag whole_tag;
```

The new image copy made from the original image copy will inherit the tag of the source image copy.

Here's an example showing how to use the backup ... copy of database command to back up image copies from disk to tape:

```
RMAN> backup as backupset
      device type sbt_tape
      tag "monthly_backup"
      copy of database;
```

The previous backup command will make a backup of the image copies of all datafiles and the control file of the target database. Since we specified a backup set as the backup type, RMAN will generate backup sets, even though you're making the copy of the database from an image copy of the database.

How It Works

Often, you may first copy a datafile to disk and then want to transfer the backup to a tape device for storing it offsite. The `backup datafilecopy` and `backup ... copy of` commands come in handy at times like this.

You can use the `noduplicates` option when backing up datafile copies to ensure that only a single copy of each datafile copy is backed up by RMAN. The following example comprising a series of `backup` commands illustrates this point:

```
RMAN> run {
backup as copy
datafile 1
format '/u01/app/oracle/backups/df1.copy';

backup as copy
datafilecopy '/u01/app/oracle/backups/df1.copy'
format '/u02/app/oracle/backups/df1.copy';

backup as copy
datafilecopy '/u01/app/oracle/backups/df1.copy'
format '/u03/app/oracle/backups/df1.copy';

backup
device type sbt
datafilecopy all noduplicates;
}
```

The first `backup` command creates an image copy of datafile 1. The second and third `backup` commands use the `datafilecopy` clause to back up the image copy of datafile 1 to two other locations on disk. The last `backup` command backs up only one of the two copies on disk to a tape drive (sbt).

7-16. Excluding a Tablespace from a Backup

Problem

You have a tablespace whose contents don't change over time or a tablespace that contains temporary data such as test data that you don't need to back up. You want to exclude such tablespaces from a whole backup of the database.

Solution

Use the `configure exclude for tablespace` command to exclude a tablespace from a whole-database backup. First use the `show exclude` command to see whether any tablespaces are already configured to be excluded from backups:

```
RMAN> show exclude;
RMAN configuration parameters are:
RMAN configuration has no stored or default parameters
RMAN>
```

By default, RMAN includes all the tablespaces in the database for a whole backup. To exclude a particular tablespace from future backups, you'd use the following command (users is the tablespace you want to exclude):

```
RMAN> configure exclude for tablespace users;

tablespace USERS will be excluded from future whole database backups
new RMAN configuration parameters are successfully stored

RMAN>;
```

Any tablespace exclusion you specify in a RMAN session through the `configure` command will last through that RMAN session.

How It Works

You may exclude any tablespace from a whole backup, except the system tablespace. You can disable tablespace exclusion and include a previously excluded tablespace in future backups by using the following command:

```
RMAN> configure exclude for tablespace users clear;

tablespace USERS will be included in future whole database backups
old RMAN configuration parameters are successfully deleted

RMAN>
```

Even after excluding a specific tablespace as shown in the previous section, you can back up that tablespace either by using the `noexclude` option in a `backup database` or `backup copy of database` command or by issuing a `backup tablespace` command. If you use the `noexclude` option as part of a `backup database` or `backup copy of database` command, RMAN will back up all tablespaces, including those tablespaces that you expressly excluded from the backup earlier with a `configure exclude` command. Here's how you use the `noexclude` option as part of a `backup database` command:

```
RMAN> backup database noexclude;
```

Since the exclusion from the RMAN backup is stored as a property of the tablespace and not of the individual datafiles in the tablespace, the exclusion will apply to any new datafiles you may add to an excluded tablespace.

7-17. Skipping Read-Only, Offline, or Inaccessible Files

Problem

You want RMAN to skip the backing up of read-only, offline, or inaccessible datafiles and archived redo log files.

Solution

You can skip the backup of offline, read-only, or inaccessible datafiles and archived redo log files by using the `skip` option, as shown in the following example:

```
RMAN> backup database
      skip inaccessible
      skip readonly
      skip offline;
```

The explicit skipping of inaccessible, read-only, and offline datafiles means that RMAN won't issue an error when it confronts a datafile that falls into one of these three categories.

How It Works

Since read-only tablespaces don't change over time, you need to back up these tablespaces only once, after you first make a tablespace read-only. Note that you can persistently skip read-only, offline, and inaccessible tablespaces by using the `configure exclude` command, as explained in recipe 7-16.

You can use the `skip inaccessible` clause with your backups to specify the exclusion of any datafiles or archived redo logs that couldn't be read by RMAN because of I/O errors. For example, some archived redo logs may have been deleted or moved and thus can't be read by RMAN. In such cases, the `skip inaccessible` clause will avoid errors during a backup.

7-18. Encrypting RMAN Backups

Problem

You want to encrypt the backups made with RMAN in order to meet your organization's security guidelines.

Solution

By default, all RMAN backups are unencrypted (encryption is turned off), but you can encrypt any RMAN backup in the form of a backup set. You can encrypt the backup sets in two ways—transparent encryption and password encryption.

Transparent Encryption

The default encryption mode in RMAN is transparent encryption. Transparent encryption uses the Oracle encryption key management infrastructure to create and restore encrypted backups. Transparent encryption is the way to go if you want to persistently configure encrypted backups. Here are the steps to encrypt backups using this method:

1. Configure the Oracle Encryption Wallet (Oracle Wallet) if it hasn't already been configured before. You can do this in several ways, including using the Oracle Wallet Manager. However, using the SQL command we show you here is probably the easiest way to create the wallet. Before you create the Oracle Wallet, first create a directory named wallet in the directory $ORACLE_BASE/admin/$ORACLE_SID. After that, issue the following statement from SQL*Plus:

   ```
   SQL> alter system set encryption key identified by "sammyy11";
   System altered.
   SQL>
   ```

The `alter system` statement will do the following for you:

- If you already have an Oracle Wallet, it opens that wallet and creates (or re-creates) the master encryption key.

- If you don't have an Oracle Wallet already, it creates a new wallet, opens the wallet, and creates a new master encryption key.

2. If you're using the encrypted wallet, open the wallet. If you're using the autologin form of the Oracle Wallet, you don't have to do this, since the Oracle Wallet is always open under this method. The SQL statement in the previous step automatically opens a new wallet after creating it.

3. Configure encrypted backups using the `configure` command, as shown in the following example:

```
RMAN> configure encryption for database on;

new RMAN configuration parameters:
CONFIGURE ENCRYPTION FOR DATABASE ON;
new RMAN configuration parameters are successfully stored

RMAN>
```

The previous command will configure automatic backup encryption for all database files using the default 128-bit key (AES128) algorithm. You can use an alternative encryption algorithm by specifying the `algorithm` parameter with the value for the alternative encryption algorithm (AES256, for example). You don't have to specify any encryption-related options or clauses with your `backup` commands when you configure encryption using the `configure` command, as shown in the example.

4. Make encrypted backups by using the usual `backup` or `backup ...` backupset command, as shown here:

```
RMAN> backup database;
```

Make sure that the Oracle Wallet is open before you issue the previous `backup` command because you've configured database encryption in the previous step, which requires the use of the Oracle wallet as explained earlier.

Password Encryption

If you don't want to configure an Oracle Wallet, you can still perform encrypted backups by using the `set encryption` command. This method is called *password encryption* of backups since the DBA must provide a password both for creating an encrypted backup and for restoring an encrypted backup.

Use the `set encryption` command in order to use password encryption, as shown here:

```
RMAN> set encryption on identified by <password> only;
```

The set encryption on command lets you make password-protected backups. If you've also configured *transparent encryption*, then the backups you make after this will be dual protected—with the password you set here as well as by transparent encryption.

How It Works

You use normal RMAN backup commands to perform backup encryption once you set up configuration using the Oracle Wallet (and the configure command) or the password encryption (and the set encryption command). Oracle uses a backup encryption key encrypted with either the password or the database master key, depending on whether you choose password-based encryption or the Oracle Wallet–based encryption.

In addition to the Transparent Encryption and Password Encryption modes, you also have the option of using a dual mode of encryption, wherein you may create the encrypted backups using a password (using the set encryption on identified by <password> command) but can decrypt the backups using either a password or Oracle Wallet credentials. This method is appropriate in cases where you may have to perform off-site restoration of encrypted backups without access to the Oracle Wallet.

It's a good idea to configure multiple channels when performing backup encryption using RMAN because of the additional demands on resources for encrypting backup data.

You can select the level (database, tablespace) of backup encryption as well as the algorithm to use for the encrypted backups through the configure command. By default, RMAN uses the 128-bit AES encryption algorithm. If you configured persistent encryption settings through the configure command, you can turn encryption off when necessary by using the following command:

```
RMAN> configure encryption for database off;
```

The following command shows a variation of the configure command, where we use the tablespace option with the configure command to specify encryption for a specific tablespace named example:

```
RMAN> configure encryption for tablespace example on;

tablespace EXAMPLE will be encrypted in future backup sets
new RMAN configuration parameters are successfully stored

RMAN>
```

When you back up the database, only the example tablespace backup will be in an encrypted form. You can disable encryption for the tablespace example by using the following command:

```
RMAN> configure encryption for tablespace example off;

Tablespace EXAMPLE will not be encrypted in future backup sets
new RMAN configuration parameters are successfully stored

RMAN>
```

If you back up an already encrypted backupset using the `backup ... backupset` command, no further encryption takes place. Oracle simply backs up the previously encrypted backup set. However, if you use transparent data encryption in some tables to encrypt selected columns, the encrypted RMAN backups will encrypt the already encrypted columns again when backing up the data.

You can look up the available encryption algorithms for encryption in the V$RMAN_ENCRYPTION_ALGORITHMS view.

7-19. Making a Compressed Backup

Problem

You want to compress RMAN backups in order to save storage space.

Solution

Specify the as `compressed backupset` option with your `backup` command to direct RMAN to produce a binary compressed backup set, as shown in the following example:

```
RMAN> backup
      as compressed backupset
      database plus archivelog;

Starting backup at 22-APR-07
current log archived
using channel ORA_DISK_1
channel ORA_DISK_1: starting compressed archive log backupset
```

The previous command will back up all datafiles and the archived redo log files as a compressed backup set. The backup may be made to disk or tape, depending on which one you configured as the default backup destination.

How It Works

RMAN's compression capabilities are especially useful when you're backing up to disk and confront a tight disk space situation. Just make sure you schedule the compressed backups during a low database usage period, because of the higher CPU overhead for compression.

You don't need to explicitly uncompress a compressed backup during recovery. RMAN recommends that you not use RMAN's backup set compression feature if you're backing up to a tape device and the media manager is using its own compression.

7-20. Parallelizing Backups

Problem

You want to make the backups complete faster by parallelizing them.

Solution

You can parallelize a backup by configuring channel parallelism using the `channel` parameter. Each `allocate channel` command you specify will dictate the files each channel should back up, along with the locations where RMAN should place those backups. Here's an example that shows how to use a parallelism of degree 2 by specifying two separate tape channels for a single backup job:

```
run
{
allocate channel ch1 device type sbt
     parms 'env=(ob_device_1=testtape1)';
allocate channel ch2 device type sbt
     parms 'env=(ob_device_2=testtape12';
backup
database channel ch1
archivelog all channel ch2;
}
```

If you're backing up to multiple disk drives, you can allocate a disk channel for each disk drive. You can use the format clause of the allocate channel command to spread the backups across multiple disks to enhance backup performance. Here's an example that shows how to spread the backup of a database across four disks:

```
run
{
  allocate channel d1 device type disk  format '/u01/%d_backups/%U';
  allocate channel d2 device type disk  format '/u02/%d_backups/%U';
  allocate channel d3 device type disk  format '/u03/%d_backups/%U';
  allocate channel d4 device type disk  format '/u04/%d_backups/%U';
  backup database;
}
```

If you want to configure persistent backup parallelism, first specify the degree of parallelism for the device type you want, as shown here:

```
RMAN> configure device type disk parallelism 4;

new RMAN configuration parameters:
CONFIGURE DEVICE TYPE DISK PARALLELISM 4 BACKUP TYPE TO BACKUPSET;
new RMAN configuration parameters are successfully stored

RMAN>
```

In the previous example, we specify a degree of parallelism of 4 for the device type disk. Once you configure the degree of parallelism, configure channels as follows (assuming you want parallelism of degree 4) using the parallelism clause to specify the degree of parallelism:

```
configure device type disk parallelism 4;
configure default device type to disk;
configure channel 1 device type disk format '/u01/%d_backups/%U';
configure channel 2 device type disk format '/u02/%d_backups/%U';
configure channel 3 device type disk format '/u03/%d_backups/%U';
configure channel 4 device type disk format '/u04/%d_backups/%U';
```

RMAN will henceforward distribute all your backups over the four disks by default. You can undo the configuration of parallelism for the disk device in the following manner:

```
RMAN> configure device type disk clear;
```

```
old RMAN configuration parameters:
CONFIGURE DEVICE TYPE DISK PARALLELISM 4 BACKUP TYPE TO BACKUPSET;
RMAN configuration parameters are successfully reset to default value
```

```
RMAN>
```

You can also specify the degree of parallelism for tape backups by using the following command:

```
RMAN> configure device type sbt parallelism 3;
```

The previous command uses a degree of parallelism of 3 for all subsequent tape backups. Once again you can use the `clear` option to revert to the default parallelism setting, as shown here:

```
RMAN> configure device type sbt clear;
```

This command will set the degree of parallelism to the default value of 1, which means future tape backups will not be parallelized.

How It Works

You can parallelize an RMAN backup by using either the `configure` command (as explained in Chapter 5) or the `allocate channel` command to manually specify multiple channels for a backup job.

The `parallelism` clause configures the number of automatic channels of a specific type, disk, or tape that RMAN allocates to a job. The default degree of parallelism is 1, and you can set the degree of parallelism for both disk and tape drives, as shown in the "Solution" section of this recipe. RMAN determines the degree of parallelism for a job based on which device type you specify as the device type for the backup.

7-21. Making Faster Backups of Large Files

Problem

You want to make faster backups of a large datafile.

Solution

You can back up a large datafile faster by dividing the backup work among multiple channels so they can back up the large datafile in parallel. To do this, you can make a *multisection backup*, wherein each channel backs up a section of a datafile, thus enhancing performance.

You perform a multisection backup by specifying the `section size` parameter in the `backup` command. Here are the steps you must follow in order to make a multisection backup:

1. Connect to the target database:

```
$ rman target sys/<sys_password>@target_db
```

2. Configure channel parallelism. In this example, we use a parallel setting 3 for the sbt device, as shown here:

```
{allocate channel c1 device type sbt
     parms 'env=(ob_device_1=testtape1)';
allocate channel c1 device type sbt
     parms 'env=(ob_device_2=testtape2)';
allocate channel c1 device type sbt
     parms 'env=(ob_device_3=testtape3)';
```

3. Execute the backup, specifying the section size parameter:

```
RMAN> backup
         section size 150m
         tablespace system;

Starting backup at 07-JUN-07
using target database control file instead of recovery catalog
allocated channel: ORA_DISK_1
channel ORA_DISK_1: SID=181 device type=DISK
channel ORA_DISK_1: starting full datafile backup set
channel ORA_DISK_1: specifying datafile(s) in backup set
input datafile file number=00001
name=C:\ORCL11\APP\ORACLE\ORADATA\ORCL11\SYSTEM
01.DBF
backing up blocks 1 through 32768
channel ORA_DISK_1: starting piece 1 at 07-JUN-07
channel ORA_DISK_1: finished piece 1 at 07-JUN-07
,,,
channel ORA_DISK_1: backup set complete, elapsed time: 00:00:02
Finished backup at 07-JUN-07

RMAN> exit
```

In this example, the tablespace system has one datafile, size 600m. The section size parameter (set to 150m) breaks up the datafile backup into four chunks of about 150m each.

How It Works

In a multisection backup, multiple channels back up a single datafile. Each of the channels you specify will back up a single file section, which is a contiguous set of blocks in a datafile. Each of the datafile sections is backed up to a different backup piece.

■**Note** You can't specify the section size parameter along with the maxpiecesize parameter.

By default, RMAN won't let you make multisection backups for any datafile smaller than 1GB, but you can override this by simply specifying a smaller size than 1GB in the `section size` parameter of the RMAN `backup` command. You can have up to 256 sections per datafile. RMAN makes uniform-sized sections, except the very last one, which may or may not be the same size as all the other sections.

Use the new (Oracle Database 11*g*) backup command clause `section size` to perform multisection backups. If you don't specify a value for the sections with the `section size` parameter, RMAN computes an internal default section size for that backup job. Multisection backups offer performance benefits, since you can back up a single datafile simultaneously in multiple sections, thus parallelizing the backup. You also don't have to back up a large file all over again, if the backup fails midway—you need to back up only those sections that weren't backed up the first time around.

You must set the initialization parameter `compatibility` to at least 11.0 when performing multisection backups, since it's not possible to restore multisection backups with a release earlier than 11.0.

You can also use the `section size` clause with the `validate datafile` command.

The `section_size` column in both the V$BACKUP_DATAFILE and RC_BACKUP_DATAFILE views shows the number of blocks in each section of a multisection backup. If you haven't performed any multisection backups, the section_size column would have a zero value. The V$BACKUP_SET and RC_BACKUP_SET views tell you which backups or multisection backups. The following example shows a query on the V$BACKUP_DATAFILE view:

```
SQL> select pieces, multi_section from V$BACKUP_SET;
PIECES      MUL
------      --------
     1      NO
     2      YES
     7      YES
     4      NO
SQL>
```

The V$BACKUP_DATAFILE shows information about control files and datafiles in backup sets. The previous command shows that datafile 7's backup is a multisection backup.

7-22. Specifying Backup Windows

Problem

The DBA has a limited window for running the RMAN backups. The backups must complete within this specified backup window every day.

Solution

By using the `duration` parameter as part of your `backup` command, you can specify a window for an RMAN backup. The backup either will complete during the time interval you specify with the `duration` parameter or will stop midway through the backup if it doesn't finish within the specified time. RMAN may or may not issue an error when an ongoing backup runs past the backup window, based on your selection of certain options.

Here's an example that shows how to limit an RMAN backup to six hours:

```
RMAN> backup duration 6:00
        database;
```

You can use the `duration` clause along with other clauses to control what happens when a backup fails to complete within the specified time interval. By default, RMAN reports an error when the backup is interrupted because of the end of the backup interval. If your backup command is part of a `run` block, that `run` block will also terminate immediately. By using the optional clause `partial`, you can suppress the RMAN error reports and instead have RMAN merely report which datafiles it couldn't back up because of a lack of time. Here's an example:

```
RMAN> backup duration 6:00 partial
        database
        filesperset 1 ;
```

In addition to not issuing any error messages, the `partial` clause also lets the other commands within a `run` block continue to execute after the termination of a backup when the window of time for backups expires. You can also use the `duration` clause along with one of two other options to control the *speed* of the backup. To perform the backup in the shortest time possible, specify the `minimize time` option, as shown here:

```
RMAN> backup
        duration 6:00 partial
        minimize time
        database
        filesperset 1;
```

On the other hand, if you think that the backup may not go over the backup window, you can reduce the overhead imposed by the backup with the `minimize load` option with the duration clause, as shown here:

```
RMAN> backup
        duration 6:00 partial
        minimize load
        database
        filesperset 1;
```

When you specify the `minimize load` clause, RMAN extends the backup (slows it down) to take advantage of all the time that's available to it.

How It Works

Each of the `backup` commands shown in the solution section specifies the `filesperset` parameter. When you specify `filesperset=1`, each file gets its own backup set. Thus, when the backup is terminated when you bump up against the backup window, only the backup of a particular datafile is lost, and all the other backups sets already made will be good. When you resume the backup afterward, you don't have to back up these datafiles again.

When you specify the `minimize load` clause, RMAN periodically estimates the completion time for a currently running backup. If RMAN estimates that a backup will complete within the backup window, it slows down the backup to fit the entire backup window so as to reduce the overhead on the database.

If you're using a tape device to make the backup, you must understand the implications of using the `minimize load` clause during backups. When you use the `minimize load` clause, tape streaming may be below the optimal level because of the slowing down of the rate of backups by RMAN. Since RMAN has the exclusive use of the tape device for the entire duration of the backup, you can't use that tape device for any other purpose during the backup. For the reasons listed here, Oracle recommends that you not use the `minimize load` option when using a tape drive to make your backups.

7-23. Reusing RMAN Backup Files

Problem

You want to reuse some existing RMAN backup files by overwriting existing backups with new backups.

Solution

You can use the `reuse` option with your backup commands to enable RMAN to overwrite existing backups, as shown in the following example:

```
RMAN> backup reuse database;
```

How It Works

When you include the `reuse` option with a `backup` command, RMAN will overwrite the existing backups with the newer backups. The existing backup files, both backup sets and image copies, will be overwritten by a file with an identical name.

7-24. Retaining Backups for a Long Time

Problem

You want to retain certain backups beyond what the retention policy for the database will allow for archival purposes.

Solution

Use the `keep` option with the `backup` command to retain backups beyond what's mandated by the retention polices that you've configured. In the following example, the `keep until time` clause tells RMAN to retain the backup for a period of six months:

```
run
{
backup database
tag quarterly
keep until time 'sysdate+180'
restore point 2007Q1;
}
```

The previous backup command with the keep until time clause ensures that RMAN exempts this backup from any configured retention polices and retains it for six months after the backup. The backup command also creates the *restore point* 2007Q1 to mark the SCN at which the backup will be consistent.

Note Backups that use the backup ... keep command are also known as *archival backups*.

You may sometimes need to retain a given backup *forever*. As long as you're using a recovery catalog, you can simply use the keep forever option during a backup command to exempt a backup copy from any retention policies:

```
run
{
backup database
tag quarterly
keep forever
restore point Y2007Q1;
}
```

One of the common uses of archival backups is to use them for creating a test database on a different server. Since you won't need the backups after you create the test database from the backups, you can set the keep parameter to sysdate+1, meaning that the backup will become obsolete a day after the backup is made, regardless of your backup retention policy. Here's an example:

```
run
{
backup database
tag quarterly
keep until time 'sysdate+1';
restore point Y2007Q1
}
```

You can then use the RMAN duplicate command to create your test database from this archival backup, as shown in Chapter 15. If you don't delete the backup after a day, it'll become obsolete anyway and thus eligible for automatic deletion by RMAN.

Once you exempt a backup from the retention policy using the keep option, you can also mark the backups as unavailable so RMAN knows that this backup can't be used for a normal restore/recovery operation. Here's an example that shows how to do this using the keyword unavailable to mark a backup as unavailable in the RMAN repository:

```
RMAN> backup database keep forever tag 'semi_annual_bkp';
RMAN> change backup tag 'semi_annual_bkp' unavailable;
```

The unavailable option of the change command changes the status of the backup to unavailable in the RMAN repository. You can use this option when a file is missing or you have moved it offsite. When you find the file or move it back to your site, you can specify the available option of the change command to make it once again available to RMAN.

How It Works

You want to exempt backups from your retention polices at times when you want to retain a backup long term for archival purposes. For example, you may want to store a historical record of the database by taking a cold backup of the database every six months. Your main purpose in creating this backup then isn't to use it in a future recovery/restore effort but rather to serve as a permanent record of the database as of the time when you made the backup.

When you issue a backup ... keep command, RMAN does the following:

- It automatically backs up all datafiles, the control file, and the server parameter file.

- To ensure that it can restore the database to a consistent state, RMAN creates an archived redo log backup automatically as well.

- You can use the optional restore point clause, which is a label or name for the particular SCN to which RMAN must recover the database to make it consistent.

In all three examples shown in the previous section, the backup ... keep command will back up both the datafiles and the archived redo log files. RMAN backs up only those archived redo logs that are necessary to restore the backups to a consistent state. Before the RMAN backup starts, the database performs an online redo log switch, thus archiving all redo that's currently in the online redo logs and that will be necessary later to make the database consistent.

The control file autobackup that RMAN automatically makes when you use the backup ... keep command has a copy of the restore point. During a restore operation, the control file is restored first. After the control file is restored, the restore point that's recorded in the control file is looked up to see what SCN the database must be restored to in order to make it consistent.

Archival backups are usually made to tape so they can be stored offsite.

7-25. Backing Up Only Those Files Previously Not Backed Up

Problem

You want to create a backup of only new files that have been recently added or those files that failed to get backed up during the normal backup schedule.

Solution

You can limit RMAN to backing up only specific files using the not backed up or since time clause within a backup command. Using the not backed up clause, you can instruct RMAN to back up only those datafiles or archived log files that were never backed up previously. Here's the backup command that shows how to back up only previously backed-up files:

```
RMAN> backup database not backed up;
Starting backup at 15-NOV-06
using channel ORA_DISK_1
skipping datafile 1; already backed up on 14-NOV-06
skipping datafile 2; already backed up on 14-NOV-06
skipping datafile 3; already backed up on 14-NOV-06
skipping datafile 4; already backed up on 14-NOV-06
```

```
skipping datafile 5; already backed up on 14-NOV-06
Finished backup at 15-NOV-06
RMAN>
```

You can also use the not backed up command with additional specifications such as the number of backups. The following example shows how to back up only those archived redo logs that were backed up less than twice on tape:

```
RMAN> backup device type sbt archivelog all not backed up 2 times;
```

RMAN considers only backups created on identical device type as the current backup when counting the number of backups it has already made. Thus, the not backed up clause is ideal for specifying the number of archived redo logs to be stored on a specific type of media. The previous example specifies RMAN to keep at least two copies of archived redo logs on *tape*.

How It Works

The backup ... not backed up command comes in handy when you add one or more new files and want to ensure that the new file's contents are backed up soon rather than waiting for the regular scheduled time for backup.

If you're making backup sets (instead of image copies), RMAN considers the completion time for any file in the backup set as the completion time for the entire backupset. That is, all files in a backup set must have the same finishing time. Let's say you're making a backup that involves multiple backup sets. If the target database crashes midway through a database backup, you don't have to start the backup from the beginning. You can use the not backed up since time command to back up only those datafiles that haven't been backed up since the specified time, as shown in the following example:

```
RMAN> backup database not backed up since time 'sysdate-31';
```

If you use the not backed up since time clause when you restart the RMAN backup, RMAN will skip backing up the files it already backed up prior to the instance failure. Recipe 7-26 explains this in more detail. If you're using the since time clause, you can specify either a date in the nls_date_format or a SQL data expression such as sysdate-7. Note that RMAN considers only backups made on the same device type as the current backup when figuring out whether a new backup ought to be made.

7-26. Restarting Backups After a Crash

Problem

The RMAN backup process fails midway through a database backup, say, because of a database instance crash or because of the unavailability of some datafiles. You want to resume the backup but save time by backing up only those parts of the database that failed to be backed up the first time.

Solution

Use the *restartable backup* feature to back up only those files that failed to be backed up the first time around. Use the not backed up since time clause of the backup command to restart a backup after it partially completes. If the time you specify for the since time clause is a more recent time than the backup completion time, RMAN backs up the database file.

Here's an example that shows how to restart an RMAN backup that failed midway through a nightly backup. You discover the backup failure in the morning and decide to back up only those parts of the database that weren't backed up by RMAN before the backup failed. Simply run the following backup command to achieve your goal.

■**Note** If you use the backup database not backed up command without the since time clause, RMAN backs up only those files that were never backed up before by RMAN.

```
RMAN> backup not backed up since time 'sysdate-1'
       database plus archivelog;
```

The previous backup command will back up all the database files and archivelogs that weren't backed up during the past 24 hours. Any database file or archivelogs that were backed up during the last 24 hours won't be backed up again. You thus avoid backing up files you already backed up. When RMAN encounters database files that it had already backed up before the backup failed, it issues messages such as these:

```
RMAN-06501: skipping datafile 1; already backed up on APR11 2007  20:12:00
RMAN-06501: skipping datafile 2; already backed up on APR 11 2007  20:13:35
RMAN-06501: skipping datafile 3; already backed up on APR 11 2007  20:14:50
```

The backup command that produced this output used a SQL expression of type date (sysdate-1). You may also specify a date string as a literal string that matches the nls_date_format environment variable setting.

How It Works

The restartable backup feature backs up only those files that weren't backed up since a specified date and uses the last completed backup set or image copy as the restart point for the new backup. By using the restartable backup feature after a backup failure, you back up the parts of the database that the failed backup didn't back up. If your backup consists of multiple backup sets and the backup fails midway, you don't have to back up the backup sets that were already backed up. However, if your backup consists only of a single backup set, a backup failure means that the entire backup must be rerun.

All the database files are affected when you place the not backed up since clause right after the backup command, as shown in our example. By placing the not backed up since clause after a specific backupset, you can limit the backup to only the objects that are part of the backup set.

It's important to understand that when considering the number of backups, RMAN takes into account only those backups made on an identical device as the device in the current backup command.

7-27. Updating Image Copies

Problem

You want to update image copies to keep them current without having to perform lengthy image copy backups of entire datafiles.

Solution

By using *incrementally updated image copies*, you can avoid making time-consuming full image copy backups of datafiles. To use the incrementally updated backups feature, you first make a full image copy backup of a datafile and, at regular intervals, update the initial image copy of the datafile with level 1 incremental backups of that datafile.

You use the backup ... for recover of copy form of the backup command to incrementally update an image copy, as shown here:

```
run {
    recover copy of database
    with tag 'incr_update';
    backup
    incremental level 1 for recover of copy with tag 'incr_update'
    database;
}
```

By running the previous script daily, you'll never have to apply more than a day's worth of redo to recover the database, thus dramatically reducing the time needed to perform a media recovery of the database.

How It Works

You can use Oracle's incrementally updated backups feature to update image copy backups. For example, you can start by making an image copy backup of the database on day one. You can then take a daily, level 1 incremental backup of that datafile and apply it to the image copy, thus updating or rolling forward the image copy on a regular basis, in this case daily. The advantage is that during a recovery situation you can simply restore the incrementally updated image copy and recover with the help of archived redo logs, just as if you were using a recent (taken at the same time as the latest incremental level 1 backup) full backup of the database. The great benefit of using incrementally updated backups is that at any given time you won't have more than a single day's worth or redo to apply. This is of course assuming that you update your image copies daily.

It's a little hard to see how our solution script implements the incrementally updated backups strategy, so we'll explain the sequence of events in more detail. We're reproducing the script here so you can follow the logic clearly:

```
RMAN> run
2> {
3> recover copy of database
4> with tag 'incr_update';
5> backup
6> incremental level 1
```

```
7> for recover of copy with tag 'incr_update'
8> database;
9> }
```

Assuming that you run the backup script shown previously on a daily basis, the following is what happens from here on:

1. The first day the backup script runs, the `recover copy of database with tag 'incr_update'` clause doesn't find anything to recover. The `backup` command that follows it will create an image copy of the disk with the tag incr_update. The first part of the `backup` command's output shows this:

```
Starting recover at 21-APR-07
using channel ORA_DISK_1
no copy of datafile 1 found to recover
no copy of datafile 2 found to recover
no copy of datafile 3 found to recover
no copy of datafile 4 found to recover
Finished recover at 21-APR-07

Starting backup at 21-APR-07
using channel ORA_DISK_1
no parent backup or copy of datafile 1 found
no parent backup or copy of datafile 3 found
no parent backup or copy of datafile 2 found
no parent backup or copy of datafile 4 found
channel ORA_DISK_1: starting datafile copy
input datafile fno=00001 name=C:\ORACLE\PRODUCT\
                         10.2.0\ORADATA\TENNER\TENNER\SYS
TEM01.DBF
```

The output also shows that the `recover` command couldn't find any copies of datafiles to recover.

2. On the second day of the script's execution, the script will create a level 1 incremental backup of the database, as shown in the following chunk from the `backup` command's output:

```
Starting recover at 21-APR-07
using channel ORA_DISK_1
no copy of datafile 1 found to recover
no copy of datafile 2 found to recover
no copy of datafile 3 found to recover
no copy of datafile 4 found to recover
Finished recover at 21-APR-07

Starting backup at 21-APR-07
channel ORA_DISK_1: starting incremental level 1 datafile backupset
channel ORA_DISK_1: backup set complete, elapsed time: 00:00:03
Finished backup at 21-APR-07

RMAN>
```

3. On the third day and on all the subsequent days, the backup script will perform both the recovery and backup steps. The script first applies the level 1 incremental backup to the datafile copy and then creates a new level 1 backup. The following output shows the two parts of the script execution:

```
Starting recover at 21-APR-07
using channel ORA_DISK_1
channel ORA_DISK_1: starting incremental datafile backupset restore
channel ORA_DISK_1: specifying datafile copies to recover
recovering datafile copy fno=00001
...
channel ORA_DISK_1: restored backup piece 1
channel ORA_DISK_1: restore complete, elapsed time: 00:00:03
Finished recover at 21-APR-07

Starting backup at 21-APR-07
channel ORA_DISK_1: starting incremental level 1 datafile backupset
channel ORA_DISK_1: specifying datafile(s) in backupset
...
channel ORA_DISK_1: backup set complete, elapsed time: 00:00:03
Finished backup at 21-APR-07


RMAN>
```

The incrementally updated backups feature is a truly powerful feature, which lets you cut back on both the daily backup duration and the time for media recovery, should you need one. RMAN also provides the incremental Roll Forward of Database Copy feature to let you synchronize a standby database with the source database by using incremental backups of the source database. RMAN applies the incremental backups of the source database to the standby database using the recover command in order to bring the standby database up-to-date with the source database.

CHAPTER 8

∎∎∎

Maintaining RMAN Backups and the Repository

To get the most out of RMAN as your main backup and recovery tool, you must master the various RMAN backup and repository maintenance tasks. Managing RMAN backups involves managing the backups themselves as well as performing the record-keeping chores for those backups in the RMAN repository. The RMAN stores its metadata in the control file of the target database, whether you use a recovery catalog or not. If you use a recovery catalog, RMAN will store its metadata in the recovery catalog as well. You don't have to have a recovery catalog to perform any of the backup maintenance tasks.

Oracle recommends that you implement the following policies as the foundation of your RMAN backup and repository maintenance strategy:

- A flash recovery area

- An archived redo log deletion policy

- A backup retention policy

If you adhere to all the recommended backup and repository maintenance tasks, RMAN will take care of creating and managing maintenance tasks such as deleting unneeded backup files and archived redo logs. Even if you have configured the recommended policies listed here, sometimes you may need to manually delete backups, say, from a tape device, or perform related tasks such as validating datafiles and backup sets. Some of the backup and repository maintenance tasks are relatively trivial, such as using the `list` and `report` commands, which help find out which backups exist and the status of those backups. Other tasks are more significant, such as the actions you must take when you manually delete a backup with an operating system utility. To avoid a discrepancy between what RMAN records in the control file and the actual backup files caused by accidental or intentional deletions of backup files, disk failures, and tape failures, you must use RMAN maintenance commands to update the repository so it accurately reflects the true state of affairs regarding your backups. Validating datafiles, backup sets, and backup copies are important tasks that ensure your RMAN backups are usable during a recovery.

From time to time, you'll have to perform some maintenance tasks to keep the flash recovery area working well. You may, for example, add more space to the flash recovery area when it's getting full or move the flash recovery area to a different location. Chapter 3 covers the flash recovery area maintenance tasks.

8-1. Adding User-Made Backups to the Repository

Problem

You've made some datafile copies on disk, which you want to add to the RMAN repository.

Solution

You can add any user-managed copies, such as a datafile copy (that you made with an operating system utility), to the RMAN repository using the `catalog` command. Here's a basic example:

```
RMAN> catalog datafilecopy '/u01/app/oracl/example1.bkp';
```

The preceding `catalog` command catalogs the datafile copy you made of the example01.dbf datafile as an RMAN-recognized backup. You can, if you want, catalog the datafile copy as an incremental level 0 backup by issuing the following command:

```
RMAN> catalog datafilecopy '/u01/app/oracle/example01.bkp' level 0;
```

There's absolutely no difference between a datafile copy you first copy and then record in the recovery catalog using the `catalog` command and an RMAN incremental level 0 backup of that datafile. You can use this cataloged file as part of your RMAN incremental backup strategy.

How It Works

To catalog a copy made by you in the RMAN repository, the copy must be available on disk, and it must be a complete image copy of a single datafile, control file, archived redo log file, or backup piece. Use the `catalog` command in the following situations:

- You use an operating system command to make copies of datafiles, archived redo log files, or control files and want to record them in the RMAN repository.

- If you change the archiving destination during a recovery, you must use the `catalog` command to catalog those archived redo logs in the RMAN repository.

- You want to use a datafile copy as a level 0 backup, in which case you can perform incremental backups with that level 0 backup as the basis, provided you catalog it in the RMAN repository. You can also use a cataloged datafile copy for block media recovery (BMR) even if you didn't back up the datafile using RMAN.

If you copy or move an RMAN backup piece manually, you can use the `catalog` command to make that backup piece usable by RMAN. The following is an example of cataloging an RMAN backup piece on tape. The `list` command shows that a certain backup piece is uncataloged.

```
RMAN> list backuppiece 'ilif2lo4_1_1';


RMAN-00571: ===========================================================
RMAN-00569: =============== ERROR MESSAGE STACK FOLLOWS ===============
RMAN-00571: ===========================================================
RMAN-03002: failure of list command at 04/13/2007 13:39:53
RMAN-06004: ORACLE error from recovery catalog database:
```

```
RMAN-20260: backup piece not found in the recovery catalog
RMAN-06092: error while looking up backup piece
RMAN>
```

Use the catalog command to make the uncataloged backup piece available to RMAN, as shown here:

```
RMAN> catalog device type sbt backuppiece 'ilif2lo4_1_1';

released channel: ORA_SBT_TAPE_1
allocated channel: ORA_SBT_TAPE_1
channel ORA_SBT_TAPE_1: sid=38 devtype=SBT_TAPE
channel ORA_SBT_TAPE_1: WARNING: Oracle Test Disk API
cataloged backuppiece
backup piece handle=ilif2lo4_1_1 recid=3878 stamp=619796430
RMAN>
```

You can check that the backup piece has been cataloged successfully by issuing the list command again, as shown here:

```
RMAN> list backuppiece 'ilif2lo4_1_1';

List of Backup Pieces
BP Key  BS Key  Pc# Cp# Status      Device Type Piece Name
------- ------- --- --- ----------- ----------- ----------------
3473331 3473326 1   1   AVAILABLE   SBT_TAPE    ilif2lo4_1_1
RMAN>
```

If you have to catalog multiple files that you had backed up to a directory, use the catalog start with command, as shown in the following example:

```
RMAN> catalog start with '/u01/app/oracle/backup' noprompt;
```

The start with clause specifies that RMAN catalog all valid backup sets, datafile copies, and archived redo logs starting with the string pattern you pass. This string pattern can be part of a filename, an Oracle managed file (OMF) directory, or an automatic storage management (ASM) disk group. By default, RMAN prompts you after every name match for a file. In this example, we used the optional noprompt clause to suppress these automatic prompts.

You can catalog all files in the flash recovery area by using the following command:

```
RMAN> catalog recovery area;
```

When you issue the catalog recovery area command, RMAN searches for all files in the recovery area and issues a message if it doesn't find any files known to the database.

8-2. Finding Datafiles and Archivelogs That Need a Backup

Problem

You want to find out which of the datafiles and archived redo logs in a database need a backup.

Solution

Use the `report need backup` form of the `report` command to find out which backups you need to make in order to conform to the retention policy you put in place. Here's how you execute the `report need backup` command to see which database files are in need of backup:

```
RMAN> report need backup;

RMAN retention policy will be applied to the command
RMAN retention policy is set to redundancy 1
Report of files with less than 1 redundant backups
File    bkps   Name
----    ------ -----------------------------------------------------
1       0      C:\ORACLE\PRODUCT\11.1.0\ORADATA\NICK\SYSTEM01.DBF
2       0      C:\ORACLE\PRODUCT\11.1.0\ORADATA\NICK\UNDOTBS01.DBF
3       0      C:\ORACLE\PRODUCT\11.1.0\ORADATA\NICK\SYSAUX01.DBF
4       0      C:\ORACLE\PRODUCT\11.1.0\ORADATA\NICK\USERS01.DBF
5       0      C:\ORACLE\PRODUCT\11.1.0\ORADATA\NICK\EXAMPLE01.DBF

RMAN>
```

The output of the `report need backup` command tells you that you must back up several database files to comply with your retention policy.

How It Works

The `report need backup` command reports which datafiles and archived redo logs need to be backed up to conform to the backup retention policy you have put in place. You must have configured your own retention policy, or at least have enabled the default retention policy, for the `report need backup` command to work. If you disable the default retention policy, RMAN won't be able to figure out which of your datafile or archived redo logs need a backup. Here's an example that shows the result of running the `report need backup` command after disabling the default retention policy, which is set to 1.

The following command shows the current retention policy:

```
RMAN> show retention policy;

RMAN configuration parameters are:
CONFIGURE RETENTION POLICY TO REDUNDANCY 1; # default

RMAN>
```

The command shows that, currently, the retention policy is configured to a redundancy of 1. Let's change the configured retention policy from one backup to none, as shown here:

```
RMAN> configure retention policy to none;

new RMAN configuration parameters:
CONFIGURE RETENTION POLICY TO NONE;
new RMAN configuration parameters are successfully stored
RMAN>
```

If you now issue the `report need backup` command, you'll see the following error:

```
RMAN> report need backup;

RMAN-00571: ============================================================
RMAN-00569: =============== ERROR MESSAGE STACK FOLLOWS ===============
RMAN-00571: ============================================================
RMAN-03002: failure of report command at 04/29/2007 15:59:14
RMAN-06525: RMAN retention policy is set to none

RMAN>
```

The error occurs because the RMAN retention policy was set to none, thus making it impossible for RMAN to figure out whether you need to make any backups.

You can specify different options with the `report need backup` command. Here are the most useful options you can use with this command:

This command shows objects that require a backup to conform to a redundancy-based retention policy:

```
RMAN> report need backup redundancy n;
```

This command shows objects that require a backup to conform to a window-based retention policy:

```
RMAN> report need backup recovery window of n days
```

This command shows datafiles that require more than *n* days worth of archived redo logs for a recovery:

```
RMAN> report need backup days=n;
```

This command shows only the required backups on disk:

```
RMAN> report need backup device type disk;
```

This command shows only required backups on tape:

```
RMAN> report need backup device type sbt;
```

8-3. Finding Datafiles Affected by Unrecoverable Operations

Problem

You want to identify which datafiles have been affected by unrecoverable operations, since RMAN needs to back up those files as soon as possible after you perform an unrecoverable operation.

Solution

Use the `report unrecoverable` command to find out which datafiles in the database have been marked unrecoverable because they're part of an unrecoverable operation. Here's an example showing how to use the `report unrecoverable` command:

```
RMAN> report unrecoverable;

Report of files that need backup due to unrecoverable operations
File    Type of Backup   Required Name
-----   --------------   ----------------------------------------
1          full          /u01/app/oracle/data/prod1/example01.dbf

RMAN>
```

The `report unrecoverable` command reveals that the example01.dbf file is currently marked unrecoverable and that it needs a full backup to make it recoverable if necessary.

How It Works

If you perform a nonrecoverable operation such as a direct load insert, the changes made won't be logged in the redo log files. You must, therefore, immediately perform either a full backup or an incremental backup of the datafiles involved in the nonrecoverable operation.

The `report unrecoverable` command tells you both the names of the datafiles that were part of a nonlogged operation (and therefore nonrecoverable by normal media recovery) and the type of backup (full or incremental) required to recover the datafile from an RMAN backup.

8-4. Identifying Obsolete Backups

Problem

You want to find out whether any backups are obsolete according to the retention policy you configured.

Solution

The `report obsolete` command reports on any obsolete backups. Always run the `crosscheck` command first in order to update the status of the backups in the RMAN repository to that on disk and tape. In the following example, the `report obsolete` command shows no obsolete backups:

```
RMAN> crosscheck backup;
RMAN> report obsolete;

RMAN retention policy will be applied to the command
RMAN retention policy is set to redundancy 1
no obsolete backups found
```

The following execution of the `report obsolete` command shows that there are both obsolete backup sets and obsolete archived redo log backups. Again, run the `crosscheck` command before issuing the `report obsolete` command.

```
RMAN> crosscheck backup;
RMAN> report obsolete;
```

```
RMAN retention policy will be applied to the command
RMAN retention policy is set to redundancy 1
Report of obsolete backups and copies
Type                   Key    Completion Time    Filename/Handle
-------------------    ------ ------------------ --------------------
Backup Set             1      07-APR-07
Backup Piece           1      07-APR-07          C:\ORCL11\APP\ORACLE\FLASH_RECOVE
RY_AREA\ORCL11\BACKUPSET\2007_04_07\01_MF_NCSNF_TAG20070407T122609
_31H01MRO_.BKP
...
Archive Log            10     09-APR-07          C:\ORCL11\APP\ORACLE\FLASH_RECOVE
RY_AREA\ORCL11\ARCHIVELOG\2007_04_09\01_MF_1_116_31N07Q44_.ARC
Archive Log            11     09-APR-07          C:\ORCL11\APP\ORACLE\FLASH_RECOVE
...
Backup Set             7      19-APR-07
Backup Piece           8      19-APR-07          C:\ORCL11\APP\ORACLE\PRODUCT\11.1
.0\DB_1\DATABASE\5TIFHU1H_1_1
Backup Set             7      19-APR-07
Backup Piece           9      19-APR-07          C:\ORCL11\APP\ORACLE\PRODUCT\11.1
.0\DB_1\DATABASE\5TIFHU1H_1_2
RMAN>
```

The report obsolete command shows all backups sets, backup pieces, and datafile copies that RMAN considers obsolete since it doesn't need them to meet the specified backup retention policy.

How It Works

As in the case of the report need backup command, you must configure a retention policy, or at least not disable the default retention policy that's preconfigured for you already, for the report obsolete command to run without an error.

When using the report obsolete command, it's always a good idea to run the crosscheck database command beforehand to ensure that RMAN has the latest information about the status of different types of backups.

When using the report obsolete command, you can also specify the redundancy and recover window options, as shown here:

```
RMAN> report obsolete recovery window of 5 days;
RMAN> report obsolete redundancy 2;
RMAN> report obsolete recovery window of 5 days device type disk;
```

Note that the last command in the preceding code examples specifies that only disk backups be considered in determining whether there are any obsolete backups. If you don't specify the device type, RMAN takes into account both disk and sbt backups in determining whether a backup is obsolete according to the configured policy.

8-5. Displaying Information About Database Files

Problem

You want to display information about all the datafiles in the target database.

Solution

You can get a report about all the datafiles in a database by using the `report schema` command, as shown in the following example. The `report schema` command in the following example reports on all datafiles:

```
RMAN> report schema;

Report of database schema
=========================================================

List of Permanent Datafiles
File Size(MB) Tablespace    RB Segs    Datafile Name
---- -------- ----------    -- ----    ------------------
1 490  SYSTEM    ***    ***  /u01/app/oracle/system01.dbf
2  30  UNDOTBS1  ***    ***  /u01/app/oracle/undotbs01.dbf
3 320  SYSAUX    ***    ***  /u01/app/oracle/sysaux01.dbf
4   5  USERS     ***    ***  /u01/app/oracle/users01.dbf
5 100  EXAMPLE   ***    ***  /u01/app/oracle/example01.dbf

List of Temporary Files
=========================================================
File Size(MB) Tablespace           Maxsize(MB) Tempfile Name
---- -------- --------------------- ----------- -------------
1    20      TEMP                   32767      ***    /u01/app/oracle/oradata/temp

RMAN>
```

The `report schema` command is helpful in finding out the names of all the datafiles of the target database.

How It Works

You can put the `report schema` command to use to get more than the routine listing of all datafiles at the current time. You can, for example, get a listing of all database files from a past point in time by using the `at time` clause, as shown in the following example:

```
RMAN> report schema at time 'sysdate-1';
```

The previous command requires that you use a recovery catalog. You can also specify the `at scn` or `at sequence` clause instead of the `at time` clause in order to get a report specific to a certain SCN or log sequence number.

8-6. Listing RMAN Backups

Problem

You want to see the backups that are recorded in the RMAN repository for a target database.

Solution

Use the list command to review RMAN backups of datafiles, archived redo logs, and control files. The list command uses the RMAN repository data in order to provide the list of backups and copies. Here's an example of the basic list command:

```
RMAN> list backup;

List of Backup Sets
===================

BS Key  Type LV Size       Device Type Elapsed Time Completion Time
------- ---- -- ---------- ----------- ------------ ---------------
94      Full    6.83M      DISK        00:00:04     07-DEC-06
  BP Key: 85   Status: AVAILABLE  Compressed: NO  Tag: TAG20061207T072539
  Piece Name: /home/oracle/product/11.1.0/db_1/flash_recovery_area/NINA/
  backupset/2006_12_07/o1_mf_ncsnf_TAG200612o6_.bkp
  Control File Included: Ckp SCN: 23698257     Ckp time: 07-DEC-06
  SPFILE Included: Modification time: 07-DEC-06
  ...
BS Key  Size       Device Type Elapsed Time Completion Time
------- ---------- ----------- ------------ ---------------
110     5.45M      DISK        00:00:01     08-JAN-07
        BP Key: 101   Status: AVAILABLE  Compressed: NO  Tag: TAG20070108T053028
        Piece Name: /home/oracle/product/11.1.0/db_1/flash_recovery_area/NINA/
                    backupset/2007_01_08/o1_mf_annnn_TAG20070108T053028_2t47b65y_.bkp
  List of Archived Logs in backup set 110
  Thrd Seq     Low SCN    Low Time  Next SCN   Next Time
  ---- ------- ---------- --------- ---------- ---------
  1    538     27837708   08-JAN-07 27844832   08-JAN-07
List of Datafiles in backup set 111
File LV Type Ckp SCN    Ckp Time  Name
---- -- ---- ---------- --------- ----
1       Full 27844836   08-JAN-07
 /home/oracle/product/11.1.0/oradata/nina/system01.dbf
...
BS Key  Type LV Size       Device Type Elapsed Time Completion Time
------- ---- -- ---------- ----------- ------------ ---------------
112     Full    6.83M      DISK        00:00:02     08-JAN-07
        BP Key: 103   Status: AVAILABLE  Compressed: NO  Tag: TAG20070108T053031
        Piece Name: /home/oracle/product/11.1.0/db_1/flash_recovery_area/NINA/
                    backupset/2007_01_08/o1_mf_ncsnf_TAG20070108T053031_2t47dz01_.bkp
  Control File Included: Ckp SCN: 27844932     Ckp time: 08-JAN-07
```

```
    SPFILE Included: Modification time: 08-JAN-07
    ...
    List of Archived Logs in backup set 113
    Thrd Seq     Low SCN    Low Time  Next SCN   Next Time
    ---- -------  ---------- --------- ---------- ---------
    1    539     27844832   08-JAN-07 27844935   08-JAN-07

RMAN>
```

The basic list command shown in the previous example lists all backups in the RMAN repository for the target database by serially listing each backup set (including the backup pieces information) and proxy copy. It also identifies all the files that are part of the backup. If you'd rather list the backups by just the backup files, you can do so by using the list backup by file command, as shown in the following example:

```
RMAN> list backup by file;

List of Datafile Backups
==============================

File Key   TY LV S Ckp SCN    Ckp Time  #Pieces #Copies Compressed Tag
---- -------  - -- - ---------- --------- ------- ------- ----------
1    115   B  F  A 27854369  08-JAN-07 1       1       NO  TAG20070108T070012

List of Archived Log Backups
==============================

Thrd Seq    Low SCN    Low Time  BS Key  S #Pieces #Copies Compressed Tag
---- -------  ---------- --------- ------- - ------- ------- -------
1    540    27844935   08-JAN-07 114     A 1      1       NO  TAG20070108T070009
1    541    27854242   08-JAN-07 117     A 1      1       NO  TAG20070108T070141

List of Control File Backups
==============================


CF Ckp SCN Ckp Time  BS Key  S #Pieces #Copies Compressed Tag
---------- --------- ------- - ------- ------- ---------- ----
27854507   08-JAN-07 116     A 1      1       NO      TAG20070108T070012
23698257   07-DEC-06 94      A 1      1       NO      TAG20061207T072539
List of SPFILE Backups
==============================

Modification Time BS Key  S #Pieces #Copies Compressed Tag
----------------- ------- - ------- ------- ---------- -------------
08-JAN-07         116     A 1      1       NO      TAG20070108T070012
07-DEC-06         94      A 1      1       NO      TAG20061207T072539
RMAN>
```

The list backup by file command groups all backups by file and lists all datafiles, their backup sets, and any proxy copies.

How It Works

You can use the list command to list the following:

- Backup pieces, image copies, and proxy copies of databases, tablespaces, datafiles, archived redo logs, and the control file

- Expired backups

- Backups classified by time period, recoverability, path name, device type, or tag

Using the list command isn't the only way to view the status of RMAN backups. You can also check backup status by querying the recovery catalog views RC_DATAFILE_COPY, RC_ARCHIVED_LOG, and V$BACKUP_FILES.

You can also get the output of the list command in a summarized form by specifying the keyword summary when using the list command, as shown here:

```
RMAN> list backup summary;       # lists backup sets, proxy copies, and image copies
RMAN> list expired backup summary;  # lists expired backups in summary form
```

You can use optional clauses with the list command to narrow down your search of backup information or to list only a specific type of backup. Here are some of the important optional clauses you can employ with the list command, with examples showing how to use those clauses.

This command lists only backup sets and proxy copies but not image copies:

```
RMAN> list backupset;
```

This command lists only datafile, archived redo log, and control file copies:

```
RMAN> list copy;
```

This command lists a particular datafile copy:

```
RMAN> list datafilecopy '/a01/app/oracle/users01.dbf';
```

This command lists backups by tag:

```
RMAN> list backupset tag 'weekly_full_db_backup';
```

This command lists backups according to when the backup was made:

```
RMAN> list copy of datafile 1 completed between '01-JAN-2007' AND '15-JAN-2007';
```

This command lists the backup by the number of times they were backed up to tape:

```
RMAN> list archivelog all backed up 2 times to device type sbt;
```

This command lists the backups of all datafiles and archivelogs of the target database:

```
RMAN> list backup of database;
```

The list command is really not limited to merely listing only the metadata about backups and copies, although that is its primary function. You can also use the list command to mine all kinds of information from the RMAN repository. For example, you can use the following versions of the list command to gather information other than that pertaining to just RMAN backups:

list incarnation: Lists all incarnations of a database (shown in recipe 8-10)

list restore point: Lists all restore points in the target database (shown in recipe 8-9)

list script names: Lists the names of all recovery catalog scripts (shown in Chapter 9)

list failure: Lists failures recorded by the Data Recovery Advisor (shown in Chapter 20)

You can run the crosscheck and delete commands against the backups and copies displayed by the list command.

8-7. Listing Expired Backups

Problem

You want to find out which of your backups are marked in the RMAN repository as expired, meaning they were not found during the execution of an RMAN crosscheck command.

Solution

The list expired backup command shows which of the backups of the target database have an expired status in the repository. Here's an example:

```
RMAN> list expired backup;
```

Of course, if there aren't any expired backups, the previous command won't return any output. You can also find out which of the archived redo log backups have the expired status by using the following command:

```
RMAN> list expired archivelog all;

specification does not match any archived log in the recovery catalog

RMAN>
```

The output of the list command shows that there are no archived redo logs with the expired status.

How It Works

The list expired backup command shows all backups not found during an RMAN crosscheck. You can use the list expired copy command to list all copies not found during a cross-check. Of course, if you haven't run the crosscheck command for quite some time, the output of the list expired command isn't going to be very useful to you! To guarantee the best results from this command, you must make it a habit of executing the crosscheck command frequently, especially if you've been manually deleting any kind of RMAN-related backup files yourself at the OS level. This is yet another reason for you to adhere to Oracle's recommendation of configuring both a backup retention policy and an archived redo log deletion policy, in addition to using the flash recovery area. When you follow the recommended maintenance strategy, RMAN backup and repository maintenance becomes more or less automatic, obviating the need for you to constantly execute commands such as crosscheck to verify your backups.

8-8. Listing Only Recoverable Backups and Copies

Problem

You want to review all datafile backups and copies that you can actually use for a restore and recovery.

Solution

Use the list backup command with the recoverable clause to restrict the list of backups to only those backups and copies whose status is listed as available. Here's an example:

```
RMAN> list recoverable backup;
List of Backup Sets
...
Backup Set Copy #2 of backup set 6
List of Backup Pieces for backup set 6 Copy #2
7   1  AVAILABLE  C:\ORCL11\APP\ORACLE\PRODUCT\11.1.0\DB_1\DIFHTAF_1_2
  Backup Set Copy #1 of backup set 6
  List of Archived Logs in backup set 11
  ...
  1    150     7570287     02-MAY-07 7570487     02-MAY-07
RMAN>
```

The recoverable clause restricts the list of backups and copies to only those that are listed as available in the repository and, as such, can be actually used for a restore and recovery operation.

How It Works

The list backup command shows all backups and copies from the repository, irrespective of their status. Since you can use the backups and copies only with the available status, it's a good idea to run the list recoverable backup command instead when you want to know what usable backups you really do have.

8-9. Listing Restore Points

Problem

You want to list all restore points or a specified restore point in the target database.

Solution

Use the `list restore point` command to view a specific restore point in a database. You can use the `all` option to view all the restore points in the database, as shown in the following example:

```
RMAN> list restore point all;

SCN               RSP Time  Type       Time      Name
----------------  --------  ---------- --------- ---------
6815212                                24-APR-07 RESTORE_1

RMAN>
```

The `list restore point all` command reports that you have a single restore point named restore_1 that covers SCN 6815212.

How It Works

You can use the `list restore point` command to effectively manage any restore points you created in a database. Any guaranteed restore points will never age out of the control file. You must manually delete a guaranteed restore point by using the `drop restore point` command. Oracle retains 2,048 most recent restore points, no matter how old they are. In addition, Oracle also saves all restore points more recent than the value of the `control_file_record_keep_time` initialization parameter. All other normal restore points automatically age out of the control file eventually.

8-10. Listing Database Incarnations

Problem

You want to find out what incarnations of a database are currently recorded in the RMAN repository so you can use this information during potential restore and recovery operations.

Solution

When you perform an `open resetlogs` operation, it results in the creation of a new incarnation of the database. When performing recovery operations on such a database, you might want to check the database incarnation. The `list incarnation` command is handy for this purpose, as shown in the following example:

```
RMAN> list incarnation;

List of Database Incarnations
DB Key  Inc Key DB Name  DB ID            STATUS  Reset SCN  Reset Time
------- ------- -------- ---------------- ------- ---------- ------
1       1       ORCL11   3863017760       PARENT  1          22-NOV-06
2       2       ORCL11   3863017760       CURRENT 909437     03-MAR-07

RMAN>
```

The list incarnation command output lists all incarnations of the target database.

How It Works

If the list incarnation command shows three incarnations of a database, for example, it means you've reset the online redo logs of this database twice. Each time you reset the online redo logs, you create a new incarnation of that database.

RMAN can use backups both from the current incarnation of a database and from a previous incarnation as the basis for subsequent incremental backups if incremental backups are part of your backup strategy. As long as all the necessary archived redo logs are available, RMAN can also use backups from a previous incarnation for performing restore and recovery operations.

8-11. Updating the RMAN Repository After Manually Deleting Backups

Problem

You have deleted some unneeded archived redo logs from disk using an operating system command instead of using the RMAN delete command. The RMAN repository, however, continues to indicate that the deleted archived redo logs are available on disk. You want to update this outdated RMAN repository information about the deleted backups.

Solution

Execute the change ... uncatalog command to update the RMAN repository after you manually delete a backup. Let's say you delete the datafile copy /u01/app/oracle/users01.dbf using the rm command from the Linux operating system. Here's an example of how you'd then use the change ... uncatalog command to change the RMAN repository information pertaining to the removed datafile copy:

```
RMAN> change datafilecopy '/u01/app/oracle/users01.dbf' uncatalog;
```

Here's another example showing how to uncatalog a specific backup piece:

```
RMAN> change backuppiece 'ilif2lo4_1_1' uncatalog;

uncataloged backuppiece
backup piece handle=ilif2lo4_1_1 recid=3876 stamp=619796229
Uncataloged 1 objects
RMAN>
```

If you're using a recovery catalog, the change ... uncatalog command will also delete the backup record you are specifying in the change ... uncatalog command from the recovery catalog.

How It Works

The change ... uncatalog command changes only the RMAN repository information pertaining to the manually deleted backups, but it doesn't actually delete the physical backups and copies of backups. The command removes all references to datafile copies, backup pieces, and archived redo logs from the recovery catalog. It also updates the status of those records in the control file to be deleted.

Run the change ... uncatalog command anytime you delete a backup or an archived redo log with an operating system command. The command removes all RMAN repository references for the file you manually deleted. Otherwise, RMAN won't know about the files you deleted unless you run the crosscheck command.

8-12. Synchronizing the Repository with the Actual Backups

Problem

You've manually removed some old archived redo logs from disk and want to make sure you update the RMAN repository (in the control file and in the recovery catalog) to match the actual backup situation both on disk and in the media management catalog.

Solution

Use the crosscheck command in order to update the RMAN repository with the correct information about available backups. If you physically remove an RMAN backup file, the crosscheck command will update the RMAN repository so its records match the physical status of the backups. The crosscheck command synchronizes the backup data in the RMAN repository (in the control file and the recovery catalog) with the actual backups both on disk and in the media management catalog.

■**Note** If you use all three of Oracle's recommended backup maintenance polices—a backup retention policy, an archived redo log deletion policy, and the flash recovery area—you don't need to resort to the crosscheck command often. If you happen to be manually deleting backup files, run the crosscheck command often to make sure the RMAN repository is current.

In the following example, we issue a delete backup command, which results in a warning that an object couldn't be deleted because of "mismatched status." That is one of the typical errors that results from manually deleting archived redo logs as described in the "Problem" section. Here's the example:

```
RMAN> delete backup;
 using channel ORA_DISK_1

List of Backup Pieces
BP Key  BS Key  Pc# Cp# Status       Device Type Piece Name
------- ------- --- --- ----------- ----------- ----------
85      94      1   1   AVAILABLE    DISK        /home/oracle/
product/11.1.0/db_1/flash_recovery_area/NINA/backupset/
2006_12_07/o1_mf_ncsnf_TAG20061207T072539_2qj283o6_.bkp
```

Do you really want to delete the above objects (enter YES or NO)? yes

```
RMAN-06207: WARNING: 1 objects could not be deleted for DISK channel(s) due
RMAN-06208: to mismatched status.  Use CROSSCHECK command to fix status
RMAN-06210: List of Mismatched objects
RMAN-06211: ===========================
RMAN-06212:   Object Type    Filename/Handle
RMAN-06213: -------------- -----------------------------------------------------
RMAN-06214: Backup Piece    /home/oracle/product/11.1.0/db_1/flash_recovery_area/
NINA/backupset/2006_12_07/o1_mf_ncsnf_TAG20061207T072539_2qj283o6_.bkp
RMAN>
```

You attempt to delete a backup with a mismatched status, which leads to a recommendation from RMAN to run the crosscheck command to fix the status of the backup in the repository. The crosscheck command will update the RMAN repository records with the correct status of the backups. If you manually delete a backup file, for example, a subsequent crosscheck command will result in RMAN marking that file status as expired in the RMAN repository. In the following example, once you issue the crosscheck command, RMAN marks the missing file as expired. Once a file is marked as expired, it's eligible for deletion from the RMAN repository (with the delete expired command), although the physical file itself may have been deleted long ago.

Here's how you run the basic crosscheck command:

```
RMAN> crosscheck backup;

using channel ORA_DISK_1
crosschecked backup piece: found to be 'EXPIRED'
backup piece handle=/home/oracle/product/11.1.0/db_1/flash_recovery_area/NINA/backu
pset/2006_12_07/o1_mf_ncsnf_TAG20061207T072539_2qj283o6_
.bkp recid=85 stamp=608542131
crosschecked backup piece: found to be 'AVAILABLE'
backup piece handle=/home/oracle/product/11.1.0/db_1/flash_recovery_area/NINA/backu
pset/2007_01_08/o1_mf_annnn_TAG20070108T070009_2t4dlcf5_.bkp recid=105
stamp=611305211
crosschecked backup piece: found to be 'AVAILABLE'
backup piece handle=/home/oracle/product/11.1.0/db_1/flash_recovery_area/NINA/backu
pset/2007_01_08/o1_mf_nnndf_TAG20070108T070012_2t4dlftx_.bkp recid=106
stamp=611305213
crosschecked backup piece: found to be 'AVAILABLE'
backup piece handle=/home/oracle/product/11.1.0/db_1/flash_recovery_area/NINA/backu
pset/2007_01_08/o1_mf_ncsnf_TAG20070108T070012_2t4do371_.bkp recid=107
stamp=611305299
crosschecked backup piece: found to be 'AVAILABLE'
backup piece handle=/home/oracle/product/11.1.0/db_1/flash_recovery_area/NINA/backu
pset/2007_01_08/o1_mf_annnn_TAG20070108T070141_2t4do6kt_.bkp recid=108
stamp=611305302
Crosschecked 5 objects
RMAN>
```

The previous crosscheck command will search for all backups on all channels with the same device type as the channel that was used to make the RMAN backups.

How It Works

The crosscheck command helps you update backup information about corrupted backups on disk and tape, as well as any manually deleted archived redo logs or other backup files. For disk backups, the crosscheck command validates the file headers, and for tape backups, it checks whether the backups are in the media management layer (MML) catalog.

It's a good strategy to always first use the list command to see what backups you have and follow it up with the crosscheck command to make sure you really do have those backups. You can use the delete expired command to remove RMAN repository data for all those backups that fail the checking performed by the crosscheck command.

The crosscheck backup command checks all backups on both disk and tape, provided you've already configured an automatic channel for your tape backups. As you know, RMAN already comes with a single preconfigured disk channel.

If you haven't configured an automatic sbt channel, you must allocate a maintenance channel within a run block before you execute the crosscheck command, as shown here:

```
RMAN> allocate channel for maintenance device type sbt;
    crosscheck backup;
```

Once you've configured an sbt channel through the configure command or manually allocate it through the allocate channel command shown previously, you can then check backups on both disk and tape with a single crosscheck command, as shown here:

```
RMAN> crosscheck backup;
```

There are three possible values for the status of a file following the execution of the crosscheck command—available, unavailable, and expired.

When the crosscheck command fails to locate the backups and copies you're looking for on disk or tape (files are absent or RMAN can't access them), it'll update the RMAN repository to show the backup record status for those backups and copies as expired. You can then consequently use the delete expired command to delete the expired backup records (metadata) from the RMAN repository. Thus, you use the following sequence of commands to delete expired backups:

```
RMAN> crosscheck backup;
RMAN> delete expired backup;
```

The crosscheck command checks whether the backups still exist. The command checks backup sets, proxy copies, and image copies. The delete expired backup command will delete the expired backups. Here's another example:

```
RMAN> crosscheck backupset of tablespace users
        device type sbt completed before 'sysdate-14';
RMAN> delete expired backupset of tablespace users
        device type sbt completed before 'sysdate-14';
```

The crosscheck command checks the media manager for expired backups of the tablespace users, and the delete command removes their repository records.

If you want to search for and check only image copies and not backup sets, you can do so by using the copy option with the crosscheck command, as shown in the following example:

```
RMAN> crosscheck copy;
```

You may want to run the crosscheck copy command when verifying the current status and the availability of image copies that you made yourself or through RMAN.

You can use various options of the crosscheck command to perform the cross-checking of a specific tablespace, datafile, archived redo log, control file, and so on. Here are some examples that show how to restrict the cross-checking to specify types of backups:

```
# cross-checking just backup sets.
RMAN> crosscheck backupset;
# cross-checking a copy of a database
RMAN> crosscheck copy of database;
# cross-checking specific backupsets;
RMAN> crosscheck backupset 1001, 1002;
# cross-checking using a backup tag
RMAN> crosscheck backuppiece tag = 'weekly_backup';
# cross-checking a control file copy;
RMAN> crosscheck controlfilecopy '/tmp/control01.ctl';
# cross-checking backups completed after a specific time
RMAN> crosscheck backup of datafile   "/u01/app/oracle/prod1/system01.dbf" completed
after 'sysdate-14';
# cross-checking of all archivelogs and the spfile;
RMAN> crosscheck backup of archivelog all spfile;
# cross-checking a proxy copy
RMAN> crosscheck proxy 999;
```

Use the completed after clause to restrict the crosscheck command to check only those backups that were created after a specific point in time. The following command will check only for backups of a datafile made in the last week:

```
RMAN> crosscheck backup of datafile 2
    completed after 'sysdate -7';
```

It's important to understand that the crosscheck command doesn't *delete* the RMAN repository records of backup files that were manually removed. It simply *updates* those records in the repository to reflect that the backup isn't available any longer by marking the file status as expired. You must use the delete command to actually remove the records of these expired backups from the RMAN repository. On the other hand, if a file was expired at one time and is now made available again on disk or on media management layer, then RMAN will mark the file's status as available.

8-13. Deleting Backups

Problem

You want to delete unwanted backups.

Solution

Use the delete or backup ... delete command to remove both archived redo logs and RMAN
backups. You can remove backup sets, image copies, proxy copies, and archive log backups
through the delete command. The most general form of the delete command is delete
backup. This command deletes all backup pieces for the target database that are recorded in
the RMAN repository. Here's an example:

```
 RMAN> delete backup;

using channel ORA_DISK_1

List of Backup Pieces
BP Key  BS Key  Pc# Cp# Status       Device Type Piece Name
------- ------- --- --- ----------- ----------- ----------
110     119     1   1   AVAILABLE    DISK
/home/oracle/oracle/product/11.1.0/db_1/flash_recovery_area/
                                           NINA/backupset/2007_01_09/
o1_mf_annnn_TAG20070109T073214_2t72ths1_.bkp
111     120     1   1   AVAILABLE    DISK
/home/oracle/product/11.1.0/db_1/flash_recovery_area/
NINA/backupset/2007_01_09/o1_mf_nnndf_TAG20070109T073231_2t72v08l_.bkp

Do you really want to delete the above objects (enter YES or NO)? yes
deleted backup piece
backup piece handle=/home/oracle/oracle/product/11.1.0/db_1/flash_recovery_area/
NINA/backupset/
2007_01_09/o1_mf_annnn_TAG20070109T073214_2t72ths1_.bkp recid=110
 stamp=611393535
deleted backup piece
backup piece handle=/home/oracle/oracle/product/11.1.0/db_1/flash_recovery_area/
NINA/backupset/2007_01_09/o1_mf_nnndf_TAG20070109T073231_2t72v08l_.bkp
recid=111 stamp=611393552
deleted backup piece
...
Deleted 2 objects

RMAN>
```

RMAN always prompts you for confirmation before going ahead and deleting the backup
files. You can issue the delete noprompt command to suppress the RMAN confirmation
prompt. You can use the delete command with various options, as shown in the following
examples:

```
RMAN> delete backuppiece 999;
RMAN> delete copy of controlfile like '/u01/%';
RMAN> delete backup tag='old_production';
RMAN> delete backup of tablespace sysaux device type sbt;
```

In some special situations, you may want to delete all backups—including backup sets, proxy copies, and image copies—belonging to a database. This can happen when you decide to drop a database and get rid of all of its backups as well. Use a pair of crosscheck commands first, one for backups and the other for the image copies, to make sure the repository and the physical media are synchronized. Then issue two delete commands, one for the backups and the other for the copies. Here are the commands:

```
RMAN> crosscheck backup;
RMAN> crosscheck copy;
RMAN> delete backup;
RMAN> delete copy;
```

If you configure a tape channel, RMAN will use both the (preconfigured) disk and the tape channels to delete the backups and copies.

How It Works

When you issue the delete backup command, RMAN does the following:

1. Removes the physical file from the backup media

2. Marks the status of the deleted backup in the control file as deleted

3. Deletes the rows pertaining to the deleted backup from the recovery catalog repository, which is actually stored in database tables, if you are using a recovery catalog and are actually connected to it while deleting the backup

If you issue the delete backup command, you may sometimes get the RMAN prompt back right away without any messages about deleted backups. However, that doesn't mean RMAN has deleted all backups. This actually means RMAN didn't find any backups to delete. Here's an example:

```
RMAN> delete backup;

using channel ORA_DISK_1

RMAN>
```

If you issue the simple delete command, without specifying the force option, the deletion mechanism works in the following manner under different circumstances:

- If the status of the object is listed as available in the repository but the physical copy isn't found on the media, RMAN doesn't delete the object and doesn't alter the repository status.

- If the status is listed as unavailable in the repository, RMAN deletes the object if it exists and removes the repository record for the object.

- If the object has the expired status and RMAN can't find the object on the media, RMAN doesn't delete the object or update its repository status.

Here are some options you can use with the `delete` command when deleting backups:

`delete force`: Deletes the specified files whether they actually exist on media or not and removes their records from the RMAN repository as well

`delete expired`: Deletes only those files marked *expired* pursuant to the issuance of the `crosscheck` command.

`delete obsolete`: Deletes datafile backups and copies and the archived redo logs and log backups that are recorded as *obsolete* in the RMAN repository

Instead of using the basic `delete backup` command, you can also use the alternative deletion command, `backup ... delete [all] input`, to first make a backup of and then delete the input files (source files) of backup sets, datafile copies, and archived redo logs. Typically, you use the `backup ... delete` command to back up the source files to tape and then delete them after a successful backup. We show you how to use the `backup ... delete` command in the next recipe, where we focus on deleting archived redo logs.

8-14. Deleting Archived Redo Logs

Problem

You want to manually delete some unneeded archived redo logs.

Solution

You can delete any eligible archived redo log by using the `delete archivelog` or `backup ... delete input` command. Here's an example showing how to delete all archived redo logs with the `delete archivelog all` command:

```
RMAN> delete archivelog all;
```

The `delete archivelog all` command deletes all archived redo logs on disk that aren't necessary to meet the configured archived redo log deletion policy. It's more likely that you'd want to use the following `delete` command, which deletes archived redo logs from disk based on whether they have been first backed up to tape a certain number of times:

```
RMAN> delete archivelog all
      backed up 3 times to sbt;
```

You can delete specific archived redo logs by using the `delete` command, as shown in the following example.

```
RMAN> delete archivelog until sequence = 999;
```

The `backup ... delete` command lets you first back up an archived redo log and then delete the source archived redo log file. In order to delete the source file, you use the additional clause `delete input`, as shown in the following example:

```
RMAN> backup device type sbt
      archivelog all
      delete all input;
```

The previous backup ... delete command backs up all the archived redo logs and then deletes all those archived redo logs (input files). The delete all input clause results in the deletion of all backed-up archived redo logs from all archived redo log destinations. If you want to delete only the specified archived redo log that you've just backed up to a backup set, use the delete input clause instead, as shown in the following example:

```
RMAN> backup archivelog  like '/arch%'
    delete input;
```

Note that it's common to use the backup ... delete command to back up archived redo logs to tape and then delete the source files.

How It Works

RMAN uses the configured archived redo log deletion policy to determine which of the archived redo logs are eligible for deletion, including those archived redo logs that are stored in the flash recovery area. RMAN automatically deletes the eligible archived redo logs from the flash recovery area. An archived redo log is considered eligible for deletion when the flash recovery area becomes full.

Suppose you have configured the following archived redo log deletion policy:

```
RMAN> configure archivelog deletion policy
    to backed up 2 times to device type sbt;
```

The previous command specifies that all archived redo log files will be eligible for deletion from all locations when those files have been backed up twice or more to tape. Once you set the archived redo log deletion policy shown here, a delete archivelog all or backup ... delete input command will delete all archived redo logs that satisfy the requirements of your configured deletion policy, which requires that RMAN back up all archived redo logs to tape twice.

If you *haven't* configured an archived redo log deletion policy (by default there is no policy set), RMAN will deem any archived redo log file in the flash recovery area eligible for deletion, if both of the following are true:

- The archived redo logs have been successfully sent to all the destinations specified by the log_archive_dest_n parameter.

- You have copied the archived redo logs to disk or to tape at least once, or the archived redo logs are obsolete per your configured backup retention policy.

Use the configure archivelog deletion policy command to specify your own archive redo log deletion criteria instead of leaving the deletion timing to RMAN. Once you configure an archived redo log deletion policy this way, it applies to all archived redo log locations, including the flash recovery area, if you've configured one.

RMAN stores the archived redo logs as long as possible in the flash recovery area. When the flash recovery area is under space pressure, RMAN tries to ensure that any flashback retention time you've set is being satisfied before automatically deleting the archived redo logs. RMAN deletes eligible archived redo logs stored in all areas other than the flash recovery area when you execute one of the two deletion commands shown in the "Solution" section of this recipe, backup ... delete input or delete archivelog.

If you execute the delete command with the force option, RMAN will ignore any configured archived redo log retention polices and delete all the specified archived redo logs.

8-15. Deleting Obsolete RMAN Backups

Problem

You want to delete just those RMAN backups that are obsolete according to the defined retention policy.

Solution

Use the obsolete option of the delete command to remove just the obsolete backups. The
following command shows how to remove all backups that are obsolete according to the
retention policy that's currently configured:

```
RMAN> delete obsolete;

RMAN retention policy will be applied to the command
RMAN retention policy is set to redundancy 1
using channel ORA_DISK_1
Deleting the following obsolete backups and copies:
Type                    Key    Completion Time    Filename/Handle
-------------------- ------ ------------------ --------------------
Backup Set              1      07-APR-07
Backup Piece        1      07-APR-07             C:\ORCL11\APP\ORACLE\FLASH_RECOVE
RY_AREA\ORCL11\BACKUPSET\2007_  TAG20070407T122609_31HO1MRO_.BKP
...
Do you really want to delete the above objects (enter YES or NO)? YES
RMAN>
```

The delete obsolete command shown here will delete all backups deemed obsolete per
your configured backup retention policy.

■**Note** The delete obsolete command relies only on the backup retention policy in force. It doesn't consider the configured archived redo log deletion policy in effect to determine which archived redo logs are
obsolete. The delete archivelog all command, on the other hand, relies entirely on the configured
archived redo log deletion policy.

The following examples show how to use either the redundancy or recovery window clause
to delete backups that are deemed obsolete according to a retention policy that you have configured:

```
RMAN> delete obsolete redundancy = 2;
```

The command shown here deletes backups that exceed the redundancy requirement of 2:

```
RMAN> delete obsolete recovery window of 14 days;
```

The previous command deletes backups and the archived redo logs that aren't necessary to recover the database to an arbitrary SCN within the last two weeks.

How It Works

Obsolete backups are any backups that you don't need to satisfy a configured retention policy. You may also delete obsolete backups according to any retention policy you may specify as an option to the `delete obsolete` command. The `delete obsolete` command will remove the deleted files from the backup media and mark those backups as deleted in both the control file and the recovery catalog.

When deleting obsolete backups, it's important to understand how the `keep until` clause impacts how RMAN deems a backup obsolete. No matter what `keep until` time you specify, RMAN will never consider a backup obsolete if that backup is needed to satisfy any retention policy you might have configured. This applies to both a recovery window–based and a redundancy-based retention policy. If you set the `keep until` time for some backups longer than a configured retention policy interval, however, RMAN will retain those backups. Regardless of any configured backup retention policy, a backup will be considered obsolete as soon as its `keep until` period expires, and the `delete obsolete` command will delete all such obsolete backups.

8-16. Changing the Status of an RMAN Backup Record

Problem

You have migrated some backups off-site and want to let RMAN know that those files aren't available to it.

Solution

Use the `change ... unavailable` command when you move backups off-site or can't find a backup for some reason. Here's an example showing how you can change the status of a backup set to unavailable because you've temporarily moved the backup set to a different location because of a lack of space on a disk:

```
RMAN> change backupset 10 unavailable;

changed backup piece unavailable
backup piece handle=C:\ORCL11\APP\ORACLE\PRODUCT\11.1.0\DB_1\
DATABASE\7QIGN5L1_1_1 RECID=32 STAMP=621516450
Changed 1 objects to UNAVAILABLE status

RMAN>
```

Use the `change ... unavailable` option when you know you don't want a particular backup or copy to be restored yet but don't want to delete that backup or copy either. If you uncatalog the backup set, it'll have a status of deleted in the repository. However, if you just use the `change` command to make the backup set unavailable, you can always make that available again when you have more space on this disk and are able to move the backup set to its original location.

How It Works

Once you mark a backup file unavailable, RMAN won't use that file in a `restore` or `recover` operation. Note that you can't mark files in the flash recovery area as unavailable. Once you find copies of the unavailable, misplaced, or lost backups and restore them, you can mark all the backups you had marked unavailable previously as available again by using the keyword `available` as part of the `change` command, as shown here:

```
RMAN> change backupset 10 available;
using channel ORA_DISK_1
changed backup piece available
backup piece handle=C:\ORCL11\APP\ORACLE\PRODUCT\11.1.0\DB_1\DATABASE\7QIGN5L1_1
_1 RECID=32 STAMP=621516450
Changed 1 objects to AVAILABLE status
RMAN>
```

When you change the status of a file to available, RMAN searches for that file and makes sure it actually exists. You can use the `change` option to modify the status of backups and copies from previous incarnations of a database.

You can use the `change` command in a Data Guard environment to update the status of backups. The command itself doesn't check whether a file is accessible on the backup media but simply changes the status of that backup in the repository to whatever you specify. For example, if you performed a backup using an NFS-mounted disk and that disk subsequently becomes inaccessible, you can connect to either the primary database or the standby database and issue the `change` command to set the status of the backup as unavailable. Later, once the disk becomes accessible again, you can change its status back to available.

8-17. Changing the Status of Archival Backups

Problem

You have made an archival backup for long-term storage to comply with some business requirements. These requirements have changed over time, and you now want to change the status of the archival backup.

Solution

Use the `change` command when you want to change the status of an archival backup pertaining to the long-term retention of that backup. You can use the `change` command in two ways to alter the retention requirements of your archival backups.

If you have previously specified the `keep forever` option to create an archival backup and have now decided to alter the status of this backup to that of a regular backup, use the `change ... nokeep` command to alter the status of the archival backup. Here's an example:

1. Use the `change` command to modify a regular consistent database backup into an archival backup:

   ```
   RMAN> change backup tag 'consistent_db_bkup'
         keep forever;
   ```

   Since this is a consistent backup, it won't need any recovery, and as such, you won't need any archived redo log backups.

2. Use the change command to change the archival backup to a normal database backup subject to the backup obsoletion policies you have in place:

```
RMAN> change backup tag 'consistent_db_backup' nokeep;
```

When you make an archival backup with the keep ... forever option, RMAN disregards the backup retention time for these backups. Once you run the change ... nokeep command, the backup set with the tag consistent_db_backup, which was previously designated as a long-term archival backup, will once again come under the purview of your configured retention policy. The backup will become obsolete per the configured retention policy and can be removed by the delete obsolete command.

How It Works

Remember that you can create archival backups (with the keep forever option) only if you're using a recovery catalog. You can't also set, and therefore, alter the keep attribute for any backup files that are stored in the flash recovery area.

If you want to modify the time period for which you want to retain the archival backups, you can do so by using the change ... keep command. Here's an example:

```
RMAN> change backupset 111 keep until time 'sysdate+180';
```

When you execute the change ... keep command as shown in the example, the previously (permanently) archived backup (backup set 111) will now be retained only for a period of 180 days starting from today. After the 180 days are up, the backup will become obsolete and is eligible for deletion by the delete obsolete command.

8-18. Testing the Integrity of an RMAN Backup

Problem

You want to test your backup operation without actually performing a backup to a disk or tape device to make sure that RMAN can indeed make good backups of your datafiles. Your goal is to ensure that all the datafiles exist in the correct locations and that they aren't physically or logically corrupt.

Solution

Use the backup validate command to perform an integrity testing of RMAN backups without actually performing the backup. Here's an example that shows how to check all the datafiles and the archived redo logs for physical corruption:

```
RMAN> backup validate database archivelog all;

Starting backup at  30-APR-07
using target database control file instead of recovery catalog
allocated channel: ORA_DISK_1
channel ORA_DISK_1: specifying archived log(s) in backup set
input archived log thread=1 sequence=151 RECID=45 STAMP=621554554
channel ORA_DISK_1: specifying datafile(s) in backup set
input datafile file number=00002 name=C:\ORCL11\APP\ORACLE\ORADATA\ORCL11\SYSAUX
```

```
01.DBF
...
Finished backup at 30-APR-07
RMAN>
```

The backup validate command shows that all the necessary datafiles and archived redo logs can be backed up successfully by RMAN. The output of this command is identical to that of an actual RMAN backup command, but as with the other validation command shown in this recipe, no actual backup takes place.

To check for logical corruption, use the following variation of the backup validate command:

```
RMAN> backup validate
        check logical
        database archivelog all;
```

The check logical clause means that RMAN will check for logical corruption only.

How It Works

The backup ... validate command confirms that all the datafiles are indeed where they are supposed to be. The command also checks for both physical and logical corruption. Look up the V$DATABASE_BLOCK_CORRUPTION view for any corruption identified by RMAN after the backup ... validate command finishes executing.

RMAN reads all the database files that are covered by the backup command without creating any backup files themselves. Since all the data blocks are examined for corruption, the backup ... validate command provides a good way to check your backup strategy without being surprised during an actual backup to find that either the necessary datafiles are missing or they are corrupt.

8-19. Validating Datafiles, Backup Sets, and Data Blocks

Problem

You aren't sure whether a particular datafile is missing and you want to run a check to validate the file(s). In addition, you may also want to check whether a particular backup set or a data block is corrupt.

Solution

You can validate datafiles, backup sets, or even individual data blocks by using the validate command. The following example shows how to validate a single backup set with the validate command:

```
RMAN> validate backupset 7;

Starting validate at 30-APR-07
using target database control file instead of recovery catalog
allocated channel: ORA_DISK_1
channel ORA_DISK_1: SID=193 device type=DISK
```

```
channel ORA_DISK_1: starting validation of datafile backup set
channel ORA_DISK_1: reading from backup piece C:\ORCL11\APP\ORACLE\PRODUCT\11.1.
0\DB_1\DATABASE\5TIFHU1H_1_1
channel ORA_DISK_1: piece handle=C:\ORCL11\APP\ORACLE\PRODUCT\11.1.0\DB_1\DATABA
SE\5TIFHU1H_1_1 tag=TAG20070419T081823
channel ORA_DISK_1: restored backup piece 1
channel ORA_DISK_1: validation complete, elapsed time: 00:00:01
Finished validate at 30-APR-07

RMAN>
```

You can also use the validate command to check all datafiles at once, as shown here:

```
RMAN> validate database;

Starting validate at 30-APR-07
using channel ORA_DISK_1
channel ORA_DISK_1: starting compressed full datafile backup set
channel ORA_DISK_1: specifying datafile(s) for validation
input datafile file number=00002 name=C:\ORCL11\APP\ORACLE\ORADATA\1\SY01.DBF
...
channel ORA_DISK_1: validation complete, elapsed time: 00:11:24
List of Datafiles
=================
File Status Marked Corrupt Empty Blocks Blocks Examined High SCN
---- ------ -------------- ------------ ---------------- ----------
1    OK     0              12542        72960            7236557
   File Name: C:\ORCL11\APP\ORACLE\ORADATA\ORCL11\SYSTEM01.DBF
   Block Type Blocks Failing Blocks Processed
   ---------- -------------- ----------------
   Data       0              48959
   Index      0              9143
   Other      0              2316
...
channel ORA_DISK_1: specifying datafile(s) for validation
including current control file for validation
channel ORA_DISK_1: validation complete, elapsed time: 00:00:02
List of Control File and SPFILE
===============================
File Type    Status Blocks Failing Blocks Examined
------------ ------ -------------- ----------------
Control File OK     0              594
Finished validate at 30-APR-07

RMAN>
```

Note that when you issue the `backup ... validate` command, the command begins with the message "Starting validate" and not "Starting backup," as is the case with the `backup ... validate` command.

How It Works

The semantics of the `validate` command are similar to those of the `backup ... validate` command, with the big advantage that the `validate` command can check at a much more granular level than the `backup ... validate` command. You can use the `validate` command with individual datafiles, backup sets, and even data blocks.

■**Note** The `validate` command checks only for intrablock corruption, which may be either physical or logical in nature.

You can speed up the validation of a large datafile by using the `section size` clause with the `validate` command after first configuring multiple channels. The allocation of multiple channels with the `section size` clause parallelizes the datafile validation, making it considerably faster. Here's an example using two disk channels, with the `section size` clause dividing up the validation work between the two channels:

```
RMAN> run
  2> {
  3> allocate channel ch1 device type disk;
  4> allocate channel ch2 device type disk;
  5> validate datafile 1 section size = 250m;
  6> }

allocated channel: ch1
channel ch1: SID=193 device type=DISK
allocated channel: ch2
channel c2: SID=191 device type=DISK

Starting validate at 30-APR-07
...
validating blocks 1 through 32768
...
validating blocks 32769 through 65536
including current control file for validation
channel ch1: validation complete, elapsed time: 00:00:17
=================================================================
File Status Marked Corrupt Empty Blocks Blocks Examined High SCN
---- ------ -------------- ------------ --------------- ----------
1    OK     0              12542        72960           7373884
    File Name: C:\ORCL11\APP\ORACLE\ORADATA\SYSTEM01.DBF
...
```

```
Finished validate at 30-APR-07
released channel: ch1
released channel: ch2

RMAN>
```

The validate command always skips all the data blocks that were never used, in each of the datafile it validates. The larger the value of the section size clause you set, the faster the validation process completes. You can use the validate command with the following options, among others:

- validate recovery area

- validate recovery files

- validate spfile

- validate tablespace <tablespace_name>

- validate controlfilecopy <filename>

- validate backupset <primary_key>

CHAPTER 9

■ ■ ■

Scripting RMAN

Although RMAN allows interactive commands to be entered from the command line, there is little use for some of them in real life, especially for the commands that back up the database. In almost all cases, you'll want to automate your processes to back up your databases, delete archived redo logs, and so on. You should set up these tasks in such a way that they can run without any human intervention. This means you need to script RMAN commands, and the scripts need to be run by some sort of automated scheduler such as cron. In this chapter, you will learn different ways to script and schedule RMAN commands, both in Unix and in Windows.

Approaches to Scripting

RMAN provides for several approaches to scripting. We discuss each approach in the following sections.

With so many options comes the natural question, what is the best approach in your case? While deciding on the exact option to use, you should consider the usage of your scripts. If yours is a Unix server and you are fairly good at shell scripting, the command file option with shell scripts might be attractive. Even if you are not that proficient at shell scripting, you can use the shell script we provide in recipe 9-1, which might be the only one you ever need. If your server is Windows, you can use the Windows batch file example in recipe 9-3.

Stored scripts, meaning scripts stored in an RMAN repository, are attractive since they store the code in the catalog database. So, you can connect from any target and run these scripts as long as you are connected to the catalog. This reduces your coding effort significantly. However, in Oracle Database 10*g* and older, stored scripts are not good at parameter passing and replacing parameters at runtime, whereas shell scripts are good at those tasks. So, stored scripts are attractive for repetitive tasks that you generally use interactively but not against a specific database, such as delete archivelog all, crosscheck backup, list copy of datafiles, and so on. Such scripts are the same regardless of the database and therefore can be executed against any target, saving you a lot of typing effort. On the other hand, shell scripts (or batch files) are better for tasks such as backing up a database, where you can write a generic script and merely substitute parameter values depending on the database target.

The Script Delimiter Approach

You can embed RMAN commands within a shell script by using input redirection along with a delimiter. For instance, here are some RMAN commands embedded within a Unix shell script:

```
... snipped ...
rman target / << EOF
... RMAN commands come here ...
... more RMAN commands
EOF
... and the rest of the script ...
```

The RMAN commands until the EOF marker are all executed.

Command File

You can create regular text files containing RMAN commands. These are regular files in the operating system's filesystem. In RMAN, you can call them in a variety of ways, one of which is putting an at (@) sign in front of them, similarly to how you execute an SQL*Plus script file. For example:

```
RMAN>@cmd.rman
```

Unlike the behavior of SQL*Plus, which expects the script file to have an extension of .sql, RMAN does not expect any extension. If your script filename includes an extension, you'll need to specify that extension when you invoke the script.

The cmdfile Option

You can use the cmdfile command-line option to call a command file while calling RMAN from the Unix shell prompt, as shown here:

```
$ rman target=/ catalog=u/p@catalog cmdfile cmd.rman
```

You can also use the cmdfile option with an equal sign:

```
$ rman target=/ catalog=u/p@catalog cmdfile=cmd.rman
```

You can use the SQL*Plus-like notation to call a script by placing an @ before the name. For example:

```
$ rman target=/ catalog=u/p@catalog @cmd.rman
```

At the RMAN command line, the @ is synonymous with cmdfile.

Stored Scripts

You can store scripts in a catalog and call them from the RMAN command prompt, as shown here:

```
RMAN> run { execute script stored_script; }
```

The stored script is in an RMAN catalog database, not on any filesystem.

Stored Scripts on the Command Line

You can also call a stored script using the `script` parameter on the command line, as shown here:

```
$ rman target=/ catalog=u/p@catalog script stored_script
```

9-1. Developing a Unix Shell Script for RMAN

Problem

You want to develop a shell script to be run by an automated process to back up the database via RMAN.

Solution

The most common platforms for Oracle databases are Unix and its variants, such as Linux, Solaris, HPUX, and so on. The presence of a shell programming language is extremely handy when using these variants. In this recipe, you will learn how to develop a complete shell script to call any RMAN script. Here are some expectations for the script:

- It should be able to be run from some automated utility such as `cron`.

- It should send an email to a set of email addresses after successful completion.

- It should send an email to another set of email addresses after a failure.

- It should back up to multiple mount points. In this example, we have assumed nine mount points.

- It should produce a log file whose name follows this format:

  `<ORACLE_SID>_<BACKUP_TYPE>_<BACKUP_MEDIA>_<TIMESTAMP>.log`

- The log file should show the time stamp in mm/dd/yy hh24:mi:ss format, not the default dd-MON-yy format.

- This log file should be copied over to a central server where all the DBA-related logs are kept. In addition, the log file should be copied to one of the backup mount points as well.

- The script should be generic enough to be called for any database. In other words, the script should not hard-code components that will be different from database to database, such as Oracle Home, SID, and so on.

- The script should have a built-in locking mechanism; in other words, if the script is running and is being called again, it shouldn't start.

With these requirements in mind, you can develop a script similar to the one that follows, which enables you to back up any database automatically and on a recurring basis by using `cron` or some other job-scheduling utility. (Our listing has line numbers to aid explanation; the actual script does not have those line numbers.) The script has a configurable section in which you can replace the variable values to suit your environment.

```
1. # Beginning of Script
2. # Start of Configurable Section
3. export ORACLE_HOME=/opt/oracle/10.2/db_1
4. export ORACLE_SID=PRODB1
5. export TOOLHOME=/opt/oracle/tools
6. export BACKUP_MEDIA=DISK
7. export BACKUP_TYPE=FULL_DB_BKUP
8. export MAXPIECESIZE=16G
9. # End of Configurable Section
10. # Start of site specific parameters
11. export BACKUP_MOUNTPOINT=/oraback
12. export DBAEMAIL="dbas@proligence.com"
13. export DBAPAGER="dba.ops@proligence.com"
14. export LOG_SERVER=prolin2
15. export LOG_USER=oracle
16. export LOG_DIR=/dbalogs
17. export CATALOG_CONN=${ORACLE_SID}/${ORACLE_SID}@catalog
18. # End of site specific parameters
19. export LOC_PREFIX=$BACKUP_MOUNTPOINT/loc
20. export TMPDIR=/tmp
21. export NLS_DATE_FORMAT="MM/DD/YY HH24:MI:SS"
22. export TIMESTAMP=`date +%T-%m-%d-%Y`
23. export LD_LIBRARY_PATH=$ORACLE_HOME/lib:/usr/lib:/lib
24. export LIBPATH=$ORACLE_HOME/lib:/usr/lib:/lib
25. export SHLIB_PATH=$ORACLE_HOME/lib:/usr/lib:/lib
26. export LOG=${TOOLHOME}/log
27. LOG=${LOG}/log/${ORACLE_SID}_${BACKUP_TYPE}_${BACKUP_MEDIA}_${TIMESTAMP}.log
28. export TMPLOG=$TOOLHOME/log/tmplog.$$
29. echo `date` "Starting $BACKUP_TYPE Backup of $ORACLE_SID \
30. to $BACKUP_MEDIA" > $LOG
31. export LOCKFILE=$TOOLHOME/${ORACLE_SID}_${BACKUP_TYPE}_${BACKUP_MEDIA}.lock
32. if [ -f $LOCKFILE ]; then
33. echo `date` "Script running. Exiting ..." >> $LOG
34. else
35. echo "Do NOT delete this file. Used for RMAN locking" > $LOCKFILE
36. $ORACLE_HOME/bin/rman log=$TMPLOG <<EOF
37. connect target /
38. connect catalog $CATALOG_CONN
39. CONFIGURE SNAPSHOT CONTROLFILE NAME TO
40.   '${ORACLE_HOME}/dbs/SNAPSHOT_${ORACLE_SID}_${TIMESTAMP}_CTL';
41. run
42. {
43. allocate channel c1 type disk
44. format '${LOC_PREFIX}1/${ORACLE_SID}_${BACKUP_TYPE}_${TIMESTAMP}_%p_%s.rman'
45. maxpiecesize ${MAXPIECESIZE};
46. allocate channel c2 type disk
47. format '${LOC_PREFIX}2/${ORACLE_SID}_${BACKUP_TYPE}_${TIMESTAMP}_%p_%s.rman'
```

```
48. maxpiecesize ${MAXPIECESIZE};
49. allocate channel c3 type disk
50. format '${LOC_PREFIX}3/${ORACLE_SID}_${BACKUP_TYPE}_${TIMESTAMP}_%p_%s.rman'
51. maxpiecesize ${MAXPIECESIZE};
52. allocate channel c4 type disk
53. format '${LOC_PREFIX}4/${ORACLE_SID}_${BACKUP_TYPE}_${TIMESTAMP}_%p_%s.rman'
54. maxpiecesize ${MAXPIECESIZE};
55. allocate channel c5 type disk
56. format '${LOC_PREFIX}5/${ORACLE_SID}_${BACKUP_TYPE}_${TIMESTAMP}_%p_%s.rman'
57. maxpiecesize ${MAXPIECESIZE};
58. allocate channel c6 type disk
59. format '${LOC_PREFIX}6/${ORACLE_SID}_${BACKUP_TYPE}_${TIMESTAMP}_%p_%s.rman'
60. maxpiecesize ${MAXPIECESIZE};
61. allocate channel c7 type disk
62. format '${LOC_PREFIX}7/${ORACLE_SID}_${BACKUP_TYPE}_${TIMESTAMP}_%p_%s.rman'
63. maxpiecesize ${MAXPIECESIZE};
64. allocate channel c8 type disk
65. format '${LOC_PREFIX}8/${ORACLE_SID}_${BACKUP_TYPE}_${TIMESTAMP}_%p_%s.rman'
66. maxpiecesize ${MAXPIECESIZE};
67. backup
68. incremental level 0
69. tag = 'LVL0_DB_BKP'
70. database
71. include current controlfile;
72. release channel c1;
73. release channel c2;
74. release channel c3;
75. release channel c4;
76. release channel c5;
77. release channel c6;
78. release channel c7;
79. release channel c8;
80. allocate channel d2 type disk format
81. '${LOC_PREFIX}8/CTLBKP_${ORACLE_SID}_${TIMESTAMP}.CTL';
82. backup current controlfile;
83. release channel d2;
84. }
85. exit
86. EOF
87. RC=$?
88. cat $TMPLOG >> $LOG
89. rm $LOCKFILE
90. echo `date` "Script lock file removed" >> $LOG
91. if [ $RC -ne "0" ]; then
92. mailx -s "RMAN $BACKUP_TYPE $ORACLE_SID $BACKUP_MEDIA Failed" \
93. $DBAEMAIL,$DBAPAGER < $LOG
94. else
```

```
95.  cp $LOG ${LOC_PREFIX}1
96.  mailx -s "RMAN $BACKUP_TYPE $ORACLE_SID $BACKUP_MEDIA Successful" \
97.  $DBAEMAIL < $LOG
98.  fi
99.  scp $LOG \
100. ${LOG_USER}@${LOG_SERVER}:${LOG_DIR}/${ORACLE_SID}/.
101. rm $TMPLOG
102. fi
```

The "How It Works" section describes the mechanics of the script.

■**Note** You don't need to type this solution script. If you want to use it or adapt it to your own use, you'll find the script in the zip file of script examples that you can download for this book from the Apress website.

How It Works

We made this script as generic as possible. All the parameters are configurable. Keeping in that spirit, pretty much everything in the script is parameter-driven. You can use the same script on any database on any Unix server. You merely need to modify the parameters appropriately.

One issue we must clarify before you start the database backup to tape based on this script is the location of the backup files. You can store the backup pieces on one mount point, such as /oraback, for example. All the backup files go there. However, sometimes it may not be advisable to store everything on a single mount point. Some tape backup systems work more efficiently if the files are spread over multiple filesystems (or mount points), since they allow for parallel backup from all those mount points. If the files are on the same filesystem, the files are backed up to tape serially. In this case, it makes sense for RMAN to create the backup pieces on multiple filesystems. Usually you define as many channels as there are mount points. So, you can have mount points such as /oraback/loc1, /oraback/loc2, and so on. In our example script, we're assuming there are eight mount points: /oraback/loc1 through /oraback/loc8. Accordingly, we have configured eight channels.

We use three types of parameters in the script:

Fixed: The parameters that are fixed for a site. Examples of such parameters are the email addresses of DBAs, the name of the central log server, and so on. These parameters do not change from database to database.

DB specific: The parameters that change between databases. Examples are the Oracle SID, the Oracle Home, the type of the backup (full, incremental, and so on), and the media such as tape and disk.

Derived: The parameters that are derived from the previous two types of parameters. Examples are the location of the rman executable in the bin directory of Oracle Home, and so on. You don't need to change these parameters.

Table 9-1 shows a line-by-line explanation of the script.

Table 9-1. *Line-by-Line Explanation of the Unix Shell Script to Back Up via RMAN*

Line Number	Explanation
3	The Oracle Home for that database. Change for another database.
4	The SID of the database being backed up.
5	The location on the server where this script is executed.
6	The media where the backup is stored, such as tape or disk. This parameter is only for naming the log file, not for directing the target of the backup.
7	The type of backup, such as full or incremental. This is only for naming the log file. This parameter does not actually cause the backup to be full or otherwise.
8	The MAXPIECESIZE parameter for RMAN. This parameter in RMAN creates the backup pieces to be limited to a certain size, which is a limitation on some operating systems. The limit should be based on the database size as well. If your database is fairly small and you want to remove any limit, just specify a very high number. In this example, we have assumed a 16GB limit.
11	The backups will be made to /oraback/loc1 through /oraback/loc8.
12	The email that says where the successful notification should be sent.
13	The email that says where the failure email should be sent, usually a pager.
14	The server where the log files of each run are stored.
15	The user ID of the log server.
16	The directory where the logs are kept on the central log server.
17	The connection string for the catalog connection. Here we assume that your catalog database connect string is catalog and you have defined a separate catalog owner for each database, where the owner's name is the same as the SID of the database being backed up and the password is the same as the owner name. This is not absolutely necessary; you can have a common owner for catalogs of all databases. Whatever your decision is, update this parameter to reflect that.
19	The mount points where the backups will be taken have a common format, such as /oraback/loc<n>, where <n> varies from 1 to 8. The format is mentioned here.
20	The directory where the temporary file log file of the script is generated. Later this temp file and the RMAN log file are merged and sent out as the log file.
21	The date format that the time stamps in the RMAN log files are shown as.
22	The time stamp; the log files are generated in this name.
23–25	Various path variables that need to be there. Remember, this script is called from a cron job, so the user's profile is not executed, and no variables are set.
26	The log file name is constructed.
27	The temporary log file is created in this name. The parameter $$ indicates the PID in the shell script. Since the PID of each process is different, a different log file will be created each time.
31	Since we want to prevent the script from starting if it is running currently, we're using a lock file. At the beginning of each run, the script checks the lock file. If it is present, it indicates the script is running now, and the current run is aborted. At the end of the run, the script deletes the lock file.
32	We check whether the lock file exists. If it does, then the script is running, so we abort this run.

Continued

Table 9-1. *Continued*

Line Number	Explanation
35	If the lock file does not exist, we create one. The contents of the file do not matter, but we put the lines "Do NOT delete this file. Used for RMAN locking" in the file, just in case someone gets curious and opens this file. The message should be crystal clear.
36	We start the RMAN command. The `<< EOF` clause at the end of the line indicates that the RMAN executable should accept all the lines until the string `EOF` is encountered.
37	We connect to the target database.
38	We connect to the catalog.
39	When RMAN starts backing up the database, it must get an exclusive lock on the control file. Since that creates the disruption of the database, RMAN takes a snapshot of the control file and uses that. Here, in this line, we decide the snapshot control file location.
43–45	We allocate the first channel, specifying the format string so that the backups go there. We also specify `MAXPIECESIZE`, which determines how big each piece should be. Note the format string: `${LOC_PREFIX}1/${ORACLE_SID}_${BACKUP_TYPE}_${TIMESTAMP}_%p_%s.rman` The location of the file will be constructed as /oraback/loc1, a mount point.
46–66	We do the same for channels 2 through 8. They go to the mount points /oraback/loc2 through /oraback/loc8.
67–71	The actual backup command comes here. You can specify any RMAN command you want here.
72–79	The channels are explicitly released, a best practice.
80–83	We take an explicit backup of the current control file. Note that in line 69 we have included the control file as part of the backup, but the control file gets embedded in the backup pieces. If you have the catalog, it is simple to get the control file from the backup pieces. But imagine the worst-case scenario where the catalog is lost and so is the control file. It will be hard to locate the control file from the many backup piece files. Therefore, as a good practice, we take an explicit backup of the control file, which has a clearly identified name.
87	After we exit the RMAN command line, we capture the return code, $?.
88	We merge the RMAN log with the script log file.
89	We remove the lock file created earlier to indicate that the script has completed its run and a new script run may be started.
87	We check the status of the RMAN execution. 0 indicates successful execution.
91	If the script fails because of any reason, the return code will not be 0. The exact return code is immaterial; the cause of the error will be captured in the RMAN log file. The error is notified to the DBA's pager. The log file is sent to the pager and the DBA's email.
95	If the RMAN execution was successful, we copy the log file to one of the locations where the backups are generated. The tape backup software will pick it up from that location.
99–100	The log file is also copied to the central log server.
101	The temporary log file is removed.

The beauty of the solution script is that it's useful for any type of RMAN run—full, incremental, merge, archivelog, and so on; it also can be applied to any database on any server. All you have to do is to change the values of the parameters in the script to reflect the correct target.

9-2. Scheduling a Unix Shell File

Problem

You want to run a backup shell script using some Unix scheduler such as `cron`.

Solution

The `cron` utility in Unix is a built-in scheduler that can kick off any shell script at a certain time. You can decide a specific day to run a script, or you can repeatedly run a script based on weekday and time, such as every Monday at 8 a.m. You enable a shell script to be run from `cron` by placing a reference to it in the crontab file. The crontab file is a text file with one line per execution. The lines have several fields indicating the execution times, with each field separated by a space. Here is an example of a crontab file:

```
00 11 * * 0 /opt/oracle/tools/rman_full.disk.sh > /opt/oracle/tools/➥
rman_full.disk.log 2>&1
00 11 * * 0 /opt/oracle/tools/rman_arc.disk.sh > /opt/oracle/tools/➥
rman_arc.disk.log 2>&1
```

These two lines show the execution properties of two programs under the `cron` scheduler: rman_full.disk.sh and rman_arc.disk.sh. The lines have several fields separated by spaces. These fields denote the execution times. Table 9-2 later in the chapter describes the fields. In general, the fields are shown as follows:

```
<minute> <hour> <date> <month> <weekday> <program>
```

The `cron` tool then runs the <program> at <hour>:<minute> on the <date> of the <month>. If <weekday> is specified, the program is run on the weekday at that time. If any of these entries have an asterisk (*) in them, the asterisk is ignored.

Direct Editing of Crontab

To schedule a program via `cron`, you have two options. One is to directly edit the crontab entries. Here is the process to follow:

1. Issue the following Unix command:

   ```
   $ crontab -e
   ```

   This opens your crontab file in the vi editor. If you don't have any entry yet in crontab, you will see an empty file. Place whatever line you want in the file. Be sure to adhere to the format described in Table 9-2 later in this chapter.

2. Save the file and exit. The line is now scheduled in crontab.

3. Check `cron` for all scheduled programs:

   ```
   $ crontab -l
   ```

This should show the line you just placed in addition to all the other `cron` entries.

Updating Crontab

Instead of directly editing the crontab entries, you can edit a different file and then replace the crontab entries with the contents of that file. Here are the steps to follow:

1. Put the contents of crontab in a temporary file by issuing this Unix command:

   ```
   $ crontab -l > crontab.txt
   ```

   This creates a text file—crontab.txt—with all the cron entries.

2. Open the file crontab.txt using vi or any other editor, and place the line you want to add there. Save this file. Remember this file does not constitute the actual crontab file.

3. Replace the system crontab entries with the contents of the temporary file by issuing the following Unix command:

   ```
   $ crontab crontab.txt
   ```

The crontab file now mirrors the contents of the temporary file.

Both ways of adding a line to crontab—editing directly and editing a work file—do the same thing, but the second option might be less risky. If you make a mistake—even a small typo—while editing the system crontab, it could be a problem. The second approach does not let the crontab entries be replaced if an error is encountered. In addition, you have a backup of the crontab entries as a text file.

Examples of Crontab Schedules

Here are several examples of scheduling times for running a program named rman.sh.

- To schedule the program to run at 10:23 p.m. every night, use the following line:

  ```
  23 22 * * * rman.sh
  ```

  Note how the date, month, and weekday entries are *, indicating that they do not matter; this should be run every day.

- To schedule it at 10:23 p.m. every Friday and Sunday, use this:

  ```
  23 22 * * 5,7 rman.sh
  ```

- To schedule it at 10:23 p.m. on March 10, use this:

  ```
  23 22 10 03 * rman.sh
  ```

- To schedule it at 10:23 p.m. on the 10th of each month, use this:

  ```
  23 22 10 * * rman.sh
  ```

- To schedule it at 10 minutes past every hour on Sunday, use this:

  ```
  10 * * * 0 rman.sh
  ```

- To schedule it every 15 minutes every day, use this:

  ```
  0,15,30,45 * * * * rman.sh
  ```

How It Works

One of the problems of cron jobs is that they are executed in background, so any output from them does not go to the screen. You must capture the output in some log file. To facilitate that, in the actual task name, you can use a notation like this:

```
<command> > log.log 2>&1
```

This notation uses two special output *streams*, 1 and 2, for standard *output* and standard *error*, respectively. The output of the command that generally goes to the screen is shown as standard output, and any error messages go to standard error. Here the standard output is redirected by the > character to the file log.log. The notation 2>&1 means that the output of standard error (denoted by 2) is being redirected to 1 (standard output), which in turn goes to the file log.log too. So, this way, all the output from the <command > can be captured in the file log.log.

Table 9-2 describes the fields of crontab entries in detail. Remember that fields are delimited from each other by whitespace (space characters, tabs, and the like).

Table 9-2. *Crontab Entries*

Field Position	Example	Description
1	20	Shows the minute of the time component. You can place multiple values here, such as 10,20,30 to execute at the 10th, 20th, and 30th minute. You can also specify a range such as 10-12 to denote the 10th, 11th, and 12th minutes.
2	12	Shows the hour of the time component in 24-hour format. For instance, to set something for 1:23 p.m., you will place 13 in this field and 23 in the minutes field (the first field). Like the minutes, you can place a range here as well. If you place an asterisk on this field, the task is executed every hour, on that minute. For instance, if fields 1 and 2 are 20 and *, the task executes every 20 minutes of every hour.
3	25	Date when this task is run, 25th in this case. An asterisk in this field means every day.
4	12	Month when the task will run. In this example, it will run on December 25. An asterisk in this field means every month on that date, shown in field 3.
4	3	Weekday, starting with 0 for Sunday. So, 3 means it will execute on Wednesday.
5	myrman.sh	The actual task name.

9-3. Developing a Windows Batch File to Run RMAN

Problem

You want to develop a Windows batch file to kick off RMAN to back up the database on a Windows server.

Solution

A batch file in Windows to script RMAN commands is similar in concept to a shell script in Unix, but you need to shift directions. In the Unix script, you used the RMAN commands inline in the script. In Windows, you will use a slightly different approach, as shown here:

1. Create a RMAN command file with all the parameters you want.

2. Call the command file from the RMAN command line.

The batch file needs some utilities outside what are available in Windows:

- A utility to get the date and time in the format you want; here we have used a tool called `realdate`. We give a source for this utility in the "How It Works" section.

- A utility to send email; here we use a tool called `bmail`. Again, see "How It Works" for where to find this utility.

Here are the steps for creating a batch file:

1. Check whether `realdate` is installed. If not, install `realdate`.

2. Install `bmail`. Again, see "How It Works" for the source of this utility.

3. Prepare the batch file as shown in the upcoming code. Please note that the lines are preceded by line numbers for easy explanation; they do not actually appear in the code.

4. Schedule the batch file for execution via any scheduler such as Windows Scheduler or the at command (described in recipe 9-6).

The following is a Windows batch file to create a full RMAN backup of a database running on Windows. This batch file will accept parameters to back up any database in any server, connecting to any catalog and to any media; after the backup, it will check for errors and email the DBA on completion or send an email to a pager in case of failure.

```
1. @ECHO OFF
2. :: Beginning of Script
3. :: Start of Configurable Section
4. set ORACLE_HOME=C:\oracle\product\10.2\db_1
5. set ORACLE_SID=MOBDB10
6. set TOOLHOME=C:\TOOLS
7. set BACKUP_MEDIA=DISK
8. set BACKUP_TYPE=FULL_DB_BKUP
9. set MAXPIECESIZE=16G
10. set BACKUP_MOUNTPOINT=c:\oracle\flash
11. set DBAEMAIL="dbas@proligence.com"
12. set DBAPAGER="dba.ops@proligence.com"
13. set CATALOG_CONN=%ORACLE_SID%/%ORACLE_SID%@catalog
14. set MS=mail.proligence.com
15. ::
16. :: end of Configurable Section
17. ::
```

```
18. set BACKUP_LOC_PREFIX=%BACKUP_MOUNTPOINT%\loc
19. set TMPDIR=C:\temp
20. set NLS_DATE_FORMAT="MM/DD/YY HH24:MI:SS"
21. realdate /d /s="set curdate=" > %TOOLHOME%\tmp_dt.bat
22. realdate /t /s="set curtime=" > %TOOLHOME%\tmp_tm.bat
23. call %TOOLHOME%\tmp_dt.bat
24. call %TOOLHOME%\tmp_tm.bat
25. ::
26. ::
27. set LOG=%TOOLHOME%\%ORACLE_SID%_%BACKUP_TYPE%_%BACKUP_MEDIA% ➥
%CURDATE%_%CURTIME%.log
28. set TMPLOG=%TOOLHOME%\tmplog.$$
29. ::
30. :: Build the Command File
31. set FORMATSTRING=%BACKUP_LOC_PREFIX%1\%ORACLE_SID%_%%u_%%p.rman
32. set CMDFILE=%TOOLHOME%\%ORACLE_SID%.rman
33. echo run { > %CMDFILE%
34. echo   allocate channel c1 type disk >> %CMDFILE%
35. echo     format '%FORMATSTRING%' >> %CMDFILE%
36. echo     maxpiecesize %MAXPIECESIZE%; >> %CMDFILE%
37. echo   backup >> %CMDFILE%
38. echo     tablespace users; >> %CMDFILE%
39. echo   release channel c1; >> %CMDFILE%
40. echo } >> %CMDFILE%
41. :: End of Command File Generation
42. ::
43. echo Starting the script > %LOG%
44. %ORACLE_HOME%\bin\rman target=/ catalog=%CATALOG_CONN% @%CMDFILE% ➥
msglog=%TMPLOG%
45. ::
46. :: Merge the Logfiles
47. type %TMPLOG% >> %LOG%
48. :: Check for errors
49. ::
50. echo THE OUTPUT WAS %ERRORLEVEL% >> %LOG%
51. findstr /i "error" %LOG%
52. if errorlevel 0 if not errorlevel 1 bmail -s %MS%  -t %DBAPAGER% ➥
-f "Database" -m %LOG%
53. @echo on
```

How It Works

The program realdate is freely available at http://www.huweb.hu/maques/realdate.htm. The program bmail is freely available at http://www.beyondlogic.org/solutions/cmdlinemail/cmdlinemail.htm. This page also details its usage.

Table 9-3 gives a line-by-line explanation of the solution batch file.

Table 9-3. *Line-by-Line Explanation of the Batch File*

Lines	Description
1	This line instructs the batch program executer to stop displaying the commands in the file; just execute them.
4	We set the Oracle Home.
5	We set the Oracle SID.
6	We set the location of this batch file.
7	We specify the type of the backup, such as disk, tape, and so on. Please note that specifying a type here merely places the type in the name of the log file; it does not impact the type of the backup created by this batch file. The RMAN backup commands in the batch file determine the nature of the backup created.
8	We specify the type of backup, such as full or incremental, so that it becomes part of the name of the log file.
9	The MAXPIECESIZE for the backup is specified here.
10	The variables that hold the location of the backup.
11–12	The email addresses where an email will be sent.
13	The catalog connection string. In this script, we have assumed that the rman repository username is the ORACLE_SID and the password is the same as the username.
14	The mail server name. You can ask your email administrator for this. In many small and medium organizations, this may be mail.organization.com.
21	We want to create a log file whose name should have the current date and time. The standard Windows date command does not easily yield a usable form of the date to be used in the log file, as is the case with the time component. Here we have used a special program called realdate. More information about realdate is provided following the table. In this line, we have extracted the current date and issued the command to set a variable curdate to hold the current date. For instance, if this program is executed on February 1, 2007, the command realdate /d /s="set curdate=" returns set curdate=20070201. This line is placed in the file tmp_dt.bat.
22	We again use realdate to extract the current time. For instance, if the program is executed at 11:15:53 p.m., the command realdate /t /s="set curtime=" yields set curtime=231553. This line places that string in the file tmp_tm.bat.
23–24	We execute the batch files we generated in the previous two lines. These set the variables curdate and curtime.
27	We set the name of the log file.
28	We create a temporary log file to hold the output of the RMAN commands.
31	We create a variable called FORMATSTRING for the name of the backup piece.
32	We create a variable called CMDFILE to hold the name of the command file that will be passed to RMAN.
33–40	We put all the RMAN commands to be executed later in the command file.
44	We call the RMAN to execute the command file created dynamically in lines 33–40. The output goes to the log file named in line 28.
47	Now that we have the output of the RMAN output, we place the contents of that RMAN log file to the main log file we have been using.
50	We place the result of the RMAN run, as captured in the variable ERRORLEVEL. If the RMAN run was successful, this variable will be 0. The result will be in the log file.
51	If there is any error, the log file will contain that error. This line shows how to use the findstr command to find out whether the log file contains the word *error* in either uppercase or lowercase.
52	If the error was found, the errorlevel variable will be nonzero, and we want to email the log file to the email address specified in the variable DBAPAGER. To send the email, we have used a program called bmail, which is described next.

After running the batch file, a log file is produced whose name is in the format <DbName>_<BackupType>_<What'sBeingBackedUp>_BKUP_<Target>_<Date>_<Time>.log. Here are the contents of the file after a test run on one of our own systems:

```
C:\TOOLS>type MOBDB10_FULL_DB_BKUP_DISK_20070201_234326.log
Starting the script

Recovery Manager: Release 10.2.0.1.0 - Production on Thu Feb 1 23:43:27 2007

Copyright (c) 1982, 2005, Oracle.  All rights reserved.

connected to target database: MOBDB10 (DBID=358194812)

RMAN> run {
2>  allocate channel c1 type disk
3>    format 'c:\oracle\flash\loc1\MOBDB10_%u_%p.rman'
4>    maxpiecesize 16G;
5>  backup
6>    tablespace users;
7>  release channel c1;
8> }
9>
using target database control file instead of recovery catalog
allocated channel: c1
channel c1: sid=133 devtype=DISK

Starting backup at MM/DD/YY HH24:MI:SS
channel c1: starting full datafile backupset
channel c1: specifying datafile(s) in backupset
input datafile fno=00004 name=C:\ORACLE\ORADATA\MOBDB10\USERS01.DBF
channel c1: starting piece 1 at MM/DD/YY HH24:MI:SS
channel c1: finished piece 1 at MM/DD/YY HH24:MI:SS
piece handle=C:\ORACLE\FLASH\LOC1\MOBDB10_0CI90LHF_1.RMAN ➡
tag=TAG20070201T234342 comment=NONE
channel c1: backup set complete, elapsed time: 00:00:03
Finished backup at MM/DD/YY HH24:MI:SS

released channel: c1

Recovery Manager complete.
THE OUTPUT WAS 0
```

The log file shows the RMAN command file as well, which confirms the actual command run.

9-4. Scheduling a Script in Windows via the GUI

Problem

You want to schedule a batch file or script in Windows to create a backup using the graphical user interface.

Solution

The Windows operating system has a task-scheduling interface that can be used to schedule tasks such as an RMAN backup. Here are the steps to follow:

1. Click Start ➤ Control Panel ➤ Scheduled Tasks ➤ Add a Scheduled Task. This opens the wizard shown in Figure 9-1.

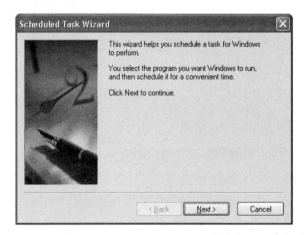

Figure 9-1. *Adding a scheduled task*

2. Click Next. This takes you to the page shown in Figure 9-2. Click the Browse button, and select the batch file you created earlier in recipe 9-3.

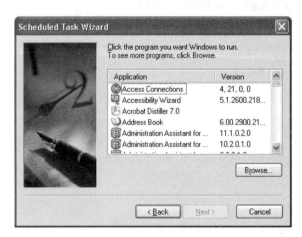

Figure 9-2. *Choosing a program to add to the scheduled tasks*

3. The next page of the wizard, shown in the Figure 9-3, allows you to enter the schedule. Choose one of the options: Daily, Weekly, and so on.

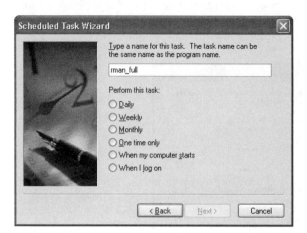

Figure 9-3. *Choosing the batch file and the schedule*

4. The next page allows you to enter the time of execution, as shown in Figure 9-4. On the same page, choose how often the program should be executed, what days the task should run, and so on.

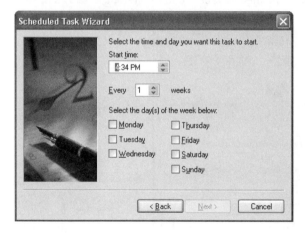

Figure 9-4. *Entering the time of execution*

5. The next page, shown in Figure 9-5, asks you to enter the user ID and password of the user who will run this task. The user ID can be the same as your usual login; otherwise, you can use a special user created just for this. In this example, we have assumed the user `oracle` will perform the backups and run the task. Enter the password of the user here, as shown in Figure 9-5.

Figure 9-5. *Specifying the user ID and password used to run the scheduled task*

6. When you click the Next button, the task is added to the system, as shown in Figure 9-6.

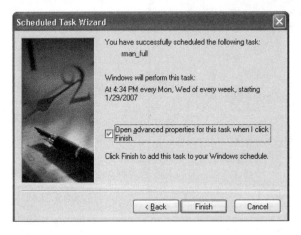

Figure 9-6. *Completion of the task addition*

That's it; the task is now scheduled.

How It Works

The Windows Task Scheduler provides a fairly straightforward way to configure scheduled jobs. The steps are self-explanatory.

Windows also provides for a way to schedule jobs via the command line. To learn how, see recipe 9-6.

9-5. Changing the Schedule of a Batch Job in the Task Scheduler

Problem

You want to change the schedule and/or other attributes of a scheduled RMAN batch job in Windows using the Task Scheduler.

Solution

In recipe 9-4, you learned how to schedule a job using the graphical Task Scheduler. That interface also lets you modify jobs. Figure 9-7 shows how to arrive at the menu item to modify the task rman_full from the Windows Start button.

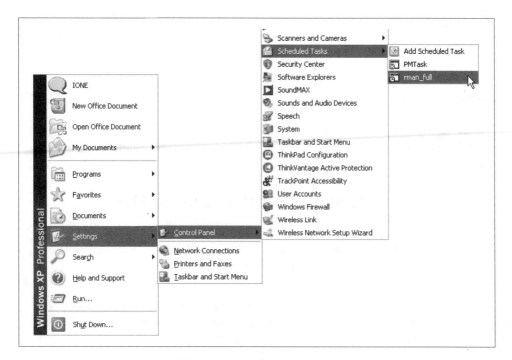

Figure 9-7. *Choosing the scheduled tasks*

From the resulting dialog box, you can change all the attributes of the job, such as the time and date of execution, the user and password being logged in as, and so on.

How It Works

When you select the RMAN job in the menu, you'll see the dialog box shown in Figure 9-8.

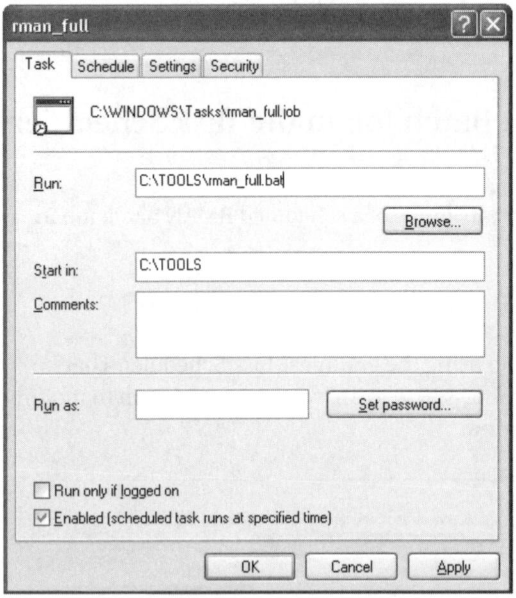

Figure 9-8. *The Task tab*

On the Task tab, you can change the advanced settings such as the password of the user who runs it and so on. We recommend you take full advantage of the Comments field to describe the purpose of this task and the expected output.

9-6. Scheduling in Windows from the Command Line

Problem

You want to schedule a task in Windows from the command line, without using the GUI.

Solution

The solution is to use a tool called at in Windows. This tool is Windows' equivalent of Unix's cron. You can schedule, display, and delete tasks using this tool. Here are some specific examples showing how to use at to schedule and manage recurring tasks:

- To schedule a batch file called rman_full.bat in the C:\TOOLS directory to be run every Tuesday and Thursday at 1:23 p.m., issue the following command from the command line:

```
C:\TOOLS>at 13:23 every:T,Th c:\tools\rman_full
Added a new job with job ID = 1
```

The command added a scheduled task with job ID 1.

- If you want the schedule to be every 1st and 2nd of the month, instead of a day of the week, put the dates after the every: parameter, as shown here:

```
C:\TOOLS>at 13:23 every:1,2 c:\tools\rman_inc
Added a new job with job ID = 2
```

This command added a new task with ID of 2.

- If you want to check how many tasks have been added, just issue the at command without any parameter:

```
C:\TOOLS>at
Status ID   Day                 Time              Command Line
-------------------------------------------------------------------------
        1   Today               1:23 PM           every:T,Th c:\tools\rman_full
        2   Today               1:23 PM           every:1,2 c:\tools\rman_inc
```

You can also examine the scheduled tasks in the Control Panel menu, as shown in recipe 9-5.

- To delete a task—say, ID 1—issue the following command:

```
C:\TOOLS>at 1 /delete
```

- To delete all tasks, issue the following command:

```
C:\TOOLS>at /delete
```

Windows will ask you for a confirmation:

```
This operation will delete all scheduled jobs.
Do you want to continue this operation? (Y/N) [N]:
```

Enter Y to delete all tasks.

How It Works

For a more complete description of the at command, see Microsoft Knowledge Base article 313565 at http://support.microsoft.com/kb/313565/en-us.

The end results of both the at command and the scheduler are the same, so there is no specific reason to choose one over the other. The choice is primarily whether you prefer using a GUI tool or a command-line tool. Another consideration is how these schedules are set up. If you want to schedule a lot of similar programs, such as backing up several tablespaces through one per script, the at command is far better than the scheduler because you can type them pretty fast.

9-7. Creating Local-Stored Scripts

Problem

You want to store often-used scripts in the RMAN catalog and call them whenever needed as local scripts. You are not worried about executing such scripts against any database other than the original target database.

Solution

A script you create, by default, can be used only against the target database against which it was created; that is why it's called a *local script*. A stored script is stored in the catalog, not in the control file of the target database. So, to create a stored script, a catalog connection is necessary. Here are the steps to create a stored script:

1. Connect to the RMAN target database and catalog:

   ```
   $ rman target=/  catalog=rman/<PasswordOfRep>@catalog

   Recovery Manager: Release 10.2.0.1.0 - Production on Mon Jan 29 18:09:50 2007

   Copyright (c) 1982, 2005, Oracle.  All rights reserved.

   connected to target database: MOBDB10 (DBID=358194812)
   connected to recovery catalog database
   ```

2. Create the stored script by enclosing it within curly braces. Here is a script named full_disk_db to create a full backup of the database (including the control file) to the disk:

   ```
   RMAN> create script full_disk_db
   2> {
   3>     allocate channel c1 type disk
   4>         format 'c:\oracle\flash\loc1\rman_%U.rman';
   5>     backup
   6>         database
   7>         include current controlfile;
   8>     release channel c1;
   9> }
   created script full_disk_db
   RMAN>
   ```

   The script is now created and stored in the catalog database.

   Once you've created a stored script, you can invoke it from the RMAN command prompt as shown at the beginning of the chapter.

How It Works

Stored scripts are stored in the catalog database, not on a filesystem. After executing the create script command in RMAN, the result came back as follows:

```
created script full_disk_db
```

This output assures you that the script was created successfully. Had there been some issue while creating the script, the output would have been an error message. For instance, imagine that while typing you made a mistake in line 8, as shown here:

```
RMAN> create script full_db_bkup
2> {
```

```
3>    allocate channel c1 type disk
4>        format 'c:\oracle\flash\loc1\rman_%U.rman';
5>    backup
6>        database
7>        include current controlfile;
8>    release c1;
```

Note the syntax error in line 8, release c1, instead of release channel c1. The moment you press Enter, RMAN immediately comes back with the following error message:

```
RMAN-00571: ===========================================================
RMAN-00569: =============== ERROR MESSAGE STACK FOLLOWS ===============
RMAN-00571: ===========================================================
RMAN-00558: error encountered while parsing input commands
RMAN-01009: syntax error: found "identifier": expecting one of: "channel"
RMAN-01008: the bad identifier was: c1
RMAN-01007: at line 8 column 9 file: standard input

RMAN-00571: ===========================================================
RMAN-00569: =============== ERROR MESSAGE STACK FOLLOWS ===============
RMAN-00571: ===========================================================
RMAN-00558: error encountered while parsing input commands
RMAN-01009: syntax error: found ";": expecting one of: "allocate, alter, ➥
backup, beginline, blockrecover, catalog, change, connect,
copy, convert, create, crosscheck, configure, duplicate, debug, delete, drop, ➥
exit, endinline, flashback, host, {, library, list,
mount, open, print, quit, recover, register, release, replace, report, ➥
renormalize, reset, restore, resync, rman, run, rpctest, set,
setlimit, sql, switch, spool, startup, shutdown, send, show, test, transport, ➥
upgrade, unregister, validate"
RMAN-01007: at line 8 column 11 file: standard input
```

There are some restrictions on the stored scripts. For example, you can't create the stored scripts within another stored script; they can be created only at the RMAN prompt. If you try to create a script within a script, as shown here, then RMAN throws an error immediately:

```
RMAN> create script parent
2> {
3>    create script child
```

You can't go far:

```
RMAN-00571: ===========================================================
RMAN-00569: =============== ERROR MESSAGE STACK FOLLOWS ===============
RMAN-00571: ===========================================================
RMAN-00558: error encountered while parsing input commands
RMAN-01009: syntax error: found "create": expecting one of: "allocate, alter, ➥
backup, beginline, blockrecover, catalog, change, copy
, convert, crosscheck, configure, duplicate, debug, delete, execute, endinline, ➥
flashback, host, mount, open, plsql, recover,
```

```
release, replicate, report, restore, resync, set, setlimit, sql, switch, startup, ➥
shutdown, send, show, transport, validate"
RMAN-01007: at line 3 column 1 file: standard input
```

The run command can't be used within the script.

```
RMAN> create script myscript
2> {
3>   run
```

RMAN immediately throws an error:

```
RMAN-00571: ============================================================
RMAN-00569: =============== ERROR MESSAGE STACK FOLLOWS ===============
RMAN-00571: ============================================================
RMAN-00558: error encountered while parsing input commands
RMAN-01009: syntax error: found "run": expecting one of: "allocate, alter, ➥
backup, beginline, blockrecover, catalog, change, copy,
convert, crosscheck, configure, duplicate, debug, delete, execute, endinline, ➥
flashback, host, mount, open, plsql, recover, release,
replicate, report, restore, resync, set, setlimit, sql, switch, startup, ➥
shutdown, send, show, transport, validate"
RMAN-01007: at line 3 column 1 file: standard input
```

The @ and @@ commands, which are the equivalent of run, also can't be put in a script.

9-8. Creating a Global-Stored Script

Problem

You want to create a global-stored script that can be called for any target database.

Solution

Stored scripts are stored in the catalog database, and you can call them by name when you want to execute. Here is the RMAN command segment to create a global script called gs_arc_disk_bkup:

```
RMAN> create global script gs_arc_disk_bkup
2> comment 'Global Script to Backup Arc Logs Delete Input'
3> {
4>    allocate channel c1 type disk
5>        format 'C:\oraback\%U.rman';
6>    backup
7>        archivelog
8>        all
9>        delete input;
10>   release channel c1;
11> }

created global script gs_arc_disk_bkup
```

Note that the syntax to create a global script is the same as a local script with one exception—the presence of the clause global before the script keyword.

How It Works

Global scripts are available to more than just the target database to which you were originally connected. After a global script is created, you can connect to any target database and execute the script. So, a natural question is, when is a global script beneficial?

A global script, as the name implies, lets you write once and execute anywhere. So, there is the biggest benefit. You do not need to write scripts for each database, and thus you save on coding and QA costs.

On the other hand, a one-size-fits-all script may not be possible or desirable in all cases. For instance, consider a full backup script. The parameters such as MAXPIECESIZE, and so on, will be different for each database, obviating the usefulness of a single global script.

So, when are these global scripts really useful? Generic, repetitive, non-database-dependent activities are the most suitable for global scripts. Common examples are listing or deleting archivelogs, cross-checking backups, and subsequently deleting expired backups.

Note The restrictions that apply to local scripts apply to local ones as well. These restrictions are described in the "How It Works" section of recipe 9-7.

9-9. Updating Stored Scripts

Problem

You want to update a stored script, one that you've stored in a recovery catalog, with new code.

Solution

There is no concept of a line-by-line update to a stored script. You have to replace the entire stored script with a new code. To update a script, issue the replace script command followed by new code that you want for the script, as shown here:

```
RMAN> replace script full_disk_db
2> {
3>    allocate channel c1 type disk
4>        format 'c:\backup\rman_%U.rman';
5>    backup
6>       database
7>       include current controlfile;
8>    release channel c1;
9> }

replaced script full_disk_db
```

The script is now replaced by the new code. Remember, you have to replace the entire script.

How It Works

The replace script action essentially re-creates the same script. Therefore, the same restrictions applicable to creating a script apply here too. Check the "How It Works" section of recipe 9-7 to learn about those restrictions.

The replace script command replaces the script in the catalog without leaving a copy behind in some manner. This may not be acceptable to you. You may want to get a copy of the script, and edit that, while the older version of the copy serves as a backup. See recipe 9-16 on how to accomplish that.

9-10. Commenting on Stored Scripts

Problem

You want to save a comment along with a stored script so you have something to help you remember what that script does when you return to it potentially months later.

Solution

To associate a comment with a script, use the optional comment clause in the command to create (or to replace) that script. Enclose your comment within single quotes, as shown here:

```
RMAN> create script full_disk_db
2> comment 'Full Backup as Backupset to Disk'
3> {
4>    allocate channel c1 type disk
5>        format 'c:\backup\rman_%U.rman';
6>    backup
7>        database
8>        include current controlfile;
9>    release channel c1;
10> }

created script full_disk_db
```

How It Works

Comments help describe the scripts more clearly than just the names you give them. The comments appear when you display or list the scripts, which amounts to a sort of metadata of the scripts.

There is no way to add a comment to an existing script. Instead, you will need to re-create the script using the replace command, as shown here:

```
RMAN> replace script full_disk_db
2> comment 'New Full Backup as Backupset to Disk'
3> {
... and so on ...
```

9-11. Displaying Stored Scripts

Problem

You want to display the code of a script stored in the catalog database.

Solution

The print script command displays the code of the script, as shown here:

```
RMAN> print script full_disk_db;
```

The output, in this case, comes back as follows:

```
printing stored script: full_disk_db
 {allocate channel c1 type disk
format 'c:\backup\rman_%U.rman';
backup
database
include current controlfile;
release channel c1;
}
```

If there are two scripts of the same name—one local and the other global—then the print script command shown earlier displays the *local* script, not the global one. If you want to display the global script, use the global keyword before the word script, as shown here:

```
RMAN> print global script full_disk_db;
```

How It Works

How the print command works should be fairly obvious. It's worth talking a bit, though, about script names having unusual characters. Usually, there are no quotes around script names. However, quotes are necessary when the following is true:

- A script name starts with a number.

- A script name contains a reserved word, such as backupset.

- A script name is in mixed case.

Suppose you have a script called 1ClickBackup and you want to display the contents. Use double quotes around the script name:

```
RMAN> print script "1ClickBackup";

printing stored script: 1ClickBackup
 {allocate channel c1 type disk
format 'c:\oracle\flash\loc1\rman_%U.rman';
backup
database include current controlfile;
release channel c1;
}
```

Note if you make a typo in the script name, say by capitalizing the letter *A*, as shown here:

```
RMAN> print script "1clickBAckup";
```

then RMAN immediately comes back with an error:

```
RMAN-00571: ===========================================================
RMAN-00569: =============== ERROR MESSAGE STACK FOLLOWS ===============
RMAN-00571: ===========================================================
RMAN-06004: ORACLE error from recovery catalog database: RMAN-20400: stored ➡
script not found
RMAN-06083: error when loading stored script 1clickBAckup
```

The names 1ClickBackup and 1ClickBAckup are not the same; the letter *A* is capitalized in the latter.

9-12. Listing Stored Scripts

Problem

You want to display a list of stored scripts in the catalog database.

Solution

The list script names command lists all the scripts in the database. For example:

```
RMAN> list script names;
```

The output comes back as follows:

```
List of Stored Scripts in Recovery Catalog


    Scripts of Target Database MOBDB10

        Script Name
        Description
        -----------------------------------------------------------------------
        full_disk_db
        Full Backup as Backupset to Disk


    Global Scripts

        Script Name
        Description
        -----------------------------------------------------------------------
        gs_arc_disk_bkup
        Global Script to Backup Arc Logs Delete Input
```

How It Works

The list script names command simply lists the scripts you've saved to your catalog database. The comments of each script, if available, are displayed in the Description column.

The command list script names shows both local and global scripts. If you want to list only global scripts, use the global keyword before the word script:

```
RMAN> list global script names;

List of Stored Scripts in Recovery Catalog


    Global Scripts


        Script Name
        Description
        -------------------------------------------------------------------------
        gs_arc_disk_bkup
        Global Script to Backup Arc Logs Delete Input
```

If you want to find out the global scripts and the local scripts of all the databases using the recovery catalog, you merely use the all qualifier before the script keyword:

```
RMAN> list all script names;
```

9-13. Dropping Stored Scripts

Problem

You want to drop a stored script from the catalog database.

Solution

The RMAN command delete script drops the script from the catalog database. Here is how you drop a script named delete_arc_logs:

```
RMAN> delete script delete_arc_logs;

deleted script: delete_arc_logs
RMAN>
```

How It Works

If you want to drop a script with some special name, such as a number at the beginning of the name or a reserved word, you need to enclose the name in quotes, as shown here:

```
RMAN> delete script "1stDelete";
```

If you have two scripts—one local and one global—in the same name, then the `delete script` command drops the local one, not the global one. If you want to drop the global script, you must use the keyword `global` in the command, as shown here:

```
RMAN> delete global script delete_arc_logs;

deleted global script: delete_arc_logs
RMAN>
```

9-14. Executing a Global Script When a Local Script of the Same Name Exists

Problem

You have two scripts of the same name—`delete_arc_logs`—one local and one global. You want to execute the global script, not the local one.

Solution

To execute the global script, you call that script with the clause `global` before it, as shown in the following RMAN command:

```
RMAN> run { execute global script delete_arc_logs; }
```

The output is as follows:

```
executing global script: delete_arc_logs

allocated channel: ORA_DISK_1
channel ORA_DISK_1: sid=141 devtype=DISK

List of Archived Log Copies
Key     Thrd Seq    S Low Time            Name
------- ---- ------- - ------------------- ----
116     1    40      A MM/DD/YY HH24:MI:SS ➥
C:\FLASH\MOBDB10\ARCHIVELOG\2007_01_22\O1_MF_1_40_2V9VWM6T_.ARC
... and so on ...
```

The global script has now executed.

How It Works

When you call a script as follows:

```
RMAN> run { execute script delete_arc_logs; }
```

the *local* script is executed, if there is a local script. RMAN looks for a local script first and executes that if it is found. Only if no local script exists will RMAN then go on to execute the global script. That is the default behavior. You can, however, add the clause `global` before the word `script` to make RMAN execute a global script no matter what.

9-15. Converting Stored Scripts to Files

Problem

You want to convert a stored script in the catalog database to an operating system file.

Solution

The print script command shown in recipe 9-11 has a clause to redirect the output to a file. If you want to store the code in the script delete_arc_logs in the file c:\tools\delete_arc_logs.rman, issue the following command:

```
RMAN> print script delete_arc_logs to file 'c:\tools\delete_arc_logs.rman';

script delete_arc_logs written to file c:\tools\delete_arc_logs.rman

RMAN>
```

This generates a file named delete_arc_logs.rman in the C:\TOOLS directory.

How It Works

Generating files from stored scripts is a good way to protect scripts. You can store the scripts on local filesystems as backups against the catalog database. The generated files also are handy while transferring scripts from one database to another. You will learn how to do the reverse—create a script from a file—in recipe 9-16.

The generated file looks exactly like the code in the script. Here is what the contents of the file look like:

```
{ delete noprompt archivelog all; }
```

However, this file by itself cannot be called from the command line of RMAN directly:

```
RMAN> @delete_arc_logs.rman
RMAN-00571: =============================================================
RMAN-00569: =============== ERROR MESSAGE STACK FOLLOWS ===============
RMAN-00571: =============================================================
RMAN-00558: error encountered while parsing input commands
RMAN-01009: syntax error: found ";": expecting one of: "exit"
RMAN-01007: at line 2 column 1 file: standard input
```

So, you need to edit the file to remove the curly braces or put a run keyword before the first curly brace:

```
RMAN> run { delete noprompt archivelog all; }
```

9-16. Creating or Replacing a Stored Script from a File

Problem

You want to create a script from an operating system file generated from a script earlier.

Solution

You can use the `create script` command with a special `from file` option. To create a script from the named file, issue the following RMAN command:

```
RMAN> create script delete_arc_logs from file 'c:\tools\delete_arc_logs.rman';

script commands will be loaded from file c:\tools\delete_arc_logs.rman
created script delete_arc_logs

RMAN>
```

This creates the stored script.

How It Works

This is an excellent way to back up and restore the stored scripts outside the database. In recipe 9-15, you learned how to create a file from a stored script. In this recipe, you learned how to create a stored script from the same file. The approach is also useful when you want to move a stored script from one database to another.

If you want to replace an *existing* stored script, you issue a modified version of the `replace` command, as shown here:

```
RMAN> replace script delete_arc_logs from file 'c:\tools\delete_arc_logs.rman';

script commands will be loaded from file c:\tools\delete_arc_logs.rman
replaced script delete_arc_logs
RMAN>
```

This replaces the script `delete_arc_logs` with the contents of the file.

9-17. Passing Parameters to Stored Scripts

Problem

You want to create a script that can accept parameters during runtime.

Solution

In Oracle Database 11g, the RMAN scripts can accept parameters. This applies to both the command file scripts and the stored scripts. To make the stored script `delete_archive_log` accept a parameter—the log sequence number—you create the script as shown here:

```
RMAN> replace script delete_archive_log { delete noprompt archivelog sequence &1 ; }
```

Note the &1 at the end. This is a placeholder for the parameter. When you execute the command, you may get a message such as the following asking you to enter a value of parameter 1. Enter any number; this does not actually execute the command.

```
Enter value for 1: 1
created script delete_archive_log
```

You can call this script to delete the archived redo log sequence 36, as shown here:

```
RMAN> run {execute script delete_archive_log using 36; }

executing script: delete_archive_log

released channel: ORA_DISK_1
allocated channel: ORA_DISK_1
channel ORA_DISK_1: SID=135 device type=DISK
List of Archived Log Copies for database with db_unique_name MOBDB11
=====================================================================

Key     Thrd Seq     S Low Time
------- ---- ------- - ---------
72      1    36      A 11-MAY-07
        Name: C:\ORACLE\FLASH\MOBDB11\ARCHIVELOG\2007_05_11\O1_MF_1_36_348WK31G_.ARC

deleted archived log
archived log file name=C:\ORACLE\FLASH\MOBDB11\ARCHIVELOG\2007_05_11\O1_MF_1_36_➡
348WK31G_.ARC RECID=1 STAMP=622287588
Deleted 1 objects
```

Similarly, to delete archived redo log sequence number 132, you will need to call the same script with the parameter 132.

How It Works

The parameterized stored scripts work with positional parameters the same way SQL*Plus does. The parameters are named &1, &2, and so on, relating to their relative positions.

If you need to pass a character value to a parameter, you should use single quotes around the value passed. Here is how you can create a script that expects a character argument:

```
RMAN> replace script delete_archive_log { delete &2 archivelog sequence &1 ; }

Enter value for 2: noprompt

Enter value for 1: 1

replaced script delete_archive_log
```

Now you can call this stored script as follows:

```
RMAN> run {execute script delete_archive_log using 36 'noprompt'; }

executing script: delete_archive_log
... and so on ...
```

If you have a need to replace the part of a string with the value of the parameter, you can use a period to separate the name from the value passed. For instance, if you want to delete archived redo logs matching a pattern, you can create the script as follows:

```
RMAN> create script del_arc_log_pattern {
2> delete archivelog like '%&1.%'; }

Enter value for 1: a

created script del_arc_log_pattern
```

Note how the pattern has been specified as %&1.%. The second % character is separated from the &1 by a period. Now, to delete the archived redo logs with the string 2007_05_11 in them, you can call the script as follows:

```
RMAN> run {execute script del_arc_log_pattern using '2007_05_11'; }

executing script: del_arc_log_pattern

released channel: ORA_DISK_1
allocated channel: ORA_DISK_1
channel ORA_DISK_1: SID=134 device type=DISK
List of Archived Log Copies for database with db_unique_name MOBDB11
======================================================================

Key     Thrd Seq     S Low Time
------- ---- ------- - ---------
75      1    38       A 11-MAY-07
        Name: C:\ORACLE\FLASH\MOBDB11\ARCHIVELOG\2007_05_11\O1_MF_1_38_348WK5OZ_.ARC

76      1    39       A 11-MAY-07
        Name: C:\ORACLE\FLASH\MOBDB11\ARCHIVELOG\2007_05_11\O1_MF_1_39_348WKBQX_.ARC

77      1    40       A 11-MAY-07
        Name: C:\ORACLE\FLASH\MOBDB11\ARCHIVELOG\2007_05_11\O1_MF_1_40_348WKCB8_.ARC

78      1    41       A 11-MAY-07
        Name: C:\ORACLE\FLASH\MOBDB11\ARCHIVELOG\2007_05_11\O1_MF_1_41_348WKJ6C_.ARC


Do you really want to delete the above objects (enter YES or NO)? no
```

Parameterized scripts help significantly in managing the infrastructure with RMAN. You can create just one script and then call it several times with different values of the parameter, which reduces the overall scripting time and potential for errors.

9-18. Creating a Parameterized Command File Script

Problem

You want to create an RMAN command file script that can accept a parameter.

Solution

In Oracle Database 11g, to create a RMAN command file in Unix (or Windows) that can accept a parameter, you simply create a file like this:

```
{ delete noprompt archivelog sequence &1 ; }
```

Note the &1 at the end, which is the positional parameter whose value you will pass later. Name this file delete_arc_logs.rman, and place it in the directory C:\TOOLS. Now, call the script to delete the archived redo log 37, as shown here:

```
C:\tools>rman target=/ @c:\tools\delete_arc_logs.rman using 37

Recovery Manager: Release 11.1.0.4.0 - Beta on Fri May 11 11:54:23 2007

Copyright (c) 1982, 2006, Oracle.  All rights reserved.

connected to target database: MOBDB11 (DBID=406156306)

RMAN>  { delete noprompt archivelog sequence 37 ; }
2>
using target database control file instead of recovery catalog
allocated channel: ORA_DISK_1
channel ORA_DISK_1: SID=170 device type=DISK
deleted archived log
archived log file name=C:\ORACLE\FLASH\MOBDB11\ARCHIVELOG\2007_05_11\O1_MF_1 ➡
37 348WK57T_.ARC RECID=3 STAMP=622287589
Deleted 1 objects


Recovery Manager complete.
```

How It Works

The parameters in the script are positional, which is similar to the parameters in a Unix shell script or a SQL*Plus script. You name the parameters &1, &2, and so on, and pass the values to these parameters in the same order. For instance, here is an example of a script file that accepts two parameters:

```
{ delete &2 archivelog sequence &1 ; }
```

Name the script file delete_arc_logs.rman. Now, call the script with the second parameter as noprompt, which is a character string. You can pass the characters by enclosing them in single quotes:

```
C:\tools>rman target=/ @c:\tools\delete_arc_logs.rman using 36 'noprompt'

Recovery Manager: Release 11.1.0.4.0 - Beta on Fri May 11 12:04:39 2007

Copyright (c) 1982, 2006, Oracle.  All rights reserved.

connected to target database: MOBDB11 (DBID=406156306)

RMAN>  { delete noprompt archivelog sequence 36 ; }
2>
using target database control file instead of recovery catalog
allocated channel: ORA_DISK_1
channel ORA_DISK_1: SID=127 device type=DISK
... and so on ...
```

If you need to replace the part of a string with the value of the parameter, you can use a period to separate the string from the value passed. For instance, if you want to delete archived redo logs matching a pattern, you can create the script file with the contents, as shown here:

```
{ delete archivelog like '%&1.%' ; }
```

Note how the pattern has been specified as %&1.%. The second % character is separated from the &1 by a period. Name this file del_arc_logs_pattern.rman. Now you can call this script file to delete the archived redo logs matching the pattern %2007_05_11%:

```
C:\tools>rman target=/ @c:\tools\del_arc_logs_pattern.rman using '2007_05_11'

Recovery Manager: Release 11.1.0.4.0 - Beta on Fri May 11 14:55:36 2007

Copyright (c) 1982, 2006, Oracle.  All rights reserved.

connected to target database: MOBDB11 (DBID=406156306)

RMAN>  { delete archivelog like '%2007_05_11%' ; }
2>
using target database control file instead of recovery catalog
allocated channel: ORA_DISK_1
channel ORA_DISK_1: SID=134 device type=DISK
deleted archived log
archived log file name=C:\ORACLE\FLASH\MOBDB11\ARCHIVELOG\2007_05_11\01_MF_1_38_➥
348WK5OZ_.ARC RECID=4 STAMP=622287589
deleted archived log
archived log file name=C:\ORACLE\FLASH\MOBDB11\ARCHIVELOG\2007_05_11\01_MF_1_39_➥
348WKBQX_.ARC RECID=5 STAMP=622287595
```

```
deleted archived log
archived log file name=C:\ORACLE\FLASH\MOBDB11\ARCHIVELOG\2007_05_11\O1_MF_1_40_ ➥
348WKCB8_.ARC RECID=6 STAMP=622287595
deleted archived log
archived log file name=C:\ORACLE\FLASH\MOBDB11\ARCHIVELOG\2007_05_11\O1_MF_1_41_ ➥
348WKJ6C_.ARC RECID=7 STAMP=622287600
Deleted 4 objects
```

```
Recovery Manager complete.
```

Parameterized scripts help significantly in managing the infrastructure with RMAN. You can create just one script and then call it several times with different values of the parameter, making many routine tasks a breeze. This strategy is especially useful in cases where the script remains the same but some output changes to match the date and month, such as when you want to name the backup pieces with the day, month, and year when they were generated. In that case, you can merely call the script with a parameter that accepts the output name. This will reduce the scripting time and the possibility of errors.

CHAPTER 10

■■■

Restoring the Control File

Your control file restore method is highly dependent on your backup strategy. The phrase "when you think of backups, think of recovery" especially applies to control files. Depending on your backup methodology, the control file restore can be effortless, or it can be complicated.

If you have enabled a flash recovery area (FRA) or are using a recovery catalog, then you'll find restoring the control file an automated and simple process. Having RMAN do all of the heavy lifting helps ensure that you'll get this critical file restored in a timely and accurate manner.

■**Note** We recommend that you enable the control file autobackup feature as described in recipe 5-4. This will ensure that you have a backup of your control file after every RMAN backup and also after making database structural changes (such as adding a datafile).

If you're neither using a flash recovery area nor using a recovery catalog, then restoring the control file requires that you perform a few manual steps. Manually performing steps is time-consuming and prone to error.

Control files aren't usually a source of failure. That's because they're usually multiplexed, which gives you a high degree of protection against failure. However, these are very critical files, and you should know how to restore them if the need arises. This chapter starts with the automated and simple methods for control file restores and then progresses to the more complicated, manual scenarios.

Before you begin, if you have a copy of your current control file, then we recommend you make a backup of it before you issue a RMAN `restore controlfile` command. In most scenarios, the `restore controlfile` command will overwrite any existing control files. See recipe 7-2 for an example of how to back up your control file.

■**Note** Anytime you restore a control file from a backup, you are required to perform media recovery on your entire database and then open it with the `open resetlogs` command. This is true even if you don't restore any datafiles (because the control file's SCN is no longer synchronized with the SCNs in the datafiles and online redo log files). This chapter covers only how to restore your control file and does not show how to restore and recover your entire database. Refer to Chapter 11 for complete recovery scenarios, and refer to Chapter 12 for incomplete recovery situations.

10-1. Restoring Control File Using Flash Recovery Area

Problem

You have wisely enabled a flash recovery area, and you use it as a repository for your control file backups. Unfortunately, you've lost all your control files, and now you need to use RMAN to restore them.

Solution

When you use the flash recovery area, you can use one of two very different methods to restore the control file depending on whether you enabled the autobackup of the control file. This recipe describes both of these scenarios.

Using the Autobackup of the Control File

When you enable the autobackup of your control file and are using a flash recovery area, then restoring your control file is fairly simple. First connect to your target database, then issue a `startup nomount` command, and lastly issue the `restore controlfile from autobackup` command:

```
RMAN> connect target /
RMAN> startup nomount;
RMAN> restore controlfile from autobackup;
```

RMAN restores the control files to the location defined by your `control_files` initialization parameter. You should see a message indicating that your control files have been successfully copied back from an RMAN backup piece. Here is a partial snippet of the output:

```
Starting restore at 02-FEB-07
allocated channel: ORA_DISK_1
channel ORA_DISK_1: sid=156 devtype=DISK
database name (or database unique name) used for search: ORCL
channel ORA_DISK_1: autobackup found in the recovery area
Finished restore at 02-FEB-07
```

You can now alter your database into mount mode and perform any additional restore and recovery commands required for your database.

Not Using the Autobackup of the Control File

If you don't use the autobackup of the control file feature, then restoring the control file becomes more difficult. If autobackup is disabled, you have to explicitly tell RMAN from which directory and backup piece to restore the control file. This example specifies a directory and a lengthy filename:

```
RMAN> connect target /
RMAN> startup nomount;
RMAN> restore controlfile from
2>   'C:\FRA\DB1\backupset\2006_09_23\01_mf_ncnnf_TAG20060923T02kc1vgsh.bck';
```

Here is a partial listing of the RMAN output when restoring your control file:

```
Starting restore at 02-FEB-07
allocated channel: ORA_DISK_1
channel ORA_DISK_1: sid=156 devtype=DISK
channel ORA_DISK_1: restoring control file
channel ORA_DISK_1: sid=156 devtype=DISK
```

As you can see, that's not nearly as easy to do as when you have the control file auto-backup enabled. You must tell RMAN to restore from a specific backup piece file.

How It Works

We highly recommend enabling autobackup of the control file. By default, the autobackup of your control file is not enabled (see recipe 5-4 for details on enabling this feature). This ensures that the backup piece is placed in a default location that RMAN can use to automatically restore your target database control file.

Autobackup Enabled

When you enable autobackups and use the flash recovery area, no recovery catalog is required, and you don't have to explicitly provide RMAN with the name and location of backup files or your target database identifier (DBID). This is the simplest method that RMAN provides for restoring a control file. However, this solution works only when you enable auto-backups of your control file and use a flash recovery area.

RMAN uses the value of your operating system ORACLE_SID variable to look in the default location for control file backups in the flash recovery area. RMAN deduces the default location of the backup file by combining the values of the db_recovery_file_dest initialization parameter and your operating system ORACLE_SID variable setting. By default RMAN will look in a directory with the following format:

```
\<FRA>\<target database SID>\autobackup\YYYY_MM_DD\<backup piece file>
```

Autobackup Not Enabled

When you don't have the autobackup of your control file enabled, then by default RMAN will place the backup of your control file in a directory path named like this:

```
\<FRA>\<target database SID>\backupset\YYYY_MM_DD\<backup piece file>
```

> **Note** RMAN will by default back up your control file anytime you back up datafile 1, regardless of whether you have the autobackup of your control file feature enabled.

When you restore your control file and when the autobackup feature has not been enabled, then RMAN is unable to determine by itself the default location. You must directly tell RMAN from which backup piece to restore the control file.

> **Note** If you are using a recovery catalog, then you should see recipe 10-2 for details about restoring your control file. In that scenario, RMAN will automatically retrieve the backup piece name and location from the recovery catalog.

If you have the RMAN output log from a backup, then you should be able to see which backup piece contains the backup of your control file. For example, here is the partial output of RMAN messages during a backup of datafile 1:

```
including current control file in backupset
including current SPFILE in backupset
channel ORA_DISK_1: starting piece 1 at 02-FEB-07
channel ORA_DISK_1: finished piece 1 at 02-FEB-07
piece handle=
C:\FRA\DB1\backupset\2006_09_23\01_mf_ncnnf_TAG20060923T02kc1vgsh.BCK
```

In this example, the correct backup piece name is as follows:

```
01_mf_ncnnf_TAG20060923T02kc1vgsh.BCK
```

> **Note** When you restore a control file from a backup, you are required to perform media recovery on your entire database and open your database with the open resetlogs command, even if you didn't restore any datafiles. You can determine whether your control file is a backup by querying the CONTROLFILE_TYPE column of the V$DATABASE view.

10-2. Restoring Control File Using Recovery Catalog

Problem

You need to restore your control file, and you use a recovery catalog when creating backups.

Solution

Restoring the control file is fairly simple when you use a recovery catalog. All you need to do is ensure that you connect to both your target database and the recovery catalog. Then issue startup nomount, and issue the restore controlfile command.

In this example, the recovery catalog owner and password are both *rcat*, and the name of the recovery catalog is *recov*. You'll have to change those values to match the username/password@service in your environment.

```
RMAN> connect target /
RMAN> connect catalog rcat/rcat@recov
RMAN> startup nomount;
RMAN> restore controlfile;
```

RMAN restores the control files to the location defined by your control_files initialization parameter. You should see a message indicating that your control files have been successfully copied back from an RMAN backup piece. Here's a partial listing of RMAN's message stack after a successful control file restore:

```
Starting restore at 07-02-02
allocated channel: ORA_DISK_1
channel ORA_DISK_1: sid=156 devtype=DISK
channel ORA_DISK_1: restoring control file
channel ORA_DISK_1: reading from backup piece
channel ORA_DISK_1: restore complete, elapsed time: 00:00:04
Finished restore at 07-02-02
```

You can now alter your database into mount mode and perform any additional restore and recovery commands required for your database. Refer to Chapter 11 for complete recovery scenarios, and refer to Chapter 12 for incomplete recovery situations.

How It Works

Using a recovery catalog makes it straightforward to restore the control file. When you issue the restore controlfile command, RMAN will retrieve from the recovery catalog the location and name of the file that contains the control file backup and restores the control file appropriately. Because the recovery catalog knows the location of the RMAN backup piece, it doesn't matter whether the backup piece is in a flash recovery area or in a configured channel location.

When you're connected to the recovery catalog, you can view backup information about your control files even while your target database is in nomount mode. To list backups of your control files, use the list command as shown here:

```
RMAN> connect target /
RMAN> connect catalog rcat/rcat@recov
RMAN> startup nomount;
RMAN> list backup of controlfile;
```

If you have registered two databases in the recovery catalog with the same name, then you might receive an error such as this when you attempt to list backups or restore the control file:

```
RMAN-06004: ORACLE error from recovery catalog database:
RMAN-20005: target database name is ambiguous
```

In this situation, you will need to first set your database identifier (DBID) before you can restore your control file. See recipe 10-3 for details on how to determine your DBID.

The database name that is stored in the recovery catalog is not guaranteed to be unique. You can verify that you have multiple databases with the same name in your recovery catalog by querying the recovery catalog RC_DATABASE view as shown here:

```
SQL> connect rcat/rcat@rcat
SQL> select db_key, dbid, name from rc_database;
DB_KEY       DBID NAME
------ ---------- ----
1       1124743449 ORCL
4241    1140772490 ORCL
```

■**Note** When you restore a control file from a backup, you are required to perform media recovery on your entire database and open your database with the open resetlogs command, even if you didn't restore any datafiles. You can determine whether your control file is a backup by querying the CONTROLFILE_TYPE column of the V$DATABASE view.

10-3. Determining the Database Identifier

Problem

Your backup strategy doesn't take advantage of either a flash recovery area or a recovery catalog. You are trying to restore a control file as follows, and you receive an error message stating that you must explicitly set the database identifier (DBID):

```
RMAN> connect target /
RMAN> startup nomount;
RMAN> restore controlfile from autobackup;
```

RMAN specifically instructs you to set the DBID first:

```
RMAN-06495: must explicitly specify DBID with SET DBID command
```

You don't know the DBID for your database, and you aren't sure how to find the DBID. Without a control file for your database, you can't mount the database and query the DBID value from the V$DATABASE view.

Solution

You can determine the DBID of your database in one of the following ways:

- You can derive the DBID from an autobackup file.

- You can retrieve the DBID from RMAN output.

- You can write the DBID to the alert.log file.

- You can derive DBID from a file dump.

Deriving the DBID from an Autobackup File

If you chose to configure the autobackup control file format, then you are required to include the format variable %F when formatting the name used for the RMAN backup piece. The format of the %F variable is a unique combination of the database identifier, the date, and a sequence, and it follows this format: c-IIIIIIIIII-YYYYMMDD-QQ. The first ten *I*s comprise your target database's DBID. For example, if the control file backup piece name is c-2601506593-20060918-01, then the DBID substring is 2601506593. Table 10-1 describes the meaning of each section of the %F format variable.

Table 10-1. *Description of %F Format Variable*

String	Meaning
c	Signifies a control file backup.
IIIIIIIIII	DBID.
YYYYMMDD	Date backup was created. Used by maxdays parameter of the restore controlfile command.
QQ	A hex sequence number that is incremented each time a control file autobackup is created for a given day. Used by the maxseq parameter of the restore controlfile command.

The default location for a control file autobackup on Unix systems is ORACLE_HOME/dbs, and on Windows platforms it's usually ORACLE_HOME\database.

Retrieving the DBID from RMAN Output

Another method for identifying your DBID is to extract it from any RMAN session output that you have previously saved to a log file. The output of an RMAN session will contain the DBID as displayed when you first connect to your target database. For example:

```
RMAN> connect target /
connected to target database: BRDSTN(DBID=2601506593)
```

Writing the DBID to the Alert.log File

Another way of recording the DBID is to make sure that it is written to the alert.log file on a regular basis using the DBMS_SYSTEM package. For example, you could have this SQL code execute as part of your backup job:

```
COL dbid NEW_VALUE hold_dbid
SELECT dbid FROM v$database;
exec dbms_system.ksdwrt(2,'DBID: '||TO_CHAR(&hold_dbid));
```

After running the previous code, you should see a text message in your target database alert.log file that looks like this:

```
DBID: 2601506593
```

The KSDWRT procedure writes a text message to your database alert.log file. In this case, the hold_dbid SQL variable is populated with the DBID. If you write your target database DBID to the alert.log file on a regular basis, you should be able to identify it easily should the need arise.

■**Caution** Writing messages to the alert.log file may result in Oracle Support's refusal to use the alert.log file when diagnosing issues.

Dumping Files

If any of the datafiles, online redo log files, or archived redo log files are physically available, you can use the SQL alter system dump statement to write the DBID to a trace file. Your database does not have to be mounted for this to work. For example, here is the syntax for taking a datafile dump:

```
SQL> connect / as sysdba
SQL> startup nomount;
SQL> alter system dump datafile '/<PATH>/system01.dbf' block min 1 block max 10;
```

Use this syntax to take a dump of an archived redo log file or online redo log file:

```
SQL> alter system dump logfile '<log file name>';
```

The trace file with the DBID will be in your user dump destination. If you search for the string "Db ID," you should find something similar to this output:

```
Db ID=2601506593=0x9b0fd721, Db Name='BRDSTN'
```

How It Works

If you're using a flash recovery area with the autobackup of your control file enabled, then you shouldn't need the DBID when restoring the control file. If you're neither using a flash recovery area nor using a recovery catalog, then you might have to know your DBID before you restore the control file.

Every Oracle database has an internal unique DBID that can be queried from V$DATABASE as follows:

```
SQL> select dbid from v$database;
DBID
------------------------------
2601506593
```

RMAN uses the DBID to uniquely identify databases. The DBID helps RMAN identify the correct RMAN backup piece from which to restore the control file. If you don't use a flash recovery area or a recovery catalog, then you should record the DBID in a safe location and have it available in the event you need to restore your control file.

10-4. Restoring Control File with No Flash Recovery Area or Recovery Catalog

Problem

You are neither using a flash recovery area nor using a recovery catalog, and you need to restore your control file using RMAN.

VERIFYING USE OF A FRA

You can verify whether you are using a flash recovery area (FRA) by issuing the following SQL statement:

```
SQL> show parameter db_recovery_file_dest;
```

If you are not using a flash recovery area, then the value of the db_recovery_file_dest initialization parameter will be null. If you are using a flash recovery area, then there will be a directory shown in the VALUE column. For example, here's the FRA for one of our test databases:

```
NAME                     TYPE          VALUE
---------------------    ----------    ------------------------------
db_recovery_file_dest    string        /oraback/FRA
```

See Chapter 3 for complete details on how to implement a FRA.

Solution

If you're not using a flash recovery area or a recovery catalog, then the location of the backup of your control file is highly dependent on how you configured your backups. We outline four scenarios next.

Using Autobackup, with RMAN Backup Piece in the Default Location

The first example shows how to restore a control file when you've enabled autobackup and have not used the configure command to specify a location for the RMAN backup piece. In this scenario, RMAN will look for the backup in the default location. You need to provide RMAN with the DBID so that it knows from which backup piece the control file should be restored.

■**Note** See recipe 10-3 for details on how to identify your DBID.

Once you know your DBID, you can connect to your target database, issue startup nomount, set the DBID, and issue the restore command. In this example, the DBID is "2601506593."

```
RMAN> connect target /
RMAN> startup nomount;
RMAN> set dbid 2601506593;
RMAN> restore controlfile from autobackup;
```

RMAN will now display output similar to the following:

```
Starting restore at 07-02-02
using channel ORA_DISK_1
channel ORA_DISK_1: looking for autobackup on day: 20070202
channel ORA_DISK_1: autobackup found: c-1140771490-20070202-05
channel ORA_DISK_1: control file restore from autobackup complete
output filename=C:\ORACLE\PRODUCT\10.2.0\ORADATA\ORCL\CONTROL01.CTL
output filename=C:\ORACLE\PRODUCT\10.2.0\ORADATA\ORCL\CONTROL02.CTL
output filename=C:\ORACLE\PRODUCT\10.2.0\ORADATA\ORCL\CONTROL03.CTL
Finished restore at 07-02-02
```

When you set the DBID, you are instructing RMAN to search outside the flash recovery area in the default location for a backup file that was formatted with the %F parameter. Part of the format for %F contains the year, month, and day.

■Note See Table 10-1 for details about the %F format variable.

RMAN will look in the default location for the RMAN backup piece file. The default location varies by operating system. On Unix, the default location is ORACLE_HOME/dbs. On Windows installations it's usually ORACLE_HOME\database.

RMAN will start with today's date and look for a control file backup with today's date as part of the backup filename. If RMAN doesn't find a backup piece with today's date as part of the filename, it will then look in the default location for a filename with yesterday's date embedded in the backup filename, and so forth.

By default, RMAN will attempt to retrieve from autobackups created within the last seven days only. If you want to modify the default behavior, use the maxdays parameter. This example instructs RMAN to look for a control file backup created in the last 20 days:

```
RMAN> connect target /
RMAN> startup nomount;
RMAN> set dbid 2601506594;
RMAN> restore controlfile from autobackup maxdays 20;
```

You can also instruct RMAN to search for control files backups by sequence number via the maxseq parameter. The sequence number used is defined by the %F format variable and is generated when the control file backup is created. This next example instructs RMAN to look for a control file backup file that has a sequence number of 10 or less:

```
RMAN> connect target /
RMAN> startup nomount;
RMAN> set dbid 2601506594;
RMAN> restore controlfile from autobackup maxseq 10;
```

■Note The maxdays and maxseq parameters are useful only when your control file backup filenames are formatted with the %F format mask. The %F format mask embeds a date and a sequence number in the backup piece name.

Using Autobackup, with RMAN Backup Piece in a Nondefault Location

If you used the `configure controlfile autobackup format` command to back up the control file to a nondefault location, then you have to tell RMAN where to find the backup file. This example tells RMAN to look in the directory C:\ODUMP for a file formatted with %F:

```
RMAN> connect target /
RMAN> startup nomount;
RMAN> set dbid 2601506594;
RMAN> set controlfile autobackup format for device type disk to 'C:\ODUMP\%F';
RMAN> restore controlfile from autobackup;
```

RMAN will now display output similar to this:

```
Starting restore at 07-02-02
allocated channel: ORA_DISK_1
channel ORA_DISK_1: sid=156 devtype=DISK
channel ORA_DISK_1: looking for autobackup on day: 20070202
channel ORA_DISK_1: autobackup found: C:\ODUMP\c-1140771490-20070202-08
channel ORA_DISK_1: control file restore from autobackup complete
output filename=C:\ORACLE\PRODUCT\10.2.0\ORADATA\ORCL\CONTROL01.CTL
output filename=C:\ORACLE\PRODUCT\10.2.0\ORADATA\ORCL\CONTROL02.CTL
output filename=C:\ORACLE\PRODUCT\10.2.0\ORADATA\ORCL\CONTROL03.CTL
Finished restore at 07-02-02
```

This next example is a slight variation of the previous example. Here, instead of using the set command, you directly instruct RMAN to restore from a specific backup piece. In this scenario, you do not need to set the DBID because you're pointing RMAN at a specific backup file.

```
RMAN> connect target /
RMAN> startup nomount;
RMAN> restore controlfile from 'C:\ODUMP\c-1140771490-20070202-08';
```

You should now see RMAN output similar to this:

```
Starting restore at 07-02-02
using target database control file instead of recovery catalog
allocated channel: ORA_DISK_1
channel ORA_DISK_1: sid=159 devtype=DISK
channel ORA_DISK_1: restoring control file
channel ORA_DISK_1: restore complete, elapsed time: 00:00:04
output filename=C:\ORACLE\PRODUCT\10.2.0\ORADATA\ORCL\CONTROL01.CTL
output filename=C:\ORACLE\PRODUCT\10.2.0\ORADATA\ORCL\CONTROL02.CTL
output filename=C:\ORACLE\PRODUCT\10.2.0\ORADATA\ORCL\CONTROL03.CTL
Finished restore at 07-02-02
```

Not Using Autobackup, with RMAN Backup Piece in the Default Location

You can use RMAN without configuring anything. You can start RMAN and back up your database out of the box with a `backup database` command. In this situation, the system datafile would be part of what gets backed up. If you don't configure anything with RMAN, the default behavior is that your control file gets backed up anytime datafile 1 is backed up.

The RMAN backup piece will be in a default location that is operating system dependent. On Unix systems it will be in ORACLE_HOME/dbs; on Windows it's usually ORACLE_HOME\database. The RMAN backup piece name won't be obvious to you; instead, it will be something cryptic like 1fh0geg_1_1.

The next example uses the output of the backup database command to determine which backup piece contains the control file. Here you need to identify the correct file and instruct RMAN to restore the control file from the specific backup piece; in this example, the backup file is in the default location on a Unix box, and the name is 1hhu0gn1_1_1:

```
RMAN> connect target /
RMAN> startup nomount;
RMAN> restore controlfile from '/ora01/app/oracle/product/10.2.0/dbs/1hhu0gn1_1_1';
```

Here is the same thing on a Windows box. The filename this time is 5IHU0G6H_1_1:

```
RMAN> connect target /
RMAN> startup nomount;
RMAN> restore controlfile from 'C:\ORACLE\PROD\10.2.0\DB_1\DATABASE\5IHU0G6H_1_1';
```

Not Using Autobackup, with RMAN Backup Piece in Nondefault Location

You can configure your RMAN backup pieces to be written to a specific location via the configure channel device command as follows:

```
RMAN> configure channel device type disk format '/orabackups/%d%U.bus';
```

This instructs RMAN to write backups to the /orabackups directory with the specified file format. When you need to restore from an RMAN backup piece directly, you need to provide RMAN with the directory and backup filename when you issue the restore command. In this example, the filename is /orabackups/BRDSTN1lhu0oi_1_1.bus:

```
RMAN> connect target /
RMAN> startup nomount;
RMAN> restore controlfile from '/orabackups/BRDSTN1lhu0oi_1_1.bus';
```

How It Works

If you've enabled the autobackup of your control file feature, RMAN will look for the backup that contains the control file in the default location. If the RMAN backup piece is not in the default location, you can tell RMAN explicitly where to retrieve it from.

When you don't use the flash recovery area or the recovery catalog, then it's more complicated to restore the control file. You need to supply RMAN information such as the DBID or the exact name and location of the backup piece to successfully restore the control file. This can be time-consuming and error prone; therefore, it is highly recommended that you use a flash recovery area or a recovery catalog when backing up your control file.

■**Note** When you restore a control file from a backup, you are required to perform media recovery on your entire database and open your database with the open resetlogs command, even if you didn't restore any datafiles. You can determine whether your control file is a backup by querying the CONTROLFILE_TYPE column of the V$DATABASE view.

10-5. Restoring Control File to Nondefault Location

Problem

You want to restore your control file to a location other than the default location specified by your control_files parameter.

Solution

Use the restore controlfile to command. The syntax varies slightly depending on whether you're using autobackups, using a recovery catalog, or manually configuring the location backups.

■**Note** Your database can be in nomount, mount, or open when you use the restore controlfile to command. If your database is mounted or open, then you must use the restore controlfile to command to restore your control file. This is because RMAN will not let you overwrite the current (open) control file. That's a good thing.

Using Autobackups

This example shows the syntax when restoring to a nondefault location and using an auto-backup of the control file:

```
RMAN> connect target /
RMAN> restore controlfile to 'C:\ctl.bk' from autobackup;
```

Here is a partial listing of RMAN's output:

```
Starting restore at 07-02-02
channel ORA_DISK_1: starting datafile backupset restore
channel ORA_DISK_1: restoring control file
output filename=C:\CTL.BK
channel ORA_DISK_1: reading from backup piece
C:\FRA\ORCL\AUTOBACKUP\2007_02_02\O1_MF_S_613497405_2W7JFGJJ_.BKP
channel ORA_DISK_1: restore complete, elapsed time: 00:00:03
Finished restore at 07-02-02
```

Using a Recovery Catalog

This example shows the syntax when restoring a control file to a nondefault location using a recovery catalog. The recovery catalog knows the location of the last good backup of the control file; therefore, you don't need to use a from autobackup clause.

```
RMAN> connect target /
RMAN> connect rmancat/rmancat@rcat
RMAN> restore controlfile to 'C:\ctl.bk';
```

Using a Manually Configured RMAN Backup Piece

This example shows how to restore to a nondefault location from a backup that was created with a manually configured location for the RMAN backup piece:

```
RMAN> restore controlfile to '/ora01/oraddata/BRDSTN/ctl.bk'
2> from '/orabackups/BRDSTN/1lhuOoi_1_1.bus':
```

How It Works

By default, the control files are restored to the location defined by the control_files initialization parameter. If you want the control files restored to a location other than what is defined by the control_files initialization parameter, then use the restore controlfile to command.

■**Note** The restore controlfile to command does not overwrite the current control file. It restores only the control file to the location you specify.

10-6. Restoring Lost Copy of Multiplexed Control File

Problem

You attempted to start your database and receive the following error:

```
ORA-00205: error identifying controlfile, check alert log for more info
```

You check your target database alert.log file and verify that Oracle can't obtain the status of one of your database control files. You wonder whether you can use a good copy of an existing control file to resolve this issue.

Solution

If you multiplex your control files, you can take a good control file and copy it right over the top of a bad or missing control file. You don't need to issue an RMAN restore controlfile command in this scenario. You have two methods to get your database restarted:

- You can modify your initialization file so that it references only the good remaining control file(s).

- You can copy a good control file to the location of the bad or missing control file.

Modifying the Initialization File

In the first example, control02.ctl is missing and the database won't start, so we've decided to modify the control_files parameter in the initialization file. This example uses an spfile:

```
SQL> startup nomount;
SQL> alter system
2    set control_files='/ora01/oradata/BRDSTN/control01.ctl' scope=spfile;

System altered.

SQL> shutdown immediate;
SQL> startup;
```

Copying a Good Control File

In this example, we're copying the good control file (control01.ctl) to the location of the bad control file (contro02.ctl). To do this, first shut down your database from either RMAN or SQL*Plus using this:

```
RMAN> shutdown immediate;
```

or using this:

```
SQL> shutdown immediate;
```

Then from the Unix operating system prompt, copy the good control file to the location of the bad or missing control file:

```
$ cp /ora01/oradata/BRDSTN/control01.ctl  /ora02/oradata/BRDSTN/control02.ctl
```

Then from RMAN or SQL*Plus you should be able to start your database normally using the startup command as follows:

```
RMAN> startup;
or
SQL> startup;
```

How It Works

Before Oracle can start up normally, it must be able to locate and open each of the control files identified by the control_files initialization parameter. The control files are identical copies of each other. If a multiplexed control file becomes damaged, you can either modify the control_files initialization parameter to match the locations of the remaining good control files or copy a good control file to the location of the damaged or missing control file.

If you have one good copy of a control file, you can use that to replace the damaged control files. This minimizes the need to restore your control file from a backup.

■Tip Multiplexing your control files minimizes the chance of failure with these critical files. We highly recommend that you multiplex your control files and try to place each copy on separate devices governed by different controllers.

10-7. Re-creating the Control File

Problem

One of the following situations applies:

- You've experienced a failure and lost all of your control files, and you belatedly realize that you don't have a good binary backup of the control file.

- You want to change a database setting that can be modified only by re-creating the control file.

- You are relocating a large number of datafiles, and you find it easier to re-create the control file with the new names and locations (instead of manually renaming the datafiles).

Solution

You can use the output of the following command to re-create your control file:

```
SQL> alter database backup controlfile to trace;
```

The previous command generates a trace file that is placed in your user dump directory. You can display the location of your user_dump_dest from SQL as follows:

```
SQL> show parameter user_dump_dest
```

You might have several trace files in that directory. Usually the most recently created trace file in that directory is the one that contains the create controlfile command. Find the correct trace file, and open it.

NAMING A TRACE FILE

If you want to specify a text string to be used as part of the trace filename, then use the tracefile_identifier parameter. This makes finding the trace file generated by your session much easier. For example, if you wanted your trace filename to contain a text string of "MYTRACE," then you would set tracefile_identifier as follows:

```
SQL> alter session set tracefile_identifier='MYTRACE';
```

Every time you modify this parameter, the next trace file that is generated by your session will have the specified value of tracefile_identifier embedded in the trace filename. The format of the trace filename will be as follows:

```
<SID><Oracle process id><tracefile_identifier>.trc
```

There are two SQL statements in the trace file: one with noresetlogs and another with resetlogs. You'll have to edit the trace file so that it contains only the appropriate SQL statement that you require. If you still have good online redo log files, then use the NORESETLOGS option. If you are missing your online redo log files, then use the resetlogs option.

After you've edited the trace file, you need to connect to your database from a sysdba privileged schema (usually sys). Since the trace file contains a startup nomount SQL statement in it, you need to ensure your database is shut down first before you attempt to run the script. In this example, the trace filename is brdstn_ora_2374.trc:

```
SQL> connect / as sysdba
SQL> shutdown immediate;
SQL> @brdstn_ora_2374.trc
```

You should now have control files re-created in every location identified by your control_files initialization parameter.

If you're using a recovery catalog, your backup information is still stored safely in your recovery catalog database. After you re-create the control files, you'll have to connect to the target database and recovery catalog and run a resync catalog command to update the recovery catalog metadata with information about the newly created control file.

```
RMAN> connect target /
RMAN> connect catalog rmancat/rmancat@rcat
RMAN> resync catalog;
```

You can now back up your target database while connected to the recovery catalog.

How It Works

For critical databases, you should always multiplex your control file and also back it up on a regular basis. This obviates the need to re-create the control file. However, as the "Problem" section makes clear, sometimes you simply must re-create your control file.

When you re-create the control file, this wipes out any RMAN backup information that was stored in your target database control file. If you need to access historical RMAN backup information (and are not using a recovery catalog), then you will have to do one of the following:

- If using Oracle Database 10g or newer, then use the catalog command to repopulate your control file with RMAN backup information (see recipe 11-19).

- If using Oracle9i Database, then use the DBMS_BACKUP_RESTORE package to extract files out of RMAN backup pieces (see recipe 11-20).

■**Note** Only the parameters you have set with the RMAN configure command are retained after you re-create the control file.

When you back up your control file to trace, Oracle will place two SQL*Plus create controlfile statements in a trace file for you. Here is an example of an edited trace file so that it contains only one create controlfile SQL*Plus statement that does not reset the online redo log files:

```
STARTUP NOMOUNT
CREATE CONTROLFILE REUSE DATABASE "ORCL" NORESETLOGS  ARCHIVELOG
    MAXLOGFILES 16
    MAXLOGMEMBERS 3
```

```
      MAXDATAFILES 100
      MAXINSTANCES 8
      MAXLOGHISTORY 292
LOGFILE
  GROUP 1 'C:\ORACLE\PRODUCT\10.2.0\ORADATA\ORCL\REDO01.LOG'  SIZE 50M,
  GROUP 2 'C:\ORACLE\PRODUCT\10.2.0\ORADATA\ORCL\REDO02.LOG'  SIZE 50M,
  GROUP 3 'C:\ORACLE\PRODUCT\10.2.0\ORADATA\ORCL\REDO03.LOG'  SIZE 50M
DATAFILE
  'C:\ORACLE\PRODUCT\10.2.0\ORADATA\ORCL\SYSTEM01.DBF',
  'C:\ORACLE\PRODUCT\10.2.0\ORADATA\ORCL\UNDOTBS01.DBF',
  'C:\ORACLE\PRODUCT\10.2.0\ORADATA\ORCL\SYSAUX01.DBF',
  'C:\ORACLE\PRODUCT\10.2.0\ORADATA\ORCL\USERS01.DBF',
  'C:\ORACLE\PRODUCT\10.2.0\ORADATA\ORCL\EXAMPLE01.DBF'
CHARACTER SET WE8MSWIN1252
;
-- Configure RMAN configuration record 1
VARIABLE RECNO NUMBER;
EXECUTE :RECNO := SYS.DBMS_BACKUP_RESTORE.SETCONFIG('CONTROLFILE AUTOBACKUP','ON');
RECOVER DATABASE
ALTER SYSTEM ARCHIVE LOG ALL;
ALTER DATABASE OPEN;
ALTER TABLESPACE TEMP
ADD TEMPFILE 'C:\ORACLE\PRODUCT\10.2.0\ORADATA\ORCL\TEMP01.DBF'
SIZE 20971520  REUSE
```

CHAPTER 11

■■■

Performing Complete Recovery

Be thankful for problems. If they were less difficult, someone else with less ability might have your job.

James A. Lovell

When an airplane is flying on autopilot through clear skies, you don't worry too much about the experience level of the pilot. It's when an engine catches on fire that you want somebody who is prepared and trained to handle the disaster. Or if the pilot isn't trained, let's hope they have a comprehensive *How to Handle Disasters* recipe book handy.

That also holds true in the database arena. When the database is up and running smoothly, nobody pays too much attention to the database and the DBA. It's when disaster strikes that companies are thankful they've invested in a DBA who has implemented a solid backup and recovery strategy. It's critical that you have a plan and understand what to do when you see messages like the following:

```
ORA-01113: file 1 needs media recovery
ORA-01110: data file 1: '/ora02/BRDSTN/system01.dbf'
```

No DBA likes to see that message. However, accidents happen. People do incorrect things. Disks fail. These are all things that can cause failures. A *media failure* occurs when Oracle can't read or write to a required database file. *Media recovery* is the process of restoring files and reapplying transactions to recover the datafiles that have experienced media failure. The next several paragraphs will explain the internals of the Oracle restore and recovery process and many terms and definitions that are used by DBAs.

Background

Most recovery scenarios have two separate phases: restore and recovery. *Restore* is the process of retrieving files from backups. Appropriately named, the RMAN `restore` command is used to retrieve datafiles, control files, archived redo log files, and server parameter files (spfiles) from backup sets. When RMAN restores a datafile, it will reconstruct an exact copy of the datafile as it was when it was backed up. RMAN is the only utility that can restore files from RMAN backup pieces.

Recovery is the process of applying transactions from redo files to the datafiles. *Complete recovery* means you can recover all transactions that were committed in your database before the failure occurred. You can use either RMAN or SQL*Plus to issue a `recover` command. Aside from a few minor differences, it doesn't matter whether you use RMAN or SQL*Plus to initiate a recovery. Both result in redo being applied to datafiles to recover transactions. This book focuses on RMAN-initiated restore and recovery examples.

For complete recovery, you do not have to restore and recover all the datafiles in your database. You have to restore and recover only those datafiles that are damaged. Depending on the type of failure, that could be all the datafiles in your database or just one datafile. Oracle detects which datafiles need media recovery by comparing the system change number (SCN) information in the control file and the corresponding SCN information in the datafile headers.

Incomplete recovery means that you cannot restore all committed transactions. Incomplete recovery is required when you don't have all the redo required to apply all transactions to the datafiles. You can also initiate incomplete recovery intentionally to restore the database to a previous state to recover data that was accidentally deleted. Incomplete recovery is initiated with the `recover database until` command. Chapter 12 discusses incomplete recovery. Chapter 13 discusses performing incomplete recovery via the flashback database feature.

To understand what type of recovery is required, it's helpful to first understand the mechanics of how Oracle handles transactions. Here's a typical transaction:

```
SQL> insert into table my_table values(1);
SQL> commit;
Commit complete.
```

When you see `Commit complete`, Oracle guarantees that a record of that transaction has been safely written to the current online redo log file on disk. That does not mean the modified block has yet been written to the appropriate datafile. The transaction information in the online redo log buffer is written very frequently to disk by the log writer background process, whereas changes to the modified blocks in the database buffer are only periodically written to disk by the database writer background process.

Periodically, all changed (dirty) block buffers in memory are written (by database writer) to the datafiles on disk. This is known as a *checkpoint*. When a checkpoint occurs, the checkpoint process records the current checkpoint SCN in the control files and the corresponding SCN in the datafile headers. A checkpoint guarantees that the datafiles are in a consistent state at a point in time.

The algorithm used by the log writer to write transaction information from the log buffer to the online redo log files is entirely different from the algorithm used by the database writer to write changed blocks from the database buffer to the datafiles. This is because the log buffer and the database buffer have entirely different goals. The purpose of the log buffer is to temporarily buffer transaction changes and get them quickly written to a safe location on disk (online redo log files), whereas the database buffer tries to keep blocks in memory as long as possible to increase the performance of processes using frequently accessed blocks.

Because the log writer's activities are not synchronized with the database writer's activities, at any point in time you could have committed transactions that exist in the online redo log file but not yet have the corresponding changed blocks written to the datafiles. Also, at any given time there might be blocks with uncommitted changes written to the datafiles. This is the expected behavior. Oracle keeps track of what has been committed (or not) and ensures that you're always presented with a read consistent and committed version of the database. In the event of an unexpected failure, Oracle is able to sort out what was committed or not via information in the redo stream and rollback segments. Figure 11-1 shows how the redo information flows from background processes to memory buffers and eventually to the redo files.

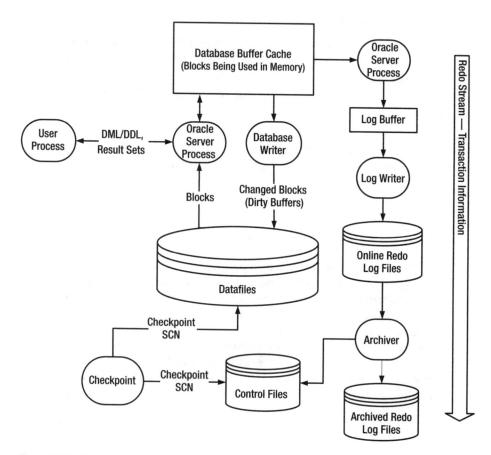

Figure 11-1. *Oracle redo stream*

If You're Still Awake...

An *instance (crash) failure* occurs when your database isn't able to shut down normally. When this happens, your datafiles could be in an inconsistent state—meaning they may not contain all committed changes and may contain uncommitted changes. Instance failures occur when the instance terminates abnormally. A sudden power failure or a `shutdown abort` are two common causes of instance failure.

Oracle uses *crash recovery* to return the database to a consistent committed state after an instance failure. Crash recovery guarantees that when your database is opened, it will contain only transactions that were committed before the instance failure occurred. Oracle's system monitor will automatically detect whether crash recovery is required.

Crash recovery has two phases: *rollforward* and *rollback*. The system monitor will first roll forward and apply to the datafiles any transactions in the online redo log files that occurred after the most recent checkpoint. Crash recovery uses redo information found in the online redo log files only. After rolling forward, Oracle will roll back any of those transactions that were never committed. Oracle uses information stored in the undo segments to roll back (undo) any uncommitted transactions.

■**Note** DBAs often use the terms *crash recovery* and *instance recovery* interchangeably. However, Oracle defines *crash recovery* as either the recovery of a single instance configuration or the crash recovery of all failed instances in an Oracle Real Application Cluster (RAC) configuration, whereas *instance recovery* is defined to be the recovery of one failed instance by an existing live instance in a RAC configuration.

When you start your database, Oracle uses the SCN information in the control files and datafile headers to determine which one of the following will occur:

- Starting up normally

- Performing crash recovery

- Determining that media recovery is required

On start-up, Oracle checks the instance thread status to determine whether crash recovery is required. When the database is open for normal operations, the thread status is OPEN. When Oracle is shut down normally (normal, immediate, or transactional), a checkpoint takes place, and the instance thread status is set to CLOSED.

When your instance abnormally terminates (such as from a shutdown abort command), the thread status remains OPEN because Oracle didn't get a chance to update the status to CLOSED. On start-up, when Oracle detects that an instance thread was abnormally left open, the system monitor process will automatically perform crash recovery. This query demonstrates how a single instance of Oracle would determine whether crash recovery is required:

```
SELECT
    a.thread#, b.open_mode, a.status,
    CASE
    WHEN ((b.open_mode='MOUNTED') AND (a.status='OPEN')) THEN 'Crash Recovery req.'
    WHEN ((b.open_mode='MOUNTED') AND (a.status='CLOSED')) THEN 'No Crash Rec. req.'
    WHEN ((b.open_mode='READ WRITE') AND (a.status='OPEN')) THEN 'Inst. already open'
    ELSE 'huh?'
    END STATUS
FROM v$thread a,
     v$database b,
     v$instance c
WHERE a.thread# = c.thread#;
```

Oracle will start up normally if the SCN information in the control files matches the SCNs in the corresponding datafiles. If the checkpoint SCN in the datafile is less than the corresponding SCN in the control file, Oracle will throw a media recovery error. For example, if you restored a datafile from a backup, Oracle would detect that the SCN in the datafile is less than the corresponding SCN in the control file. Therefore, a recovery is required to apply changes to the datafile to catch it up to the SCN in the control file. Table 11-1 summarizes the checks that Oracle performs to determine whether crash or media recovery is required.

Table 11-1. *SCN Oracle Start-up Checks*

Condition on Start-Up	Oracle Behavior	DBA Action
CF checkpoint SCN < Datafile checkpoint SCN	"Control file too old" error	Restore a newer control file.
CF checkpoint SCN > Datafile checkpoint SCN	Media recovery required	Most likely a datafile has been restored from a backup. Recovery is now required.
(CF checkpoint SCN = Datafile SCN)	Start up normally	None.
Database in mount mode, instance thread status = OPEN	Crash recovery required	None.

The following SQL query demonstrates the internal checks that Oracle performs to determine whether media recovery is required:

```
SELECT
  a.name,
  a.checkpoint_change#,
  b.checkpoint_change#,
  CASE
  WHEN ((a.checkpoint_change# - b.checkpoint_change#) = 0) THEN 'Startup Normal'
  WHEN ((a.checkpoint_change# - b.checkpoint_change#) > 0) THEN 'Media Recovery'
  WHEN ((a.checkpoint_change# - b.checkpoint_change#) < 0) THEN 'Old Control File'
  ELSE 'what the ?'
  END STATUS
FROM v$datafile a,        -- control file SCN for datafile
     v$datafile_header b -- datafile header SCN
WHERE a.file# = b.file#;
```

■**Tip** The V$DATAFILE_HEADER view uses the physical datafile on disk as its source. The V$DATAFILE view uses the control file as its source.

Media recovery requires that you perform manual tasks to get your database back in one piece. This usually involves a combination of restore and recover commands. You will have to issue an RMAN restore command if your datafiles have experienced media failure. This could be because of somebody accidentally deleting files or a disk failure.

When you issue the restore command, RMAN will automatically determine how to extract the datafiles from any of the following available backups:

- Full database backup

- Incremental level 0 backup

- Image copy backup generated by the backup as copy command

After the files are restored from a backup, you are required to apply redo to them via the `recover` command. When you issue the `recover` command, Oracle will examine the SCNs in the affected datafiles and determine whether any of them need to be recovered. If the SCN in the datafile is less than the corresponding SCN in the control file, then media recovery will be required.

Oracle will retrieve the datafile SCN and then look for the corresponding SCN in the redo stream to determine where to start the recovery process. If the starting recovery SCN is in the online redo log files, then the archived redo log files are not required for recovery.

During a recovery, RMAN will automatically determine how to apply redo. First, RMAN will apply any incremental backups available that are greater than zero, such as the incremental level 1. Next, any archived redo log files on disk will be applied. If the archived redo log files do not exist on disk, then RMAN will attempt to retrieve them from a backup set.

■**Note** An RMAN incremental backup contains copies of only those database blocks that have changed from the previous incremental backup. RMAN can more efficiently recover a datafile using an incremental backup over applying redo from an archived redo log file.

This chapter guides you through several different common (and not so common) restore and recovery scenarios. Now that you understand the mechanics, you are much better prepared to determine which steps you should take to restore and recover your database.

11-1. Determining How to Restore and Recover

Problem

You just experienced a media failure, and you're not sure what commands you'll need to restore and recover your database.

Solution

To be able to perform a complete recovery, all of the following conditions need to be true:

- Your database is in archivelog mode.

- You have a good baseline backup of your database.

- You have any required redo that has been generated since the backup (archived redo log files, online redo log files, or incremental backups that RMAN can use for recovery instead of applying redo).

There are a wide variety of restore and recovery scenarios. How you restore and recover depends directly on your backup strategy and what files have been damaged. Listed next are the general steps to follow when facing a media failure:

1. Determine what files need to be restored.

2. Depending on the damage, set your database mode to nomount, mount, or open.

3. Use the `restore` command to retrieve files from RMAN backups.

4. Use the `recover` command for datafiles requiring recovery.

5. Open your database.

Your particular restore and recovery scenario may not require that all of the previous steps be performed. For example, you may just want to restore your spfile, which doesn't require a recovery step.

The first step in a restore and recovery process is to determine what files have experienced media failure. You can usually determine what files need to be restored from three sources:

- Error messages displayed on your screen, either from RMAN or SQL*Plus

- Alert.log file and corresponding trace files

- Data dictionary views

■**Note** See Chapter 20 for details on using the Data Recovery Advisor to determine how to restore and recover your database. The Data Recovery Advisor feature is new with Oracle Database 11*g*.

Once you identify which files are damaged or missing, then you need to determine what steps to take to restore and recover. Table 11-2 contains general guidelines on what to do when presented with a media failure. You'll have to tailor these guidelines to your type of failure and then find the applicable recipe for specific instructions.

Table 11-2. *Where to Look for Restore and Recovery Instructions*

Files Needing Media Recovery	Action	Chapter/Recipe
Datafiles with all required redo available.	Complete recovery.	Chapter 11
Datafiles without all required redo available.	Incomplete recovery.	Chapter 12 or Chapter 13
Control files.	Restore control file.	Chapter 10
Online redo log files.	Combination of clearing and/or re-creating online redo log files and possibly performing incomplete recovery.	Chapter 14
Spfile.	Restore spfile.	Recipe 11-15
Archived redo log files.	Restore archived redo log files from another location or from RMAN backup.	Recipe 11-16
Control file has no information about RMAN backup piece.	Use the `catalog` command or the DBMS_BACKUP_ RESTORE package.	Recipes 11-19 and 11-20

How It Works

When faced with a media failure, you need to have a good understanding of your backup strategy and how that will enable you to restore and recover your database. You should periodically test your backups so that you can confidently recover your database when faced with a media failure. When you architect your backup strategy, you should also architect a corresponding restore and recovery strategy. A sound backup strategy should minimize the risk of you losing data and minimize the downtime of your database.

If you are missing any required redo or incremental backups required for recovery, then you need to see Chapter 12 for details on how to perform an incomplete recovery. You can also perform an incomplete recovery using the flashback database feature (described in Chapter 13).

If your database has experienced media failure, you'll see a fairly descriptive message when you attempt to start the database. Usually, it's obvious from the error message as to what files are experiencing problems. For example, this next error message shows that users01.dbf needs media recovery:

```
RMAN> connect target /
RMAN> startup;
ORA-01157: cannot identify/lock data file 4 - see DBWR trace file
ORA-01110: data file 4: 'C:\ORACLE\BRDSTN\USERS01.DBF'
```

■**Tip** When Oracle displays errors indicating there has been a media failure, we *always* recommend you look in the alert.log file for more details. There may be more than one datafile that needs to be restored and recovered, and you won't get all of that information from error messages displayed on your screen. Oracle will often just display on your screen the first file that it detects is missing or damaged.

Often there will be a corresponding trace file that contains information that Oracle Support will request when helping diagnose problems. Here's an example of what type of information you'll find in the alert.log file and related trace file when you have a media failure:

```
Errors in file c:\oracle\product\10.2.0\admin\orcl\bdump\orcl_dbw0_5416.trc:
ORA-01157: cannot identify/lock data file 4 - see DBWR trace file
ORA-01110: data file 4: 'C:\ORACLE\BRDSTN\USERS01.DBF'
ORA-27041: unable to open file
OSD-04002: unable to open file
O/S-Error: (OS 2) The system cannot find the file specified.
```

■**Tip** Before you restore the datafile from the RMAN backup, verify whether the missing datafile physically exists at the OS level, as well confirm that the Oracle software owner has the appropriate read and write privileges on the missing datafile and directory.

We also recommend querying the data dictionary for more information. The V$DATAFILE_HEADER view derives its information from the datafile headers and reports in the ERROR and RECOVER columns any potential problems. For example, a YES or null value in the RECOVER column indicates that you have a problem:

```
SQL> select file#, status, error,recover from v$datafile_header;
    FILE# STATUS  ERROR                        REC
---------- ------- ------------------------- ---
        1 ONLINE                                NO
        2 ONLINE                                NO
        3 ONLINE                                NO
        4 ONLINE  FILE NOT FOUND
        5 ONLINE                                NO
```

The V$RECOVER_FILE reads from the control file and displays information about files needing media recovery:

```
SQL> select file#, error from v$recover_file;
    FILE# ERROR
---------- -------------------------
        4 FILE NOT FOUND
```

■**Note** If you restore a control file from a backup, the V$RECOVER_FILE view will not contain accurate information.

11-2. Previewing Backups Needed for Restore

Problem

Before you perform a restore and recovery, you would like to view which backups will be required for the restore operation.

Solution

Use the restore ... preview command to query the RMAN repository for the most recent backup sets and corresponding files that will be used for a restore operation. Three restore ... preview modes are available:

- Normal
- Summarized
- Recall (MML only)

Normal Mode

In normal mode, you'll get a full listing of the information contained in the repository. The following example shows how to preview the restore of the system tablespace:

```
RMAN> restore tablespace system preview;
```

As you can see, the output from this command displays information from the repository about backup sets that RMAN will use when performing the restore operation.

■**Note** The output of the `preview` command is similar in format to the RMAN `list` command output.

```
Starting restore at 12-OCT-06
allocated channel: ORA_DISK_1
channel ORA_DISK_1: sid=145 devtype=DISK
List of Backup Sets
===================
BS Key  Type LV Size        Device Type Elapsed Time Completion Time
------- ---- -- ---------- ----------- ------------ ---------------
187     Full    843.50M   DISK        00:03:10     11-OCT-06
BP Key: 187    Status: AVAILABLE  Compressed: NO  Tag: TAG20061011T12380
Piece Name: C:\DK61HVIRPC_1_1.BUS
List of Datafiles in backup set 187
File LV Type Ckp SCN    Ckp Time  Name
---- -- ---- ---------- --------- ----
1       Full 4813354    11-OCT-06 C:\ORACLE\ORCL\SYSTEM01.DBF
using channel ORA_DISK_1
archive logs generated after SCN 4813354 not found in repository
Media recovery start SCN is 4813354
Recovery must be done beyond SCN 4813354 to clear data files fuzziness
Finished restore at 12-OCT-06
```

The following examples show how to use the `preview` command with a variety of restore operations:

```
RMAN> restore database preview;
RMAN> restore database from tag TAG20060927T183743 preview;
RMAN> restore datafile 1, 2, 3, 4 preview;
RMAN> restore archivelog all preview;
RMAN> restore archivelog from time 'sysdate - 1' preview;
RMAN> restore archivelog from scn 3243256 preview;
RMAN> restore archivelog from sequence 29 preview;
```

Summarized Mode

You can use the `preview summary` command to summarize the lengthy output. This next example shows summarized information about the backup set(s) RMAN will use to restore your entire database:

```
RMAN> restore database preview summary;

Starting restore at 12-OCT-06
using channel ORA_DISK_1
List of Backups
```

```
================
Key  TY LV S Device Type Completion Time #Pieces #Copies Compressed Tag
---- -- -- - ----------- --------------- ------- ------- ---------- ---
187  B  F  A DISK          11-OCT-06       1       1        NO         TAG200610
archive logs generated after SCN 4813354 not found in repository
Media recovery start SCN is 4813354
Recovery must be done beyond SCN 4813354 to clear data files fuzziness
Finished restore at 12-OCT-06
```

Recall Mode

If you use a media manager that supports vaulted backups, then you can use preview recall to recall media from remote storage. This next example will request that any media needed to restore the database be recalled from remote storage.

```
RMAN> restore database preview recall;
```

How It Works

You can use preview with any type of restore command. When you use the preview command, no datafiles are actually restored. The restore ... preview command queries the repository only to report on the most recent information about what backup files will be needed for the specified restore operation. It does not check to see whether the RMAN backup files physically exist or that they are accessible.

■ **Tip** If you want to verify that backup files are physically available, use the restore validate command as described in recipe 11-3.

You can preview output in the normal verbose mode, or you can have it summarized. Also, if you use a media management layer (MML) that supports recalling vaulted backups, you can use the preview recall command to request media to be recalled from remote storage.

11-3. Verifying Integrity of Backups

Problem

You need to perform a restore and recovery, but first you want to validate only that the backup pieces are available and structurally sound before you actually restore any datafiles.

Solution

You can use either the restore ... validate or validate command to verify the availability and integrity of backup pieces required by RMAN to perform the restore operation. These commands do not restore datafiles. You can additionally specify the check logical clause to instruct RMAN to check for logical corruption.

Using restore ... validate

The validate clause works with any restore command. Here are several examples of using restore ... validate:

```
RMAN> restore database validate;
RMAN> restore database from tag MON_BCK validate;
RMAN> restore datafile 1 validate;
RMAN> restore archivelog all validate;
RMAN> restore controlfile validate;
RMAN> restore tablespace users validate;
```

If successful, you'll see text similar to the following near the bottom of the output:

```
channel ORA_DISK_1: validation complete, elapsed time: 00:00:45
Finished restore at 10-AUG-06
```

By default, RMAN checks only for physical corruption when validating. You can also instruct RMAN to check for logical corruption with the check logical clause:

```
RMAN> restore database validate check logical;
```

If a backup piece is missing or corrupt, the restore ... validate command will automatically check for the availability of previously taken backups.

Using validate

When using the validate command, you need to know the primary key of the backup set that you want to validate. First, use the list backup command to find the appropriate primary key.

```
RMAN> list backup;
```

Here are the relevant lines from the output:

```
BS Key  Type LV Size       Device Type Elapsed Time Completion Time
------- ---- -- ---------- ----------- ------------ ---------------
193     Full    129.48M    DISK         00:01:05     16-AUG-06
BP Key: 193   Status: AVAILABLE  Compressed: YES  Tag: TAG20061014T13291
```

After determining the backup set key, validate as follows:

```
RMAN> validate backupset 193;
```

If the validate command works, you should see a message similar to this one at the bottom of the message stack:

```
channel ORA_DISK_1: validation complete, elapsed time: 00:00:45
```

If the validation process discovers a problem, it will display an error message and stop processing. By default the validate command checks only for physical corruption. Use the check logical parameter if you want the validation process to also check for logical corruption:

```
RMAN> validate backupset 193 check logical;
```

New in Oracle Database 11*g*, you can use the `validate` command to validate all backup pieces in the flash recovery area with the following command:

```
RMAN> validate recovery area;
```

How It Works

We recommend that you use `restore ... validate` on a regular basis as part of testing the viability of your backups. This command works with any type of restore operation.

You can also use the `validate` command to verify a specific backup set. Both the `restore ... validate` and `validate` commands will check to see whether the required backup piece is available and additionally whether it is free from physical corruption. The `restore ... validate` command will also check to verify whether any required archived redo log file backup sets are available and intact. These commands do not actually restore any files.

■Note Physical corruption is when the block contents don't match the physical format that Oracle expects. By default, RMAN checks for physical corruption when backing up, restoring, or validating datafiles. Logical corruption is when the block is in the correct format but the contents aren't consistent with what Oracle expects. Logical corruption would be issues such as corruption in a row piece or an index entry.

You can instruct RMAN to check for logical corruption with the `check logical` clause of the `restore` command. When RMAN detects logical corruption, it will write relevant error messages to your target database's alert.log file and also reflect this information in the V$DATABASE_BLOCK_CORRUPTION view.

You can see whether a corrupt block is either physically or logically corrupt by querying the CORRUPTION_TYPE column of the V$DATABASE_BLOCK_CORRUPTION view. RMAN can perform block media recovery only on physically corrupt blocks. Blocks tagged with type LOGICAL corruption cannot be recovered by RMAN (through block-level recovery). To recover logically corrupt blocks, restore the datafile from a backup and perform media recovery.

When you issue `restore ... validate`, RMAN will look in the repository, get the latest backup information, and look for the relevant backup pieces. When RMAN can't find a backup piece or when RMAN detects corruption, it will then issue a "failover to previous backup" message and automatically search for a previously taken backup. RMAN will stop looking when it finds a good backup or until it has searched through all known backups without finding one.

■Note RMAN's behavior of searching sequentially back through backups until a good backup is found is called *restore failover*.

11-4. Testing Media Recovery

Problem

You need to perform a database recovery, but you suspect one of your archived redo log files is bad. You want to perform a test to see whether all of the redo is available and can be applied.

Solution

The recover ... test command instructs Oracle to apply the redo necessary to perform recovery but does not make the changes permanent in the datafiles. When you recover in test mode, Oracle applies the required redo but rolls back the changes at the end of the process.

This example starts up the database in mount mode, restores the entire database, and then does a test recovery:

```
RMAN> connect target /
RMAN> startup mount;
RMAN> restore database;
RMAN> recover database test;
```

Here is a partial snippet of the output showing that the test recovery was successful:

```
ORA-10574: Test recovery did not corrupt any data block
ORA-10573: Test recover tested redo from change 847960 to 848243
ORA-10570: Test recovery complete
```

You can test a recovery with most recover commands. Here are some examples:

```
RMAN> recover tablespace users, tools test;
RMAN> recover datafile 1 test;
```

■**Note** Before performing a test recovery, ensure that the datafiles being recovered are offline. Oracle will throw an ORA-01124 error for any one line datafiles being recovered in test mode.

How It Works

The test command allows you to test drive the redo application process without making any permanent changes to the datafiles. Running this command is particularly useful for diagnosing problems that you're having with the application of redo during the recovery process. For example, you can use the test command with the until clause to test up to a specific trouble point:

```
RMAN> recover database until time 'sysdate - 1/48' test;
RMAN> recover database until scn 2328888 test;
RMAN> recover database until sequence 343 test;
```

■Caution If you attempt to issue a `recover tablespace until ... test`, RMAN will attempt to perform a tablespace point-in-time recovery (TSPITR).

If you're missing archived redo log files or online redo log files that are needed for recovery, you'll receive a message similar to this:

```
ORA-06053: unable to perform media recovery because of missing log
```

If you can't locate the missing redo, then you'll most likely have to perform incomplete recovery. See Chapter 12 for details on how to perform an incomplete recovery.

ALLOWING CORRUPTION

In Oracle Database 10*g* and lower, the syntax `recover ... test allow n corruption` does not work from within RMAN. If you want to run the `test` command with the `allow n corruption` clause, then you must issue that command from inside SQL*Plus, as shown here:

```
SQL> connect sys/muft as sysdba
SQL> recover tablespace system test allow 5 corruption;
```

When using the `recover ... test allow n corruption` command, you can specify integers greater than 1 for n. If you are using `recover ... allow n corruption` (and not using the `test` command), then n can be 1 only.

11-5. Performing Database-Level Recovery

Problem

You've lost all of your datafiles but still have your online redo log files. You want to perform complete recovery.

Solution

You can perform a complete database-level recovery in this situation with either the current control file or a backup control file.

Use Current Control File

You must first put your database in mount mode to perform a database-wide restore and recovery. This is because the system tablespace datafile(s) must be offline when being restored and recovered. Oracle won't allow you to operate your database in open mode with the system datafile offline.

In this situation, we simply start up the database in mount mode, issue the restore and recover commands, and then open the database:

```
RMAN> connect target /
RMAN> startup mount;
RMAN> restore database;
RMAN> recover database;
RMAN> alter database open;
```

If everything went as expected, the last message you should see is this:

```
database opened
```

Use Backup Control File

This solution uses an autobackup of the control file retrieved from the flash recovery area. If you're using a different strategy to back up your control file, then see Chapter 10 for details on restoring your control file.

In this example, we first restore the control file before issuing the restore and recover database commands:

```
RMAN> connect target /
RMAN> startup nomount;
RMAN> restore controlfile from autobackup;
RMAN> alter database mount;
RMAN> restore database;
RMAN> recover database;
RMAN> alter database open resetlogs;
```

If everything went as expected, the last message you should see is this:

```
database opened
```

■**Note** You are required to open your database with the open resetlogs command anytime you use a backup control file during a recovery operation.

How It Works

The restore database command will restore every datafile in your database. The exception to this is when RMAN detects that datafiles have already been restored, then it will not restore them again. If you want to override that behavior, then use the force command as explained in recipe 11-12.

When you issue the `recover database` command, RMAN will automatically apply redo to any datafiles that need recovery. The recovery process includes applying changes found in the following:

- Incremental backup pieces (applicable only if using incremental backups)

- Archived redo log files (generated since the last backup or last incremental backup that is applied)

- Online redo log files (current and unarchived)

You can open your database after the restore and recovery process is complete. If you restore from a backup control file, you are required to open your database with the `open resetlogs` command.

Complete database recovery works only if you have good backups of your database and have access to all redo generated after the backup was taken. You need all the redo required to recover the database datafiles. If you don't have all the required redo, then you'll most likely have to perform an incomplete recovery. See Chapter 12 for details on performing an incomplete recovery.

■**Note** Your database has to be at least mounted to restore datafiles using RMAN. This is because RMAN reads information from the control file during the restore and recovery process.

11-6. Performing Tablespace-Level Recovery

Problem

You're seeing a media error associated with several datafiles contained in one tablespace. You want to perform complete recovery on all datafiles associated with that problem tablespace.

Solution

Use the `restore tablespace` and `recover tablespace` commands to restore and recover all the datafiles associated with a tablespace. You can either place the database in mount mode or have the database open. In the first scenario, we'll place the database in mount mode for the restore and recovery.

Recover While Database Not Open

This solution works for any tablespace in your database. In this example, we restore the user_data and user_index tablespaces:

```
RMAN> connect target /
RMAN> startup mount;
RMAN> restore tablespace user_data, user_index;
RMAN> recover tablespace user_data, user_index;
RMAN> alter database open;
```

If everything was successful, the last message you should see is this:

```
database opened
```

Recover While Database Is Open

You can take a tablespace offline, restore, and recover it while your database is open. This works for any tablespace except the system and undo tablespaces. This example takes data_ts offline and then restores and recovers before bringing it back online:

```
RMAN> connect target /
RMAN> sql 'alter tablespace data_ts offline immediate';
RMAN> restore tablespace data_ts;
RMAN> recover tablespace data_ts;
RMAN> sql 'alter tablespace data_ts online';
```

After the tablespace is brought online, you should see a message similar to this:

```
sql statement: alter tablespace data_ts online
```

How It Works

The RMAN `restore tablespace` and `recover tablespace` commands will restore and recover all datafiles associated with the specified tablespace(s). It's appropriate to perform this type of complete recovery when you only have datafiles from a tablespace or set of tablespaces missing. If your database is open, then all datafiles in the tablespace(s) being recovered must be offline.

11-7. Performing Datafile-Level Recovery

Problem

You have one datafile that has experienced media failure. You don't want to restore and recover the entire database or all datafiles associated with the tablespace. You just want to restore and recover the datafile that experienced media failure.

Solution

Use the `restore datafile` and `recover datafile` commands to restore and recover one or more datafiles. The database can be mounted or open to restore datafiles.

Recover While Database Not Open

In this scenario we mount the database and then restore and recover the missing datafile. You can restore and recover any datafile in your database while the database is not open. This example shows restoring the datafile 1, which is associated to the system tablespace:

```
RMAN> connect target /
RMAN> startup mount;
RMAN> restore datafile 1;
RMAN> recover datafile 1;
RMAN> alter database open;
```

You can also specify the filename when performing a datafile recovery:

```
RMAN> connect target /
RMAN> startup mount;
RMAN> restore datafile '/ora01/brdstn/system_01.dbf';
RMAN> recover datafile '/ora01/brdstn/system_01.dbf';
RMAN> alter database open;
```

Recover While Database Open

For nonsystem and non-undo datafiles, you have the option of keeping the database open while performing the recovery. When your database is open, you're required to take offline any datafiles you're attempting to restore and recover.

```
RMAN> connect target /
RMAN> sql 'alter database datafile 3, 4 offline';
RMAN> restore datafile 3, 4;
RMAN> recover datafile 3, 4;
RMAN> sql 'alter database datafile 3, 4 online';
```

■**Tip** Use the RMAN report schema command to list datafile names and file numbers. You can also query the NAME and FILE# columns of V$DATAFILE to take names and numbers.

You can also specify the name of the datafile that you want to restore and recover:

```
RMAN> sql "alter database datafile ''/ora01/BRDSTN/data_ts01.dbf'' offline";
RMAN> restore datafile '/ora01/BRDSTN/data_ts01.dbf';
RMAN> recover datafile '/ora01/BRDSTN/data_ts01.dbf';
RMAN> sql "alter datafile ''/ora01/BRDSTN/data_ts01.dbf'' online";
```

■**Note** When using the RMAN sql command, if there are single quote marks within the SQL statement, then you are required to use double quotes to enclose the entire SQL statement and then also use two single quote marks where you would ordinarily just use one quote mark.

How It Works

A datafile-level restore and recovery works well when you want to specify which datafiles you want recovered. With datafile-level recoveries, you can use either the datafile number or the datafile name. For nonsystem and non-undo datafiles, you have the option of restoring and recovering while the database is open. While the database is open, you have to first take offline any datafiles being restored and recovered.

11-8. Restoring Datafiles to Nondefault Locations

Problem

You've just experienced a serious media failure and won't be able to restore datafiles to their original locations. In other words, you need to restore datafiles to a nondefault location.

Solution

Use the `set newname` and `switch` commands to restore datafiles to nondefault locations. Both of these commands must be run from within an RMAN run{} block. This example changes the location of datafiles 4 and 5, which are in the data_ts tablespace:

```
RMAN> connect target /
RMAN> startup mount;
RMAN> run{
2> set newname for datafile 4 to '/ora01/BRDSTN/data_ts01.dbf';
3> set newname for datafile 5 to '/ora01/BRDSTN/data_ts02.dbf';
4> restore tablespace data_ts;
5> switch datafile all; # Updates repository with new datafile location.
6> recover tablespace data_ts;
7> alter database open;
8> }
```

This is a partial listing of the output:

```
Starting recover at 08-FEB-07
using channel ORA_DISK_1
starting media recovery
media recovery complete, elapsed time: 00:00:37
Finished recover at 08-FEB-07
database opened
```

If the database is open, you can place the datafiles offline and then set their new names for restore and recovery:

```
RMAN> run{
2> sql 'alter database datafile 4, 5 offline';
3> set newname for datafile 4 to '/ora01/BRDSTN/data_ts01.dbf';
4> set newname for datafile 5 to '/ora01/BRDSTN/data_ts02.dbf';
5> restore datafile 4, 5;
5> switch datafile all; # Updates repository with new datafile location.
6> recover datafile 4, 5;
7> sql 'alter database datafile 4, 5 online';
8> }
```

You should now see a message similar to the following:

```
starting media recovery
media recovery complete, elapsed time: 00:00:57
Finished recover at 08-FEB-07
sql statement: alter database datafile 4, 5 online
```

■**Tip** Use the RMAN report schema command to list datafile names and file numbers. You can also query the NAME and FILE# columns of V$DATAFILE to take names and numbers.

You can also use datafile names instead of numbers. However, you have to be careful about which name you use and where it comes in the script. This is because the control file doesn't consider the new location to be the current location until you issue the switch command.

```
RMAN> run{
2> sql "alter database datafile ''/ora02/BRDSTN/data_ts01.dbf'' offline';
3> set newname for datafile '/ora02/BRDSTN/data_ts01.dbf'
4>    to '/ora01/BRDSTN/data_ts01.dbf';
5> restore datafile '/ora02/BRDSTN/data_ts01.dbf';
6> switch datafile all; # Updates repository with new datafile location.
7> recover datafile '/ora01/BRDSTN/data_ts01.dbf';
8> sql "alter database datafile ''/ora01/BRDSTN/data_ts01.dbf'' online";
9> }
```

■**Tip** When using the RMAN sql command, if there are single quote marks in the SQL command, then you are required to use double quotes to enclose the entire SQL statement and use two single quote marks where you would ordinarily use just one quote mark.

How It Works

You can use a combination of the set newname and switch commands to restore and recover a datafile to a nondefault location. You must run the set newname command and the switch command from within a run{} block.

The switch command updates the target database control file with the new location of the datafile. It's OK to use switch datafile all, which updates all datafile locations. The only datafile names that will actually change are the ones that you have specified. Alternatively, you can use switch datafile <number> to update the repository with a specific datafile number.

■**Note** If you don't run the `switch` command, then RMAN marks the restored datafile to be a valid datafile copy that can be used for subsequent restore operations.

11-9. Performing Block-Level Recovery

Problem

When performing daily backups, you notice that RMAN is reporting in your target database alert.log file that there is a corrupt block in a large datafile. It could take a significant amount of time to perform the traditional restore and recover of a large datafile. You wonder whether there is a method for just recovering the corrupt block and not the entire datafile.

Solution

If you're using Oracle Database 11g or newer, use the `recover datafile ... block` command to recover individual blocks within a datafile.

■**Note** If you're using Oracle Database 10g or Oracle9i Database, then use the `blockrecover` command to perform block media recovery. The block recovery examples in this recipe use the `recover` command. You can substitute the `blockrecover` command for the `recover` command in the examples in this recipe if you're using Oracle Database 10g or Oracle9i Database.

You can instruct RMAN to recover blocks in two ways:

- Use the `corruption list` clause.

- Specify individual datafiles and blocks.

When RMAN detects corrupt blocks, it writes an error to the alert.log file and also populates the V$DATABASE_BLOCK_CORRUPTION view. You can instruct RMAN to recover the blocks listed as corrupt in that view as follows:

```
RMAN> recover corruption list;
```

The other way to recover blocks is to specify particular datafiles and blocks. Here are several examples:

```
RMAN> recover datafile 5 block 24;
RMAN> recover datafile 7 block 22 datafile 8 block 43;
RMAN> recover datafile 5 block 24 from tag=tues_backup;
RMAN> recover datafile 6 block 89 restore until sequence 546;
RMAN> recover datafile 5 block 32 restore until 'sysdate-1';
RMAN> recover datafile 5 block 65 restore until scn 23453;
```

If you attempt to use the `recover` command on a datafile that RMAN does not know about, you'll receive an error similar to this:

```
RMAN-06023: no backup or copy of datafile 6 found to restore
```

If you have a user-managed backup of the datafile that you've taken outside RMAN, you can use the `catalog datafilecopy` command to create metadata about the file in the RMAN repository, as shown here:

```
RMAN> catalog datafilecopy '/orabackups/BRDSTN/index_ts01.dbf';
```

If all the required redo (online or archived) is available, you can now issue the `recover` command, as shown here:

```
RMAN> recover datafile 6 block 25;
```

How It Works

Block-level corruption is rare and is usually caused by some sort of I/O error. However, if you do have an isolated corrupt block within a large datafile, it's nice to have the option of performing a block-level recovery. Block-level recovery is useful when a small number of blocks are corrupt within a datafile. Block recovery is not appropriate if the entire datafile needs media recovery.

RMAN will automatically detect corruption in blocks whenever a `backup` or `backup validate` command is issued. These blocks are reported as corrupt in the alert.log file and the V$DATABASE_BLOCK_CORRUPTION view.

Here are the various locations that Oracle will record block-level corruption:

- RMAN backup populates V$DATABASE_BLOCK_CORRUPTION.

- Trace files.

- Alert.log file.

- Output of `dbverify` utility.

- Output of SQL `analyze ... validate structure` command.

- V$BACKUP_CORRUPTION and V$COPY_CORRUPTION will list corrupt blocks in backup piece files.

Your database can be either mounted or open when performing block-level recovery. You do not have to take the datafile being recovered offline. Block-level media recovery allows you to keep your database available and also reduces the mean time to recovery since only the corrupt blocks are offline during the recovery.

■**Note** RMAN cannot perform block-level recovery on block 1 (datafile header) of the datafile.

Your database must be in archivelog mode for performing block-level recoveries. In Oracle Database 11g, RMAN can restore the block from the flashback logs (if available). If the flashback logs are not available, then RMAN will attempt to restore the block from a full backup, a level 0 backup, or an image copy backup generated by backup as copy command. After the block has been restored, any required archived redo logs must be available to recover the block. RMAN can't perform block media recovery using incremental level 1 (or higher) backups.

CREATING AND FIXING BLOCK CORRUPTION

The purpose of this sidebar is to show you how to corrupt a block so that you can test recovering at the block level. *Do not* perform this test exercise in a production environment.

In a Unix environment, you can corrupt a specific block in a datafile using the dd command. For example, the following dd command populates the 20th block of the tools01.dbf datafile with zeros:

```
$ dd if=/dev/zero of=tools01.dbf bs=8k conv=notrunc seek=20 count=1
```

Now if we attempt to back up the tools tablespace using RMAN, we receive an error indicating there is a corrupt block:

```
RMAN> backup tablespace tools;

RMAN-03009: failure of backup command on ORA_DISK_1 channel
ORA-19566: exceeded limit of 0 corrupt blocks for file /ora01/BRDSTN/tools01.dbf
```

We additionally use the dbverify utility to validate that the tools01.dbf datafile has a corrupt block:

```
$ dbv file=/ora01/BRDSTN/tools01.dbf blocksize=8192
```

Here is the partial output of the dbverify command:

```
DBVERIFY - Verification starting : FILE = tools01.dbf
Page 20 is marked corrupt
Corrupt block relative dba: 0x01400014 (file 5, block 20)
```

The dbverify utility indicates that block 20 in file 5 is corrupt. We can corroborate this by viewing the contents of V$DATABASE_BLOCK_CORRUPTION, as shown here:

```
SQL> select * from v$database_block_corruption;

    FILE#      BLOCK#      BLOCKS CORRUPTION_CHANGE# CORRUPTIO
---------- ---------- ---------- ------------------- ---------
        5         20           1                   0 ALL ZERO
```

We can now use the RMAN recover command to restore block 20 in datafile 5, as shown here (if you're using Oracle Database 10g or Oracle9i, then use the RMAN blockrecover command):

```
RMAN> recover datafile 5 block 20;
```

11-10. Recovering Read-Only Tablespaces

Problem

You issued a `restore database` command and notice that the datafiles associated with read-only tablespaces were not restored.

Solution

Use the `check readonly` command to instruct RMAN to restore datafiles associated with read-only tablespaces.

```
RMAN> connect target /
RMAN> startup mount;
RMAN> restore database check readonly;
RMAN> recover database;
RMAN> alter database open;
```

Another alternative is to explicitly restore the read-only tablespaces after you have restored the regular datafiles. In this example, two read-only tablespaces are restored after the entire database has been restored:

```
RMAN> connect target /
RMAN> startup mount;
RMAN> restore database;
RMAN> restore tablespace MAR05DATA, JUN05DATA;
RMAN> recover database;
RMAN> alter database open;
```

How It Works

By default, the `restore` command skips datafiles associated with read-only tablespaces. If you want read-only tablespaces restored, then you must use the `check readonly` command or explicitly restore each read-only tablespace.

■**Note** If you are using a backup that was created after the read-only tablespace was placed into read-only mode, then no recovery is necessary for the read-only datafiles. In this situation, there is no redo that has been generated for the read-only tablespace since it was backed up.

11-11. Restoring Temporary Tablespaces

Problem

RMAN doesn't back up locally managed temporary tablespace tempfiles, and you want to ensure that they're restored as part of your backup strategy.

Solution

Starting with Oracle Database 10g, you don't have to restore or re-create missing locally managed temporary tablespace tempfiles. When you open your database for use, Oracle automatically detects and re-creates locally managed temporary tablespace tempfiles.

When Oracle automatically re-creates a temporary tablespace, it will log a message to your target database alert.log file similar to the following:

```
Re-creating tempfile <your temporary tablespace filename>
```

How It Works

When you open your database, Oracle will check to see whether any locally managed temporary tablespace tempfiles are missing. If Oracle detects missing temporary tempfiles, it will automatically re-create them using information from the control files.

■**Note** Oracle's feature of automatically re-creating temporary tablespace tempfiles applies only to missing locally managed temporary tablespace tempfiles. This feature does not apply to a dictionary-managed temporary tablespace.

If for any reason your temporary tablespace becomes unavailable, you can also re-create it yourself. Since there are never any permanent objects in temporary tablespaces, you can simply re-create them as needed. Here is an example of how to create a locally managed temporary tablespace:

```
SQL> CREATE TEMPORARY TABLESPACE temp TEMPFILE
2    '/ora03/oradata/BRDSTN/temp01.dbf' SIZE 5000M REUSE
3    EXTENT MANAGEMENT LOCAL UNIFORM SIZE 512K;
```

If your temporary tablespace exists but the temporary datafiles are missing, you can simply add the temporary datafile(s) as shown here:

```
SQL> alter tablespace temp
2    add tempfile '/ora03/oradata/BRDSTN/temp01.dbf' SIZE 5000M REUSE;
```

11-12. Forcing RMAN to Restore a File

Problem

As part of a test exercise, you attempt to restore a datafile twice and receive this RMAN message:

```
restore not done; all files readonly, offline, or already restored
```

In this situation, you want to force RMAN to restore the datafile again.

Solution

Use the force command to restore datafiles and archived redo log files even if they already exist in a location. This command forces RMAN to restore files, even if RMAN determines that they don't need to be restored. This first example uses the force to restore the obiwan01.dbf datafile:

```
RMAN> restore datafile '/ora01/yoda/obiwan01.dbf' force;
```

You should see a message similar to this at the bottom of your RMAN messages stack:

```
channel ORA_DISK_1: restore complete, elapsed time: 00:00:15
Finished restore at 09-FEB-07
```

Or if you know the particular datafile number, you can use the force command this way:

```
RMAN> restore datafile 42 force;
```

Similarly, you can use the force command on a tablespace. Here we use the force command to restore all datafiles associated with the star_wars tablespace:

```
RMAN> restore tablespace star_wars force;
```

To force RMAN to restore all datafiles in the database, issue this command:

```
RMAN> restore database force;
```

By default, RMAN won't restore archived redo log files if they already exist on disk. You can override this behavior as follows:

```
RMAN> restore archivelog from sequence 343 force;
```

How It Works

By default, RMAN will not restore a datafile that is in the correct location and contains the expected information in the datafile header. This is known as *restore optimization*. To override RMAN's default behavior, use the power of the force command. The force command works with any restore command.

11-13. Restoring from an Older Backup

Problem

You want to specifically instruct RMAN to restore from a backup set that is older than the last backup that was taken.

Solution

You can restore an older backup a couple of different ways: using a tag name or using the restore ... until command.

Specify a Tag Name

Use the `list backup` to find the tag name of the backup set. Every backup set has a tag name, either the default or one you specified. For example, here's the partial output of a `list backup` command that shows the desired tag name:

```
BP Key: 159 Status: AVAILABLE Compressed: NO  Tag: MON_BACK
```

Once you've identified the tag, you can instruct RMAN to use that as follows:

```
RMAN> startup mount;
RMAN> restore database from tag MON_BACK;
RMAN> recover database;
RMAN> alter database open;
```

You can also use a tag to restore specific tablespaces or datafiles as follows:

```
RMAN> restore tablespace users from tag INCUPDATE;
RMAN> restore datafile 2, 3 from tag AUG_FULL;
```

Using restore ... until

You can also tell RMAN to restore datafiles from a point in the past using the `until` clause of the `restore` command in one of the following ways:

- Until SCN

- Until sequence

- Until restore point

- Until time

■**Caution** This recipe uses the `restore ... until` command with the `recover` command to perform complete recovery. If you need to perform an incomplete recovery, then you will need to use the `recover ... until` command (not just the `recover` command by itself). See Chapter 12 for details on incomplete recoveries using `recover until` in conjunction with the `restore ... until` command.

If you know the SCN in a backup piece that you want to restore from, you can specify the SCN as follows:

```
RMAN> startup mount;
RMAN> restore database until SCN 1254174;
RMAN> recover database;
RMAN> alter database open;
```

Or if you know the log sequence number that you want to restore up to, the syntax is as follows:

```
RMAN> startup mount;
RMAN> restore database until sequence 17;
RMAN> recover database;
RMAN> alter database open;
```

If you've created restore points, then you can also use the restore point name as follows:

```
RMAN> startup mount;
RMAN> restore database until restore point FRI_RS;
RMAN> recover database;
RMAN> alter database open;
```

You can also specify a point in time from which you want RMAN to restore an older backup. This example instructs RMAN to retrieve the first backup it finds that is more than 10 days old:

```
RMAN> startup mount;
RMAN> restore database until time 'sysdate - 10';
RMAN> recover database;
RMAN> alter database open;
```

Here we're specifically instructing RMAN to restore from a date and time. Since we don't instruct RMAN to recover to a point in time, this example will perform a complete recovery:

```
RMAN> startup mount;
RMAN> restore database until time
2>     "to_date('05-oct-2006 14:00:00', dd-mon-rrrr hh24:mi:ss')";
RMAN> recover database;
RMAN> alter database open;
```

How It Works

You can easily instruct RMAN to restore from backups older than the most recent backup set. You can do this by specifying a tag or using the restore ... until command. In versions prior to Oracle Database 10g, this was the only way you could instruct RMAN to restore from a backup older than the most recent one recorded in the repository.

New with Oracle Database 10g, by default RMAN will look in older backups if it can't find a backup piece or if corruption is detected. RMAN will search through backup history until it locates a good backup or until it exhausts all possibilities. This feature is called *restore failover*.

In this example, RMAN cannot find the expected backup piece and automatically searches for a prior backup. Here is the backup operation and its corresponding partial output indicating that RMAN is initiating a restore failover:

```
RMAN> restore database;
ORA-27041: unable to open file
OSD-04002: unable to open file
O/S-Error: (OS 2) The system cannot the file specified.
failover to previous backup
```

11-14. Recovering Through Resetlogs

Problem

You recently performed an incomplete recovery that required you to open your database with the open resetlogs command. Before you could back up your database, you experienced another media failure. Prior to Oracle Database 10g, it was extremely difficult to recover using a backup of a previous incarnation of your database. You now wonder whether you can get your database back in one piece.

Solution

Beginning with Oracle Database 10g, you can restore a backup from a previous incarnation and recover through a resetlogs command. You simply need to restore and recover your database as required by the type of failure. In this example, the control files and all datafiles are restored:

```
RMAN> connect target /
RMAN> startup nomount;
RMAN> restore controlfile from autobackup;
RMAN> alter database mount;
RMAN> restore database;
RMAN> recover database;
RMAN> alter database open resetlogs;
```

When you issue the recover command, you should see redo being applied from the previous incarnation of the database and then the current incarnation. In this example, the previous incarnation has logs 77 through 79, and the current incarnation has logs 1 and 2:

```
archive log filename … thread=1 sequence=77
archive log filename … thread=1 sequence=78
archive log filename … thread=1 sequence=79
archive log filename … thread=1 sequence=1
archive log filename … thread=1 sequence=2
```

How It Works

Anytime you perform an incomplete recovery or recover with a backup control file, you are required to open your database with an open resetlogs command. Prior to Oracle Database 10g, you were required to take a backup of your database immediately after you reset the online redo log files. This is because resetting the online redo log files creates a new incarnation of your database and resets your log sequence number back to 1. Any backups taken before resetting the logs could not be easily used to restore and recover your database.

Starting with Oracle Database 10g, there is a new feature known as *simplified recovery through resetlogs*. This feature allows you to restore from a backup from a previous incarnation of your database and issue restore and recovery commands as applicable to the type of failure that has occurred.

Oracle keeps track of log files from all incarnations of your database. The V$LOG_HISTORY view is no longer cleared out during a resetlogs operation and contains information for the current incarnation as well as any previous incarnations.

The default format of the archived redo log files is now arch_%R_%T_%S.arc. The format character %R is a resetlogs identifier that ensures that unique names are used for the archived redo log files across different database incarnations.

You can view the incarnation of your database using the list incarnation command:

```
RMAN> list incarnation;

using target database control file instead of recovery catalog
List of Database Incarnations
DB Key  Inc Key DB Name  DB ID            STATUS   Reset SCN  Reset Time
------- ------- -------- ---------------- ---      ---------- ----------
1       1       ORCL     1109210542       PARENT   3605284    25-AUG-06
2       2       ORCL     1109210542       PARENT   7349364    07-FEB-07
3       3       ORCL     1109210542       CURRENT  7652413    08-FEB-07
```

■**Note** The simplified recovery through resetlogs feature works both with RMAN and with user-managed recoveries.

11-15. Restoring the Spfile

Problem

You might need to restore the spfile for one of several reasons:

- You accidentally deleted your server parameter file.

- You want to view an old copy of the spfile.

- You can't start your instance with the current spfile.

Solution

First you need to have enabled the autobackup of your control file. For details on enabling the autobackup of your control file, see recipe 5-4. Once autobackup of your control file is enabled, then you can restore your spfile from an autobackup. All of the following examples assume that there is not an spfile located in the default location. The approach varies slightly depending on whether you're using a recovery catalog, using a flash recovery area, or using default locations for backups of the spfile.

■**Note** If you can't start your instance with the current spfile, first rename or move your spfile and then restore the spfile from a backup.

Using a Recovery Catalog

If you're using a recovery catalog, then restoring the spfile is fairly straightforward. This example connects to the recovery catalog and then restores the spfile:

```
RMAN> connect target /
RMAN> connect catalog rmancat/rmancat@rcat
RMAN> startup nomount;
starting Oracle instance without parameter file for retrieval of spfile
RMAN> restore spfile;
RMAN> startup force; # startup using restored spfile
```

Not Using a Recovery Catalog, RMAN Autobackup in Default Location

If you aren't using a recovery catalog, then you need to know your database identifier before you can proceed. See recipe 10-3 for details about determining your DBID.

This recipe assumes that you have configured your autobackups of the spfile to go to the default location. The default location depends on your operating system. For Unix, the default location is ORACLE_HOME/dbs. On Windows systems, it's ORACLE_HOME\database or ORACLE_HOME\dbs.

```
RMAN> connect target /
RMAN> shutdown immediate;
RMAN> startup force nomount; # start instance for retrieval of spfile
RMAN> set dbid 260150593;
RMAN> restore spfile from autobackup;
RMAN> startup force; # startup using restored spfile
```

You should now see your instance start normally:

```
Oracle instance started
database mounted
database opened
```

When the autobackup is located in the default location, you can use the parameters maxseq and maxdays to alter the default behavior of RMAN. These parameters also apply to control file restores from the default location. See recipe 10-4 for examples on how to use maxseq and maxdays.

Not Using a Recovery Catalog, RMAN Autobackup Not in Default Location

If you're either using a flash recovery area (FRA) or have the autobackup of your control file configured to a nondefault location, then the spfile will not be backed up to what Oracle calls the *default location*. In these situations, you have to specifically tell RMAN where to retrieve the backup from.

If you're using a FRA, your spfiles will be backed up in an autobackup directory in your flash recovery area. You'll have to find that directory and backup piece name before you can restore your spfile. You'll also need to know your database identifier before you can proceed. See recipe 10-3 for determining your DBID. Once you know your DBID, you can restore the spfile as follows:

```
RMAN> connect target /
RMAN> shutdown immediate;
RMAN> set dbid 260150593;
RMAN> startup force nomount;  # start instance for retrieval of spfile
RMAN> restore spfile from '/ora02/FRA/BRDSTN/autobackup/2006_10_02/o1_mf_s_62.bkp';
RMAN> startup force; # startup using restored spfile
```

You should now see your instance start normally:

```
Oracle instance started
database mounted
database opened
```

How It Works

If you're using an spfile, then you can have it automatically backed up for you by enabling the autobackup of the control file. If you're using a recovery catalog, restoring the spfile is simple. The recovery catalog maintains information about what backup piece contains the latest copy of the spfile.

If the autobackups have been configured to create a backup piece in the default location, then you need to set the DBID and issue the `restore from autobackup` command. When the autobackup is in the default location, you can also use the values `maxseq` and `maxdays` to direct RMAN to look at specific ranges of backup files.

If you're not using a recovery catalog and the autobackups are created either in the FRA or in a nondefault location, then you will specifically set your DBID and tell RMAN where the backup files are located. This is because when you start your database in nomount mode and if it doesn't have access to a parameter file, there is no way for RMAN to know where the FRA is located. If RMAN doesn't know where the FRA is located, then there is no way for it to determine where the autobackups are stored.

11-16. Restoring Archived Redo Log Files

Problem

RMAN will automatically restore any archived redo log files that it needs during a recovery process. You almost *never* need to manually restore archived redo log files. However, you may want to manually restore the archived redo log files if any of the following situations apply:

- You want to restore archived redo log files in anticipation of later performing a recovery; the idea is that if the archived redo log files are already restored, this will speed up the recovery operation.

- You need to restore the archived redo log files to a nondefault location, either because of media failure or because of storage space issues.

- You need to restore specific archived redo log files because you want to inspect them via LogMiner.

Solution

This recipe is divided into two sections: restoring to the default location and restoring to a nondefault location.

Restoring to Default Location

The following command will restore all archived redo log files that RMAN has backed up:

```
RMAN> restore archivelog all;
```

If you want to restore from a specified sequence, use the from sequence clause. This example restores all archived redo log files from sequence 50:

```
RMAN> restore archivelog from sequence 50;
```

If you want to restore a range of archived redo log files, use the from sequence and until sequence clauses or the sequence between clause, as shown here. These commands restore archived redo log files from sequence 5170 through 5178 using thread 1.

```
RMAN> restore archivelog from sequence 5170 until sequence 5178 thread 1;
RMAN> restore archivelog sequence between 5170 and 5178 thread 1;
```

By default, RMAN won't restore an archived redo log file if it is already on disk. You can override this behavior via the force option:

```
RMAN> restore archivelog from sequence 1 force;
```

Restoring to Nondefault Location

Use the set archivelog destination clause if you want to restore archived redo log files to a different location than the default. The following example restores to the nondefault location of /ora01/archrest. The set command must be run from within the RMAN run{} block.

```
RMAN> run{
2> set archivelog destination to '/ora01/archrest';
3> restore archivelog from sequence 5200;
4> }
```

How It Works

If you've enabled a flash recovery area, then RMAN will by default restore archived redo log files to the destination defined by the initialization parameter db_recovery_file_dest. Otherwise, RMAN uses the log_archive_dest_1 initialization parameter to determine where to restore the archived redo log files.

If you restore archived redo log files to a nondefault location, RMAN knows the location they were restored to and automatically finds these files when you issue any subsequent recover commands. RMAN will not restore archived redo log files that it determines are already on disk. Even if you specify a nondefault location, RMAN will not restore an archived redo log file to disk if it already exists. In this situation, RMAN will simply return a message stating that the archived redo log file has already been restored. Use the force command to override this behavior.

If you are uncertain of the sequence numbers to use during a restore of log files, you can query the V$LOG_HISTORY view or issue an RMAN list backup command for more information.

■**Note** When restoring archived redo log files, your database can be either mounted or open.

11-17. Recovering Datafiles Not Backed Up

Problem

You recently added a datafile to a tablespace and had a failure before the datafile was backed up. You wonder how you're going to restore and recover a datafile that was never backed up.

Solution

For this solution to work, you need to have a good baseline backup of your database and any subsequently generated redo up to the point where the datafile was created. If you have your current control file, then you can restore and recover at the datafile, tablespace, or database level. If you're using a backup control file that has no information about the datafile, then you must restore and recover at the database level.

■**Note** In Oracle9*i* Database and previous releases, the DBA had to perform some manual steps to restore a datafile not backed up yet. This usually involved re-creating the missing datafile and then restarting the recovery process.

Using a Current Control File

In this example, we use the current control file and are recovering the user_idx01.dbf datafile in the user_idx tablespace:

```
RMAN> connect target /
RMAN> startup mount;
RMAN> restore tablespace user_idx;
```

You should see a message like the following in the output as RMAN re-creates the datafile:

```
creating datafile fno=5 name=/ora01/oradata/BRDSTN/user_idx01.dbf
```

Now issue the `recover` command and open the database:

```
RMAN> recover tablespace user_idx;
RMAN> alter database open;
```

Using a Backup Control File

This scenario is applicable anytime you use a backup control file to restore and recover a datafile that has not yet been backed up. First, we restore a control file from an older backup:

```
RMAN> connect target /
RMAN> startup nomount;
RMAN> restore controlfile from '/orafra/BRDSTN/autobackup/2006_10_11/01_mfn_.bkp';
```

When the control file has no record of the datafile, RMAN will throw an error if you attempt to recover at the tablespace or datafile level. In this situation, you must use the `restore database` and `recover database` commands as follows:

```
RMAN> startup mount;
RMAN> restore database;
RMAN> recover database;
```

Next, you should see quite a bit of RMAN output. Near the end of the output you should see a line similar to this indicating that the datafile has been re-created:

```
creating datafile fno=9 name=/ora02/BRDSTN/data_ts06.dbf
```

Since you restored using a backup control file, you are required to open the database with the `resetlogs` command:

```
RMAN> alter database open resetlogs;
```

How It Works

Starting with Oracle Database 10g, there is enough information in the redo stream for RMAN to automatically re-create a datafile that was never backed up. It doesn't matter whether the control file has a record of the datafile. It doesn't matter whether the datafile was added as part of a `create database datafile` command or a `create tablespace` command.

Prior to Oracle Database10g, manual intervention from the DBA was required to recover a datafile that had not been backed up yet. If Oracle identified that a datafile was missing that had not been backed up, the recovery process would halt, and you would have to identify the missing datafile and re-create it. After re-creating the missing datafile, you had to manually restart the recovery session.

In Oracle Database 10g and newer, this is no longer the case. RMAN automatically detects that there isn't a backup of a datafile being restored and re-creates the datafile from information retrieved from the control file and/or redo information as part of the restore and recovery operations.

11-18. Deleting Archived Redo Log Files During Recovery

Problem

You know that you're going to be applying many archived redo log files during a recovery process. You want RMAN to automatically delete the archived redo logs after they're applied.

Solution

Use the `recover ... delete archivelog` command as shown here:

```
RMAN> recover database delete archivelog;
```

You should see a message like the following in the output after RMAN successfully applied an archived redo log:

```
archived log file name=/usr/oracle/flash_recovery_area/DB11G/archivelog
/2007_04_20/o1_mf_1_740_32jmotgx_.arc thread=1 sequence=740
channel default: deleting archived log(s)
archived log file name=/usr/oracle/flash_recovery_area/DB11G/archivelog
/2007_04_20/o1_mf_1_740_32jmotgx_.arc RECID=1724 STAMP=620357134
```

How It Works

If you know you're going to restore and apply many archived redo log files, then you can use the `delete archivelog` clause of the `recover` command. This will cause RMAN to automatically remove any archived redo log files that have been applied and are not needed for recovery any longer. RMAN will not delete any archived redo log files that were already on disk at the time the `recover` command was issued.

■**Note** If your archived redo log files are restored to a flash recovery area, then RMAN will automatically enable the `delete archivelog` feature.

You can also instruct RMAN to use a specified amount of space for keeping restored archived redo logs on disk. For example, if you want RMAN to use at most 500MB disk space for restored archived redo log files, then you would specify that maximum size, as shown here:

```
RMAN> recover database delete archivelog maxsize 500m;
```

If you don't specify a maximum size, then RMAN deletes archived redo log files after they are applied. If you do specify a maximum size, then be careful not to specify a size smaller than your largest archived redo log file. RMAN will throw an error if it encounters an archived redo log file smaller than the specified maximum size and halt the restore process, as shown here:

```
RMAN-06557: unable to restore archived log thread 1, sequence 361
RMAN-06558: archived log size of 7546 kb is bigger than available space of 5120 kb
```

11-19. Restoring from Uncataloged Backup Pieces in Oracle Database 10*g* and Newer

Problem

You had to re-create your control file and you are not using a recovery catalog. Afterward, you attempted to restore datafiles using RMAN but received the following errors:

```
RMAN-06026: some targets not found - aborting restore
RMAN-06023: no backup or copy of datafile 10 found to restore
RMAN-06023: no backup or copy of datafile 5 found to restore
RMAN-06023: no backup or copy of datafile 3 found to restore
RMAN-06023: no backup or copy of datafile 2 found to restore
RMAN-06023: no backup or copy of datafile 1 found to restore
```

You want to restore control files, datafiles, and archived redo logs from RMAN backup pieces, but your control file now contains no information whatsoever about previously taken backups.

Solution

Use the `catalog` command to add RMAN metadata directly to your control file about backup pieces.

Using a Flash Recovery Area

You can have RMAN repopulate the control file with all file information in the flash recovery. The following command will catalog all backup sets, datafile copies, and archived redo log files located in the flash recovery area:

```
RMAN> catalog recovery area;
```

Using a Directory

You can also instruct RMAN to catalog all the backup pieces and image copies located under a starting directory path. This example instructs RMAN to record metadata in the repository for any backup pieces and image copies located under the /oradump01/FRA directory:

```
RMAN> catalog start with '/oradump01/FRA';
```

Using a Backup Piece

For a backup set to be usable, you must catalog all backup pieces in the backup set. In this example, there is only one backup piece in the backup set:

```
RMAN> catalog backuppiece
2> 'C:\FRA\ORCL\BACKUPSET\2007_01_03\O1_MF_NNNDF_TAG20070103T160632_2SRFQSG2_.BKP';
```

This writes metadata information about that backup piece into the control file. If successful, you should see output similar to this:

```
cataloged backuppiece
backup piece handle=C:\FRA\ORCL\BACKUPSET\
2007_01_03\O1_MF_NNNDF_TAG20070103T160632_2SRFQSG2_.BKP recid=2 stamp=610911396
```

How It Works

New with Oracle Database 10*g*, you can now add metadata about backup pieces directly to your control file via the `catalog` command. If you're not using a recovery catalog, this can be particularly useful if you ever have to re-create your control file. This is because when re-creating the control file, all of your RMAN information is wiped out.

You can use the `catalog` command to add the following types of information to your control file:

- Backup pieces

- Archived redo log files

- Control file copies

- Datafile copies

- Files in the flash recovery area

If you're using a database version prior to Oracle Database 10*g*, then see recipe 11-20 on how to use DBMS_BACKUP_RESTORE to extract files from backup pieces for which your control file has no information.

■**Note** You cannot use the `catalog` command for backup pieces on a tape device.

11-20. Restoring from Uncataloged Backup Pieces in Oracle9*i* Database and Older

Problem

You had to re-create your control file, and you are not using a recovery catalog. You want to restore control files, datafiles, and archived redo logs from RMAN backup pieces, but your control file now contains no information whatsoever about previously taken backups.

■**Note** If you are using Oracle Database 10*g* or newer, we strongly recommend that you use the `catalog` command and *do not* use DBMS_BACKUP_RESTORE. See recipe 11-19 for details on how to add metadata to your control file for uncataloged backup pieces.

Solution

Use the DBMS_BACKUP_RESTORE package to restore files from backup pieces. This recipe has several examples:

- Restoring a control file

- Restoring datafiles contained in a single backup piece

- Restoring datafiles contained in several backup pieces

- Applying incremental backups to datafiles

- Restoring archived redo log files

■**Note** You can use the DBMS_BACKUP_RESTORE package with any version of Oracle that supports RMAN.

Restoring a Control File

You can use the PL/SQL package DBMS_BACKUP_RESTORE to restore a control file. You need to know the name of the backup piece that contains the backup of the control file before you begin. Modify the following anonymous block of PL/SQL to use your backup piece name and control file name:

```
DECLARE
  finished BOOLEAN;
  v_dev_name VARCHAR2(75);
BEGIN
  -- Allocate a channel, when disk then type = null, if tape then type = sbt_tape.
  v_dev_name := dbms_backup_restore.deviceAllocate(type=>null, ident=>'d1');
  --
  dbms_backup_restore.restoreSetDatafile;
  dbms_backup_restore.restoreControlFileTo(
    cfname=>'C:\oracle\product\10.2.0\oradata\ORCL\CONTROL01.CTL');
  --
  dbms_backup_restore.restoreBackupPiece(
    'C:\oracle\product\10.2.0\flash_recovery_area\ORCL\AUTOBACKUP\
    2006_12_06\O1_MF_N_608466281_2QFZ6TNJ_.BKP', finished);
  --
  if finished then
    dbms_output.put_line('Control file restored.');
  else
    dbms_output.put_line('Problem');
  end if;
  --
  dbms_backup_restore.deviceDeallocate('d1');
END;
/
```

If the previous code was stored in a file named rc.sql, then you would execute it as follows:

```
SQL> connect / as sysdba
SQL> startup nomount;
SQL> @rc.sql
```

Restoring Datafiles in a Single Backup Piece

If you have output logs from your backups, then you can visually inspect those and determine the names of the datafiles within a backup piece. If you don't have any output logs, then you'll have to figure out through trial and error which datafiles are in which backup piece.

In this example, we know from our RMAN backup output logs that there are four datafiles contained within this backup piece. You'll need to modify this anonymous block of PL/SQL code to specify the files in your environment:

```
SET SERVEROUTPUT ON
DECLARE
  finished BOOLEAN;
  v_dev_name  VARCHAR2(75);
BEGIN
  -- Allocate channels, when disk then type = null, if tape then type = sbt_tape.
  v_dev_name := dbms_backup_restore.deviceAllocate(type=>null, ident=> 'd1');
  --
  -- Set beginning of restore operation (does not restore anything yet).
  dbms_backup_restore.restoreSetDatafile;
  --
  -- Define datafiles and their locations for datafiles in first backup piece.
  dbms_backup_restore.restoreDatafileTo(dfnumber=>1,toname=>'C:\ORCL\SYSTEM01.DBF');
  dbms_backup_restore.restoreDatafileTo(dfnumber=>3,toname=>'C:\ORCL\SYSAUX01.DBF');
  dbms_backup_restore.restoreDatafileTo(dfnumber=>4,toname=>'C:\ORCL\USERS08.DBF');
  dbms_backup_restore.restoreDatafileTo(dfnumber=>9,toname=>'C:\ORCL\ORA02.DBF');
  --
  -- Restore the datafiles in this backup piece.
  dbms_backup_restore.restoreBackupPiece(done => finished,
  handle=>'C:\FRA\ORCL\BACKUPSET\2006_12_26\
  O1_MF_NNNDF_TAG20061226T174632_2S3JM9NJ_.BKP', params=>null);
  --
  IF finished THEN
    dbms_output.put_line('Datafiles restored');
  ELSE
    dbms_output.put_line('Problem');
  END IF;
  --
  dbms_backup_restore.deviceDeallocate('d1');
END;
/
```

If you put the prior code into a file named dbr.sql, then you would run it as follows:

```
SQL> connect / as sysdba
SQL> startup mount;
SQL> @dbr.sql
```

Restoring Datafiles in Multiple Backup Pieces

If you have output logs from your backups, then you can visually inspect those and determine the names of the datafiles within a backup piece. If you don't have any output logs, then you'll have to figure out through trial and error which datafiles are in which backup piece.

In this example, we know from our RMAN backup output logs that there are two datafiles contained within three separate backup pieces. You'll need to modify this anonymous block of PL/SQL code to specify the files in your environment.

```
SET SERVEROUTPUT ON
DECLARE
  finished     BOOLEAN;
  v_dev_name   VARCHAR2(75);
  TYPE v_filestable IS TABLE OF varchar2(500) INDEX BY BINARY_INTEGER;
  v_filename   V_FILESTABLE;
  v_num_pieces NUMBER;
BEGIN
  -- Allocate channels, when disk then type = null, if tape then type = sbt_tape.
  v_dev_name := dbms_backup_restore.deviceAllocate(type=>null, ident=> 'd1');
  --
  -- Set beginning of restore operation (does not restore anything yet).
  dbms_backup_restore.restoreSetDatafile;
  --
  -- Define backup pieces in backup set.
  v_filename(1) :=
  'C:\FRA\ORCL\BACKUPSET\2006_12_29\01_MF_NNNDF_TAG20061229T175720_2SCGCR59_.BKP';
  v_filename(2) :=
  'C:\FRA\ORCL\BACKUPSET\2006_12_29\01_MF_NNNDF_TAG20061229T175720_2SCGG2J0_.BKP';
  v_filename(3) :=
  'C:\FRA\ORCL\BACKUPSET\2006_12_29\01_MF_NNNDF_TAG20061229T175720_2SCGHSC4_.BKP';

  -- There are 3 backup pieces in this backup set.
  v_num_pieces := 3;

  -- Define datafiles and locations.
  dbms_backup_restore.restoreDatafileTo(dfnumber=>1,toname=>'C:\ORCL\SYSTEM01.DBF');
  dbms_backup_restore.restoreDatafileTo(dfnumber=>10,toname=>'C:\ORCL\DS_TS01.DBF');

  -- Restore the datafiles in this backup set.
  FOR i IN 1..v_num_pieces LOOP
    dbms_backup_restore.restoreBackupPiece(done => finished, handle=> v_filename(i),
    params=>null);
```

```
  END LOOP;
  --
  IF finished THEN
    dbms_output.put_line('Datafiles restored');
  ELSE
    dbms_output.put_line('Problem');
  END IF;
  --
  dbms_backup_restore.deviceDeallocate('d1');
END;
/
```

If you put the prior code into a file named dbr.sql, then you would run it as follows:

```
SQL> connect / as sysdba
SQL> startup mount;
SQL> @dbr.sql
```

Applying Incremental Backups

Here's an example that shows how to apply an incremental backup. This example assumes that the datafile has already been restored and is now ready to have an incremental backup applied to it. You'll need to modify this anonymous block of PL/SQL to specify the filenames in your environment.

```
SET SERVEROUTPUT ON
DECLARE
  finished     BOOLEAN;
  v_dev_name   VARCHAR2(75);
BEGIN
  -- Allocate channels, when disk then type = null, if tape then type = sbt_tape.
  v_dev_name := dbms_backup_restore.deviceAllocate(type=>null, ident=> 'd1');
  --
  -- Set beginning of apply operation (does not restore anything yet).
  dbms_backup_restore.applySetDatafile;
  --
  -- Define file to apply incremental to.
  dbms_backup_restore.applyDatafileTo(dfnumber=>10,toname=>'C:\ORCL\DATA_TS.DBF');
  --
  -- Apply incremental backup to datafile.
  dbms_backup_restore.applyBackupPiece(done=>finished,

handle=>'C:\FRA\ORCL\BACKUPSET\2006_12_31\O1_MF_NNND1_TAG20061231T130613_2SJ61T4S_.B
KP');
  --
  IF finished THEN
    dbms_output.put_line('Incremental applied.');
  ELSE
    dbms_output.put_line('Problem');
```

```
  END IF;
  --
  dbms_backup_restore.deviceDeallocate('d1');
END;
/
```

If you put the prior code into a file named dbr.sql, then you would run it as follows:

```
SQL> connect / as sysdba
SQL> startup mount;
SQL> @dbr.sql
```

Restoring Archived Redo Log Files

Here is an anonymous block of PL/SQL that shows how to restore archived redo log files using DBMS_BACKUP_RESTORE. Before using this, you'll have to change this code to match your environment. This example restores two archived redo log files that are stored in one backup piece.

```
SET SERVEROUTPUT ON
DECLARE
  finished      BOOLEAN;
  v_dev_name    VARCHAR2(75);
BEGIN
  -- Allocate channels, when disk then type = null, if tape then type = sbt_tape.
  v_dev_name := dbms_backup_restore.deviceAllocate(type=>null, ident=> 'd1');
  --
  -- Set beginning of restore operation (does not restore anything yet).
  dbms_backup_restore.restoreSetArchivedlog;
  --
  -- Define archived redo log files to be restored.
  dbms_backup_restore.restoreArchivedlog(thread=>1, sequence=> 354);
  dbms_backup_restore.restoreArchivedlog(thread=>1, sequence=> 355);
  --
  dbms_backup_restore.restoreBackupPiece(done=>finished, handle=>
  'C:\FRA\ORCL\BACKUPSET\2006_12_30\O1_MF_ANNNN_TAG20061230T100354_2SF7055R_.BKP',
   params=>null);
  --
  IF finished THEN
    dbms_output.put_line('Archived redo log files restored');
  ELSE
    dbms_output.put_line('Problem');
  END IF;
  --
  dbms_backup_restore.deviceDeallocate('d1');
END;
/
```

If you put the prior code into a file named dbr.sql, then you would run it as follows:

```
SQL> connect / as sysdba
SQL> @dbr.sql
```

How It Works

Normally you will never need to know about or use DBMS_BACKUP_RESTORE. You would use it only if you couldn't accomplish a backup and recovery task through the regular RMAN interface. The PL/SQL package does come in handy once in a while if you're exclusively using a control file for your repository and find yourself in the circumstance where the control file doesn't contain any information about your RMAN backups.

Before you can use the DBMS_BACKUP_RESTORE package, you need to know the following:

- Location and names of files in a backup set

- Location and names of backup pieces in the backup set

We recommend that when you create your RMAN backups that you always spool out a log file (see recipe 17-7 for details). That will ensure that you can determine which datafiles, control files, and archived redo log files are in which backup pieces. If you don't know what datafiles are in which backup pieces, then you'll have to do some trial-and-error restore operations (guess which datafile is in which backup piece).

The basic approach to restore a datafile using DBMS_BACKUP_RESTORE is to use an anonymous block of PL/SQL as follows:

1. Allocate a channel with deviceAllocate.

2. Inform Oracle that you're going to restore datafiles using restoreSetDatafile.

3. Use restoreDatafile to specify datafiles to be restored.

4. Use restoreBackupPiece to specify the backup piece(s) and perform the actual restore operation.

5. Deallocate the channel with deviceDeallocate.

Interestingly, most of the work that RMAN performs is accomplished through calls to DBMS_BACKUP_RESTORE. Oracle does not readily provide documentation for this package. We suggest that you contact Oracle Support if you need more details on how to use this undocumented package for your particular situation.

■**Tip** If you want to view what calls RMAN makes to DBMS_BACKUP_RESTORE, enable PL/SQL debugging as described in recipe 17-9.

From within SQL*Plus, if you describe DBMS_BACKUP_RESTORE, you'll see that it contains more than 150 procedures and functions. You'll need to use only a small subset of those. Table 11-3 contains a brief description of the functions and procedures in DBMS_BACKUP_RESTORE that you are most likely to use. The most common uses of this package are to restore control files, datafiles, and archived redo log files.

Table 11-3. *Useful Procedures and Functions in DBMS_BACKUP_RESTORE*

Procedure/Function	Description
deviceAllocate	Allocates a device to be used
restoreSetDatafile	Tells Oracle that you're going to be restoring from an RMAN backup set
restoreControlfileTo	Instructs Oracle where the control file is to be restored
restoreDatafileTo	Defines a datafile and where it should be restored
restoreBackupPiece	Defines a backup piece and initiates the actual restore operation
deviceDeallocate	Deallocates device that was allocated by the deviceAllocate function
restoreArchivedLog	Defines an archived redo log file thread and sequence to be restored
applySetDatafile	Tells Oracle that you're going to be applying an incremental to a datafile
applyDatafileTo	Tells Oracle to which datafile that the incremental will be applied
ApplyBackupPiece	Defines which backup piece has the incremental backup and applies the incremental

CHAPTER 12

■■■

Performing Incomplete Recovery

One of us once worked in a place where a system administrator saw some *.log files in several directories and decided that since they were just log files, they could be deleted:

```
$ rm *.log
```

The log files that were removed were all of our online redo log files for the database. Oops! Big mistake—we had to perform an incomplete database recovery to get our database back online.

Incomplete database recovery means that you cannot recover all committed transactions. Incomplete means that you do not apply all redo to restore to the point of the last committed transaction that occurred in your database. In other words, you are restoring and recovering to a point in time in the past. For this reason, incomplete database recovery is also called *database point-in-time recovery* (DBPITR). Usually you perform incomplete database recovery because of one of the following reasons:

- You don't have all the redo required to perform a complete recovery. You're missing either archived redo log files or online redo log files that are required for complete recovery. This situation could arise because the required redo files are damaged or missing.

- You purposely want to roll the database back to a point in time. For example, you would do this in the event somebody accidentally truncated a table and you intentionally wanted to roll the database back to just before the truncate table command was issued.

■**Tip** To minimize the chance of failure with your online redo log files, we highly recommend you multiplex them with at least two members in each group and have each member on separate physical devices governed by separate controllers.

Background

Incomplete database recovery consists of two steps: restore and recovery. The restore step will re-create datafiles, and the recover step will apply redo up to the specified point in time. The restore process can be initiated from RMAN in several ways:

- `restore database until`

- `restore tablespace until`

- `flashback database`

For the majority of incomplete database recovery circumstances, you'll use the `restore database until` command to instruct RMAN to retrieve datafiles from the RMAN backup files. This type of incomplete database recovery is the main focus of this chapter. The `until` portion of the `restore database` command instructs RMAN to retrieve datafiles from a point in the past based on one of the following methods:

- Time

- Change (sometimes called *system change number* [SCN])

- Log sequence number

- Restore point (Oracle Database 10*g* Release 2 and newer versions)

The RMAN `restore database until` command will retrieve all datafiles from the most recent backup set or image copy. RMAN will automatically determine from the `until` clause which backup set contains the required datafiles. If you omit the `until` clause of the `restore database` command, RMAN will retrieve datafiles from the latest available backup set or image copy. In some situations, that may be the behavior you desire. We recommend you use the `until` clause to ensure that RMAN restores from the correct backup set. When you issue the `restore database until` command, RMAN will determine how to extract the datafiles from any of the following:

- Full database backup

- Incremental level 0 backup

- Image copy backup generated by the `backup as copy` command

You cannot perform an incomplete database recovery on a subset of your database's online datafiles. When performing incomplete database recovery, all of the checkpoint SCNs for all online datafiles must be synchronized before you can open your database with the `alter database open resetlogs` command. You can view the datafile header SCNs and the status of each datafile via this SQL query:

```
SQL> select file#, status, checkpoint_change#,
2    to_char(checkpoint_time,'dd-mon-rrrr hh24:mi:ss')
3    from v$datafile_header;
```

The only exception to this rule of not performing an incomplete recovery on a subset of online database files is a tablespace point-in-time recovery (TSPITR), which uses the `recover tablespace until` command. TSPITR is used in rare situations and restores and recovers only the tablespace(s) you specify. This type of recovery is described in recipe 12-10 and involves many steps to achieve the desired result.

The recovery portion of an incomplete database recovery is always initiated with the `recover database until` command. RMAN will automatically recover your database to the point specified with the `until` clause. Just like the `restore` command, you can recover until a time, change/SCN, log sequence number, or restore point. When RMAN reaches the specified point, it will automatically terminate the recovery process.

■**Note** Regardless of what you specify in the `until` clause, RMAN will convert that into a corresponding `until scn` clause and assign the appropriate SCN. This is to avoid any timing issues, particularly those caused by daylight saving time.

During a recovery, RMAN will automatically determine how to apply redo. First, RMAN will apply any incremental backups available. Next, any archived redo log files on disk will be applied. If the archived redo log files do not exist on disk, then RMAN will attempt to retrieve them from a backup set. If you want to apply redo as part of an incomplete database recovery, the following conditions must be true:

- Your database must be in archivelog mode.

- You must have a good backup of all datafiles.

- You must have all redo required to restore up to the specified point.

■**Tip** Starting with Oracle Database 10*g*, you can perform parallel media recovery by using the `recover database parallel` command (see recipe 16-8 for more details).

When performing an incomplete database recovery with RMAN, you must have your database in mount mode. RMAN needs the database in mount mode to be able to read and write to the control file. Also, with an incomplete database recovery, the system datafile is always one of the datafiles being recovered. The system datafile must be offline while it is being recovered. Oracle will not allow your database to be open while this is happening.

■**Note** After incomplete database recovery is performed, you are required to open your database with the `alter database open resetlogs` command.

Depending on your scenario, you can use RMAN to perform a variety of incomplete recovery methods. The first recipe in this chapter discusses how to determine what type of incomplete recovery to perform.

12-1. Determining Type of Incomplete Recovery

Problem

You want to perform an incomplete recovery but don't know which method to use.

Solution

Use Table 12-1 to determine which type of incomplete recovery to perform.

Table 12-1. *Deciding Type of Incomplete Recovery to Perform*

Situation	Instructions Location
You know approximately what time you want to stop the recovery process.	Recipe 12-2
You know the particular log file for which you want to stop the recovery process.	Recipe 12-3 or recipe 12-4
You know the SCN at which you want to end the recovery process.	Recipe 12-6
You want to restore to a defined restore point.	Recipe 12-7
You want to restore one tablespace to a point in time.	Recipe 12-10
You want to restore and recover a subset of your database's datafiles.	Recipe 12-11
You have enabled the flashback database feature and want to flash back your database.	Chapter 13

■ **Tip** Consider using a flashback drop, flashback table, or flashback query to restore and recover an erroneously dropped table or deleted data. Chapter 13 describes these flashback techniques in full detail.

How It Works

Time-based restore and recovery is commonly used when you know approximately the date and time to which you want to recover your database. For example, you may know approximately the time you want to stop the recovery process but not a particular SCN.

Log sequence–based and cancel-based recovery work well in situations where you have missing or damaged log files. In such scenarios, you can recover only up to your last good archived redo log file.

SCN-based recovery works well if you can pinpoint the SCN at which you want to stop the recovery process. You can retrieve SCN information from views such as V$LOG and V$LOG_HISTORY. You can also use tools such as LogMiner to retrieve the SCN of a particular SQL statement.

Restore point recoveries work only if you have established restore points. In these situations, you restore and recover up to the SCN associated with the specified restore point.

Tablespace point-in-time recovery is used in situations where you can restore and recover just a few tablespaces. You can use RMAN to automate many of the tasks associated with this type of incomplete recovery.

Flashing back your database works only if you have enabled the flashback database feature. Chapter 13 covers this topic in detail.

12-2. Performing Time-Based Recovery

Problem

You want to restore your database to a previous date and time.

Solution

You can restore your database to a previous time in one of two ways:

- Specify the time as part of the `restore` and `recover` commands.

- Use the `set until time` command, and then issue unqualified `restore` and `recover` commands.

The following example specifies a time when issuing the `restore` and `recover` commands:

```
RMAN> connect target /
RMAN> startup mount;
RMAN> restore database until time
2> "to_date('05-oct-2006 14:00:00', 'dd-mon-rrrr hh24:mi:ss')";
RMAN> recover database until time
2> "to_date('05-oct-2006 14:00:00', 'dd-mon-rrrr hh24:mi:ss')";
RMAN> alter database open resetlogs;
```

If everything went well, you should now see output similar to this:

```
Database altered
```

■**Tip** For time-based incomplete database recovery, we recommend using the TO_DATE function and explicitly specifying the date format. This eliminates any ambiguity about what date format is being used.

You can also specify the time by using the `set until time` command. This command and the subsequent `restore` and `recover` must be executed from within a `run{}` block:

```
RMAN> connect target /
RMAN> startup mount;
RMAN> run{
RMAN> set until time "to_date('05-oct-2006 14:00:00', 'dd-mon-rrrr hh24:mi:ss')";
RMAN> restore database;
RMAN> recover database;
RMAN> }
RMAN> alter database open resetlogs;
```

If everything went well, you should now see output similar to this:

```
Database altered
```

How It Works

To restore and recover your database back to a point in time, you can use either the `until time` clause of the `restore` and `recover` commands or the `set until time` clause within a `run{}` block. RMAN will restore and recover the database up to, but not including, the specified time. In other words, RMAN will restore any transactions committed prior to the time specified. RMAN automatically stops the recovery process when it reaches the time you specified.

The default date format that RMAN expects is YYYY-MM-DD:HH24:MI:SS. However, we recommend using the TO_DATE function and specifying a format mask. This eliminates ambiguities with different national date formats and having to set the operating system NLS_DATE_FORMAT variable.

When performing time-based recoveries, sometimes you'll see this error:

```
RMAN-03002: failure of restore command at ...
RMAN-20207: UNTIL TIME or RECOVERY WINDOW is before RESETLOGS time
```

This usually means you're trying to restore from a backup that belongs to a previous incarnation of the database. In other words, the backup that RMAN is trying to use was created prior to the database being opened with the `alter database open resetlogs` command. See recipe 12-9 for details on how to restore from a previous incarnation.

12-3. Performing Log Sequence–Based Recovery

Problem

You want to use RMAN to restore up to, but not including, a certain archived redo log file.

Solution

RMAN allows you to apply redo up to (but not including) a specific archived redo log file by specifying its sequence number when restoring and recovering. You can do this in one of two ways:

- Specify `until sequence` as part of the `restore` and `recover` commands.

- Use the `set until sequence` command.

The following example restores and recovers the target database up to, but not including, log sequence number 50:

```
RMAN> connect target /
RMAN> startup mount;
RMAN> restore database until sequence 50;
RMAN> recover database until sequence 50;
RMAN> alter database open resetlogs;
```

If everything went well, you should now see output similar to this:

```
Database altered
```

You can also use the set until command from within a run{} block to perform a log sequence–based recovery. The following examples restores and recovers up to but not including log sequence number 125 of thread 1:

```
RMAN> connect target /
RMAN> startup mount;
RMAN> run{
2> set until sequence 125 thread 1;
3> restore database;
4> recover database;
5> }
RMAN> alter database open resetlogs;
```

If everything went well, you should now see output similar to this:

```
Database altered
```

How It Works

Usually this type of incomplete database recovery is initiated because you have a missing or damaged archived redo log file. If that's the case, you can recover only up to your last good archived redo log file, because you cannot skip a missing archived redo log file.

How you determine which archived redo log file to restore up to (but not including) will vary by situation. For example, if you are physically missing an archived redo log file and if RMAN can't find it in a backup set, then you'll receive the following message when trying to apply the missing file:

```
RMAN-06053: unable to perform media recovery because of missing log
RMAN-06025: no backup of log thread 1 seq 45 lowscn 2149069 found to restore
```

Based on the previous error message, you would restore up to (but not including) log sequence 45.

Another common way to determine which archived redo log file you need to restore up to (but not including) is if files can't be restored from a bad tape. In this situation, you'll work with your system administrator to restore all available archived redo log files and then determine which sequence number to restore up to (but not including) based on what files were restorable.

Each time an online redo log file is generated, it is assigned a sequential log sequence number. When the online redo log file is copied to an archived redo log file, the log sequence number is preserved in the file header. You can view log sequence numbers by querying the SEQUENCE# column of the V$LOG_HISTORY and V$ARCHIVED_LOG views. Both of these views are based on information stored in the control file. You can query sequence number information from V$LOG_HISTORY, as shown here:

```
SQL> select sequence#, first_change#, first_time
2  from v$log_history
3  order by first_time;
```

And here's the corresponding query for V$ARCHIVED_LOG:

```
SQL> select sequence#, first_change#, first_time
2   from v$archived_log
3   order by first_time;
```

■**Tip** If you're using a flash recovery area (FRA), the sequence number is automatically embedded in the archived redo log filename. When an archived redo log file is created in the FRA, it uses the Oracle Managed File (OMF) format for the filename. The OMF format for an archived redo log file is O1_MF_<thread number>_<sequence number>_%u.arc.

If you're not using a FRA, then you must specify the file format of the archived redo log file via the log_archive_format initialization parameter. The default format is ARC%S_%R.%T. The %S specifies the log sequence number, %R specifies the resetlogs ID, and %T is the thread number.

■**Note** In Oracle Database 10g and newer, when not using a FRA, the log_archive_format initialization parameter must contain the format parameters %S, %R, and %T.

If any of your archived redo log files or online redo log files are physically available, you can also view the sequence number by dumping the file contents to a trace file with the dump logfile command as follows:

```
SQL> alter system dump logfile '<log file>';
```

This creates a trace file in the user dump destination. You can search that trace file for the string Seq#, which shows the sequence number for the log file that you dumped. Here's a sample of what you should see in the dump file:

```
descrip: Thread 0001, Seq# 0000000390, SCN 0x00000047bd5b-0x00000047db63
```

In this case, the sequence number is 390.

12-4. Performing Cancel-Based Recovery

Problem

You desire to perform a cancel-based incomplete database recovery first using RMAN to restore the datafiles and then using SQL*Plus to recover the datafiles. A cancel-based recovery is one that proceeds until you manually stop it.

Solution

The following example restores from the latest RMAN backup in preparation for a SQL*Plus cancel-based recovery:

```
RMAN> connect target /
RMAN> startup mount;
RMAN> restore database; # restore database from last backup
```

Once your database is restored, you can start a SQL*Plus session and initiate a cancel-based recovery, as shown here:

```
SQL> connect / as sysdba
SQL> recover database until cancel;
```

You will now be prompted by SQL*Plus to manually apply each archived redo log file. The following is the prompt that you'll get for each log file:

```
Specify log: {<RET>=suggested | filename | AUTO | CANCEL}
```

Hit the Return/Enter key until you arrive at the archived redo log file where you want to stop the recovery process. When you want to stop the recovery process, type the CANCEL keyword, as shown in Figure 12-1.

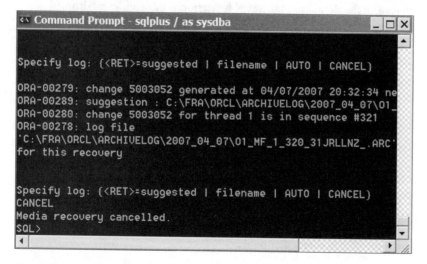

Figure 12-1. *Performing cancel-based recovery*

You should see a message indicating media recovery has been canceled:

```
Media recovery cancelled.
```

You can now open your database with the open resetlogs command:

```
SQL> alter database open resetlogs;
```

How It Works

SQL*Plus cancel-based incomplete database recovery is similar to the RMAN log sequence–based incomplete database recovery described in recipe 12-3. The only difference is that you're using SQL*Plus to initiate the recovery process.

Sometimes it's desirable to use SQL*Plus cancel-based recovery. For example, you may want to view the name and location of each log file before it is applied. Why would you want to view each filename? Sometimes DBAs are paranoid and stressed out in recovery situations, and they feel a little warmer and fuzzier when they can first view the archived redo log filename before applying it.

■Note With cancel-based recovery, you also have the option of manually entering an archived redo log file or online redo log filename and location.

12-5. Using LogMiner to Find an SCN

Problem

A user accidentally dropped a table. You want to find the SCN associated with that drop statement so that you can restore the database to the SCN just prior to the accidental drop.

■Note To be able to mine redo for DML statements, you must have database supplemental logging enabled prior to when the archived redo log file was generated. However, LogMiner can search for DDL statements without having supplemental logging enabled.

Solution

Here are the steps for instructing LogMiner to analyze a specific set of archived redo log files for an SCN associated with a SQL statement:

1. Specify a set of archived redo log files for LogMiner to analyze.

2. Start LogMiner, and specify a data dictionary.

3. Perform analysis.

4. Stop the LogMiner session.

First you need to tell LogMiner which online redo log files or archived redo log files you want to analyze. In this scenario, we know the SQL statement that we're looking for is in the archived redo log file with a sequence number of 7.

```
SQL> connect sys/foo as sysdba
SQL> exec dbms_logmnr.add_logfile(-
logfilename=>'/ora01/BRDSTN/arc00007_0605867201.001', -
options=>dbms_logmnr.addfile);
```

If you want to mine multiple online redo log files, you can add more using DBMS_LOGMNR.ADD_LOGFILE as follows:

```
SQL> exec dbms_logmnr.add_logfile(-
logfilename=>'/ora01/BRDSTN/arc00008_0605867201.001', -
options=>dbms_logmnr.addfile);
```

■**Note** You can view which log files will be analyzed by the current LogMiner session by querying the V$LOGMNR_LOGS view.

LogMiner needs access to the data dictionary to translate object IDs into object names. This example starts LogMiner and specifies that we want to use the current data dictionary for metadata information:

```
SQL> exec dbms_logmnr.start_logmnr(options=>dbms_logmnr.dict_from_online_catalog);
```

After you've started LogMiner, you can query the V$LGMNR_CONTENTS view for the SCN of the transaction of interest. This example queries for an SCN associated with a drop of the PAYROLL table:

```
SQL> select operation, scn
2  from v$logmnr_contents
3  where table_name='PAYROLL'
4  and operation='DROP';
OPERATION SCN
--------- -------
DROP      1047474
```

After you've found the SCN of interest, you can end your LogMiner session by calling dbms_logmnr as follows:

```
SQL> exec dbms_logmnr.end_logmnr();
```

How It Works

You can use LogMiner to find SCNs associated with DML and DDL statements. LogMiner requires supplemental logging to be enabled to be able to display information about DML statements. Enable supplemental logging by issuing the following SQL:

```
SQL> connect sys/foo as sysdba
SQL> alter database add supplemental log data;
```

By default, Oracle is not enabled with supplemental logging. LogMiner requires that supplemental logging be enabled prior to the log files being created so it can extract SCNs associated with DML commands. Once supplemental logging is enabled, you can use LogMiner to analyze and retrieve information such as an SCN associated with a particular DML statement.

You can analyze redo logs based on a time range, schema, SCN range, and so on. See the Oracle Database Utilities Guide for full details on how to use LogMiner. You can download all of Oracle's documentation from the `http://otn.oracle.com` website.

■**Tip** Consider using flashback drop, flashback table, or flashback query to restore and recover an erroneously dropped table or deleted data. Chapter 13 describes these flashback techniques in full detail.

12-6. Performing Change/SCN-Based Recovery

Problem

You want to perform an incomplete database recovery to a particular database SCN.

Solution

After establishing the SCN to which you want to restore, use the `until scn` clause to restore up to, but not including, the SCN specified. The following example restores all transactions that have an SCN that is less than 950:

```
RMAN> connect target /
RMAN> startup mount;
RMAN> restore database until scn 950;
RMAN> recover database until scn 950;
RMAN> alter database open resetlogs;
```

If everything went well, you should now see output similar to this:

```
Database altered
```

You can also use `set until scn` within a `run{}` block to perform SCN-based incomplete database recovery without having to repeat the SCN number for each command:

```
RMAN> connect target /
RMAN> startup mount;
RMAN> run{
2> set until scn 950;
3> restore database;
4> recover database;
5> }
RMAN> alter database open resetlogs;
```

If everything went well, you should now see output similar to this:

```
Database altered
```

How It Works

SCN-based incomplete database recovery works in situations where you know the SCN value up to where you want to end the restore and recovery session. RMAN will recover up to, but not including, the specified SCN. RMAN automatically terminates the restore process when it reaches the specified SCN.

You can view your database SCN information in several ways:

- As detailed in recipe 12-5, you can use LogMiner to determine an SCN associated with a DDL or DML statement.

- You can look in the alert.log file.

- You can look in your trace files.

- You can query the FIRST_CHANGE# column of VLOG, VLOG_HISTORY, and V$ARCHIVED_LOG.

If you have set the initialization parameter `log_checkpoints_to_alert` to TRUE, then every time a log switch occurs, Oracle will write the SCN of each checkpoint to your target database alert.log file. This feature can be handy when trying to determine historical checkpoint SCN activity. Here's an excerpt from the alert.log file that shows the SCN of a checkpoint for a database that has `log_checkpoints_to_alert` set to TRUE:

```
Completed checkpoint up to RBA [0xb.2.10], SCN: 7757450
```

You can also view SCN information by querying data dictionary views. For example, you can query V$ARCHIVED_LOG to display the first SCN and time that it was generated, as shown here:

```
SQL> select sequence#, first_change#, first_time
2   from v$archived_log
3   order by first_time;
```

Once you determine the SCN to which you want to recover, then you can use the `until scn` clause of the `restore` and `recover` commands to perform incomplete database recovery.

12-7. Recovering to a Restore Point

Problem

You want to restore and recover to a restore point.

Solution

Before you can restore to a restore point, you must have previously created a restore point via the `create restore point` command. Once you've done this, you can use the `until restore point` clause of the `restore` command.

CREATING A NORMAL RESTORE POINT

There are two types of restore points: normal and guaranteed. Guaranteed restore points require that you have the flashback database feature enabled. See Chapter 13 for more details on how to use flashback database with guaranteed restore points.

You can create a normal restore point using SQL*Plus as follows:

```
SQL> create restore point MY_RP;
```

This command creates a restore point named MY_RP that is associated with the SCN of the database at the time the command was issued. You can view the current SCN of your database as shown here:

```
SQL> select current_scn from v$database;
```

You can also view the SCN assigned to your restore point(s):

```
SQL> select name, scn from v$restore_point;
```

This example restores and recovers to the MY_RP restore point:

```
RMAN> connect target /
RMAN> startup mount;
RMAN> restore database until restore point MY_RP;
RMAN> recover database until restore point MY_RP;
RMAN> alter database open resetlogs;
```

Alternatively, you can use the set until command within a run{} block to specify a target restore point. The restore and recover commands will perform the incomplete database recovery up to the specified restore point:

```
RMAN> connect target /
RMAN> startup mount;
RMAN> run{
RMAN> set until restore point MY_RP;
RMAN> restore database;
RMAN> recover database;
RMAN> }
RMAN> alter database open resetlogs;
```

How It Works

A restore point records the SCN of the database at the time the restore point was created. The restore point acts like a synonym for the particular SCN. It allows you to restore and recover to an SCN without having to specify a number. RMAN will restore and recover up to, but not including, the SCN associated with the restore point.

You can view restore point information in the V$RESTORE_POINT view. That view contains information such as NAME, SCN, TIME, and DATABASE_INCARNATION#.

12-8. Restoring a Noarchivelog Mode Database

Problem

You used RMAN to back up a database in noarchivelog mode. You now need to restore this database from an RMAN backup.

Solution

When you restore a noarchivelog database, you can choose to use a backup control file or the current control file. You can run the following query to verify the type of control file you used to mount your database:

```
SQL> select open_mode, controlfile_type from v$database;
OPEN_MODE  CONTROL
---------- -------
MOUNTED    CURRENT
```

Using Backup Control File

Our recommended approach is to first restore the control file that was backed up at the same time your noarchivelog mode database was backed up. This way the control file has an SCN that is consistent with the datafile SCNs. After you restore the control file, you can then restore the datafiles and open your database with the open resetlogs command. For example:

```
RMAN> connect target /
RMAN> startup nomount;
RMAN> restore controlfile from autobackup;
RMAN> alter database mount;
RMAN> restore database;
RMAN> alter database open resetlogs;
```

You should see the following message after opening your database with the resetlogs option:

```
Database altered.
```

■**Note** In this scenario, if you don't restore the control file, then you won't be able to open your database. This is because the control file needs to be in sync with the datafiles.

Using Current Control File

If you don't restore your control file, you will have to perform a few extra steps. This example does not restore the control file and uses SQL*Plus to cancel out of the recovery session:

```
RMAN> connect target /
RMAN> startup mount;
RMAN> restore database;
RMAN> alter database open resetlogs;
```

At this point, you'll get an error message indicating that the resetlogs option is valid only after an incomplete database recovery:

```
ORA-01139: RESETLOGS option only valid after an incomplete database recovery
```

Perform the following steps from SQL*Plus to open your database:

```
SQL> recover database until cancel;
```

You should now be prompted as follows:

```
Specify log: {<RET>=suggested | filename | AUTO | CANCEL}
```

Immediately type CANCEL (as demonstrated in Figure 12-1). At this point, you should see a message indicating media recovery has been canceled, as shown here:

```
Media recovery cancelled.
```

You can now open your database with the alter database open resetlogs command, as shown here:

```
SQL> alter database open resetlogs;
```

You should see the following message after opening your database with the resetlogs option:

```
Database altered.
```

How It Works

You can restore a noarchivelog database only to the point at which it was backed up. There is no roll forward of transactions because there are no archived redo log files to apply. This type of restore and recovery is commonly used to reset a test environment database to a baseline point in time.

Since the online redo log files are not included in the RMAN backup, then you must issue alter database open resetlogs to create new online redo log files, as well as to synchronize the control files and datafiles in terms of their checkpoint SCNs.

12-9. Recovering to a Previous Incarnation

Problem

You recently opened your database with the alter database open resetlogs command, and you have now decided that you want to perform an incomplete restore and recovery to a time prior to the time when the database was opened with the resetlogs option. When restoring datafiles, you receive the following error:

```
RMAN-03002: failure of restore command ...
RMAN-20207: UNTIL TIME or RECOVERY WINDOW is before RESETLOGS time
```

The Oracle documentation indicates that in this situation you must restore and recover to a previous incarnation of your database.

The Solution

You have to restore a control file that knows about the incarnation of the database to which you want to restore. The following example assumes you're using a flash recovery area and have enabled the autobackup of the control file feature. See Chapter 10 for details with other control file restore scenarios.

ENABLING AUTOBACKUP OF CONTROL FILE

Enabling the autobackup of the control file is fairly straightforward. To enable this feature, use the `configure` command as follows:

```
RMAN> configure controlfile autobackup on;
```

See recipe 5-4 for more details about the autobackup feature.

If you have the control file autobackup feature enabled, then you just have to determine a date and time to which to go back to when you restore the control file. In this example, we opened the database with the `resetlogs` command on September 4, 2006. We also know that we want to restore the database to September 3, 2006. This means we'll have to restore our database to a previous incarnation.

Then you can restore the old control file as of that date and time, place your database in mount mode, and list the available incarnations:

```
RMAN> connect target /
RMAN> startup nomount;
RMAN> restore controlfile from autobackup until time
2> "to_date('03-sep-2006 00:00:00', 'dd-mon-rrrr hh24:mi:ss')";
RMAN> alter database mount;
RMAN> list incarnation of database;
```

You should now see a list of the incarnations stored in the control file.

DB Key	Inc Key	DB Name	DB ID	STATUS	Reset SCN	Reset Time
1	1	BSTN102	2601506593	PARENT	1	15-JUN-06
2	2	BSTN102	2601506593	CURRENT	33550336	04-SEP-06

■**Tip** If you want to see the time portion of the "Reset Time" output of the `list` command, first set the OS variable NLS_DATE_FORMAT to a format that includes the time stamp.

Choose the incarnation you want to use. In this case, we can reset our database to incarnation 1 as follows:

```
RMAN> reset database to incarnation 1;
```

It's critical that you restore and recover your database so that the datafiles are restored to a point where they are aware of incarnation 1. If the datafiles are restored to a different incarnation than the control files, then you most likely won't be able to open your database after recovery. Since we restored the control file from September 3, 2006, we must do the same with the restore and recover commands for the target database datafiles:

```
RMAN> restore database until time
2> "to_date('03-sep-2006 00:00:00', 'dd-mon-rrrr hh24:mi:ss')";
RMAN> recover database until time
2> "to_date('03-sep-2006 00:00:00', 'dd-mon-rrrr hh24:mi:ss')";
RMAN> alter database open reset logs;
```

The database is now as it was on September 3, 2006 at 12 a.m.

■**Note** You can restore until a time, SCN, sequence, or restore point.

How It Works

Anytime you restore your database with a backup control file or perform an incomplete database recovery, you are required to use the alter database open resetlogs command to open your database. This resets the online redo log sequence to 1 and creates a new version of your database. Oracle calls this fresh version of your database a *new incarnation*.

You can view incarnation information by querying the V$DATABASE_INCARNATION view. You can also view database incarnation data from within RMAN by issuing the following:

```
RMAN> connect target /
RMAN> list incarnation of database;
using target database control file instead of recovery catalog
List of Database Incarnations
```

DB Key	Inc Key	DB Name	DB ID	STATUS	Reset SCN	Reset Time
1	1	BRDSTN	1109210542	PARENT	1	04-SEP-05
2	2	BRDSTN	1109210542	PARENT	120462	04-DEC-05
3	3	BRDSTN	1109210542	PARENT	3141592	10-AUG-06
4	4	BRDSTN	1109210542	PARENT	3579884	16-AUG-06
5	5	BRDSTN	1109210542	CURRENT	3581321	31-OCT-06

In rare situations, you may find that you need to restore to a previous incarnation of your database. For example, there may be data that is contained only in a prior incarnation, and the only way to retrieve it is to restore and recover to that previous incarnation of your database.

When you restore and recover to a previous incarnation, you need to ensure that your control file that you restore is aware of the particular database incarnation that you want to restore.

> **■Tip** If you are using an Oracle9*i* Database or prior, we recommend you immediately perform an RMAN backup after the database is opened with the `resetlogs` command. This is because with previous versions of Oracle, it is difficult to recover a database through a `resetlogs` operation (and often requires the assistance of Oracle Support).

12-10. Performing Tablespace Point-in-Time Recovery

Problem

A rogue developer thought they were in a test environment and issued commands to delete data from several tables in one tablespace. It turns out they were in the production environment. You want to use tablespace point-in-time recovery (TSPITR) to restore your tablespace to the point in time just before the erroneous DML was issued.

Solution

This recipe shows how to perform fully automated RMAN tablespace point-in-time recovery. Here are the steps:

1. Determine and resolve any dependencies to objects in tablespaces not included in the TSPITR.

2. Determine whether there are objects that will not be recovered.

3. Create a destination on disk to temporarily hold the auxiliary database.

4. Run the `recover tablespace until` command.

5. Back up the restored tablespace and alter it online.

Step 1: Determine and Resolve Dependencies

If objects in the tablespaces involved with the TSPITR have constraint relationships to objects not in tablespaces included in the TSPITR, you will not be able to perform a successful TSPITR.

You can use the TS_PITR_CHECK view to help you determine whether there are constraint dependencies to objects in tablespaces not included in the TSPITR. Here's a sample query that checks to see whether there are any dependencies to the users tablespace:

```sql
SQL> SELECT *
2  FROM sys.ts_pitr_check
3  WHERE(ts1_name =  'USERS'  AND ts2_name != 'USERS')
4  OR   (ts1_name != 'USERS'  AND ts2_name =  'USERS');
```

If there are dependencies, consider including dropping or disabling the constraints. Another option would be to include the dependent tablespace in the TSPITR.

Step 2: Determine Which Objects Will Not Be Recovered

For objects in tablespaces involved with the TSPITR, you'll lose any transactions that were created prior to the point to which you restore. If you need to preserve objects created after the time to which you are going to restore, then you'll need to use the DataPump utility or the export utility to save them. After you have performed TSPITR, then you can import these objects.

You can query the TS_PITR_OBJECTS_TO_BE_DROPPED view to help identify objects that need to be preserved. This query identifies objects created after the time to which the TSPITR will be performed:

```
SQL> SELECT owner, name, tablespace_name
  2  FROM ts_pitr_objects_to_be_dropped
  3  WHERE tablespace_name ='USERS'
  4  AND creation_time > to_date('12-nov-2006 16:00:00','dd-mon-rrrr hh24:mi:ss');
```

Step 3: Create an Auxiliary Destination

First ensure that you have an area on disk that will serve as a temporary container for an auxiliary database. This area will need enough space for a system, undo, and temporary tablespace. We recommend you have at least 1GB of space in your auxiliary destination.

```
C:\> mkdir c:\auxx
```

Step 4: Run the recover Command

You can now perform a fully automated TSPITR. You can restore until a time, SCN, or sequence. Notice that your database is open during the TSPITR. In this example, we restore the users tablespace up to, but not including, the time specified:

```
RMAN> connect target /
RMAN> recover tablespace users until time
2> "to_date('12-nov-2006 16:00:00','dd-mon-rrrr hh24:mi:ss')"
3> auxiliary destination 'c:\auxx';
```

■**Caution** Make sure you use the recover command (and not restore)! You can recover to an SCN, log sequence number, or time.

Also, don't forget to specify the auxiliary destination. RMAN will now perform a fully automated TSPITR recovery of the specified tablespaces.

You should see a *large* amount of output as RMAN creates an auxiliary database and automatically performs all steps associated with TSPITR. After successful completion, you should see message output similar to the following:

```
Removing automatic instance
Automatic instance removed
Finished recover at 07-02-17
```

Step 5: Back Up the Tablespace and Alter It Online

Once the TSPITR completes, you must back up the recovered tablespace and bring it online:

```
RMAN> backup tablespace users;
RMAN> sql 'alter tablespace users online';
```

How It Works

RMAN TSPITR allows you to recover one or more tablespaces back to a time that is different from the other tablespaces in your database. Performing TSPITR is useful in the following situations:

- When you have a tablespace or set of them that contains objects owned by only one schema. If there are undesired DML statements that affect several of the schema's objects, then you have the option of using TSPITR to restore the schema's objects to a previous point in time.

- There have been erroneous DML statements that affect only a subset of tables isolated to a few tablespaces.

For example, say you have two tablespaces, p_dt and p_idx, and all of the objects in those two tablespaces are owned by prod_own. If there were undesirable DML statements that were issued against tables owned by prod_own, then you could use TSPITR to restore and recover to just prior to when the bad SQL was run. In this example, we restore the two tablespaces back to just before SCN 1432:

```
C:\> mkdir c:\auxx
RMAN> connect target /
RMAN> recover tablespace p_dt, p_idx until SCN 1432 auxiliary destination 'c:\auxx';
```

You should now see quite a number of RMAN messages displaying the status of each operation. Once complete, back up the recovered tablespaces and bring them online:

```
RMAN> backup tablespace p_dt, p_idx;
RMAN> sql 'alter tablespace p_dt online';
RMAN> sql 'alter tablespace p_idx online';
```

■**Caution** If you are not using a recovery catalog, you can perform TSPITR only once on a tablespace. You will be allowed to perform another TSPITR only from a backup taken after the first TSPITR was performed. This is because after performing TSPITR, the control file has no record of the previous incarnation of the tablespace you recovered. Therefore, you won't be able to recover this tablespace again from the backup taken before TSPITR was performed. However, when using a recovery catalog, you can "cry mulligan" and perform multiple TSPITRs if you discover that you restored your tablespace(s) to the wrong point. Therefore, we recommend you use a recovery catalog if you foresee the need to perform multiple TSPITRs on a tablespace.

RMAN does many complicated tasks for you with automated TSPITR. Here are the steps that RMAN performs for you:

1. Creates an auxiliary instance, starts it, and connects to it

2. Takes offline tablespaces that are involved with TSPITR

3. Restores the backup control file that corresponds to the target restore time

4. Restores datafiles to a destination specified by your AUXILIARY DESTINATION

5. Recovers restored datafiles in an auxiliary location

6. Opens an auxiliary database with the `open resetlogs` command

7. Exports the auxiliary data dictionary metadata about recovered tablespaces and shuts down the auxiliary database

8. Issues a `switch` command on the target database to update the control file to point at the recovered auxiliary datafiles

9. Imports objects associated with recovered tablespaces into the target database

10. Deletes the auxiliary datafiles

After step 10 is complete, your target database should have the tablespaces recovered to the point listed in the `recover` command. The rest of the tablespaces in your database should be as they were before you initiated the TSPITR. You need to back up any tablespaces involved in the TSPITR and then alter them online.

Many limitations are involved with TSPITR. Here are some situations where you cannot use TSPITR:

- Tablespaces contain objects owned by `sys`.

- Tablespaces containing undo segments or rollback segments.

- Recovering dropped tablespaces.

- Tables with nested tables or `varray` columns.

- Tables that reference external files.

- Tables that have snapshot logs.

- If a table is partitioned across multiple tablespaces, then you cannot recover just one of its tablespaces; you must recover all tablespaces associated with the partitioned table.

■**Tip** A wide variety of features are available with TSPITR. This recipe covers only the automated RMAN tablespace point-in-time recovery. For complete details on all features of TSPITR, see the Oracle Backup and Recovery Advanced User's Guide.

12-11. Recovering a Subset of Datafiles

Problem

You want to perform incomplete recovery on a subset of datafiles in your database.

Solution

The basic procedure is to determine which datafiles you don't want to restore and recover and then use `alter database datafile ... offline for drop` for the datafiles to be excluded.

■**Caution** The datafiles you offline drop using this procedure will not be available for subsequent restore and recovery operations.

Here are the RMAN commands to perform an incomplete recovery on a subset of datafiles in your database:

```
RMAN> connect target /
RMAN> startup mount;
```

Use the RMAN `report schema` command to identify which datafiles you do not want to restore and recover. You can also query V$DATAFILE for the datafile details. In this example, the datafiles 7, 8, and 9 are taken offline and are not restored and recovered:

```
RMAN> sql 'alter database datafile 7, 8, 9 offline for drop';
RMAN> restore database until SCN 314159;
RMAN> recover database until SCN 314159;
RMAN> alter database open resetlogs;
```

How It Works

This type of recovery is used sometimes if you need to restore and recover only part of your database. For example, if some data is accidentally modified in your production database, you can use this recovery to do the following:

1. Copy production RMAN backup files to a nonproduction database server.

2. On the non-production database server, restore and recover just the system, sysaux, undo, and other datafiles that you're interested in to a point in time just before the data was erroneously modified.

3. Export the data out of the database's tablespaces to a point in time.

4. Use the exported data to fix data in your production database.

■**Note** Consider using a tablespace point-in-time recovery to restore and recover specific tablespaces to a previous point in time (see recipe 12-10 for details).

12-12. Troubleshooting Incomplete Recovery

Problem

You're attempting to perform an incomplete recovery, and RMAN is returning the following error:

```
ORA-01139: RESETLOGS option only valid after an incomplete database recovery
```

You wonder how to go about determining what is wrong.

Solution

In many situations, problems with incomplete recovery are caused by omitting one of the required steps. Here is the correct sequence of steps for most incomplete recovery scenarios:

1. `restore database until <specified point>;`

2. `recover database until <specified point>;`

3. `alter database open resetlogs;`

The specified point in steps 1 and 2 should be identical. The specified point can be an SCN, a time, a log sequence number, or a restore point.

How It Works

Listed in Table 12-2 are some of the more common incorrect actions performed during an incomplete recovery. If you receive an error listed in the Result column, then ensure you are performing the correct steps for incomplete recovery (detailed in the "Solution" section of this recipe).

Table 12-2. *Incomplete Recovery Incorrect Action and Result*

Incorrect Action	Result
Issue restore database until and attempt to open database without issuing a corresponding recover database until command.	ORA-01139: RESETLOGS option only valid after an incomplete database recovery
Restored all datafiles but performed recovery only on a subset of restored online datafiles.	ORA-01139: RESETLOGS option only valid after an incomplete database recovery
Issue restore database until, and then attempt to open database with alter database open command.	ORA-01113: file 1 needs media recovery
Issue the alter database open command after performing incomplete recovery.	ORA-01589: must use RESETLOGS or NORESETLOGS option for database open
The restore database until <specified point> command is greater than recover database until <specified point>.	RMAN-06556: datafile must be restored from backup older than scn

When performing an incomplete recovery, before you can open the database with a resetlogs option, the checkpoint SCN for all online datafiles must be identical. You can view the datafile checkpoint SCNs via this query:

```
SQL> select file#, status, checkpoint_change#,
2    to_char(checkpoint_time,'dd-mon-rrrr hh24:mi:ss')
3    from v$datafile_header;
```

After you open your database with the resetlogs clause, the checkpoint SCN in the control file will be synchronized with the checkpoint SCN in the datafile headers.

■■■

Performing Flashback Recovery

In Oracle Database 10g Release 1, Oracle introduced a new feature: *flashback*. Actually, the term is used in three different contexts, making the usage somewhat confusing. There is also a similar-sounding feature—*flashback queries*—in Oracle9i Database, and this doesn't help matters much.

The flashback concepts introduced in Oracle Database 10g are different from the ones introduced in Oracle9i Database. The 10g version of the term—flashback—actually refers to an aid to recoverability. In this chapter, you will learn about the various flavors of flashback and how to use each one.

Introducing Flashback

There are three flavors of flashback:

- Flashing back a database

- Undropping a table

- Flashing back a table

Flashing Back a Database

Many times, you might need to roll back the database to a point in time in the past. In earlier releases, this functionality was present but in a very different way. For instance, in Oracle9i Database and prior versions, you would reinstate an older backup and then roll it forward to a point in time in the past. For instance, suppose today is January 21 and the time is 10 a.m. The database backups are taken at 5 a.m. every day. If you wanted to roll the database back to 10 p.m. on January 20, you would restore the backup taken at 5 a.m. on January 20 and then apply all the archived redo logs to restore it to 10 p.m. But what if you made a mistake in your calculation and the data you wanted to recover was deleted at 9 p.m.? After you recover the database up to 10 p.m., all your work was in vain. There is no going back to 9 p.m.; you would have to start the process again from the beginning—restore the backup of 5 a.m. and then roll forward all the changes by applying logs up to 9 p.m.

Oracle Database 10g changes all that by introducing a new feature called *flashback database*. You enable flashback on the database. This causes additional logs to be created during the database operation. These logs, called *flashback logs*, are generated along with the regular archived logs. The flashback logs record changes to the database blocks exclusively for the purpose of rolling back the block changes, so they are different from archived logs. When you flash the database back to a point in the past, these flashback logs are read and applied to the database blocks to undo the changes. The entire database is transported to that point in time.

Note The entire database is rolled back; you can't perform flashback on individual tables or tablespaces.

Undropping a Table

This has happened to the best of us—you dropped a very important table. What can you do? In versions prior to Oracle Database 10g Release 1, there wasn't any choice other than to restore the backup of the corresponding tablespace to another database, recover the table-space, export the table, and import the table to the production database. These tasks are time-consuming and risky, and the table is unavailable throughout them.

In Oracle Database 10g, the process is less threatening. When the table is dropped, it's not really erased from the database; rather, it is renamed and placed in a logical container called the *recycle bin*, similar to the Recycle Bin found in Windows. After you realize the mistake, you can reinstate the dropped table using only one simple command. Who says you can't revive the dead?

Flashing Back a Table

The Oracle9i Database introduced a new feature called *flashback query*. When the data in the database changes, the past images of the changed data are stored in special segments called *undo segments*. The reason for storing this data is simple—if the changed data is not commit-ted yet, the database must reconstruct the prechange data to present a read-consistent view to the other users selecting the same data item. When the change is committed, the need for the past image is gone, but it's not discarded. The space is reused if necessary. The reason for keeping it around is simple too.

The read consistency requirement does not stop after the data changes are committed. For instance, a long-running query needs a read-consistent view when the query started, which could be well in the past. If the query refers to the data that might have been changed and committed in the recent past, after the query has started, the query must get the past image, not the image now, even though it is committed. If the query finds that the past data is no longer available, it throws the dreaded ORA-1555 Snapshot Too Old error.

Anyway, what does the ORA-1555 error have to do with flashback operation? Plenty. Since the past image of the data is available in the undo segment for a while, why should a long-running query be the only one to have fun? You can benefit from that past image too. That thought gave rise to flashback queries in Oracle9i Database where you could query data as of a time in the past. In Oracle Database 10g, that functionality was made richer with flashback version queries, where you can pull the changes made to the row data from the undo seg-ments, as long as they are available in the undo segments, of course. And, when you pull the older versions of the table, you can effectively reinstate the entire table to a point in time in the past using these past images. This is known as *flashing back the table*.

In this chapter, you will learn to use all three types of flashback technology.

13-1. Checking the Flashback Status of a Database

Problem

You want to check whether your database is flashback enabled.

Solution

The data dictionary view V$DATABASE contains information about the flashback status of the database. Check the column FLASHBACK_ON on that view to ascertain the flashback status:

```
SQL> select flashback_on from v$database;

FLASHBACK_ON
------------------
YES
```

The output shows that the value of the column FLASHBACK_ON is set to YES, which means the database is running in flashback mode. If the database is not in flashback mode, the query would have returned NO.

How It Works

If the database is running in flashback mode, it generates additional files known as *flashback logs*, which record changes to the data blocks. These files are recorded in the flash recovery area, which was described in Chapter 3. In addition, the FLASHBACK_ON column will return a YES indicator so that you know for sure that flashback mode is enabled.

13-2. Enabling Flashback on a Database

Problem

You want to enable a database to flash back to a point in time in the past.

Solution

The database must be running in archivelog mode to enable flashback. The flashback-enabled database generates flashback logs, which are stored only in the flash recovery area (FRA), so the FRA must be configured prior to enabling the flashback. These flashback logs are generated in addition to the archived logs. Here are the steps to then follow to enable flashback on the database:

1. Make sure the FRA is defined in the database. To set up the FRA, check out recipe 3-1. To find out whether the FRA is set, execute the following command via SQL*Plus while logged in as sys or any other sysdba account:

   ```
   SQL> show parameter db_recovery_file_dest
   ```

If the value of the parameter db_recovery_file_dest is set, then the FRA is defined to that location. Here is a sample output:

```
NAME                                    TYPE         VALUE
------------------------------------    ----------   ------------------------------
db_recovery_file_dest                   string       C:\oracle\product\10.2\db_1➥
\flash_recovery_area
db_recovery_file_dest_size              big integer  2G
```

From the output, you'll notice that the parameter db_recovery_file_dest is set to C:\oracle\product\10.2\db_1\flash_recovery_area, which is the location of the flash recovery area. The second parameter, db_recovery_file_dest_size, shows the size of the flash recovery area.

2. Make sure the database is in archivelog mode. You check the mode by issuing the following SQL:

```
SQL> select log_mode from v$database;

LOG_MODE
------------
ARCHIVELOG
```

The value of the column LOG_MODE is ARCHIVELOG, which indicates the database is running in archivelog mode.

3. If the result of the query is different, as in the example shown here, then the database is not running in archivelog mode:

```
SQL> select log_mode from v$database;

LOG_MODE
------------
NOARCHIVELOG
```

4. To enable archivelog mode, follow these steps:

   a. Shut down the database by issuing the following SQL statement:

   ```
   SQL> shutdown immediate
   Database closed.
   Database dismounted.
   ORACLE instance shut down.
   ```

   b. Start the database in mount mode by issuing the following SQL statement:

   ```
   SQL> startup mount
   ORACLE instance started.

   Total System Global Area  289406976 bytes
   Fixed Size                  1248576 bytes
   Variable Size              83886784 bytes
   ```

```
Database Buffers           197132288 bytes
Redo Buffers                 7139328 bytes
Database mounted.
```

    c. Enable archivelog mode by issuing the following command:

```
SQL> alter database archivelog;
```

```
Database altered.
```

    d. At this point, you can open the database for business, but since your objective is to enable flashback, go to the next step.

5. Make sure the database is in mounted state by issuing the following SQL statement:

```
SQL> select OPEN_MODE from v$database;
```

```
OPEN_MODE
----------
MOUNTED
```

6. If the database is in any other state, then shut it down and restart it in mounted mode:

```
SQL> shutdown immediate
Database closed.
Database dismounted.
ORACLE instance shut down.
SQL> startup mount
ORACLE instance started.

Total System Global Area  289406976 bytes
Fixed Size                  1248576 bytes
Variable Size              83886784 bytes
Database Buffers          197132288 bytes
Redo Buffers                7139328 bytes
Database mounted.
```

The final line confirms that the database is now mounted.

7. Enable flashback for the database by issuing the following SQL statement:

```
SQL> alter database flashback on;
```

```
Database altered.
```

8. Open the database:

```
SQL> alter database open;
```

```
Database altered.
```

The database is now in flashback mode.

How It Works

When the database is in flashback mode, it generates flashback logs as a result of changes to the data. These flashback logs are later used to roll the database to a previous state. However, the flashback logs capture only the changes to the data blocks, which may not be enough for rebuilding a consistent database. In addition to the flashback logs, the rollback process needs archived logs. Therefore, the database must also be in archivelog mode to enable flashback.

The flashback logs are stored in the flash recovery area, which is described in Chapter 3. The flash recovery area is the only place the flashback logs can be stored. Therefore, it's necessary to enable flash recovery area with the appropriate size to enable flashback in the database. You can learn how to size the flash recovery area in recipe 3-16. One of the inputs to the calculations is the estimated size of the total flashback logs generated. You will learn how to estimate that value in recipe 13-8.

13-3. Disabling Flashback on a Database

Problem

You want to disable flashback mode for a database.

Solution

Disable flashback mode by issuing the following SQL statement:

```
SQL> alter database flashback off;
```

```
Database altered.
```

Now the database is running in nonflashback mode.

How It Works

When the database is taken out of flashback mode, the flashback logs are not generated anymore. You can check that the database has indeed been taken off flashback mode by issuing the following query:

```
SQL> select flashback_on from v$database;
```

```
FLASHBACK_ON
------------------
NO
```

The result shows NO, confirming that the database is not running in flashback mode now.

13-4. Flashing Back a Database from RMAN

Problem

You want to flash a database back to a point in time in the past through RMAN.

Solution

When you want to flash the database back to a time in the past, you have a few choices in deciding when to flash back to. You can flash back to the following:

- A specific point in time, specified by date and time

- A specific SCN number

- The last `resetlogs` operation

- A named restore point

We describe each of these scenarios in the following sections. Each of the solutions, however, has some common tasks before and after the actual flashback.

Common Presteps

The following are the "common presteps" to follow for any type of full database flashback procedure:

1. Check how far back into the past you can flash back to. Refer to recipe 13-6.

2. Connect to RMAN:

```
rman target=/
```

3. Shut the database down:

```
RMAN> shutdown immediate

database closed
database dismounted
Oracle instance shut down
```

4. Start the database in mount mode:

```
RMAN> startup mount

connected to target database (not started)
Oracle instance started
database mounted

Total System Global Area    289406976 bytes

Fixed Size                    1248576 bytes
Variable Size                83886784 bytes
Database Buffers            197132288 bytes
Redo Buffers                  7139328 bytes
```

This completes the preflashback steps.

Common Poststep

After the flashback operation, you will open the database with the clause resetlogs, as shown in the following actions in RMAN:

```
RMAN> alter database open resetlogs;

database opened
```

It's important to open the database in resetlogs mode since the flashback operation performs a point-in-time recovery, which is a form of incomplete recovery. For more information about incomplete recovery, refer to Chapter 12.

Solution 1: Flashing Back to a Specific SCN

In this example, you will see how to flash back a database to a specific SCN, which is the most precise flashback procedure possible. Here are the steps to follow:

1. First, check the SCN of the database now. Connecting as sys or any other DBA account, issue the following SQL statement:

   ```
   SQL> select current_scn
     2  from v$database;

   CURRENT_SCN
   -----------
      1137633
   ```

   The output shows the current SCN is 1,137,633. You can flash back to an SCN prior to this number only.

2. Execute the "common presteps" 1 through 4.

3. Flash the database back to your desired SCN. For instance, to flash back to SCN 1,050,951, issue the following RMAN command:

   ```
   RMAN> flashback database to scn 1050951;

   Starting flashback at 24-JAN-07
   using target database control file instead of recovery catalog
   allocated channel: ORA_DISK_1
   channel ORA_DISK_1: sid=154 devtype=DISK


   starting media recovery
   media recovery complete, elapsed time: 00:00:35

   Finished flashback at 24-JAN-07
   ```

   This command flashed the database back to the desired SCN.

4. You can open the database now for regular operations by executing the "common poststep."

5. However, you may not be certain whether you have flashed back to the exact point in time you wanted to be at. To determine whether you have, you can open the database in read-only mode:

```
RMAN> alter database open read only;
```

```
Database opened.
```

6. Check the data in the table. For instance, the purpose of the flashback was to undo the changes done to the interest calculation table, so you can check the interest table to see whether the values are 0.

7. If you have not gone far back into the past, you can start the flashback process again to flash back to a different SCN. Start with step 2—shut down the database, start up in mount mode, and then flash back.

```
RMAN> flashback database to scn 1050900;
```

8. Again, open the database in read-only mode, and check the data to make sure you are at a point you want to be. If you are not there, you can redo the steps.

9. Once you are satisfied you have arrived at a point where you want to be, follow step 2 of the "common poststeps" to open the database for regular operation.

Now the database is at the point in time in the past you want to be.

Solution 2: Flashing Back to a Specific Time

You want to flash the database to a specific time, not an SCN. Here are the steps to follow:

1. Follow common steps 1 through 4.

2. Use the following command to flash back to a time just two minutes ago:

```
RMAN> flashback database to time 'sysdate-2/60/24';
Starting flashback at 24-JAN-07
using channel ORA_DISK_1


starting media recovery

archive log thread 1 sequence 1 is already on disk as file ➥
C:\ORACLE\PRODUCT\10.2\DB_1\FLASH_RECOVERY_AREA\MOBDB10\ARCHIVELOG\2007_0➥
1_22\01_MF_1_1_2VBFN3MF_.ARC
... and so on ...
archive log  thread 1 sequence 3 is already on disk as file ➥
:\ORACLE\PRODUCT\10.2\DB_1\FLASH_RECOVERY_AREA\MOBDB10\ARCHIVELOG\2007_0➥
1_24\01_MF_1_3_2VH3MF89_.ARC
media recovery complete, elapsed time: 00:00:40
Finished flashback at 24-JAN-07
```

3. If you want to flash back to a specific time, not in reference to a time such as `sysdate`, you can use the time stamp instead of a formula:

```
RMAN> flashback database to time "to_date('01/23/07 13:00:00','mm/dd/yy➥
hh24:mi:ss')";
```

This flashes the database to that specific time stamp.

4. Like the first solution, you can open the database in read-only mode at this time to check whether you have traversed far enough into the past.

5. If you haven't, you can start the process once again—shut down immediately, start in mount mode, flash back to a different time, and then open the database in read-only mode.

6. Once you are satisfied you have arrived at the desired point in time, shut the database down, and follow the "common poststep" to open the database for regular operation.

The database is now as January 23 at 13:00:00.

Solution 3: Flashing Back to a Restore Point

In this solution, you will learn how to flash back the database to a restore point. You can learn about creating restore points in recipe 13-9 and recipe 13-10. Here are the steps to follow to flash back to a restore point:

1. Follow "common presteps" 1 through 4.

2. To flash back to a restore point named rp6, issue the following SQL:

```
RMAN> flashback database to restore point rp6;

Starting flashback at 24-JAN-07
using channel ORA_DISK_1


starting media recovery

archive log thread 1 sequence 1 is already on disk as file ➥
C:\ORACLE\PRODUCT\10.2\DB_1\FLASH_RECOVERY_AREA\MOBDB10\➥
ARCHIVELOG\2007_01_24\01_MF_1_1_2VH3MG3X_.ARC
media recovery complete, elapsed time: 00:00:07
Finished flashback at 24-JAN-07
```

3. At this time you can open the database in read-only mode and check the data, as described in the first solution of this recipe. If the flashback is not far enough in the past, or too far, you can flash back to another restore point—rp5, for instance. In that case, you repeat the steps—shut down, start, and flash back. To flash back to a restore point rp5, you issue the following RMAN command:

```
RMAN> flashback database to restore point rp5;
```

```
Starting flashback at 24-JAN-07
using channel ORA_DISK_1


starting media recovery

archive log thread 1 sequence 1 is already on disk as file ➥
C:\ORACLE\PRODUCT\10.2\DB_1\FLASH_RECOVERY_AREA\MOBDB10\ARCHIVELOG\➥
2007_01_24\O1_MF_1_1_2VH3MG3X_.ARC
media recovery complete, elapsed time: 00:00:07
Finished flashback at 24-JAN-07
```

4. Execute the "common poststep" to open the database for normal operation.

The database is now as of the time when the restore point rp5 was created.

Solution 4: Flashing Back to Before the Last resetlogs Operation

You have opened the database with the resetlogs clause, and that was probably a mistake. Now you want to revert the changes to the last resetlogs operation. Here are the steps to accomplish that:

1. Execute the "common presteps" 1 through 4.

2. Use the following command to flash back the database to the last resetlog operation:

```
RMAN> flashback database to before resetlogs;

Starting flashback at 24-JAN-07
allocated channel: ORA_DISK_1
channel ORA_DISK_1: sid=155 devtype=DISK


starting media recovery
media recovery complete, elapsed time: 00:00:07

Finished flashback at 24-JAN-07
```

3. The database has now been flashed back to the last restore point. Execute the "common poststep" to open the database for normal operation.

How It Works

When the database is in flashback mode, it generates special log files called *flashback logs* that can be used to flash back the database to a prior point in time. The flashback logs carry the SCN, allowing you to use the SCN as a measuring point to which to flash back. But SCNs are akin to the internal clock of the database, and they also relate to the wall clock. Therefore, when you issue the commands to flash back to a specific time stamp, Oracle automatically determines the SCN associated with the time stamp and rolls back to that SCN.

Similarly, restore points are merely pointers to specific SCNs so when you flash back to a specific restore point, the database actually issues a flashback to the SCN associated with that restore point. Finally, the database records the SCN when the database was opened with resetlogs; so, again, your flashback command to the last resetlogs operations is merely the same as issuing the flashback to that SCN. You can check the SCN during the last resetlogs operation by issuing the following query:

```
SQL> select resetlogs_change#
  2  from v$database;


RESETLOGS_CHANGE#
-----------------
          1070142
```

Flashback does not work in only one direction; it works both back and forth from a point. Of course, you can't go to a point in time in the future, and you can go only as far back into the past as the flashback logs are available. Figure 13-1 shows how the flashback works in both forward and reverse directions from a point.

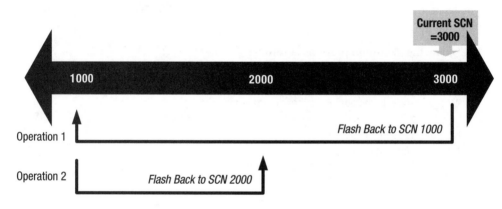

Figure 13-1. *Flashback operations*

Note that Operation 1 flashed the database from the current SCN (3,000) to SCN 1,000. After that is done, before the database opened for read/write access, Operation 2 flashed the database back from SCN 1,000 to SCN 2,000, which is akin to rollforward operations, but we still call it *flashback*. You can do this operation up to any SCN less than 3,000 any number of times to get to the precise position in time. The lower limit of SCN you can flash back to depends on how much flashback log data is available in the flash recovery area.

■**Note** To guarantee the ability to flash back to a point in time, you can create guaranteed restore points, discussed in recipe 13-10.

13-5. Flashing Back a Database from SQL

Problem

You want to flash the database back to a point in time in the past by using SQL statements, not RMAN.

Solution

Like the RMAN approach, several options are available to you in deciding on a reference point to flash back to. You can flash back to the following:

- A specific point in time, specified by date and time

- A specific SCN

- A named restore point

Common Presteps

We'll describe each option's solution in the following sections. All the solutions have some common steps, just like the RMAN approach described in recipe 13-4. Here are those common tasks:

1. Check how far back into the past you can flash back to. Refer to recipe 13-6.

2. Connect as a sysdba user, and shut down the database:

```
SQL> shutdown immediate
database closed
database dismounted
Oracle instance shut down
```

3. Start the database in mount mode:

```
SQL> startup mount
Oracle instance started
database mounted
Total System Global Area     289406976 bytes
Fixed Size                     1248576 bytes
Variable Size                 83886784 bytes
Database Buffers             197132288 bytes
Redo Buffers                   7139328 bytes
```

This completes the preflashback steps.

Common Poststep

After the flashback operation, you will open the database with the clause resetlogs:

```
SQL> alter database open resetlogs;

database opened
```

It's important to open the database in resetlogs mode since the flashback operation performs a point-in-time recovery, which is a form of incomplete recovery. For more information on incomplete recovery, refer to Chapter 12.

Solution 1: Flashing Back to a Time

You have a specific time—such as January 21, 2007, at 10 p.m.—that you want to flash back to. This time must be in the past. Here are the steps to follow:

1. Perform the "common presteps" 1 through 3.

2. Flash the database to your desired time stamp by issuing the following SQL statement:

```
SQL> flashback database to timestamp
  2> to_date('1/22/2007 00:00:00','mm/dd/yyyy hh24:mi:ss');

Flashback complete.
```

The message "Flashback complete" confirms that the database has been flashed back.

3. As described in the RMAN approach, you can open the database now for regular operations by executing the "common poststep."

4. However, you may not be certain that you have flashed back to the exact point in time at which you wanted to be. To determine whether you have, you can open the database in read-only mode:

```
SQL> alter database open read only;

Database opened.
```

5. Check the data in the tables so you can figure out whether you have flashed back enough in the past or you need to go even further. For instance, the purpose of the flashback was to undo the changes to the interest calculation table, so you can check the interest table to see whether the values are 0.

6. If you have not gone far back into the past, you can start the flashback process again to flash back to a different SCN. Start with step 2, and execute the "common presteps" and flashback:

```
SQL> flashback database to scn 1050900;
```

7. Again, open the database in read-only mode, check the data to make sure you are at the point at which you want to be. If you are not there, you can reexecute step 2 through step 6.

8. Once you are satisfied that you have arrived at a point where you want to be, follow the "common poststep" to open the database for regular operation.

The flashback to the time stamp is now complete.

Solution 2: Flashing Back to a Specific SCN

You have a specific SCN to flash back to. This SCN must be less than the current SCN. The steps are the same as for the first solution, except for step 6 in which you substitute the SCN with the time stamp:

1. Find out the current SCN by issuing this query:

```
sql> select current_scn from v$database;

CURRENT_SCN
-----------
    1044916
```

   From the output, you know that the current SCN is 1,044,916. You can flash back only to a SCN less than this number. These are the steps to flash back to the SCN 1,000,000.

2. Follow the "common presteps" 1 through 3.

3. Issue the following SQL statement to flash back to SCN 1,000,000:

```
SQL> flashback database to scn 1000000;

Flashback complete.
```

4. After the flashback is complete, you can open the database in read-only mode to check the contents.

```
SQL> alter database open read only;

Database altered.
```

5. After the database is opened, you can check the data and determine whether the flash-back was done to a time far back enough. If not, you can flash it back once more by repeating the steps: shut down, start up, flash back, and open as read-only.

6. When you want the database to be at a point in time you want, follow the "common poststep" to open the database for normal use.

The database is now flashed back and ready for use.

Solution 3: Restoring to a Restore Point

You can also use the flashback feature to roll a database back to a named restore point. See recipe 13-9 to learn how to create a restore point. Then use the following steps to revert to such a restore point:

1. Follow the "common presteps."

2. Issue the following SQL statement to flash the database back to, in this example, restore point rp1:

```
SQL> flashback database to restore point rp1;

Flashback complete.
```

3. Similar to the second solution, you can open the database in read-only mode to check whether you have flashed back to a correct place in time:

```
SQL> alter database open read only;

Database altered.
```

4. After the database is opened, you can check the data and determine whether the flashback was done to a time far back enough. If not, you can flash it back once more by repeating the steps: shut down, start up in mount mode, flash back, and open as read-only.

5. When you want the database to be at a point in time you want, follow the "common poststep" to open the database for normal use.

The database is now flashed back and ready for use.

How It Works

The SQL approach works exactly like the RMAN approach described in recipe 13-4. Refer to the "How It Works" section of that recipe for details.

13-6. Finding Out How Far Back into the Past You Can Flash Back

Problem

You want to flash back the database, and you want to find out how far into the past you can go.

Solution

Query the V$FLASHBACK_DATABASE_LOG view to find out how far into the past you can flash back. For example:

```
SQL> select * from v$flashback_database_log;

OLDEST_FLASHBACK_SCN OLDEST_FL RETENTION_TARGET FLASHBACK_SIZE
-------------------- --------- ---------------- --------------
ESTIMATED_FLASHBACK_SIZE
-----------------------
            1050956 22-JAN-07             1440       91914240
                12115968
```

The value of the column OLDEST_FLASHBACK_SCN is 1050956, which indicates you can flash back to the SCN up to that number only, not before that.

The column OLDEST_FLASHBACK_TIME shows the earliest time you can flash back to when you use the time stamp approach shown in recipe 13-4 and recipe 13-5. The default display format of a datetime column is just a date, and it does not yield enough information. To see the exact time, you issue the following SQL statement:

```
SQL> select to_char(oldest_flashback_time,'mm/dd/yy hh24:mi:ss')
  2  from v$flashback_database_log;
```

```
TO_CHAR(OLDEST_FL
-----------------
01/22/07 16:19:39
```

The output shows that you can flash back to at most January 22 at 4:19:39 p.m. when you flash back using the time stamp option.

How It Works

You can flash back the database to any point in the past as long as the required flashback logs are available and as long as the required archived logs are available. The archived logs can be either online or on backup, but they must be available.

Information on flashback logs is available on the data dictionary view V$FLASHBACK_DATABASE_LOG.

The dynamic performance view V$FLASHBACK_DATABASE_LOG shows some of the information on flashback operations. Table 13-1 describes the columns of this view.

Table 13-1. *Columns of V$FLASHBACK_DATABASE_LOG*

Column Name	Description
OLDEST_FLASHBACK_SCN	The minimum SCN to which you can flash back the database.
OLDEST_FLASHBACK_TIME	The earliest time to which you can flash back the database.
RETENTION_TARGET	The initialization parameter db_flashback_retention_target determines how long the flashback logs are retained, in minutes. The same parameter is shown in this column. See the note after this table for more information.
FLASHBACK_SIZE	The size of flashback logs as of now.
ESTIMATED_FLASHBACK_SIZE	This column is interesting and explained in detail after this table.

■**Note** To find the value of the db_flashback_retention_target parameter, you can also issue this SQL:

```
SQL> show parameter db_flashback_retention_target

NAME                                    TYPE        VALUE
------------------------------------- ----------- --------
db_flashback_retention_target           integer     1440
```

Note that the database initialization parameter db_flashback_retention_target sets the target for the flashback operation. Since this is set to 1440 in the solution example, the database tries to keep the logs for 1,440 minutes. The important word here is "tries," not "guarantees." The actual number of logs kept depends on the size of the flash recovery area, which is determined by another database initialization parameter: db_recovery_file_dest_size. When the flashback logs fill up the flash recovery area, the database removes the oldest logs to make room for the new ones. The age of the oldest logs removed may potentially be less than 1,440 minutes, which is why 1,440 minutes is merely a target, not a guaranteed value of retention.

So, if the database were to retain the flashback logs for the entire 1,440 minutes, what would the combined size of those flashback logs have been?

The column ESTIMATED_FLASHBACK_SIZE answers the question. In the example shown here, the value of this column is 12,115,968, or about 12MB, while the column FLASHBACK_SIZE is 91,914,240, or about 91MB, more than the estimated size. This occurred since the flash recovery area has plenty of space and the older flashback logs are still retained in the flash recovery area. Normally, on a small flash recovery area and very active database, this output would be reversed—the estimated size will be more than the actual size.

13-7. Estimating the Amount of Flashback Logs Generated at Various Times

Problem

You want to find out how much space the flashback logs are expected to consume in the database at various points of time.

Solution

The solution is rather simple. The Oracle database already has a view that shows the estimated database changes and flashback changes in a one-hour period. This view is V$FLASHBACK_DATABASE_STAT. Here is a sample of how to use the view to identify how much flashback and database changes are generated in hour-long intervals:

```
SQL> alter session set nls_date_format = 'mm/dd/yy hh24:mi:ss';

Session altered.


SQL> select * from v$flashback_database_stat
  2  order by begin_time
  3  /

BEGIN_TIME         END_TIME          FLASHBACK_DATA    DB_DATA   REDO_DATA➡
ESTIMATED_FLASHBACK_SIZE
----------------- ----------------- --------------- ---------- ----------➡
-----------------------
01/25/07 21:53:08 01/25/07 22:59:40       27860992   33284096   21613056➡
194224128
01/25/07 22:59:40 01/25/07 23:16:56        2138112    2285568     749056➡
0
... and so on ...
```

The data of interest is the column ESTIMATED_FLASHBACK_SIZE, which shows the expected flashback log generated in the time period shown by the columns BEGIN_TIME and END_TIME. Using this view, you can see an hour-by-hour progress of the flashback data generation. Issue the following query to find out the estimated total size of the flashback logs at the end of each period:

```
SQL> select end_time, estimated_flashback_size
  2  from v$flashback_database_stat
  3  order by 1
  4  /
```

Here is the output:

```
END_TIME            ESTIMATED_FLASHBACK_SIZE
----------------    ------------------------
01/25/07 19:58:00                   73786720
01/25/07 20:53:10                  164890123
01/25/07 21:57:37                  287563456
01/25/07 22:59:40                  194224128
... and so on ...
```

Studying the output, you can see the demand for flashback logs went up at 21:57 to 287,563,456, or about 287MB. If you estimate the total size of flashback logs as 190MB, then the older logs will be deleted to make room for the new ones at 21:57. This information helps you when deciding the optimal value of the flashback logs.

How It Works

This view V$FLASHBACK_DATABASE_STAT shows the estimated flashback data within hour-long intervals. Table 13-2 describes the columns of the view.

Table 13-2. *Columns of V$FLASHBACK_DATABASE_STAT*

Column Name	Description
BEGIN_TIME	The beginning of the interval
END_TIME	The end time of the interval
FLASHBACK_DATA	The amount of flashback data generated in bytes in this time interval
DB_DATA	The amount of database change data generated in bytes in this time interval
REDO_DATA	The amount of redo generated in bytes in this time interval
ESTIMATED_FLASHBACK_SIZE	The estimated size of the total flashback logs retained to satisfy the retention target at the end of this time interval, shown in the column END_TIME

13-8. Estimating the Space Occupied by Flashback Logs in the Flash Recovery Area

Problem

You want to estimate how much space will be needed for the flashback logs to be retained enough to flash back by a time period specified by the retention target.

Solution

To estimate the total size of all flashback logs required for the retention target, follow these steps:

1. Check the dynamic performance view V$FLASHBACK_DATABASE_LOG:

    ```
    SQL> select * from v$flashback_database_log;

    OLDEST_FLASHBACK_SCN OLDEST_FL RETENTION_TARGET FLASHBACK_SIZE➡
    ESTIMATED_FLASHBACK_SIZE
    -------------------- --------- ---------------- --------------➡
    -----------------------
                1050956 22-JAN-07             1440       91914240➡
                92430336
    ```

2. Note the value of ESTIMATED_FLASHBACK_SIZE, which is 92,430,336, or about 92MB in this case. This should ideally be your size of the flashback logs.

How It Works

It is not necessary for the database to hold on to the flashback logs. If the space inside the flashback recovery area is under pressure, Oracle automatically deletes the oldest flashback logs to make room for the new ones. Even though the retention target is set, there is no guarantee that Oracle can actually flash back to that point in the past. Since flashback logs are removed only when there is no space, if you size the flashback recovery area large enough, no flashback logs that are required to flash the database back by the retention target need to be deleted. In this recipe, you have identified how many flashback logs would need to be retained to meet the retention target requirement.

13-9. Creating Normal Restore Points

Problem

You want to create normal (or nonguaranteed) restore points that you can later flash back to.

Solution

Execute a statement such as the following, which creates a restore point named rp1:

```
SQL> create restore point rp1;

Restore point created.
```

The restore point is now created. You can flash back to the rp1 restore point later, as explained in recipe 13-4 and recipe 13-5.

How It Works

Restore points are named positions in time. While flashing a database back, you can specify a restore point as a destination instead of specifying an SCN or time stamp. However, flashing back to a restore point is possible only if the flashback logs are available for the time associated with the restore point. Because the restore points created by following this recipe are not guaranteed, they are known as *unguaranteed* or *normal* restore points. Normal restore points are the default type.

13-10. Creating Guaranteed Restore Points

Problem

You want to create guaranteed restore points to ensure that you can flash back to them as needed. You want to require the database to retain any needed logs to support those points.

Solution

Add the `guarantee` keyword to your `create restore point` command. For example:

```
SQL> create restore point rp2 guarantee flashback database;

Restore point created.
```

Restore point rp2 is now created as a *guaranteed* restore point.

How It Works

For a description of restore points and how they work, refer to the "How It Works" section of recipe 13-9. As described in that recipe, merely defining a restore point does not mean you can flash back to the associated point in time. Flashback logs are deleted by the database automatically when the space in the flash recovery area is inadequate for an incoming backup. It's entirely possible then for the logs required by a given restore point to be deleted, making that restore point useless.

If you try to flash the database to a point for which no flashback logs are available, you will see the following error message:

```
ORA-38729: Not enough flashback database log data to do FLASHBACK.
```

This message means the database does not have the flashback logs needed to go back to the restore point (or time or SCN) that you've specified. By adding the word `guarantee` to your `create restore point` command, you prevent the database from deleting any needed logs for whatever restore point you are creating.

■**Caution** When a guaranteed restore point is defined, the associated flashback logs are never deleted unless the restore point is dropped. This will reduce the available space in the flash recovery area. A filled-up flash recovery area will cause the database instance to abort, with the failure in the recovery writer (RVWR) process. So, create guaranteed restore points only when you need to go back to them after some preestablished event to be completed in the near future, such as doing a test run of the application and then reverting to the starting data sets. After the test is completed, you will drop the guaranteed restore points.

13-11. Listing Restore Points

Problem

You want to list the various restore points in the database and the information about them.

Solution

Query the view V$RESTORE_POINT. For example:

```
SQL> col time format a32
SQL> col name format a10
SQL> select * from v$restore_point
  2  order by 2,1;

       SCN DATABASE_INCARNATION# GUA STORAGE_SIZE TIME                             NAME
---------- --------------------- --- ------------ -------------------------------- ----
   1047095                     2 NO             0 22-JAN-07 01.57.14.00 PM         RP1
   1049764                     2 YES      4096000 22-JAN-07 03.40.55.00 PM         RP2
   1051267                     2 YES            0 22-JAN-07 04.32.55.00 PM         RP3
   1051276                     2 NO             0 22-JAN-07 04.33.05.00 PM         RP4
   1047289                     3 NO             0 22-JAN-07 05.13.55.00 PM         RP5
   1047301                     3 YES      3981312 22-JAN-07 05.14.17.00 PM         RP6
... and so on ...
```

The various columns of the view are described in the "How It Works" section.

How It Works

When you create a restore point as guaranteed, the database marks the flashback logs as not to be removed when the flash recovery area runs out of space. The space occupied by these specially marked flashback logs is shown under the column STORAGE_SIZE in the view V$RESTORE_POINT.

Table 13-3 describes the columns of the view V$RESTORE_POINT.

Table 13-3. *Columns of V$RESTORE_POINT*

Column Name	Description
SCN	This is the SCN of the database when the restore point was created.
DATABASE_INCARNATION#	This column displays the incarnation of the database when this restore point was created. If the database was flashed back and then opened with resetlogs, it creates a new incarnation of the database.
GUARANTEE_FLASHBACK_DATABASE	If the restore point is a guaranteed one, this column holds the value YES.
STORAGE_SIZE	This is the storage occupied by the flashback logs of the guaranteed restore points. In case of normal restore points, this value is 0.

Column Name	Description
TIME	This is the time stamp when the restore point was created.
NAME	This is the name of the restore point.
PRESERVED	This is a new column in Oracle Database 11*g*. It shows whether the restore point must be explicitly deleted.
RESTORE_POINT_TIME	This shows whether you specified a specific time when the restore point was supposed to be taken. If you didn't specify a time, it's NULL.

13-12. Dropping Restore Points

Problem

You want to drop a specific restore point.

Solution

To drop a restore point named rp2, whether normal or guaranteed, simply execute the following SQL statement:

```
SQL> drop restore point rp2;

Restore point dropped.
```

To list the restore points defined in the database, use recipe 13-11.

How It Works

Normal restore points are merely pointers to the SCNs at the time they were defined. They do not consume any space. Guaranteed restore points mark the flashback logs necessary to enable flashback to a specific point in time, and those flashback logs do take up space. When you drop a guaranteed restore point, you will see an immediate increase in the available space in the flash recovery area. To check the available space in the flash recovery area, refer to recipe 3-4.

13-13. Recovering a Dropped Table

Problem

You accidentally dropped a table that should not have been dropped. You want to reinstate the table without doing a database recovery.

Solution

If you dropped the table just moments ago, it is not actually dropped; it is placed in the recycle bin. Assume that you dropped the table ACCOUNTS and want to revive it. You can resurrect that table from the recycle bin by following these steps:

1. Log on to the database as the table owner.

2. Check whether the table exists in the recycle bin. Issue the SQL*Plus command show recyclebin:

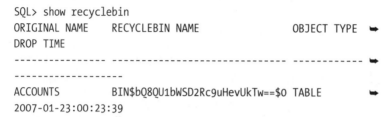

```
SQL> show recyclebin
ORIGINAL NAME    RECYCLEBIN NAME                OBJECT TYPE  ➡
DROP TIME
--------------- ----------------------------- ------------ ➡
------------------
ACCOUNTS           BIN$bQ8QU1bWSD2Rc9uHevUkTw==$0 TABLE        ➡
2007-01-23:00:23:39
```

The presence of the table ACCOUNTS under the column ORIGINAL_NAME indicates that the table is still present in the recycle bin and can be revived. If you see multiple entries with the same ORIGINAL_NAME, it indicates the table was dropped, another table was created with the same name, that table was dropped too, and so on, for however many duplicate entries you have. Recipe 13-14 shows how to handle a situation in which you have duplicate names in the recycle bin.

3. Revive the table from the recycle bin by issuing the following SQL*Plus command:

```
SQL> flashback table accounts to before drop;

Flashback complete.
```

The table is now available in the database.

How It Works

In Oracle Database 10g, when you drop a table, the table is not really dropped. Rather, the table is renamed. For instance, in the example in this recipe, when the table ACCOUNTS was dropped, the table was actually renamed to BIN$bQ8QU1bWSD2Rc9uHevUkTw==$0. That name is cryptic enough that it would never be used and thus would never conflict with a real name by any user. Since the table is merely renamed and not dropped, the data in the table is still available. When you issue the flashback command in step 2, Oracle Database 10g merely renames the table to the original name. However, the dropped table does not show up in the data dictionary views USER_TABLES and ALL_TABLES.

```
SQL> select table_name
  2  from user_tables;

no rows selected
```

However, the view TAB shows this renamed table:

```
SQL> select *
  2  from tab;

TNAME                           TABTYPE  CLUSTERID
------------------------------- -------- ----------
BIN$bQ8QU1bWSD2Rc9uHevUkTw==$0  TABLE
```

If you check the USER_SEGMENTS dictionary view, the segments will be there:

```
SQL> col segment_name format a30
SQL> select segment_type, segment_name
  2  from user_segments;

SEGMENT_TYPE       SEGMENT_NAME
-----------------  -----------------------------
TABLE              BIN$bQ8QU1bWSD2Rc9uHevUkTw==$0
INDEX              BIN$FPl4bnVgTH2ZIr1uc310Hg==$1
INDEX              BIN$c7f1XmKBQjiVXy2j/NcJqA==$1
```

The indexes are those of the table. When the table was dropped, the indexes were not dropped. They were renamed, just like the table.

If you make a mistake in identifying the correct table, Oracle Database returns an ORA-38305 error, as shown in the following example where you are trying to revive a table named ACCOUNTS1 that does not exist in the recycle bin:

```
SQL> flashback table accounts1 to before drop;
flashback table accounts1 to before drop
*
ERROR at line 1:
ORA-38305: object not in RECYCLE BIN
```

The error says it all.

■**Tip** If you want to delete a table permanently, without sending it to the recycle bin, then use the purge clause in the drop statement. For example:

```
SQL> drop table accounts purge;

Table dropped.
```

The table is now completely dropped; similar to the pre-10*g* behavior, it does not go to the recycle bin.

13-14. Undropping a Table When Another Exists with the Same Name

Problem

You had a table called ACCOUNTS that was dropped, and you created another table called ACCOUNTS. Now you want to reinstate the first table ACCOUNTS from the recycle bin.

Solution

There are two potential solutions:

- Drop the existing table so there will be no conflict for the name of the table undropped.

- Undrop the table but reinstate it to a different name.

Here are the solutions in detail.

Solution 1: Dropping the Existing Table

The easiest approach is, of course, to drop the existing table. The flashed-back table then comes on the database without any problems.

Solution 2: Renaming the Reinstated Table

The alternative approach is safer because you do not need to drop anything. When you flash back a table to undrop it, you can optionally rename it. In this case, when you flash back the table ACCOUNTS, you want to reinstate it as NEW_ACCOUNTS.

```
SQL> flashback table accounts to before drop rename to new_accounts;

Flashback complete.
```

The existing table still remains as ACCOUNTS, but the reinstated table is renamed to NEW_ACCOUNTS.

How It Works

When you flash back a table from the recycle bin, a table with that name must not already exist in the database. Suppose you are trying to revive a table called ACCOUNTS but it already exists. In that case, the flashback statement returns with an error—ORA-38312:

```
SQL> flashback table accounts to before drop;

Flashback complete.

SQL> flashback table accounts to before drop;
flashback table accounts to before drop
*
ERROR at line 1:
ORA-38312: original name is used by an existing object
```

■**Note** Suppose there are two tables in the recycle bin with the same name—ACCOUNTS, as shown here:

```
SQL> show recyclebin
ORIGINAL NAME    RECYCLEBIN NAME                  OBJECT TYPE  DROP TIME
---------------  -------------------------------  -----------  -------------------
ACCOUNTS         BIN$VKGbC+r/Qjqg3avhlpBpqw==$0 TABLE          2007-01-23:00:46:50
ACCOUNTS         BIN$bQ8QU1bWSD2Rc9uHevUkTw==$0 TABLE          2007-01-23:00:23:39
```

Now you issue this:

```
SQL> flashback table accounts to before drop;
```

Which table ACCOUNTS will be reinstated?

The table that was dropped last will be reinstated; that is, the table that shows up first will be reinstated. Pay attention to this behavior while reinstating a table from the recycle bin.

13-15. Undropping a Specific Table from Two Dropped Tables with the Same Name

Problem

You had a table called ACCOUNTS, which you dropped. Later you created a table, again called ACCOUNTS, and dropped that too. Now you want to revive the table ACCOUNTS, the one that was dropped first.

Solution

To reinstate a specific dropped table, follow the steps:

1. First find out the presence of these objects in the recycle bin:

   ```
   SQL> show recyclebin
   ORIGINAL NAME RECYCLEBIN NAME                  OBJEC  DROP TIME
   ------------- -------------------------------  ------ -------------------
   ACCOUNTS      BIN$VKGbC+r/Qjqg3avhlpBpqw==$0 TABLE   2007-01-23:00:46:50
   ACCOUNTS      BIN$bQ8QU1bWSD2Rc9uHevUkTw==$0 TABLE   2007-01-23:00:23:39
   ```

   Note there are two different tables with the same name—ACCOUNTS.

2. Decide which of the two accounts tables to revive. The column DROP_TIME helps in your decision; it shows when each table was dropped. In your case, you want to recover the one that was dropped earlier. If you issue the statement flashback table accounts to before drop, the more recently dropped table will be revived—not what you want in this scenario.

3. To revive the earlier table, the one that was dropped first, issue the `flashback table` command, giving the recycle bin name as the table name:

```
SQL> flashback table "BIN$bQ8QU1bWSD2Rc9uHevUkTw==$0" to before drop;

Flashback complete.
```

Be sure to put the recycle bin name—BIN$bQ8QU1bWSD2Rc9uHevUkTw==$0—in double quotes. The double quotes are necessary because of the presence of special characters in the name.

4. Check the recycle bin. You will see only one table now:

```
SQL> show recyclebin
ORIGINAL NAME    RECYCLEBIN NAME                        OBJECT DROP TIME
-------------    -----------------------------    ------  -------------------
ACCOUNTS         BIN$VKGbC+r/Qjqg3avhlpBpqw==$0 TABLE   2007-01-23:00:46:50
```

There is just one table in the recycle bin. You have successfully restored the earlier version of the table.

How It Works

As mentioned in recipe 13-13, a `drop table` command in Oracle Database 10*g* does not actually drop a table; it merely renames it to a name with a lot of special characters. An example of such a name is the `"BIN$VKGbC+r/Qjqg3avhlpBpqw==$0"` name shown in this recipe. While reviving a table in the recycle bin, you can use its original name or the special recycle bin name.

In most cases, you can use the original name. Sometimes, though, you can't use the original name. One such example could be when you drop a table and create another with the *same* name. When you re-create a table that was dropped before and then drop the re-created one, the table name is same—ACCOUNTS, in this example—but the recycle bin names for each of those two tables are unique. To reinstate a specific dropped table, you should specify the recycle bin name instead of the real name.

13-16. Checking the Contents of the Recycle Bin

Problem

You want to see the objects in the recycle bin.

Solution

You can display the objects in your own recycle bin in two ways:

- Use the SQL*Plus command `show recyclebin`:

```
SQL> show recyclebin
ORIGINAL NAME    RECYCLEBIN NAME                         OBJECT TYPE  DROP TIME
-------------    ----------------------------------    ------------  -----------------
C                BIN$SUhZujR9R5SjV3ujnYa82w==$0 TABLE        2007-01-28:12:54:03
```

The command SHOW RECYCLEBIN shows some pertinent details for all tables in the recycle bin. However, the command does not show corresponding indexes, triggers, and so on.

- To get information on *all* objects in the recycle bin, including indexes and triggers, query the view USER_RECYCLEBIN, as shown in the following example:

```
SQL> select * from user_recyclebin;
```

OBJECT_NAME	ORIGINAL_NAME	OPERATION
TYPE	TS_NAME	CREATETIME
DROPTIME	DROPSCN PARTITION_NAME	CAN CAN
RELATED BASE_OBJECT PURGE_OBJECT	SPACE	
BIN$ROMlhUf5SCGLUnqmsAxMoA==$0	IN_ACC_02	DROP
INDEX	USERS	2007-01-23:12:25:03
2007-01-23:12:25:36 1068318		NO YES
51888 51888 51891 256		
BIN$oyuX86OoRjWa2KYaWiY4zw==$0	PK_ACCOUNTS	DROP
INDEX	USERS	2007-01-23:12:24:01
2007-01-23:12:25:36 1068321		NO YES
51888 51888 51889 88		
BIN$UawCFy69TUyc9DgR50AEMw==$0	ACCOUNTS	DROP
TABLE	USERS	2007-01-23:12:24:01
2007-01-23:12:25:36 1068325		YES YES
51888 51888 51888 384		
BIN$V1wmU6mRTsyQFLvbPQKMnQ==$0	IN_ACC_01	DROP
INDEX	USERS	2007-01-23:12:25:02
2007-01-23:12:25:36 1068315		NO YES
51888 51888 51890 88		

To check the recycle bin of all users, check the view DBA_RECYCLEBIN:

```
SQL> select * from dba_recyclebin;
```

The columns are the same as user_recyclebin, except the additional column—OWNER—that shows the owner of the dropped object.

How It Works

When a table is dropped in Oracle Database 10*g* Release 1 and newer, it is not actually dropped. It's merely renamed to a different name, such as BIN$UawCFy69TUyc9DgR50AEMw==$0. A record is placed in the table RECYCLEBIN$ (in the sys schema) for that table. The view USER_RECYCLEBIN is a join between, among other tables, the OBJ$ (the objects in the database) and RECYCLEBIN$ tables in the sys schema.

13-17. Restoring Dependent Objects of an Undropped Table

Problem

You want to recover all the subordinate objects such as the indexes, constraints, and so on, of a table that has been undropped.

Solution

Here are the steps to restore the dependent objects:

1. First, check the contents of the recycle bin to get an inventory of what is available. This is an important step; do not skip it. The following is the query you want to execute:

```
SQL> col type format a5
SQL> col original_name format a15
SQL> select original_name, object_name, type, can_undrop
  2  from user_recyclebin;

ORIGINAL_NAME   OBJECT_NAME                      TYPE    CAN
--------------- -------------------------------- ------- ---
IN_ACC_03       BIN$mc3jkDZRR42mswWBROXPyA==$0   INDEX   NO
IN_ACC_02       BIN$B8BgSIvWTweFyZv/y57GHg==$0   INDEX   NO
IN_ACC_01       BIN$t8poR1f4SIKTOTpH2vYKSQ==$0   INDEX   NO
TR_ACC_01       BIN$dt6tBSIWSn+F5epvjybKmw==$0   TRIGGER NO
ACCOUNTS        BIN$laonDjIDS6macycHgAjP1Q==$0   TABLE   YES
```

   The most important column is the column CAN_UNDROP. If this column is YES, then you can undrop an object cleanly without any additional efforts. Objects with CAN_UNDROP = NO can still be reinstated, but you have to change their names to the original names manually.

■**Tip** The ORIGINAL_NAME column shows the original names. Once a table is undropped, the recycle bin information is removed, and you will never be able to see the original names of the dependent objects such as triggers and indexes of that table. So, save the output of this query before you go to the next step.

---

2. Now undrop the table ACCOUNTS by executing the following SQL statement:

```
SQL> flashback table accounts to before drop;

Flashback complete.
```

   The table is now available in the database.

3. Display the constraints of the table:

```
SQL> select constraint_type, constraint_name
  2  from user_constraints
  3  where table_name = 'ACCOUNTS';
```

```
C CONSTRAINT_NAME
- ------------------------------
P BIN$ncFOiaduRZeURXatWq8lyA==$0
C BIN$782qhcPvQbajusPeAEiR3Q==$0
```

The flashback (or the undrop) brought back the primary key and check constraints but not the foreign keys, if there were any. The foreign keys are lost forever.

4. Change the names of the reinstated objects to their original names, if you know what they were. For example, if you know the original name of the constraint BIN$ncFOiaduRZeURXatWq8lyA==$0 was pk_accounts, you can issue the following query to restore the original name:

```
SQL> alter table accounts rename constraint "BIN$ncFOiaduRZeURXatWq8lyA==$0" ➥
to pk_accounts;

Table altered.

SQL> alter table accounts rename constraint "BIN$782qhcPvQbajusPeAEiR3Q==$0" ➥
to ck_acc_01;

Table altered.
```

If you don't have the names, use any human-readable name you consider appropriate.

5. Now check the indexes of the newly reinstated table:

```
SQL> select index_name
  2  from user_indexes
  3  where table_name = 'ACCOUNTS';

INDEX_NAME
------------------------------
BIN$9POlL6gfQK6RBoOK4klc3Q==$0
BIN$PookVi5nRpmhmPaVOThGQQ==$0
BIN$fzY77+GmTzqz/3u4dqac9g==$0
```

6. Note the names, and compare them to the names you got in step 1. It's not easy, but you can make a clear connection. Using the output from step 1, rename the indexes:

```
SQL> alter index "BIN$9POlL6gfQK6RBoOK4klc3Q==$0" rename to IN_ACC_01;

Index altered.

SQL> alter index "BIN$PookVi5nRpmhmPaVOThGQQ==$0" rename to SYS_C005457;

Index altered.

SQL> alter index "BIN$fzY77+GmTzqz/3u4dqac9g==$0" rename to in_acc_02;

Index altered.
```

7. Finally, make sure the indexes are in place and have correct names:

```
SQL> select index_name
  2  from user_indexes
  3  where table_name = 'ACCOUNTS';

INDEX_NAME
------------------------------
IN_ACC_01
SYS_C005457
IN_ACC_02
```

8. Check the triggers on the reinstated table:

```
SQL> select trigger_name
  2  from user_triggers;

TRIGGER_NAME
------------------------------
BIN$dt6tBSIWSn+F5epvjybKmw==$0
```

9. Rename triggers to their original names:

```
SQL> alter trigger "BIN$dt6tBSIWSn+F5epvjybKmw==$0" rename to tr_acc_01;

Trigger altered.
```

10. Check the triggers now to make sure they are named as they were originally:

```
SQL> select trigger_name
  2  from user_triggers;

TRIGGER_NAME
------------------------------
TR_ACC_01
```

This confirms you reinstated all the dependent objects.

How It Works

In Oracle Database 10*g* Release 1 and newer, when a table is dropped, the table is not actually dropped; it is merely renamed to a system-generated name and marked as in the recycle bin. Likewise, all the dependent objects of the table—triggers, constraints, indexes—are also not dropped; they are renamed as well and continue to exist on the renamed table. When you flash back the table to before the drop, or *undrop* the table, these dependent objects are not undropped. But those objects do exist, and you can rename them to their original names. The only exceptions are foreign key constraints, which are lost when a table is dropped.

13-18. Turning Off the Recycle Bin

Problem

You want to turn off the recycle bin behavior; that is, you want behavior like in Oracle9i where a dropped table just gets dropped permanently.

Solution

You can modify the recycle bin behavior so that dropped objects do not go to the recycle bin. Instead, they simply get dropped permanently. The parameter that influences this is recyclebin. You can set this parameter at the session level or the system level.

Set the session parameter to disable the recycle bin at the session level:

```
SQL> alter session set recyclebin = off;
```

```
Session altered.
```

After setting recyclebin to off, if you drop a table, the table is completely dropped:

```
SQL> drop table accounts;
```

```
Table dropped.
```

Now, if you check the recycle bin:

```
SQL> show recyclebin
```

the command returns no output, indicating that the recycle bin is empty.

You can turn off the recycle bin for the entire database by executing this:

```
SQL> alter system set recyclebin = off;
```

```
System altered.
```

If the recycle bin is turned off at the system level, you can turn it on at the session level, and vice versa.

How It Works

In Oracle Database 10g Release 1 and newer, when the tables are dropped, they are really not dropped. Instead, they are renamed and marked to be in the recycle bin. This is the default behavior. By executing the statement alter session/system set recyclebin = off at the session or system level, the behavior is changed to the pre-10g one; that is, the table is actually dropped as a result of the drop command, not renamed to be placed in the recycle bin.

SHOULD YOU TURN OFF THE RECYCLE BIN?

Even though you can turn off the recycle bin at the system level, there is no valid reason to do so in our opinion. Here are some arguments against recycle bins:

- They take up space, since the dropped objects are not actually dropped.

- They make the free-space calculations erroneous because they are dropped but still counted as occupied space.

- They show up in a user's list of tables, which can be confusing. And the names are confusing.

- In some environments, such as data warehouses, a lot of tables are created and dropped rapidly. Dropping those tables is permanent, and there is never a need to undrop them.

Each of these arguments can be countered, as shown here:

- They take up space, but the space is immediately deallocated and given to the segment that needs it, if there is a space pressure in the tablespace. So, the space is not taken up in a practical sense.

- The free-space calculations exclude the recycle bin objects, so the free space reported is accurate.

- The recycle bin object shows up in TAB but not in the view USER_TABLES. Most scripts are written against USER_TABLES, not against TAB, so this is not a real concern.

- The last argument has some merit. Ordinarily, this should not cause any issues, since the recycle bin objects are not counted toward the user's total used space. But if you would rather not see the recycle bin objects, you can turn it off for that session only.

So, as you can see, there is no real reason behind turning off the recycle bin at the system level (or mimicking the 9*i* behavior). On the other hand, if you disable it, you will lose a valuable feature—a safety net of sorts while dropping tables. So, we strongly recommend against turning off the recycle bin.

13-19. Clearing the Recycle Bin

Problem

You want to remove all dropped objects from the recycle bin.

Solution

You can clean up the recycle bin using the purge statement, which clears the recycle bin of the currently logged on user. For example:

```
SQL> purge recyclebin;

Recyclebin purged.
```

Each user has a logically individual recycle bin. If you want to clear the recycle bins of all users in the database, you should purge dba_recyclebin, as shown here:

```
SQL> purge dba_recyclebin;

DBA Recyclebin purged.
```

This clears all the data from all the recycle bins.

How It Works

Note from the earlier recipes that when a table is dropped, it's not really dropped. Instead, the table is renamed and marked to be in the recycle bin. The statement purge recyclebin merely drops all the objects that were marked to be in the recycle bin.

CALLING PURGE IN PL/SQL

purge is a DDL statement, not a DML statement. The difference is not significant when you use it in the SQL*Plus command line as shown in the examples, but it is important to understand the difference when writing a PL/SQL routine. You can't call it in PL/SQL code as shown here:

```
SQL> begin
  2      purge recyclebin;
  3  end;
  4  /
    purge recyclebin;
          *
ERROR at line 2:
ORA-06550: line 2, column 10:
PLS-00103: Encountered the symbol "RECYCLEBIN" when expecting one of the
following:
:= . ( @ % ;
The symbol ":=" was substituted for "RECYCLEBIN" to continue.
```

To call purge in a PL/SQL code, you will need to call it as a parameter to execute immediate, as shown here:

```
SQL> begin
  2      execute immediate 'purge recyclebin';
  3  end;
  4  /

PL/SQL procedure successfully completed.
```

13-20. Querying the History of a Table Row (Flashback Query)

Problem

You want to find how the values of the columns in a row have changed over a period of time.

Solution

To find all the changes to the row for ACCNO 3760 in table ACCOUNTS, issue the following query:

```
SQL> select
  2      acc_status,
  3      versions_starttime,
  4      versions_startscn,
  5      versions_endtime,
  6      versions_endscn,
  7      versions_xid,
  8      versions_operation
  9  from accounts
 10      versions between scn minvalue and maxvalue
 11  where accno = 3760
 12  order by 3
 13  /
```

The result comes back as follows:

```
A VERSIONS_STARTTIME    VERSIONS_STARTSCN VERSIONS_ENDTIME       VERSIONS_ENDSCN➥
VERSIONS_XID     V
- -------------------- ----------------- ---------------------- ----------------➥
---------------- -
A 23-JAN-07 04.38.57 PM           1076867 23-JAN-07 04.39.03 PM          1076870➥
02002F00D8010000 U
I 23-JAN-07 04.39.03 PM           1076870 23-JAN-07 04.39.12 PM          1076874➥
08001B00DB010000 U
A 23-JAN-07 04.39.12 PM           1076874                                       ➥
07002B0068010000 U
A                                         23-JAN-07 04.38.57 PM          1076867
```

The results show how the values of the column ACC_STATUS were changed at different points in time. Note the column VERSIONS_OPERATION, which shows the DML operation that modified the value of the corresponding row. The values are as follows:

I: Insert

U: Update

D: Delete

In the example output, you can see that on January 23, 2007, at 4:38:57 p.m. (the value of the column VERSIONS_STARTTIME), someone updated the value of a row by using an Update operation. The SCN at that time was 1076867. The ACC_STATUS column was changed to A at that time. This value was unchanged until January 23, 2007, at 4:39:03 p.m. (the value of column VERSIONS_ENDTIME).

As shown in the second record of the output, on January 23, 2007, at 4:39:03 p.m. and at SCN 1076870, another update operation updated the ACC_STATUS to I. This is how you read the changes to the table row where ACCNO is 3760.

Note the line where VERSIONS_ENDTIME is null. This indicates the current row, which has not been changed yet.

In addition to the SCN, you can also use timestamp as a predicate, as shown here:

```
SQL> select
  2      acc_status,
  3      versions_starttime,
  4      versions_startscn,
  5      versions_endtime,
  6      versions_endscn,
  7      versions_xid,
  8      versions_operation
  9   from accounts
 10      versions between timestamp minvalue and maxvalue
 11   where accno = 3762
 12   order by 3;
```

In the previous example, you specified the predicate to get all the available records. Note line 10:

```
versions between timestamp minvalue and maxvalue
```

This predicate indicates the minimum and maximum values of the time stamps available. You can specify exact values for these as well. To get the versions on January 23 between noon and 3 p.m., you need to rewrite the query by modifying line 10 to this:

```
versions between timestamp to_date('1/23/2007 12:00:00', 'mm/dd/yyyy hh24:mi:ss')
and to_date('1/23/2007 15:00:00', 'mm/dd/yyyy hh24:mi:ss')
```

Instead of using time stamps, you can use SCNs, such as between 1000 and 2000, to get the versions of the row. In that case, line 10 becomes this:

```
versions between SCN 1000 and 2000
```

If you don't see any data under the pseudocolumns, the reasons could be one of the following:

- The information has aged out of the undo segments.

- The database was recycled after the changes occurred.

How It Works

When a row is updated, the database records the relevant change details in the database blocks, in addition to some other related details such as the SCN of when the change occurred, the time stamp, the type of operation that resulted in the change, and so on—a sort of "metadata" about the changes, if you will. This metadata is stored in pseudocolumns and can be queried afterward.

Table 13-4 describes the flashback query pseudocolumns. The pseudocolumns that start with VERSIONS, such as VERSIONS_STARTTIME, are not actually part of the table. They are computed and shown to the user at runtime. A good everyday example of such a pseudocolumn is ROWNUM, which denotes the serial number of a row in the returned result set. This column is not stored in the table but is computed and returned to the user when the query is executed. Since these columns are not part of the table's definition, they are called *pseudocolumns*.

Table 13-4. *Flashback Query Pseudocolumns*

Pseudo Column Name	Description
VERSIONS_STARTTIME	This is the time stamp when this version of the row became effective. This is the commit time after the row was changed.
VERSIONS_STARTSCN	This is the SCN when this version became effective.
VERSIONS_ENDTIME	This is the time stamp when the version became old, replaced by a new version. This is the time of commit after the row was changed.
VERSIONS_ENDSCN	This is the SCN when the row's version was changed.
VERSIONS_XID	This is the transaction ID that changed the row's version. This can be joined with the XID column of the dictionary view FLASHBACK_TRANSACTION_QUERY to show the transaction that made this change. The view FLASHBACK_TRANSACTION_QUERY also shows other relevant details of the transaction such as who did it, when, and so on.
VERSIONS_OPERATION	This is the abbreviated activity code—I, U, or D—for Insert, Update, or Delete that resulted in this version of the row.

13-21. Flashing Back a Specific Table

Problem

You want to flash back a specific table, not the entire database, to a point in time in the past.

Solution

The table can be flashed back with a specialized adaptation of flashback queries. Here are the steps on how to do it:

1. Make sure the table has row movement enabled:

```
SQL> select row_movement
  2  from user_tables
  3  where table_name = 'ACCOUNTS';

ROW_MOVE
--------
ENABLED
```

2. If the output comes back as DISABLED, enable them by issuing this SQL statement:

```
SQL> alter table accounts enable row movement;
```

```
Table altered.
```

This prepares the table for flashback.

3. Check the table to see how far into the past you can flash it back. Use recipe 13-6 to determine how far back into the past you can go.

4. Flash the table back to a specific time stamp:

```
SQL> flashback table accounts to timestamp to_date ('23-JAN-07 18.23.00',➥
'dd-MON-YY hh24.mi.ss');
```

```
Flashback complete.
```

You can flash back to a specific SCN as well:

5. Check the data in the table to make sure you have flashed back to the exact point you want. If the flashback was not enough, you can flash the table back once more to a point even further in the past. For instance, the previous step reinstated the table as of 6:23 p.m., which was not enough. In this step, you will flash it back to one more minute in the past—to 6:22 p.m.

```
SQL> flashback table accounts to timestamp to_date ('23-JAN-07 18.22.00', ➥
'dd-MON-YY hh24.mi.ss');
```

```
Flashback complete.
```

6. If you have gone too far into the past, you can flash "forward" using the same flashback statement:

```
SQL> flashback table accounts to timestamp to_date ('23-JAN-07 18.24.00',➥
'dd-MON-YY hh24.mi.ss');
```

```
Flashback complete.
```

As you can see, you can flash the table back and forth until you arrive at the exact point.

The flashback is complete. Since the table was not dropped, all dependent objects such as triggers and indexes remain unaffected.

How It Works

Table flashback is entirely different from the database flashback you saw earlier in the chapter. When a table's data changes, the past information is stored in undo segments. Oracle uses this information to present a read-consistent view of the data later. Even if the changes were committed, the undo data is important for the read-consistent image needed by a query that started after the data was changed but before it was committed.

The flashback versions query in recipe 13-20 uses the information in the undo segments to display past versions of the data at multiple points in time. Flashing back a table uses the same undo data to reconstruct the data at whatever point in the past you specify. If sufficient information is not available in the undo segments, you will get the following error:

```
SQL> flashback table accounts to timestamp to_date ('23-JAN-07 15.23.00',➥
'dd-MON-YY hh24.mi.ss');
flashback table accounts to timestamp to_date ('23-JAN-07 15.23.00',➥
'dd-MON-YY hh24.mi.ss')
                 *
ERROR at line 1:
ORA-00604: error occurred at recursive SQL level 1
ORA-12801: error signaled in parallel query server P003
ORA-01555: snapshot too old: rollback segment number 4 with name "_SYSSMU4$" ➥
too small
```

This error may not be that intuitive to interpret, but it conveys the message—the undo segment does not have information the flashback operation needs.

Contrast this operation to the flashback database operation. In flashback database, the changes at the block level to the entire database are captured in flashback logs, and the flashback operation undoes the block changes. Any database change—the creation of new objects, truncation, and so on—is captured by the logs and can be played back. In a flashback query, the data is reconstructed from the undo segments. Any DDL operations are not reinstated. So if you have added a column at 1:30 p.m. and flash back to 1:25 p.m., the added column is not dropped. By the way, the DDL operation does not restrict your ability to perform a flashback beyond that point.

During the flashback operation, the database might have to move the rows from one block to another. This is allowed only if the table has the property row movement enabled. Therefore, you had to enable that as the first step of the process.

You can flash back a table owned by another user, but to do so you need SELECT, INSERT, DELETE, and ALTER privileges on the table, as well as one of the following:

- FLASHBACK ANY TABLE system privilege

- FLASHBACK privilege on that particular table

Table flashback does not work on the following types of tables:

- Advanced queuing (AQ) tables

- Individual table partitions or subpartitions

- Materialized views

- Nested tables

- Object tables

- Remote tables

- Static data dictionary tables

- System tables

- Tables that are part of a cluster

There are some important points you should know when you flash back a table. To make our description of those points easier to understand, suppose the following is a timeline of events:

```
Time -> -------------------------------------------------------------------------
SCN ->         1,000            2,000           3,000           4,000
Events ->    DDL Occurred     Index Dropped   Table Data
```

The SCNs corresponding to each event are shown on the scale. The current SCN is 4,000. Given this scenario, the following limitations and caveats are true:

- You can't flash back the table to an SCN prior to SCN 1,000 (when a specific type of DDL occurred). These DDL operations are as follows:

  - Adding a constraint to the table.

  - Adding the table to a cluster.

  - Adding, dropping, merging, splitting, coalescing, or truncating a partition or sub-partition. Adding a range partition is acceptable.

  - Dropping columns.

  - Modifying columns.

  - Moving the table to a different (or even the same) tablespace.

  - Truncating the table.

- When you flash back the table to a SCN prior to 2,000 (when the index was dropped), the index is not reinstated. Remember, the flashback operation is a data movement operation, not DDL, so dropped objects are not created.

- When you flash back a table, the statistics on the table are not reinstated. When you flash back the table to SCN 1,500, the statistics on the table are as of SCN 4,000.

■■■

Handling Online Redo Log Failures

One of us worked for a company that had just implemented an expensive database server with redundancy built into every component, or so we thought. We were using RAID disks for all database files and the online redo log groups. We were confident that there was minimal risk of failure with these disks.

Therefore, we decided not to multiplex the online redo log groups. A few days later, an inexpensive battery that maintained the cache for a disk controller failed. This caused corruption in the current online redo log group. As a result, we lost data, experienced downtime, and had to perform an incomplete recovery.

How Redo Logs Work

Online redo logs store a record of transactions that have occurred in your database. Online redo logs exist solely to provide a mechanism for you to recover your database in the event of a failure. You are required to have at least two *online redo log groups* in your database. Each online redo log group must contain at least one *online redo log member*. The member is the physical file that exists on disk. You can create multiple members in each redo log group, which is known as *multiplexing* your online redo log group.

■**Tip** We highly recommend that you multiplex the online redo log groups with at least two members in each group and have each member on separate physical devices governed by separate controllers.

The log writer is the background process responsible for writing transaction information from the redo log buffer to the online redo log files. The online redo log group that the log writer is actively writing to is the *current online redo log* group. The log writer writes simultaneously to all members of a redo log group. The log writer needs to successfully write to only one member for the database to continue operating. Your database will cease operating if the log writer cannot write successfully to at least one member of the current group.

When the current online redo log group fills up, a *log switch* occurs, and the log writer starts writing to the next online redo log group. The log writer writes to the online redo log groups in a round-robin fashion. Since you have a finite number of online redo logs groups, eventually the contents of each online redo log group will be overwritten. If you want to save a history of the transaction information, then you must place your database in *archivelog mode* (see recipe 2-3 for details on how to enable archiving).

When your database is in archivelog mode, after every log switch, the archiver background process will copy the contents of the online redo log file to an *archived redo log file*. In the event of a failure, the archived redo log files allow you to restore the complete history of transactions that have occurred since your last database backup.

Figure 14-1 displays a typical setup for the online redo log files. This figure shows three online redo log groups, with each group containing two members. The database is in archivelog mode. In this figure, group 2 has recently filled with transactions, a log switch has occurred, and the log writer is now writing to group 3. The archiver process is copying the contents of group 2 to an archived redo log file. When group 3 fills up, another log switch will occur, and the log writer will begin writing to group 1. At the same time, the archiver process will copy the contents of group 3 to archive log sequence 3 (and so forth).

Figure 14-1. *Typical online redo log configuration*

The online redo log files aren't intended to be backed up. These files contain only the most recent redo transaction information generated by the database. When you enable archiving, the archived redo log files are the mechanism for protecting your database transaction history.

The contents of the current online redo log files are not archived until a log switch occurs. This means that if you lose all members of the current online redo log file, then you'll lose transactions. Listed next are several mechanisms you can implement to minimize the chance of failure with the online redo log files:

- Multiplex groups to have multiple members.

- Never allow two members of the same group to share the same controller.

- Never put two members of the same group on the same physical disk.

- Ensure operating system file permissions are set appropriately.

- Use physical storage devices that are redundant (that is, RAID).

- Appropriately size the log files so that they switch and are archived at regular intervals.

- Set the `archive_lag_target` initialization parameter to ensure that the online redo logs are switched at regular intervals.

■**Note** The only tool provided by Oracle that can protect you and preserve all committed transactions in the event you lose all members of the current online redo log group is Oracle Data Guard implemented in Maximum Protection Mode.

The online redo log files are never backed up by an RMAN online backup or by a user-managed hot backup. If you did back up the online redo log files, it would be meaningless to restore them. The online redo log files contain the latest redo generated by the database. You would not want to overwrite them from a backup with old redo information. For a database in archivelog mode, the online redo log files contain the most recently generated transactions that are required to perform a complete recovery.

■**Tip** Use the RMAN `backup database plus archivelog` command to ensure that your current online redo log files of all the threads are switched and archived before and after the backup of the database.

Since RMAN doesn't backup online redo log files, you can't use RMAN to restore these critical files. Given their criticality, we thought it was important to include a chapter on how to deal with failures with online redo log files. We first start by detailing how to decide how and what to restore.

14-1. Determining How to Restore

Problem

You've experienced a problem with your online redo log files and need to determine what shape they are in and what course of action to take.

Solution

Follow these steps when dealing with online redo log file failures:

1. Inspect the alert.log file to determine which online redo log files have experienced a media failure.

2. Query V$LOG and V$LOGFILE to determine the status of the log group and degree of multiplexing.

3. If there is still one functioning member of a multiplexed group, then see recipe 14-2 for details on how to fix the remaining failed member(s).

4. Depending on the status of the log group, use Table 14-1 to determine what action to take.

Inspect your target database alert.log file to determine which online redo log file member is unavailable. Oracle error messages related to online redo log file failures are ORA-00312 and ORA-00313. Here's an example of errors written to the alert.log file when there are problems with an online redo log file:

```
Errors in file c:\oracle\product\10.2.0\admin\orcl\bdump\orcl_lgwr_5800.trc:
ORA-00313: open failed for members of log group 1 of thread 1
ORA-00312: online log 1 thread 1'C:\ORACLE\PRODUCT\10.2.0\ORADATA\ORCL\REDO01B.LOG'
ORA-27041: unable to open file
OSD-04002: unable to open file
O/S-Error: (OS 2) The system cannot find the file specified.
```

Query V$LOG and V$LOGFILE views to determine the status of your log group and the member files in each group:

```
SQL> select
2     a.group#, a.thread#,
3     a.status grp_status,
4     b.member member,
5     b.status mem_status
6     from v$log      a,
7          v$logfile b
8     where a.group# = b.group#
9     order by a.group#, b.member;
GROUP# THREAD# GRP_STAT MEMBER                                            MEM_STA
------ ------- -------- ------------------------------------------------- -------
     1       1 CURRENT  C:\ORACLE\PRODUCT\10.2.0\ORADATA\ORCL\REDO01.LOG
     1       1 CURRENT  C:\ORACLE\PRODUCT\10.2.0\ORADATA\ORCL\REDO01B.LOG
     2       1 INACTIVE C:\ORACLE\PRODUCT\10.2.0\ORADATA\ORCL\REDO02.LOG
     2       1 INACTIVE C:\ORACLE\PRODUCT\10.2.0\ORADATA\ORCL\REDO02B.LOG
```

If only one member of a multiplexed group has experienced a failure, then proceed to recipe 14-2.

If all members of a redo log group have experienced a failure and if your database is open, it will hang (cease to allow transactions) as soon as the archiver background process cannot successfully copy the failed online redo log file members. If your database is closed, Oracle will not allow you to open it if all members of one online redo log group are experiencing a media failure. When you attempt to open your database, you'll see a message similar to this:

```
ORA-00313: open failed for members of log group...
```

Depending on the status reported in V$LOG for the failed group, use Table 14-1 to determine what action to take.

Table 14-1. *Determining the Action to Take*

Type of Failure	Status Column of V$LOG	Action	Recipe
One member failed in multiplexed group	N/A	Re-create member.	Recipe 14-2
All members of group	INACTIVE	Clear logfile.	Recipe 14-3
All members of group	ACTIVE	Attempt checkpoint, and if successful, clear logfile. If checkpoint is unsuccessful, perform incomplete recovery.	Recipe 14-4
All members of group	CURRENT	Attempt to clear log, and if unsuccessful, perform incomplete recovery.	Recipe 14-5

How It Works

Your target database's alert.log file contains the best information for figuring out what type of failure has occurred. If only one member of a multiplexed group fails, then you will be able to detect this only by inspecting the alert.log file. You can also try to stop and start your database. If all members of a group have experienced media failure, then Oracle will not let you open the database and will display an ORA-00313 error message.

The alert.log file will also tell you where additional error messages have been written to trace files:

```
Errors in file c:\oracle\product\10.2.0\admin\orcl\bdump\orcl_lgwr_5800.trc:
ORA-00313: open failed for members of log group 1 of thread 1
```

The trace file will contain additional information such as this:

```
*** SERVICE NAME:() 2007-02-24 10:07:31.605
*** SESSION ID:(166.1) 2007-02-24 10:07:31.589
ORA-00313: open failed for members of log group 1 of thread 1
ORA-00312: online log 1 thread 1:
'C:\ORACLE\PRODUCT\10.2.0\ORADATA\ORCL\REDO01B.LOG'
```

When diagnosing online redo log issues, the V$LOG and V$LOGFILE views are particularly helpful. You can query these views while the database is mounted or open. Table 14-2 briefly describes each view.

Table 14-2. *Useful Views Related to Online Redo Logs*

View	Description
V$LOG	Displays the online redo log group information stored in the control file.
V$LOGFILE	Displays online redo log file member information.

The STATUS column of the V$LOG view is particularly useful when working with online redo logs groups. Table 14-3 describes each status and meaning for the V$LOG view.

Table 14-3. *Status for Online Redo Log Groups in the V$LOG View*

Status	Meaning
CURRENT	The log group that is currently being written to by the log writer.
ACTIVE	The log group is required for crash recovery and may or may not have been archived.
CLEARING	The log group is being cleared out by an `alter database clear logfile` command.
CLEARING_CURRENT	The current log group is being cleared of a closed thread.
INACTIVE	The log group isn't needed for crash recovery and may or may not have been archived.
UNUSED	The log group has never been written to; it was recently created.

The STATUS column of the V$LOGFILE view also contains useful information. This view contains information about each physical online redo log file member of a log group. Table 14-4 provides descriptions of the status of each log file member.

Table 14-4. *Status for Online Redo Log File Members in the V$LOGFILE View*

Status	Meaning
INVALID	The log file member is inaccessible, or it has been recently created.
DELETED	The log file member is no longer in use.
STALE	The log file member's contents are not complete.
NULL	The log file member is being used by the database.

It's important to differentiate between the STATUS column in V$LOG and the STATUS column in V$LOGFILE. The STATUS column in V$LOG reflects the status of the *log group*. The STATUS column in V$LOGFILE reports the status of the physical *online redo log file* member. Refer to these tables when diagnosing issues with your online redo logs.

14-2. Restoring After Losing One Member of the Multiplexed Group

Problem

You notice this message in your alert.log file:

```
Errors in file c:\oracle\product\10.2.0\admin\orcl\bdump\orcl_lgwr_5800.trc:
ORA-00321: log 1 of thread 1, cannot update log file header
ORA-00312: online log 1 thread 1:'C:\ORACLE\PRODUCT\10.2.0\ORADATA\ORCL\REDO01B.LOG'
```

You are experiencing media failure with one member of a multiplexed online redo log group and need to restore the damaged online redo log file member.

Solution

If your online redo log file members are multiplexed, the log writer will continue to function as long as it can successfully write to one member of the current log group. If the problem is temporary, then as soon as the online redo log file becomes available, the log writer will start to write to the online redo log file as if there was never an issue.

If the media failure is permanent (such as a bad disk), then you'll need to replace the disk and drop and re-create the bad member to its original location. If you don't have the option of replacing the bad disk, then you'll need to drop the bad member and re-create it in an alternate location.

For permanent media failures, here are the instructions for dropping and re-creating one member of an online redo log group:

1. Identify the online redo log file experiencing media failure.

2. Ensure that the online redo log file is not part of the current online log group.

3. Drop the damaged member.

4. Add a new member to the group.

To begin, open your alert.log file and look for an ORA-00312 message that identifies which member of the log group is experiencing media failure. You should see lines similar to these near the bottom of your alert.log file:

```
Errors in file c:\oracle\product\10.2.0\admin\orcl\bdump\orcl_lgwr_5800.trc:
ORA-00313: open failed for members of log group 1 of thread 1
ORA-00312: online log 1 thread 1:'C:\ORACLE\PRODUCT\10.2.0\ORADATA\ORCL\REDO01B.LOG'
ORA-27041: unable to open file
OSD-04002: unable to open file
O/S-Error: (OS 2) The system cannot find the file specified.
Sat Feb 24 10:07:31 2007
Errors in file c:\oracle\product\10.2.0\admin\orcl\bdump\orcl_lgwr_5800.trc:
ORA-00321: log 1 of thread 1, cannot update log file header
ORA-00312: online log 1 thread 1:'C:\ORACLE\PRODUCT\10.2.0\ORADATA\ORCL\REDO01B.LOG'
Thread 1 opened at log sequence 40
```

This message tells you which log member has failed. The alert.log file output also specifies that a trace file has been generated. You'll find additional information about the bad member in the specified trace file:

```
*** SERVICE NAME:() 2007-02-24 10:07:31.605
*** SESSION ID:(166.1) 2007-02-24 10:07:31.589
ORA-00313: open failed for members of log group 1 of thread 1
ORA-00312: online log 1 thread 1:
'C:\ORACLE\PRODUCT\10.2.0\ORADATA\ORCL\REDO01B.LOG'
ORA-27041: unable to open file
OSD-04002: unable to open file
O/S-Error: (OS 2) The system cannot find the file specified.
ORA-00321: log 1 of thread 1, cannot update log file header
ORA-00312: online log 1 thread 1:'C:\ORACLE\PRODUCT\10.2.0\ORADATA\ORCL\REDO01B.LOG'
```

Once you've identified the bad online redo log file, execute the following query to check whether that online redo log file's group has a CURRENT status:

```
SQL> select
2  a.group#, a.thread#,
3  a.status grp_status,
4  b.member member,
5  b.status mem_status
6  from v$log  a,
7       v$logfile b
8  where a.group# = b.group#
9  order by a.group#, b.member;
```

■Note If you attempt to drop a member of a current log group, Oracle will throw an ORA-01609 error specifying that the log is current and you cannot drop one of its members.

If the failed member is in the current log group, then use the `alter system switch logfile` command to make the next group the current group. Then drop the failed member as follows:

```
SQL> alter database drop logfile member '<\directory\member>';
```

Then re-create the online redo log file member:

```
SQL> alter database add logfile member '<\new directory\member>' to group <group#>;
```

If an unused log file already happens to exist in the target location, you can use the reuse parameter to overwrite and reuse that log file. The log file must be the same size as the other log files in the group.

```
SQL> alter database add logfile member '\directory\member>' reuse to group <group#>;
```

How It Works

Oracle will continue to operate as long as it can write to at least one member of a multiplexed redo log group. An error message will be written to the alert.log file when the log writer is unable to write to a current online redo log file.

You should periodically inspect your alert.log file for Oracle errors. This may be the only way that you'll discover a member of a group has experienced a media failure. We recommend that you run a periodic batch job that searches the alert.log file for any errors and automatically notifies you when it finds potential problems.

SEARCHING FOR ERRORS IN THE ALERT.LOG FILE

Here's a simple Unix Korn shell script that greps for "ORA-" and "ERROR" in the alert.log file. Before you run this shell script, you'll have to change the setup variables at the top to match your environment. The DBS variable stores the databases on a box. The ADIR variable stores the base directory for the database. The DIRS variable stores the actual directories that you want to search for the alert.log file. The MAILLIST variable stores the email address to where the error findings will be sent.

```ksh
#!/bin/ksh
export DBS="PATCH50 PATCH60"
export ADIR="/ora01/app/oracle/admin"
export DIRS="bdump udump cdump"
export MAILLIST=" uncleLarry@oracle.com "
export BOX=`uname -a | awk '{print$2}'`
export MAILX="/usr/ucb/Mail"
#-------------------------------------------------------------
for instance in $DBS
do
  for directories in $DIRS
    do
    if [ -r $ADIR/$instance/$directories/alert*.log ]
    then
      grep -ic error $ADIR/$instance/$directories/alert*.log
      if [ $? = 0 ]
      then
        $MAILX -s "Error in $instance log file" $MAILLIST <<EOF
Error in $instance log file on $BOX...
Check $ADIR/$instance/$directories/alert*.log
EOF
      fi # $?
      grep -ic ORA- $ADIR/$instance/$directories/alert*.log
      if [ $? = 0 ]
      then
        $MAILX -s "ORA- Error in $instance log file" $MAILLIST <<EOF
Error in $instance log file on $BOX...
Check $ADIR/$instance/$directories/alert*.log
```

Continued

```
EOF
      fi # $?
    fi # -r
  done # for directories
done # for instance
exit
```

Once you've identified the bad member of an online redo log group, then you can drop and re-create the online redo log file. The newly created online redo log file will display an INVALID status in V$LOGFILE until it becomes part of the CURRENT log group. Once the newly created member becomes part of the CURRENT log group, its status should change to NULL. A NULL member status (as described in Table 14-4) indicates that the database is using the online redo log file.

You can drop and add online redo log file members while your database is in either a mounted state or an open state. While dropping and re-creating log members, we recommend that you have your database in a mounted state. This will ensure that the status of the log group doesn't change while dropping and re-creating members. You cannot drop an online redo log file member that is part of the CURRENT group.

■**Note** When using the `alter database drop logfile member` command, you will not be allowed to drop the last remaining online redo log file member from a redo log group. If you attempt to do this, Oracle will throw an `ORA-00361` error stating that you cannot remove the last standing log member. If you need to drop all members of a log group, use the `alter database drop logfile group` command.

14-3. Recovering After Loss of All Members of the INACTIVE Redo Log Group

Problem

You're attempting to open your database and receive this message:

```
Database mounted.
ORA-00313: open failed for members of log group 1 of thread 1
ORA-00312: online log 1 thread 1:'C:\ORACLE\PRODUCT\10.2.0\ORADATA\ORCL\REDO01.LOG'
ORA-00312: online log 1 thread 1:'C:\ORACLE\PRODUCT\10.2.0\ORADATA\ORCL\REDO01B.LOG'
```

The message indicates that two members of an online redo log group in your database have experienced a media failure. You wonder how you're going to get your database open again.

Solution

To recover when you've lost all members of an inactive redo log group, perform the following steps:

1. Verify that all members of a group have been damaged.

2. Verify that the log group status is INACTIVE.

3. Re-create the log group with the clear logfile command.

4. If the re-created log group has not been archived, then immediately back up your database.

If all members of an online redo log group are damaged, you won't be able to open your database. In this situation, Oracle will allow you to only mount your database.

Inspect your alert.log file, and verify that all members of a redo log group are damaged. You should see a message indicating that all members of an online redo log group are damaged and database cannot open:

```
ORA-00313: open failed for members of log group 1 of thread 1
ORA-00312: online log 1 thread 1:'C:\ORACLE\PRODUCT\10.2.0\ORADATA\ORCL\REDO01B.LOG'
ORA-00312: online log 1 thread 1:'C:\ORACLE\PRODUCT\10.2.0\ORADATA\ORCL\REDO01.LOG'
O/S-Error: (OS 2) The system cannot find the file specified.
ORA-313 signalled during: alter database open...
```

Next, ensure that your database is in mount mode:

```
SQL> connect / as sysdba
SQL> startup mount;
```

Next, run the following query to verify that the damaged log group is INACTIVE and determine whether it has been archived:

```
SQL> select group#, status, archived, thread#, sequence# from v$log;
GROUP# STATUS   ARC THREAD# SEQUENCE#
------ -------- --- ------- ----------
     1 INACTIVE YES       1         44
     3 INACTIVE YES       1         45
     2 CURRENT  NO        1         46
```

If the status is INACTIVE, then this log group is no longer needed for crash recovery (as described in Table 14-3). Therefore, you can use the clear logfile command to re-create all members of a log group. The following example re-creates all log members of group 1:

```
SQL> alter database clear logfile group 1;
```

If the log group has not been archived, then you will need to use the clear unarchived logfile command as follows:

```
SQL> alter database clear unarchived logfile group 1;
```

If the cleared log group had not been previously archived, it's critical that you immediately create a backup of your database. See Chapter 7 for details on taking a complete backup of your database.

How It Works

If the online redo log group is inactive and archived, then its contents aren't required for crash or media recovery. Use the `clear logfile` command to re-create all online redo log file members of a group.

■**Note** The `clear logfile` will drop and re-create all members of a log group for you. You can issue this command even if you have only two log groups in your database.

If the online redo log group has not been archived, then it may be required for media recovery. In this case, use the `clear unarchived logfile` command to re-create the logfile group members. Back up your database as soon as possible in this situation.

The unarchived log group may be needed for media recovery if the last database backups were taken before the redo information in the log was created. This means if you attempt to perform media recovery, you won't be able to recover any information in the damaged log file or any transactions that were created after that log.

If the `clear logfile` command does not succeed because of an I/O error and it's a permanent problem, then you will need to consider dropping the log group and re-creating it in a different location.

DROPPING AND ADDING A REDO LOG GROUP

A log group has to have an inactive status before you can drop it. You can check the status of the log group, as shown here:

```
SQL> select group#, status, archived, thread#, sequence# from v$log;
```

If you attempt to drop the current online log group, Oracle will return an ORA-01623 error stating that you cannot drop the current group. Use the `alter system switch logfile` command to switch the logs and make the next group the current group.

After a log switch, the log group that was previously the current group will retain an active status as long as it contains redo that Oracle requires to perform crash recovery. If you attempt to drop a log group with an active status, Oracle will throw an ORA-01624 error stating that the log group is required for crash recovery. Issue an `alter system checkpoint` command to make the log group inactive.

Additionally, you cannot issue a `drop logfile group` command if it leaves you with only one log group left in your database. If you attempt to do this, Oracle will throw an ORA-01567 error and inform you that dropping the log group is not permitted because it would leave you with less than two logs groups for your database (Oracle minimally requires two log groups to function).

> You can drop a log group with the drop logfile group command:
>
> ```
> SQL> alter database drop logfile group <group #>;
> ```
>
> You can add a new log group with the add logfile group command:
>
> ```
> SQL> alter database add logfile
> 2    group <group_#> ('\directory\file') SIZE <bytes> K|M;
> ```
>
> You can specify the size of the log file in bytes, kilobytes, or megabytes. The following example adds log group 4 with two members sized at 50MB:
>
> ```
> SQL> alter database add logfile group 4
> 2   ('C:\ORADATA\ORCL\RED004A.LOG',
> 3    'D:\ORADATA\ORCL\RED004B.LOG') SIZE 50M;
> ```

14-4. Recovering After Loss of All Members of the ACTIVE Redo Log Group

Problem

All the members of an active online redo log group in your database have experienced media failure.

Solution

Perform the following steps when restoring an active online redo log group:

1. Verify the damage to the members.

2. Verify that the status is ACTIVE.

3. Attempt to issue a checkpoint.

4. If the checkpoint is successful, the status should now be INACTIVE, and you can clear the log group.

5. If the log group that was cleared was unarchived, back up your database immediately.

6. If the checkpoint is unsuccessful, then you will have to perform incomplete recovery (see recipe 14-5 for options).

Inspect your target database alert.log file, and verify the damage. You should see a message near the bottom of the alert.log file identifying the bad members:

```
ORA-00313: open failed for members of log group 1 of thread 1
ORA-00312: online log 1 thread 1:'C:\ORACLE\PRODUCT\10.2.0\ORADATA\ORCL\RED001B.LOG'
ORA-00312: online log 1 thread 1:'C:\ORACLE\PRODUCT\10.2.0\ORADATA\ORCL\RED001.LOG'
O/S-Error: (OS 2) The system cannot find the file specified.
ORA-313 signalled during: alter database open...
```

Next, verify that the damaged log group has an ACTIVE status as follows:

```
SQL> connect / as sysdba
SQL> startup mount;
SQL> select group#, status, archived, thread#, sequence# from v$log;
GROUP# STATUS    ARC THREAD#  SEQUENCE#
------ --------- --- ------- ----------
     1 ACTIVE    YES       1         47
     2 INACTIVE  YES       1         46
     3 CURRENT   NO        1         48
```

If the status is ACTIVE, then attempt to issue an `alter system checkpoint` command, as shown here:

```
SQL> alter system checkpoint;
```

If the checkpoint completes successfully, then the active log group should be marked as INACTIVE. A successful checkpoint ensures that all modified database buffers have been written to disk, and at that point, only transactions contained in the CURRENT online redo log will be required for crash recovery.

■**Note** If the checkpoint is unsuccessful, you will have to perform incomplete recovery. See recipe 14-5 for a full list of options in this scenario.

Verify the status of the log group to see whether it is now INACTIVE with this query:

```
SQL> select group#, status, archived, thread#, sequence# from v$log;
GROUP# STATUS    ARC THREAD#  SEQUENCE#
------ --------- --- ------- ----------
     1 INACTIVE  YES       1         47
     2 INACTIVE  YES       1         46
     3 CURRENT   NO        1         48
```

If the status is inactive and the log has been archived, you can use the `clear logfile` command to re-create the log group, as shown here:

```
SQL> alter database clear logfile group <group#>;
```

If the status is inactive and the log group has not been archived, then re-create it with the `clear unarchived logfile` command, as shown here:

```
SQL> alter database clear unarchived logfile group <group#>;
```

If the cleared log group had not been previously archived, it's critical that you immediately create a backup of your database. See Chapter 7 for details on creating a complete backup of your database.

How It Works

An online redo log group with an ACTIVE status is still required for crash recovery. If all members of an active online redo log group experience media failure, then you must attempt to issue a checkpoint. If the checkpoint is successful, then you can clear the log group. If the checkpoint is unsuccessful, then you will have to perform an incomplete recovery.

If the checkpoint is successful and if the log group has not been archived, then the log may be required for media recovery. Back up your database as soon as possible in this situation. The unarchived log group may be needed for media recovery if the last database backups were taken before the redo information in the log was created. This means if you attempt to perform media recovery, you won't be able to recover any information in the damaged log file or any transactions that were created after that log.

14-5. Recovering After Loss of All Members of the CURRENT Redo Log Group

Problem

All of the members of a current online redo log group in your database have experienced media failure.

Solution

Unfortunately, your alternatives are limited when you lose all members of a current online redo log group. Here are some possible options:

- Perform an incomplete recovery up to the last good SCN.

- If flashback is enabled, flash your database back to the last good SCN.

- If you're using Oracle Data Guard, fail over to your physical or logical standby database.

- Contact Oracle Support for suggestions.

In preparation for an incomplete recovery, first determine the last good SCN by querying the FIRST_CHANGE# column from V$LOG. In this scenario, you're missing only the current online redo logs. Therefore, you can perform an incomplete recovery up to, but not including, the FIRST_CHANGE# SCN of the current online redo log.

```
SQL> shutdown immediate;
SQL> startup mount;
SQL> select group#, status, archived, thread#, sequence#, first_change# from v$log;
GROUP# STATUS    ARC THREAD#  SEQUENCE# FIRST_CHANGE#
------ --------- --- ------- ---------- -------------
     1 INACTIVE YES       1         50       1800550
     2 INACTIVE YES       1         49       1800468
     3 CURRENT  NO        1         51       1800573
```

In this case, you can restore and recover up to, but not including, SCN 1800573. Here's how you'd do that:

```
RMAN> restore database until scn 1800573;
RMAN> recover database until scn 1800573;
RMAN> alter database open resetlogs;
```

For complete details on incomplete recovery, see Chapter 12. For details on flashing back your database, see Chapter 13.

How It Works

Losing all members of your current online redo log group is arguably the worst thing that can happen to your database. If you experience media failure with all members of the current online redo group, then you will lose any transactions contained in those logs. In this situation, you will have to perform incomplete recovery before you can open your database.

■**Tip** If you are desperate to restore transactions lost in damaged current online redo log files, then contact Oracle Support to explore all options.

■■■

Duplicating Databases and Transporting Data

Oracle DBAs routinely create duplicate databases by using the source database backup files or by using the new Oracle Database 11g feature *active database duplication*, which lets you duplicate a database without any prior backups of the source database. You can make an exact replica of the source database or omit some of the tablespaces if you want. These duplicate databases help you test database upgrades and application changes and serve as reporting databases under some circumstances. You also have the option, if you want, of duplicating a database to a past point in time. Duplicating a database comes in handy when you need to test a backup and recovery strategy. You also use the duplicate database process when you accidentally lose a table and must recover it from the backups. You can simply create a duplicate database in this case and export the table you need and then import it into the production database.

Besides duplicating databases, RMAN also helps you set up *standby databases*, which are not merely one-time copies of the production databases like the duplicate database but are continually updated versions of the production database. The primary purpose of a standby database is its ability to serve as the production server during recovery and failover situations. You can't use a duplicate database to perform a standby recovery and failover job. To create a duplicate database, RMAN uses what's called an *auxiliary database instance*.

Several options are available to you when performing database duplication with the help of RMAN. You can do the following:

- You can duplicate a database without even making a backup of the source database first by using the new Oracle Database 11g technique of network-enabled duplication.

- You can register in the same recovery catalog as the primary database, since the duplicate database will have its own unique DBID.

- You can exclude certain tablespaces, such as the read-only tablespaces.

- You can duplicate the database on the same server or on a remote host.

- You can duplicate a database to a past point in time if you want.

Any database duplication you make with the help of preexisting RMAN backups is called *backup-based duplication*. Prior to the Oracle Database 11g release, this was your only means of duplicating a database with RMAN, either as a testing database or for creating a standby database. You needed a source database and a backup copy of that source database, either on the source database host or on tape. You then needed to transfer these source database backups to the destination system for the duplication process. You may transfer disk backups of database files and the archived redo logs in various ways:

- Manually transfer backups from the target host to the host on which you are duplicating the database by using identical directory paths. For example, if the backups are stored in /u01/backup on the source host, move them to the /u01/backup directory on the destination host.

- Manually transfer backups from the target host to the duplicate host using different directory paths (to a different location on the host where you're creating the duplicate database). For example, if the backups are in the /u01/backup directory on the source host, copy them to the /u02/backup directory on the destination host.

  You must then update the source database control file using the `catalog` (`"catalog start with <directory>"`) command so it's aware of the new location of the backups. You must do this because RMAN checks the backup metadata in the control file for the location of the backup files and archived redo logs. Of course, this means that for the `catalog` command to work you must have the /u02/backup directory on the source host as well!

- Use a network file system (NFS), and ensure that the source and destination hosts can both access the same NFS mount point.

In the previous releases of the database, RMAN helped you duplicate databases by using the source database's backups, and thus, you used a backup-based duplication method. Oracle Database 11*g* provides a new method of duplicating databases, which duplicates a live database without using any preexisting backups. This database duplication, performed directly over the network, is called *active database duplication*. In this chapter, we show you how to perform duplicate databases using both the older backup-based duplication method and the new Oracle Database 11*g* innovation: active database duplication.

Also in this chapter, we talk about using RMAN to move data with transportable tablespaces. Oracle's transportable tablespaces feature lets you move large amounts of data much faster than an export and import of data. This is because the transportable tablespace operation requires that you copy only those datafiles pertaining to a tablespace and merely export and import the metadata concerning the tablespaces. The transportable tablespace feature is highly useful when archiving historical data, performing tablespace point-in-time recovery, and exporting and importing large data warehouse table partitions. You can transport tablespaces across platforms, which means you can use this feature to easily migrate Oracle databases from one platform to another or move data from data warehouses to data marts running on smaller platforms.

15-1. Renaming Files in a Duplicate Database

Problem

You are planning to duplicate a database and learn that there are multiple ways to specify filenames for the duplicate database. You want to find out which file-renaming method is best for you.

Solution 1: Specify the spfile Clause in the duplicate Command

The simplest way to generate filenames for the duplicate database is to specify the spfile clause in the duplicate command to set all the filename-related parameters except the db_file_name_convert and the log_file_name_convert parameters, as shown here:

```
duplicate database
...
spfile
...
```

If you're using the backup-based duplication method, RMAN restores the server parameter file from a backup of the source database server parameter file. If you are using the active database duplication method, on the other hand, RMAN will copy the server parameter file currently being used by the source database. When you specify the keyword spfile during database duplication, RMAN copies or restores the source database's spfile to the default location for the auxiliary instance on the host where it's running. If you don't specify the spfile clause, you must copy the server parameter file yourself and edit it by using new values for the initialization parameters in the source databases. You must specify this spfile when you start the new auxiliary instance in nomount mode, as well as when you open the new duplicate database from the RMAN prompt.

Note that you can also specify a normal text-based initialization parameter (*pfile*) by specifying the pfile parameter instead of the spfile parameter as part of the duplicate command.

■**Tip** Oracle recommends specifying the spfile clause in the duplicate command for both backup-based and active database duplication techniques to set all the necessary parameters involving filenames for the duplicate database.

Once you specify the spfile parameter during the database duplication, you can provide your list of initialization parameters and the values for them through the parameter_value_convert clause and the set clause. It's easiest to use the parameter_value_convert clause in the duplicate database command to specify all parameters that specify a directory path. You can specify all such directory-related parameter values through the parameter_value_convert parameter, except for the db_file_name_convert and log_file_name_convert parameters. Here's an example showing how to use the parameter_value_convert clause and the set clause to specify various initialization parameter values for the duplicate instance right when you issue the duplicate database command:

```
duplicate target database
  to dupdb
  from active database  spfile
    parameter_value_convert '/a01', '/a20'
    set sga_max_size = 800m
    set sga_target = 700m
    set log_file_name_convert = '/a01','/a20',
    db_file_name_convert '/a01','/a20';
```

The multiple `set` clauses have the same effect as issuing an `alter system set param=value scope=spfile` command, and there's no limit on how many of these `set` commands you can use. Using the `spfile` parameter during database duplication amounts to interrupting the duplication process after the spfile is restored and editing it with multiple `alter system set` commands, one for each of the initialization parameters you specify as attributes for the `parameter_value_convert` clause as well as the multiple `set` clauses, before mounting the database. The real purpose of the `parameter_value_convert` clause is to set the values of a bunch of directory-related initialization parameters when creating the duplicate database. RMAN will update the initialization parameter values in the spfile it copied (or the backed-up spfile if using the backup method of duplication) from the source database, based on the values you provide for the `parameter_value_convert` and `set` parameters. RMAN will then start the new duplicate (auxiliary) instance with the updated server parameter values.

If you specify the `spfile` clause with the `duplicate database` command, you must have started the auxiliary instance already with a text-based initialization parameter file (with one required parameter, `db_name`). If you haven't specified the `from active database` clause in the `duplicate database` command, RMAN will copy the binary server parameter file and restart the auxiliary instance based on the modified settings gathered from the `spfile` clause. If you specify the `from active database` clause in the `duplicate database` command, then the target instance must be using a server parameter file.

Solution 2: Name Duplicate Files with Alternative Techniques

If you don't want to use the `spfile` clause technique for naming the duplicate files, you can use alternative file-naming techniques. You can also choose to use the `spfile` clause to name the files and supplement that technique with one or more of the alternative techniques. The following sections summarize the available alternative file-naming techniques for different types of database files such as the online redo logs, the data files, the control files, and the temp files for the duplicate database.

Online Redo Logs

The following is the order of precedence for online redo log filename creation:

1. By specifying the `logfile` clause of the `duplicate` command, you can make RMAN create online logs according to your specification.

2. By setting the `log_file_name_convert` initialization parameter (as in the following recipe), you can create new filenames for the duplicate database that are transformations of the source database filenames, such as changing from log_* to duplog_*.

3. Set one or more of the OMF initialization parameters—db_create_file_dest, db_create_online_dest_n, and db_recovery_file_dest—to transform the target database filenames.

The three methods specified here have the same order of precedence as their numbers in this list. You can avoid using any of the three methods listed here by simply using filenames identical to those of the target database. You can do that, however, only if you're duplicating a database to a different server from that of the primary database. You must specify the nofilenamecheck option if you choose to go this route.

Datafiles

The following is the order of precedence for using new names for the datafiles of the duplicate database:

1. Use the set newname for datafile clause with the duplicate command by enclosing it in a run block.

2. Run a configure auxname command prior to running the duplicate command to set the new names for the datafiles.

3. You can also use the db_file_name_convert parameter in the duplicate command to convert filenames for datafiles that you didn't rename with the set newname or configure auxname command.

4. You can set the db_file_name_convert initialization parameter (as in the following recipe) to specify rules for naming datafiles. If you use the db_create_file_dest initialization parameter, RMAN will create OMF datafiles.

If you don't use any of the methods listed here, RMAN will simply reuse the parent database's datafile locations for the duplicate database.

Control Files

If you use the control_files initialization parameter, the Oracle Database will create a control file in the location you specify for the control_files initialization parameter. Otherwise, the database will create an OMF-based control file in a default location, which is determined in the following order of precedence:

1. The location specified by the db_create_online_log_dest_n initialization parameter.

2. If you set values for the db_create_file_dest and db_recovery_file_dest initialization parameters (but not the db_create_online_log_dest_n parameter), the Oracle database will create control files in both locations.

3. If you set values only for the db_create_file_dest parameter, the database will create a single control file in that location.

4. If you set values only for the db_recovery_file_dest parameter, the database will create a single control file in that location.

If you omit all the previously specified parameters, the Oracle Database will create a control file in the default location for that operating system.

Temp Files

Here are the different ways in which you can specify locations for the duplicate database temp files, listed in the order of precedence:

1. Use the set newname for tempfile command within a run block.

2. Specify the db_file_name_convert clause in the duplicate command to specify filename conversion for temp files not converted with the set newname for tempfile command.

3. Use the db_file_name_convert initialization parameter to specify the temp file location.

4. Use the db_create_file_dest initialization parameter if you want to create OMF-based temp files.

How It Works

When you duplicate a database, RMAN has to generate names for the duplicate database's database files. If you're using the same directory structure on a different host than the source host, there's no problem in using identical database filenames as the source database. Simply specify the nofilenamecheck clause in the duplicate database command to do this.

If the duplicate host uses a different directory structure or you want to rename the database files anyway, you must adopt a strategy to generate the new datafile names during the database duplication process. You're concerned with renaming the following types of files:

- Datafiles
- Control files
- Online redo log files
- Temp files

You can adopt two basic strategies to generate names for the duplicate database files. You can use the spfile clause, or you can name the duplicate database files with a set of alternative techniques. The latter method requires more manual effort on your part.

Use the Oracle-recommended spfile clause in the new Oracle 11g duplicate database command to set all necessary parameters involving filenames for the duplicate database. This is by far the more straightforward and easier of the two filename-generating techniques available to you during database duplication.

- Use spfile ... parameter_value_convert 'string_pattern' to specify conversion strings for all initialization parameters specifying directory path names, except two: db_file_name_convert and log_file_name_convert. The parameter_value_convert clause helps you specify strings to convert the old initialization parameters copied from the source database parameter file. Note that you can also use the parameter_value_convert parameter to update the string value of any initialization parameter, not just path names.

■**Note** You use the set clause in the duplicate database command to set the values for the log_file_name_convert and db_file_name_convert parameters.

- Use the set clause to set initialization parameters to specific values. The set subclause lets you specify initialization parameters to the values you want. For example, you can use the set command to specify initialization parameters such as sga_target or turn off replication options. In essence, the set functionality amounts to temporarily stopping the database duplication process in midstream after restoring the server parameter file and issuing the alter system set statement to change the initialization parameter values. The parameter_value_convert clause is processed before the set clauses, and the set values for an initialization parameter will override the setting specified by the parameter_value_convert clause.

- Use the `log_file_name_convert` *'string_pattern'* to specify the filename rules for creating the online redo log files.

- Use `db_file_name_convert` *'string_pattern'* to specify filename rules for creating data files and temp files.

You must be aware of the different ways you can go about naming the online redo log files, data files, control files, and temp files, especially when you're duplicating a database onto the same server, since you may mistakenly overlay the production database files if you're not careful. In the duplicate database example shown in the previous recipe, we used the `db_file_name_convert` and `log_file_name_convert` initialization parameters to specify rules for transforming the database files and online redo log files from the source database to the primary database. However, you can name the duplicate database files in other ways.

You must specify new filenames for datafiles and online redo logs when you're duplicating a database on the same host as the primary database. If you don't do this, RMAN will reuse the existing target datafile names and thus overwrite the target database files.

■**Note** *Always* back up the source database prior to running the RMAN `duplicate` command, especially if the auxiliary database is hosted on the same machine/server as the source database. This is to ensure you can always restore and recover the source database in case your database duplication process goes awry.

Use caution when specifying filenames. For example, when you're duplicating a database on the same host, make sure the duplicate database's redo logs aren't named the same as the online logs of the parent database. Often, the `configure auxname`, `set newname`, and `db_file_name_convert` parameters may generate filenames that are in use by the target database, leading to an error. However, if you're duplicating a database to a different host, obviously identical filenames shouldn't matter. To avoid RMAN errors, use the `nofilenamecheck` option, as shown here:

```
RMAN> run
{
  set newname for datafile 1 to '/u01/app/oracle/testdata/file1.dbf';
  set newname for datafile 2 to '/u01/app/oracle/testdata/file2.dbf';
  ...
  duplicate target database to newdb nofilenamecheck;
}
```

You have fewer filename-generating options when duplicating databases when the source database files are in the OMF format. Since OMF files are uniquely generated by the database, you can't use the `db_file_name_convert` and `log_file_name_convert` parameters to generate new filenames for the duplicate database. You can, however, use both parameters in the special case when you're changing ASM disk group names. RMAN will then convert the ASM disk group name and generate new filenames based on the new disk group name.

15-2. Creating a Duplicate Database on the Same Host

Problem

You want to use RMAN to create a duplicate database on the same server by using RMAN backups.

Solution

In this sequence of steps to create a duplicate database using RMAN backups, the target database is named prod1, and the duplicate database, also known as the *auxiliary database* in RMAN parlance, is named test1. We'll use the control file instead of a recovery catalog to show the database duplication process. Here are the steps to duplicate a database to the same server (the target or source database name is prod1, and the auxiliary or duplicate database name is test1):

1. Back up the target database as follows:

   ```
   RMAN> connect target /
   RMAN> backup database plus archivelog;
   ```

   You'll use these backups as the source for the database duplication later. Of course, if you already have made backups of the source database, you can skip this step.

2. Use a dedicated listener configuration for RMAN by making the following additions to your listener.ora file:

   ```
   SID_LIST_LISTENER =
       (SID_LIST =
           (SID_DESC =
               (GLOBAL_DBNAME = prod1)
               (ORACLE_HOME = /u01/app/oracle/product/11g/)
               (SID_NAME =prod1)
           )
           (SID_DESC =
               (GLOBAL_DBNAME = test1)
               (ORACLE_HOME = /u01/app/oracle/product/11g/)
               (SID_NAME =test1)
           )
       )
   ```

3. Add the following information to the tnsnames.ora file, located in the $ORACLE_HOME/network/admin directory:

   ```
   test1 =
   (DESCRIPTION =
   (ADDRESS_LIST =
   (ADDRESS = (PROTOCOL = TCP)(HOST = prod1)(PORT = 1521))
   ```

```
      )
(CONNECT_DATA =
(SERVER = DEDICATED)
(SERVICE_NAME = test1)
    )
  )
```

4. Create the init.ora file for the new duplicate database, test1. During the database duplication process, RMAN will create the control files, the data files, and the redo log files for the duplicate database with the filename structure you provide through the db_file_name_convert and log_file_name_convert initialization parameters. The database duplication process will create a control file for the new duplicate database in the location specified by the control_files initialization parameter.

```
db_name = test1
db_block_size = 8192
compatible = 11.1.0.1.0
remote_login_passwordfile = exclusive
control_files = ('/u01/app/oracle/test1/control01.ctl',
'/u01/app/oracle/test1/control02.ctl')
db_file_name_convert = ('/u01/app/oracle/oradata/prod1',
 '/u05/app/oracle/oradata/test1')
log_file_name_convert = ('/u01/app/oracle/oradata/prod1',
 '/u05/app/oracle/oradata/test1')
```

Note that only the db_name and control_files initialization parameters are required. The db_block_size parameter is also required if this parameter is set in the target database. All the other initialization parameters are optional. In this example, the init.ora file for the duplicate database is named inittest1.ora. Save this file in the appropriate location. (On Linux/Unix, the default location is $ORACLE_HOME/dbs, and on Windows, it is %ORACLE_HOME%\database.)

5. Start the new auxiliary database (duplicate database) instance. You must start the new instance in nomount mode since you don't have a control file for this new database yet.

```
$ export ORACLE_SID=test1
$ sqlplus /nolog
SQL> connect / as sysdba
Connected to an idle instance
SQL> startup nomount pfile=$ORACLE_HOME/dbs/inittest1.ora
Oracle Instance started.
Total System Global Area      113246208 bytes
Fixed Size                      1218004 bytes
Variable Size                  58722860 bytes
Database Buffers               50331648 bytes
Redo Buffers                    2973696 bytes
SQL> exit
```

The previous start-up command will start the auxiliary instance and mount the new control file. Once you create a new Oracle instance as shown here, the listener utility will automatically register the new database.

6. Start RMAN, and connect to the target database after making sure you first set the ORACLE_SID environmental variable to the source database, prod1. Note that the target database can be mounted or open.

```
$  rman

Recovery Manager: Release 11.1.0.1.0 - Beta on Sat Jun 9 14:03:42 2007
Copyright (c) 1982, 2005, Oracle.  All rights reserved.
RMAN> connect target
connected to target database: prod1 (DBID=2561840016)
```

7. Connect to the duplicate database using the keyword auxiliary through a SQL*Net connection:

```
RMAN> connect auxiliary sys/<sys_password>@test1
connected to auxiliary database: test1 (not mounted)
RMAN>
```

■**Note** If you're duplicating a database to the same host, as is the case in this example, you don't have to use a password file. You can simply choose to use operating system authentication to connect to the auxiliary instance. If you're performing active database duplication, on the other hand, you must use a password file for both the target and auxiliary instances, and they must use the same sysdba password. You must use an Oracle Net service name to connect to the auxiliary instance.

---

8. Issue the duplicate target database command to start the database duplication process:

```
RMAN> duplicate target database to test1;
Starting Duplicate Db at 09-JUN-07
allocated channel: ORA_TEST1_DISK_1
contents of Memory Script:
{
set until scn  23697974;
set newname for datafile  1 to
"/u05/app/oracle/CATDB/system01.dbf";
...
restore
check readonly
clone database
   ;
}
executing Memory Script
```

```
executing command: SET until clause
...
Starting restore at 09-JUN-07
...
Finished restore at 09-JUN-07
...
contents of Memory Script:
{
switch clone datafile all;
}
executing Memory Script
contents of Memory Script:
{
set until scn  23697974;
recover
clone database
delete archivelog
   ;
}
executing Memory Script
executing command: SET until clause
Starting recover at 09-JUN-07
starting media recovery
...
executing Memory Script
database dismounted
Oracle instance shut down
connected to auxiliary database (not started)
Oracle instance started
...
executing command: SET NEWNAME
contents of Memory Script:
{
Alter clone database open resetlogs;
}
executing Memory Script
database opened
Finished Duplicate Db at 09-JUN-07
RMAN>
```

The duplicate database command creates the duplicate datafiles for the new database and recovers them with the help of incremental backups (if you have any) and archived redo logs. The database duplication is successfully completed. You now have an identical copy of the source database.

How It Works

These prerequisites apply to all database duplication jobs:

- You must connect to both the target (source) database and the auxiliary (destination) instance.

- You must start the auxiliary instance with the nomount option.

- You can't use a standby database as the target database.

- You'll need the password file for the auxiliary instance only if you're using the RMAN client on a different host than the auxiliary host or if you duplicate from an active database (see recipe 15-3 and recipe 15-4).

- The target database can be open or closed.

- Both the source and destination databases must be on the same operating system platform (32-bit and 64-bit versions of a platform are considered identical). However, when duplicating from a 32-bit platform to a 64-bit platform, you must run the utlrp.sql script (located in the $ORACLE_HOME/rdbms/admin directory) to convert the code to the new operating system format.

If you're using disk-based backups, you can speed up the database duplication by allocating more channels. If you're using tape backups, however, you can have only as many channels as the number of tape devices you have available.

You can optionally specify the password file option with the duplicate database command when duplicating a database using the backup-based method if you want to make multiple passwords from your target database available on the new duplicate database. Specifying this option will overwrite any existing auxiliary instance password file with the source database password file.

■**Note** You don't need a password file for performing backup-based database duplication. Use operating system authentication for connecting to the auxiliary instance when you're duplicating a database on the same host as the source database.

It's your job to ensure that the auxiliary channel can access all the necessary datafile backups and the archived redo logs necessary to create the duplicate database. You may use a mix of full and incremental backups for this purpose. You can also use the backups of the archived redo log files or the actual archived redo log files during the database duplication process. By default, RMAN will duplicate a database from the most recent available backups of the source database and will recover the duplicate database to the latest SCN contained in the archived redo logs. RMAN can't recover the duplicate database to the latest SCN, since it doesn't use the online redo logs as part of the database duplication. The RMAN client can run on any host as long as it can connect to the source and the auxiliary instances. You must ensure that all the necessary backup files and archived redo log files are accessible by the server session on the duplicate host. The auxiliary channel performs the bulk of the duplication work through the server session it starts on the host where you are duplicating the database. The auxiliary channel restores the backups of the primary database and starts the recovery process as part of the database duplication.

During the database duplication, RMAN does the following:

1. Generates a unique DBID for the new duplicate database.

2. Creates a new control file for the duplicate database.

3. Restores the backups and performs an incomplete recovery using all backups and archived redo logs. The recovery must be an incomplete recovery since you don't back up the online redo logs on the target database. Therefore, you can't apply the online redo logs to the duplicate database, and thus you can recover only to the latest archived redo log.

4. Shuts down and starts up the auxiliary instance.

5. Opens the duplicate database with the resetlogs option, thus clearing the online redo logs.

As part of the duplication process, RMAN re-creates the control file for the duplicate database using information from the target database. RMAN knows which backups (including incremental backups) and archived redo logs it needs for the duplication from the backup metadata for the target database's control file. If you don't ensure that all auxiliary channels can access all backups and archived redo logs, the backup will fail.

Once the duplicate database is started, you can comment out or delete the db_file_name_convert and log_file_name_convert parameters from the init.ora file for the duplicate database. You can restart the duplicate database for normal use at this point.

Once you've duplicated the source database, you can register the duplicate database in the same recovery catalog as the primary database, since the two databases will have unique DBIDs.

If you are duplicating a database to the same Oracle home as the primary database, you must use a different database name for the duplicate database. You must also convert the filenames so they are different from the source database filenames. Make sure you don't specify the nofilenamecheck clause while duplicating the database on the same host, because this may cause the duplicate command to overwrite the primary database files.

■**Tip** Make sure you don't use the `nofilenamecheck` clause with the `duplicate` command when duplicating a database on the same host as the source database, as is the case in this recipe. The `nofilenamecheck` clause keeps RMAN from checking whether the source and target filenames are identical, and you use it only when duplicating a database to a different host.

If you get an error such as PLS-561, it means the duplicate database doesn't have the same value for the `nls_lang` parameter as the source database. In this case, you must set the correct `nls_lang` environment variable to get past the error. Use the following query to find out the value of the `nls_lang` parameter in the source database:

```
SQL> select parameter, value from nls_database_parameters
     where parameter in
     ('NLS_LANGUAGE','NLS_TERRITORY','NLS_CHARACTERSET'
     ,'NLS_NCHAR_CHARACTERSET');
```

To change the value of the `nls_lang` variable, use the `export` or `setenv` command (in Linux/Unix) to set the value for the variable you get from the previous query.

To avoid problems because of inadequate SGA memory, you may use a higher memory for the duplicate database when you're duplicating it. You can always reduce the memory allocation afterward if you don't have sufficient RAM on your server.

The previous example showed you basic backup-based database duplication. A *backup-based database duplication* works the following way regarding the various types of source database files:

- Data files are restored from backups.

- Control files are re-created but are restored from backups if you specify `for standby`.

- Temp files are re-created in the location set by the `db_create_file_dest` parameter.

- Online redo log files are re-created.

- Archived redo logs are restored from backups, but only if needed for duplication.

- Server parameter files are restored from backup if you use the `spfile` clause only.

- Flash recovery area files aren't copied, and flashback log files, password files, and block change tracking files are not re-created.

15-3. Duplicating a Database Without Any RMAN Backups

Problem

You want to duplicate a database from a source database but realize you don't have any backups of the source database.

Solution

In Oracle Database 11g, you can duplicate a source database entirely without any premade source database backups whatsoever by using the new network-enabled backup feature. The steps are essentially still the same as those we showed for the older backup-based database duplication techniques earlier in this chapter.

You can use the source database files to duplicate a database directly to the auxiliary instance by using the new active database duplication feature. In an active database duplication process, the service name of the auxiliary instance is utilized to copy the source database online image copies and archived redo log copies to the duplicate instance. There's absolutely no need for any preexisting backups whatsoever to duplicate the source database.

Here's an example showing how to perform an active database duplication with Oracle Database 11g by using the active database clause of the RMAN duplicate command. Notice that you don't need any preexisting backups to start the database duplication process. In the example, the source and duplicate databases are on the *same host*, so you do have to use different database filenames for the two databases.

1. Use a dedicated listener configuration for RMAN by making the following additions to your listener.ora file:

```
SID_LIST_LISTENER =
(SID_LIST =
    (SID_DESC =
          (GLOBAL_DBNAME = prod1)
          (ORACLE_HOME = /u01/app/oracle/product/11g/)
          (SID_NAME =prod1)
    )
    (SID_DESC =
          (GLOBAL_DBNAME = test1)
          (ORACLE_HOME = /u01/app/oracle/product/11g/)
          (SID_NAME =test1)
    )
)
```

2. Add the following information to the tnsnames.ora file, located in the $ORACLE_HOME/network/admin directory:

```
test1=
(DESCRIPTION =
(ADDRESS_LIST =
(ADDRESS = (PROTOCOL = TCP)(HOST = prod1)(PORT = 1521))
    )
(CONNECT_DATA =
(SERVER = DEDICATED)
(SERVICE_NAME = test1)
    )
  )
```

We're going to use the spfile technique for naming the duplicate files. Therefore, you need only one parameter, in there, db_name, to denote the name of your new duplicate database. You don't need to set the initialization parameters such as db_file_name_convert and log_file_name_convert, because you're going to set these parameters directly in the duplicate database command itself. So, here's how your spfile will look for the duplicate database:

```
db_name = test1
```

In this example, the init.ora file for the duplicate database is named inittest1.ora. Save this file in the appropriate location. (On Linux/Unix, the default location is $ORACLE_HOME/dbs, and on Windows, it is %ORACLE_HOME%\database.)

3. Create a password file for connecting remotely to the duplicate database with the sysdba privilege. This is because when you perform active database duplication, the target database instance must connect directly to the auxiliary database instance. Note that the password file connection requires the same sysdba password as that of the source database. Create the password file manually with the orapwd utility, as shown here, with just a single password to start the auxiliary instance:

```
$ orapwd password=<sys_pwd> file=orapwtest1 entries=20
```

4. Start the auxiliary database (duplicate database) instance. You must start the new instance in nomount mode since you don't have a control file for this new database yet.

```
$ export ORACLE_SID=test1
$ sqlplus /nolog
SQL> connect / as sysdba
Connected to an idle instance
SQL> startup nomount
Oracle Instance started.
Total System Global Area      113246208 bytes
Fixed Size                       218004 bytes
Variable Size                  58722860 bytes
Database Buffers               50331648 bytes
Redo Buffers                    2973696 bytes
SQL> exit
```

The previous startup command will start the auxiliary instance in nomount mode. If you're using a Windows server, you create a new instance by using the oradim utility.

5. Start up RMAN, and connect to the target database after making sure you first set the ORACLE_SID environmental variable to the source database, prod1. Note that the target database can be mounted or open.

```
$rman target sys/sammyy1@eleven
Recovery Manager: Release 11.1.0.3.0 - Beta on Mon Mar 19 08:07:53 2007
Copyright (c) 1982, 2006, Oracle.  All rights reserved.
connected to target database: ELEVEN (DBID=3481681133)
```

■**Note** If you're duplicating a database to the same host, as is the case in this example, you don't have to use a password file. You can simply choose to use operating system authentication to connect to the auxiliary instance. If you're performing active database duplication, on the other hand, you must use a password file for both the target and auxiliary instances, and they must use the same `sysdba` password. You must use an Oracle Net service name to connect to the auxiliary instance.

6. Connect to the duplicate database using the keyword `auxiliary` through a SQL*Net connection:

```
RMAN> connect auxiliary sys/sammyy1@auxdb
connected to auxiliary database: AUXDB (not mounted)
RMAN>
```

7. Issue the `duplicate target database` command to start the database duplication process:

```
RMAN> duplicate target database
    2> to auxdb
    3> from active database
    4> spfile
    5> parameter_value_convert =
        '/u01/app/oracle/eleven/eleven','/u01/app/oracle/eleven/auxdb'
    6> set log_file_name_convert =
        '/u05/app/oracle/eleven/eleven','/u05/app/oracle/eleven/auxdb'
    7> db_file_name_convert =
        '/u05/app/oracle/eleven/eleven','/u05/app/oracle/eleven/auxdb';

Starting Duplicate Db at 19-MAR-07
using target database control file instead of recovery catalog
...
}
executing Memory Script
executing command: SET NEWNAME
Starting backup at 19-MAR-07
...
Finished backup at 19-MAR-07

sql statement: alter system archive log current
...
Finished recover at 19-MAR-07
connected to auxiliary database (not started)
Oracle instance started
contents of Memory Script:
{
    Alter clone database open resetlogs;
}
executing Memory Script
```

```
database opened
Finished Duplicate Db at 19-MAR-07

RMAN>
```

How It Works

Make sure you follow these guidelines for network-enabled database duplication:

- Both the source and destination databases must be known to Oracle Net.

- The source database can be mounted or open.

- If the source database is mounted, you must have shut it down cleanly prior to starting it up in mount mode.

- If the source database is open, it must be running in archivelog mode.

- You can continue to use the source database normally while the database duplication is going on, but be aware that there is an overhead cost of CPU and network bandwidth consumption for sending the data.

You start the active database duplication process by using the `from active database` clause of the RMAN `duplicate` command. The inter-instance network connection is used to copy the source database files to the specified destination on the auxiliary instance. At the end of the datafile copying process, RMAN uses a "memory script" to complete the recovery before opening the new duplicate database. RMAN decides the end time for the duplication based on when it completes the copying of the online data files.

If you were to perform the active database duplication on a different host with the same directory structure, your database duplication command would be much simpler, as shown here:

```
RMAN> duplicate database
         to newdb
         from active database
         spfile
         nofilenamecheck;
```

Note that you still have to specify the `nofilenamecheck` clause, just as in the case of a backup-based duplication, since you're going to the use identical directory structures and filenames for both the source and destination databases. You also could use the optional password file option as part of the `duplicate database` command, if you wanted RMAN to copy the entire source database password file to the duplicate database. We actually chose to create the password file manually in this recipe.

An *active database duplication* works the following way regarding the various types of source database files:

- Data files are copied from the source database.

- Control files are re-created but will be copied from the source database if you specify the `for standby` clause.

- Temp files are re-created in the location set by the `db_create_file_dest` parameter.

- Online redo log files are re-created.

- Archived redo logs are copied from the source database, but only if needed for duplication.

- Server parameter files are copied from the source database if you use the `spfile` clause only.

- Password files are copied for standby databases always, but for a duplicate database, they're copied only if you specify the password file option in the `duplicate database` command.

- Flash recovery area files aren't copied, and flashback log files, password files, and block change tracking files are not re-created.

If you'd rather create a standby database instead of a duplicate database, all you have to do is replace the `to auxdb` part of the `duplicate database` command with the `for standby` clause, as shown here:

```
RMAN> duplicate target database
        for standby
        from active database
        spfile
```

It's easy to duplicate a non-ASM file based database to an ASM file system–based database. Here we'll show you a simple example to demonstrate how to do this. First create an ASM disk group, named +DISK1. Here's the database duplication command to create an ASM file system–based duplicate database:

```
RMAN> duplicate target database
        to newdb
        from active database
        spfile
        parameter_value_convert
'/u01/app/oracle/oradata/sourcedb/','+DISK1'
set db_create_file_dest = +DISK1;
```

This `duplicate database` command will create a database whose datafiles, control files, and online redo logs are all in the ASM disk group +DISK1.

You can speed up active database duplication by increasing the parallelism setting of disk channels on the source database, which leads to the parallel copying of the source database files over the network

15-4. Creating a Duplicate Database on a Remote Host with the Same File Structure

Problem

You want to duplicate a database from one server to another using RMAN.

■**Note** You are limited to the same operating system platform when performing database duplication to a different host.

Solution

Let's call our primary database PROD, the duplicate database AUX, and the RMAN catalog database CATDB (the catalog is purely optional). Here are the steps to duplicate the primary database on a different server:

1. Back up the primary database. You must take a full backup and include all the archive logs as well as the control file.

   ```
   [oracle@linux] rman target=/ catalog rman/rman@catdb

   RMAN> run {
   allocate channel d1 type disk;
   backup format '/backups/PROD/df_t%t_s%s_p%p' database;
   backup format '/backups/PROD/al_t%t_s%s_p%p' archivelog all;
   release channel d1;
   }
   ```

2. Ensure that the source database backups are available for the duplication process. You can get a complete list of the necessary backups by running the list backup command, as shown here:

   ```
   RMAN>list backup;
   ```

3. Create the necessary directories for the duplicate database, and then create the initialization parameter file for the duplicate database, as shown in the following example:

   ```
   audit_file_dest =/oradata/AUX/adump
   background_dump_dest =/oradata/AUX/bdump
   core_dump_dest =/oradata/AUX/cdump
   user_dump_dest =/oradata/AUX/udump
   db_name ="AUX"
   instance_name =AUX
   control_files =('/oradata/AUX/control01.ctl',
   '/oradata/AUX/control02.ctl','/oradata/AUX/control03.ctl')

   #the following sets the source and target location for data files
   db_file_name_convert =("/oradata/PROD/", "/oradata/AUX/")

   #the following sets the source and target location for redo log files
   log_file_name_convert =("/oradata/PROD/", "/oradata/AUX/")

   #the following lines must be the same as those on the target instance
   undo_management =AUTO
   undo_retention =10800
   undo_tablespace =UNDOTBS1
   ```

```
db_block_size = 8192
compatible = 11.1.0.1.0
```

4. Start up the auxiliary instance in nomount mode:

```
$ export ORACLE_SID=AUX
$ sqlplus '/as sysdba'
SQL> startup nomount;
```

5. Check the Oracle Net connections to the primary database and the recovery catalog. The production database can be open or in a mounted state. The catalog database, if you're using it, must be open. Make sure you can connect to the primary database on server A from the target server. Make sure you can also connect to the RMAN catalog from the target server..

```
$ sqlplus 'sys/oracle@PROD as sysdba'
$ rman catalog  rman/rman@catdb      # not mandatory
```

6. Execute the duplicate command after first setting the environment variables:

```
$ export ORACLE_SID=AUX
$ rman target sys/sys@PROD catalog rman/rman@catdb auxiliary /
RMAN> duplicate target database to AUX
       nofilenamecheck;
```

Once the duplicate database command finishes executing, your new database is ready for your use as an exact replica of the source database.

How It Works

If you're duplicating a database to a new host and use an identical directory structure, you don't need to set new filenames for the duplicate database. You can also use an identical initialization parameter file. You must specify the nofilenamecheck clause with the duplicate command, as shown in the "Solution" section, so RMAN doesn't issue any errors because of identical filenames on the two servers.

When the source and the destination database datafiles and online redo log files have identical filenames and the two databases are on two different hosts, you must specify the nofilenamecheck clause with the duplicate database command. This will keep RMAN from checking whether the source and destination filenames for the datafiles and the online redo log files are the same. If you're creating the duplicate database on a different host but with the same disk configuration, directory structure, and database filenames as the source database, you must use the nofilenamecheck clause.

Before you start the duplication of the primary database, you must first determine the amount of disk space you'll need by running a query such as the following:

```
SQL> select DF.TOTAL/1048576 "DataFile Size Mb",
LOG.TOTAL/1048576 "Redo Log Size Mb",
CONTROL.TOTAL/1048576 "Control File Size Mb",
(DF.TOTAL + LOG.TOTAL + CONTROL.TOTAL)/1048576 "Total Size Mb" from dual,
(select sum(a.bytes) TOTAL from dba_data_files a) DF,
(select sum(b.bytes) TOTAL from v$log b) LOG,
```

```
(select sum((cffsz+1)*cfbsz) TOTAL from x$kcccf c) CONTROL;

DataFile Size Mb Redo Log Size Mb Control File Size Mb Total Size Mb
---------------- ---------------- -------------------- -------------
900              150              20.34375             1070.34375
```

Of course, you must also ensure that you have the necessary space on the target server to accommodate the copy of the primary database. You can do this by executing a command such as df -kh, for example, on a Linux server.

15-5. Duplicating a Database with Several Directories

Problem

You want to duplicate a source database with data spread out over several directories.

Solution

If the source database files are spread over multiple directories, you must use the set newname parameter instead of the db_file_name_convert parameter to rename the files in the duplicate database.

The following example shows how to create a duplicate database when the target database uses several different directories:

```
RMAN> run
{set newname for datafile 1 to '/u01/app/oracle/testdata/system01.dbf';
set newname for datafile 2 to '/u01/app/oracle/testdata/sysaux01.dbf';
set newname for datafile 3 to '/u01/app/oracle/testdata/data01.dbf';
set newname for datafile 4 to '/u01/app/oracle/testdata/index01.dbf';
set newname for datafile 5 to '/u01/app/oracle/testdata/undotbs01.dbf';
duplicate target database to newdb
logfile
    group 1 ('/u01/app/oracle/testdata/logs/redo01a.log',
      ('/u01/app/oracle/testdata/logs/redo01b.log') size 10m reuse,
    group 2 ('/u01/app/oracle/testdata/logs/redo02a.log',
      ('/u01/app/oracle/testdata/logs/redo02b.log') size 10m reuse;
}
```

The run block duplicates the target database and supplies filenames for both the datafiles and the online redo log files for the duplicate database.

How It Works

You must use a run block when duplicating database with the set newname for datafile clause, since that's a requirement for using the set newname clause. Before you run the duplicate database command, copy the source database initialization file from host1 to host2, where you're creating the duplicate database. Specify a path name in this initialization parameter file for all parameters that end with _dest. However, you mustn't set any values for the db_file_name_convert and log_file_name_convert parameters, because the run command specifies filenames for both the datafiles and the online redo log files.

15-6. Creating a Standby Database on a New Host

Problem

You want to create a standby database on a different host than the production database.

Solution

Use the `for standby` clause in the `duplicate database` command to specify that the database you're going to duplicate is meant for use as a standby database. As in the case of database duplication, it isn't mandatory to use a recovery catalog to create a standby database. In the following example, the Oracle SID for both the primary and standby databases is identical (PROD). The primary (target) database is on Host A, and the server hosting the standby (auxiliary) database is called Host B. Here are the steps for creating the standby database:

1. Perform a full backup of the primary database, including all the archive logs and the current control file.

2. Calculate the disk space necessary for the standby database by summing up the size of all the datafiles in the database.

3. Ensure there is enough space on the target host to accommodate the standby database by using an operating system command such as `df -kh`.

4. Back up the target database as shown here with the `'backup current controlfile for standby format'` command:

```
RMAN> run {
allocate channel d1 type disk;
backup format '/backups/PROD/df_t%t_s%s_p%p' database;
sql 'alter system archive log current';
backup format '/backups/PROD/al_t%t_s%s_p%p' archivelog all;
backup current controlfile for standby format '/backups/PROD/sb_t%t_s%s_p%p';
release channel d1;
}
```

5. Copy the backups from Host A to Host B to make them available to the standby creation process. Make sure you place the backups in identically named directories on Host B. For example, if your source backup files are in /backups/PROD, those backup files must be copied to the /backups/PROD directory on Host B. If you decide to place them in a different directory, as explained at the beginning of this chapter, you must run the `catalog` command (`"catalog start with <directory>"`) to update the source database control file with the location of the backups. For the `catalog` command to work, make sure you have the different directory structure on the source database as well.

   You must also move the archive log backups to the target server. If you're performing a point-in-time recovery, you may need only some of the archived redo logs:

```
RMAN> list backup;
List of Backup Sets
```

```
BS Key  Type LV Size       Device Type Elapsed Time Completion Time
------- ---- -- ---------- ----------- ------------ ---------------
534     Full    80.00K     DISK         00:00:02     06-DEC-06
        BP Key: 535   Status: AVAILABLE  Compressed: NO  Tag:
TAG20061206T073326
Piece Name: /home/oracle/product/11.1.0/db_1/flash_recovery_area/NINA/
backupset/2006_12_06/o1_mf_nnsnf_TAG20061206T073326_2qfg83xd_.bkp
SPFILE Included: Modification time: 06-DEC-06
List of Archived Logs in backup set 693
Thrd Seq    Low SCN    Low Time   Next SCN   Next Time
---- ------- ---------- ---------- ---------- ---------
  1   458    23543278   06-DEC-06 23544242    06-DEC-06
  1   459    23544242   06-DEC-06 23544537    06-DEC-06
  1   460    23544537   06-DEC-06 23618584    06-DEC-06

List of Datafiles in backup set 1409
File LV Type Ckp SCN    Ckp Time   Name
---- -- ---- ---------- ---------- -------------------------
  1     Full 24913456   19-DEC-06
/home/oracle/product/11.1.0/oradata/nina/system01.dbf
  2     Full 24913456   19-DEC-06
/home/oracle/product/11.1.0/oradata/nina/undotbs01.dbf
  3     Full 24913456   19-DEC-06
/home/oracle/product/11.1.0/oradata/nina/sysaux01.dbf
  4     Full 24913456   19-DEC-06
/home/oracle/product/11.1.0/oradata/nina/users01.dbf
  5     Full 24913456   19-DEC-06
/home/oracle/product/11.1.0/oradata/nina/example01.dbf


RMAN>
```

6. Create an initialization file (init.ora) for the standby database in the $ORACLE_HOME/dbs
   directory. Use the primary database's initialization file as the source for the initialization
   parameter settings:

```
audit_file_dest =/apps/oracle/admin/PROD/adump
background_dump_dest =/apps/oracle/admin/PROD/bdump
core_dump_dest =/apps/oracle/admin/PROD/cdump
user_dump_dest =/apps/oracle/admin/PROD/udump
db_name ="PROD"
instance_name =PROD
# Set the following to the location of the standby clone control file.
control_files=('/u01/PROD/control01.ctl','/u02/PROD/control02.ctl',
'/u03/PROD/control03.ctl')
# Set the following for the from and to location for all data files / redo
# logs to be cloned. This is set if the location differs from Primary.
db_file_name_convert =("/u01/oradata/PROD","/u02/oradata/PROD")
log_file_name_convert =("/u01/oradata/PROD","/u02/oradata/PROD")
```

```
#Set the following to the same as the production target
undo_management =AUTO
undo_retention =10800
undo_tablespace =UNDOTBS1
db_block_size = 8192
compatible = 11.1.0.1.0
```

7. Run the following command on the standby database server to start the auxiliary instance in nomount state:

```
$ export ORACLE_SID=AUX
$ sqlplus '/ as sysdba'
SQL> startup nomount;
```

8. Test the SQL*Net connections to the primary database and the RMAN catalog. The production database must be open or mounted, and the recovery catalog must be open. Run the following commands on the standby database server:

```
$ sqlplus 'sys/oracle@prod1 as sysdba'
$ sqlplus rman/rman@catdb
```

Test that you're connecting to the correct SID/service_name and the hostname by executing the tnsping command for both the prod and rman connections.

9. Connect to the production database (target) and the auxiliary instance, and run the RMAN duplicate command for the standby database, as shown here (again, you'll be running these commands on the standby database server):

```
$ export ORACLE_SID=PROD
$ rman target sys/sys@PROD auxiliary /
RMAN> run {
        allocate channel C1 device type disk;
        allocate auxiliary channel C2 device type disk;
        duplicate target database for standby nofilenamecheck;
        }
```

The standby database is created when the run block completes executing. The duplicate database ... for standby command restores a standby control file and mounts that control file, thus creating the standby database.

How It Works

You can't connect to a standby database when issuing the duplicate ... for standby command. You can use this command only when connected to the original primary database. When duplicating a database on a different server, you can do any of the following:

- Send the backups to an identical path on the remote host.

- Send the backups to a new location on the remote host.

- Use a network file system (NFS) to make the same path accessible from the remove host. That is, the same NFS mount point—for example, /home/file_server—can be accessible to both hosts.

If you're using tape backups, make sure the backup tapes are accessible to the remote host by moving the tape to a drive connected to that remote host or by placing the tapes in a tape server that can be accessible through the network.

In the example shown here, we are assuming you want to create a standby database that is identical with the primary database. If you want to restore and recover the standby database to a previous point in time, you can do so by using the set until time clause while performing the database duplication for the standby database. You must have backups for all the archivelogs you want to use in the recovery of the standby database.

As with the regular databases, you can create a standby database either by using the source database backup files or by using the active database method (live, with no backups). To create a standby database over the network without any preexisting backup files, simply add the active database clause to the duplicate database command, as shown here:

```
duplicate target database for standby
from active database;
...
```

15-7. Duplicating a Database to a Past Point in Time

Problem

You want to create a duplicate database to a past point in time.

Solution

To create an auxiliary database to a past point in time, you use essentially the same steps as shown in recipe 15-2 (for duplication on the same host) and recipe 15-4 (for different hosts). The only difference comes at the end, during the execution of the duplicate command. You must use the until time clause to create an auxiliary database to a past period in time. Here's an example that shows how to duplicate the database to a past point in time using the until time clause:

```
RMAN> connect target sys/<sys_password>@targdb
RMAN> connect auxiliary sys/<sys_password.@dupdb
RMAN> duplicate target database
      to dupdb
      spfile
      nofilenamecheck
      until time 'sysdate-1';
```

The duplicate ... until time command shown here will create a duplicate database that'll be in the same state as the source database 24 hours ago.

How It Works

Use the until time clause when you want to specify a database duplication but don't want the duplicate database to be up-to-date as the source database. You can provide the archived logs in the form of an already backed up RMAN backup set or in their original form from the archived log destination.

You can also perform incomplete database duplication to a past point in time by placing the `set until time` clause before the `duplicate database` command, as shown in the following example:

```
run
{
  allocate channel C1 device type disk;
  allocate auxiliary channel C2 device type disk
  set until time "to_date('July 16 2007 12:00:00',
  'Mon DD YYYY HH24:MI:SS')";
  duplicate target database to aux;
}
```

The `set until time` clause will ensure that the duplicate target database won't be up-to-date but rather be current only to the July 16 point in time that you specified in the `duplicate database` command.

■**Note** The `until` or `to restore point` clause, which allows you to perform an incomplete recovery when duplicating a database, is usable only in *backup-based duplication*. You can't use these incomplete duplication techniques when using *active database duplication*, which doesn't use any preexisting backups.

Note that in addition to specifying a point in time (`until time`), you can also specify an SCN or a log sequence number for an incomplete database duplication job. Or, you may specify the `to restore point` clause, which results in an incomplete database duplication with the SCN corresponding to the restore point as the inclusive limit point for the database duplication.

15-8. Skipping Tablespaces During Database Duplication

Problem

You want to skip certain tablespaces when duplicating a database.

Solution

Use the `skip tablespace` clause to omit specific tablespaces when duplicating a database. In the following example, the `skip tablespace` clause leads to the omission of the users and tools tablespaces from the duplicate database aux:

```
run
{
  allocate channel C1 device type disk;
  allocate auxiliary channel C2 device type disk;
  duplicate database to aux
  skip tablespace users, tools;
}
```

The result of this command will be a duplicate database but without the tools and users tablespaces.

How It Works

As soon as RMAN opens the new auxiliary database, it'll start dropping all tablespaces that are part of the `skip tablespace` command. The tablespace drop is done using the option `including contents cascade constraints`. RMAN drops the tablespaces in a reverse sorted list of tablespace names. You'll get errors if you try to exclude tablespaces that contain indexes used for enforcing unique or primary keys.

You don't have to specify the temporary tablespaces as part of the excluded tablespaces since RMAN doesn't back up the temporary tablespace. Since leaving out LOBs may cause a database duplication to fail, it's a good idea not to exclude tablespace containing LOBs. You can't exclude the default permanent tablespace (such as the users tablespace in most Oracle databases). If you do, RMAN will get an error because it'll try to drop the default permanent tablespace from the new duplicate database. One way around this is to change the default permanent tablespace to a different tablespace and then drop the tablespace.

15-9. Duplicating a Database with a Specific Backup Tag

Problem

You want to specify a particular backup tag during the duplication of a database.

Solution

You can "force" RMAN to use a specific backup during a database duplication process by simply making other backups unavailable. Here are the steps to follow:

1. Use the `list backup of database` command to find out the primary key of the backup set you plan to use in the duplication process:

   ```
   RMAN> list backup of database;
   ```

2. Make all the backup sets except the one you choose unavailable to RMAN during the database duplication process by using the following command for each of the backups you want to make inaccessible to RMAN:

   ```
   RMAN> change backupset <primary key> unavailable;
   ```

3. Follow the steps in recipe 15-2 or recipe 15-3 to duplicate the source database.

4. Once the database duplication is finished, make all the backups available to RMAN again by issuing the following command for each of the backup sets you made unavailable prior to the database duplication:

   ```
   RMAN> change backupset <primary key> available;
   ```

All the backup sets are once again "available" for use by RMAN.

How It Works

The ability to specify a particular tag to back up a database is handy when you're moving a production database to a test platform. You may have multiple backups of the production database available to RMAN, and you may not necessarily want the latest backup to be the basis of a database duplication. In such cases, you can choose a specific version of the production database by picking the backup based on the backup tag and make only that backup available to RMAN for duplicating the database.

15-10. Resynchronizing a Duplicate Database

Problem

You want to synchronize a duplicate database with its parent database.

Solution

Once you create a duplicate database from a source database, you can periodically "update" or synchronize the duplicate database by simply rerunning the duplicate command over again, in essence re-creating the duplicate database (reduplicating the target database). In the following example, we first perform a one-time setup of the new datafile names by using the configure auxname clause, as shown here:

```
RMAN> connect target /
RMAN> connect catalog rman/cat@catdb
RMAN> connect auxiliary sys/sammyy1@dupdb
RMAN> run {
configure auxname for datafile 1 to '/oradata1/system01.dbf';
configure auxname for datafile 2 to '/oradata2/sysaux01.dbf';
configure auxname for datafile 3 to '/oradata3/undotbs01.dbf';
configure auxname for datafile 4 to '/oradata4/drsys01';
configure auxname for datafile 5 to '/oradata5/example01.dbf';
configure auxname for datafile 6 to '/oradata6/indx01.dbf';
configure auxname for datafile 7 to '/oradata7/users01.dbf';
}
```

Synchronize the duplicate database with the source database by periodically executing the duplicate target database command to re-create the duplicate database. For example:

```
RMAN> connect target /
RMAN> connect catalog rman/cat@catdb
RMAN> connect auxiliary sys/sammyy1@dupdb
RMAN> duplicate target database to dupdb
logfile
group 1 ('/duplogs/redo01a.log',
'/duplogs/redo01b.log') size 200k reuse,
group 2 ('/duplogs/redo02a.log',
'/duplogs/redo02b.log') size 200k reuse;
```

You can schedule this script for running on a daily or a weekly basis, thus creating a new and up-to-date duplicate database on a continuous basis.

How It Works

To synchronize a duplicate database with the parent database, you must in essence re-create the duplicate database by transferring the latest copies of the source database files to the duplicate database.

To set up a database for periodic synchronization, you must first use the `configure` command to set persistent new names for the datafiles. Once you set the persistent datafile names, the filenames will be recorded in the control file, and RMAN will use the same file-names each time you synchronize the duplicate database by using the `duplicate` command.

Remember that you have to employ the `configure` auxname clause only once—the first time you duplicate the database. RMAN will reuse the same persistent filenames anytime you execute the `duplicate` command after configuring the auxiliary filenames to synchronize the duplicate database.

15-11. Transporting Tablespaces on the Same OS Platform

Problem

You want to transport tablespaces using RMAN backups instead of performing the trans-portable tablespaces operation on the "live" production database.

Solution

You create a transportable tablespace set by executing the RMAN command `transport tablespace`. The following example shows how to transport tablespaces on identical operating system platforms by utilizing RMAN backups. Here are the steps you must follow to transport the tablespaces:

1. Make sure the tablespaces you plan to transport are *self-contained*. To be considered self-contained, the tablespace set you want to transport mustn't contain references pointing outside those tablespaces, such as an index on a table that doesn't belong to one of the tablespaces you're transporting. In the following example, the transportable tablespace set consists of two tablespaces—test1 and test2. Use the `transport_set_check` procedure of the DBMS_TTS package to verify whether the two tablespaces are self-contained, as shown here:

   ```
   SQL> execute sys.dbms_tts.transport_set_check('test1, test2',TRUE);
   PL/SQL procedure successfully completed.
   SQL>
   ```

   To confirm that there are no errors because of the tablespaces, you can also query the `sys.transport_set_violations` table after running the `sys.dbms_tts.transport_set` procedure to verify the results and view error messages if there are any.

■**Note** You don't have to manually make the tablespaces you are transporting read-only. RMAN will do this as part of the `transport tablespace` command.

---

2. Generate the transportable tablespace set by issuing the `transport tablespace` command. During regular (without RMAN) tablespace transport, you use an operating system utility such as the `cp` or `copy` command to copy the database files that belong to the tablespaces in the transportable tablespace set. Here, however, since we're using RMAN to transport the tablespaces, we use the RMAN backups for this purpose:

```
RMAN> transport tablespace test1,test2
   2> tablespace destination '/u05/app/oracle/transportdest'
   3> auxiliary destination '/u05/app/oracle/auxdest';

Creating automatic instance, with SID='aux'
db_name=NINA
db_unique_name=tspitr_NINA_aux
...
starting up automatic instance NINA
Oracle instance started
contents of Memory Script:
{
# restore the controlfile
restore clone controlfile;
# mount the controlfile
sql clone 'alter database mount clone database';
...
}
executing command: SET until clause
Starting restore at 20-JUN-07
...
Finished restore at 20-JUN-07
sql statement: alter database mount clone database
alter clone database open resetlogs;
executing command: SET until clause
executing command: SET NEWNAME
...
Starting restore at 20-JUN-07
...
Finished restore at 20-JUN-07
...
Starting recover at 20-JUN-07
...
Finished recover at 20-JUN-07
database opened
# export the tablespaces in the recovery set
host 'expdp userid=\"/@\(DESCRIPTION=\(ADDRESS=\(PROTOCOL=beq\)
\(PROGRAM=/home/oracle/product/11.1.0/db_1/bin/oracle\)
\(ARGV0=oracleaux\)\(ARGS=^'\(DESCRIPTION=\(LOCAL=YES\)
\(ADDRESS=\(PROTOCOL=beq\)\)\)^'\)\(ENVS=^'ORACLE_SID=aux^'\)\)
\(CONNECT_DATA=\(SID=aux\)\)\) as sysdba\" transport_tablespaces=
TEST1,
```

```
TEST2 dumpfile=
dmpfile.dmp directory=
STREAMS_DIROBJ_DPDIR logfile=
explog.log';
}
sql statement: alter tablespace TEST1 read only
sql statement: alter tablespace TEST2 read only
sql statement: create or replace directory STREAMS
DIROBJ_DPDIR as "/u05/app/oracle/transportdest"
...
Removing automatic instance
shutting down automatic instance
Oracle instance shut down
Automatic instance removed
...
RMAN>
Export: Release 11.1.0.1.0 - Beta on Tuesday, 20 June, 2007 2:27:03
Copyright © 2003, 2005, Oracle.  All rights reserved.
Connected to: Oracle Database 11g Enterprise Edition
Release 11.1.0.1.0- Beta
Starting "SYS"."SYS_EXPORT_TRANSPORTABLE_01":  userid="/********@
(DESCRIPTION=(ADDRESS=(PROTOCOL=beq)
(PROGRAM=/home/oracle/product/11.1.0/db_1/bin/oracle)
(ARGV0=oracleaux)(ARGS=\(DESCRIPTION=\(LOCAL=YES\)\
(ADDRESS=\(PROTOCOL=beq\)\)\))(ENVS=ORACLE_SID=aux))
(CONNECT_DATA=(SID=aux))) AS SYSDBA"
transport_tablespaces= TEST1, TEST2
dumpfile=dmpfile.dmp directory=STREAMS_DIROBJ_DPDIR logfile=explog.log
Processing object type TRANSPORTABLE_EXPORT/PLUGTS_BLK
Processing object type TRANSPORTABLE_EXPORT/POST_INSTANCE/PLUGTS_BLK
Master table "SYS"."SYS_EXPORT_TRANSPORTABLE_01" successfully
loaded/unloaded********************************************************
Dump file set for SYS.SYS_EXPORT_TRANSPORTABLE_01 is:
/u05/app/oracle/transportdest/dmpfile.dmp
Job "SYS"."SYS_EXPORT_TRANSPORTABLE_01" successfully completed at 02:27:54
RMAN>
```

3. You now have the export file with the necessary metadata to transport the two table-spaces, test1 and test2. You also have the datafiles for the two tablespaces you're going to transport.

4. Import the tablespace set into the target database. You can perform the import by using the Data Pump Import utility from the command line, but it's a whole lot simpler to use the import script prepared for you by RMAN, with the default name impscrpt.sql.

```
SQL> @impscrpt.sql
Directory created.
```

```
Directory created.
PL/SQL procedure successfully completed.
Directory dropped.
Directory dropped.
SQL>
```

5. Use the DBA_TABLESPACES view to check that the two tablespace test1 and test2 have been currently imported to the newdb database.

How It Works

In this recipe, we showed you how to transport tablespaces to the same operating system platform using RMAN backups. The next recipe shows how to do this on different platforms.

You can also transport tablespaces from a "live" database using an alternative transport tablespace technique explained in the Oracle manual. However, the big disadvantage in that method is that the transportable tablespaces must be put in a "read-only" mode, thus affecting database availability. It not only may be time-consuming to put the tablespaces into read-only mode, but users can't write to those tablespaces for the duration of the tablespace transport. You don't have any of these limitations when you use RMAN backups as the basis of your transportable tablespace operation.

You can create transportable tablespace sets from RMAN backups. You must have a prior backup of all the datafiles that belong to the transportable tablespace set and the archived redo logs, so RMAN can use them to recover to the target point in time.

You may use this capability of RMAN for creating transportable tablespace sets for reporting purposes. Transportable tablespace sets are also highly useful during the instantiation of streams. The one big requirement for using RMAN backups to create transportable tablespaces is that your RMAN backups must be recoverable to the SCN at which you want the transportable tablespaces.

RMAN creates an auxiliary database instance through which it creates the transportable tablespace sets. RMAN does quite a few things in order to prepare the transportable table set. Here's a summary of the actions set off when you execute the transport tablespace command:

1. RMAN starts an auxiliary instance in nomount mode first. You don't have to specify a parameter file for this auxiliary instance, since RMAN automatically creates the file. The name of the auxiliary instance is also made up by RMAN. In our example shown in the previous section, the ORACLE_SID of the auxiliary instance is aux (Creating automatic instance, with SID='aux').

2. RMAN restores a backup of the target database control file and uses it to mount the auxiliary database.

3. Using the switch operation, RMAN restores all datafiles from the target database for the auxiliary instance. These files are restored to the location specified by the auxiliary destination clause in the transport tablespace command.

4. RMAN also stores the files pertaining to the tablespaces in the transportable tablespace set in the location specified by the tablespace destination parameter in the transport tablespace command.

5. Once the datafiles from the target database are all restored to the auxiliary database location, RMAN performs a point-in-time recovery of the auxiliary instance. In our example, since we didn't specify a target time, a complete database recovery is performed. Note that all applicable archived redo logs are also automatically restored and applied by RMAN during the recovery process. Once the recovery is finished, an open resetlogs operation is performed on the auxiliary database by RMAN.

6. RMAN invokes the Data Pump Export utility (in the transportable tablespace mode) to create the export dump file containing the tablespaces in the transportable tablespace set. By default, the export dump file is placed in the location specified by the `tablespace destination` clause of the `transport tablespace` command.

7. RMAN also simultaneously generates a Data Pump Import script you can use to plug in the transported tablespaces into the target database. The default script name is impscrpt.sql, and this script is located in the directory specified by the `tablespace destination` clause of the `transport tablespace` command.

8. RMAN shuts down the auxiliary instance and automatically deletes all the files created and used during the transport tablespace process. The only files that remain are the transportable set files, the Data Pump Export log, and the sample Data Pump Import script.

In the example shown in the solution, the RMAN-created impscrpt.sql script was used to import the tablespaces into the target database. The script utilizes a PL/SQL script to import the tablespaces.

Alternatively, you can use the following Data Pump `import` command to import the tablespaces. For example:

```
$ impdp sys/sammyy1

directory=exp_data_dir

dumpfile= 'dmpfile.dmp'
transport_datafiles= /u05/app/oracle/transportdest/test1_01.dbf,
/u05/app/oracle/transportdest/test2_01.dbf
```

■**Note** You can even use non-RMAN backups to create transportable tablespace sets, as long as you record the datafile copies and archived redo logs in the RMAN repository using the `catalog` command.

You can also use the `transport tablespace` command to perform a tablespace transport to a past point in time. Simply add the `unit1 scn` clause to the `transport tablespace` command, as shown here:

```
RMAN> transport tablespace test1,test2
   2> tablespace destination '/u05/app/oracle/transportdest'
   3> auxiliary destination '/u05/app/oracle/auxdest'
   4> until SCN 259386;
```

The preceding command will recover the transportable tablespaces only up to the specified SCN. Instead of the SCN, you can also specify a target point in time or a restore point as well.

15-12. Transporting Tablespaces Across Different Operating System Platforms

Problem

You want to transport one or more tablespaces to another Oracle Database running on a different operating system platform using RMAN-made backups.

Solution

You can transport a tablespace to a host running on a different operating system platform than the source database basically by using the same transport tablespace command, as shown in recipe 15-11. The crucial thing to do here is to determine the *endian formats* of the two platforms—the source and the target. If the two server platforms have the same endian format, then the transport tablespace operation will be identical to the one described in recipe 15-11. If the two operating systems' endian formats differ, say one is big and the other is little, then you have to *convert the tablespaces* either before or after moving the tablespace's datafiles to the target server platform.

To find out the endian formats of the two platforms, use the following query:

```
SQL> select platform_name, endian_format from
  2* v$transportable_platform;
```

PLATFORM_NAME	ENDIAN_FORMAT
Solaris[tm] OE (32-bit)	Big
Solaris[tm] OE (64-bit)	Big
Microsoft Windows IA (32-bit)	Little
Linux IA (32-bit)	Little
AIX-Based Systems (64-bit)	Big
HP-UX (64-bit)	Big
HP Tru64 UNIX	Little
HP-UX IA (64-bit)	Big
Linux IA (64-bit)	Little
HP Open VMS	Little
Microsoft Windows IA (64-bit)	Little
IBM zSeries Based Linux	Big
Linux 64-bit for AMD	Little
Apple Mac OS	Big
Microsoft Windows 64-bit for AMD	Little
Solaris Operating Sy stem (x86)	Little
IBM Power Based Linux	Big

```
17 rows selected.
SQL>
```

If the endian formats of the two platforms (source and target) are different, you must convert the endian format of the datafiles in the transportable tablespace set to match the endian format of the target operating system platform. You must use the `convert tablespace` command if you want to convert on the source host or the `convert datafile` command if you want to perform the conversion on the destination host.

In our example, we are transporting a tablespace from the HP-UX (64-bit) operating system platform to a Linux (32-bit) platform. Since the HP-UX (64-bit)'s endian format is big and the Linux platform's is small, the endian formats aren't identical, and we must convert the datafiles belonging to the source platform before we can perform the transport tablespace operation.

The following are the steps you must take to transport a tablespace across different platforms when the endian formats of the two platforms are different:

1. Place the tablespaces you want to transport in read-only mode:

```
SQL> alter tablespace myspace read only;
Tablespace altered.
SQL>
```

2. Use the `convert tablespace` command to convert the source (HP-UX in this case) datafiles in the transportable tablespace set to the target (Linux in this case) platform:

```
RMAN> convert tablespace myspace
    2> to platform 'Linux IA (32-bit)'
    3> format='/tmp/dba/%U';
Starting backup at 02-JAN-07
using channel ORA_DISK_1
channel ORA_DISK_1: starting datafile conversion
input datafile fno=00064 name=/pasu61/oradata/pasu/myspace01.dbf
converted datafile=/tmp/dba/data_D-PASU_I-877170026_TS-MYSPACE_FNO-64_02i6g1vs
channel ORA_DISK_1: datafile conversion complete, elapsed time: 00:00:03
channel ORA_DISK_1: starting datafile conversion
input datafile fno=00066 name=/pasu61/oradata/pasu/myspace02.dbf
converted datafile=/tmp/dba/data_D-PASU_I-877170026_TS-MYSPACE_FNO-66_03i6g200
channel ORA_DISK_1: datafile conversion complete, elapsed time: 00:00:03
Finished backup at 02-JAN-07
RMAN>
```

3. Verify that you have the two datafiles that are part of the myspace tablespace in the /tmp/dba directory:

```
$ ls -altr /tmp/dba
data_D-PASU_I-877170026_TS-MYSPACE_FNO-64_02i6g1vs
data_D-PASU_I-877170026_TS-MYSPACE_FNO-66_03i6g200
```

Note that the two files listed here are converted to the endian format of the Linux IA (32-bit) platform.

4. Use the Data Pump Export utility to create the export dump file with the metadata for the myspace tablespace:

```
$ expdp pasowner/orbiter1 directory=direct1 transport_tablespaces=myspace
Export: Release 11.1.0.1.0 - 64bit Production on Tuesday, 26 June,
2007 10:18
Connected to: Oracle Database 11g Enterprise Edition Release 11.1.0.1.0 -
64bit Beta
Starting "PASOWNER"."SYS_EXPORT_TRANSPORTABLE_01":  pasowner/********
 directory=direct1 transport_tablespaces=myspace dumpfile=myspace.dmp
logfile=myspace.log
Processing object type TRANSPORTABLE_EXPORT/TABLE
Master table "PASOWNER"."SYS_EXPORT_TRANSPORTABLE_01" successfully
 loaded/unloaded

Dump file set for PASOWNER.SYS_EXPORT_TRANSPORTABLE_01 is:
/u01/app/oracle/dba/myspace.dmp
Job "PASOWNER"."SYS_EXPORT_TRANSPORTABLE_01" successfully completed at 10:19

$
```

5. Move both the converted datafiles from step 2 and the export dump file (myspace.dmp) from step 3 to the target host, as shown here:

```
$ rcp data_D-PASU_I-877170026_TS-MYSPACE_FNO-64_02i6g1vs prod1:/tmp/dba
$ rcp data_D-PASU_I-877170026_TS-MYSPACE_FNO-66_03i6g200 prod1:/tmp/dba
$ rcp myspace.dmp prod1:/tmp/dba
```

6. Import the tablespace metadata for the transported tablespaces into the target database, as shown here:

```
$ impdp system/sammyy1 directory=data_dump_dir2
dumpfile='myspace2.dmp'
transport_datafiles='/u05/app/oracle/data_D-PASU_I-877170026_TS-YSPACE_FNO-➡
64_02i6g1v,
'/u05/app/oracle/ data_D-PASU_I-877170026_TS-MYSPACE_FNO-66_03i6g200'
Import: Release 11.1.0.1.0 - Beta on Tuesday, 26 June, 2007
5:10:17
Copyright © 2003, 2005, Oracle.  All rights reserved.
Connected to: Oracle Database 10g Enterprise Edition Release
11.1.0.1.0 - Beta
With the Partitioning, OLAP and Data Mining options
ORA-31655: no data or metadata objects selected for job
Master table "SYSTEM"."SYS_IMPORT_TRANSPORTABLE_01" successfully ➡
loaded/unloaded
Starting "SYSTEM"."SYS_IMPORT_TRANSPORTABLE_01":  system/********
directory=data_dump_dir2 dumpfile=myspace2.dmp
transport_datafiles=/u05/app/oracle/data_D-PASU_I-877170026_TS-
MYSPACE_FNO-64_02i6g1v,/u05/app/oracle/ data_D-PASU_I-877170026_TS-
MYSPACE_FNO-66_03i6g200 Job "SYSTEM"."SYS_IMPORT_TRANSPORTABLE_01"
 successfully completed at 05:10:29
$
```

Once the import completes successfully as shown here, the tablespace transport process is complete.

How It Works

Contrary to its name, the `convert` command doesn't actually *convert* the source database files—it merely *prepares* duplicate files in the correct format for use on the target platform. The source files remain untouched by this conversion operation.

In the example shown in this recipe, we converted the source datafiles on the source platform by using the `convert tablespace` command. However, you can convert the datafiles that belong to the tablespaces in the transportable tablespace set on the target system as well by using the `convert datafile` command, as shown here:

```
RMAN> connect target /
RMAN> convert datafile=
'/u01/transport_solaris/sales/sales01.dbf',
'/u01/transport_solaris/sales/sales02.dbf'
from platform 'Solaris[tm] OE (32-bit)'
db_file_name_convert
'/u01/transport_solaris/sales','/u05/newdb/sales';
```

You'll end up with the following pair of files on the target server after the datafile conversion:

```
/u05/newdb/sales01.dbf
/u05/newdb/sales02.dbf
```

You follow the same general procedure for transporting tablespaces. After the conversion, use the Data Pump Import utility to plug the converted tablespaces into the target database.

15-13. Transporting an Entire Database to a Different Platform

Problem

You want to transport an entire Oracle database to another host that is using a different operating system platform.

Solution

Use the `convert database` command to move an Oracle database from one platform to another. The only requirement is that the two platforms share an identical endian format. You can perform the `convert database` operation on the source platform or the destination platform. In our example here, we perform the datafile conversion process on the source database platform. The next recipe shows you how to perform the datafile conversion on the target database platform.

The following are the steps to transport an Oracle database from a Windows XP platform to the Linux platform:

1. Make sure the source database is eligible for transporting to the destination operating system platform by executing the dbms_tdb.check_db procedure, as shown here. The source database is running on a Windows XP platform, and the target database is running on a Linux 32-bit platform.

```
SQL> connect sys/sammyy1 as sysdba
Connected.
SQL> set serveroutput on
SQL> declare
  2> db_ready boolean;
  3> begin
  4> db_ready := dbms_tdb.check_db('Linux IA(32-bit)',
     dbms_tdb.skip_readonly);
  5* end;
SQL> /
PL/SQL procedure successfully completed.
SQL>
```

If you see the message "PL/SQL procedure successfully completed," as is the case in this example, it means you can migrate from the specified operating system platform to the destination platform.

2. Since external tables aren't automatically transported to the target platform, you must invoke the dbms_tdb.check_db procedure again to get a list of the external tables, which you can then use to re-create those tables on the destination platform after the database transportation.

```
SQL> declare
   2> external boolean;
   3> begin
   4> external :=dbms_tdb.check_external;
   5*  end;
SQL> /
PL/SQL procedure successfully completed.
SQL>
```

Again, the output of the execution of the dbms_tdb package shows you don't have any external tables in the parent database that you'll have to worry about.

3. Put the target database in the read-only mode after shutting it down first and restarting it in mount state:

```
SQL> connect sys/sammyy1 as sysdba
Connected.
SQL> shutdown immediate;
Database closed.
Database dismounted.
ORACLE instance shut down.
SQL>
SQL> startup mount;
ORACLE instance started.
Total System Global Area  612368384 bytes
Fixed Size                  1250452 bytes
Variable Size             180357996 bytes
Database Buffers          427819008 bytes
```

```
Redo Buffers                     2940928 bytes
Database mounted.
SQL> alter database open read only;
Database altered.
SQL>
```

4. Execute the convert database command, which creates a transport script you'll subsequently use in the transportation process:

```
RMAN> convert database new database 'mydb'
    2> transport script 'c:\temp\mydb_script'
    3> to platform 'Linux IA (32-bit)'
    4> db_file_name_convert 'c:\oracle\product\11.1.0\oradata\nick\'
     'c:\temp\';
Starting convert at 15-FEB-07
using channel ORA_DISK_1
External table SH.SALES_TRANSACTIONS_EXT found in the database
Directory SYS.SUBDIR found in the database
Directory SYS.XMLDIR found in the database
Directory SYS.MEDIA_DIR found in the database
Directory SYS.LOG_FILE_DIR found in the database
Directory SYS.DATA_FILE_DIR found in the database
Directory SYS.WORK_DIR found in the database
Directory SYS.ADMIN_DIR found in the database
Directory SYS.DATA_PUMP_DIR found in the database
BFILE PM.PRINT_MEDIA found in the database
User SYS with SYSDBA and SYSOPER privilege found in password file
channel ORA_DISK_1: starting datafile conversion
input datafile fno=00001
name=C:\ORACLE\PRODUCT\11.1.0\ORADATA\NICK\SYSTEM01.DBF
converted datafile=C:\TEMP\SYSTEM01.DBF
channel ORA_DISK_1: datafile conversion complete, elapsed time:
00:00:35
...
Edit init.ora file
C:\ORACLE\PRODUCT\11.1.0\DB_1\DATABASE\INIT_00IA4IO1_1_0.ORA.
This PFILE will be used to create the database on the target platform
To recompile all PL/SQL modules, run utlirp.sql and utlrp.sql on the target ➥
platform
To change the internal database identifier, use DBNEWID Utility
Finished backup at 15-FEB-07
RMAN>
```

Once the source database files are converted, you must move them to the target platform and place them in the location specified for the datafiles in the pfile of the target database. You must also copy the mydb_script file and the pfile for the new database to the target platform.

5. On the target platform, first set the ORACLE_SID environment variable pointing to the new database:

```
$ export ORACLE_SID=newdb
```

The ORACLE_HOME environment variable must point to the same version of Oracle software as on the source platform.

Execute the mydb_script file after logging in to SQL*Plus as the user sys:

```
$ sqlplus /nolog
SQL> connect sys/sammyy1 as sysdgba
Connected to an idle instance.
SQL> @mydb
ORACLE instance started.
Total System Global Area  243269632 bytes
Fixed Size                  1218748 bytes
Variable Size              79693636 bytes
Database Buffers          159383552 bytes
Redo Buffers                2973696 bytes
...
Control file created.
Database altered.
Tablespace altered.

• Your database has been created successfully!
• There are many things to think about for the new database. Here
• is a checklist to help you stay on track:
• 1 You may want to redefine the location of the directory objects.
• 2.You may want to change the internal database identifier (DBID)
•    or the global database name for this database. Use the
• NEWDBID Utility (nid).

Database closed.
Database dismounted.
ORACLE instance shut down.
ORACLE instance started.
Total System Global Area  243269632 bytes
Fixed Size                  1218748 bytes
Variable Size              79693636 bytes
Database Buffers          159383552 bytes
Redo Buffers                2973696 bytes
Database mounted.
Database opened.
SQL>
SQL> Rem invalidate all pl/sql modules and recompile standard and ➥
dbms_standard
SQL>  @/u01/app/oracle/product/11.1.0/db_3/rdbms/admin/utlrp.sql
DOC>   utlirp.sql completed successfully. All PL/SQL objects in the
```

```
DOC>    database have been invalidated.
DOC>    Shut down and restart the database in normal mode and run utlrp.sql to
DOC>    recompile invalid objects.
SQL> SHUTDOWN IMMEDIATE
Database closed.
Database dismounted.
ORACLE instance shut down.
SQL> STARTUP
ORACLE instance started.
...
Database mounted.
Database opened.
SQL> -- The following step will recompile all PL/SQL modules.
SQL> -- It may take several hours to complete.
SQL> @/home/oracle/product/11.1.0/db_3/rdbms/admin/utlrp.sql
```

When the utlrp.sql script completes, your database transport is complete. You now
have a functioning copy of the target database on the new platform.

6. Check to make sure there are no invalidated objects left in the database:

```
SQL> select count(*) from dba_objects where
     status='INVALID';

no rows selected
SQL>
```

Sometimes, several invalid objects are in the database after the utlrp.sql script finishes
executing. To recompile the leftover invalid objects, you can run the utlrp.sql script multiple
times.

How It Works

It's important to understand that although you can use the RMAN backups from the source
database as the basis for the target database, you must still create the new instance first. As
part of the database transport, you have to move all the datafiles belonging to the permanent
tablespaces, as well as the initialization parameter file (pfile), from the source platform to the
destination platform.

If you're using a pfile for your source database, the conversion process will migrate the
pfile to the new database. If you're using an spfile instead, Oracle will first create a pfile from
this spfile and then use the pfile as the basis for creating a new spfile for the transported database (destination database).

The transportation process won't transport the following items:

- Redo logs and control files.

- Bfiles.

- Temp files. You must create a new temporary tablespace on the target platform after the
  transport is done.

- External tables and directories. You must redefine these on the target platform.

- Password files. Using the information provided in the output of the convert database command, you must create a new password file on the destination database.

Running utlrp.sql as part of the transportation script (mydb_script in our example) recompiles all the invalidated objects in the database. Even if you don't recompile the objects with this script, it is OK, since Oracle dynamically recompiles any invalidated object when you try to access it. The utlrp.sql script is invoked really to reduce latencies caused by on-the-fly recompilation of objects. Once the new database is created, it'll automatically be registered by the currently running Oracle listener process.

15-14. Transporting a Database by Converting Datafiles on the Target Platform

Problem

You want to perform a database transport but perform the datafile conversion on the target database platform instead of the source database platform.

Solution

Performing a database transport by performing the file conversion on the target platform is similar in many ways to the database transport shown in recipe 15-14, where we performed the datafile conversion on the target platform. Here are the steps:

1. Make sure the source database is eligible for transporting to the destination operating system platform by executing the dbms_tdb.check_db procedure, as shown here. The source database is running on a Windows XP platform, and the target database is running on a Linux 32-bit platform.

```
SQL> connect sys/sammyy1 as sysdba
Connected.
SQL> set serveroutput on
SQL> declare
  2> db_ready boolean;
  3> begin
  4> db_ready := dbms_tdb.check_db('Linux IA(32-bit)',
  5> dbms_tdb.skip_readonly);
  6* end;
SQL> /
PL/SQL procedure successfully completed.
SQL>
```

   If you see the message "PL/SQL procedure successfully completed," as is the case in this example, it means you can migrate from the specified operating system platform to the destination platform.

2. Since external tables aren't automatically transported to the target platform, you must invoke the dbms_tdb.check_external procedure again to get a list of the external tables that you can then use to re-create those tables on the destination platform after the database transportation.

```
SQL> declare
  2> external boolean;
  3> begin
  4> external :=dbms_tdb.check_external;
  5> end;
  6> /
PL/SQL procedure successfully completed.
SQL>
```

Again, the output of the execution of the dbms_tdb package shows that you don't have any external tables in the parent database you'll have to worry about.

3. Put the target database in read-only mode after shutting it down first and restarting it in the mount state:

```
SQL> connect sys/sammyy1 as sysdba
Connected.
SQL> shutdown immediate;
Database closed.
Database dismounted.
ORACLE instance shut down.
SQL>
SQL> startup mount;
ORACLE instance started.
Total System Global Area   612368384 bytes
Fixed Size                   1250452 bytes
Variable Size              180357996 bytes
Database Buffers           427819008 bytes
Redo Buffers                 2940928 bytes
Database mounted.
SQL> alter database open read only;
Database altered.
SQL>
```

4. Execute the convert database command on the source database platform with the on target platform clause, as shown here:

```
RMAN> convert database on target platform
  2> convert script 'c:\temp\convert\convertscript.rman'
  3> transport script 'c:\temp\convert\transportscript.sql'
  4> new database 'youdb'
  5> format 'c:\temp\convert\%U'
  6> ;

Starting convert at 21-FEB-07
```

```
using channel ORA_DISK_1
External table SH.SALES_TRANSACTIONS_EXT found in the database
Directory SYS.SUBDIR found in the database
Directory SYS.XMLDIR found in the database
Directory SYS.MEDIA_DIR found in the database
Directory SYS.LOG_FILE_DIR found in the database
Directory SYS.DATA_FILE_DIR found in the database
Directory SYS.WORK_DIR found in the database
Directory SYS.ADMIN_DIR found in the database
Directory SYS.DATA_PUMP_DIR found in the database
BFILE PM.PRINT_MEDIA found in the database
User SYS with SYSDBA and SYSOPER privilege found in password file
channel ORA_DISK_1: starting to check datafiles input datafile fno=00001
name=C:\ORACLE\PRODUCT\11.1.0\ORADATA\NICK\SYSTEM01.DBF
channel ORA_DISK_1: datafile checking complete, elapsed time: 00:00:00
...
Run SQL script C:\TEMP\CONVERT\TRANSPORTSCRIPT.SQL on the target
platform to create database
Edit init.ora file C:\TEMP\CONVERT\INIT_OOIAKAV1_1_0.ORA. This PFILE
will be used to create the database on the target platform
Run RMAN script C:\TEMP\CONVERT\CONVERTSCRIPT.RMAN on target platform
to convert datafiles
To recompile all PL/SQL modules, run utlirp.sql and utlrp.sql on the
target platform
To change the internal database identifier, use DBNEWID Utility
Finished backup at 21-FEB-07
RMAN>
```

The convert database command shown here creates three files to help in the database transport:

- A pfile to create the new database on the target platform, with identical parameters as the source database.

- A SQL script named transportscript.sql with SQL*Plus commands to create the new database. This script will first create the new instance using the pfile created here.

- A datafile conversion script named convertscript.rman to help convert the source datafiles on the target platform so they can be used by the new database you're going to create on that platform.

It's important to understand that although you use a convert database command here, no actual conversion of the datafiles takes place. That step will come after you transport the original datafiles to the target platform.

5. Copy the datafiles of the source database while that database is still in the read-only mode and move them to the target database platform.

6. Run the `convertscript.rman` script on the target database after first transporting all the source database files to the target platform. Once you copy the necessary files, you can put the source database in a read-write mode again.

7. You use a separate `convert datafile` command for each datafile you need to convert from the source to the target platform. The `format` parameter of the `convert datafile` command specifies the location of each file on the target platform.

```
$ rman target / cmdfile=CONVERTSCRIPT.RMAN
Recovery Manager: Release 11.1.0.1.0 - Beta on Thu Feb 22 11:13:09 2007
Copyright © 1982, 2005, Oracle.  All rights reserved.
connected to target database: MYDB (DBID=2561840016)
RMAN> run
2>     {
3>     convert datafile '/u01/app/oracle/youdb/temp/SYSTEM01.DBF'
4>     from platform 'Microsoft Windows IA (32-bit)'
5>     format '/u01/app/oracle/youdb/SYSTEM01.DBF';
6>
7>     convert datafile '/u01/app/oracle/youdb/temp/SYSAUX01.DBF'
8>     from platform 'Microsoft Windows IA (32-bit)'
9>   format '/u01/app/oracle/youdb/SYSAUX01.DBF';
10>
11>    convert datafile '/u01/app/oracle/youdb/temp/EXAMPLE01.DBF'
12>    from platform 'Microsoft Windows IA (32-bit)'
13>    format '/u01/app/oracle/youdb/EXAMPLE01.DBF';
14>
15>    convert datafile '/u01/app/oracle/youdb/temp/UNDOTBS01.DBF'
16>    from platform 'Microsoft Windows IA (32-bit)'
17>    format '/u01/app/oracle/youdb/UNDOTBS01.DBF';
18>
19>    convert datafile '/u01/app/oracle/youdb/temp/USERS01.DBF'
20>    from platform 'Microsoft Windows IA (32-bit)'
21>    format '/u01/app/oracle/youdb/USERS01.DBF';
22>    }

Starting backup at 22-FEB-07
using target database control file instead of recovery catalog
allocated channel: ORA_DISK_1
channel ORA_DISK_1: sid=150 devtype=DISK
channel ORA_DISK_1: starting datafile conversion
input filename=/u01/app/oracle/youdb/temp/SYSTEM01.DBF
converted datafile=/u01/app/oracle/youdb/SYSTEM01.DBF
channel ORA_DISK_1: datafile conversion complete, elapsed time: 00:00:36
Finished backup at 22-FEB-07
Starting backup at 22-FEB-07
using channel ORA_DISK_1
channel ORA_DISK_1: starting datafile conversion
input filename=/u01/app/oracle/youdb/temp/SYSAUX01.DBF
```

```
converted datafile=/u01/app/oracle/youdb/SYSAUX01.DBF
channel ORA_DISK_1: datafile conversion complete, elapsed time: 00:00:26
Finished backup at 22-FEB-07
Starting backup at 22-FEB-07
using channel ORA_DISK_1
channel ORA_DISK_1: starting datafile conversion
input filename=/u01/app/oracle/youdb/temp/EXAMPLE01.DBF
converted datafile=/u01/app/oracle/youdb/EXAMPLE01.DBF
channel ORA_DISK_1: datafile conversion complete, elapsed time: 00:00:16
Finished backup at 22-FEB-07
Starting backup at 22-FEB-07
using channel ORA_DISK_1
channel ORA_DISK_1: starting datafile conversion
input filename=/u01/app/oracle/youdb/temp/UNDOTBS01.DBF
converted datafile=/u01/app/oracle/youdb/UNDOTBS01.DBF
channel ORA_DISK_1: datafile conversion complete, elapsed time: 00:00:04
Finished backup at 22-FEB-07
Starting backup at 22-FEB-07
using channel ORA_DISK_1
channel ORA_DISK_1: starting datafile conversion
input filename=/u01/app/oracle/youdb/temp/USERS01.DBF
converted datafile=/u01/app/oracle/youdb/USERS01.DBF
channel ORA_DISK_1: datafile conversion complete, elapsed time: 00:00:02
Finished backup at 22-FEB-07
RMAN>
```

When the convertscript.rman script finishes executing, all your source database files are converted into the target database format and are ready for use by the new instance you're going to create in the next step.

8. Make the necessary changes in the pfile and the transportscript.sql script produced by the convert database script. Execute the transportscript.sql script from SQL*Plus to produce a new database instance, and create the new database (named youdb in the example):

```
$ sqlplus /nolog
SQL> @transportscript
```

The transportscript.sql script invokes the pfile to start a new instance and create the control files to open the new database youdb. The script also invokes the utlrp.sql script to recompile all the invalidated objects. When the script finishes executing, you'll have your new database on the target platform.

How It Works

If you are copying a database from the source platform to several different operating system platforms, you must convert the source database datafiles on each of the target platforms. If you're copying a production database to multiple test platforms, converting the datafiles of the parent database on each of the target platforms also eliminates the performance overhead on the production system.

Once you finish executing the convert script, the database is ready for use, and the Oracle listener process will automatically register your new instances and will accept connection requests. You must transport the unconverted, original source data files to the target platform. These datafiles are still in the format of the original platform and hence aren't suitable for use in the target platform unless they are converted to the target operating system format. The convert script (convertscript.rman) contains the actual convert datafile commands for converting each of the datafiles you transport to the target platform.

CHAPTER 16

■■■

Tuning RMAN

For most backup and recovery scenarios, you'll find that RMAN's out-of-the-box performance is quite acceptable. RMAN is a reliable and efficient tool for backing up, restoring, and recovering your database. However, sometimes (especially with large databases), you will be required to tune and increase the performance of RMAN jobs.

Listed next are the most common reasons you'll encounter for needing to tune RMAN:

- Your backups are taking too long.

- The performance of the overall system is unacceptable during backups.

- Restore and recovery operations take too long.

Before you start the tuning process, you must first clearly identify what it is that you want to accomplish and how to measure success. If you can't measure performance, then it is difficult to manage it. Without specific criteria, you won't know when you have successfully improved the job being tuned.

For example, your business may have the requirement that the production database cannot be down for more than six hours. As part of your backup and recovery strategy, you have regularly been testing how long a complete restore and recovery of your database will take. If you discover that the test environment restore times have been steadily increasing and are now taking close to six hours, you should start the tuning process.

In the situation we've just described, you would have a specific requirement that the restore and recovery operation must take less than six hours. You also have been testing and gathering metrics and can show a historical trend toward unacceptable performance. Having specific goals and a way to measure performance are the first steps toward being able to tune successfully (RMAN or otherwise).

Here are the general steps that we recommend when trying to improve backup and recovery performance:

1. Identify measurable business performance requirements.

2. Collect data and measure performance.

3. Identify bottlenecks.

4. Make adjustments that will alleviate the worst bottleneck.

5. Repeat steps 1–4 until your performance goals are achieved.

You'll have to work with your business to figure out what the specific and measurable performance goals are for your backup and recovery processes. This chapter will assist you with steps 2, 3, and 4 in the tuning process.

Before going any further, we feel compelled to point out the obvious, which is that isolated tuning of single components of your system will not necessarily lead to a holistic optimized result. Your backup and recovery performance will be impacted by the architecture of your entire system. This includes components such as the following:

- CPU

- Memory

- Operating system

- Disk layout

- Network

- Database architecture

- Tape technology and vendor

- Application design

- Design of data model and its physical implementation

- Robustness of SQL statements

In reality, you rarely have control over all aspects of your system. However, you should be aware of the system as a whole and do everything you can to work with the appropriate personnel to identify and address performance issues that aren't directly related to RMAN or Oracle. You'll also find yourself in the position of trying to convince other people (managers, evil application developers, and so on) that Oracle and RMAN are not the cause of the system performance issues. If you're not holistically aware of your system, then you won't know who else you can blame when performance issues (outside your control) crop up. Having said that (and now seriously), the primary focus of this chapter is on tuning RMAN backup and recovery operations. We'll begin by introducing you to several views that Oracle provides to monitor and measure performance. The data dictionary views described in Table 16-1 will be referenced throughout the chapter.

Table 16-1. *Useful V$ Views for RMAN Performance Tuning*

View Name	Description
V$RMAN_BACKUP_JOB_DETAILS	Reports information about backup jobs
V$BACKUP_ASYNC_IO	Displays RMAN asynchronous I/O performance information for currently running and recently completed backup and restore operations
V$BACKUP_SYNC_IO	Displays RMAN synchronous I/O performance information for currently running and recently completed backup and restore operations
V$PROCESS	Lists currently active processes

View Name	Description
V$SESSION	Displays session information for current sessions
V$SESSION_LONGOPS	Shows progress of RMAN backup, restore, and recovery operations
V$RECOVERY_PROGRESS	Shows progress of RMAN or user-managed recovery operations
V$SESSION_WAIT	Displays events or resources for which sessions are currently waiting

16-1. Identifying RMAN Processes

Problem

An RMAN backup job is running too long. You would like to identify and monitor the RMAN processes associated with the backup job.

Solution

Inspect RMAN's output messages to your terminal to identify your session identifier (SID). If you're sending output to a log file, then look for the session ID in that file.

When you start an RMAN job, you should see output similar to this on your screen. In this example, the SID is 146:

```
allocated channel: ORA_DISK_1
channel ORA_DISK_1: sid=146 devtype=DISK
```

Next, use the V$SESSION and V$PROCESS views to identify which database server sessions correspond to RMAN channels:

```
SQL> SELECT b.sid, b.serial#, a.spid, b.client_info
2  FROM v$process a, v$session b
3  WHERE a.addr = b.paddr
4  AND    b.client_info LIKE '%rman%';
```

This output shows that there is currently one RMAN channel allocated:

```
   SID    SERIAL# SPID         CLIENT_INFO
---------- ---------- ------------ --------------------------
   146        29 4376         rman channel=ORA_DISK_1
```

How It Works

When you first connect to RMAN, Oracle will start two sessions and two corresponding OS processes. There will also be a session and process started for each subsequent channel that is allocated. You can monitor and view these channel processes via the V$SESSION and V$PROCESS views.

The SID and SERIAL# values are useful when querying from other V$ views where you want to select and return rows just for your session identifier or serial number (and not hundreds of unrelated rows). The SPID column in V$PROCESS identifies the OS process ID.

You can also use set command id to label a process. This will help you identify a channel process if you have many RMAN jobs running at the same time. You must put set command id after the allocate channel command, or your specified identifier will not be included in the CLIENT_INFO output. This example sets the command ID to my_session:

```
RMAN> run{
2> allocate channel d1 type disk;
3> set command id to 'my_session';
4> backup database;
5> }
```

The output (of the previous SQL statement) now includes the ID of my_session:

```
    SID    SERIAL# SPID          CLIENT_INFO
---------- ---------- ------------ ------------------------------
    146        29 4376          id=my_session,rman channel=d1
```

16-2. Measuring Backup Performance

Problem

You want to determine whether backups are taking longer and longer.

Solution

Use information in V$RMAN_BACKUP_JOB_DETAILS for statistics on backups. The following query displays the time taken for recent backup jobs:

```
SQL> SELECT session_recid, input_bytes_per_sec_display,
2    output_bytes_per_sec_display,
3    time_taken_display, end_time
4    FROM v$rman_backup_job_details
5    ORDER BY end_time;
```

You should see output similar to the following:

```
SESSION_RECID INPUT_BYTES_PER OUTPUT_BYTES_PE TIME_TAKEN_DISPLAY   END_TIME
------------- --------------- --------------- -------------------- ---------
         1096    8.60M           7.69M           00:14:25             20-DEC-06
         1101    1.88M           1.78M           00:42:03             21-DEC-06
         1110    9.59M           8.56M           00:14:56             22-DEC-06
         1114    9.75M           8.71M           00:14:52             23-DEC-06
         1116   10.73M           9.58M           00:14:31             24-DEC-06
```

This output indicates that there might have been some sort of a snafu on December 21, possibly related to the sun being directly over the tropic of Capricorn at the time of the backup. Seriously, the job showing a duration of 42 minutes is most likely the result of a DBA doing some experimentation and running several backups interactively, from the command prompt, during one connected session, whereas the other sessions were small backup jobs that connected, ran the backup, and then disconnected from RMAN.

How It Works

Measuring the duration of your backups provides a good starting point from which you can begin tuning your RMAN backups. The V$RMAN_BACKUP_JOB_DETAILS view contains a plethora of information about backup durations and I/O rates.

■**Note** If you're using a recovery catalog, you can query RC_RMAN_BACKUP_JOB_DETAILS for the same information as found in V$RMAN_BACKUP_JOB_DETAILS. The view RC_RMAN_BACKUP_JOB_DETAIL may contain a longer history than what's available in V$RMAN_BACKUP_JOB_DETAILS.

The rows in V$RMAN_BACKUP_JOB_DETAILS are aggregated for all backup jobs that have run during a connection to RMAN. That means the first time stamp recorded is for the first backup operation that the session performs, and the last time stamp recorded is for the last backup job that was run during a session. Table 16-2 describes all the columns of V$RMAN_BACKUP_JOB_DETAILS.

Be careful about interpreting the contents of the view. The view records statistics such as the aggregated duration and number of bytes, but it does not report on what actual backup or restore commands were executed during a session.

Table 16-2. *Column Descriptions of V$RMAN_BACKUP_JOB_DETAILS*

Column	Description
SESSION_KEY	Session identifier.
SESSION_RECID	Used in combination with SESSION_STAMP to identify corresponding records in V$RMAN_OUTPUT.
SESSION_STAMP	Used in combination with SESSION_RECID to identify corresponding records in V$RMAN_OUTPUT.
COMMAND_ID	Unique command ID generated by RMAN or specified by the user with set command id.
START_TIME	Start time of first backup job run by the session.
END_TIME	End time of the last backup job run by the session.
INPUT_BYTES	Sum of all files backed up during a session.
OUTPUT_BYTES	Output size of backup pieces created during a session.
STATUS_WEIGHT	Used by Enterprise Manager.
OPTIMIZED_WEIGHT	Used by Enterprise Manager.
OBJECT_TYPE_WEIGHT	Used by Enterprise Manager.
OUTPUT_DEVICE_TYPE	DISK or SBT. If both, then *.
AUTOBACKUP_COUNT	Number of autobackups run during a session.
AUTOBACKUP_DONE	Displays YES or NO, depending on whether a control file autobackup was taken during a session.
STATUS	Status of backup job.

Continued

Table 16-2. *Continued*

Column	Description
INPUT_TYPE	Displays the file type. This won't necessarily show the last file type backed up. For example, if you run a backup database command, the type will remain DB FULL, even if you back up a different file after the backup database command was run.
OPTIMIZED	Displays YES or NO depending on whether backup optimization has been enabled and applied.
ELAPSED_SECONDS	Number of seconds.
COMPRESSION_RATIO	Compression ratio.
INPUT_BYTES_PER_SEC	Input I/O rate per second.
OUTPUT_BYTES_PER_SEC	Output I/O rate per second.
INPUT_BYTES_DISPLAY	Input bytes formatted with M for megabytes, G for gigabytes, and so on.
OUTPUT_BYTES_DISPLAY	Output bytes formatted with M for megabytes, G for gigabytes, and so on.
INPUT_BYTES_PER_SEC_DISPLAY	Input bytes/second formatted with M for megabytes, G for gigabytes, and so on.
OUTPUT_BYTES_PER_SEC_DISPLAY	Output bytes formatted with M for megabytes, G for gigabytes, and so on.
TIME_TAKEN_DISPLAY	Time for backup operation shown in the format of hours:minutes:seconds.

Refer to Table 16-3 for the view that you should use if you need to analyze backup performance information on a more granular basis than what's available in V$RMAN_BACKUP_JOB_DETAILS. The view names in Table 16-3 describe each view's content. For example, if you want to analyze what is happening at the backup set level, then V$BACKUP_SET or V$BACKUP_SET_DETAILS will provide information at that level. The RC views are available only in your recovery catalog database. The RC views can be more valuable to you in that they are capable of providing a longer history of information than the V$ views.

Table 16-3. *Description of Detailed Performance Views*

View Name	Recovery Catalog View
V$RMAN_BACKUP_SUBJOB_DETAILS	RC_RMAN_BACKUP_SUBJOB_DETAILS
V$BACKUP_SET	RC_BACKUP_SET
V$BACKUP_SET_DETAILS	RC_BACKUP_SET_DETAILS
V$BACKUP_SET_SUMMARY	RC_BACKUP_SET_SUMMARY
V$BACKUP_PIECE	RC_BACKUP_PIECE
V$BACKUP_PIECE_DETAILS	RC_BACKUP_PIECE_DETAILS
V$BACKUP_DATAFILE	RC_BACKUP_DATAFILE
V$BACKUP_DATAFILE_DETAILS	RC_BACKUP_DATAFILE_DETAILS
V$BACKUP_DATAFILE_SUMMARY	RC_BACKUP_DATAFILE_SUMMARY
V$BACKUP_FILES	RC_BACKUP_FILES

View Name	Recovery Catalog View
V$BACKUP_COPY_DETAILS	RC_BACKUP_COPY_DETAILS
V$BACKUP_COPY_SUMMARY	RC_BACKUP_COPY_SUMMARY
V$BACKUP_REDOLOG	RC_BACKUP_REDOLOG
V$BACKUP_ARCHIVELOG_DETAILS	RC_BACKUP_ARCHIVELOG_DETAILS
V$BACKUP_ARCHIVELOG_SUMMARY	RC_BACKUP_ARCHIVELOG_SUMMARY
V$BACKUP_CONTROLFILE_DETAILS	RC_BACKUP_CONTROLFILE_DETAILS
V$BACKUP_CONTROLFILE_SUMMARY	RC_BACKUP_CONTROLFILE_SUMMARY
V$BACKUP_SPFILE	RC_BACKUP_SPFILE
V$BACKUP_SPFILE_DETAILS	RC_BACKUP_SPFILE_DETAILS
V$BACKUP_SPFILE_SUMMARY	RC_BACKUP_SPFILE_SUMMARY

QUERYING FROM RC_BACKUP_FILES

If you get an ORA-20021 error when querying RC_BACKUP_FILES, you'll need to call the
DBMS_RCVMAN.SETDATABASE procedure to resolve this problem. Follow the steps outlined
in this sidebar to do this. These steps are also documented in Oracle's MetaLink note 363125.1.

1. First connect to SQL*Plus in your recovery catalog database as the recovery catalog owner:

```
SQL> connect rcat/rcat@rcat
SQL> select count(*) from rc_backup_files;
*
ERROR at line 1:
ORA-20021: database not set
```

2. To fix this issue, call the DBMS_RCVMAN package. The fourth parameter to the SETDATABASE
procedure needs to be your *target* database ID:

```
SQL> call dbms_rcvman.setdatabase(null, null, null, 378401810, null);
SQL> select count(*) from rc_backup_files;

  COUNT(*)
----------
       205
```

16-3. Monitoring RMAN Job Progress

Problem

You have a long-running RMAN job, and you wonder how much longer it will take to complete.

Solution

To monitor the progress of an RMAN backup or restore command, query V$SESSION_
LONGOPS via SQL*Plus while connected as a schema with sysdba privileges:

```
SQL> select sid, serial#, sofar, totalwork, opname,
2        round(sofar/totalwork*100,2) "% Complete"
3    from   v$session_longops
4    where  opname LIKE 'RMAN%'
5    and    opname NOT LIKE '%aggregate%'
6    and    totalwork != 0
7    and    sofar <> totalwork;
```

You should now see some output similar to the following:

```
SID SERIAL#    SOFAR  TOTALWORK OPNAME                           % Complete
--- -------  -------- --------- ------------------------------ ----------
136       7      3259     51840 RMAN: full datafile backup           6.29
141      57     28671     74880 RMAN: full datafile backup          38.29
```

Oracle also provides a view, V$RECOVERY_PROGRESS, that reports on just the recovery operations (either RMAN or user-managed). This view is a subview of the V$SESSION_
LONGOPS view. To report on the progress of a recover command, you can run a SQL query as shown here:

```
SQL> select type, item, units, sofar, total from v$recovery_progress;
```

The following output shows (amongst other things) that only 3 out of 229 archive redo logs have been applied in the recovery process:

```
TYPE            ITEM                     UNITS          SOFAR      TOTAL
--------------- ------------------------ ---------- ---------- ----------
Media Recovery  Log Files                Files               3        229
Media Recovery  Active Apply Rate        KB/sec           3425          0
Media Recovery  Average Apply Rate       KB/sec           3861          0
Media Recovery  Redo Applied             Megabytes         449          0
Media Recovery  Last Applied Redo        SCN+Time      1415101          0
Media Recovery  Active Time              Seconds            81          0
Media Recovery  Apply Time per Log       Seconds             0          0
Media Recovery  Checkpoint Time per Log  Seconds             0          0
Media Recovery  Elapsed Time             Seconds           119          0
```

How It Works

The V$SESSION_LONGOPS view contains information about long-running jobs (SQL statements, RMAN operations, and so on) in your database. You can use this view to monitor the progress of RMAN backup, restore, and recovery operations.

Often it's useful to join V$SESSION_LONGOPS to both V$SESSION and V$PROCESS. This query allows you to see the RMAN channel session ID and the OS process ID:

```
select s.client_info,
       sl.opname,
       sl.message,
       sl.sid, sl.serial#, p.spid,
       sl.sofar, sl.totalwork,
       round(sl.sofar/sl.totalwork*100,2) "% Complete"
from   v$session_longops sl, v$session s, v$process p
where  p.addr = s.paddr
and    sl.sid=s.sid
and    sl.serial#=s.serial#
and    opname LIKE 'RMAN%'
and    opname NOT LIKE '%aggregate%'
and    totalwork != 0
and    sofar <> totalwork;
```

For RMAN jobs, the view V$SESSION_LONGOPS contains two types of rows:

- Aggregate

- Detailed

Aggregate rows capture the progress of the backup or restore operation as each job step completes. A job step is the creation or restore of a backup set or image copy. Aggregate rows are updated only after the completion of each job step in the backup or restore operation.

Detailed rows show the progress of individual job steps. Typically several datafiles are associated with one job step. Detailed rows are updated after every buffer I/O associated with the restore or recover operation.

If your backup or restore command is interacting with several backup sets, then you may want to report at an aggregate level. To report at the aggregate level, run a query similar to the one shown next:

```
SQL> select sid, serial#, sofar, totalwork,opname,
  2         round(sofar/totalwork*100,2) "% Complete"
  3  from   v$session_longops
  4  where  opname LIKE 'RMAN%aggregate%'
  5  and    totalwork != 0
  6  and    sofar <> totalwork;
```

Table 16-4 describes several of the columns of V$SESSION_LONGOPS that you will find useful in relation to RMAN jobs.

Table 16-4. *Column Descriptions of V$SESSION_LONGOPS Applicable to RMAN*

Column	Description
SID	The server session identifier that corresponds to an RMAN channel
SERIAL#	The server session serial number
OPNAME	Description of the operation being performed
SOFAR	The units of work completed so far
TOTALWORK	The total units of work to be completed
UNITS	Unit of measurement (blocks, files, seconds, KB/sec, and so on)
START_TIME	The time the job started
TIME_REMAINING	Estimate in seconds of time remaining for job to complete
ELAPSED_SECONDS	The number of elapsed seconds since the job began
MESSAGE	Message describing job and progress
USERNAME	User who started the job, which is always sys for RMAN operations because you can connect to the target database only using an account with the sysdba privilege

You can use the V$RECOVERY_PROGRESS view to monitor the progress of recovery operations (either RMAN or user-managed). Table 16-5 shows all the columns of this view.

Table 16-5. *Column Descriptions of all Columns in V$RECOVERY_PROGRESS*

Column	Description
START_TIME	Time the recovery operation was initiated.
TYPE	Type of recovery.
ITEM	Item being monitored.
UNITS	The unit of measurement. This varies by operation. Common units for restore operations are files and seconds.
SOFAR	Amount of work done so far for the operation.
TOTAL	Total amount of work expected for the operation.
TIMESTAMP	Time stamp.

16-4. Identifying I/O Bottlenecks

Problem

You want to determine I/O bottlenecks in your RMAN backup and recovery jobs.

Solution

Query V$BACKUP_ASYNC_IO and V$BACKUP_SYNC_IO to determine I/O bottlenecks. Ideally, the EFFECTIVE_BYTES_PER_SECOND column should return a rate that is close to the capacity of the backup device. The following query returns statistics for asynchronous I/O for backup and restore operations that have occurred within the last seven days:

```
SQL> SELECT sid, serial, filename, type, elapsed_time, effective_bytes_per_second
2  FROM v$backup_async_io
3  WHERE close_time > sysdate - 7;
```

If you have identified your SID and SERIAL number (see recipe 16-1), you can specifically query for records associated with your current session:

```
SQL> SELECT filename, sid, serial, close_time, long_waits/io_count as ratio
2  FROM    v$backup_async_io
3  WHERE   type != 'AGGREGATE'
4  AND     SID = &SID
5  AND     SERIAL = &SERIAL
6  ORDER BY ratio desc;
```

If you are using tape drives, then query the EFFECTIVE_BYTES_PER_SECOND column of V$BACKUP_SYNC_IO. If the effective rate is less than the tape device's maximum throughput, then this may indicate that your tape device is not streaming (continuously writing).

For tape devices, you can also identify bottlenecks by using the backup validate command. You can compare the time it takes for a regular backup job to tape versus just a backup validate command. A backup validate command performs the same reads as a regular backup but does not write to tape. If the time to perform a backup validate is significantly less than a regular backup job to tape, then writing to tape is most likely the bottleneck.

How It Works

Most operating systems now support asynchronous I/O. When backing up to disk, asynchronous I/O is advantageous because a server process can perform more than one I/O operation at a time. Contrast that to synchronous I/O, where the server process has to wait for each I/O operation to complete before starting the next I/O operation.

The initialization parameter disk_asynch_io controls Oracle's asynchronous behavior. If your operating system supports asynchronous I/O, then Oracle recommends that you leave this parameter set to its default value of TRUE. Oracle will take advantage of asynchronous I/O if it's available. If asynchronous I/O is not available with your operating system, then you can tune I/O performance by setting the dbwr_io_slaves initialization parameter to a nonzero value.

■**Note** Enabling multiple I/O slaves will increase the number of processes that your database uses. You will need to adjust the processes initialization parameter accordingly.

You can use two views to monitor asynchronous and synchronous I/O. As its name implies, V$BACKUP_ASYNC_IO contains information for asynchronous backup or restore operations. Likewise, V$BACKUP_SYNC_IO contains information for synchronous operations. For each backup or restore operation, you will see a row in the view for the following events:

- Each datafile read or written

- Each backup piece read or written

- An aggregate record for overall performance of files read or written during an operation

The TYPE column of V$BACKUP_ASYNC_IO and V$BACKUP_SYNC_IO can have the following values: INPUT for files read, OUTPUT for files written, and AGGREGATE for aggregated rows.

The EFFECTIVE_BYTES_PER_SECOND column specifies the read/write rate for the backup or restore operation. For aggregated rows, the EFFECTIVE_BYTES_PER_SECOND should be close to the maximum throughput of the backup device. If the value of EFFECTIVE_BYTES_PER_SECOND is significantly less than the backup device's maximum I/O rate, then you probably have a system performance issue with something other than your database (like a busy CPU).

■**Note** The V$BACKUP_ASYNC_IO and V$BACKUP_SYNC_IO views have information only since the last time your instance was started.

RMAN will record information about asynchronous backup operations to V$BACKUP_ASYNC_IO. Table 16-6 describes the columns of this view.

Table 16-6. *Column Descriptions of V$BACKUP_ASYNC_IO*

Column	Description
SID	ID of the session doing backup or restore operation.
SERIAL	The use count for the session doing the backup or restore.
USE_COUNT	Identifies rows from different backup sets.
RMAN_STATUS_RECID	Record ID that corresponds to the record in V$RMAN_STATUS.
RMAN_STATUS_STAMP	Record stamp that corresponds to the record in V$RMAN_STATUS.
DEVICE_TYPE	Device type of where the file being backed up or the restore is located.
TYPE	INPUT, OUTPUT, or AGGREGATE.
STATUS	NOT STARTED, IN PROGRESS, or FINISHED.
FILENAME	Name of file used in read/write operation.
SET_COUNT	Set count of the backup set.
SET_STAMP	Set stamp of the backup set.
BUFFER_SIZE	Size of buffer (in bytes) used to read/write the file.
BUFFER_COUNT	Number of buffers used for read/write.
TOTAL_BYTES	Total number of bytes used for read/write.
OPEN_TIME	Time file was opened. If TYPE is AGGREGATE, then this is the time the first file was opened.
CLOSE_TIME	Time file was closed. If TYPE is AGGREGATE, then this is the time the last file was closed.
ELAPSED_TIME	Time (in hundredths of seconds) that the file was open.
MAXOPENFILES	When TYPE is AGGREGATE, this is the number of open files.

Column	Description
BYTES	Number of byes read/written.
EFFECTIVE_BYTES_PER_SECOND	Read/write rate for device during backup or restore.
IO_COUNT	Number of reads/writes to file.
READY	Number of asynchronous requests for which a buffer was immediately ready.
SHORT_WAITS	Number of times a buffer was not immediately ready but became available after nonblocking poll for read/write completion.
SHORT_WAIT_TIME_TOTAL	Time (in hundredths of seconds) taken by nonblocking polls for read/write completion.
SHORT_WAIT_TIME_MAX	Maximum time (in hundredths of seconds) for a nonblocking poll for read/write completion.
LONG_WAITS	The number of times a buffer wasn't immediately available and became available after blocking wait issued.
LONG_WAIT_TIME_TOTAL	Total time (in hundredths of seconds) taken by blocking wait for read/write completion.
LONG_WAIT_TIME_MAX	Maximum time (in hundredths of seconds) taken for a blocking wait for read/write completion.

If your operating system or backup device (such as a tape drive) doesn't support asynchronous I/O, then you can use V$BACKUP_SYNC_IO for diagnosing I/O bottlenecks.

■**Note** Refer to Oracle's operating system–specific documentation to determine whether your operating system supports asynchronous I/O.

Table 16-7 describes the columns of V$BACKUP_SYNC_IO. Many of the columns are the same as V$BACKUP_ASYNC_IO, but there are several notable differences.

Table 16-7. *Column Descriptions of V$BACKUP_SYNC_IO*

Column	Description
SID	ID of the session doing backup or restore operation.
SERIAL	The use count for the session doing the backup or restore.
USE_COUNT	Identifies rows from different backup sets.
RMAN_STATUS_RECID	Record ID that corresponds to the record in V$RMAN_STATUS.
RMAN_STATUS_STAMP	Record stamp that corresponds to the record in V$RMAN_STATUS.
DEVICE_TYPE	Device type of where the file being backed up or restore is located.
TYPE	INPUT, OUTPUT, or AGGREGATE.
STATUS	NOT STARTED, IN PROGRESS, or FINISHED.

Continued

Table 16-7. *Continued*

Column	Description
FILENAME	Name of file used in read/write operation.
SET_COUNT	Set count of the backup set.
SET_STAMP	Set stamp of the backup set.
BUFFER_SIZE	Size of buffer (in bytes) used to read/write the file.
BUFFER_COUNT	Number of buffers used for read/write.
TOTAL_BYTES	Total number of bytes used for read/write.
OPEN_TIME	Time file was opened. If TYPE is AGGREGATE, then this is the time the first file was opened.
CLOSE_TIME	Time file was closed. If TYPE is AGGREGATE, then this is the time the last file was closed.
ELAPSED_TIME	Time (in hundredths of seconds) that the file was open.
MAXOPENFILES	When TYPE is AGGREGATE, this is the number of open files.
BYTES	Number of byes read/written.
EFFECTIVE_BYTES_PER_SECOND	Read/write rate for device during backup or restore.
IO_COUNT	Number of reads/writes to file.
IO_TIME_TOTAL	Total time (in hundredths of seconds) for I/O on a file.
IO_TIME_MAX	Maximum time taken for an I/O.
DISCRETE_BYTES_PER_SECOND	Average transfer rate for a file.

16-5. Improving Tape I/O Performance

Problem

You have identified your tape drive as an I/O performance bottleneck (see recipe 16-4). You want to improve RMAN's I/O performance with your tape device.

Solution

We have two recommendations for improving RMAN's I/O performance with tape devices:

- Use an incremental backup strategy with block change tracking.

- Adjust multiplexing of backup sets.

The RMAN incremental block change tracking backup strategy is detailed in recipe 7-11. For information about multiplexing backup sets, refer to recipe 16-6.

How It Works

Improving tape I/O can be difficult because many of the variables are not dependent on RMAN. Some factors are dependent on the tape device and Media Management Layer (MML) software. Here are some variables to consider when tuning tape I/O:

- MML software configuration

- Network configuration

- Level of tape compression

- Tape streaming

- Tape block size

Variables that you can control from RMAN are your incremental backup strategy and the level of multiplexing. If your tape device is not streaming (continuously writing), then consider using an incremental backup strategy. Incremental backups usually have fewer writes than full backups and therefore should lessen the bottleneck writing to tape.

The block change tracking feature enables RMAN to quickly identify which blocks have changed since the last incremental backup. This feature can significantly improve the performance of incremental backups.

Also, consider altering the default multiplexing behavior of RMAN. Setting filesperset high and maxopenfiles low may increase the efficiency of writing to your tape device. You can also use the diskratio parameter to instruct RMAN to balance the load if datafiles are distributed across several different disks. See recipe 16-6 for details on how to adjust the multiplexing of backup sets.

■**Note** In Oracle9*i* Database and older, you can set the RMAN blksize parameter to manually adjust the block size that RMAN uses to write to tape. See MetaLink note 107213.1 for more details. This parameter has been deprecated in RMAN in Oracle Database10*g*.

16-6. Maximizing Throughput to Backup Device

Problem

You suspect that your backup device is a bottleneck for backup operations. You want to adjust the throughput to the backup device.

Solution

You can tune the throughput to backup devices by adjusting RMAN's level of multiplexing. RMAN multiplexing is controlled by three parameters:

- filesperset

- maxopenfiles

- diskratio

Using filesperset

Use the `fileperset` clause of the `backup` command to limit the number of datafiles in each backup set. For example, if you wanted to limit the number of files being written to a backup set to only two files, you would use `filesperset`, as shown here:

```
RMAN> backup database filesperset 2;
```

Using maxopenfiles

Use the `maxopenfiles` clause of the `configure channel` command or the `allocate channel` command to limit the number of files that can be simultaneously open for reads during a backup. If you want to limit the number of files being read by a channel to two files, use `maxopenfiles` as follows:

```
RMAN> configure channel 1 device type disk maxopenfiles 2;
```

To reset the channel `maxopenfiles` back to the default setting, use the `clear` parameter as shown here:

```
RMAN> configure channel 1 device type disk clear;
```

Using diskratio

The `diskratio` parameter of the `backup` command instructs RMAN to read datafiles from a specified number of disks. For example, if you wanted RMAN to include datafiles located on at least four different disks into one backup set, then use `diskratio` as follows:

```
RMAN> backup database diskratio 4;
```

If you specify `filesperset`, and not `diskratio`, then `diskratio` will default to the value of `filesperset`. The `diskratio` parameter works only on operating systems that can provide RMAN with information such as disk contention and node affinity.

How It Works

Multiplexing backup sets is RMAN's ability to read multiple datafiles simultaneously and write them to the same physical backup piece file. The *level of multiplexing* is defined by the number of files read simultaneously.

As of Oracle Database 10*g*, RMAN will automatically tune the level of multiplexing of your backup sets. RMAN will automatically divide the files being read during a backup across the available channels. Therefore, under most conditions you will not be required to tune throughput. If you're working with tape devices, you may need to adjust the parameters described in this recipe to ensure that writes to tape are continuously streaming. Setting `filesperset` high and `maxopenfiles` low may increase the efficiency of writing to your tape device.

You can alter the default levels of multiplexing by using the `filesperset` and `maxopenfiles` parameters. The value of `filesperset` specifies the maximum number of files in each backup set. The default value of `filesperset` is as follows:

```
MIN(64, # of files to be backed up divided by the numbers of channels allocated)
```

For example, if you had 12 datafiles in your database and allocated two channels, then the number of files in each backup piece would be 6.

The default value of maxopenfiles is as follows:

```
MIN(8, # files being backed up)
```

This places a limit on the number of files that RMAN can read in parallel. For example, if you set maxopenfiles for a channel to 2, then only two datafiles would be read and then written to the backup piece at a time (for that channel).

16-7. Setting Large Pool Memory Size

Problem

You're using I/O slaves, and you're aware that RMAN can take advantage of memory in the large pool when using I/O slaves. You want to ensure that the large pool is sized correctly.

Solution

Use the Automatic Shared Memory Management (ASMM) feature to have Oracle automatically manage the allocation of memory pools. To enable ASMM, do the following:

1. Ensure that the initialization parameter statistics_level is set to TYPICAL (the default) or ALL.

2. Set sga_target to an appropriate nonzero value for your database not exceeding the sga_max_size.

3. Set the following initialization parameters to zero:

    - shared_pool_size

    - large_pool_size

    - java_pool_size

    - db_cache_size

    - streams_pool_size

Once you enable ASMM, Oracle will automatically size and adjust those memory pools for you. You can set any of these values manually to enforce a minimum amount of memory used for the specified pool.

If you want to manually set the large pool size, here is Oracle's recommended formula for sizing it:

```
large_pool_size = num_of_allocated_channels * (16 MB + (4 * size_of_tape_buffer ))
```

How It Works

You need to set the large pool size only if you've enabled I/O slaves via one of the following parameters: dbwr_io_slaves or backup_tape_io_slaves. If you are not using those parameters, then you don't need to worry about setting up an area for the large pool.

When I/O slaves are enabled, RMAN will use memory in the large pool if it is allocated; otherwise, it will allocate memory in the shared pool. If you're using I/O slaves, we recommend that you enable a large pool to avoid contention in the shared pool. If you're not using I/O slaves, then RMAN will not use the large pool.

Normally, you would not enable I/O slaves because most operating systems now support asynchronous I/O. You would enable I/O slaves only if you're working with devices that don't support asynchronous I/O.

We recommend that you use Oracle's ASMM feature and have Oracle automatically allocate memory to the large pool (and other memory pools) for you. This way, you avoid having to manually set and adjust memory components.

16-8. Tuning Media Recovery

Problem

You want to manually adjust the degree of parallelism that Oracle uses for media recovery to match the number of CPUs on your database server.

Solution

Starting with Oracle Database 10g, when you issue an RMAN recover command from either within RMAN or within SQL*Plus, Oracle's default behavior is to automatically perform media recovery operations in parallel. However, if you want to override this default behavior, you can use the recover parallel or recover noparallel command. This next line of code instructs Oracle to spawn four parallel processes to apply redo:

```
RMAN> recover database parallel 4;
```

If you don't want Oracle to recover in parallel, then specify the noparallel clause as shown here:

```
RMAN> recover database noparallel;
```

How It Works

Ordinarily you don't need to adjust the degree of parallelism for media recovery. This is because Oracle automatically parallelizes media recovery for you. Oracle determines the number of parallel processes to spawn for media recovery from the initialization parameter cpu_count. This parameter is set by default to the number of CPUs on your database server.

For example, if your server has two CPUS, then by default cpu_count will be set to 2 when you create your database. For this server, Oracle will spawn two processes to apply redo anytime you issue a recover command (from either RMAN or SQL*Plus).

Oracle's documentation states that systems with efficient asynchronous I/O see little benefit from parallel media recovery. You should test whether adjusting the degree of parallelism improves performance before you attempt this in a production environment.

■**Note** The initialization parameter `recovery_parallelism` has no effect on media recovery. The `recovery_parallelism` parameter affects only crash recovery.

16-9. Tuning Crash Recovery

Problem

You want to ensure that your database comes up as efficiently as possible after you issue a `shutdown abort` command or experience a hard crash. You want to specify a target duration time for any crash recovery that is needed as a result of an instance crash or a `shutdown abort` command.

Solution

The `fast_start_mttr_target` initialization parameter allows you to specify a target value in seconds that denotes the amount of time that you want Oracle to take to perform crash recovery. To determine an appropriate value for this parameter, follow this procedure:

1. Disable the initialization parameters that interfere with `fast_start_mttr_target`.

2. Determine the lower bound for `fast_start_mttr_target`.

3. Determine the upper bound for `fast_start_mttr_target`.

4. Select a value within the upper and lower bounds.

5. Monitor and adjust.

The following subsections provide more detail on this procedure.

■**Note** Although you can specify a target duration using `fast_start_mttr_target`, be aware that the database software treats that target as a "best-effort" target. Depending upon the circumstances, the actual time to perform crash recovery might be more or less than the target.

Step 1: Disable Parameters

Ensure that `fast_start_io_target`, `log_checkpoint_interval`, and `log_checkpoint_timeout` are all set to 0. These parameters will interfere with `fast_start_mttr_target`.

Step 2: Determine the Lower Bound

Set `fast_start_mttr_target` to a value of 1, and then stop and start your database. This example assumes you are using an spfile; if you aren't, then you will have to manually modify your init.ora file.

```
SQL> alter system set fast_start_mttr_target=1;
SQL> shutdown immediate;
SQL> startup;
```

Immediately query the TARGET_MTTR value from V$INSTANCE_RECOVERY, as shown here:

```
SQL> select target_mttr from v$instance_recovery;

TARGET_MTTR
-----------
         52
```

For this database, 52 seconds is a practical lower bound for fast_start_mttr_target.

Step 3: Determine the Upper Bound

Set fast_start_mttr_target to a value of 3600, and then stop and start your database. This example assumes you are using an spfile; if you aren't, then you will have to manually modify your init.ora file.

```
SQL> alter system set fast_start_mttr_target=3600;
SQL> shutdown immediate;
SQL> startup;
```

Immediately query the TARGET_MTTR value from V$INSTANCE_RECOVERY, as shown here:

```
SQL> select target_mttr from v$instance_recovery;

TARGET_MTTR
-----------
        377
```

For this database, 377 seconds is a practical upper bound for fast_start_mttr_target.

Step 4: Select a Value

Choose a value that is between the lower and upper bounds. In this example, we would probably choose a value of 60 seconds because we want to minimize the mean time to recovery after a database crash.

Step 5: Monitor and Adjust

Use the MTTR advisor to monitor and adjust the setting for fast_start_mttr_target. To enable the MTTR advisor, ensure that the following are in place:

- The statistics_level initialization parameter is set to TYPICAL (default) or ALL.

- The fast_start_mttr_target initialization parameter is set to a nonzero value.

After your database has experienced a normal amount of activity, you can query V$MTTR_TARGET_ADVICE as follows:

```
SQL> SELECT
2    mttr_target_for_estimate, advice_status, estd_cache_writes, estd_total_ios
3    from v$mttr_target_advice
4    order by 1;
```

The following output shows values of writes and I/O for each estimated value of fast_start_mttr_target:

MTTR_TARGET_FOR_ESTIMATE	ADVIC	ESTD_CACHE_WRITES	ESTD_TOTAL_IOS
52	ON	1811	11030
130	ON	1575	10794
209	ON	1575	10794
288	ON	1575	10794
377	ON	1575	10794

Notice that the practical values for the lower and upper bounds are populated in this view along with four other records of possible values for fast_start_mttr_target. This output shows that the estimated number of total I/Os required for crash recovery goes down slightly as you move upward from the lower bound. This indicates that there won't be a large penalty in terms of I/O for setting the value of fast_start_mttr_target to a value close to the lower bound.

How It Works

The fast_start_mttr_target parameter allows you to configure how many seconds you want to allow for your database to perform crash recovery after an instance crash (like after a shutdown abort). This parameter takes a range of values from 0 to 3600 seconds (60 minutes).

Setting fast_start_mttr_target enables Oracle's *fast-start fault recovery* feature. For this feature to work properly, you must disable these initialization parameters (by setting them to zero): fast_start_io_target, log_checkpoint_interval, and log_checkpoint_timeout. If for any reason you don't want to use fast-start checkpointing, then simply set these parameters back to their nonzero values.

Fast-start fault recovery relies heavily on *fast-start checkpointing*. Conventional checkpointing uses bulk writes of modified blocks from memory to disk. Fast-start checkpointing incrementally writes modified buffers to disk, thus eliminating I/O spikes and providing a more predictable time used for crash recovery.

To monitor and tune fast-start checkpointing, use the V$MTTR_TARGET_ADVICE view. Table 16-8 describes all the columns of V$MTTR_TARGET_ADVICE.

Table 16-8. *Column Descriptions of V$MTTR_TARGET_ADVICE*

Column	Description
MTTR_TARGET_FOR_ESTIMATE	Mean time to recovery setting being simulated
ADVICE_STATUS	Status of MTTR advice (ON, READY, or OFF)
DIRTY_LIMIT	Dirty buffer limit for estimated MTTR
ESTD_CACHE_WRITES	Estimated number of physical cache writes for estimated MTTR
ESTD_CACHE_WRITE_FACTOR	Ratio of estimated cache writes to number of cache writes for current MTTR
ESTD_TOTAL_WRITES	Estimated number of physical writes for estimated MTTR
ESTD_TOTAL_WRITE_FACTOR	Ratio of estimated writes to total number of writes for current MTTR
ESTD_TOTAL_IOS	Estimated number of total I/Os for estimated MTTR
ESTD_TOTAL_IO_FACTOR	Ratio of estimated total number of I/Os to total number of I/Os for current MTTR

16-10. Slowing RMAN Down

Problem

You've noticed that your application performance degrades when the RMAN backups are running. You want to reduce RMAN's I/O rate so that it spreads out its impact on the system over a period of time.

Solution

Use one of the following to control RMAN's I/O rate:

- The backup duration ... minimize load command

- The rate clause of the allocate channel or configure channel command

Using backup duration ... minimize load

Use the backup duration ... minimize load command to evenly distribute RMAN I/O over a period of time. This example shows how to spread the I/O of an RMAN backup over a 45-minute period:

```
RMAN> backup duration 00:45 minimize load database;
```

RMAN will report the time taken for the backup operation in the output, as shown in this snippet:

```
channel ORA_DISK_1: throttle time: 0:44:43
Finished backup at 10-MAR-07
```

Using rate

You can also use the rate clause of the allocate channel command or the configure channel command to control RMAN's I/O rate. This example configures channel 1 to have a maximum read rate of 5MB per second:

```
RMAN> configure channel 1 device type disk rate=5M;
```

The rate can be set using M, K, or G (for megabytes, kilobytes, and gigabytes).

How It Works

The duration clause specifies the amount of time you want an RMAN backup to take. When you use the minimize load clause, this instructs RMAN to spread out the I/O load over the duration of the specified time. When minimizing the load, RMAN will monitor and adjust the I/O rate so that the resources are consumed evenly across the duration of the backup. The format for the time value of the duration clause is HH:MM (HH is hours and MM is minutes). You must specify the hour and colon components of the time even if the hour component is zero.

If a backup does not complete within the specified duration period, then RMAN will abort the backup. If you are running backup commands from within a run{} block, then RMAN will not execute subsequent commands. You can use the partial clause to instruct RMAN to continue running subsequent commands within a run{} block (even if the backup doesn't finish in the specified time).

In this example, the partial clause instructs RMAN to execute all subsequent commands in the run{} block even if the first command doesn't finish within the specified time:

```
RMAN {
2>  backup duration 1:00 partial minimize load database;
3>  backup archivelog all;
3>  backup current controlfile;
4>  }
```

Whether you use the partial clause or not, RMAN will still consider any backup sets that were created successfully (before the time limit was exceeded) to be usable for restore operations. If you want to force RMAN to include only one datafile per backup set, then you can use the filesperset parameter as shown here:

```
RMAN> backup duration 01:00 minimize load database filesperset 1;
```

When you set the filesperset parameter to 1, it forces RMAN to create each backup set with only one datafile within it. Any backup sets that complete before the duration time is exceeded will be marked as successful.

■**Note** Oracle does not recommend using backup duration ... minimize load when using tape devices. When using minimize load, RMAN could reduce its I/O to a rate that is too low to keep the tape device streaming.

You can also instruct to minimize the time that RMAN takes to perform a backup. This example instructs RMAN to try to complete the backup in two minutes or less:

```
RMAN> backup duration 0:02 minimize time database;
```

Minimizing time is default behavior, and this instructs RMAN to back up as quickly as possible within the specified time. When you use the `minimize time` clause, RMAN will prioritize the files to be backed up, giving the most recently backed up datafile the lowest priority.

■Tip If you use Oracle Data Guard, consider a strategy where you use RMAN to take backups of the physical standby database. This will give the same protection as backing up your primary database but will offload the impact of RMAN backups from the primary database server to the standby database server.

16-11. Improving Performance Through Parallelism

Problem

You want to improve RMAN performance by utilizing multiple I/O channels.

Solution

Use the `parallel` clause of the `configure` command to instruct RMAN to allocate multiple channels for backup and restore operations. The following command instructs RMAN to automatically allocate four channels for the default disk device:

```
RMAN> configure device type disk parallelism 4;
```

How It Works

An easy way to improve performance is to allocate multiple channels for backup and restore operations. If your database has datafiles that physically exist across different disks, then using multiple channels can significantly reduce the time required to back up and restore your database.

The default degree of parallelism for a channel is 1 (and can be up to 254). If you change the degree of parallelism, RMAN will start the number of server sessions to match the degree of parallelism that you specify. For example, if you specify a degree of parallelism of 4, then RMAN will start four server sessions for that channel.

A good rule of thumb to follow is to have the degree of parallelism match the number of physical devices. For example, if you have datafiles distributed over four physical drives, then a parallelism degree of 4 would be appropriate. If you have only one physical drive, then setting the degree of parallelism to a higher value generally does not help improve performance.

To view the degree of parallelism for the default device type, use the `show device type` command as shown here:

```
RMAN> show device type;

RMAN configuration parameters are:
CONFIGURE DEVICE TYPE DISK PARALLELISM 4 BACKUP TYPE TO BACKUPSET;
```

You can configure channel devices to back up to different locations on disk as shown here:

```
RMAN> configure channel 1 device type disk format '/ora01/backup/rman%U.bak';
RMAN> configure channel 2 device type disk format '/ora02/backup/rman%U.bak';
RMAN> configure channel 3 device type disk format '/ora03/backup/rman%U.bak';
RMAN> configure channel 4 device type disk format '/ora04/backup/rman%U.bak';
```

In this case, if you configure the degree of parallelism to 4, then RMAN will spread the backup pieces across the four configured channels. If you set the degree of parallelism to 1, then RMAN will back up only to the first channel device defined (even though you have configured four channels).

You can view the channel configuration information as shown here:

```
RMAN> show channel;
```

■**Note** If you are using a flash recovery area and manually configuring channels, then you may end up with some backup pieces in your flash recovery area and some backup pieces located in the directories specified during manual channel configuration. For example, if you manually configure two channels and specify a degree of parallelism of 4 (and are using a flash recovery area), then RMAN will write backup pieces to the two manually configured disk locations as well as creating two backup pieces in the flash recovery area.

16-12. Improving Performance Using Incremental Features

Problem

You wonder whether you can improve performance by using one or more of RMAN's incremental backup features.

Solution

RMAN provides three main incremental backup features:

- Incremental backups
- Change tracking
- Incremental update

Table 16-9 describes how each feature can improve performance with backup and restore operations. You'll have to test these features in your environment to see whether they give you the desired performance boost.

Table 16-9. *Matrix of Incremental Features Available to Increase RMAN Performance*

	Incremental Backups	Change Tracking	Incremental Update
Backup	Reduces disk space and time writing to the backup device. This is a good choice when most of your blocks aren't updated often. See recipe 7-10 for details.	Significantly improves performance when using incremental backups. See recipe 7-11 for details.	Backup time becomes proportional to amount of redo generated. See recipe 7-27 for details.
Restore	Dependent on number of incremental backups taken since Level 0 backups.	N/A	Significantly decreases time required to restore database.

How It Works

Incremental backups are a good choice for databases in which a small percentage of blocks are updated from one backup to next. Incremental backups would be less ideal for databases in which most of the blocks are updated between backups.

You can significantly improve the performance of incremental backups by using change tracking. Change tracking can slightly decrease the performance of your database activities (because Oracle has to keep track of which blocks are changing). However, if the performance of backups is paramount, then you should consider implementing this feature.

If you want to minimize the mean time to recovery, you should consider using the RMAN incremental update feature. Incremental updates use image copies as a basis for the backup. Restoring a datafile from an image copy is much more efficient than restoring from a backup set. This is because an image copy is an identical copy of the datafile and RMAN can simply copy the image to the location from where it was backed up.

Troubleshooting RMAN

Not many things are more vexing to a DBA than experiencing problems when backing up and recovering a mission-critical database. The good news is that RMAN is a tried-and-true backup and recovery tool. RMAN has been available since version 8.0. Many companies now use RMAN as their backup and recovery (B&R) solution. As a result, vast sources of RMAN information are available (websites, white papers, presentations, forums, user groups, and so on). This means you can *usually* find somebody else who has already encountered the problem you're facing.

For example, if you visit Oracle's RMAN technical forum website, you'll see that there have been thousands of postings for problems that DBAs have encountered. We can't cover all these potential RMAN issues and corresponding solutions in a book. However, we can cover helpful RMAN troubleshooting techniques and some of the more common types of problems you'll encounter. We begin by helping you determine where to look for answers when facing an RMAN issue.

17-1. Determining Where to Start

Problem

You just issued an RMAN command, and it returned a long error stack message. You wonder where to start to resolve the issue.

Solution

When dealing with RMAN issues, here are the general steps that we recommend you follow to resolve problems:

1. Start at the bottom of the error stack and work your way back up until you spot the most relevant error message(s).

2. If you suspect the problem is a syntax error, use the checksyntax option as described in recipe 4-15, or look in Oracle's RMAN Reference Guide for syntax descriptions.

3. Look for relevant error messages in these files: the alert log, trace files (usually in a location defined by user_dump_dest), and sbtio.log (if using an MML).

4. Follow a recipe in this book that helps resolve the issue.

5. Use your favorite search engine to search the Web for information from other DBAs who have encountered similar situations.

6. Ask other DBAs for help.

7. Search Oracle's RMAN backup and recovery documentation at `http://otn.oracle.com`.

8. Search Oracle's MetaLink website at `http://metalink.oracle.com`.

9. Search for an answer or post a question on Oracle's RMAN forum at `http://forums.oracle.com`.

10. Open a service request (SR) with Oracle Support.

11. Enable more output logging and debugging (see recipes 17-7, 17-8, and 17-9).

12. When all else fails, send an email to `lellison@oracle.com`.

■**Note** Before you can use Oracle's MetaLink website to open a service request, you must first purchase a valid Oracle support license.

How It Works

With RMAN troubleshooting, usually you start with the error message displayed on your terminal or recorded in a log file. This section discusses a typical RMAN error stack. To begin with, you'll almost always see the following text as the first part of the output when there's an RMAN error:

```
RMAN-00571: ===========================================================
RMAN-00569: =============== ERROR MESSAGE STACK FOLLOWS ===============
RMAN-00571: ===========================================================
```

RMAN error messages can sometimes be frustrating to interpret. Even for something as simple as an incorrectly typed RMAN command, you'll be presented with a lengthy output describing the error. For example, you might receive the following message stack:

```
RMAN-01009: syntax error: found ";": expecting one of: "allocate, alter, backup,
beginline, blockrecover, catalog, change, connect, copy, convert, create, cross
check, configure, duplicate, debug, delete, drop, exit, endinline, flashback, ho
st, {, library, list, mount, open, print, quit, recover, register, release, repl
ace, report, renormalize, reset, restore, resync, rman, run, rpctest, set, setli
mit, sql, switch, spool, startup, shutdown, send, show, test, transport, upgrade
, unregister, validate"
RMAN-01007: at line 1 column 16 file: standard input
```

When presented with an RMAN error message stack, follow the steps outlined in the "Solution" section of this recipe. You'll have to vary the steps depending on your scenario. For example, if you have a priority-one (P1) production problem, you may want to open an SR with Oracle Support as your first step. For most other situations, you'll use a subset of the solution steps and resolve the problem on your own.

17-2. Resolving Connection Permission Issues

Problem

You're trying to log in to RMAN from the command prompt, and you receive the following message:

```
c:\> rman target /

RMAN-00571: ============================================================
RMAN-00569: =============== ERROR MESSAGE STACK FOLLOWS ===============
RMAN-00571: ============================================================
RMAN-00554: initialization of internal recovery manager package failed
RMAN-04005: error from target database:
ORA-01031: insufficient privileges
```

Solution

If you're attempting to use OS authentication (not supplying a username and password) when starting RMAN, you need to ensure that your OS user account is part of the privileged DBA OS group. If you're not using OS authentication, then you need to make sure that you have correctly enabled a password file.

Using OS Authentication

In Unix, the privileged OS group is usually named dba or oinstall. This is the group you specified when installing the Oracle software. To verify that your OS account belongs to the proper group, use the Unix id command:

```
$ id
uid=100(oracle) gid=101(oinstall)
```

In a Windows environment, here is the process to verify that your OS user is part of the Oracle DBA group:

1. Go to Control Panel, and then go to Administrative Tools.

2. Click Computer Management.

3. Click Local Users and Groups, then click Groups.

4. You should see a group named ora_dba; double-click it.

5. Make sure your OS user is a member of the Oracle DBA group.

Using a Password File

If you're not using OS authentication, then you must supply a username and password combination that is recorded in the password file:

```
$ rman target sys/<your password>
```

If you don't supply a correct username and password, you'll get an ORA-01031 "insufficient privileges" error. Ensure that you use a correct username and password when using a password file.

How It Works

RMAN requires that you connect to the target database with a user who has the sysdba database privilege. You can connect to your target database with sysdba privilege in one of two ways:

- Use an OS-authenticated account.

- Use a password file that contains the username and password information of schemas granted the sysdba privilege.

■**Tip** Recipe 2-1 has complete details on how to use OS authentication and also how to implement a password file.

Another way to help determine the root cause of an ORA-01031 error is to attempt to log in to SQL*Plus with the same authentication information as when trying to connect through RMAN. This will help verify either that you are using an OS-authenticated account or that the username and password are correct.

If OS authentication is working, then you should be able to log in to SQL*Plus as follows:

```
$ sqlplus / as sysdba
```

If you're using a password file, then you can verify that the username and password are correct by logging in as shown here:

```
$ sqlplus sys/<your password> as sysdba
```

If you receive an ORA-01031 error from attempting to log in to SQL*Plus, then either you aren't using an OS-authenticated account or your username and password combination does not match what is stored in the password file.

■**Note** If you are using an OS-authenticated account, it doesn't matter what you specify for the username and password. You can specify any text strings for the username and password, and Oracle will allow you to connect.

17-3. Handling Disk Space Issues

Problem

You're attempting to create a backup, and you receive an error similar to the following:

```
ORA-19504: failed to create file "/oraback/BRDSTN/bsi2phe7_1_1"
ORA-27004: unable to write the header block of file
```

Solution

This error is usually caused by a lack of disk space. Verify from the operating system that the location you're backing up to is indeed full. In a Unix environment, you can use the df command to verify this. In a Windows environment, you can right-click the backup directory and view its properties.

If your backup location is full, you can do one of the following to correct the problem:

- Change the backup location to an area that has more space.

- Add disk space to the backup location.

- If using a flash recovery area (FRA), then either move the FRA or increase its size.

- Change the retention policy to fewer days or fewer backups.

- Delete old backup files that are no longer required.

Changing your backup location and deleting old backup files are trivial tasks to perform, and you'll need to see your system administrator about adding space to your backup location. The other two options, though, require a bit more explanation.

Moving and/or Resizing the FRA

The following SQL statement uses the alter system command to move the flash recovery area to /orabackup02/FRA:

```
SQL> alter system set db_recovery_file_dest='/oraback02/FRA';
```

If disk space is available, you can increase the size of the flash recovery area to an appropriate value. This example changes the flash recovery area size to 100GB:

```
SQL> alter system set db_recovery_file_dest_size=100g;
```

■**Note** If you're not using an spfile, make sure you update the new initialization settings in your init.ora file.

You can verify what the new flash recovery area settings are with this query:

```
SQL> select * from v$recovery_file_dest;
```

■**Note** See Chapter 3 for complete details on how to manage your flash recovery area.

Changing Retention Policy and Deleting Old Backups

This section shows how to change a retention policy and use the `delete obsolete` command to free up space being used by obsolete backups. First use the `report obsolete` command to view backups that are candidates to be deleted:

```
RMAN> report obsolete;
```

This command will show the retention policy and which backups and archived redo log files are obsolete. Here is what the output might look like:

```
RMAN retention policy will be applied to the command
RMAN retention policy is set to redundancy 6
no obsolete backups found
```

In this example, no obsolete backups were reported. We'll use the `configure` command to change the retention policy from a redundancy policy of six down to two:

```
RMAN> configure retention policy to redundancy 2;
```

Now the `report obsolete` command shows that there are several obsolete files:

```
RMAN> report obsolete;

RMAN retention policy will be applied to the command
RMAN retention policy is set to redundancy 2
Report of obsolete backups and copies
Type                 Key    Completion Time Filename/Handle
-------------------- ------ --------------- --------------------
Backup Set           19     04-JAN-07
  Backup Piece       19     04-JAN-07       C:\FRA\ORCL\BACKUPSET\2006_10_14\
01_MF_NNNDF_TAG20061014T140221_2M2JLM1Y_.DK.BKP
Archive Log          2      04-JAN-07       C:\FRA\ORCL\ARCHIVELOG\2007_01_04\
01_MF_1_133_2STQTT89_.ARC
```

Now we can use the `delete obsolete` command to have RMAN remove the backups from the backup media and also update the repository:

```
RMAN> delete obsolete;
```

How It Works

If you're encountering disk space issues, the error message will vary depending on whether you're using a flash recovery area. When you're using a flash recovery area, the error message will look something similar to this:

```
RMAN-03009: failure of backup command on ORA_DISK_2 channel at 08/10/2006
ORA-19809: limit exceeded for recovery files
ORA-19804: cannot reclaim 52528800 bytes disk space from 85899345892 limit
```

If you're not using a flash recovery area, the error message will be slightly different:

```
RMAN-03009: failure of backup command on ORA_DISK_2 channel at 08/10/2006
ORA-19504: failed to create file "/oraback/BRDSTN/bsi2phe7_1_1"
ORA-27004: unable to write the header block of file
SVR4 Error 2: No space left on device
Additional information: 3
```

You can resolve disk space issues in a number of ways. If you're in an emergency situation, the quickest way to resolve the issue may be to change the location of the backup directory. If you're looking for a long-term solution, you'll probably want to consider adding more disk space to the backup location and/or changing your RMAN retention policy.

If you're using a flash recovery area, then you can dynamically issue an `alter system` command to change the location and size of the backup directory. If you're not using a flash recovery area, you can use the `configure` command to change the location of the backups (see recipe 5-16 for an example of how to do this).

If there are old archived redo log files, consider backing them up and then deleting them from disk. You can use commands such as `report obsolete` to show which RMAN backup files and archived redo log files are no longer required as per the retention policy. If there are obsolete files, then you can use the `delete obsolete` command to have RMAN remove them from the backup media.

17-4. Dealing with the RMAN-06059 Error

Problem

You've just switched from user-managed backups to using RMAN backups and attempt to run the following command:

```
RMAN> backup database plus archivelog;
```

Your backup process doesn't get very far when RMAN throws this error:

```
RMAN-03002: failure of backup command ...
RMAN-06059: expected archived log not found, loss of archived log compromises
recoverability
```

Your boss happens to be in your office when you were attempting to back up the database and lets you know that "compromised recoverability" will translate into "compromised job security."

Solution

You must update RMAN's repository to reflect that archived redo log files either have been physically deleted or have been moved to another location on disk. Use the `crosscheck` command to inform RMAN that archived redo log files have been physically removed from disk, as shown here:

```
RMAN> crosscheck archivelog all;
```

Now run your backup command again; this time it should succeed:

```
RMAN> backup database plus archivelog;
```

If the archived redo log files have been physically moved to a different location on disk, then use the `catalog` command to update the RMAN repository with the new location of the files:

```
RMAN> catalog start with '/oradump01/oldarchive';
```

The `start with` clause of the `catalog` command instructs RMAN to look in the specified directory and update its repository with any archived redo log files, backup pieces, or image copies located within that directory (and its subdirectories).

How It Works

When you switch from user-managed backups to RMAN backups, you will most likely have many historical archived redo log files that have been generated and removed from disk by your user-managed backup scripts. In situations where you have used operating system commands to remove or move archived redo log files, you must inform RMAN that files have been deleted or moved.

You can tell RMAN to back up datafiles and archived redo log files with the `backup database plus archivelog` command, or you can just back up archived redo log files via the `backup archivelog all` command. Both of these commands instruct RMAN to back up any archived redo log files that have an AVAILABLE status in the V$ARCHIVED_LOG view. You can query the STATUS column of V$ARCHIVED_LOG as follows:

```
SQL> select sequence#,
2 decode(status,'A','available','D','deleted','U','unavailable','X','expired')
3 from v$archived_log;
```

If RMAN can't find on disk an archived redo log file that has an AVAILABLE status, then it will throw the RMAN-06059 error and abort the backup. If you are not using RMAN to delete archived redo log files from disk, then the archived redo log file status remains AVAILABLE, even though the file isn't in the expected location.

■**Tip** We recommend that you always use RMAN to delete archived redo log files and backup pieces from the backup media. If you use an OS command to delete files, then RMAN is unaware that the files have been removed from the backup media. When RMAN is unaware that the files are removed, then you will have to run a `crosscheck` command to update the target database control file and recovery catalog (if using one).

When running the `crosscheck archivelog all` command, RMAN will change the status of an archived redo log file to EXPIRED if it cannot locate the file. RMAN will not attempt to back up an archived redo log file with an EXPIRED status.

The `catalog` command is handy because you can use it to update the RMAN repository with information about relocated archived redo log files, RMAN backup pieces, and image copies. Use the `catalog start with` command to tell RMAN which directory to look in for your relocated files. Alternatively, you can tell RMAN to catalog just one archived redo log file, as shown here:

```
RMAN> catalog archivelog '/oldarchvies/arch1_3144_234562.arc';
```

Now you can select the NAME column from V$ARCHIVED_LOG, and it will reflect the new location of the archived redo log file.

17-5. Terminating RMAN Processes

Problem

You have an RMAN job that appears to be hung. You want to terminate the job.

Solution

You can terminate an RMAN job by using one of the following techniques:

- Press Ctrl+C from the RMAN interface. This approach, of course, works only if performed from the online session responsible for the process you want to terminate.

- Manually kill the OS process.

- Terminate the server session corresponding to an RMAN channel using an `alter system kill` SQL statement.

Pressing Ctrl+C from the RMAN interface is the easiest way to terminate a job (when it works). If that isn't successful or if you did not initiate the job interactively, then you'll have to try one of the following solutions.

Terminating a Unix Process

In a Unix environment, you can identify an RMAN operating system process number using the Unix ps command as follows:

```
$ ps -ef | grep -v grep | grep -i rman
```

The process number is displayed in the second column of the output:

```
oracle 25010 24946 0 15:42:57 pts/2 0:01 rman target /
```

In this example, the process to terminate is 25010. You can then use the Unix `kill` command, as shown here:

```
$ kill -9 25010
```

Terminating a Windows Process

On a Windows server, you can use the Task Manager utility to identify background processes. You can start Task Manager in one of the following ways:

- Ctrl+Alt+Delete.

- Ctrl+Shift+Esc.

- Right-click an empty space in the taskbar, and choose Task Manager.

From the Task Manager, click Applications, and select the RMAN process you want to terminate. Click End Task to terminate the process.

Using SQL to Terminate an RMAN Channel

Use the `alter system kill session` SQL statement to terminate a hung RMAN job. To do this, you need to first identify the serial ID and serial number:

```
SQL> SELECT
2    s.sid
3    ,s.serial#
4    ,p.spid
5    ,s.client_info
6  FROM v$process p,
7       v$session s
8  WHERE p.addr = s.paddr
9  AND client_info LIKE '%rman%';

  SID    SERIAL# SPID          CLIENT_INFO
  ----- ---------- ------------ -------------------------
  157     18030 7344          rman channel=ORA_DISK_1
```

In this case, the SID is 157, and the serial number is 18030. You can then use the `alter system kill session` SQL statement as follows:

```
SQL> alter system kill session '157,18030';
```

If multiple RMAN jobs are running, then you'll have to identify the serial ID number of the particular job you are interested in terminating. You can do this by viewing the RMAN output from the terminal:

```
Starting backup at 14-DEC-06
using target database control file instead of recovery catalog
allocated channel: ORA_DISK_1
channel ORA_DISK_1: sid=145 devtype=DISK
```

From the previous text, you can see that the serial ID is 145. After you have identified the serial ID that you want to terminate, you can run the previous SQL query in this example to identify the corresponding serial number to use in your `alter system kill session` command.

How It Works

On rare occasions, you might encounter the need to terminate a hung RMAN job. For example, when backing up to tape, RMAN jobs might sometimes hang because of problems with the media manager. In these situations, you'll have to manually kill the appropriate RMAN job with one of the techniques shown in this recipe.

■**Note** We recommend that before terminating an RMAN job you first query the V$SESSION_LONGOPS view to see whether the job is making any progress. You can find full details on how to monitor RMAN jobs in recipe 16-3.

17-6. Diagnosing NLS Character Set Issues

Problem

You're trying to connect to RMAN, and you get an NLS error similar to the following:

```
ORA-12705: Cannot access NLS data files or invalid environment specified
```

Solution

There are usually two reasons for NLS character set problems:

- There's a mismatch between the NLS character set of the client and that of the database server.

- You have an NLS-related operating system variable that has been set incorrectly.

To determine whether there is an NLS character set mismatch, compare your target database character set to your client character set. To display your target database character set, issue the following SQL statement:

```
SQL> select value from v$nls_parameters where parameter = 'NLS_CHARACTERSET';

VALUE
-----------
WE8ISO8859P1
```

Compare that to the operating system NLS_LANG setting on your client. In Unix, use the echo command to display the relevant NLS parameters:

```
$ echo $NLS_LANG
```

In Windows, search the Registry Editor for the value of NLS_LANG as shown here: Start ➤ run ➤ regedit ➤ Edit ➤ Find ➤ NLS_LANG.

If you find that there is an NLS_LANG mismatch, then you can override the OS variable manually. For example, in a Unix C shell environment, use the setenv OS command:

```
$ setenv NLS_LANG american_america.we8iso8859p1
```

In a Unix Korn shell environment, use the OS export command as follows:

```
$ export NLS_LANG=american_america.we8iso8859p1
```

In a Windows environment, use the set command, as shown here:

```
c:\> set NLS_LANG=american_america.we8iso8859p1
```

If you set NLS_LANG to a value that RMAN doesn't recognize, then you will receive an error like this:

```
RMAN-00554: initialization of internal recovery manager package failed
RMAN-04005: error from target database:
ORA-12705: Cannot access NLS data files or invalid environment specified
```

If you receive an error like that, ensure that your NLS_LANG operating system parameter is set to a valid value.

■Tip To view valid NLS values, query the V$NLS_VALID_VALUES view.

How It Works

When faced with potential NLS character set issues, first verify the settings on both your target server and your client. The value of NLS_LANG should match between the client OS and the target database server. To troubleshoot this, you can manually override the client setting and force it to match your target database NLS_LANG setting.

When troubleshooting NLS issues, it can sometimes be difficult to pin down where the NLS values are being set. This is because you can have variables set at the database, instance, session, and client OS. Table 17-1 describes useful NLS views that can help verify at what level the NLS parameters have been set.

Table 17-1. *Useful NLS Troubleshooting Views*

NLS View Name	Description
V$NLS_VALID_VALUES	Lists all valid values for NLS settings.
NLS_SESSION_PARAMETERS	Contains NLS values for the current session.
V$NLS_PARAMETERS	Contains current values of NLS parameters.
NLS_INSTANCE_PARAMETERS	Contains NLS values set at the instance level. These values are set through the initialization file or an alter system command.
NLS_DATABASE_PARAMETERS	Contains NLS values defined when your database was created. These can be overridden by the instance, client OS, or client session.

17-7. Logging RMAN Output

Problem

You're trying to debug a difficult issue and want to capture the output of an RMAN session.

Solution

You can enable RMAN logging in two ways:

- From the OS prompt
- From the RMAN command line

From the OS Prompt

From the OS prompt you can use the log parameter to instruct RMAN to send any output to an OS file (instead of to your screen):

```
$ rman target / log=rman_output.log
```

■**Note** The keyword `msglog` has been deprecated in favor of the keyword `log`.

From the RMAN Command Line

You can also spool the output to a log file from the RMAN command line, as shown here:

```
RMAN> spool log to rman_output.log
RMAN> set echo on
RMAN> backup database;
```

To turn off logging, use the `log off` parameter, as shown here:

```
RMAN> spool log off;
```

You should now have captured in your log file all the output associated with the `backup database` command.

■**Tip** We recommend that when you capture the output to a log file that you also use the `set echo on` command. This will ensure that the RMAN command is displayed before actually running it.

USING THE UNIX SCRIPT COMMAND

If you're in a Unix environment, you can use the `script` command to record everything printed to your screen. For example, if you wanted to capture all output from an RMAN session in a file named rman.log, then use the Unix `script` command as shown here:

```
$ script rman.log
Script started, file is rman.log

$ rman target /
RMAN> backup database;
```

You should see several RMAN output messages at this time:

```
RMAN> exit
```

Now press Ctrl+D or type `exit` to end the script session. After you press Ctrl+D or type `exit`, you should see this message:

```
$ Script done, file is rman.log
```

You should now see all the output from your `backup database` command in the rman.log file.

How It Works

You can use the RMAN command-line `log` option or the `spool` command to capture output in a log file. When you are troubleshooting RMAN, it's often helpful to capture all the output in a log file so that it can be later analyzed. If you request assistance from Oracle Support, they will often ask you to capture the complete RMAN session output and send it to them.

If the log file that you specify already exists, then by default RMAN will overwrite the file. If you want RMAN to append to an existing file, use the `append` parameter. Here's how to append to a file from the OS command line:

```
$ rman target / log=rman_output.log append
```

Here's how you would append to a file from the RMAN prompt:

```
RMAN> spool log to rman_output.log append
```

You cannot use the `spool` command from within a `run{}` block. You must set spooling outside the `run{}` block, as shown here:

```
RMAN> spool log to rman_output.log
RMAN> set echo on
RMAN> run{ allocate channel d1 type disk;
2> backup database;
3> release channel d1;
4> }
```

17-8. Viewing RMAN Command History

Problem

You didn't log your output to an OS file, and you now wonder whether there is a way to view the RMAN command stack output.

Solution

Use V$RMAN_OUTPUT to view the text messages that RMAN produces when performing tasks. Run this query to view the historical RMAN command messages:

```
SQL> select
2  sid,
3  recid,
4  output
5  from v$rman_output
6  order by recid
7  /
```

The output looks like this:

```
SID RECID OUTPUT
------ ----- -----------------------------------------------------------------
   154    31 Starting backup at 14-JAN-07
   154    32 using target database control file instead of recovery catalog
```

```
154    33 allocated channel: ORA_DISK_1
154    34 channel ORA_DISK_1: sid=144 devtype=DISK
154    35 channel ORA_DISK_1: starting full datafile backupset
154    36 channel ORA_DISK_1: specifying datafile(s) in backupset
154    37 input datafile fno=00001 name=C:\ORACLE\10.2\ORADATA\ORCL\SYSTEM01.DBF
154    38 input datafile fno=00003 name=C:\ORACLE\10.2\ORADATA\ORCL\SYSAUX01.DBF
154    39 input datafile fno=00002 name=C:\ORACLE\10.2\ORADATA\ORCL\UNDOTBS01.DBF
154    40 input datafile fno=00005 name=C:\ORACLE\10.2\ORADATA\ORCL\TOOLS01.DBF
154    41 input datafile fno=00004 name=C:\ORACLE\10.2\ORADATA\ORCL\USERS01.DBF
154    42 channel ORA_DISK_1: starting piece 1 at 14-JAN-07
154    43 channel ORA_DISK_1: finished piece 1 at 14-JAN-07
154    44 piece handle=C:\ORACLE\PRODUCT\10.2.0\FLASH_RECOVERY_AREA\ORCL\
          BACKUPSET\2007_01_13\01_MF_NNNDF_TAG20070113T160913_2TLSNTNZ_.BKP
154    45 channel ORA_DISK_1: backup set complete, elapsed time: 00:02:35
154    46 Finished backup at 14-JAN-07
```

You can also join V$RMAN_OUTPUT to V$RMAN_STATUS to get additional information. This useful query shows the type of command RMAN is running, its current status, and its associated output messages:

```
SQL> select
2  a.sid,
3  a.recid,
4  b.operation,
5  b.status,
6  a.output
7  from v$rman_output a,
8      v$rman_status b
9  where a.rman_status_recid = b.recid
10   and   a.rman_status_stamp = b.stamp
11   order by a.recid
12   /
```

How It Works

The V$RMAN_OUTPUT view contains messages recently reported by RMAN. It is an in-memory view that can hold up to a maximum of 32,768 rows. Information in this view is cleared out when you stop and restart your database. The OUTPUT column of V$RMAN_OUTPUT contains the messages that RMAN logs to your terminal when running commands.

Another handy use of this view is to query the output in the event that you are using a log file. If you are writing RMAN output to a log file, then RMAN will not display messages to your terminal. In this situation, you can query V$RMAN_OUTPUT to check on the status of your RMAN operations.

Table 17-2 describes all the columns of V$RMAN_OUTPUT.

Table 17-2. *Description of V$RMAN_OUTPUT Columns*

Column	Description
SID	ID number of session running the RMAN command
RECID	Sequential ID for each record
STAMP	Timestamp number for output record
SESSION_RECID	Record identifier of the session
SESSION_STAMP	Time stamp of the session
OUTPUT	Output message of RMAN operation
RMAN_STATUS_RECID	Corresponds to the record ID in V$RMAN_STATUS
RMAN_STATUS_STAMP	Corresponds to the status stamp in V$RMAN_STATUS
SESSION_KEY	Session record identifier

17-9. Enabling RMAN's Debug Output

Problem

You want to turn on debugging output for an RMAN session.

Solution

You can turn on debugging in several different ways:

- From the OS prompt

- When allocating a channel

- When configuring a channel

- From the RMAN command-line prompt

From the OS Prompt

This first example enables all debugging and captures the output in a log file:

```
$ rman target / debug=all log=rman_output.log
```

The following example enables debugging just for I/O activities:

```
$ rman target / debug=io
```

When Allocating a Channel

This example uses debug with the trace parameter. Tracing at level 1 gives you the least amount of information, and tracing at level 5 gives you the most verbose output. Run the allocate command from within the run{} block, as shown here:

```
RMAN> run{
2    allocate channel d1 type disk debug=5 trace=5;
3    backup database;
```

```
4   release channel d1;
5   }
```

You should now have a trace file located in the directory specified by the user_dump_dest initialization parameter.

When Configuring a Channel

This example configures a channel to debug and trace at level 5:

```
RMAN> configure channel device type disk debug=5 trace=5;
```

Anytime this channel is used, it will generate a trace file in the directory specified by the user_dump_dest initialization parameter. To clear the channel debug settings, use the clear parameter as shown here:

```
RMAN> configure channel device type disk clear;
```

From Within RMAN

This example turns on debugging and then turns off debugging after the backup command has run:

```
RMAN> spool log to rman_output.log
RMAN> debug on
RMAN> set echo on
RMAN> backup database;
RMAN> debug off
RMAN> spool log off
```

How It Works

The debug command produces a detailed report of internal operations being performed by RMAN. You'll notice that the performance of RMAN will suffer when debugging is enabled. Therefore, we don't recommend running commands in debug mode on a production database. You should turn on debugging only in test environments or at the recommendation of Oracle Support.

The debug on command is equivalent to debug all. Both of those commands turn on all available types of debugging. You also have the option of just enabling debugging for certain types of operations. Listed next are specific areas for which you can turn on debugging:

- io

- sql

- plsql

- rcvman

- rpc

For example, if you wanted to just debug I/O-related operations when backing up your users tablespace, then you would enable I/O debugging as shown here:

```
RMAN> spool log to rman_output.log
RMAN> set echo on
RMAN> debug io
RMAN> backup tablespace users;
RMAN> debug off
RMAN> spool log off
```

Your output file should now have messages that start with "DBGIO" that are related to RMAN I/O activities:

```
DBGIO:    channel ORA_DISK_1: blocks=2880 block_size=8192 [11:55:39.843]
RMAN-08038: channel ORA_DISK_1: starting piece 1 at 01-JAN-07
DBGIO:    Type %Comp Blocks Tot Blocks Blksize    ElpTime(s) IO Rt(b/s)
DBGIO:    ---- ----- ---------- ---------- ---------- ---------- ----------
DBGIO:    IN   100.0 2880       2880       8192       2          11796480
C:\>ORACLE\PRODUCT\10.2.0\ORADATA\ORCL\USERS01.DBF [11:55:47.000] (krmkqio)
DBGIO:    OUT        2389                  8192       2          9785344
C:\>FRA\ORCL\BACKUPSET\2007_01_01\O1_MF_NNNDF_TAG20070101T115539_%U_.BKP
DBGIO:    AGG        2880                  8192       2          11796480
```

The default level for debugging is 9. Valid ranges of debug levels are from 1 to 15, with level 1 the least verbose and level 15 generating the most output. Usually the default debugging level of 9 is sufficient. You can alter the default level of debugging by using the level parameter. For example, this sets the debug level of PL/SQL operations to the maximum level of 15:

```
RMAN> debug plsql level=15
```

17-10. Enabling Granular Time Reporting

Problem

You're troubleshooting an issue, and you notice that the output from the list command specifies the date but without an hours:minutes:time component. You want to capture the exact second when your RMAN operations started and finished.

Solution

Use the operating system NLS_DATE_FORMAT variable to specify a date format that includes a time component. In a Unix C shell environment, use the setenv OS command as shown here:

```
$ setenv NLS_DATE_FORMAT 'dd-mon-yyyy hh24:mi:ss'
```

In a Unix Korn shell environment, use the OS export command as follows:

```
$ export NLS_DATE_FORMAT='dd-mon-yyyy hh24:mi:ss'
```

In a Windows environment, use the set command as shown here:

```
c:\> set NLS_DATE_FORMAT=dd-mon-yyyy hh24:mi:ss
```

How It Works

We recommend that you always set your NLS_DATE_FORMAT variable so that you see the hour, minute, and second components of the date when issuing RMAN commands. If you spool a log file when issuing backup, restore, and recovery commands, then this will ensure that a timestamp component is displayed. This can be useful when trying to troubleshoot RMAN issues.

If you don't set the NLS_DATE_FORMAT, then you won't see the hour, minute, and second component of the date columns. Here's a snippet of output from a list command without NLS_DATE_FORMAT set:

```
BS Key  Type LV Size       Device Type Elapsed Time Completion Time
------- ---- -- ---------- ----------- ------------ ---------------
201     Full    18.66M     DISK         00:00:03     01-JAN-07
```

Here's the same output when the NLS_DATE_FORMAT is set. Notice how the hours, minutes, and seconds are now displayed:

```
BS Key  Type LV Size       Device Type Elapsed Time Completion Time
------- ---- -- ---------- ----------- ------------ --------------------
201     Full    18.66M     DISK         00:00:03     01-jan-2007 12:11:25
```

You can verify the value of NLS_DATE_FORMAT from your OS environment with the echo command. In Unix, use echo as follows:

```
$ echo $NLS_DATE_FORMAT
```

Here is a Windows example of displaying NLS_DATE_FORMAT using the echo command:

```
C:\> echo %NLS_DATE_FORMAT%
```

■**Caution** If you accidentally set NLS_DATE_FORMAT to an invalid Oracle date format, RMAN will complain and not let you start a session. Refer to Oracle's SQL Reference Guide for valid Oracle date formats. The SQL Reference Guide is available for download at Oracle's http://otn.oracle.com website.

To unset an OS variable, simply make it blank. For example, to unset NLS_DATE_FORMAT in a Unix C shell environment, use the unsetenv OS command:

```
$ unsetenv NLS_DATE_FORMAT
```

In a Unix Korn shell environment, use the OS export command as follows:

```
$ export NLS_DATE_FORMAT=
```

In a Windows environment, use the set command as shown here:

```
c:\> set NLS_DATE_FORMAT=
```

17-11. Working with Oracle Support

Problem

You ran into an RMAN problem, and you want to get help from Oracle Support.

Solution

Go to Oracle's MetaLink website (`http://metalink.oracle.com`), and open a service request (SR), which was formally known as a technical assistance request (TAR). When working with Oracle Support, you'll get a faster and better response by providing the following documentation when you open a request for service:

- Test case that illustrates step-by-step details to reproduce the problem

- Complete RMAN script or command(s) that were run

- Complete RMAN output log

- Database alert.log file

- Remote Diagnostic Agent (RDA) output (optional)

How It Works

If you've purchased a support license from Oracle, then you should open an SR when you run into an RMAN problem that you can't solve. You'll need your customer support identifier (CSI) number when you open a service request.

From our experience, documenting steps to reproduce the problem at hand is perhaps the most useful task when requesting help from Oracle Support. We know that not all problems are easily reproducible. However, if at all possible, document clearly the conditions and steps that produce the problem and send those to Oracle Support when you first request help.

Usually we'll open an SR as soon as we first suspect that we may have run into an issue that won't be easily resolved. This way we get a support person working on our issue in parallel with our own efforts. Then if we can't solve the problem, we already have Oracle in the loop and working on a solution.

■Tip It doesn't hurt to open an SR early in your problem resolution process. In many cases, you may solve the problem before Oracle Support gets a chance to look at it. However, for the cases that you don't solve quickly, the sooner you get Oracle Support involved, the greater chance you'll have to escalate your SR and get a more experienced support analyst working on your request.

17-12. Resolving RMAN Compatibility Issues

Problem

Your RMAN executable is version 8.1.6, and you're trying to connect to a version 10.2 database. You are receiving this error message:

```
database not compatible with this version of RMAN
```

You wonder which versions of the RMAN executable are compatible with which versions of your target database.

Solution

Table 17-3 lists Oracle's RMAN compatibility matrix. The easiest way to use this matrix is to find the version of your database in the "Target DB" column and then use that row for determining the compatibility required for other RMAN components in your environment.

Table 17-3. *RMAN Compatibility Matrix*

Target DB	Auxiliary DB	RMAN Executable	Catalog DB	Catalog Schema
8.1.7.4	8.1.7.4	8.1.7.4	>= 8.1.7	8.1.7.4 or >= 9.0.1.4
9.0.1	9.0.1	9.0.1	>= 8.1.7	>= RMAN executable
9.2.0	9.2.0	>= 9.0.1.3 and <= Target DB	>= 8.1.7	>= RMAN executable
10.1.0	10.1.0	>= 9.0.1.3 and <= Target DB	>= 9.0.1	>= RMAN executable
10.2.0	10.2.0	>= 9.0.1.3 and <= Target DB	>= 9.0.1	>= RMAN executable
11.1.0	11.1.0	TBD	TBD	>= RMAN executable

■**Note** You can also find the RMAN compatibility matrix information in MetaLink note 73431.1.

How It Works

Ideally, you'd like all your environments to be at the same Oracle version. In reality, that rarely is the case. Therefore, in most environments, you will have to deal with some RMAN compatibility issues. Here are the general rules of thumb when dealing with RMAN compatibility problems:

- Whenever possible, the version of the rman executable should be the same as your target/auxiliary database version.

- The version of the catalog schema must be at the same version or newer than the rman executable.

- The version of the catalog database is backward compatible with earlier versions of the target database.

If you're not sure which version of the catalog you are using, then connect via SQL*Plus to the recovery catalog as the catalog owner and run this query:

```
SQL> select * from rcver;
```

17-13. Dealing with an ORA-19511 Error

Problem

You're receiving an ORA-19511 error message from your media management layer (MML).

Solution

Inspect the contents of the sbtio.log file. It should have more detailed information about the root cause of the problem. The sbtio.log file is usually located in the directory defined by the user_dump_dest initialization variable or in the $ORACLE_HOME/rdbms/log directory.

How It Works

When your MML returns the ORA-19511 error, this is usually an indication of one of the following:

- The MML software has not been configured or installed correctly.

- An OS variable related to the MML has not been set correctly.

In this situation, Oracle is only passing back the error from the MML. If the text of message ORA-19511 does not provide enough information to resolve the problem, then you should contact the third-party MML vendor and engage their assistance to resolve the problem.

When you receive an ORA-19511 error message, it will typically be accompanied by other media management layer or OS error messages. Table 17-4 lists the error messages and their meanings.

■**Note** You can find additional information about media management layer errors in MetaLink note 149068.1.

Table 17-4. *Media Management Layer Error Messages*

Message Number	Description
sbtopen 7000	Backup file not found
sbtopen 7001	File exists
sbtopen 7002	Bad mode specified
sbtopen 7003	Invalid block size specified
sbtopen 7004	No tape device found
sbtopen 7005	Device found, but busy
sbtopen 7006	Tape volume not found
sbtopen 7007	Tape volume in use
sbtopen 7008	I/O error
sbtopen 7009	Can't connect with Media Manager
sbtopen 7010	Permission denied
sbtopen 7011	OS error
sbtopen 7012	Invalid argument to sbtopen
sbtclose 7020	Invalid file handle or file not open
sbtclose 7021	Invalid flags to sbtclose
sbtclose 7022	I/O error
sbtclose 7023	OS error

Message Number	Description
sbtclose 7024	Invalid argument to sbtclose
sbtclose 7025	Can't connect with Media Manager
sbtwrite 7040	Invalid file handle or file not open
sbtwrite 7041	End of volume reached
sbtwrite 7042	I/O error
sbtwrite 7043	OS error
sbtwrite 7044	Invalid argument to sbtwrite
sbtread 7060	Invalid file handle or file not open
sbtread 7061	EOF encountered
sbtread 7062	End of volume reached
sbtread 7063	I/O error
sbtread 7064	OS error
sbtread 7065	Invalid argument to sbtread
sbtremove 7080	Backup file not found
sbtremove 7081	Backup file in use
sbtremove 7082	I/O error
sbtremove 7083	Can't connect with Media Manager
sbtremove 7084	Permission denied
sbtremove 7085	OS error
sbtremove 7086	Invalid argument to sbtremove
sbtinfo 7090	Backup file not found
sbtinfo 7091	I/O error
sbtinfo 7092	Can't connect with Media Manager
sbtinfo 7093	Permission denied
sbtinfo 7094	OS error
sbtinfo 7095	Invalid argument to sbtinfo
sbtinit 7110	Invalid argument to sbtinit
sbtinit 7111	OS error

17-14. Dealing with an ORA-27211 Error

Problem

When attempting to allocate a channel for tape I/O, you receive an ORA-27211 error.

Solution

The ORA-27211 error is usually indicative of the media management library not loading properly. When you receive this error, usually a corresponding trace file is generated. Look for a trace file in the location specified by your user_dump_dest location. The trace file should have additional information about MML errors or OS errors.

How It Works

The ORA-27211 error is usually thrown when you have not correctly installed your MML. Consult your vendor's MML documentation, and ensure that you have correctly integrated the software with Oracle.

■**Tip** See Chapter 18 on how to use the sbttest utility to verify whether your MML is integrated correctly.

17-15. Dealing with an ORA-04031 Error

Problem

You're using I/O slaves and are getting an ORA-04031 error written to your alert.log file.

Solution

Set up a large pool memory area on your database. If you are using Oracle Database 10g or newer, then consider using automatic shared memory management (ASMM) to have Oracle automatically allocate memory to the large pool.

If you're not comfortable with using ASMM, then you can manually set the initialization parameter large_pool_size. If you want to manually set the large pool size, here is Oracle's recommended formula for sizing it:

```
large_pool_size = num_of_allocated_channels * (16 MB + (4 * size_of_tape_buffer ))
```

■**Tip** You can display the component name and associated memory area (shared, large, Java, or streams pool) of structures using the SGA by querying the V$SGASTAT view.

How It Works

If you have enabled the use of I/O slaves, we recommend that you set up a large pool memory area. When using I/O slaves for synchronous I/O, RMAN will use memory in the large pool if it is available. If a large pool memory is not available, RMAN will allocate memory from the shared pool. If RMAN cannot allocate enough memory, it will acquire memory from the PGA and write an ORA-04031 message to your alert.log file.

Using I/O slaves can improve performance when performing I/O to synchronous devices such as tape drives. You enable tape I/O slaves by setting the backup_tape_io_slaves parameter to TRUE. This causes an I/O server processes (slaves) to be assigned to each tape channel being used.

■**Tip** See MetaLink note 73354.1 for details on how the use of I/O slaves can affect RMAN's use of memory buffers for backup and recovery operations.

If you are working with an OS that doesn't support asynchronous I/O, then you can enable disk I/O slaves via the dbwr_io_slaves parameter. If you set this parameter to a nonzero value, RMAN will use four server processes to perform backup and recovery operations.

17-16. Managing Files in an ASM Environment

Problem

You're using Oracle's automatic storage management (ASM) to manage your disks. You want to view the datafiles and RMAN backup pieces that are stored on ASM diskgroups.

Solution

Use the ASMCMD utility to manage RMAN files and database files when using ASM-managed disks. Ensure that your ORACLE_SID and ORACLE_HOME environment variables are set properly for your ASM instance. Type asmcmd -p from the operating system to invoke the utility:

```
C:\> asmcmd -p
```

You should now see the ASMCMD prompt:

```
ASMCMD [+]>
```

The -p option will set your prompt to display the current working directory as part of the prompt. For example, the ASMCMD prompt changes as we use the cd command to change the current directory:

```
ASMCMD [+] > cd +data/prmy/datafile
ASMCMD [+data/prmy/datafile] >
```

If you are familiar with Unix commands, it should be easy for you to manage your ASM environment using ASMCMD commands. For example, the ls command will list the files in an ASM directory. Table 17-5 lists all the options available with ASMCMD.

Table 17-5. *ASMCMD Commands*

Command	Description
cd	Changes the current directory to the specified directory
du	Displays the total disk space occupied by ASM files in the specified ASM directory and all its subdirectories, recursively
exit	Exits ASMCMD
find	Lists the paths of all occurrences of the specified name (with wildcards) under the specified directory
help	Displays the syntax and description of ASMCMD commands
ls	Lists the contents of an ASM directory, the attributes of the specified file, or the names and attributes of all disk groups
lsct	Lists information about current ASM clients
lsdg	Lists all disk groups and their attributes
mkalias	Creates an alias for a system-generated filename

Continued

Table 17-5. *Continued*

Command	Description
mkdir	Creates ASM directories
pwd	Displays the path of the current ASM directory
rm	Deletes the specified ASM files or directories
rmalias	Deletes the specified alias, retaining the file to which the alias points
md_backup	Creates a metadata backup script of mounted disk groups (Oracle Database 11*g* only)
md_restore	Restores a disk group backup (Oracle Database 11*g* only)
lsdsk	Lists the ASM disks (Oracle Database 11*g* only)
repair	Repairs range of physical blocks on the ASM disk (Oracle Database 11*g* only)

How It Works

You can view and manage ASM diskgroups and ASM files via one of the following tools:

- Enterprise Manager

- SQL*Plus

- ASMCMD

The focus of this recipe is on using the ASMCMD utility. See Chapter 19 for details on how to use RMAN with Enterprise Manager. If you're familiar with SQL*Plus, the following query is useful for viewing files within your ASM environment:

```
SQL> SELECT concat('+'||gname, sys_connect_by_path(aname, '/')) full_alias_path FROM
2    (SELECT g.name gname, a.parent_index pindex, a.name aname,
3    a.reference_index rindex FROM v$asm_alias a, v$asm_diskgroup g
4    WHERE a.group_number = g.group_number)
5    START WITH (mod(pindex, power(2, 24))) = 0
6    CONNECT BY PRIOR rindex = pindex;
```

The ASMCMD utility will also allow you to view and display information about your ASM environment. Before running the asmcmd, ensure that you set the ORACLE_SID variable of the ASM instance as follows:

```
C:\> set ORACLE_SID=+ASM
```

If the ORACLE_SID variable is not properly set to the correct ASM instance, then you will get the following error message:

```
asmcmd: command disallowed by current instance type
```

Also ensure that ORACLE_HOME is set properly. If it isn't, then Oracle will display an error such as this:

```
asmcmd: the environment variable ORACLE_HOME is not set.
```

Once you set your environment variables, you should be able to invoke the ASMCMD utility and use its Unix-like commands to manage your ASM environment. If you want to view more information about ASM commands, use the `help` option:

```
ASMCMD> help
ASMCMD> help md_backup
```

■**Note** The `asmcmd` is not available by default in Oracle Database 10*g* Release 1, but you can copy the two required files from the Oracle Database 10*g* Release 2 installation, namely, asmcmdcore and asmcmd for Unix/Linux or asmcmd.bat for Windows. You can find these files in the $ORACLE_HOME/bin directory.

CHAPTER 18

■ ■ ■

Using a Media Management Layer

RMAN comes preconfigured to work with a single disk channel. To back up and restore from a tape device, you need to configure a media management layer (MML), which works with the actual storage devices. When you instruct RMAN to work with a tape device, RMAN sends the media management layer the necessary information so the MML can send instructions to the actual storage media. In other words, RMAN doesn't deal directly with the tape devices. You can use Oracle's own freely available Oracle Secure Backup (OSB) as your media management layer, or you can choose to go with a third-party MML. The OSB is an excellent product that can make both database and operating system file backups, but it has limitations in the number of storage devices it can handle and therefore is an ideal solution for small enterprises.

In this chapter, we'll provide recipes for three MML products—Oracle Secure Backup, Veritas NetBackup, and EMC NetWorker. If you're planning on using OSB, please refer to the Oracle's manuals for Oracle Secure Backup to learn how to install and configure the OSB product as well as how to set up RMAN for use with OSB. If you're using either of the third-party products, please refer to the product-specific installation and configuration information.

Your first step in using an MML is to install it and configure RMAN to work with it. Before you can use any of the MMLs to make backups, you must first configure RMAN to make backups to the media manager. Each of the MML products comes with a media management module consisting of a media management library that works with the Oracle database. When you're configuring channels for RMAN to use with a media manager, you use the `sbt_library` parameter in the `allocate channel` or `configure channel` command to specify the path name to the media management library. You use vendor-specific values for the `parms` parameter inside a command such as `configure channel` to send instructions to the media manager.

Once you install and configure the media manager library to work with RMAN and your databases, test to confirm that RMAN can successfully be backed up to the media manager. Make a test backup and restore it before you start using the media manager with RMAN. After you make the test backups, issue the `list backup` command, which shows you whether your backup really went to the media manager. The easiest way to perform a backup to a media manager is by configuring automatic sbt channels and setting the default device type to sbt.

■**Tip** See recipe 18-22 for details on testing your MML installation.

Using Oracle Secure Backup

Oracle provides a free media management layer as part of its OSB server software. OSB offers an easy way to implement a tape backup strategy without having to go through the trials and tribulations that may be part of a full-scale MML configuration (not to mention the additional licensing fees you have to cough up). OSB is ideal for small environments where you have one or a few databases, and it offers all the essential features of a full-fledged MML while avoiding some of the drawbacks of its industrial-strength brethren. If you have just a single server, you can use Oracle Secure Backup Express to back up your Oracle database. If you have a large environment, you must use the full-fledged Oracle Secure Backup, which is available as a separate licensable product to back up multiple database servers.

OSB acts as a media management layer for RMAN by providing a built-in media management software library that RMAN uses to make tape backups. This software library is also called an *sbt interface*. Although it's a free product, note that OSB provides advantages you can't get from other MMLs, such as the ability to directly make RMAN-encrypted backups to tape. You can use OSB with Oracle9*i* Database, Oracle Database 10*g*, and Oracle Database 11*g*. Please refer to the documentation for the relevant MML product you're using to get a list of the platforms that are compatible as client, media, and administrative servers.

Understanding the Advantages of Using OSB

OSB costs much less than other third-party products in terms of license costs. The other products need you to license each client such as the host, the application, the storage device, the media server, and the administrative server separately. OSB licensing is strictly based on the number of physical tape drives you use, and you can use an unlimited number of clients without licensing costs.

Here are the other advantages of using OSB:

- It offers automatic integration with Oracle products such as real application clusters, automatic storage management, and Data Guard.

- The OSB encryption module is within the Oracle database and encrypts the data before it's recorded on media. In addition, the data on tape is stored in encrypted form, providing you a secure backup of your data.

- OSB can back up both database files and the operating system files.

- Because of OSB's tight integration with RMAN, it helps optimize storage access, resulting in a 15 to 30 percent performance improvement over other third-party products, according to Oracle.

Introducing the OSB Architecture

OSB divides its tasks into three components, called *domains*:

Administrative server: Each OSB domain contains one administrative server, which manages the entire backup and recovery information that's stored in a special OSB catalog. On a Linux server, for example, the catalog is stored in the /usr/local/oracle/backup directory by default.

Media server: This is the OSB component that manages the actual media devices, such as the physical tape drives, virtual tape libraries, and physical tape libraries. OSB supports a variety of tape backup devices made by third-party vendors such as NetApp and EMC.

Client: Client applications are mostly the Oracle databases you want to back up and recover with OSB. OSB also supports backup appliances such as network-attached storage (NAS) as clients.

The obtool command-line program is the main OSB command-line interface. You can use obtool to back up and recover filesystems and to configure and manage OSB. To invoke the obtool interface, just type obtool at the command line. You can use obtool on any host that's part of the administrative domain. Please refer to the *Oracle Secure Backup Reference* for details about obtool.

Understanding How OSB and RMAN Work Together

The process of RMAN backup and recovery operations with OSB is straightforward, as summarized in the following steps:

1. When you initiate a backup or restore command through RMAN (using the command line or Enterprise Manager) and allocate a tape channel, generically known as a *system backup to tape* (sbt) channel for it, a server session starts on the target database.

2. The server session on the target database makes a request to the OSB to execute the backup or restore job.

3. OSB creates the backup or restore job and assigns it a unique identifier.

4. OSB reserves the tape drive to perform the backup job and starts the tape-loading process in motion. If no tape drives are available, OSB queues the job request.

5. OSB creates the backup or restores the backup pieces, as per the backup or restore request.

Managing Backup and Recovery with RMAN and OSB

You can run RMAN backup and recovery commands in three ways using OSB:

- You can use the normal RMAN client. Note the following:

  - You must install OSB on the target host where the target database is running.

  - The client can be run from any Oracle Home, even if it's not a member of the OSB administrative domain.

  - The database host must be part of the administrative domain.

- You can use the Oracle Enterprise Manager (OEM) Database Control. Database Control must be running on the administrative server of OSB. In addition, the target database must be running on the same host as well.

- You can use the OEM Grid Control. Grid Control is the way to go if you want to perform tape backups of several databases through a centralized control interface. Grid Control can run on any host in the administrative domain.

These three tools provide you with an interface for performing database backup and recovery functions when working with RMAN and OSB. If you want to work with file system backups, you can do so by using the following tools:

- You can use the OSB web interface, called the *web tool*, for OSB-related tasks.

- You can use the obtool utility, which you invoke by typing obtool at the command line.

■ **Note** You can determine the version of obtool on your server by executing the command obtool --version/-V.

We assume you've already installed OSB before trying to use the OSB-related recipes in this chapter. We also assume that you've configured the OSB environment and set up your tape devices and virtual tape libraries. The following OSB-related recipes focus strictly on how to configure and use an OSB tape device as part of an RMAN backup and recovery strategy.

18-1. Configuring RMAN Access to the Oracle Secure Backup sbt Library

Problem

You want to configure RMAN access to Oracle Secure Backup.

Solution

The easiest way to make RMAN backups through the OSB interface is to use the Enterprise Manager Grid Control or Database Control. In this recipe, we show you how to use Database Control to manage RMAN tape backups through OSB.

You must follow these steps to configure RMAN access to Oracle Secure Backup through Database Control:

1. Log in to Database Control as a user with sysdba privileges.

2. Click the Availability tab on the Home page of Database Control.

3. In the Oracle Secure Backup section, click Oracle Secure Backup Device and Media.

4. On the Add Administrative Server page that appears, perform the following two steps to register the administer server with Database Control:

   a. In the Oracle Secure Backup Home directory, enter the full Oracle Secure Backup Home directory. This is the same directory in which you originally installed OSB. By default, this is the /usr/local/oracle/backup directory on Unix/Linux and the C:\Program Files\Oracle\Backup directory on Windows.

    b. Enter an OSB administrator name and password in the Username and Password boxes, respectively.

5. On the Host Credentials Page that appears next, enter the credentials (needs root privileges on Unix/Linux) for the administrative user on the administrative server.

6. The *hostname* page appears next, which you can use to load tapes.

Once you've registered the administrative sever by following these steps, you're ready to work with OSB through the OEM Database Control or through manual commands.

How It Works

When you install OSB on a Linux/Unix platform, the installer automatically copies the sbt library to the subdirectory named lib, under the OSB home, which is the /usr/local/oracle/backup directory on Unix/Linux systems and the C:\Program Files\Oracle\Backup directory on Windows. You can use the parameter sbt_library to specify a location to replace the default sbt library location. When you allocate an sbt channel, RMAN will automatically load the OSB sbt library. Here's an example showing how to configure a default media management library using the sbt_library parameter:

```
configure default device type to sbt;
configure channel device type sbt parms="sbt_library=?/lib/med_li1.so";
backup database;
```

The backup database command backs up the database using the media management library you configured in the previous command. The following example shows how to set a value for the sbt_library parameter by using the keyword parms:

```
run
{
  allocate channel device type sbt
  parms="sbt_library=?/lib/med_lib1.so";
  backup database;
}
```

The previous run block backs up the database using the media management library specified by the sbt_library parameter.

18-2. Managing Authorized OSB Accounts

Problem

You want to create and manage an operating system user account to perform backup and recovery tasks with OSB.

Solution

You can create the special OSB user and perform the necessary preauthorization during the OSB installation. However, we don't cover OSB installation in this book, so we'll show you how to handle user management after the installation is complete by using obtool, the OSB command-line interface. Execute the `obtool` command `mkuser` to create the OSB user, as shown in the following example:

```
ob> mkuser --class oracle --preauth prod1:+rman obuser
```

The previous command creates the account named `obuser`. Note the following about the `mkuser` command that creates the new OSB user:

- `obuser` is the name of the new OSB user.

- `class` denotes that the new user `obuser` is assigned to the `oracle` class.

- The `preauth` option `+rman` preauthorizes sbt backups through RMAN. The `prod1` here stands for the host of the operating system user who has been granted preauthorized access to OSB.

You've now successfully configured an RMAN preauthorization, wherein you authorized an operating system user to make RMAN tape backups using OSB.

In addition to the `mkuser` command, `obtool` provides several other commands that help you manage OSB accounts. The following are examples showing how to use the most useful of these commands.

Listing Users

Use the `lsuser` command to list the names and attributes of one or more users. The simple `lsuser` command provides the names of the users:

```
ob> lsuser
```

Use the `lsuser` command with the `--long` option to get a user's attributes, as shown here:

```
ob> lsuser --long salapati
```

Changing User Attributes

Use the `chuser` command to change an OSB user's attributes, as shown in the following example:

```
ob> chuser --password sammyy1 --email salapati@netbsa.org
```

Renaming Users

The `renuser` command lets you rename an OSB user, as shown here:

```
ob> renuser salapati sam_alapati
```

The previous command renames user `salapati` to `sam_alapati`.

Removing Users

You can remove an OSB user with the `rmuser` command, as shown here:

```
ob> rmuser -nq salapati
```

The rmuser command in this example removes the OSB user salapati from the administrative domain after displaying a confirmation message. The nq option is optional and specifies that there is no need for a prompt.

How It Works

You must "preauthorize" an OS user to access OSB and perform backup and recovery actions. Your OSB interaction will be successful only if you've first authenticated the operating system user who starts the Oracle server session as an Oracle Secure Backup user. The server session can use only the OSB user account that you create to perform backup and recovery jobs.

You can also use the browser-based Oracle Secure Backup web tool to configure RMAN preauthorization. The OSB web tool helps you configure an administrative domain, browse the backup catalog, and back up and restore the filesystem. Once you configure a preauthorized OSB user account, the easiest way to make a connection between this OSB account and RMAN is to simply use Database Control for that purpose.

18-3. Creating OSB Media Families for RMAN Backups

Problem

You want to create separate groups of tape volumes for different types of RMAN backup sets.

Solution

You can create named groups of tape volumes called *media families* that share common characteristics. You can create separate media families for the datafiles and the archived redo logs, and you can assign them different expiration and recycling policies, for example.

You can create a media family using the Enterprise Manager, the Oracle Secure Backup web tool, or the mkmf command in obtool. In this recipe, we show you how to create a media family using the mkmf command.

You can create two types of media families—time-managed and content-managed. We provide an example showing how to create a time-managed media family first. Here's the example:

```
ob> mkmf --vidunique --writewindow 14days --retain 28days family_time
```

You can use the mkmf command with numerous options. In the simple example here, the options are as follows:

- vidunique creates a unique volume ID for the new media family.

- writewindow specifies a time window for the *write window*, which is the time during which you can update the volume set by adding backup images to it. OSB can use the volume family for backups until the write window remains open. In the example here, the write window is set to 14, which means all volumes in this media family will be available for update for 14 days.

- retain specifies the amount of time for which the volumes in the media family are retained before being possibly overwritten. In the example, the retention parameter is set to 28 days. However, each volume in the backup expires only after 42 days after the first time OSB makes a backup to the volume, since OSB adds the write window duration (14 days) to volume retention time (28 days) to arrive at the volume expiration time (42 days).

The last item in the command, `family_time`, is the name of the media family. The next example shows how to create a content-managed media family, again by executing the `mkmf` command:

```
ob> mkmf --vidunique --writewindow forever family_content_1
```

By giving the value `forever` for the `writewindow` parameter, you're specifying that OSB can update all volumes in this media family indefinitely. The name of the media family is `family_content_1`.

How It Works

Create media families to separate your OSB tape volumes into meaningful groups. For example, if you want to retain a set of tape volumes for six months, you can do so by using a time-based media family and specifying 180 days as the value for the `retain` parameter.

The key thing to understand is that all volumes that are members of a media family share the same retention and other characteristics. Note that this applies to all volumes, no matter when they were created.

The default volume expiration policy for a media family is the content-managed policy. A volume that's a member of such a family expires when the status of all the backup pieces stored on that volume is set to deleted. Media volumes that belong to time-managed policy-based media families, on the other hand, will expire only when the expiration time is reached, as explained in the "Solution" section of this recipe.

18-4. Creating an OSB Database Backup Storage Selector

Problem

You want to create a database backup storage selector for OSB.

Solution

You can configure a database backup storage selector by using the web tool or the `mkssel` command in `obtool` or by using the Enterprise Manager. In this recipe, we show you how to create a database backup storage selector using the `mkssel` command in `obtool`.

Execute the `mkssel` command to create database backup storage selectors for OSB. Make sure you have the right to modify the administrative domain's configuration. The `mkssel` command has several options you can use. Here's a simple example showing how to create a backup storage selector named `stor_sel1`:

```
ob> mkssel --dbid 2233353479 --host prod1 --content full --family med_fam1 stor_sel1
```

The storage selector `stor_sel1` applies to the database with a specific DBID on the prod1 host. If you want this storage selector to all databases, specify an asterisk (*) instead of the DBID. The content option specifies that full rather than incremental backups can be made with this storage selector. The media family `med_fam1` will be used for backups under this storage selector.

You can use other commands from the obtool utility to manage database backup storage selectors, as shown in the following sections.

Changing a Database Storage Selector

Once you create backup storage selector, you can modify it with help from the chssel command, shown here:

```
ob> chssel --dbid 5123449812 --host prod1 --content full --family f1 ssel_new
```

The previous command replaces the current media family with the new media family ssel_new.

Renaming a Database Storage Selector

You can use the renssel command to rename a backup storage selector, as shown in the following example:

```
ob> renssel ssel_old ssel_new
```

The command shown here renames the ssel_old storage selector to ssel_new.

Removing a Database Storage Selector

Use the rmssel command to remove a database backup storage selector, as shown in this example:

```
ob> rmssel ssel_old
```

This command deletes the database backup storage selector ssel_old.

How It Works

OSB uses the database backup storage selectors to represent the backup attributes of an Oracle database. The backup storage attributes that are required are as follows:

- Database name or ID

- Host name

- Name of the media family to use for the backups

Optionally, you can specify settings of backup storage selectors indicating the backup contents (full/incremental) and the copy number of duplexed backups.

18-5. Configuring OSB Parameters in RMAN

Problem

You want to configure Oracle Secure Backup (OSB) media management parameters in RMAN.

Solution

You can specify the following OSB parameters in a backup or restore job in RMAN:

- ob_media_family [_n] specifies the media family to use for a job.

- ob_device [_n] specifies the tape drive to be used for the job.

- ob_resource_wait_time specifies the length of time for which a job should wait for a necessary resource to become available.

You can specify media management parameters in RMAN in two ways. You can use environment variables via the configure or allocate channel command. Or you can use the send command. We'll illustrate both methods in this solution.

Using the configure or allocate channel Command

Use the parms parameter to send instructions to the media manager from RMAN. In the following example, we use the configure channel command to specify values for the ob_device and ob_media_family parameters:

```
RMAN> configure channel device type sbt
      parms='env=(ob_device=drive3,
      ob_media_family=med_fam1)';
```

The previous command specifies the ob_device parameter to direct the backup to the tape drive drive3 and the ob_media_family parameter to specify the media family med_fam1 for the backup.

You can also use the allocate channel command to specify media management parameters, as shown in the following example:

```
RMAN> run
      {
      allocate channel ch1 device type sbt
      parms 'env=(ob_device=drive3, ob_media_family=med_fam1)';
      ,,,
      }
```

This allocate channel command uses the env parameter of the parms option to specify the media family med_fam1 for the backup.

Using the send Command

The RMAN send command lets you send a vendor-specific string to a channel that's supported by a media manager. The following example shows how to issue the send command to specify a tape drive by sending the value for the ob_device parameter to Oracle Secure backup:

```
RMAN> run
      {
      allocate channel device type sbt;
      send 'ob_device drive3';
      send 'ob_media_family med_fam1';
      backup database;
      }
```

This `run` command will back up the spfile of the target database to the tape device drive3. The `send` command specifies the tape drive device3 as the value for the `ob_device` parameter for channel ch1, which communicates with the media manager.

How It Works

When you use the `send` command, if you don't specify a channel for a backup or restore job, RMAN uses all allocated channels for the job. The `send` command will accept only those commands that are supported by the specific media manager you are using. The database has nothing to do with the interpretation of the strings that you enter as input to the `send` command strings—that's left entirely to the MML.

18-6. Backing Up Using Oracle Secure Backup

Problem

You want to perform a backup using Oracle Secure Backup and RMAN.

Solution

You use the same `backup` commands as you would when you back up to disk, but you specify a tape channel when using Oracle Secure Backup. Here's a simple example of a command to back up the database and the archivelogs:

```
RMAN> run
      {
      allocate channel device type sbt
      parms 'env=(ob_media_family=med_fam1)';
      backup database plus archivelog;
      }
```

This command will back up the database and the archived redo logs to the media family med_fam1, as specified by the env parameter of the parms option.

How It Works

You can configure either a content-based or a time-based backup expiration policy for backups made to tape. If you delete any backup made through the sbt interface by using RMAN's `delete` command, OSB updates its catalog automatically to account for the deleted backups pieces. However, when you delete a backup piece from tape using an OSB command (`rmpiece`) or when you overwrite a backup piece on tape, RMAN's repository won't be automatically updated. Always make it a policy to use RMAN's `crosscheck` command to avoid discrepancies between the actual backups on tape and RMAN's repository backup metadata.

You can also use the `obtool` tool's `backup` command set to create an OSB-based operating system file backup. For example, the `backup --go` command starts a scheduled backup.

18-7. Restoring Using Oracle Secure Backup

Problem

You want to restore and recover a datafile with Oracle Secure Backup and RMAN.

Solution

Once you configure the OSB sbt interface, restoring datafiles requires using the same RMAN commands as you would for disk-based restore operations. Here's an example showing how to restore a datafile from tape and recover it using the recover command. You are missing a datafile or it's corrupted, so when you start the database, you're getting error message ORA-01157 saying that a file can't be identified. Follow these steps to perform a media recovery:

1. Start the database in the mount mode.

2. Run the following query to see exactly which datafiles are missing and need to be restored:

   ```
   SQL> select * from v$recover_file;
   ```

3. The restore preview command shows you what RMAN backups you need for restoring a missing datafile, as shown in the following example:

   ```
   RMAN> restore preview datafile 1;
   ```

4. Next, restore the datafile using the restore command, and then perform a media recovery of the restored datafile by using the recover command, as shown here:

   ```
   RMAN> run
          {
            allocate channel device type sbt
            parms 'env=(ob_media_family=test_mf)';
            restore datafile 1;
            recover datafile 1;
          }
   ```

   The run block shown here will restore datafile 1 from tape and recover it.

5. Open the database:

   ```
   SQL> alter database open;
   ```

   The recovery is successful because the database opens without any errors.

How It Works

You can perform all RMAN restore and recover commands with OSB-based tape backups. You can also use the obtool utility's restore command set to restore operating system files from an OSB backup of operating system files. The lsrestore command lets you see the restore jobs that have been submitted.

18-8. Accessing RMAN Backup Data in Oracle Secure Backup

Problem

You want to access and manage information about RMAN backups made with the OSB sbt interface.

Solution

You can use various commands in obtool to view important information about backup and restore jobs made through the OSB interface. For example, the lsjob command lists the information about backup and restore jobs for a database. Here's a typical lsjob command:

```
ob> lsjob --all
Job ID  Sched time   Contents              State
------------------------------------------------------------------------------
admin/1   none       incremental backup    completed successfully at 2005/06➥
/22/07:05:20
admin/2   none       backup prod1          completed successfully at 20075/06➥
/22.11:44
...
```

The lsjob command shows the backup job IDs, the contents (datafile backup, restore piece, and so on), and their *states*, which tell you whether they completed successfully. The lsbackup command shows what OSB backups currently exist:

```
ob> lsbackup --long

    Dataset:            prod1.ds
    Media family:       (null)
    Backup level:       full
    Priority:           2
    Privileged op:      yes
    Eligible to run:    2007/06/21.21:50:00
    Job expires:        2007/06/24.12:00:00
    Restriction:        any device
```

Use the catxcr command (again, in obtool) to obtain job transcripts, which provide detailed information such as the media family and volume information for an RMAN job. Here's a typical catxcr command:

```
ob> catxcr --noninput  --follow  --level warning  sbt/1.2
```

The example shown here disables any input requests and displays all warning and error messages for the job sbt/1.2. The follow option specifies that the job be monitored continually and new lines be shown as they appear. Instead of using the catxcr command, you can use the web tool to obtain job transcripts that contain information about RMAN jobs.

How It Works

OSB's catalog of backup metadata is maintained separately from RMAN'S recovery catalog and is directly managed by OSB. OSB's administrative server stores the backup catalog. Instead of using the `obtool` commands shown in the "Solution" section, you can also use the OSB web tool to view OSB's backup catalog metadata.

Of course, you can also use all RMAN commands such as the `list backup` command to view both disk-based and tape-based backups, including those made through the OSB interface.

Using Veritas NetBackup

The following set of recipes show how to use the Veritas NetBackup MML to perform backup and recovery operations with RMAN.

18-9. Installing the NetBackup Agent for Oracle

Problem

You want to install the NetBackup agent for Oracle.

Solution

Installing NetBackup is a rather involved affair with a lot of variables depending on the exact configuration chosen and the options installed. Here is a high-level task list for installing the NetBackup agent for Oracle:

1. Make sure you have all the software for the installation:

    • NetBackup license (you can't install without one)

    • NetBackup server software for your platform (the current version is 6.0)

    • NetBackup agent for Oracle software

2. Prepare the necessary hardware for the installation:

    • Master server

    • Media server

    • Tape library

3. Install the NetBackup software on the master server, the media servers, and the database (client) server. Test the communication from the master server to the database server by issuing the following command:

    ```
    $ cd /usr/openv/netbackup/bin
    $ ./bpclntcmd -pn
    expecting response from server hounbupbs01-nbu
    houcrspdb02-nbu.cce.star houcrspdb02-nbu 172.22.1.121 42546
    $
    ```

    The output shows that the master server (hounbupbs01-nbu) can be reached from the client (houcrspdb02-nbu) where the database is running.

4. Check the master server and other parameters to make sure everything is correct:

```
$ cd /usr/openv/netbackup
$ ls
bin bp.conf client dbext ext help logs nblog.conf nblog.conf.template
$ cat bp.conf
SERVER = hounbupbs01-nbu
SERVER = hounbupbs01
MEDIA_SERVER = hounbupms01-nbu
SERVER = houjmp1w-nbu
SERVER = hounbupbs01-nbu.cce.starwoodhotels.com
MEDIA_SERVER = hounbupms02
CLIENT_NAME = houcrspdb02-nbu
```

5. Verify that the NetBackup daemons are running:

```
$ netstat -a | grep bpcd
tcp        0      0 *:bpcd                    *:*              LISTEN
$ netstat -a | grep vnetd
tcp        0      0 *:vnetd                   *:*              LISTEN
```

The presence of the lines with LISTEN at the end indicates that the NetBackup daemons bpcd and vnetd are listening to the client requests.

6. Verify that the licenses are all installed. Run the following command:

```
$ /usr/openv/netbackup/bin/jnbSA
```

This will open the Admin Console. Check the license, and make sure you have it.

7. Insert the installation CD for NetBackup for Oracle, and mount the CD-ROM.

8. Log in as root on the database server.

9. Run the script ./install.

10. From the menu, choose the option NetBackup Database Agent.

11. When prompted, choose Y for local installation.

12. From the menu, choose NetBackup for Oracle.

13. Check the log files for any installation-related errors.

14. Now link Oracle to the NetBackup client. Log in to the database server box as the Oracle software owner.

15. Shut down all the Oracle Databases running on the server under the Oracle Home.

16. Relink Oracle by running the script oracle_link:

```
$ cd /usr/openv/netbackup/bin
$ ./oracle_link
```

17. This creates an output in the file /tmp/make_trace.<pid>. Check the file for errors.

The NetBackup agent for Oracle is now installed and ready to use.

How It Works

In this section, we will briefly explain the architecture of the NetBackup configuration. Figure 18-1 shows the various components of the NetBackup configuration and how they interact.

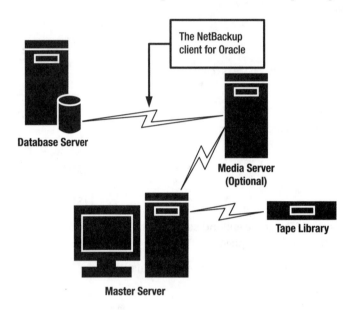

Figure 18-1. *NetBackup for Oracle architecture*

The primary software component is the *master server*, which actually acts as a master of the NetBackup processes, similar to the SMON of the Oracle instance. It schedules jobs, executes when the schedule comes up, and so on. It also manages the most important part of the system—the metadata repository—that is needed to catalog the tapes and chase the files to be restored. This is the critical component of the NetBackup system.

The *media server* is optional. This is used to take a local file backup. You can have more than one media server. In an Oracle database system, you can run the media server on the same host as the database runs.

The actual backup is taken from the *client server*, which, in your case, is the database server. NetBackup for the Oracle client software is installed on this server.

The relink operation integrates the NetBackup client libraries with the Oracle binary.

18-10. Maintaining Policies for the RMAN Backups

Problem

You want to create a new NetBackup policy or update an existing policy to make RMAN backups.

Solution

When NetBackup is installed, a policy is created by default. To add a new policy, follow these steps:

1. Start the Admin Console by issuing the following program:

   ```
   $ /usr/openv/netbackup/bin/jnbSA
   ```

   This opens a screen similar to the one shown in Figure 18-2.

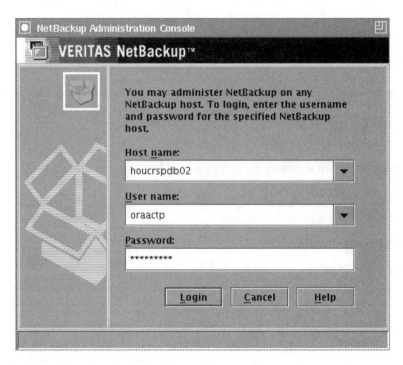

Figure 18-2. *NetBackup Admin Console login screen*

2. After you log in, you'll see the main console. From the console, choose the tab Policies.

3. In the All Policies pane, right-click the master server, and click New to create a new policy.

4. In the Policy Name field, type the name for the new policy.

5. From the Policy Type menu, choose Oracle.

6. Choose all the other options, and click OK. The policy will be created.

7. In the same pane, you can also update an existing policy.

How It Works

To create backups with RMAN via the NetBackup agent for Oracle, you must define a policy. The policy sets the parameters for the backup such as when they are created, where they are saved to, how many tape libraries are used, and so on. Without a policy, the RMAN job cannot proceed with the NetBackup as a media management library.

18-11. Scheduling NetBackup RMAN Jobs

Problem

You want to create schedules for NetBackup agent for Oracle.

Solution

The schedule is associated with a policy. To define a schedule for the policy, follow these steps:

1. Start the Admin Console by issuing the following program:

   ```
   $ /usr/openv/netbackup/bin/jnbSA
   ```

   This opens the screen shown earlier in Figure 18-2. Log in.

2. Choose the tab Policies.

3. Click the tab Schedules.

4. Click Default-Application-Backup.

5. Enter the relevant details of the schedule.

How It Works

The NetBackup policies are driven by schedules, which are required for automated backups. However, RMAN backups are not automated through the policies; rather, they are separately scheduled either through cron jobs or through other mechanisms. Therefore, the RMAN backups follow what is known as an *application backup schedule*. This schedule is automatically created when you create an Oracle policy. In step 4, you actually updated this application backup schedule.

18-12. Defining Client Databases in NetBackup

Problem

You want to define a database as a client of the NetBackup policy.

Solution

To add a database server as a client of the NetBackup system, follow these steps:

1. Start the Admin Console by issuing the following program:

   ```
   $ /usr/openv/netbackup/bin/jnbSA
   ```

This opens the screen shown earlier in Figure 18-2. Log in.

2. Click the Policies tab.

3. Click the Clients tab.

4. Click the New button.

5. In the Client Name field, enter a name.

6. Enter the Hardware and Operating System Type fields, and click the Add button.

The policy now has a new client.

How It Works

For a database to use the NetBackup client as its RMAN media management library, you must add the client to the NetBackup media server. You can add a number of clients to the same policy if the other characteristics are the same. For instance, if most of the databases use the same number of tape libraries and should have the same priority, you can choose only one policy for all the databases. Otherwise, group the clients, and choose the policy attributes according to their needs.

18-13. Checking for NetBackup Files on Tape

Problem

You want to check which backups are available on tape.

Solution

To find out which backups are available on the tape, query the control file of the Oracle database. Here are the steps:

1. Connect to RMAN client from the client server (which is the database server):

```
$ rman target=/

Recovery Manager: Release 10.2.0.1.0 - Production on Tue May 29 18:19:35 2007

Copyright (c) 1982, 2005, Oracle.  All rights reserved.


connected to target database: ACTPRD (DBID=2679297151)
RMAN>
```

2. Create a special channel for maintenance to query the tape:

```
RMAN> allocate channel for maintenance type sbt_tape;

using target database control file instead of recovery catalog
allocated channel: ORA_MAINT_SBT_TAPE_1
channel ORA_MAINT_SBT_TAPE_1: sid=361 devtype=SBT_TAPE
```

```
channel ORA_MAINT_SBT_TAPE_1: VERITAS NetBackup for Oracle - Release 6.0➥
   (2006110304)
```

3. Find out the backups available:

```
RMAN> list backup of database summary;
```

```
List of Backups
===============
```

Key	TY	LV	S	Device Type	Completion Time	#Pieces	#Copies	Compressed	Tag
1	B	F	A	SBT_TAPE	05-MAY-06	1	1	NO	TAG➥
20060505T155954									
2	B	F	A	SBT_TAPE	08-JUN-06	1	1	NO	TAG➥
20060608T213344									
3	B	0	A	SBT_TAPE	20-JUN-06	1	1	NO	LEVEL0
4	B	0	A	SBT_TAPE	20-JUN-06	1	1	NO	LEVEL0
8	B	1	A	SBT_TAPE	20-JUN-06	1	1	NO	LEVEL1
9	B	1	A	SBT_TAPE	20-JUN-06	1	1	NO	LEVEL1
11	B	0	A	DISK	18-JAN-07	1	1	NO	LVL0➥
_DB_BKP									
12	B	0	A	DISK	18-JAN-07	1	1	NO	LVL0➥
_DB_BKP									
13	B	0	A	DISK	18-JAN-07	1	1	NO	LVL0➥
_DB_BKP									
14	B	0	A	DISK	18-JAN-07	1	1	NO	LVL0➥
_DB_BKP									
16	B	0	A	DISK	18-JAN-07	1	1	NO	LVL0➥
_DB_BKP									
66	B	0	A	DISK	21-JAN-07	1	1	NO	LVL0➥
_DB_BKP									
67	B	0	A	DISK	21-JAN-07	1	1	NO	LVL0➥
_									
_DB_BKP									
68	B	0	A	DISK	21-JAN-07	1	1	NO	LVL0➥
_									
_DB_BKP									
69	B	0	A	DISK	21-JAN-07	1	1	NO	LVL0➥
_									
_DB_BKP									
74	B	0	A	DISK	28-JAN-07	1	1	NO	LVL0➥
_DB_BKP									
75	B	0	A	DISK	28-JAN-07	1	1	NO	LVL0➥
_DB_BKP									
76	B	0	A	DISK	28-JAN-07	1	1	NO	LVL0_DB
_BKP									

77 _DB_BKP	B	O	A DISK	28-JAN-07	1	1	NO	LVLO➥
79 _DB_BKP	B	O	A DISK	28-JAN-07	1	1	NO	LVLO➥
83 _DB_BKP	B	O	A *	21-JAN-07	1	2	NO	LVLO➥
84	B	O	A SBT_TAPE	07-FEB-07	1	1	NO	LEVEL0
85	B	O	A SBT_TAPE	07-FEB-07	4	1	NO	LEVEL0
86	B	O	A SBT_TAPE	07-FEB-07	1	1	NO	LEVEL0
87	B	O	A SBT_TAPE	07-FEB-07	1	1	NO	LEVEL0
89	B	O	A SBT_TAPE	07-FEB-07	1	1	NO	LEVEL0
92	B	O	A SBT_TAPE	12-FEB-07	1	1	NO	LEVEL0
93	B	O	A SBT_TAPE	12-FEB-07	4	1	NO	LEVEL0
94	B	O	A SBT_TAPE	12-FEB-07	1	1	NO	LEVEL0
95	B	O	A SBT_TAPE	12-FEB-07	1	1	NO	LEVEL0
97	B	O	A SBT_TAPE	12-FEB-07	1	1	NO	LEVEL0

4. This shows the summary of all the backups available. To find out the backups on tape only, see those with sbt_tape in the Device Type column.

How It Works

This RMAN command queries the control file to check the availability of the backups and reports them.

18-14. Configuring NetBackup Parameters in RMAN

Problem

You want to configure the NetBackup client to be called by RMAN to write directly to tape.

Solution

To set the NetBackup parameters that will be used every time the client is called, you can set the parameters permanently using the configure command, as shown here:

```
RMAN> configure channel DEVICE TYPE sbt_tape PARMS  'ENV=(NB_ORA_SERV=hounbupbs➥
01-nbu,NB_ORA_CLIENT=houcrspdb02-nbu,NB_ORA_POLICY=T2_HOU_CRS_P_ORACLE_PDB02,➥
SBT_LIBRARY=/logprd/oracle/app/oracle/product/10.2.0/db1/lib/libobk.so)';

new RMAN configuration parameters:
CONFIGURE CHANNEL DEVICE TYPE 'SBT_TAPE' PARMS  'ENV=(NB_ORA_SERV=hounbupbs01-➥
nbu,NB_ORA_CLIENT=houcrspdb02-nbu,NB_ORA_POLICY=T2_HOU_CRS_P_ORACLE_PDB02,➥
SBT_LIBRARY=/logprd/oracle/app/oracle/product/10.2.0/db1/lib/libobk.so)';
new RMAN configuration parameters are successfully stored

RMAN>
```

How It Works

To configure the Oracle Database backups in RMAN using NetBackup, you have to set some parameters that instruct the RMAN client to search for different settings such as the library and client server name. You do this by using the `configure` command.

To verify what settings have been set up for tape, use the following command:

```
RMAN> show channel;

RMAN configuration parameters are:
CONFIGURE CHANNEL 1 DEVICE TYPE 'SBT_TAPE' PARMS  'ENV=(NB_ORA_SERV=hounbupbs01-➡
nbu,NB_ORA_CLIENT=houcrspdb02-nbu,NB_ORA_POLICY=T2_HOU_CRS_P_ORACLE_PDB02,➡
SBT_LIBRARY=/logprd/oracle/app/oracle/product/10.2.0/db1/lib/libobk.so)';
CONFIGURE CHANNEL DEVICE TYPE 'SBT_TAPE' PARMS  'ENV=(NB_ORA_SERV=hounbupbs01-➡
nbu,NB_ORA_CLIENT=houcrspdb02-➡
nbu,NB_ORA_POLICY=T2_HOU_CRS_P_ORACLE_PDB02,SBT_LIBRARY=/logprd/oracle/app/➡
oracle/product/10.2.0/db1/lib/libobk.so)';

RMAN>
```

If you do not want to store these settings permanently, you need not issue the `configure` command. In that case, you need to set some environmental variables prior to issuing the RMAN commands. Here are the variables:

```
export NB_ORA_POLICY=T2_HOU_CRS_P_ORACLE_PDB01
export NB_ORA_SERV=hounbupbs01-nbu
export NB_ORA_CLIENT=houcrspdb01-nbu
export SBT_LIBRARY=$ORACLE_HOME/lib/libobk.so
```

18-15. Backing Up Using NetBackup

Problem

You want to back up an Oracle database using the NetBackup client.

Solution

To back up the database through RMAN using the NetBackup client, follow these steps:

1. Configure the NetBackup client parameters, as shown in recipe 18-14.

2. Call the RMAN backup commands as usual, but allocate a different type of channel in the beginning, as shown here:

```
RMAN> run
2> {
3>    allocate channel c1 type sbt_tape;
4>    backup database;
5> }
```

```
    allocated channel: c1
    channel c1: sid=359 devtype=SBT_TAPE
    channel c1: VERITAS NetBackup for Oracle - Release 6.0 (2006110304)

    Starting backup at 29-MAY-07
    channel c1: starting full datafile backupset
    channel c1: specifying datafile(s) in backupset
    input datafile fno=00004 name=/actprd/oracle/u01/actprd/actional_data01.dbf
    input datafile fno=00007 name=/actprd/oracle/u02/actprd/actional_data02.dbf
    channel c1: starting piece 1 at 29-MAY-07
    ... and so on ...
```

The backup is now complete.

How It Works

When RMAN backs up the database, it needs to write the output to a channel. Normally, the default is to write to a disk area. By specifying the allocate channel command in line 3, you instructed RMAN to write to the library called sbt_tape. This action in turn called the Net-Backup libraries to write to the tape with the parameters specified in the configure command shown in recipe 18-14.

If you didn't set the parameters, either by environmental variables or by the configure command, you will need to set them in the RMAN command itself. Here is an example how you can set the parameter in the run block:

```
RMAN> run
2> {
3>     allocate channel c1 type 'sbt_tape' parms='SBT_LIBRARY=/logprd/oracle/app/➡
oracle/product/10.2.0/db1/lib/libobk.so' maxpiecesize ${MAXPIECESIZE};
4>     backup database;
5> }
```

18-16. Restoring Using NetBackup

Problem

You want to restore a tablespace, a data file, or even the entire database through the Net-Backup MML.

Solution

To restore a tablespace, follow these steps:

1. Check whether a backup of the tablespace exists on the tape. You can issue the RMAN command list backup:

   ```
   RMAN> list backup of tablespace xmldb1;
   ```

```
List of Backup Sets
===================

BS Key  Type LV Size       Device Type Elapsed Time Completion Time
------- ---- -- ---------- ----------- ------------ ---------------
28      Full    256.00K     SBT_TAPE    00:01:13     13-JUN-07
        BP Key: 64    Status: AVAILABLE  Compressed: NO  Tag: ➥
TAG20070613T033536
          Handle: 14ik51o8_1_1   Media: 900116
    List of Datafiles in backup set 28
    File LV Type Ckp SCN    Ckp Time  Name
    ---- -- ---- ---------- --------- ----
    24      Full 9773915687 13-JUN-07 /logprd/oracle/u01/logprd/xmdb1_01.dbf
```

The presence of the last line indicates that at least one backup of the tablespace exists.

2. Then, take the tablespace offline, if it's not already:

```
RMAN> sql 'alter tablespace xmldb1 offline';

sql statement: alter tablespace xmldb1 offline
```

3. The tablespace is now ready to be restored. Issue the following commands in RMAN:

```
RMAN> restore tablespace xmldb1;

Starting restore at 13-JUN-07
configuration for SBT_TAPE channel 2 is ignored
configuration for SBT_TAPE channel 3 is ignored
allocated channel: ORA_SBT_TAPE_1
channel ORA_SBT_TAPE_1: sid=378 devtype=SBT_TAPE
channel ORA_SBT_TAPE_1: VERITAS NetBackup for Oracle - Release 6.0 ➥
(2006110304)
allocated channel: ORA_DISK_1
channel ORA_DISK_1: sid=283 devtype=DISK

channel ORA_SBT_TAPE_1: starting datafile backupset restore
channel ORA_SBT_TAPE_1: specifying datafile(s) to restore from backup set
restoring datafile 00024 to /logprd/oracle/u01/logprd/xmdb1_01.dbf
channel ORA_SBT_TAPE_1: reading from backup piece 14ik51o8_1_1
channel ORA_SBT_TAPE_1: restored backup piece 1
piece handle=14ik51o8_1_1 tag=TAG20070613T033536
channel ORA_SBT_TAPE_1: restore complete, elapsed time: 00:00:46
Finished restore at 13-JUN-07
```

■**Note** This `restore` command shown here assumes you have already configured the channels for both tape and disk so that the `restore` command can find the backup in either place. If this is not the case, you will need to issue two commands prior to the `restore` command: the `allocate channel for tape ...` command and the `allocate channel for disk ...` command. You can avoid that by simply configuring channels for tape and disk, as shown in recipe 18-14.

---

    4. Recover the tablespace:

```
RMAN> recover tablespace xmldb1;

Starting recover at 13-JUN-07
using channel ORA_SBT_TAPE_1
using channel ORA_DISK_1

starting media recovery
media recovery complete, elapsed time: 00:00:05

Finished recover at 13-JUN-07
```

    5. After the recovery is complete, bring the tablespace online:

```
RMAN> sql 'alter tablespace xmldb1 online';

sql statement: alter tablespace xmldb1 online
```

    The restore and recovery is now complete.

How It Works

When you back up a tablespace, actually its data files are backed up, and the information is recorded in the control file. When you issue the `list backup` command, RMAN queries the control file to check for the presence of backups. Later, when you issue the `restore tablespace` command, RMAN checks the data dictionary to get information about the data files of the tablespace, gets the backup name from the control file, and instructs the MML to execute a NetBackup command to get the specified file from the tape. Once the restore is complete, you need to recover the data file to apply all archived log files and any changes recorded in online redo log files. This opens the data file to be most up-to-date.

Using EMC NetWorker

The following recipes show how to use EMC NetWorker to perform backup and recovery operations with RMAN. Here are the prerequisite steps you must perform before you can use RMAN with the NetWorker software:

    1. Install and configure EMC NetWorker.

    2. Install and configure EMC NetWorker Module for Oracle (NMO).

EMC NetWorker is a suite of tools that provides data storage management services such as backup and recovery. The EMC NetWorker Module for Oracle component (formerly known as Legato NetWorker for Oracle) contains the application programming interfaces (APIs) that allow RMAN to interact with the MML and the NetWorker server. The NetWorker server and NMO work together to enable RMAN to perform backup and restore operations to and from a tape device. Figure 18-3 shows the basic architecture of NetWorker, NMO, and RMAN.

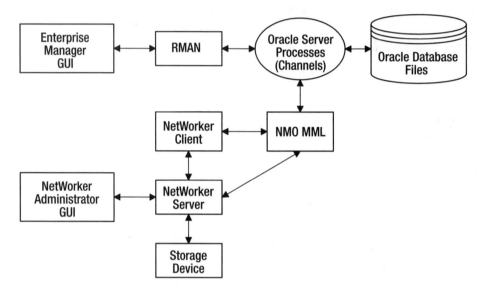

Figure 18-3. *Architecture of EMC NetWorker, NMO, and RMAN*

We don't cover all the possible hardware configurations and methods for using EMC NetWorker and NMO. We recommend that you refer to EMC's complete documentation for configuration details for the various versions of hardware, operating systems, and EMC NetWorker.

18-17. Configuring EMC NetWorker

Problem

You are required to configure EMC NetWorker before you can use NetWorker Module for Oracle (NMO).

Solution

This solution assumes you have already installed the EMC NetWorker software. Once EMC NetWorker is installed, then you will need to configure it so it can be used with NMO and RMAN. Here are the steps you need to perform:

1. Set up an Oracle administrator.

2. Configure a storage device.

3. Label and mount a tape.

Next we provide the details of the previous steps. You should perform these steps before you attempt to use the NMO MML and RMAN to back up your database.

Step 1: Setting Up an Oracle Administrator

From the NetWorker Administrator GUI, click Configuration. Next, right-click the host of interest, and choose Properties. You should see a screen similar to Figure 18-4.

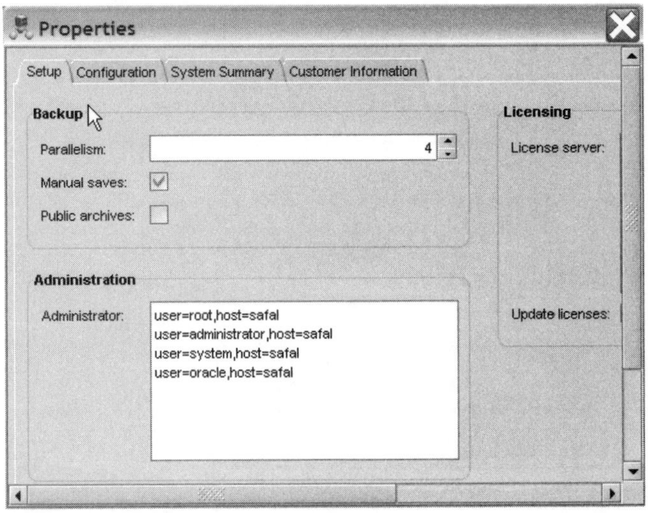

Figure 18-4. *Setting up an Oracle administrator*

The most critical property to set up is the administrator. You will need to add an administrator in the Administration pane. The user that you add as administrator is the owner of the Oracle binaries (on Unix systems this is usually the `oracle` operating system account).

Here are some typical entries in the Administration pane. In this example, we're adding the user `oracle`, and the server name is `safal`:

```
user=root,host=safal
user=administrator,host=safal
user=system,host=safal
user=oracle,host=safal
```

From the configuration screen, you can also set the degree of parallelism. This specifies the number of backup save streams that NetWorker uses to write to the backup device.

Step 2: Configuring a Storage Device

You must configure a storage device to be used for backup and recovery operations. The specific configuration will vary by device. You must first have a storage device connected to your backup server. The storage device can be a single tape drive or a multitape autochanger.

From the NetWorker Administrator GUI, click Devices. Select the host for which you want to specify a device. Right-click Devices. Next, choose Scan for Devices. You should see a screen similar to Figure 18-5.

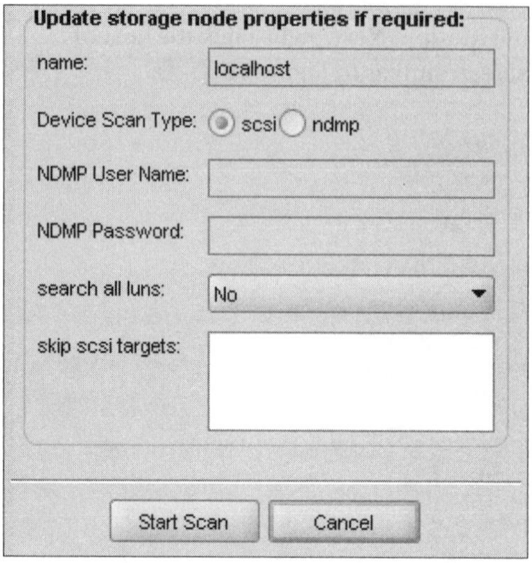

Figure 18-5. *Scanning for devices*

You can now choose the Start Scan option. When the scanning is complete, you should be able to view all detected devices.

Step 3: Labeling and Mounting a Tape

From the NetWorker Administrator GUI, click Devices. Select the appropriate host. Next click Devices for that host. Right-click the device of interest, and select Label. This will take you through the steps to label and mount a tape for the device.

How It Works

This recipe outlines the basic setup steps that need to be completed before you can use NMO with RMAN for backup and recovery. The exact setup will vary depending on how your environment is configured.

■**Note** Refer to the EMC NetWorker Module for Oracle administrator's guide for complete details on how to configure your environment.

18-18. Installing EMC NetWorker Module for Oracle
Problem

You want to install and use EMC NetWorker Module for Oracle (NMO).

Solution

Listed next are the general steps for installing and using NMO:

1. Log in as root on Oracle server.

2. Change directories to where the NMO installation software resides.

3. Use the appropriate software for your operating system to install NMO.

4. Log in as the owner of the Oracle binaries (usually oracle).

5. Link the NMO software with Oracle.

■**Note** We recommend you review the EMC NetWorker Module for Oracle installation guide for complete installation details for your operating system environment.

Step 1: Logging In As Root

Log in as root on the Oracle sever where NMO is going to be installed.

Step 2: Locating the NMO Installation Software

Change directories to where the NMO installation files reside. In this example, the NMO installation media is in directory /cdrom/solaris_64:

```
$ cd /cdrom/solaris_64
```

Step 3: Using OS Commands to Install NMO

On Solaris, use the pkgadd utility to install the appropriate packages (on HP, use swinstall; on Linux use rpm). This example shows a Solaris example of using pkgadd:

```
$ pkgadd -d /ora01/ebs/modules/oracle/solaris_64 LGTOnmo
```

You should see some output similar to the following:

```
*** Important Information for Completing your NMO Installation ***
--------------------------------------------------------------------------------
Depending on the Oracle version you are running,
you may have to link the Oracle executable
and/or shutdown and restart Oracle
before you are ready to use NMO.
Please, consult your Installation Guide for complete instructions.
```

After the installation is complete, you should see a message similar to this:

```
Installation of  <LGTOnmo> was successful.
```

Step 4: Logging In As an OS Oracle Account

Next, log in as the operating system oracle user account. On Unix, you can do this with the su command, as shown here:

```
$ su - oracle
```

Step 5: Linking NMO to Oracle

Now you need to link the NMO library file to Oracle. The procedure for linking varies by operating system. The following shows the procedure for Solaris and Linux:

```
$ cd $ORACLE_HOME/lib
$ ln -s /usr/lib/libnwora.so libobk.so
```

The key point for this step is that the libnwora.so file that is included with your NMO installation must be linked to the libobk.so file in the $ORACLE_HOME/lib directory.

How It Works

EMC NetWorker Module for Oracle is an add-on component to the EMC NetWorker software suite. NMO works with RMAN to enable backup and recovery operations via tape. NMO interacts with RMAN through the Oracle System Backup to Tape (SBT) application programming interface (API).

The EMC NetWorker client and NetWorker server need to be installed prior to installing NetWorker Module for Oracle. The NMO component must be installed on the same server as your EMC NetWorker client and your Oracle server. You can install the EMC NetWorker server on a separate server.

This recipe does not cover how to install and configure the EMC NetWorker suite of software. See EMC's documentation for full details on how to implement NetWorker modules.

18-19. Backing Up Using the EMC NetWorker Module for Oracle

Problem

You want to back up your database using EMC NetWorker Module for Oracle.

Solution

After NMO has been configured, you can begin to use RMAN to manually back up to tape. For basic functionality, you can simply allocate a channel of type sbt_tape and begin to back up your database, as shown here:

```
RMAN> connect target /
RMAN> run {
2>    allocate channel c1 type sbt_tape;
3>    backup database;
4>    release channel c1;}
```

Listed next is a partial snippet of the output you can expect to see:

```
channel c1: backup set complete, elapsed time: 00:03:26
channel c1: starting full datafile backupset
channel c1: specifying datafile(s) in backupset
including current control file in backupset
channel c1: starting piece 1 at 18-JUN-07
channel c1: finished piece 1 at 18-JUN-07
piece handle=18ikjuds_1_1 tag=TAG20070618T190726
comment=API Version 2.0,MMS Version 4.2.0.0
channel c1: backup set complete, elapsed time: 00:00:04
Finished backup at 18-JUN-07
released channel: c1
```

You can also use the RMAN send command to specify NSR variables to be used by NMO during a backup operation. The send command allows you to send vendor-specific commands to a channel when using an MML. In this example, the host name is shrek, and the default NetWorker group is used with compressed backup sets:

```
RMAN> connect target /
RMAN> run {
2>    allocate channel c1 type sbt_tape;
3>    send 'NSR_ENV=(NSR_SERVER=shrek,NSR_GROUP=Default,NSR_COMPRESSION=TRUE)';
4>    backup database;
5>    release channel c1;}
```

■Note Consult with the NMO administrator's guide for complete details on how to use NMO to run a scheduled RMAN backup job.

How It Works

You can use a wide variety of methods to back up your database files. This recipe showed only how to run the backup database command. See Chapter 7 for complete details on various options when using RMAN to back up database files.

After NMO has been installed, you can manually run backup and restore operations that use tape devices. You can govern the behavior of NMO by setting NSR parameters through the send command. Table 18-1 describes the NSR environment variables that control the behavior of NMO backup and restore operations.

Table 18-1. *NSR Parameter Descriptions and Values*

NSR Parameter	Description	Valid Values
nsr_checksum	Specifies whether NetWorker performs a checksum on backups.	Valid values are FALSE (default) and TRUE.
nsr_client	Specifies NetWorker client used for backup and recovery operations.	NetWorker client hostname.
nsr_compression	Specifies whether NetWorker compresses backups.	Valid values are FALSE (default) and TRUE.
nsr_data_volume_pool	Controls name of volume pool for backups.	A NetWorker pool name.
nsr_data_volume_pool*n*	*n* can be 1, 2, or 3. Specifies name of volume pool for duplexed backups.	A NetWorker pool name.
nsr_debug_file	Specifies a filename and path of file to which debugging output can be logged.	Valid path name and file on database server.
nsr_debug_level	Specifies the level of debugging. Use this with the parms parameter (not the send command).	Valid values are 0 (default), 1, and 2.
nsr_dprintf_file	Specifies filename and path of the file for the debugging output of the NetWorker dbprintf() function. Use this with the parms parameter (not the send command).	Valid pathname and file on database server.
nsr_encryption	Controls whether encryption is performed on the backup.	Valid values are FALSE (default) and TRUE.
nsr_group	Specifies the NetWorker group to be used by RMAN.	Valid NetWorker group. The Default NetWorker group is the default (you probably could have guessed that).
nsr_no_busy_errors	Controls whether a backup fails immediately in the event the server is busy.	Valid values are FALSE (default) and TRUE.
nsr_no_multiplex	Specifies whether multiplexing is disabled for the backup device.	Valid values are FALSE (default) and TRUE.
nsr_nwpath	Specifies the directory path for nsrmm and nsrsnapck binaries.	Valid directory path for nsrmm and nsrsnapck binaries.
nsr_proxy_file	Specifies path of PowerSnap configuration settings.	Valid directory path for configuration file.
nsr_retention_disabled	Specifies whether NetWorker policies of browse and retention are disabled.	Valid values are FALSE (default) and TRUE.
nsr_saveset_browse	Specifies a date at which a backup is to be removed from the NetWorker client.	Valid date nsr_getdate(3) format.
nsr_saveset_retention	Specifies a date at which a saveset can be recycled.	Valid date nsr_getdate(3) format.
nsr_server	Specifies server name of NetWorker server.	A valid NetWorker server name.

18-20. Restoring Using the EMC NetWorker Module for Oracle

Problem

You want to restore and recover your database using EMC NetWorker Module for Oracle (NMO).

Solution

When using NMO to restore and recover your database, use the RMAN send command to specify the appropriate NSR parameters and then issue the restore and recover commands, as shown here:

```
RMAN> connect target /
RMAN> startup mount;
RMAN> run {
2>    allocate channel c1 type sbt_tape;
3>    send 'NSR_ENV=(NSR_SERVER=shrek,NSR_GROUP=Default)';
4>    restore database;
5>    recover database;
6>    alter database open;
7>    release channel c1;}
```

Here is a partial listing of the output you can expect to see:

```
channel c1: starting datafile backupset restore
channel c1: specifying datafile(s) to restore from backup set
restoring datafile 00001 to /ora01/BRDSTN/system01.dbf
restoring datafile 00002 to /ora02/BRDSTN/undotbs01.dbf
restoring datafile 00003 to /ora02/BRDSTN/sysaux01.dbf
restoring datafile 00004 to /ora04/BRDSTN/users01.dbf
channel c1: reading from backup piece 17ikju7e_1_1
channel c1: restored backup piece 1
piece handle=17ikju7e_1_1 tag=TAG20070618T190726
channel c1: restore complete, elapsed time: 00:03:25
Finished restore at 18-JUN-07
Starting recover at 18-JUN-07
starting media recovery
media recovery complete, elapsed time: 00:00:08
Finished recover at 18-JUN-07
database opened
released channel: c1
```

How It Works

Performing a restore and recovery using NMO requires that you allocate a channel of type sbt_tape. Similar to backup operations, you can also specify NSR parameters to govern the behavior of the restore and recovery operations (see Table 18-1 for valid NSR parameters).

You can specify any valid restore and recovery commands when using an MML. This recipe showed an example of performing a complete restore and recovery of your database.

For full details on various restore and recovery scenarios, see Chapters 10, 11, and 12 of this book.

18-21. Uninstalling the EMC NetWorker Module for Oracle

Problem

You want to uninstall the EMC NetWorker Module for Oracle (NMO) software.

Solution

Follow these steps to uninstall NMO from your Oracle database server:

1. Ensure that no database backups are currently running.

2. Log in as the Oracle operating system account.

3. Use the appropriate operating system command to remove the symbolic link.

4. Log in as the root user.

5. Follow the instructions for your operating system to remove the NMO software.

■**Note** We recommend that you review the EMC NetWorker Module for Oracle installation guide for complete instructions on uninstalling NMO from your OS environment.

Step 1: Ensuring That No Backups Are Running

If you have any Oracle database backups running, you should either wait until they complete or manually stop them.

Step 2: Logging In As an Owner of the Oracle Software

Log in as the operating system account with which you installed the Oracle software. This operating system account is usually named oracle.

Step 3: Removing the Symbolic Link

This step will vary by operating system. On Solaris or Linux, use the rm command to remove the libobk.so symbolic link, as shown here:

```
$ cd $ORACLE_HOME/lib
$ rm libobk.so
```

Step 4: Logging In As the Root User

On a Unix, log in as the operating system root user account for the box.

Step 5: Removing the NMO Software

This step will vary by operating system. The following example shows how to use `pkgrm` on Solaris (use `swremove` on HP, and use `rpm` on Linux):

```
$ pkgrm LGTOnmo
```

How It Works

Sometimes you are required to remove software from a server. The NMO software is fairly easy to remove. This recipe documents the basic steps you have to perform to remove NMO.

18-22. Verifying the MML Installation

Problem

You want to verify that your media manager layer (MML) has been installed correctly.

■**Note** This recipe is valid for any Oracle environment that ships with the `sbttest` utility. The `sbttest` utility works with any media management layer (Oracle Secure Backup, Veritas NetBackup, EMC NetWorker Module for Oracle, IBM Tivoli, HP OmniBack, and so on).

Solution

On some Unix platforms there is an `sbttest` utility that can be used to verify that your MML has been installed and configured correctly. From the Unix command line, run the `sbttest` utility. To run this utility, you must specify a dummy file for the utility to interact with. In this example, the filename is mml.tst:

```
$ sbttest mml.tst
```

If the test is successful, you should see lights blinking on your tape device and output on the screen similar to the following:

```
The sbt function pointers are loaded from libobk.so library.
-- sbtinit succeeded
-- sbtinit (2nd time) succeeded
sbtinit: Media manager supports SBT API version 2.0
sbtinit: vendor description string=NMO v4.2.0.0
```

If your MML has not been installed correctly, then the utility will report errors such as the following:

```
libobk.so could not be loaded.  Check that it is installed.
```

If you receive the previous message, ensure that the libnwora file is in the correct directory and is correctly linked to the libobk file (this will vary by MML vendor).

How It Works

The sbttest utility is designed to test whether you can use your MML to back up and restore files to and from tape. This utility will test functionality such as the following:

- Is MML installed correctly?

- Can you write files to tape through the RMAN SBT API?

- Can you read files from tape via the RMAN SBT API?

This utility is located in your $ORACLE_HOME/bin directory. If you don't find it there, check with Oracle Support for the availability of sbttest for your operating system.

The sbttest utility requires that you list a filename for it to use as part of the test. This file does not have to exist before you run the test. If you want to view all options available with the sbttest utility, then don't specify any parameters on the command line, as shown here:

```
$ sbttest
```

You should now see a long listing of the parameters available with the sbttest utility. Table 18-2 describes these parameters.

Table 18-2. *Description of* sbttest *Parameters*

Parameter Name	Purpose
backup_file_name	The only required parameter. If this file doesn't exist, the sbttest utility will create it for use during the test and then delete it upon completion.
dbname	The database name that sbt uses to identify the backup file (the default is sbtdb).
trace	The trace filename where the MML software writes diagnostic messages.
remove_before	When specified, the backup file will be deleted before it is opened. This is useful when a previous run of sbttest didn't complete successfully and didn't delete the backup file.
noremove_after	Instructs sbttest to not remove the backup file after successful completion.
read_only	When specified a backup file must already exist. Instructs sbttest to validate the backup file contents.
no_regular_backup_restore	Instructs sbttest to skip the nonproxy backup and restore.
no_proxy_backup	Instructs sbttest to skip proxy copy backup.
no_proxy_restore	Instructs sbttest to skip proxy copy restore.
file_type	File type can be 1, 2, or 3.
copy_number	Specifies the copy_number parameter to sbtpcbackup.
media_pool	Specifies the media_pool parameter to sbtpcbackup.
os_res_size	Determines the size of the operating system reserved block (in bytes).
pl_res_size	Determines the size of the platform reserved block (in bytes).
block_size	Determines the size of blocks written to the backup file (default is 16,384 bytes).

Parameter Name	Purpose
block_count	Specifies number of blocks written to back up file (default is 100).
proxy_file	Specifies the operating system filename, backup filename, operating system reserved size, block size, and block count for the proxy file.
libname	Determines the sbt library to test. The default library is libobk.so. You can specify oracle.disksbt for Oracle's disk sbt library.

Listed next is an example showing how to specify parameters when running the sbttest utility. This example shows how to limit the number of blocks written to tape to 10:

```
$ sbttest mml.tst -block_count 10
```

The next example shows how to store the diagnostic messages in a file named mml.trc:

```
$ sbttest mml.tst -trace /orahome/mml.trc
```

You can also test the backup of an existing datafile. This example instructs the sbttest utility to use an existing datafile with the name of data_ts06.dbf in the BRDSTN database:

```
$ sbttest data_ts06.dbf -dbname BRDSTN
```

■**Note** There is no sbttest utility for the Windows environment. However, you can request that Oracle Support provide you with the loadsbt.exe utility for Windows. The loadsbt.exe utility isn't as robust as sbttest, but it does provide you with a way to troubleshoot your media management layer in a Windows environment.

Performing Backup and Recovery with Enterprise Manager

This chapter shows you the basics of using Enterprise Manager (EM) for backup and recovery. EM provides you with an interface to RMAN through several screens. You can access most of RMAN's many features via these screens. The main goal of this chapter is to show you how to successfully perform fundamental backup and recovery tasks via EM.

Note It is beyond the scope of this book to show you how to implement and use all the features available through EM. Oracle has a whole set of books on how to implement and use EM. You can download EM documentation from Oracle's OTN website at http://otn.oracle.com.

We assume that you have either EM Grid Control or EM Database Control installed and running. This chapter shows backup and recovery examples using screen shots from EM Database Control. The EM Database Control screens shown in this chapter are nearly identical to the screens found in EM Grid Control. Therefore, you should be able to follow the examples in this chapter using either Grid Control or Database Control.

The screen shots in this chapter are based on Enterprise Manager 11g. These screens and process flows are similar to those used in Enterprise Manager 10g. You should be able to follow the EM 11g screens even if you are using EM 10g.

19-1. Getting Started with RMAN and Enterprise Manager

Problem

You want to use RMAN through EM Database Control. You wonder where to start.

Solution

Here are the steps for getting started with EM Database Control:

1. Install EM Database Control.

2. Ensure the Database Control process is running.

3. Access EM Database Control from your favorite web browser.

Step 1: Install EM Database Control

By default, Enterprise Manager Database Control is included with every installation of Oracle Database 10g or newer. It will be installed for you unless you explicitly deselect it during the installation of the Oracle RDBMS software (binaries).

If for some reason EM Database Control hasn't been installed, then use the Oracle Universal Installer to install it. Refer to the EM installation documentation that is specific to your OS for instructions on how to install Enterprise Manager. Figure 19-1 is a partial snapshot of the Oracle Universal Installer screen showing that Enterprise Manager has already been installed.

Components	Install Status
☐ Oracle Net Listener 11.1.0.3.0	Installed (v.11.1.0.3.0)
☐ Oracle Connection Manager 11.1.0.3.0	Not Installed
■ Oracle Enterprise Manager Console DB 11.1.0.2.0	Installed (v.11.1.0.2.0)
☐ Oracle Call Interface (OCI) 11.1.0.3.0	Installed (v.11.1.0.3.0)
☐ Oracle Programmer 11.1.0.3.0	Installed (v.11.1.0.3.0)
☐ Oracle XML Development Kit 11.1.0.3.0	Installed (v.11.1.0.3.0)
☐ Oracle ODBC Driver 11.1.0.3.0	Installed (v.11.1.0.3.0)
☐ Oracle Configuration Manager 10.2.4.0.0	Installed (v.10.2.4.0.0)

Figure 19-1. *Installing the Enterprise Manager Database Control*

Step 2: Ensure the Console Process Is Running

The EM Database Control console process must be running before you can connect to EM via your web browser. If you had the Oracle Installer automatically create a starter database, then you probably already have a console process running on your database server. In Unix or Windows, you can start, stop, and check on the status of the console process via the emctl utility.

The emctl utility is located in ORACLE_HOME/bin (just like all other Oracle utilities). Ensure that ORACLE_HOME/bin is included in your OS PATH variable. Also verify that the ORACLE_SID operating system variable is set to your target database SID. Once you've established your database-related operating system variables, you can then run emctl commands.

■**Note** See recipe 2-1 for details on how to establish your OS variables.

Log in to the OS account that you installed the Oracle software with (usually named oracle), and start the EM console as shown here:

```
$ emctl start dbconsole
```

To check on the status of the EM console, run the following command:

```
$ emctl status dbconsole
```

To stop the EM console, run the following command:

```
$ emctl stop dbconsole
```

■ **Note** In Windows, you can start, stop, and check on the console status from the Services utility. You can view Windows services by running the `services.msc` utility, or you can also navigate to the Services utility by going to your Windows Control Panel and then to Administrative Tools. Once you are in the utility, you should see an OracleDBConsole<SID> service. Additionally, you can use the Windows `net start` and `net stop` OS commands to start and stop services, respectively.

Step 3: Accessing Enterprise Manager from Browser

Once your console process is running, you can access EM Database Control via your favorite web browser via the following URL:

```
http://<hostname>:<port number>/em
```

For example, if your hostname is mycomp and your port number is 1158, your URL to access EM would be as follows:

```
http://mycomp:1158/em
```

Once you launch EM, you should be presented with the screen shown in Figure 19-2.

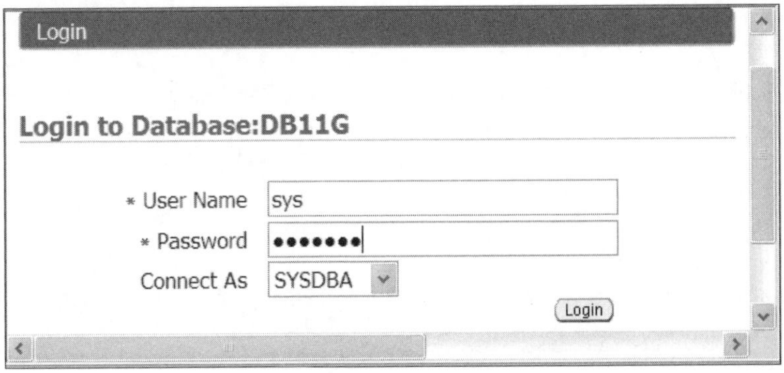

Figure 19-2. *Logging in to the EM Database Control*

You can now log in as sys or another user who you've set up to do database maintenance tasks. Use the password that you specified for the sys schema when installing the Oracle RDBMS software. If you don't know the sys password or how to change it, then contact another DBA on your team or Oracle Support.

How It Works

EM Database Control is installed by default with Oracle Database 10*g* (and newer). EM Database Control is easily accessed through a web browser. Remember to bookmark your browser with the correct EM Database Control URL. That way you don't have to try to remember the URL long after you've installed and forgotten the port and host information.

If you have forgotten your port number, then you can find it in the ORACLE_HOME/install/portlist.ini file. In that file, you can find entries similar to this:

```
iSQL*Plus HTTP port number =5560
Enterprise Manager Console HTTP Port (orcl) = 1158
Enterprise Manager Agent Port (orcl) = 3938
Enterprise Manager Console HTTP Port (ASMDB) = 5500
Enterprise Manager Agent Port (ASMDB) = 1830
```

Notice from the output that the Enterprise Manager Console HTTP port for the ORCL database is 1158. The value of 1158 is usually the default EMC port in both Windows and Unix environments.

If you don't remember your hostname, in Unix you can determine your server name by using the hostname command or by looking in your /etc/hosts file. On Windows you can determine your server computer name by using the DOS hostname command or by navigating to Start ➤ Control Panel ➤ System and then clicking the tab Computer Name.

USING EM CONFIGURATION ASSISTANT

If you need to configure your database for Database Control, then use the emca utility. Through this utility you can add or remove databases from Database Control. Here is an example of adding a database in a Unix environment to Database Control:

```
$ emca -config dbcontrol db -repos create
```

You will be prompted for information such as the SID, passwords, port number, and email address. The EM configuration assistant will create a repository owner schema for you and populate it with the necessary objects.

This example shows how to remove your database from Database Control:

```
$ emca -deconfig dbcontrol db -repos drop
```

This example instructs the EM configuration assistant to enable Database Control and configure backups for your database:

```
$ emca -config dbcontrol db -repos create -backup
```

The emca utility has numerous features. To view all options for emca, use the -help switch, as shown here:

```
$ emca -help
```

19-2. Setting Up a Credentialed OS User

Problem

Before you can run a backup job from Enterprise Manager, you must set up an OS credentialed user. You wonder how to do that task.

Unix Solution

If you're in a Unix environment, then all you need is access to an OS user account that belongs to the privileged OS group (usually dba or oinstall). Typically this is the oracle Unix account that you used to install the Oracle RDBMS software (binaries). To verify that your OS user account belongs to the proper group, use the Unix id command:

```
$ id
uid=100(oracle) gid=101(oinstall)
```

You don't need to do any further setup. You can use this operating system account as your credentialed OS user.

Windows Solution

In a Windows environment, the OS user who you use to run EM jobs must belong to the Oracle dba group and must also have the privilege to run batch jobs.

Adding a User to the DBA Group

Your credentialed OS user must belong to the dba group. Users who belong to the dba group have the privileges required to run RMAN jobs. Here are the steps for adding a Windows OS user to the dba group:

1. Go to Control Panel and then Administrative Tools.

2. Click Computer Management.

3. Click Local Users and Groups, and then click Groups.

4. Make sure your OS user is a member of the Oracle group (usually named ora_dba).

Granting Privileges to Run Batch Jobs

In Windows, your credentialed OS user must have the privilege to run batch jobs. Without this privilege, you won't be able to run RMAN jobs from Enterprise Manager. Here are the steps for granting an OS user the privilege to run batch jobs:

1. Go to Control Panel and then Administrative Tools.

2. Click Local Security Policy and then Local Policies.

3. Click User Rights Assignments and then Log On As Batch Job.

4. Click Add User or Group, and type the OS username you want to run backup jobs.

How It Works

When using Enterprise Manager for backup and recovery, you must have access to a credentialed OS user account and password. In Unix, this is usually the `oracle` operating system account you used to install the binaries. The OS account must belong to a privileged OS group that was created when you installed the Oracle binaries.

In Windows, the OS user who you specify to run Enterprise Manager backup and recovery jobs must belong to the Oracle group (usually named `ora_dba`) and must have privileges to run batch jobs. If either of these required privileges are missing, then you will not be able to successfully run an RMAN backup. If you attempt to run an Enterprise Manager backup and recovery job without a credentialed OS user, then you will be presented with an error similar to that shown in Figure 19-3.

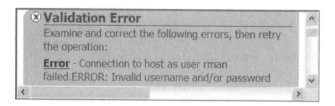

Figure 19-3. *Getting an invalid username/password message*

If you receive this error, ensure that you have correctly set up a credentialed OS user as described in this recipe.

19-3. Creating a Backup

Problem

You want to use Enterprise Manager to back up your database.

Solution

Ensure you have the following in place before you begin:

- EM Grid Control or EM Database Control installed

- Target database created and running

- A credentialed OS user created (see recipe 19-2)

If all of the previous items are available, then you are ready to begin with step 1.

Step 1: Log in and Navigate to Availability

Log in to Enterprise Manager 11*g*, and click the Availability tab. This will take you to a screen where you can set up backup and recovery jobs. If you are using Enterprise Manager 10*g*, then you will need to click the Maintenance tab for this step. Figure 19-4 shows the backup and recovery options available from this screen.

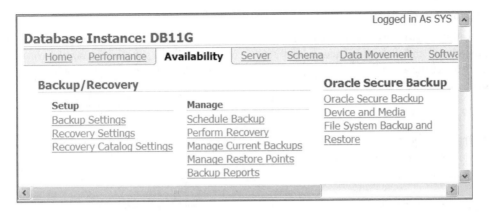

Figure 19-4. *Viewing the EM Backup and Recovery screen*

Step 2: Enter Host Credentials

Next click the Schedule Backup link. You should now see a screen similar to Figure 19-5 that allows you to schedule backups. The key task on this screen is to enter your host credentials. The host credentials are the OS username and password you set up in recipe 19-2.

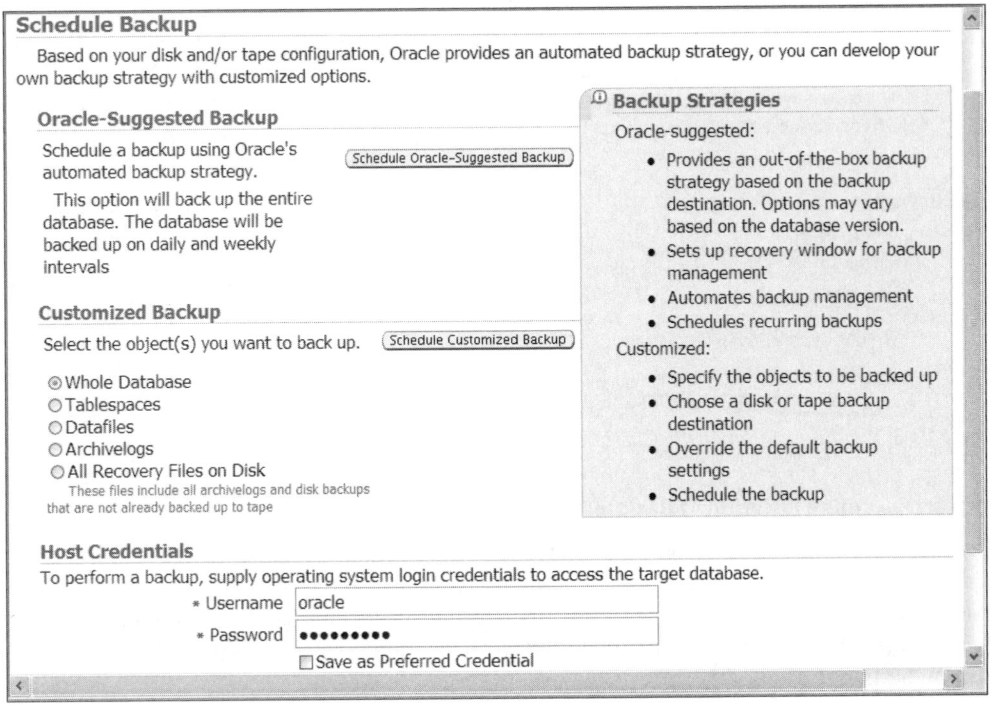

Figure 19-5. *Viewing the Schedule Backup screen*

Step 3: Choose Backup Options

In this example, we'll walk you through scheduling a customized backup. Once you fill in the host credentials, click Schedule Customized Backup. You should now see a screen similar to Figure 19-6. For this example, we're just going to use the defaults. This will be a full and online backup.

■**Note** Ensure that your database is in archivelog mode before taking an online backup. See recipe 2-3 for details on how to toggle the archivelog mode of your database.

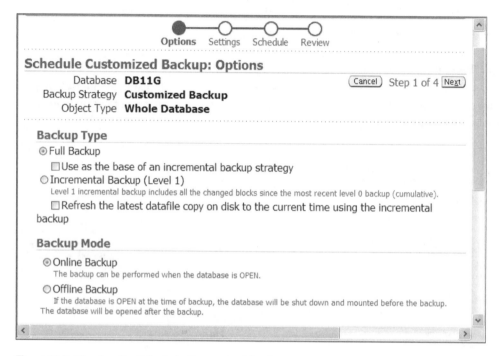

Figure 19-6. *Viewing the Schedule Customized Backup: Options screen*

Step 4: Determine Location of Backups

Click the Next tab. You should now see a screen similar to Figure 19-7. On this screen, you can choose to back up to disk or tape. We recommend using a flash recovery area when backing up to disk. See Chapter 3 for details on setting up a flash recovery area. If you don't have a flash recovery area set up, then you can directly specify a location on disk by clicking the Override Current Settings button.

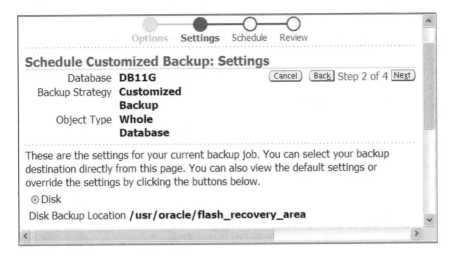

Figure 19-7. *Viewing the Schedule Customized Backup: Settings screen*

Step 5: Schedule a Backup Time

Click Next, and you should see a screen similar to Figure 19-8. Here you can choose when you want the job to start and to have the backup run at regular intervals. In this example, we accept the defaults of having the backup job run immediately and just one time.

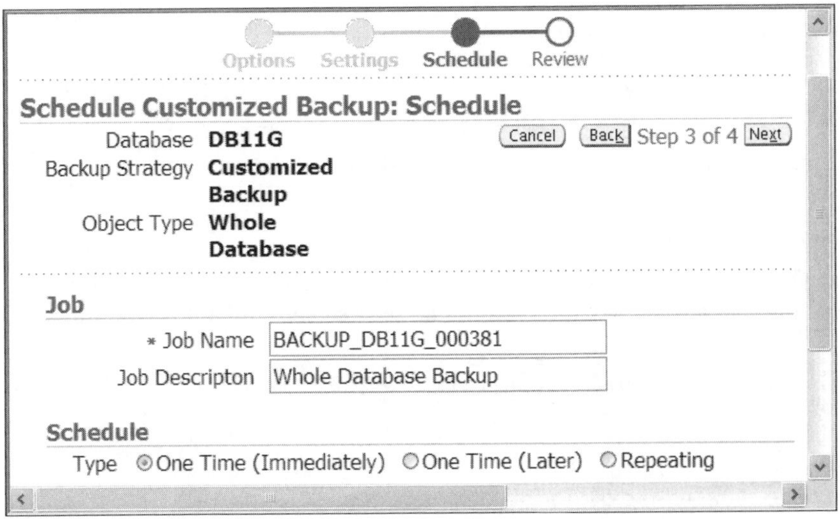

Figure 19-8. *Scheduling the backup time*

Step 6: Review RMAN Backup Scripts

Click the Next tab. You should now see a screen similar to Figure 19-9. From here you can review the details of your RMAN backup job before you submit it to run. You can see the actual RMAN commands that Enterprise Manager will submit to run.

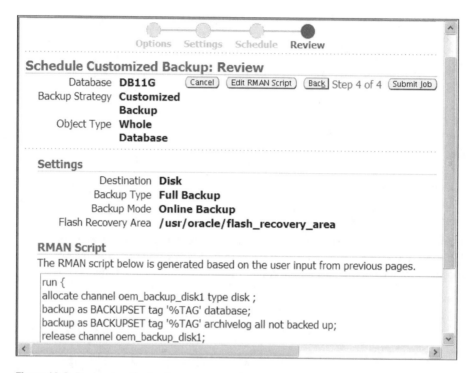

Figure 19-9. *Reviewing the backup commands*

Step 7: Review Status of Backup Job

If you're satisfied with the backup setup, click the Submit Job button to run the backup command(s). If everything goes as planned, then you should see a screen similar to Figure 19-10.

Figure 19-10. *Reviewing the status of submitting the job*

Click the View Job button to check on the status of your backup job. You should see a screen similar to Figure 19-11.

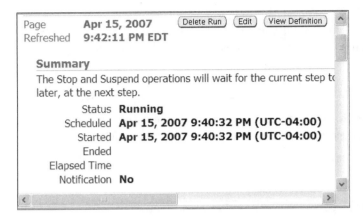

Figure 19-11. *Reviewing the status of the backup job*

How It Works

Enterprise Manager is fairly easy to use to back up your database. The default configuration is sufficient to get you going. The tricky part is ensuring that you have set up a credentialed OS user (described in recipe 19-2) before attempting to run a backup job.

This recipe just introduces you to the basics of how to use Enterprise Manager for backups. Many other features and options are available for you. We don't describe all of them in this recipe or chapter. We do encourage you to look at Oracle's documentation at http://otn.oracle.com for full details on using Enterprise Manager.

19-4. Restoring and Recovering

Problem

You want to restore and recover a damaged datafile in your database. You have current control files and all redo required to perform complete recovery.

■**Note** See Chapter 20 for details on using the Data Recovery Advisor for automated restore and recovery.

Solution

In general, the steps for completely recovering your whole database are as follows:

1. Shut down your database.

2. Start up the database in mount mode.

3. Issue the restore and recovery commands.

4. Open your database for general access.

Enterprise Manager will walk you through all of these steps via several screens. If your database isn't in mount mode, EM will guide you through the process of shutting down your database and placing it in mount mode. This example starts with the database already in mount mode.

■**Note** The example in this recipe shows how to restore one datafile in your database. The actual screens used in a restore and recovery operation will vary by quite a bit depending on the type of failure and your backup strategy.

Step 1: Log In to Enterprise Manager and Navigate to Recovery Screen

To perform recovery tasks using Enterprise Manager, first log in to the EM database console (see Figure 19-2), and then click Perform Recovery. You may be prompted for your host credentials. This is the credentialed OS user that you setup in recipe 19.2. You may also be prompted for your database login information. You must use a schema (usually sys) that has sysdba privileges.

You should see a screen similar to Figure 19-12. Select the Recover to Current Time option. In this example, we're restoring and recovering only one datafile; therefore, Datafiles is chosen from the Object Type drop-down list. Make sure your host credentials are entered, and then click Perform Customized Repair.

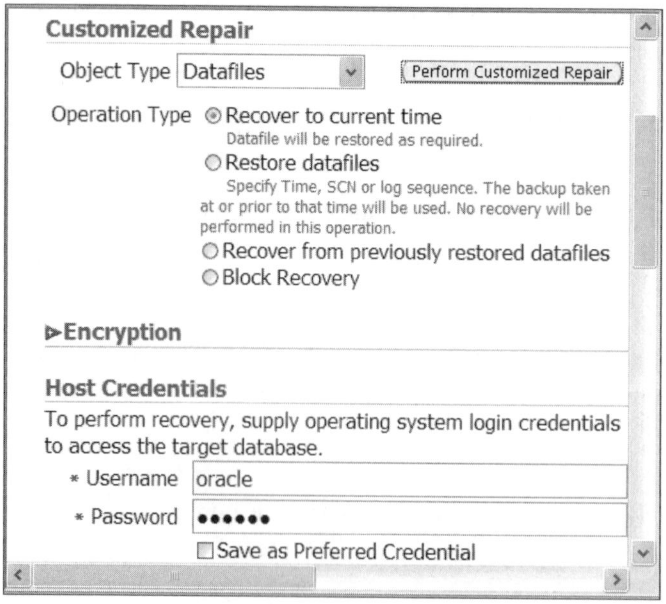

Figure 19-12. *Performing a customized repair*

Step 2: Choose Objects to Recover

You should now see a screen similar to Figure 19-13. You have the option of adding datafiles to be restored. In this example, only one datafile is missing. Now click the Next button.

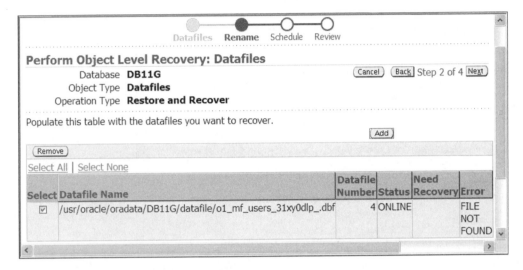

Figure 19-13. *Performing object-level recovery*

Step 3: Determine Where to Restore Datafiles

You should now see a screen similar to Figure 19-14. In this example, we're restoring the datafile to the default location. Click the Next button.

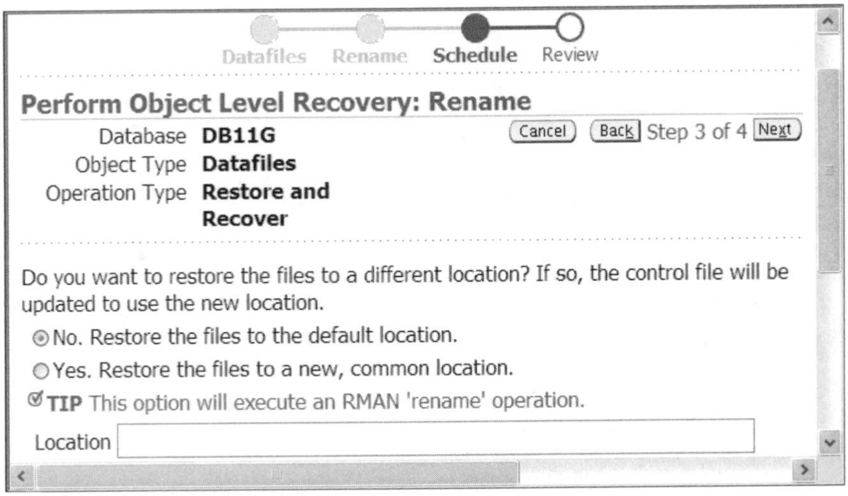

Figure 19-14. *Restoring datafiles to the default location*

Step 4: Review RMAN Commands

You now are presented with a review page, as shown in Figure 19-15. From here you can review the actual RMAN commands that will be run for the restore and recovery operations. Click Edit RMAN Script to view the RMAN commands.

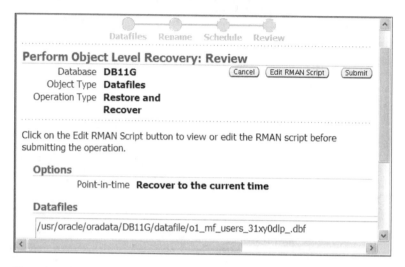

Figure 19-15. *Reviewing the recovery*

We recommend that you review the RMAN commands to verify that it is going to do what you want it to do. Here are the actual RMAN commands that will be run in this recipe:

```
run {
restore datafile 4;
recover datafile 4;
}
```

Step 5: Run the Restore and Recovery Script

If you are satisfied with the RMAN script, click the Submit button. You will now see a screen similar to Figure 19-16.

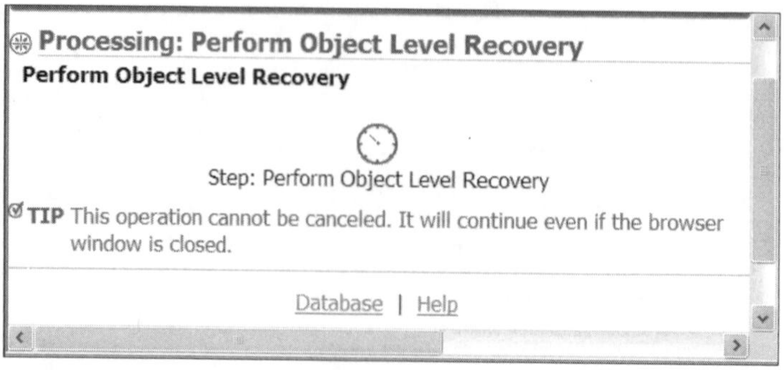

Figure 19-16. *Processing RMAN commands*

Step 6: Review the Status of Restore and Recovery

If everything goes well, you should see a screen similar to Figure 19-17. This screen shows the status of your restore and recovery operation. You can scroll through the entire stack of output.

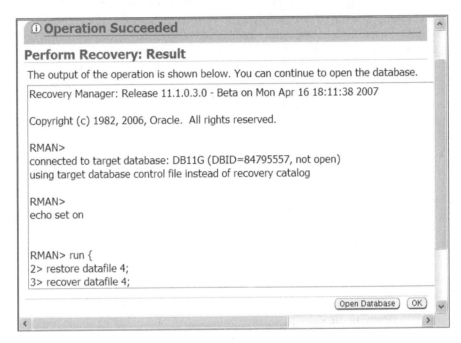

Figure 19-17. *Viewing the output of the restore and recovery operation*

Step 7: Open Your Database

If the operation was successful, click the Open Database button to open your database for use. After you open your database, you should see a screen similar to Figure 19-18 indicating that opening your database was successful.

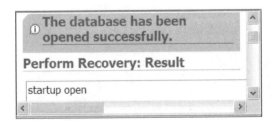

Figure 19-18. *Successfully opening the database*

How It Works

A *whole recovery* means that you're restoring and recovering all datafiles in your database. A *complete recovery* means that you were able to restore all damaged files and recover all committed transactions. In this example, we restored and recovered one datafile and performed a complete recovery. We used the current control file and had all redo required to recover the datafiles up to the last transaction that was committed in the database.

You can use Enterprise Manager to perform almost every restore and recovery scenario. It is beyond the scope of this book to describe every different restore and recovery scenario available through Enterprise Manager. The main point of this recipe is to give you enough information to get you successfully started with restore and recovery. Enterprise Manager is pretty good at displaying what options are available and how to use them.

■**Note** If you want to restore your control file, then ensure that your database is in nomount mode before you start the process described in this recipe. Enterprise Manager will display control file restore options only if your database is first placed in nomount mode.

19-5. Viewing Backup Reports

Problem

You want to view information regarding your Enterprise Manager backups.

Solution

From the EM Backup and Recovery screen (see Figure 19-4), click Backup Reports. You should see a screen similar to Figure 19-19. From this screen, you can view information about your RMAN backups.

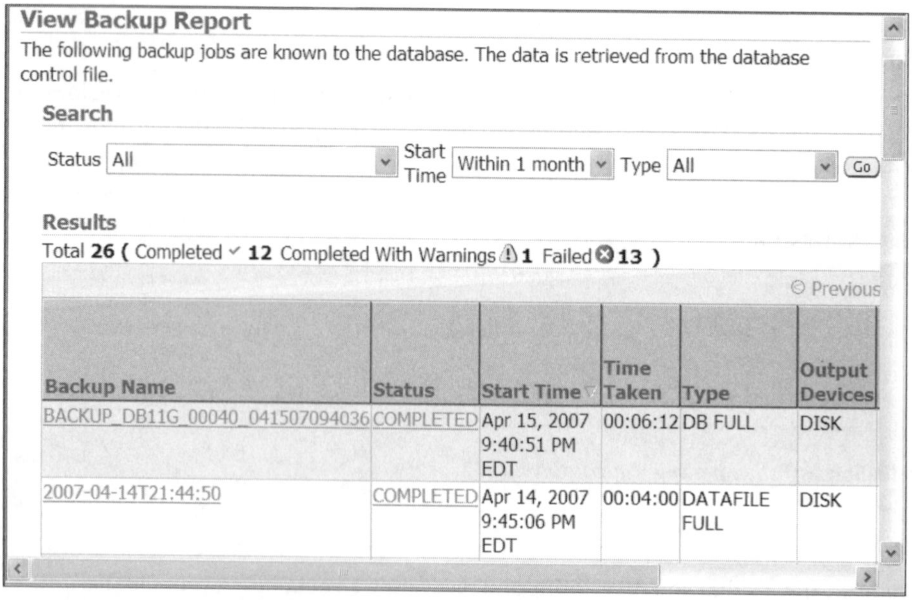

Figure 19-19. *Viewing backup reports*

How It Works

Once you are in the backup report screen, you can drill down into a backup by clicking the backup name. This presents you with a wealth of information about a particular backup. You'll notice right away that the format and content of this report is much nicer than using the output of the RMAN `report` or `list` command.

Notice also that backups are listed here regardless of whether you ran the RMAN backup from EM. The backup report is querying your target database control file or the recovery catalog (if using) for its information.

19-6. Performing Routine RMAN Maintenance Tasks

Problem

You want to perform routine RMAN maintenance tasks such as cross-checking or deleting obsolete backups.

Solution

From the EM Backup and Recovery screen (see Figure 19-4), click Manage Current Backups. You should see a screen similar to Figure 19-20. From this screen, you can perform RMAN maintenance tasks.

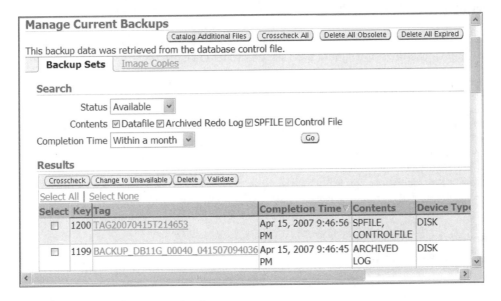

Figure 19-20. *Managing current backups*

How It Works

The Manage Current Backups screen shown in Figure 19-20 allows you to perform tasks such as the following:

- Cross-checking files

- Deleting obsolete and expired files

- Changing the status of backups

- Validating backup sets

- Cataloging files

The buttons on the Manage Current Backups screen are fairly self-explanatory. You can switch back and forth between managing image copies and backup sets by clicking either the Backup Sets tab or the Image Copies tab. You can also view backups by a date range. For example, you can use the Completion Time drop-down list to work with just a subset of your backup files.

The Manage Current Backups screen retrieves the data that it displays about backups from the control file or from the recovery catalog (if you are using one). Therefore, you will see information for all RMAN backups whether or not a given backup was initiated from Enterprise Manager.

19-7. Configuring a Recovery Catalog

Problem

You want to configure a recovery catalog using Enterprise Manager.

Solution

First you need to create another database to contain the recovery catalog (see Chapter 6 for details). Once your recovery catalog database has been created, then you can use EM to configure a recovery catalog. From the EM Backup and Recovery screen (see Figure 19-4), click Recovery Catalog Settings. You should see a screen similar to Figure 19-21.

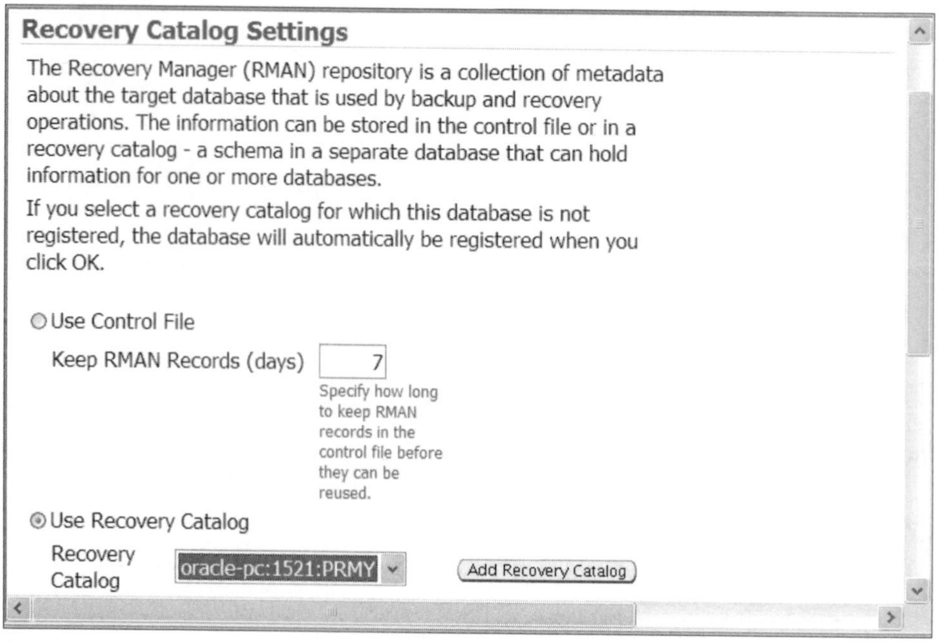

Recovery Catalog Settings

The Recovery Manager (RMAN) repository is a collection of metadata about the target database that is used by backup and recovery operations. The information can be stored in the control file or in a recovery catalog - a schema in a separate database that can hold information for one or more databases.

If you select a recovery catalog for which this database is not registered, the database will automatically be registered when you click OK.

○ Use Control File

Keep RMAN Records (days)   [7]

Specify how long to keep RMAN records in the control file before they can be reused.

◉ Use Recovery Catalog

Recovery Catalog   [oracle-pc:1521:PRMY ⌄]   (Add Recovery Catalog)

Figure 19-21. *Configuring a recovery catalog*

From the screen displayed in Figure 19-21, you can configure your recovery catalog. Select the Use Recovery Catalog option. Next click the Add Recovery Catalog button to navigate to the screen displayed in Figure 19-22.

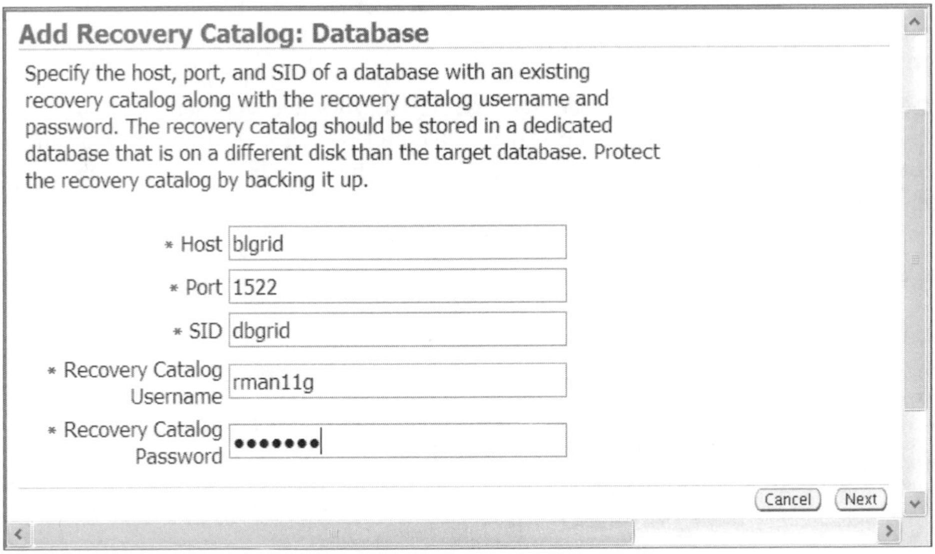

Add Recovery Catalog: Database

Specify the host, port, and SID of a database with an existing recovery catalog along with the recovery catalog username and password. The recovery catalog should be stored in a dedicated database that is on a different disk than the target database. Protect the recovery catalog by backing it up.

```
                    * Host  blgrid
                    * Port  1522
                     * SID  dbgrid
      * Recovery Catalog  rman11g
              Username
      * Recovery Catalog  •••••••
              Password
```

Cancel   Next

Figure 19-22. *Adding a recovery catalog*

Enter the details of your recovery catalog, and click Next. If all the information looks correct, click Finish to add the recovery catalog.

■**Tip** See recipe 6-1 for details on configuring a recovery catalog schema.

How It Works

By default, Enterprise Manager will use the control file as the repository for RMAN metadata. If you want EM to use a recovery catalog, then follow the steps outlined in this recipe. Once configured, be aware that EM will attempt to connect to the recovery catalog for every backup and recovery operation.

If Enterprise Manager cannot connect RMAN to the recovery catalog, it will still proceed with the operation, and RMAN will record its activities in your target database control file. If EM cannot connect to the recovery catalog, it may report an operation as failed, even though it was able to complete the primary task that you specified.

■**Note** RMAN always records its backup and recovery operations in the control file. If you are using a recovery catalog, RMAN will additionally write its activities to that repository.

19-8. Configuring Instance Recovery

Problem

You want to configure instance recovery settings using Enterprise Manager.

Solution

From the EM Backup and Recovery screen (see Figure 19-4), click Recovery Settings. You should now see a screen similar to the one shown in Figure 19-23. From this screen, you can configure an estimated time (amongst other things) for how long you want Oracle to take to perform crash recovery.

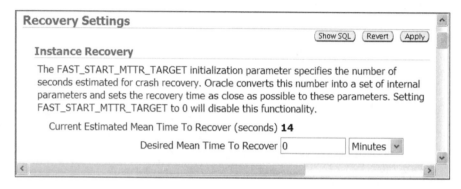

Figure 19-23. *Configuring instance recovery*

How It Works

The Instance Recovery screen shown in Figure 19-23 allows you to adjust the value for your target database `fast_start_mttr_target` initialization parameter. This parameter controls approximately how long Oracle will take to perform crash recovery. You can specify values of anywhere from 0 to 60 minutes or from 0 to 3600 seconds.

■**Note** See recipe 16-9 for complete details on the inner workings of crash recovery.

19-9. Configuring the Flash Recovery Area

Problem

You want to use Enterprise Manager to configure your target database flash recovery area.

Solution

From the EM Backup and Recovery screen (see Figure 19-4), click Recovery Settings, and scroll to the bottom of the screen. You should see a screen similar to what is shown in Figure 19-24. From this screen, you can specify a location and size for your target database flash recovery area.

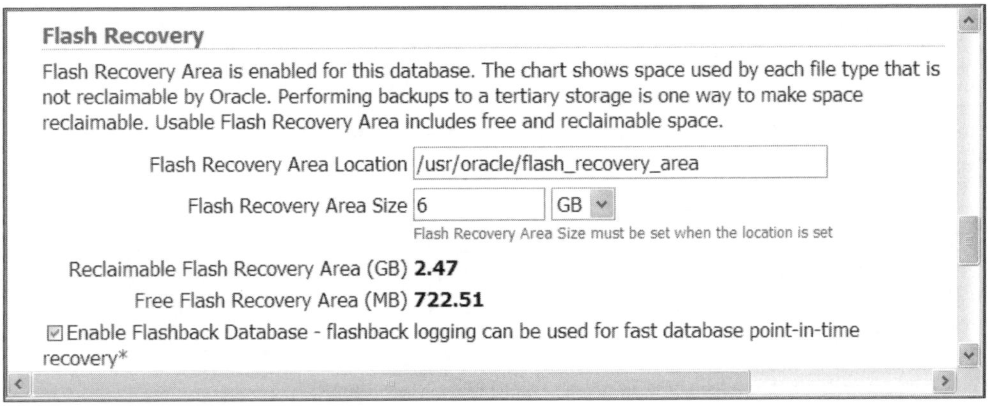

Figure 19-24. *Configuring flash recovery*

How It Works

Enterprise Manager provides a nice visual interface to manage your target database flash recovery area. You can dynamically change the flashback recovery area location and size on the screen displayed in Figure 19-24.

■**Tip** See Chapter 3 for complete details on flash recovery area internals.

You can also configure flash back logging from the screen displayed in Figure 19-24. This feature allows you to flash back your database to a previous point in time. If you do implement flash back logging, be aware that you will be required to stop and start your database as part of that operation.

■**Tip** See Chapter 13 for instructions on how to perform flashback recovery.

19-10. Configuring Restore Points

Problem

You want to use EM to configure restore points in your target database.

Solution

From the EM Backup and Recovery screen (see Figure 19-4), click Manage Restore Points. You should see a screen similar to the one shown in Figure 19-25. Use this screen to view, create, and delete restore points.

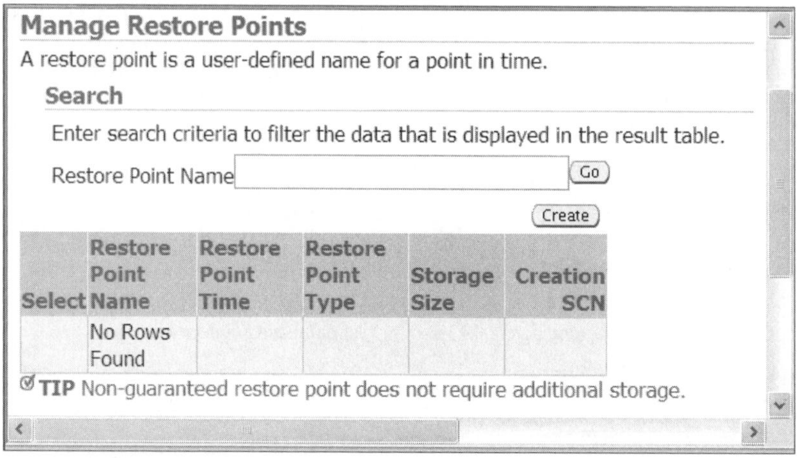

Figure 19-25. *Managing restore points*

How It Works

A restore point is a pointer to the SCN of the database as it was at the time the restore point was created. The buttons displayed on the screen shown in Figure 19-25 are self-explanatory. For example, to create a restore point, simply click the Create button. You must be logged into EM with a schema that has sysdba privileges to create and delete restore points.

19-11. Running Custom RMAN Scripts

Problem

You want to write a custom RMAN and script and schedule it to run as an EM job.

Solution

You will need to navigate through several screens to create and run your custom RMAN script. Here are the steps:

1. Navigate to the Job Activity screen.

2. Create the RMAN script job.

3. Create the RMAN script.

4. Enter your credentials.

5. Schedule the job.

Step 1: Navigate to Job Activity Screen

Navigate to the EM Backup and Recovery screen (see Figure 19-4). At the bottom of this screen is a Related Links section. In this section, click Jobs. You should now see a screen similar to Figure 19-26. In the Create Job drop-down list, pick RMAN Script. Click the Go button (just to the right of the Create Job drop-down list).

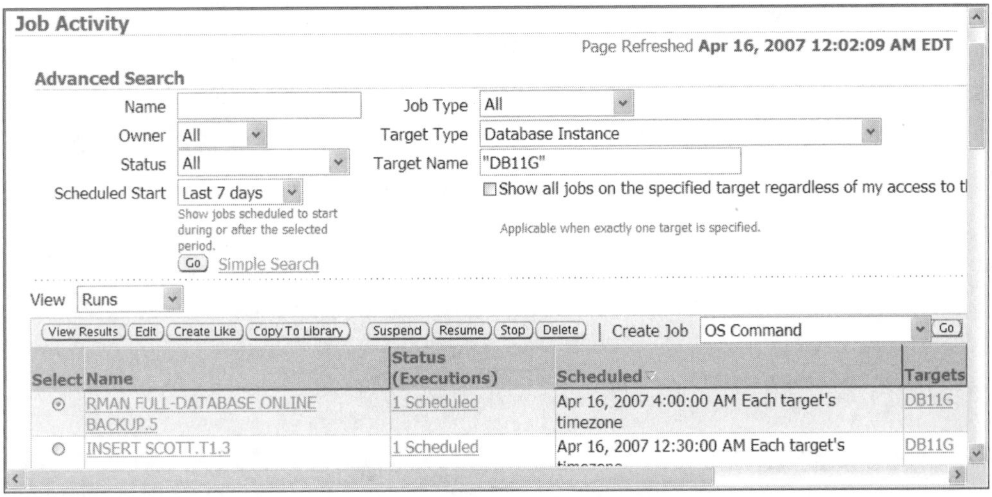

Figure 19-26. *Viewing job activity*

Step 2: Create RMAN Script Job

You will now see a screen similar to Figure 19-27. Fill in a name and description for your job. You will also need to specify your target database information. To do this, click the Add button to select your database as the target of this job. You can click the Search button to find your target database, then click the Select box, and finally click the Select button to finish specifying your target database information.

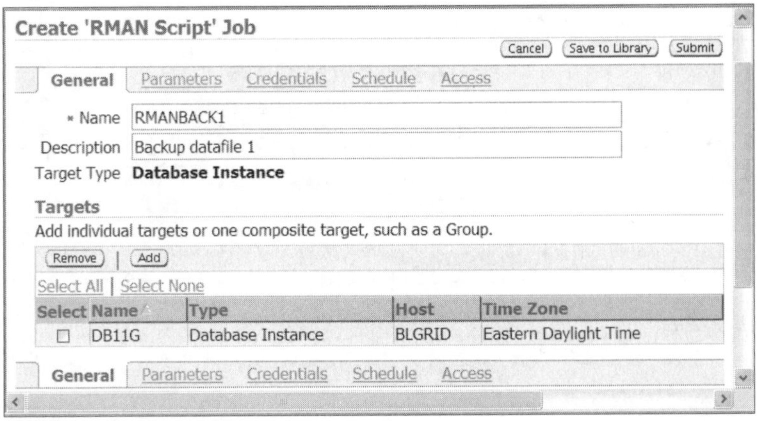

Figure 19-27. *Creating the RMAN script job*

Step 3: Create RMAN Script

Next click the Parameters link. You should now see a screen similar to Figure 19-28. Enter the RMAN commands you want to run. In this example, we're just backing up datafile 1.

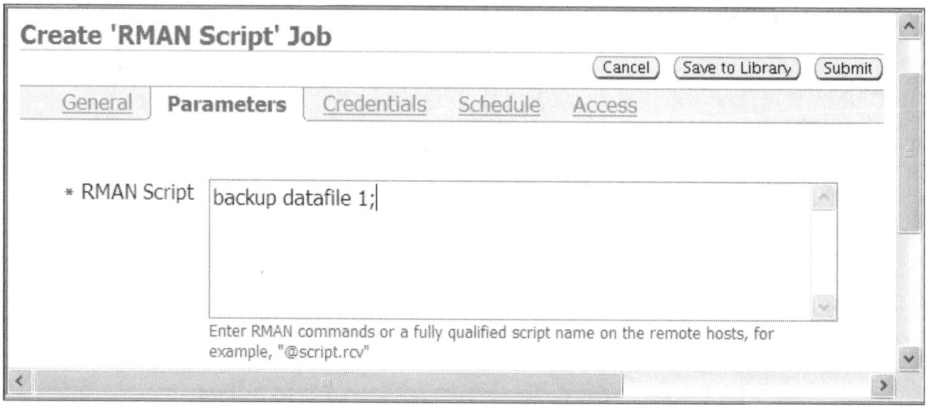

Figure 19-28. *Creating the RMAN script*

Step 4: Enter Credentials

Next click the Credentials link. You should see a screen similar to Figure 19-29. You can choose to use host credentials that you have previously saved or manually enter them by clicking Override Preferred Credentials. Ensure that you pick the sysdba role for your database credentials.

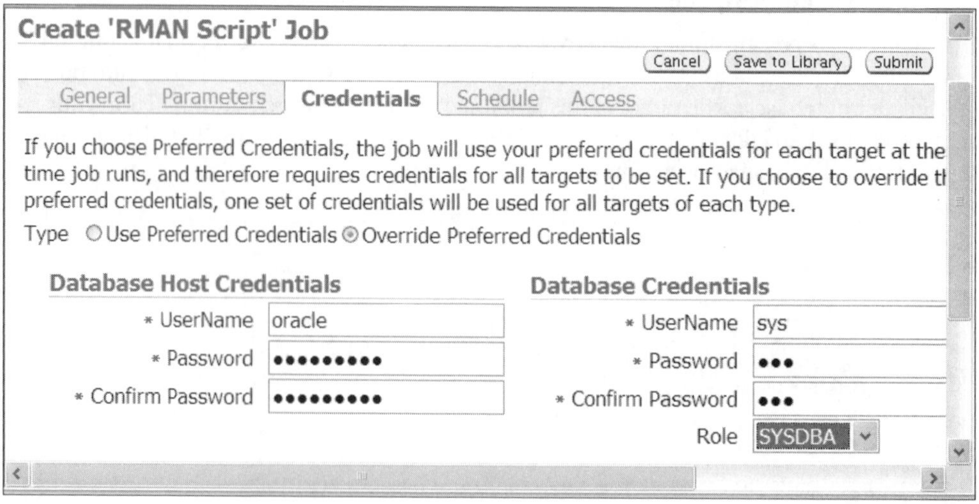

Figure 19-29. *Entering credentials*

Step 5: Schedule Job

Next click the Schedule link. You should see a screen similar to Figure 19-30. From here you can schedule your custom RMAN job to run at a specific time and frequency. In this example, we're scheduling the job to run immediately. Click the Submit button to have the script submitted to run.

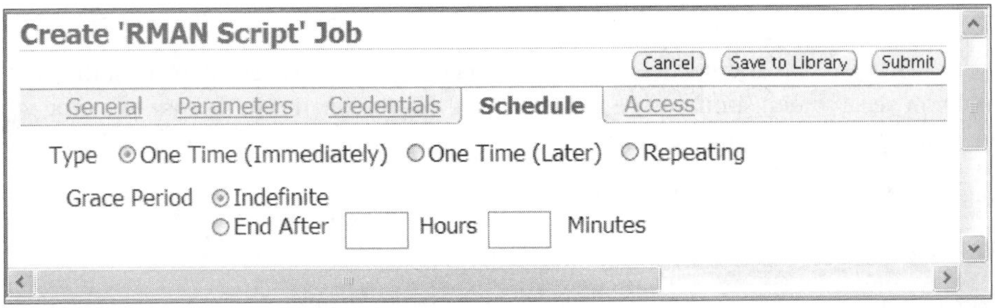

Figure 19-30. *Scheduling the RMAN job*

You should now be returned to the Job Activity screen shown in Figure 19-26. You should see a message confirming that your job has been created. Also from the Job Activity screen, you can check on the status of submitted jobs by clicking the job of interest.

How It Works

It's fairly easy to schedule custom RMAN scripts through Enterprise Manager. You need to navigate to the appropriate screens, create the custom RMAN job, and then schedule the job to be run.

You can view job information from the Job Activity screen shown in Figure 19-26, or you can also query the Enterprise Manager repository directly. To view job information from SQL*Plus, connect as the repository owner (usually named sysman), and query the MGMT_JOB table:

```
SQL> connect sysman/<your password>
SQL> select job_name, job_description from mgmt_job;

JOB_NAME                         JOB_DESCRIPTION
-------------------------------  -------------------------------
RMAN_BACK                        RMAN full backup
RMANBACK1                        Backup Datafile 1
REFRESH_FROM_METALINK_JOB        Out Of The Box Job. Do Not Delete This Job!
BACKUP_ORCL_000002               Oracle-suggested Disk Backup
BACKUP_ORCL_000001               Oracle-suggested Disk Backup
```

19-12. Configuring Backup Settings

Problem

You want to configure backup settings such as degree of parallelism, backup location, default backup type, and MML settings.

Solution

Navigate to the EM Backup and Recovery screen (see Figure 19-4), and click Backup Settings. You should now see a screen similar to Figure 19-31. On this screen, it is fairly easy to configure settings such as the following:

- Degree of backup and restore parallelism

- Backup location

- Backup type

- Tape and Media Management Layer configuration

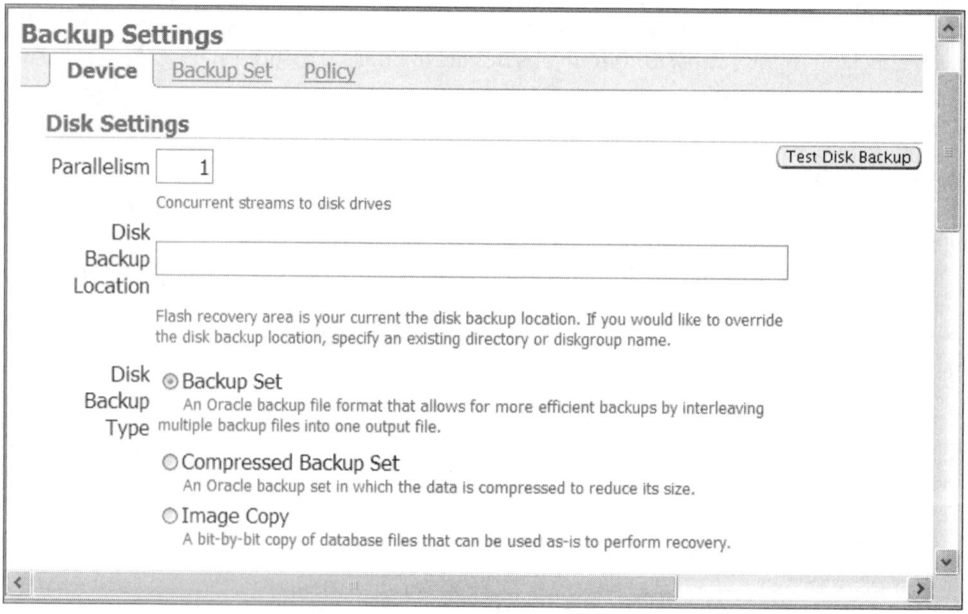

Figure 19-31. *Viewing the Backup Settings screen*

How It Works

From the screen displayed in Figure 19-31, you can perform tasks such as enabling multiple degrees of parallelism for RMAN channels, setting the backup location on disk, specifying the default backup type (backup set, compressed, or image copy), and specifying the MML settings.

You can query backup setting details from the EM repository owner's (usually the sysman schema) MGMT_BACKUP_CONFIGURATION table, as shown here:

```
SQL> connect sysman/<your password>
SQL> select use_disk, disk_location, disk_parallelism
  2  from mgmt_backup_configuration;

USE_ DISK_LOCATION        DISK_PARALLELISM
---- -------------------- ----------------
YES                                      1
```

19-13. Configuring Backup Policies

Problem

You want to configure your RMAN autobackup control file and retention policies.

Solution

Navigate to the EM Backup and Recovery screen (see Figure 19-4), and click Backup Settings. You should see a screen similar to Figure 19-31 (shown in recipe 19-12). From this screen, click the Policy tab.

You should now see a screen similar to Figure 19-32. On this screen, you can configure RMAN policies such as the following:

- Backing up the control file and server initialization file automatically

- Not backing up files that haven't changed since the previous backup

- Enabling block change tracking

- Excluding tablespaces from backups

- Establishing retention policies

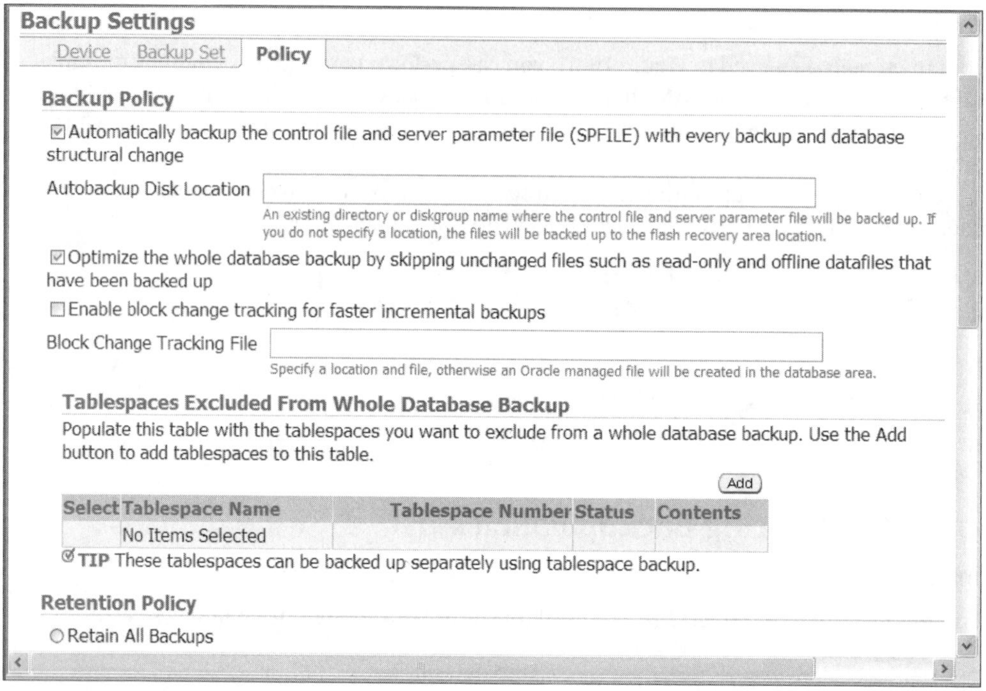

Backup Settings

Device   Backup Set | **Policy**

Backup Policy

☑ Automatically backup the control file and server parameter file (SPFILE) with every backup and database structural change

Autobackup Disk Location [   ]

An existing directory or diskgroup name where the control file and server parameter file will be backed up. If you do not specify a location, the files will be backed up to the flash recovery area location.

☑ Optimize the whole database backup by skipping unchanged files such as read-only and offline datafiles that have been backed up

☐ Enable block change tracking for faster incremental backups

Block Change Tracking File [   ]

Specify a location and file, otherwise an Oracle managed file will be created in the database area.

Tablespaces Excluded From Whole Database Backup

Populate this table with the tablespaces you want to exclude from a whole database backup. Use the Add button to add tablespaces to this table.

(Add)

Select	Tablespace Name	Tablespace Number	Status	Contents
	No Items Selected			

☞ **TIP** These tablespaces can be backed up separately using tablespace backup.

Retention Policy

○ Retain All Backups

Figure 19-32. *Setting up backup policies*

How It Works

Enterprise Manager allows you to perform RMAN tasks such as enabling the automatic backup of your control file, backup optimization, and retention polices. The Backup Policy screen shown in Figure 19-32 provides an easy point-and-click interface for configuring your RMAN policies.

CHAPTER 20

■ ■ ■

Using the Data Recovery Advisor

If your database experiences a failure and the subsequent stress causes you to have a heart attack, let's hope you'll have time to call for an emergency medical technician (EMT) or paramedic to assist you with your heart problems. If your heart goes into ventricular fibrillation, the EMT or the paramedic has the option of using an automatic defibrillator machine to shock you back to normal.

Interestingly, an EMT doesn't have the same options that a paramedic has when operating a defibrillator. The EMT is limited to pushing the power button followed by pressing the analyze button. The defibrillator then generates a message from the machine recommending whether to press the shock button. If the machine recommends a shock, then the EMT is free to give you a good zap.

The paramedic typically has more training and experience than an EMT. The paramedic has the option of running the defibrillator in manual mode, which means they can tell the machine when to perform certain actions. The difference between an EMT and a paramedic in this situation is who is making the calls. For an EMT, the defibrillator machine instructs them what to do; the machine is in charge. For a paramedic, it's the other way around. The paramedic can instruct the machine when to perform certain actions.

Assuming either the EMT or the paramedic saves you (if they don't, stop here), you can now return to trying to resolve the issue with your database. You've heard about a new feature with RMAN in Oracle Database 11g called the Data Recovery Advisor. This tool automatically detects problems with your database that may require you to perform restore and recovery operations. The Data Recovery Advisor will list failures, give you advice on how to resolve issues, and allow you to push the button that instructs RMAN to run the commands required to fix the problem.

When using the Data Recovery Advisor, it helps to have a combination of EMT (junior DBA) and paramedic skills (senior DBA). At an entry level, you should be trained in backup and recovery concepts and know how to use RMAN to restore and recover your database.

On a higher level, you also want to be able to determine whether the advice you're getting from the tool will correctly resolve the failure. You want the option of manually overriding anything the tool recommends. You might choose to override the tool because of training, prior experience with a particular type of failure, or knowledge about your environment.

The Data Recovery Advisor tool can assist with diagnosing media failures, making recommendations, and providing the RMAN commands to resolve the problem. You can use the Data Recovery Advisor from either the RMAN command line or Enterprise Manager. We'll detail how to use both the command line and GUI interfaces in this chapter. You can invoke the Data Recovery Advisor from the RMAN command line with the following three commands:

- `list failure`
- `advise failure`
- `repair failure`

The first three recipes in this chapter discuss in detail each of these new RMAN commands. Recipe 20-4 shows how to use the Data Recovery Advisor to repair a failure using Enterprise Manager. Recipe 20-5 discusses how to change the status of a failure.

20-1. Listing Failures

Problem

You suspect you have a media failure in your database. You want to use the Data Recovery Advisor to list media failures.

Solution

Use the `list failure` command as shown here:

```
RMAN> list failure;

List of Database Failures
=========================

Failure ID Priority Status    Time Detected        Summary
---------- -------- --------- -------------------- -------
15         HIGH     OPEN      31-MAR-2007 16:09:39 one or more datafiles are missing
```

How It Works

When using the Data Recovery Advisor, `list failure` is the first command you should run. This will alert you to any problems with database files such as control files, datafiles, and online redo logs.

The Data Recovery Advisor stores its information outside the database in the Automatic Diagnostic Repository (ADR). This allows you to run the `list failure` command regardless of the mount mode of your database or the availability of the recovery catalog (if using one). You can determine the location of the base directory for the ADR by viewing the `diagnostic_dest` initialization parameter. You can view the names and values of directories in the ADR with this query:

```
SQL> select name, value from v$diag_info;
```

If you suspect there is a problem with your database and the Data Recovery Advisor is not reporting a failure, you can proactively initiate a database health check by running the following RMAN command:

```
RMAN> validate database;
```

If a failure is detected, it will be recorded in the ADR. Once a failure is recorded in the ADR, then you can use the advise failure and repair failure commands to resolve the issue.

Failures with a CRITICAL status are those that usually make your database unavailable and are typically diagnosed when attempting to start the database. For example, a missing control file would be considered a CRITICAL failure. A HIGH failure is an issue that makes your database partially unavailable, such as a damaged or missing datafile.

If you want to see more detail about a given failure, then use the list failure ... detail command. In this example, we are listing more details on a failure with an ID of 15:

```
RMAN> list failure 15 detail;

List of Database Failures
=========================

Failure ID Priority Status    Time Detected        Summary
---------- -------- --------- -------------------- -------
15         HIGH     OPEN      31-MAR-2007 16:09:39 one or more datafiles are missing
  List of child failures for parent failure ID 15
  Failure ID Priority Status    Time Detected        Summary
  ---------- -------- --------- -------------------- -------
  47         HIGH     OPEN      04-APR-2007 15:05:27 datafile 4:
'/usr/oracle/oradata/DB11G/datafile/o1_mf_users_30xj0dws_.dbf' is missing
Impact: tablespace USERS is unavailable
```

If you want to see all failures that have been resolved and closed, then use the closed clause:

```
RMAN> list failure closed;
```

Table 20-1 describes the types of failures that can be reported from the list failure command.

Table 20-1. *Data Recovery Advisor List Failure Options*

Failure Type	Description
ALL	Lists all failures
CRITICAL	Lists only critical failures with an OPEN status
HIGH	Lists only high-priority failures with an OPEN status
LOW	Lists only low-priority failures with an OPEN status
CLOSED	Lists failures with a CLOSED status
EXCLUDE FAILURE	Excludes failures by a specified failure number
DETAIL	Provides verbose description of the failure

20-2. Getting Advice

Problem

You've experienced a media failure. You want to get advice from the Data Recovery Advisor about how to restore and recover your database.

Solution

First use the list failure command to display all failures (see recipe 20-1 for details). If you have only one failure associated with your database, then you can run the advise failure command without any parameters:

```
RMAN> advise failure;
```

The output will vary quite a bit depending on the failure. Here's a partial snippet of the output for a media failure that has occurred with a datafile in the users tablespace:

```
analyzing automatic repair options; this may take some time
allocated channel: ORA_DISK_1
channel ORA_DISK_1: SID=155 device type=DISK
allocated channel: ORA_SBT_TAPE_1
channel ORA_SBT_TAPE_1: SID=139 device type=SBT_TAPE
channel ORA_SBT_TAPE_1: WARNING: Oracle Test Disk API
analyzing automatic repair options complete

Manual Checklist
================
1. If file /usr/oracle/oradata/DB11G/datafile/o1_mf_users_30xj0dws_.dbf was
unintentionally renamed or moved, restore it.

Automated Repair Options
========================
Option Strategy      Repair Description
------ ------------  ------------------
1      no data loss Restore and recover datafile 4.
Repair script: /usr/oracle/diag/rdbms/db11g/DB11G/hm/reco_1169262405.hm
```

How It Works

The advise failure command gives advice about how to recover from potential problems detected by the Data Recovery Advisor. If you have multiple failures with your database, then you can directly specify the failure ID to get advice on a given failure. You obtain the failure ID by viewing the output of the list failure command. This example gets advice on the failure ID of 15:

```
RMAN> advise failure 15;
```

If you have a combination of CRITICAL, HIGH, and LOW failures, you must use the advise failure command to obtain advice about CRITICAL failures before you can get advice about lower-priority failures. You can get specific advice about the priority of failure by specifying one of the following keywords: ALL, CRITICAL, HIGH, or LOW. This example displays advice about just the critical errors:

```
RMAN> advise failure critical;
```

Depending on your situation, the advise failure output will contain one or both of the following sections:

- Manual Checklist

- Automated Repair Options

The Manual Checklist section gives you advice for manually resolving the issue at hand. For example, you may not have the required backups to restore a file, so the advice might be to find a copy of the file and restore it manually.

The Automated Repair Options section provides you with RMAN commands that you can use to mend the problem. Table 20-2 describes the columns contained in the Automated Repair Options output.

Table 20-2. *Descriptions of Automated Repair Options*

Column	Description
Option	An identifying number for a repair operation
Strategy	A complete recovery strategy (no data loss) or an incomplete recovery (data loss) strategy
Repair Description	A brief description of the proposed repair operation
Repair Script	A script that contains the proposed commands to resolve the problem

The Automated Repair Options section will list the location and name of a repair script that contains RMAN commands to resolve the problem. You can view and edit this script if necessary. If you want to edit the script, you can then run it manually to resolve the issue. If you want RMAN to automatically repair the failure, then run the repair failure command as described in recipe 20-3.

20-3. Repairing Failures

Problem

You've experienced a media failure. You want to use the Data Recovery Advisor to perform a restore and recovery.

Solution

We recommend that you always run the following RMAN commands in this order:

1. list failure

2. advise failure

3. repair failure

By running list failure and advise failure, you will gain an understanding as to what the problem is and how to fix it. You can use the repair failure command to run the repair script generated by the Data Recovery Advisor:

```
RMAN> repair failure;

Strategy      Repair script
------------ --------------
no data loss /usr/oracle/diag/rdbms/db11g/DB11G/hm/reco_3911438726.hm
contents of repair script:
# restore and recover datafile
sql 'alter database datafile 4 offline';
restore check readonly datafile 4;
recover datafile 4;
sql 'alter database datafile 4 online';
```

You will be prompted to specify whether you want to run the repair script:

```
Do you really want to execute the above repair (enter YES or NO)?
```

If you're satisfied with the repair script commands, then enter YES and hit Enter. The output will vary based on the type of restore and recovery that is performed. Here's a partial snippet of the output of restoring and recovering just one datafile:

```
media recovery complete, elapsed time: 00:00:02
Finished recover at 04-APR-2007 19:05:03
sql statement: alter database datafile 4 online
repair failure complete
```

How It Works

We recommend that you run the repair failure command only after you have run the list failure and advise failure commands. Repairing the problem should be the last step performed. You should use the Data Recovery Advisor to repair failures only after you thoroughly understand what the failure is and what commands will be run to repair the failure.

If you want to inspect what the repair failure command will do without actually running the commands, then use the preview clause:

```
RMAN> repair failure preview;
```

The preview clause instructs RMAN to display only the commands that it recommends be run to resolve the failure. If you want to spool the output of a preview command to a file, then use the spool command:

```
RMAN> spool log to rmanout.txt;
RMAN> repair failure preview;
```

If you don't want to be prompted during a repair session, then use the noprompt clause:

```
RMAN> repair failure noprompt;
```

■**Caution** Use the noprompt clause with caution. We recommend you use this only when you're sure you know exactly what the repair failure command will execute.

20-4. Using the Data Recovery Advisor Through Enterprise Manager

Problem

You've experienced a failure with a single datafile. You want to use the Data Recovery Advisor screens in Enterprise Manager to repair the failure.

Solution

Log on to Enterprise Manager with a schema that has sysdba privileges. Click the Availability tab, and then navigate to the Backup and Recovery section of Enterprise Manager. Click Perform Recovery. If a failure has been detected, you should now see a screen similar to Figure 20-1. The Oracle Suggested Repair section of this screen is the starting point for the Data Recovery Advisor in Enterprise Manager.

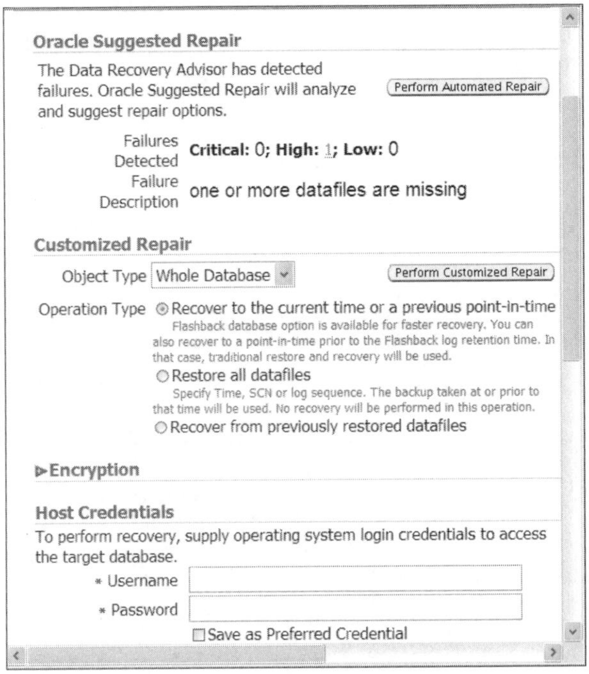

Figure 20-1. *Using the Data Recovery Advisor*

In this example, you can see in Figure 20-1 that Oracle has detected a failure displaying the message "one or more datafiles are missing."

Enter your host credentials near the bottom of the screen (see recipe 19-2 if you're not sure what to enter for host credentials). Next click Perform Automated Repair to have the Data Recovery Advisor begin the repair process.

You should now see a screen similar to Figure 20-2. Select the check box for the failures you need advice on how to fix.

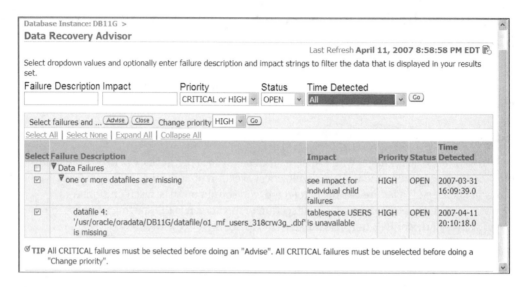

Figure 20-2. *Listing the failures*

Next click the Advise button. You should now see a screen similar to Figure 20-3.

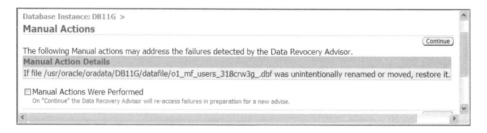

Figure 20-3. *Viewing the Manual Actions screen*

At this point, you can either attempt to manually resolve the problem or click Continue. In this example, we clicked the Continue button and are presented with a screen similar to Figure 20-4.

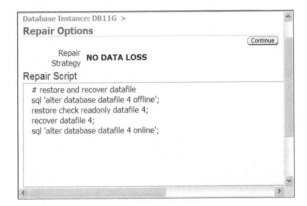

Figure 20-4. *Viewing the Repair Options screen*

Inspect the RMAN commands that will be run. If you agree with the Data Recovery Advisor, then click Continue. You will now see a screen similar to Figure 20-5.

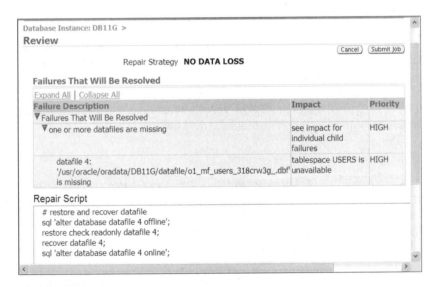

Figure 20-5. *Viewing the Review options*

You now have one final chance to review the details of the failure repair script. If you think the repair actions are appropriate, click the Submit Job button.

No, wait!!!

Just kidding. Keep going. If the job was successfully submitted, you should see a screen similar to Figure 20-6.

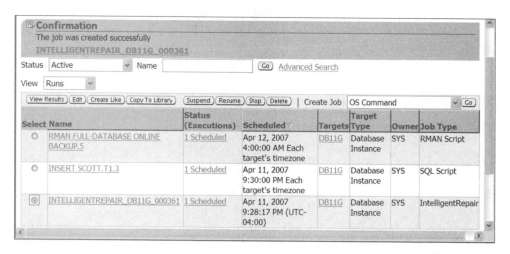

Figure 20-6. *Getting a submit confirmation*

To verify that the job ran successfully, click the radio button that matches your job. In this example, the job name is INTELLIGENTREPAIR_DB11G_000361. You can now click the View Results button to see whether your job successfully completed.

We recommend that you navigate to the Data Recovery Advisor screen shown in Figure 20-1. This screen will display any failures that the Data Recovery Advisor has detected. If your problem has been solved, this screen should now report no problems or issues.

How It Works

This recipe showed a simple example of how to use the Data Recovery Advisor via Enterprise Manager screens to repair a failure with one datafile. Obviously there are a wide variety of more complicated scenarios than the one detailed in this recipe. When you use the Data Recovery Advisor for different scenarios, you'll have to carefully evaluate the options presented in each screen and choose what you think are the right choices for your situation.

■**Note** See Chapter 19 if you need more information about how to use Enterprise Manager for backup and recovery tasks.

20-5. Changing Failure Status

Problem

You have a failure that is listed with a HIGH priority. However, you know that the failure isn't that critical for your particular database. You want to use the Data Recovery Advisor to change the priority of a failure from HIGH to LOW.

Solution

Use the change failure command to alter the priority of a failure. In this example, we have a missing datafile that belongs to a noncritical tablespace. First, obtain the failure priority via the list failure command:

```
RMAN> list failure;
```

```
Failure ID Priority Status    Time Detected        Summary
---------- -------- --------- -------------------- -------
15         HIGH     OPEN      07-JUL-2007 07:07:07 one or more datafiles are missing
```

Second, change the priority from HIGH to LOW with the change failure command:

```
RMAN> change failure 15 priority low;
```

You will be prompted to confirm that you really do want to change the priority:

```
Do you really want to change the above failures (enter YES or NO)?
```

If you do want to change the priority, then type YES, and hit the Enter key. If you run the list failure command again, you'll see that the priority has now been changed to LOW:

```
RMAN> list failure low;
```

```
Failure ID Priority Status    Time Detected        Summary
---------- -------- --------- -------------------- -------
15         LOW      OPEN      07-JUL-2007 07:07:07 one or more datafiles are missing
```

How It Works

For most problems, you should never have to change the priority or status of a failure. The priority of a failure can be one of the following: CRITICAL, HIGH, or LOW. The status of failure can be OPEN or CLOSED.

If you fix a problem manually without using the repair failure command, the Data Recovery Advisor will detect that the problem has been resolved when the next list failure command is issued. At that time, the Data Recovery Advisor will change the status of any fixed failures to CLOSED.

However, sometimes you want to change the status or priority of a failure. In those cases, you can use the change failure command. For example, you may have a datafile missing that is in a tablespace that you know is not being used. In that case, you can change the priority to LOW.

If you want to manually change the status of a failure from OPEN to CLOSED, then you can use the `closed` clause as shown here:

```
RMAN> change failure 15 closed;
```

Table 20-3 lists all the options of the `change failure` command.

Table 20-3. *Options of Change Failure*

Option	Description
ALL	Changes all failures with an OPEN status
CRITICAL	Changes all failures with a CRITICAL status
HIGH	Changes all failures with a HIGH status
LOW	Changes all failures with a LOW status
FAILURE NUMBER	Changes a specific failure
EXCLUDE FAILURE <FAILURE NUMBER>	Excludes a failure from the operation
CLOSED	Changes the status to CLOSED
PRIORITY HIGH	Changes the priority to HIGH
PRIORITY LOW	Changes the priority to LOW

CHAPTER 21

■■■

Using RMAN on Windows

Microsoft Windows has always been a favorite platform for many people and organizations—for personal and business applications including Oracle Database. There are a sizable number of production databases, estimated at about 25 percent by Oracle Corporation, running on Windows. Needless to say, where there is a production Oracle Database, there is a need to protect it, and there is a place for RMAN. That's the purpose of this chapter—to help you put the power of RMAN to the most effective use on the Windows platform.

We will start with a general discussion on Oracle on Windows. Since we have covered some of the Windows-related issues regarding RMAN in other chapters, you may already be familiar with them. In this chapter, instead of repeating the content applicable for the Windows environment, we will point out the relevant recipes in other chapters and mention only the differences or important points to consider.

Oracle on Windows

Most readers may already be familiar with the Oracle architecture on Unix platforms and its flavors such as HPUX, AIX, and Linux. In the following sections, we will explain some of the subtle but crucial differences of using an Oracle architecture on Windows.

Oracle Architecture on Windows

To begin understanding how to use Oracle on Windows, it's helpful to review the Oracle architecture in general. Most people look at Oracle on Unix as the general case, and we do the same in this book. One of the key differences between Oracle on Unix and Oracle on Windows is that Oracle on Windows is organized into threads rather than processes.

An Oracle instance is a collection of processes such as the System Monitor (SMON), the Process Monitor (PMON), the database writer (DBWn), and so on, and a bunch of memory areas such as a system global area (SGA) and a program global area (PGA). The SGA is further broken into the database buffer cache, shared pool, and log buffer memory areas. Figure 21-1 shows the memory structures and the processes for the Oracle Database instance on Windows.

The *buffer cache* is a memory area to hold the blocks of the table data retrieved from the database datafiles. When the user requests a piece of data from a table, the Oracle database gets it from the disk and places it in the buffer cache. The data is then served from the buffer cache to the user. If another user requests the same data, the database gets it from the buffer cache instead of getting it from the disk again.

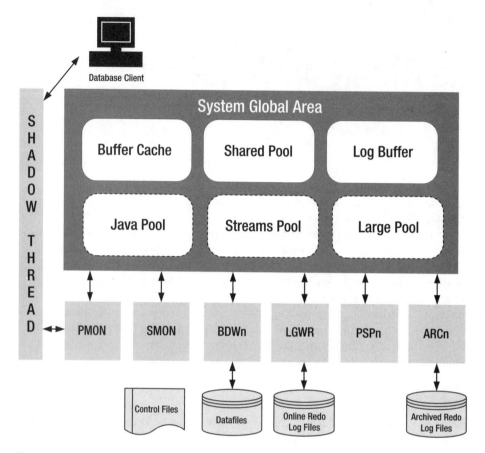

Figure 21-1. *Oracle architecture on Windows*

When the user sessions make changes to the database, the pre-change and post-change images of the data are written to a memory area called the *log buffer*. When the user commits, the contents of log buffer are written to the disk to special files called *online redo log files*. If the instance crashes, all the memory areas disappear. By examining the online redo log files, the database can find out which operations have been successful and which ones need to be discarded. The log buffer contents are flushed to the online redo log files by a process known as the *log writer* (LGWR). The flushing occurs when any one of the following happens:

- The log buffer is one-third full.

- It has been three seconds since the last flush.

- The log buffer is 1MB full.

- A session commits.

- The checkpoint occurs.

When a user changes the data, the change occurs in the buffer cache only, not on the disk. This way, the slowest operation—the physical I/O to the disk—does not become the bottleneck as the database changes. The changed blocks in the buffer cache—known as *dirty blocks*—are written to the datafiles by a process known as the *database writer* (DBWn). There can be more than one DBWn process; hence, they are named DBW0, DBW1, and so on. On Windows, however, there is no need to define multiple DBWn processes, because the I/O is asynchronous anyway and one database writer is enough. The event of flushing data from the cache to the datafiles is called *checkpointing*.

The third most important memory area is called *shared pool*, which houses several types of memory areas such as the library cache and the row cache. The *library cache* is a shared memory area that holds the parsed object definition as well as SQL queries. The *row cache* is an area that holds information on data dictionary objects.

In addition to these, the instance may also have some optional memory areas such as *large pool*, *Java pool*, and *streams pool* (Oracle Database 10*g* Release 2 and newer). These areas appear in Figure 21-1 in dotted boxes.

Now let's turn to the processes. In addition to the processes described already—DBWn and LGWR—there are several other processes. PMON monitors all other processes. SMON performs process cleanups, among other things. If the database is in archivelog mode, the online redo log files are written to a special type of file called *archived redo log files* before they are overwritten. The process that writes the online redo log files to the archived redo log files is called the *archiver* (ARCn). There can be more than one archiver process; hence, they are named ARC0, ARC1, and so on.

All these processes are not Windows processes; they are threads. You will learn later in this chapter the significance of Oracle on Windows being designed that way. All these threads are under the same Windows process called ORACLE.EXE, the main Oracle Database executable.

When a client connects to the database, it connects to a shadow thread, which in turn connects to the database instance, or more specifically the PMON thread. The client process communicates to the shadow thread only, and the shadow thread does all the work. This is why the Oracle architecture is sometimes called a *two-task* architecture.

Services

Unlike Unix, where the Oracle instance starts as a number of processes, on Windows the Oracle database starts as a service. A *service* allows the database instance to start without a user being logged in. A service is conceptually similar to, though not quite the same as, a Unix daemon.

So, an Oracle instance consists of two parts: the Windows service and the instance itself. The service has to start first before you can connect to it and start the instance. Contrast this with Unix, where you make a connection first to start the instance. When you install the Oracle database software, this service is automatically created. To check for the service, select Start ➤ Programs ➤ Administrative Tools ➤ Services. This opens the main services screen. Figure 21-2 shows part of this screen.

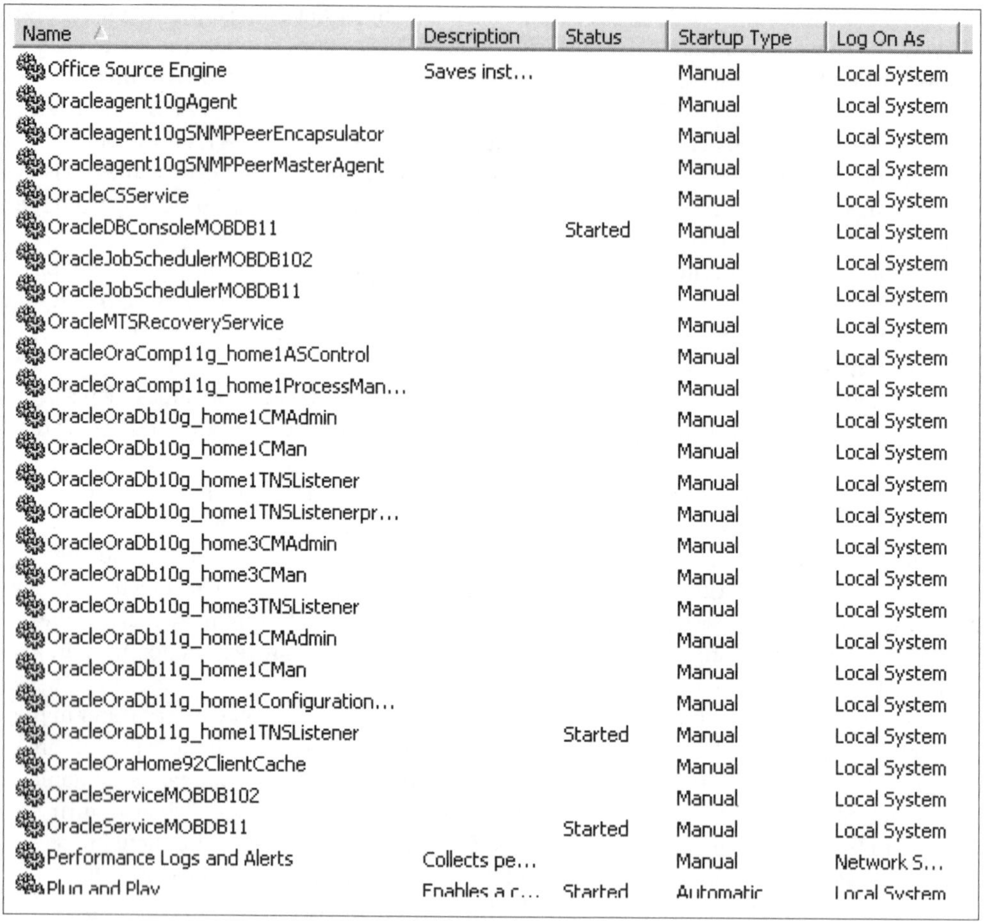

Name	Description	Status	Startup Type	Log On As
Office Source Engine	Saves inst...		Manual	Local System
Oracleagent10gAgent			Manual	Local System
Oracleagent10gSNMPPeerEncapsulator			Manual	Local System
Oracleagent10gSNMPPeerMasterAgent			Manual	Local System
OracleCSService			Manual	Local System
OracleDBConsoleMOBDB11		Started	Manual	Local System
OracleJobSchedulerMOBDB102			Manual	Local System
OracleJobSchedulerMOBDB11			Manual	Local System
OracleMTSRecoveryService			Manual	Local System
OracleOraComp11g_home1ASControl			Manual	Local System
OracleOraComp11g_home1ProcessMan...			Manual	Local System
OracleOraDb10g_home1CMAdmin			Manual	Local System
OracleOraDb10g_home1CMan			Manual	Local System
OracleOraDb10g_home1TNSListener			Manual	Local System
OracleOraDb10g_home1TNSListenerpr...			Manual	Local System
OracleOraDb10g_home3CMAdmin			Manual	Local System
OracleOraDb10g_home3CMan			Manual	Local System
OracleOraDb10g_home3TNSListener			Manual	Local System
OracleOraDb11g_home1CMAdmin			Manual	Local System
OracleOraDb11g_home1CMan			Manual	Local System
OracleOraDb11g_home1Configuration...			Manual	Local System
OracleOraDb11g_home1TNSListener		Started	Manual	Local System
OracleOraHome92ClientCache			Manual	Local System
OracleServiceMOBDB102			Manual	Local System
OracleServiceMOBDB11		Started	Manual	Local System
Performance Logs and Alerts	Collects pe...		Manual	Network S...
Plug and Play	Enables a r...	Started	Automatic	Local System

Figure 21-2. *The Windows services screen*

This screen shows the name of the various services on the left side. Note the service names related to Oracle; they all start with the word *Oracle*. In particular, note the service OracleServiceMOBDB11, which is the service for the database instance named MOBDB11. When you install Oracle, this service is created, and the start-up property is set to Automatic; that is, the service starts automatically when Windows starts. This functionally is similar to the placement of files in the /etc/init.d directory in Unix. You may decide to change it so you have to start it manually. To change the start-up option to Manual, right-click the service name, and choose Properties. In the dialog box that appears, choose Manual from the Startup Type drop-down list, and click the button Apply.

Another way to check the service name command is to use the SC command. Here is how you can check the database service:

```
C:\>sc query OracleServiceMOBDB11
```

This returns with the following output, which shows the status of the service:

```
SERVICE_NAME: OracleServiceMOBDB11
        TYPE                 : 10  WIN32_OWN_PROCESS
        STATE                : 4  RUNNING
                                (STOPPABLE,PAUSABLE,ACCEPTS_SHUTDOWN)
        WIN32_EXIT_CODE  : 0  (0x0)
        SERVICE_EXIT_CODE : 0  (0x0)
        CHECKPOINT       : 0x0
        WAIT_HINT        : 0x0
```

If the service is set to Manual, then you must start it. To start it, you can right-click the name of the service and click Start. Alternatively, you can execute the following command from the command prompt:

```
C:> net start OracleServiceMOBDB11
```

This command starts the service OracleServiceMOBDB11. Typically it also starts up the instance.

Another command used on Windows is `oradim`. This command is used for a variety of things—from creating an Oracle service to starting/stopping and even removing the services. Here is how you can start the Oracle service using this tool:

```
C:\> oradim -startup -sid MOBDB11 -starttype srvc,inst
```

You can also use the `oradim` command to stop the service. To see a complete list of `oradim` commands and options, type `oradim` at the command line without any arguments; this gives you the syntax, as shown here:

```
C:\>oradim
ORADIM: <command> [options].  Refer to manual.
Enter one of the following command:
Create an instance by specifying the following options:
    -NEW -SID sid | -SRVC srvc | -ASMSID sid | -ASMSRVC srvc [-SYSPWD pass]
 [-STARTMODE auto|manual] [-SRVCSTART system|demand] [-PFILE file | -SPFILE]
 [-SHUTMODE normal|immediate|abort] [-TIMEOUT secs] [-RUNAS osusr/ospass]
Edit an instance by specifying the following options:
    -EDIT -SID sid | -ASMSID sid [-SYSPWD pass]
 [-STARTMODE auto|manual] [-SRVCSTART system|demand] [-PFILE file | -SPFILE]
 [-SHUTMODE normal|immediate|abort] [-SHUTTYPE srvc|inst] [-RUNAS osusr/ospass]
Delete instances by specifying the following options:
    -DELETE -SID sid | -ASMSID sid | -SRVC srvc | -ASMSRVC srvc
Startup services and instance by specifying the following options:
    -STARTUP -SID sid | -ASMSID sid [-SYSPWD pass]
 [-STARTTYPE srvc|inst|srvc,inst] [-PFILE filename | -SPFILE]
Shutdown service and instance by specifying the following options:
    -SHUTDOWN -SID sid | -ASMSID sid [-SYSPWD pass]
 [-SHUTTYPE srvc|inst|srvc,inst] [-SHUTMODE normal|immediate|abort]
 Query for help by specifying the following parameters: -? | -h | -help
```

If you use ASM, you can use `oradim` to manage ASM instances too.

Threads, Not Processes

An Oracle instance under Unix is a collection of several processes such as PMON, SMON, LGWR, and so on, running on the server and several areas of memory. In Unix, these are operating system processes, and you can find them by entering the following command at the Unix command line:

```
$ ps -aef | grep ora_
oracle 11221     1  0  May  7  ?       31:04   ora_lck0_PRODB1
oracle 10723     1  0  May  7  ?      221:11   ora_lmon_PRODB1
oracle 11306     1  0  May  7  ?        3:43   ora_asmb_PRODB1
oracle 10775     1  0  May  7  ?        8:50   ora_dbw1_PRODB1
oracle 10785     1  0  May  7  ?      332:07   ora_lgwr_PRODB1
oracle 11312     1  0  May  7  ?        0:43   ora_rbal_PRODB1
... and so on ...
```

In the output, the first column shows the owner of the process, that is, oracle. The second column shows the Unix process ID (the numbers 11221, 10723, and so on) for those processes. Being processes, they can be killed and monitored independently.

Why Threads on Windows?

On the Windows platform, however, the Oracle server processes are not shown as Windows processes but as *threads* inside a single Oracle process. Threads are separate execution paths inside a process.

Why is it important for Oracle on Windows to run instance background processes as threads rather than as regular Windows processes? Here are the reasons:

- On Windows, programs can either run as processes or run as threads. When run as processes, they can potentially affect the Windows kernel code and crash Windows. You might have seen, probably more than once, the dreaded Blue Screen of Death, which occurs when some application performs an illegal operation. That is an example of an illegal operation performed by an application process that compromised the Windows kernel stability, and hence the kernel just had to crash. Threads, however, are different; they don't attach to the kernel, and nothing happening in a thread will affect kernel stability.

- When a process needs to call another process, significant time is wasted in context switching between different processes. This context switching is less expensive between multiple threads of the same process.

- When the Oracle instance creates a new server process to serve a client, it's easier and faster to create a thread than a Windows process.

- Solving the problem of allocating memory for an Oracle SGA in a threaded architecture does not require shared memory, while in the processes model it does. This important difference helps Windows manage its overall memory in a much better way compared to the processes model, where each process has to have its own shared memory segment that is just not efficient.

Therefore, the Oracle Database architecture on Windows is based on threads and not processes.

Monitoring Threads on Windows

You can use a number of tools that show threads. There is one that comes with the Windows Resource Kit, but this is not part of the Windows distribution; you have to buy it from Microsoft as a separate product. In addition to the threads viewer, the Windows Resource Kit has other cool tools too, such as tail.exe, which is similar in functionality to the tail command in Unix. You can also find tools to view threads from third parties on the Internet.

We searched the Internet and downloaded a tool called Process Viewer for Windows from http://www.teamcti.com/pview/prcview.htm. Using Process Viewer, you can see the Windows processes, as shown in Figure 21-3. This is pretty similar to what you would expect to see in the Task Manager that comes with Windows. Note the process called ORACLE.EXE. This is the single Oracle process, and all the server processes inside an Oracle instance run within this process as threads.

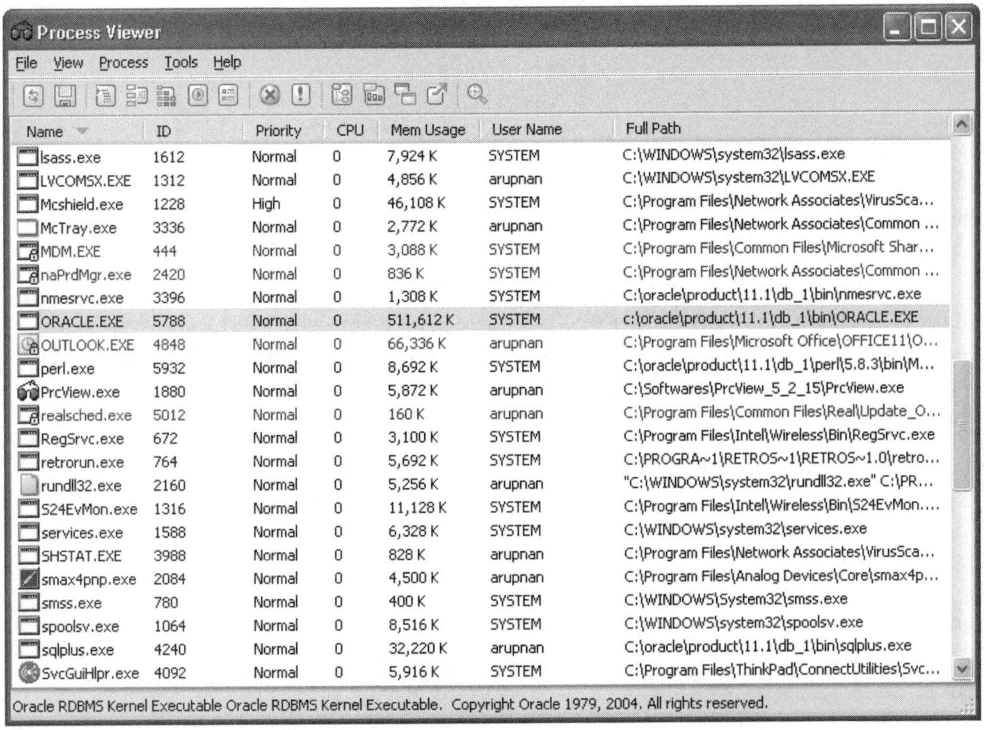

Name	ID	Priority	CPU	Mem Usage	User Name	Full Path
lsass.exe	1612	Normal	0	7,924 K	SYSTEM	C:\WINDOWS\system32\lsass.exe
LVCOMSX.EXE	1312	Normal	0	4,856 K	arupnan	C:\WINDOWS\system32\LVCOMSX.EXE
Mcshield.exe	1228	High	0	46,108 K	SYSTEM	C:\Program Files\Network Associates\VirusSca...
McTray.exe	3336	Normal	0	2,772 K	arupnan	C:\Program Files\Network Associates\Common ...
MDM.EXE	444	Normal	0	3,088 K	SYSTEM	C:\Program Files\Common Files\Microsoft Shar...
naPrdMgr.exe	2420	Normal	0	836 K	SYSTEM	C:\Program Files\Network Associates\Common ...
nmesrvc.exe	3396	Normal	0	1,308 K	SYSTEM	C:\oracle\product\11.1\db_1\bin\nmesrvc.exe
ORACLE.EXE	5788	Normal	0	511,612 K	SYSTEM	c:\oracle\product\11.1\db_1\bin\ORACLE.EXE
OUTLOOK.EXE	4848	Normal	0	66,336 K	arupnan	C:\Program Files\Microsoft Office\OFFICE11\O...
perl.exe	5932	Normal	0	8,692 K	SYSTEM	C:\oracle\product\11.1\db_1\perl\5.8.3\bin\M...
PrcView.exe	1880	Normal	0	5,872 K	arupnan	C:\Softwares\PrcView_5_2_15\PrcView.exe
realsched.exe	5012	Normal	0	160 K	arupnan	C:\Program Files\Common Files\Real\Update_O...
RegSrvc.exe	672	Normal	0	3,100 K	SYSTEM	C:\Program Files\Intel\Wireless\Bin\RegSrvc.exe
retrorun.exe	764	Normal	0	5,692 K	SYSTEM	C:\PROGRA~1\RETROS~1\RETROS~1.0\retro...
rundll32.exe	2160	Normal	0	5,256 K	arupnan	"C:\WINDOWS\system32\rundll32.exe" C:\PR...
S24EvMon.exe	1316	Normal	0	11,128 K	SYSTEM	C:\Program Files\Intel\Wireless\Bin\S24EvMon....
services.exe	1588	Normal	0	6,328 K	SYSTEM	C:\WINDOWS\system32\services.exe
SHSTAT.EXE	3988	Normal	0	828 K	arupnan	C:\Program Files\Network Associates\VirusSca...
smax4pnp.exe	2084	Normal	0	4,500 K	arupnan	C:\Program Files\Analog Devices\Core\smax4p...
smss.exe	780	Normal	0	400 K	SYSTEM	C:\WINDOWS\System32\smss.exe
spoolsv.exe	1064	Normal	0	8,516 K	SYSTEM	C:\WINDOWS\system32\spoolsv.exe
sqlplus.exe	4240	Normal	0	32,220 K	arupnan	C:\oracle\product\11.1\db_1\bin\sqlplus.exe
SvcGuiHlpr.exe	4092	Normal	0	5,916 K	SYSTEM	C:\Program Files\ThinkPad\ConnectUtilities\Svc...

Oracle RDBMS Kernel Executable Oracle RDBMS Kernel Executable. Copyright Oracle 1979, 2004. All rights reserved.

Figure 21-3. *Process Viewer for Windows main screen*

To find out the threads, right-click the process ORACLE.EXE to open the menu shown in Figure 21-4.

From this menu, choose Threads, which opens the threads viewer, as shown in Figure 21-5.

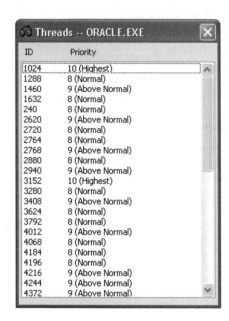

Figure 21-4. *Process submenu*   **Figure 21-5.** *Threads viewer*

This viewer shows the various threads under the Windows process ORACLE.EXE. You can find these threads in the view V$PROCESS as Oracle instance processes. The following is one example, taken from the threads viewer, of the thread 5852. If you look in V$PROCESS for a process whose ID is 5852, you will identify the instance process that is associated with this Windows thread.

```
SQL> select * from v$process
  2  where spid = 5852;

ADDR            PID SPID                    USERNAME         SERIAL#
--------  ---------- ----------------------- --------------- ----------
TERMINAL
----------------
PROGRAM
-------------------------------------------------------------------
TRACEID
--------------------------------------------------------------------------------
B LATCHWAI LATCHSPI PGA_USED_MEM PGA_ALLOC_MEM PGA_FREEABLE_MEM PGA_MAX_MEM
- -------- -------- ------------ ------------- ---------------- -----------
5AA754CC         2 5852                    SYSTEM                   1
STARUPNANT60
ORACLE.EXE (PMON)

1                        708318        859134               0      859134
```

This SPID column, which shows the operating system process ID, actually shows the thread ID on Windows, not the process ID. The only process related to Oracle is ORACLE.EXE, and its process ID is 5788.

Oracle Home and SID

In Unix-based systems, you are familiar with the environmental variables that define the Oracle SID and Oracle Home, where the Oracle binaries are stored. If you want to change the Oracle SID or Home, all you have to do is to export the variables. For example:

```
$ export ORACLE_SID=PROBE2
$ export ORACLE_HOME=/opt/oracle/products/10.2/db_1
```

On Windows, however, this technique will not necessarily work. So, let's see how the Oracle Home and other details are set on Windows.

On Windows, the information is kept in a place called the *registry*, which is sort of the brain of the Windows operating system. To check the Oracle Home and the location of the installation, check the registry. Select Start ➤ Run. In the text box, type **regedit**, and press the Enter key. This action opens the Registry Editor. Open HKEY_LOCAL_MACHINE/SOFTWARE/ORACLE. Figure 21-6 shows part of the screen.

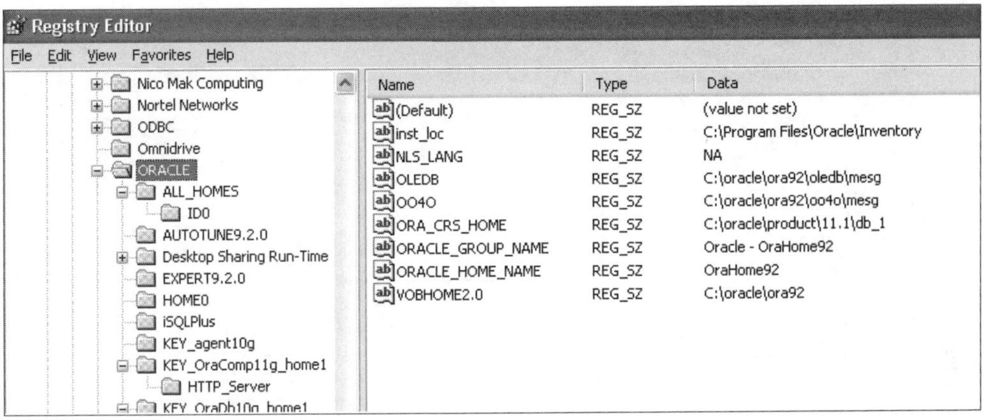

Figure 21-6. *Registry Editor for Oracle Home*

The right pane shows the information about Oracle Home and other details. Note the key named inst_loc. In Figure 21-6, the data value of that key is C:\Program Files\Oracle\Inventory, which is the location of the Oracle software inventory.

When the Oracle software is installed, the installer creates the directory C:\Program Files\Oracle\Inventory. This is where the inventory of the Oracle software is stored. In this directory you will find a file called oui.loc, which stores the location of the Oracle Universal Installer. Here is some example output of the file:

```
InstLoc=C:/Program Files/Oracle/oui
InstVer=2.2.0.12.0
```

The first line indicates that the installation location is C:/Program Files/Oracle/oui, which indicates the location of the installer files. This directory has a subdirectory called HomeSelector. In that subdirectory you will see a file called ohsel.exe. That file is used to choose a different Oracle Home. So, unlike Unix, where you export the variable ORACLE_HOME to change the Oracle Home, you will need to execute this program and choose the Oracle Home.

Oracle Groups

In Unix, the users belonging to the operating system group called dba have the sysdba privilege. In the Windows environment, this group is usually called ORA_DBA. When the Oracle Database software is installed, the group is automatically created, and the user doing the installation is placed in that group. To add a user to the group, follow these steps:

1. To locate the group, you have to use the Local Groups and User Administration screen. To go there, select Start ➤ Programs ➤ Administrative Tools ➤ Computer Management. This opens a screen similar to the one shown in Figure 21-7.

2. In the left pane, you will see several items. Click the + sign next to the Local Users and Groups item, and then click Groups. On the right side you will see all the groups defined on this computer, as shown in Figure 21-7. The last group is ORA_DBA.

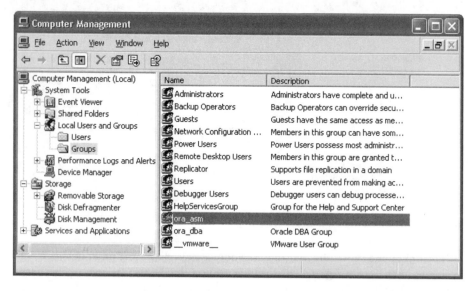

Figure 21-7. *The DBA group on Windows*

3. Once in that screen, double-click the group ORA_DBA to open the properties of the group, as shown in Figure 21-8. From the output, note that only two users are part of the ORA_DBA group. Suppose you want to put a local user called arup in this group too. To do that, click the Add button, which opens the dialog box shown in Figure 21-9.

Figure 21-8. *Viewing the properties of the group* ORA_DBA

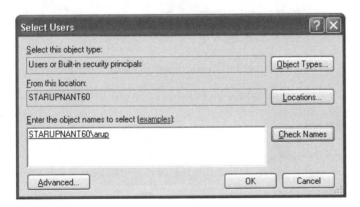

Figure 21-9. *Adding a local user to the* ORA_DBA *group*

4. In this dialog box, click the Locations button, and choose the name of this machine instead of the network name. In this example, the machine name is STARUPNANT60.

5. Type **arup** in the Enter the Object Names to Select box, and click the Check Names button, which will validate the presence of the user. If the user actually exists, the name will be highlighted by an underline under its name in the box, as shown in Figure 21-9. Click the OK button.

6. Now, make sure the user is indeed part of the ORA_DBA group by checking the group properties again. The dialog box should look something like Figure 21-10.

Figure 21-10. *Checking for user* arup *in the group* ORA_DBA

You can also use the following command to see the users in the ORA_DBA group:

```
c:\work\orascripts>net localgroup ora_dba
Alias name      ora_dba
Comment         Oracle DBA Group

Members

-------------------------------------------------------------------------
arup
CORP\arupnan
NT AUTHORITY\SYSTEM
The command completed successfully.
```

From now on, the user arup can log in to Oracle as sysdba without entering a password, as shown here:

```
C:\> sqlplus / as sysdba
```

Ideally, you would want to create separate Windows user IDs for each of the DBAs and place each in the ORA_DBA group.

Location of Oracle Binaries

In Unix, the Oracle binaries are located in the directory ORACLE_HOME/bin, and this directory is placed in the PATH variable of the user oracle. If you change the Oracle Home, all you have to do is to put the new directory in the PATH variable, as shown here:

```
$ export PATH=$PATH:$ORACLE_HOME/bin
```

On Windows, paths are usually global and apply to all users, not just locally in a session. To check for the PATH set for a Windows environment, follow these steps:

1. Go to the Desktop, right-click My Computer, and choose Properties. This opens the System Properties dialog box, as shown in Figure 21-11.

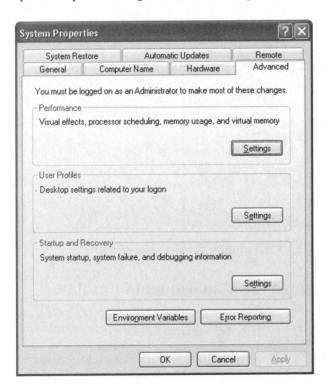

Figure 21-11. *Windows system properties*

2. Now select the Advanced tab.

3. Click the Environment Variables button, which opens the Environment Variables dialog box, as shown in Figure 21-12.

4. The lower part of the screen shows the system variables. Scroll down the list until you see the Path variable, as shown in Figure 21-12.

■**Note** You may want to click the Edit button to see the complete path. If you want to change the path, you can do so in this dialog box.

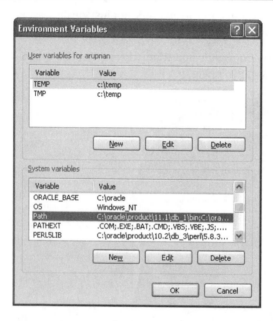

Figure 21-12. *Checking for the PATH variable for the Oracle executable*

Managing Oracle Through the Management Console

Windows provides a tool called the Management Console that allows you to control certain administrative functions through a GUI. It is handy for performing repetitive commands fairly easily and quickly. In the console, you as the user can create and add stand-alone console add-ins, also known as *snap-ins*. Oracle takes advantage of the tool and provides a snap-in for managing Oracle Databases. However, it is not installed by default. While installing Oracle Database software, choose a custom installation rather than an express one, and explicitly choose the Management Console for Oracle.

After the database is installed, you can configure this Management Console plug-in. Follow these steps to configure the Management Console for Oracle:

1. Click Start ➤ Run, enter **mmc** in the Run window, and press Enter.

2. This action opens the Management Console, similar to the window shown in Figure 21-13. Select File ➤ Add/Remove Snap-In.

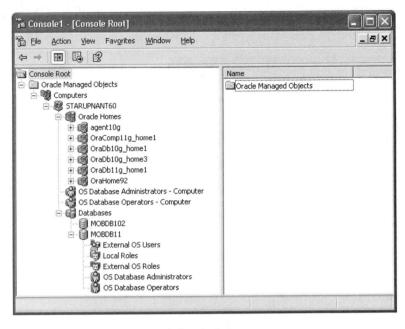

Figure 21-13. *Management Console window*

3. This opens the Add/Remove Snap-In dialog box, as shown in Figure 21-14. In this dialog box, click the Add button near the bottom-left corner. Please note that in this figure you can already see the Oracle Management Console in the dialog box, which shows up as Oracle Managed Objects. This is because we have already added it.

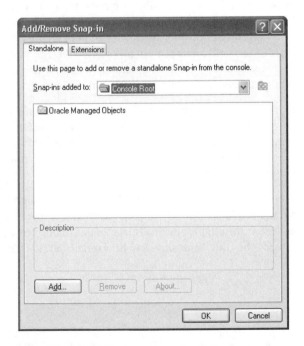

Figure 21-14. *Add/Remove Snap-In dialog box*

4. Clicking the Add button opens the Add Standalone Snap-in dialog box, as shown in Figure 21-15. Scroll down, and select Oracle Primary MMC Snap-In. Then click Add.

Figure 21-15. *Adding the Oracle Management Console snap-in*

5. From the File menu, choose Save As, and when prompted, enter **Oracle Management Console** as the name of the console.

6. From this point onward, you can directly access this MMC from the menu. Choose Start ➤ Programs ➤ Administrative Tools ➤ Oracle Management Console. Choosing the menu item opens the Oracle Management Console, as shown earlier in Figure 21-13. From this console, you can perform several management tasks as a DBA. The first action will be to connect to the database. Right-click the database name, which in this example is MOBDB11. This action opens the pop-up menu shown in Figure 21-16.

7. Click Connect Database, and it will connect to the database as the sysdba user. From this menu you can perform several administrative tasks such as stopping the Oracle service. The most useful, in our opinion, is perhaps the item called Process Information. Clicking Process Information will open a dialog box with information on the threads related to Oracle, as shown in Figure 21-17.

The dialog box shown in Figure 21-17 shows the threads of the Oracle-related programs and processes. Note how all the programs and background processes are listed. Thread 7320 is the Enterprise Manager agent, while 7588 is the job process in Oracle. In this dialog box you can monitor the processes running inside the Oracle instance and how much CPU each is consuming.

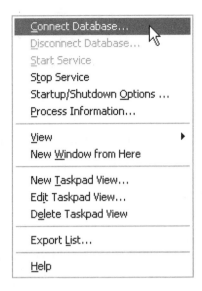

Connect Database...

Disconnect Database...

Start Service

Stop Service

Startup/Shutdown Options ...

Process Information...

View   ▶

New Window from Here

New Taskpad View...

Edit Taskpad View...

Delete Taskpad View

Export List...

Help

Figure 21-16. *Pop-up menu for database*

Process Information for MOBDB11

This list displays information about Oracle threads.

Name	Type	User	Thread ID	CPU	%	
OMS	Foreground	SYSMAN	7736	0:15:24	0%	
emagent.exe	Foreground	DBSNMP	7320	0:04:11	0%	
OMS	Foreground	SYSMAN	7468	0:01:55	0%	
ORACLE.EXE (W000)	Background	SYS	1680	0:00:00	0%	
OMS	Foreground	SYSMAN	1684	0:00:20	0%	
ORACLE.EXE (J000)	Foreground	SYS	7588	0:00:12	0%	
emagent.exe	Foreground	DBSNMP	6976	0:03:35	0%	

Kill Thread   OK   Help

Figure 21-17. *Oracle threads information*

Killing the Threads

From time to time, you may want to kill a runaway process or thread in the Oracle instance. In Unix, it's rather simple to kill a process by issuing the kill command. On Windows, this becomes a little complicated. You can kill the processes by opening the Task Manager, right-clicking the process to be killed, and choosing End Process. However, remember, the process is the entire Oracle instance; you don't want to kill that. You want to kill only a specific thread. So, you can't use the Task Manager's End Process approach.

Oracle provides a utility to kill Oracle threads, called orakill. Type orakill on the command line to see how to use this tool:

```
C:\>orakill

Usage:  orakill sid thread
```

```
where sid    = the Oracle instance to target
      thread = the thread id of the thread to kill
```

The thread id should be retrieved from the spid column of a query such as:

```
select spid, osuser, s.program from
v$process p, v$session s where p.addr=s.paddr
```

The usage is pretty straightforward. To kill thread 6776 in SID MOBDB11, you issue the following command:

```
C:\>orakill MOBDB11 6776
```

```
Kill of thread id 6776 in instance MOBDB11 successfully signalled.
```

Another way to kill the thread is to do it from the Oracle Management Console, as explained earlier in this chapter. Choose Process Information from the pop-up menu shown in Figure 21-16, highlight the thread 6776, and click the Kill Thread button in the lower-left corner.

Copying Files

On Windows, the file copy utilities are copy and xcopy, both similar to the cp utility in Unix. Although you can use copy or xcopy for many occasions, you can't use them to copy files that are held open by a process. When performing hot backups, when you place tablespaces into backup mode, the files are still used by Oracle; hence, the copy and xcopy commands may not be used to copy those files to a backup destination.

To avoid this issue, Oracle provides a utility called ocopy available in ORACLE_HOME\bin folder. You can use ocopy to copy any file, not just Oracle datafiles, but it's especially useful when making hot backups. Here is the basic syntax of ocopy:

```
C:\> ocopy <SourceFile> <DestinationFile>
```

In addition to copying files for hot backup, you can also use ocopy for other open file copies such as copying the Oracle Cluster Ready Services voting and quorum disks.

RMAN Recipes for Windows

Now that you have a basic understanding of Oracle Database on Windows, you'll learn how you can use RMAN on Windows. Most of the recipes have been described in other chapters, and we point you to those recipes for more information.

21-1. Connecting As sysdba Using OS Authentication

To enable operating system authentication for sysdba—that is, to let a Windows user connect to the database as sysdba without entering a password—follow these steps:

1. Make sure the Windows user is part of the group ORA_DBA. You can see the exact steps to accomplish this in the section "Oracle Groups" earlier in this chapter.

2. Place the following line in the file SQLNET.ORA in the directory network\admin in the Oracle Home directory. The line may already exist in the file SQLNET.ORA.

```
SQLNET.AUTHENTICATION_SERVICES = (NTS)
```

3. Now the user can connect to the database as sysdba merely by executing the following:

```
C:\> sqlplus / as sysdba
```

There is no need to enter the password.

21-2. Simulating a Failure

If you want to simulate a failure in the Windows environment and use RMAN to recover the database or datafile, all the details are available in recipe 2-6.

21-3. Creating a Flash Recovery Area

If you want to create a flash recovery area, refer to recipe 3-1. On the Windows environment, merely replace the Unix directory name with a Windows folder. For instance, to define the flash recovery area on the folder c:\flash, issue the following SQL statement:

```
alter system set db_recovery_file_dest = 'c:\flash';
```

All other details are the same as described in recipe 3-1.

21-4. Placing Datafiles, Control Files, and Online and Archived Redo Log Files in the FRA

To place the datafiles, control files, online redo log files, and archived redo log files in the flash recovery area, follow the steps shown in recipe 3-8 and recipe 3-9.

21-5. Switching Back from Image Copies

In recipe 3-13, you can learn how to reinstate the image copy of the datafile in the flash recovery area to cut down the time significantly during recovery. In recipe 3-14, you can learn how to switch back to the main datafile location from the flash recovery area. The steps are all the same in the Windows environment, except you remove the files by using the del command instead of rm. For example:

```
C:\> del c:\oradata\flash\sys01.dbf
```

21-6. Using the Flash Recovery Area

The tasks of creating and using the flash recovery area for various tasks—such as enabling the flashback for the database, storing database backups, and creating other supporting files such as control files and online/archived redo log files—have been described in Chapter 3 in various recipes. These recipes also apply to Windows platforms. In Real Application Clusters (RACs) on Windows, there is another way to define the location of the FRA. Recall from the recipes in Chapter 3 that the location must be visible to all nodes of the RAC, and it can't be a raw device. On Windows, however, it can be a raw partition, which is the Windows equivalent of the raw device in Unix. Of course, you can use a clustered file system such as OCFS or ASM, and Oracle recommends using ASM.

Raw files are typically named as a drive letter. For instance, you can specify the drive letter Z for a physical or logical partition. To use the raw files in flash recovery area, issue the following statement:

```
SQL> alter system set db_recovery_file_dest = '\\.\Z:';
```

Note the backslashes before the drive letter; these are necessary when specifying a raw partition.

21-7. Developing a Windows Batch File

You may need to develop a Windows batch file to automate various tasks including RMAN backup. In recipe 9-3 you can learn how to develop a complete batch file that accepts parameters as database names, input types, and so on, so that it can be used in many databases with little or no modification. This batch file also checks for errors and sends out notification in both success and failure cases.

21-8. Scheduling Windows Jobs

After developing a batch file on Windows, you will nevertheless want to schedule it through some mechanism so that it can be run automatically. In recipe 9-4, you can learn how to schedule a batch file or an executable through a command-line utility called at.

Schedules are not cast in stone; they need to be changed to reflect business conditions. If you prefer a GUI version instead, recipe 9-5 shows how to change a schedule through a GUI tool. To learn how to change a schedule through the command line, see recipe 9-6.

21-9. Transporting Tablespaces to/from Windows

When you want to transport a tablespace from one database to the other across multiple platforms, Oracle Database starting with version 10*g* makes it easier. If both the source and target databases are on the same platform, then it's as simple as copying the datafiles to the target server. Even if they are not on the same platform, you can still copy the datafiles if the byte order (or *endianness*) of the platforms is the same. For instance, both Linux x86 and Windows are little endian, so transporting a tablespace merely requires copying the files between them. You can learn all about that activity in recipe 15-12.

If the operating systems are not of the same endianness—that is, you are transporting between Windows and an operating system that is big endian (such as HPUX)—you will need to convert the datafiles before plugging them into the target system. Recipe 15-12 shows you how to perform the conversion through RMAN. To convert the datafiles on the target system, instead of the source system, refer to recipe 15-14.

21-10. Transporting an Entire Database to/from Windows

Sometimes you want to transport an entire database, not just a few tablespaces, to or from Windows. Oracle Database 10*g* Release 2 provides the functionality to enable that. Like when transporting tablespaces, if the platforms of both the source and target databases are the same, the task is reduced to merely copying the files. Even if they are not the same platform, if the byte order (or the *endianness*) of the platforms is the same, then you can merely copy the datafiles to the target environments as well. For instance, to transport to or from a Window environment where the source or target platform is little endian, you merely copy the files. Recipe 15-13 shows you how to perform that operation.

If you want to transport a database from Windows to another platform that is a big-endian platform or you want to transport a database from a platform like that to Windows, you will need to use RMAN to convert the datafiles. You will find the relevant details in recipe 15-13.

Index

Find it faster at http://superindex.apress.com/

Find it faster at http://superindex.apress.com/

Find it faster at http://superindex.apress.com/

You Need the Companion eBook

Your purchase of this book entitles you to buy the companion PDF-version eBook for only $10. Take the weightless companion with you anywhere.

We believe this Apress title will prove so indispensable that you'll want to carry it with you everywhere, which is why we are offering the companion eBook (in PDF format) for $10 to customers who purchase this book now. Convenient and fully searchable, the PDF version of any content-rich, page-heavy Apress book makes a valuable addition to your programming library. You can easily find and copy code—or perform examples by quickly toggling between instructions and the application. Even simultaneously tackling a donut, diet soda, and complex code becomes simplified with hands-free eBooks!

Once you purchase your book, getting the $10 companion eBook is simple:

❶ Visit **www.apress.com/promo/tendollars/**.

❷ Complete a basic registration form to receive a randomly generated question about this title.

❸ Answer the question correctly in 60 seconds, and you will receive a promotional code to redeem for the $10.00 eBook.

Offer valid through 11/07.